Shakespeare in Germany in the Sixteenth and Seventeenth Centuries

An Account of English Actors in Germany and the Netherlands and of the Plays Performed by Them During the Same Period

Albert Cohn

Alpha Editions

This edition published in 2019

ISBN : 9789353607807

Design and Setting By
Alpha Editions
email - alphaedis@gmail.com

This book is a reproduction of an important historical work. Alpha Editions uses the best technology to reproduce historical work in the same manner it was first published to preserve its original nature. Any marks or number seen are left intentionally to preserve its true form.

SHAKESPEARE IN GERMANY

IN THE

SIXTEENTH AND SEVENTEENTH CENTURIES:

AN ACCOUNT

OF

ENGLISH ACTORS IN GERMANY

AND THE NETHERLANDS

AND OF THE

PLAYS PERFORMED BY THEM DURING THE SAME PERIOD.

BY

ALBERT COHN.

WITH TWO PLATES OF FACSIMILES.

LONDON:
ASHER & Co. 13, BEDFORD STREET, COVENT GARDEN,
AND AT BERLIN: 20, UNTER DEN LINDEN.
1865.

PREFACE.

If the wishes expressed by numerous competent judges may be regarded as a sufficient criterion for the utility of an undertaking, I am justified in hoping that the essay now presented to the reader will not altogether fail of its proposed object. For some time past, indeed, whoever has had occasion to speak of the so-called English Comedians and their relation to the old German and English stages, has always complained of the want of a documentary history relating to them.

In the year 1849, having been fortunate enough to make the personal acquaintance of Ludwig Tieck, I obtained from him so much interesting information regarding the appearance of English Actors in Germany, as to cause the liveliest desire to follow up the traces of those strolling players. The remarks by which Tieck in his 'Old German Theatre' first directed attention to this subject in the year 1817, are calculated to stimulate the student to further investigations in the same field rather than to satisfy him; and in the historians of literature who have succeeded Tieck, I have only met with contradictory views, based more on conjecture than on research. One fact alone seemed to be fully evident: that the whole subject of the actors, their origin, their objects, and also the pieces which they performed, was veiled in obscurity. It was the custom to speak of them as of a myth, in the consideration of which we were to base all information regarding them on legendary rather than on historical ground. Nor indeed was there any firm footing to be obtained in the materials which had become known up to that time. Since then, I endeavoured to throw some light upon the question in a few scattered articles, which at distant intervals appeared in the Athenaeum. These were followed up by valuable contributions from other quarters; but quite recently only a few happy discoveries have put me in possession of materials which several of my literary friends considered as calculated to give a certain degree of

completeness to the results of previous researches. In saying this, however, I must not be understood as intending to state that I believe the subject to be exhausted in the present essay. So far from entertaining such an opinion, I on the contrary am well aware that in many parts of my attempt the matter offered is incomplete, and that I can lay claim to nothing more than having made my contributions to a structure, the superstructure upon which, I hope, will be continued by abler hands than mine. Nor should I have ventured to publish matter thus casually collected, had I not entertained the conviction, that any essay however imperfect, if throwing any light upon a question connected with Shakespeare, cannot be altogether useless. I had also originally intended to avail myself of an external incident as a motive for the publication of the present pages, and to found on it a claim to the reader's indulgence, as I had hoped to publish it as a contribution to the Shakespeare Tercentenary Festival; but circumstances over which I had no control deprived me of this advantage. The work was nearly through the press, when its further progress had to be interrupted for more than six months.

Four out of the six old German Plays, the first four pieces of the present work — which constitute its most important part, were to have been published more than twenty years ago by the Shakespeare Society in London, as may be gathered from the list of their intended publications; the Society however was dissolved without having carried its intention into effect. To these four pieces two others are added which possess no less interest for the present purpose. In all the six pieces, here presented to the reader in the original language with an English translation annexed, the old printed editions or manuscripts have been faithfully adhered to. In the second piece alone, 'The Beautiful Phaenicia' by Jacob Ayrer, I have confined myself to extracts, because the whole piece, which is extremely long, contains a great deal of matter entirely foreign to the object of the present essay. For the translation of these pieces I am indebted to friends, who kindly granted me their valuable assistance and to whom it is a special pleasure for me to express here publicly my sincerest thanks. The 'Beautiful Sidea' and the 'Phaenicia' have been translated by Professor Thomas Solly. Any one who has made the attempt to give a nearly literal translation in another language of the concise and pithy style of the German poets of the sixteenth century, preserving moreover the metre of the original, will be able to appreciate the difficulties of his task, and will agree with myself in admiring the skill of the translator. It would have been an easier problem for him to give the verses a somewhat more poetical colouring than the originals themselves can boast of having. Our object, however, was not

to offer any improvement on the original, but a faithful reflex of it, both as regards matter and form. The translation of the four succeeding pieces will be found not to be less meritorious. 'Julius and Hyppolita', as also 'Hamlet' have been translated by Miss Georgina Archer; 'Titus Andronicus' by Mr. Moritz Lippner; and 'Romeo and Juliet' by Mr. Lothar Bucher.

Documents scattered far and wide, which had hitherto lain hidden in public libraries, state archives, and similar depositories, were necessary for the introductory and historical part of the work. For their kind and ready aid in enabling me to procure such materials I have sincerely to thank several personal friends as well as other gentlemen whose personal acquaintance I have not had the advantage to enjoy. My especial obligations are due to Mr. Friedrich Culemann of Hanover, Mr. Moritz Fürstenau of Dresden, Professor Hoffmann von Fallersleben of Corvey, Baron Wendelin von Maltzahn. of Berlin, Mr. Ernst Pasqué of Darmstadt, Mr. W. B. Rye of the British Museum, Mr. C. W. Sack of Brunswick, Dr. A. Tobias of Zittau, and Dr. Ferdinand Wolf of the Imperial Library of Vienna.

Berlin, October 1864.

CONTENTS.

PART I: HISTORICAL ACCOUNT.

CHAPTER I.

Early connection of Theatrical Productions in Germany and England. — German travellers in London and their relation to the Theatres. — English Actors go to Germany and other Foreign Countries. The places visited by them . . . . i.

CHAPTER II.

English Actors at the Court of Duke Henry Julius of Brunswick. — The Plays composed under their influence by the Duke. — English Actors at the Court of Landgrave Maurice of Hesse. — Other places visited by them towards the end of the Sixteenth Century . . . . xxxvi.

CHAPTER III.

Jacob Ayrer and the Plays composed by him under the influence of English Actors . . . . lxi.

CHAPTER IV.

An account of the English Comedians in Germany and the Netherlands in the Seventeenth Century . . . lxxv.

CHAPTER V.

The Plays acted by the English Comedians . . . . civ.

PART II: TEXTS.

Comedy of the Beautiful Sidea, by Jacob Ayrer of Nuremberg (about 1595), the only drama extant which points to the plot of Shakespeare's *Tempest* . . . . 1.
[See also Part I, p. lxviii].

Comedy of the Beautiful Phaenicia, by Jacob Ayrer of Nuremberg (about 1595), containing the plot of Shakespeare's *Much ado about Nothing* . . . . 77.
[See also Part I, p. lxxi].

Tragedy of Julius and Hyppolita, acted in Germany about the year 1600 by English Players, containing part of the plot of Shakespeare's *Two Gentlemen of Verona* . . . . 113.
[See also Part I, p. cxi].

Tragedy of Titus Andronicus, acted in Germany about the year 1600 by English Players, supposed to be an imitation of the old *Titus Andronicus* . . . . 156.
[See also Part I, p. cxii].

Tragedy of Fratricide punished, or Prince Hamlet of Denmark, acted in Germany about the year 1603 by English Players . . . . 237.
[See also Part I, p. cxx].

Tragedy of Romeo and Juliet, acted in Germany in (and perhaps before) the year 1629 by English Players. 305.
[See also Part I, p. cxxiii].

PART I:

HISTORICAL ACCOUNT.

SHAKESPEARE IN GERMANY

IN THE SIXTEENTH AND SEVENTEENTH CENTURIES.

CHAPTER I.

So completely has Shakespeare become for us the representative, — the Alpha and Omega, of the modern drama, that we are accustomed to regard the works of all ages in this department of literature, mainly with reference to him alone. We are ready to resuscitate the dead, and to refine the coarse, wherever we succeed in discovering a trace of him, be it only a mere breath of his genius, and we go back centuries before his times in our researches after the earliest monuments of the culture which produced him as its most glorious fruit. It appears to us therefore, a circumstance of peculiar significance, that our attention is directed towards him at the very threshold of modern European Literature, at the first step which we take in the history of the modern drama. The Plays, which the learned nun Hrotsvita composed in the tenth century in the nunnery of Gandersheim, in the Hartz mountains, those firstlings of German dramatic art, which on their first appearance in print in the year 1501[1] were hailed by the learned of that day as the work of a tenth muse, a Christian Sappho,[2] although written in Latin, contain among numerous traces of their genuine Germanic Saxon origin, many passages which remind one strongly of Shakespeare. Perhaps it was this circumstance which suggested to Laurence Humphrey the unhappy idea of metamorphosing the Saxon nun into Hilda Heresvida, a British poetess of the seventh century.[3] Neither in the dramatic productions of the immediately succeeding

---

[1] *Hrosvite illustris virginis et monialis germane gente saxonica orte* (opera) *nuper a Conrado Celte inventa. Norimbergae, anno Christi, quingentesimo primo super millesimum* (1501). fol. With woodcuts. — The contemporary Manuscript from which this edition has been printed is in the Royal Library at Munich. — Another edition is by H. L. Schurtzfleisch, 4to, Wittenberg 1717 (1707 in tit.), a third by J. Bendixen, 12mo, Lübeck 1858, and a fourth by K. A. Barack, 8vo, Nürnberg 1858. A French translation (with the Latin text opposite) is by Ch. Magnin: *Théâtre de Hrotsvitha*. 8vo. Paris 1845. A German one by J. Bendixen, see below.

[2] Bilibald Pirkheimer amongst others. See J. Bendixen, *Das älteste Drama in Deutschland, oder die Comoedien der Nonne Hrotsvitha von Gandersheim, übersetzt und erläutert*. 2 Parts. 8vo. Altona 1850-53. Part i, p. 3.

[3] The unhappy conjecture of Laurence Humphrey has been refuted by Martin Friedr. Seidel in his *Icones et elogia virorum aliquot praestantium etc.* fol. 1670, and by other writers, but none of them has indicated in which of Humphrey's works it has been put forward. See also Magnin, *Théâtre* etc., p. xix. The following

centuries does this spirit disappear entirely, for in the ecclesiastical plays which are also composed in Latin, and which since the twelfth century rather follow French models, the long dawdling formal course of the action is often interrupted by a trait of German feeling.

are some of the coincidences between Hrotsvita and Shakespeare:

HROTSVITA'S GALLICANUS, Sc. X.

Gall. Behold how, at our entrance in Rome all the citizens come forth and, according to the custom, present us with the signs of victory.

SHAKESPEARE'S HENRY V, ACT V.

Chor. But now behold — how London doth pour out
                               her citizens
The mayor and all his brethren in best sort,
Like to the senators of antique Rome
With the plebeians swarming at their heels,
Go forth and fetch their conquering Cæsar in.

IBID. Sc. X.

Paul. No, verily; to the true God alone we must ascribe our victory.

. . . .

Gall. Let us then enter the church of the holy apostles as becometh the humble confessors of the faith.

IBID. ACT IV, Sc. 7.

Hen. O God thy arm was here —
And not to us, but to thy arm alone
Ascribe we all . . . .

. . . .

Do we all holy rites.

HROTSVITA'S DULCITIUS, Sc. XII.

Irene. I prefer giving up the body to all kinds of outrages, to allowing my soul to be polluted by the worship of idols.

SHAKESPEARE'S MEASURE FOR MEASURE, ACT II, Sc. 4.

Isab. Sir believe this, — I had rather give my body than my soul.

A most striking resemblance is to be noticed between Hrotsvita's *Callimachus* and Shakespeare's *Romeo and Juliet,* not only in parts of the dialogue but also with respect to characters and situations. Here are some passages from the opening scenes of both plays:

HROTSVITA'S CALLIMACHUS, Sc. I AND II.

Call. I wish, my friends, to say a few words to you.

Friends. We are at your service as long as you please.

Call. If you don't object, we would avoid the multitude.   [*They step aside.*

. . . .

Friends. Reveal then, the cause of thy grievance.

. . . .

Call. I love.
Friends. What?
Call. An object fair and graceful.
Friends. . . . But by your answer it does not appear what particular being it is you love.
Call. Well then, a woman!

. . . .

Friends. The wife of prince Andronicus?
Call. Yes, herself.

. . . .

Friends. . . . She has devoted herself entirely to the service of the Lord, and she even refuses her bed to her husband Andronicus.

SHAKESPEARE'S ROMEO AND JULIET, ACT I, Sc. 3.

Benv. . . . So please you step aside.
I'll know his grievance, or be much denied.
. . . What sadness lengthens Romeo's hours?
Rom. Not having that, which having makes them
                               short.
Benv. In love?
Rom. Dost thou not laugh?
Benv. No coz, I rather weep — —

. . . .

Tell me in sadness, who she is you love?

. . . .

Rom. In sadness cousin I do love a woman.
Benv. I aim'd so near.
Rom. And she is fair, I love.
. . . . . she'll not be hit
With Cupid's arrow . . . . . .
. . . . in strong proof of chastity well arm'd.
Benv. Then she has sworn, that she will still live
                               chaste?

The concluding scenes present almost the same picture in both plays: A sepulchral cavern, an open woman's tomb, a young woman dead, a young lover dead at the foot of the coffin of his love. This tragic scene

We meet with the first attempt to develop a drama in the German language towards the end of the thirteenth or beginning of the fourteenth century, in the 'War of Wartburg.'[1] But if we pass by this work as a failure, we must recognise the true commencement of the German Drama in the ecclesiastical plays composed in German, of the fourteenth and fifteenth centuries. The employment of the vernacular tongue soon took this department of literature out of the hands of the clergy, who were no longer the exclusive authors of these plays, as is sufficiently evident from the satirical and humorous passages which we meet with in them. The introduction of profane scenes, which were always comic, into the tragedy of these pieces, which were properly speaking only intended for ecclesiastical purposes, is their peculiar characteristic from the first, and forms the transition to the profane dramatic representations of the laity, and the Shrove-tide Plays which first appeared in Nuremberg about the middle of the fifteenth century.[2] Their authors, Hans Rosenblut and Hans Foltz,[3] are the earliest dramatic poets of Germany who appeared before the public

---

is witnessed in both pieces by two men, deeply afflicted, in *Romeo and Juliet* by the father and friar Laurence, in *Callimachus* by the husband and Saint Joan the apostle. See Magnin, *Théâtre* etc. p. xlvii, who remarks: "Ce sont là, il faut l'avouer, des coïncidences de personnages et de situations incontestables, mais qui ne sont, après tout, peut-être que secondaires et accidentelles. Ce qui mérite d'être vraiment et serieusement remarqué, c'est le ton de mysticité sophistique, qui donne aux plaintes amoureuses de Callimaque un air de si proche parenté avec celles de Romeo." — See also Philar. Chasles, *Hrosvitha, naissance du drame chrétien au Xme siècle*, in his *Études sur les premiers temps du Christianisme*. 8vo. Paris 1847.

The play of *Gallicanus* offers many points of contact with *Titus Andronicus* in the opening scenes. In both plays the scene lies in Rome, we meet the same enemies of the commonwealth (the Scythians), the same acting characters (a victorious captain and his Emperor), the same object of deliberation, the same intended relationship between them, and the same frustration of this plan. See J. Bendixen, *Das älteste Drama* etc. p. 23 and the same work for other points of similarity.

[1] See Wilh. Wackernagel, *Geschichte der deutschen Litteratur*. 8vo. Basel 1848. p. 305. It is much to be regretted that this excellent work remains unfinished. — Gottsched, in his introduction to *Nöthiger Vorrath zur Geschichte der deutschen Schaubühne*. 2 vol. 8vo. Leipzig 1757-65 pretends having read in an old chronicle which he cannot name however, that a play in the old Friesic dialect by Angilbert, a monk, has been represented before Charlemagne. Gottsched's authority has never been discovered, and the assertion is doubtful.

[2] E. A. Hagen, *Geschichte des Theaters in Preufsen*, 8vo. Königsberg 1854, speaks of Shrove-tide plays, given at the same period in Prussia. He also says that such plays were given in the open air and extempore. I believe that the plays to which he alludes are no real Shrove-tide plays. — A. Keller has given a collection of all the (121) German Shrove-tide plays of the fifteenth century: *Fastnachtspiele aus dem fünfzehnten Jahrhundert, gesammelt von A. Keller*. 3 vol. 8vo. Stuttgart 1853.

[3] The only play bearing Rosenblut's name, is *Des Künig von Engellant Hochzeit* (*The nuptials of the King of England*). Keller No. 100. Eight heralds announce that the King of England will celebrate on the 8th of May the nuptials of his daughter with the Duke of Orleans. Each herald promises a precious present: Each guest receives a florin for each mile that he has travelled; the winner in the tournament receives a horse, worth 52 marks of gold; the second prize is a necklace of Greek gold, the third a precious sword, the fourth a miraculous ring; the most skilful and most decent dancing girl receives a garland of pearls; a richly ornamented ass is promised to the laziest amongst the guests. Finally a letter of the King is read, by which twelve citizens are named to testify the truth of the promises. (See Karl Goedeke, *Grundrifs zur Geschichte der deutschen Dichtung*, 8vo, Hannover 1859, pag. 97.) Can this play be traced to an English source?

For Hans Folz see Keller, Vol. iii, and Goedeke, p. 99.

as such, under their own names. The subjects which they treated are always of a humorous and generally of a local character, taken fresh from actual life, and their own immediate surroundings. This remarkably early transition to representations of an entirely profane character, in which Germany was considerably more than half a century in advance of England,[1] had no influence on the further development of the drama. It is true, the Shrove-tide Plays were raised from their earlier and cruder form by one highly gifted genius, but they soon sank into eternal obscurity; and although their secular character might have led us to conjecture that they would form one step in the process of development to the true artistic drama, yet such a conjecture would not be justified by the fact. This process was interrupted for centuries, and Germany did not arrive at the true Art-Drama, till long after Western Europe.

The Shrove-tide Pieces were of a less public nature than the Passion-Plays; for while the latter were performed in the churches before the assembled people, or on public squares and in the open streets, the former migrated from house to house among the private citizens. This explains the immorality and want of taste pervading the humour of these plays, which abound in coarseness and indecency;[2] for although this tendency to licence met with a ready response in the popular tone of thought and feeling, publicity would have confined it within narrower limits. From the private character of the Shrove-tide Plays we may also deduce the extreme poverty of the theatrical apparatus employed in their representation. In this respect there was a retrograde movement, for in the Passion-Plays, which were often put upon the stage with great magnificence and very complicated machinery, the merely theatrical part of the representation was a very important element of the whole, while the dramatic life in the Shrove-tide Plays was almost confined to the distribution of the dialogue among several persons, the monotony of which was only interrupted by the above-mentioned jokes. Towards the close of the century, the revival of classical antiquity exercised some influence, at least upon the form of the drama; the horizon of the invention displayed in it, however, still remained exceedingly circumscribed.

Hans Sachs (born 1494, died 1576)[3] was the first who turned the studies of the

---

[1] The earliest and at the same time the only English drama of the fifteenth century, founded neither on a biblical narrative nor on the life of a saint, and the characters of which, instead of being allegorical, are taken from a popular legend, is the lately discovered *Play of the Sacrament*, composed, as it appears, during the reign of Edward iv. But though secular in form, it is thoroughly ecclesiastical in matter, its principal tendency being to prove the doctrine of the real presence. See *The Play of the Sacrament, a Middle-English Drama ed. from a Manuscript in the Library of Trinity College, Dublin,* by W(hitley) S(tokes). Published by the Philological Society. 8vo. 1862. — See also J. P. Collier's *History of the stage* in his edition of Shakespeare, in 8 vols. 8vo. 1844. Vol. i, p. xiv.

[2] "The coarse rudeness of manners, displayed in these plays, is beyond all description, and it is impossible to give an idea of it." Goedeke, *Grundriſs* etc., p. 95. Foltz, who wrote many years later than Rosenblut, outdoes his predecessor in filthiness.

[3] Hans Sachs himself has given a collective edition of his works in three folio volumes, and two other volumes were added after his death. Vol. i, 1558 (and four later editions: 1560, 1570, 1589 and 1590), Vol. ii,

learned in the ancient drama to good account for the people's stage. This poet is of very great value for the history of German Literature, as he enables us to comprehend the tone and character of popular thought during his century to which moreover he gave expression in a manner at once noble and energetic. The drama advanced with him with gigantic strides, both as regards matter as well as form. It is true, he also treated sacred subjects, and composed a great number of Shrove-tide Plays, but both these species of composition had nothing in common with the productions of his predecessors beyond the name. Neither did he confine himself to these alone. His great importance for the German Drama consists in his having emancipated its form from its previous coarseness, and its subject matter from the narrow limits which had hitherto been imposed on it. The traditions of Antiquity and of the Middle Ages, of his home and of foreign countries, Italian novels, History, sacred and profane, the events of the time and place in which he lived, all these sources offered him welcome materials in the choice of his matter. Only about a quarter of all his pieces treat of sacred subjects, in any form whatever, and even in these there is no longer any question of religious ideas and symbols, and ecclesiastical objects, but human conduct and human relations are the centre on which all the action turns. Whoever compares some of the best of his 208 dramas with those of his immediate predecessors and contemporaries, must be astonished at the contrast which results in favour of the Nuremberg shoemaker. This great revolution in the drama was effected partly through the lofty genius of the man himself, but partly also through the new energy infused into the public and political life of the nation by the Reformation, the cause of which was espoused by Hans Sachs with the most zealous enthusiasm. Ecclesiastics as well as Laymen had now become citizens of the State, who required for other excitements than any which could be afforded by the sacred dramas devoted to the service of the church, or by the low indecencies of the Shrove-tide Plays. Even at the very commencement, the indissoluble nature of the connection of the stage with the life of the Nation became very evident. In Hans Sachs everything is popular, and even in his treatment of foreign matter, we find the reflection of the German mind. Never has there been another poet whose spirit was so completely identified with that of the people, as his. He does not tower indeed over the heads of all times, like the great heroes in the field of intellect — he only aims at being understood and recognized in his own time; but it is just in his being a true reflection of his age, that his importance for us consists. We become best acquainted with him in his Shrove-tide Plays, and his humorous pieces generally.[1] Here he moves on popular ground, in which alone the new tendencies could strike root. Where he makes an incursion upon the field of Tragedy or the Antique, he very soon reaches the utmost limits of his powers.

1560 (and three later editions: 1560, 1570, 1590), Vol. iii, 1561 (and three later editions: 1577, 1588, 1589), Vol. iv, 1578, Vol. v, 1579. All of them printed and published at Nuremberg. Another edition 5 vol. 4to. Kempten 1612 et seq. The same edition with another title-page: 5 vol. 4to. Augsburg 1712. A chronological list of the plays will be found in Karl Goedeke's *Grundrifs*, p. 345.

[1] See Wilh. Wackernagel, *Geschichte* etc., p. 410.

In spite however of the important place which we must concede to Hans Sachs in the process of the development of the German Drama, he accomplished but little for dramatic art. We seek in vain in his works for an action resting on internal harmony and consistency, — for a drama constructed in conformity with the laws of human nature. Stage-management moreover, and the whole of the technical side of the drama remained for him a perfectly unknown field. And if he distinguished between Tragedy and Comedy, which had not been done before, and divided his pieces into acts and scenes, these innovations were of a merely external nature. A perfectly unmotived arrangement of the order of the scenes, and an arbitrary division into Acts even up to the number of twelve, are characteristics of him just as much as of his predecessors.[1] Neither did his immediate successors accomplish anything more for the furtherance of dramatic art. Notwithstanding the great fertility of his invention, he wanted the dramatic power to produce theatrical effects. For this a more highly gifted genius was necessary; but none such appeared. Both scholars and laymen expended their efforts on translations of antique dramas, for the most part unsuccessful ones, by which nothing was gained; while on the other hand they entirely lost the one popular element, the pure unsophisticated comedy, as practised by Hans Sachs. The Shrove-tide Plays, which in their more refined form were by far the best thing that dramatic literature had been able to shew up to that time, were obliged to yield more and more, partly to those worthless translations from the Antique, and partly to other subjects for the most part taken from the Bible. The latter found some standing ground

---

[1] Only in one of his numerous plays does he take a higher position, but here he is more imitator than inventor, and his source is an English work. His *Comedi von dem reichen sterbenden Menschen Hecastus genannt* 1549, is undoubtedly an imitation of the English Morality of *Every Man* (first printed by Pynson before 1531 and twice by Skot before 1537. Reprinted in Hawkin's *English Drama*, i, p. 27). A reprint in L. Tieck's *Deutsches Theater*, 2 vol. 8vo. Berlin 1817, Vol. i. Tieck says pag. xiii: "Here Sachs is delightful in his innocence, he probably follows his model step by step." This piece seems to be the first link between the English and the German stage. — The nearest source of Hans Sachs is perhaps a Latin version of *Every Man*. See E. A. Hagen, p. 31, and Floegel, *Geschichte der komischen Litteratur*, Vol. iv, p. 199. The first Latin version is by Georg. Macropedius, Coloniae 1539; reprinted ib. 1540, Tremon. 1549, Francofurti 1571, Argentorati 1586. A later version, probably founded on Macropedius, is by Laurentius Rappolt, which was represented at Nuremberg 1550. In 1556 a latin *Hecastus* was represented at Basle. A German version of Rappolt's play has been represented at Nuremberg in 1549: *Ein schön christlich Spiel, Hecastus genañt*, Nürnberg, Joh. Daubmann, 1552. — Other German versions are by Cyr. Spangenberg, 1564; Henr. Petr. Rebenstock, *Hecastus, ein geistlich Spiel vom Ampt vnd Beruf eines jeden Menschen*. Franckf., N. Bassens, 1568; Joh. Schreckenberger, *Georg. Macropedii Hecastus verteutscht*. Strassburg. A. Bertram, 1589; M. Abr. Saurius, *Comoedia germánica Hecastos seu Homulus*. Marpurgi 1591. The German *Hecastus* has been represented at Annaberg in 1569. — Another play, called *Homulus*, is derived from *Every Man*. This however seems to have come from the Low countries: Petrus Diesthemiius, *Homulus comoedia inprimis lepida et pia, in rem christiani hominis adprime faciens, Antverpiae quondam in publico civitatum Brabanticarum conventu vulgariter acta palmamque adepta*. Coloniae, ex off. Jasparis Gennepei, 1536; ib. 1537; Antverp. 1538; ib. 1546. — Translated into German by Jaspar von Gennep: *Comedia Homuli gemehrt vnd gebessert etc. Cöllen*, Jasp. v. Gennep, 1540, 4to; ib. 1548, 8vo; ib. 1554, 8vo; ib. 1592; Magdeburgk. J. Franck, n. d.; Erfurt 1624. Another German version by Heinr. Wettengang, *Homulus, in ietz neu übliche teutsche Reimarten übersetzet*. Bremen 1665; Nürnberg 1669. — The German version of Jaspar von Gennep has given rise to a Dutch translation: Nimmeghen 1556; Amsterdam 1632, 1656, 1661, n. d., 1701.

in the religious struggle which then agitated the nation, and as, with few exceptions, they were intended to serve satirical and didactic but not dramatic objects, they entirely failed of all theatrical effect. Such subjects as were offered by romance, tradition, and the history of the country, subjects to which English writers had had recourse at a very early period, remained almost entirely neglected. One of the results of this moralising tendency, which from the intimate connection between church questions and politics, often encroached upon the field of the latter, was soon to render the drama an affair of the state, or of the towns. We constantly meet with the civil and municipal authorities as the patrons of the stage. This perhaps may be the reason, that while dramatic art was at a far lower ebb in Germany than in England, the former country possessed permanent theatres at a far earlier period than the latter.[1] For the management of the stage and arrangements of the theatre in Germany naturally corresponded to the very imperfect condition of its dramatic literature. At a time when England was already traversed in all directions by innumerable troops of strolling players, and dramatic art had attained a high stage of development, Germany could not yet boast of any actors by profession. Nuremberg and Augsburg already possessed their permanent theatres, consisting of a large broad stage with a deep proscenium, surrounded by an unroofed amphitheatre intended for the spectators. In the other cities, just as at the time of Rosenblut's, the representations took place in the houses of the citizens, and in the inns and taverns, on a 'podium', or platform, constructed of benches and casks. But here, just as in the above-mentioned theatres, the actors continued to consist of honest citizens, and merry young fellows and scholars, who drawled out their lesson in stiff traditional forms, without any other variation than the coarse humour of the pieces, and far more for their own amusement than from any very earnest endeavour to satisfy the public. In short the play was more for the sake of the actors than the spectators. Hence arose the endeavour on the part of the authors to let as many persons as possible appear upon the stage; and there were pieces indeed with as many as a hundred characters who spoke, as well as a still larger number of mutes.[2] Occasionally indeed, for the grati-

---

[1] The first German theatre was erected at Nuremberg in 1550, by the corporation of master-singers; another followed soon at Augsburg. See Ed. Devrient, *Geschichte der deutschen Schauspielkunst*. 3 vol. 8vo. Leipzig 1848. Vol. i, p. 114. England saw her first theatre (The Blackfriars) in London in 1576. "Until then the various companies of actors had been obliged to content themselves with churches, halls, with temporary erections in the streets, or with inn-yards, in which they raised a stage, the spectators standing below, or occupying the galleries that surrounded the open space." J. P. Collier's *History of the English stage to the time of Shakespeare*, in his edition of Shakespeare's works, 8 vols. 8vo, Vol. i, p. xxxv. As early as 1398 France possessed a playhouse, built by the 'frères de la passion' in the village of St. Maur-des-Fossés near Vincennes. The same body erected the 'Théâtre de la trinité' at Paris in 1442. In 1550 a second theatre, called 'Table de marbre,' was granted to the 'Confrérie de la Bazoche.' In Italy the ancient Amphitheatres were used as playhouses; in 1264 the Passion-brothers *del Gonfalone* gave representations at the Coliseum. In the sixteenth century the Italian princes had theatres in their palaces. In Spain the first theatres were built in 1574. Up to that time the courts of private houses were used for representations. — See Devrient, ibid. Vol. i, p. 114.

[2] *e. g.* 105 persons in Jacob Rueff's *Adam und Heva*, 1550 — 158 in Valentin Boltz's *Weltspiegel*, 1550 — 162 in Joh. Rasser's *Comoedie aus Evang. Matth. 21 und 22*, — 100 acting and 200 mute persons in Math. Holzwart's *Saul*, 1571. — See W. Wackernagel, *Geschichte* etc., p. 456. — As late as 1591 a play with 106 persons

fication of the many, they again had recourse to the spectacle of the Middle Ages, to the gay, noisy processions on foot and horseback, with devils and other monsters, who amused the multitude sometimes with harmless, and sometimes with bitter jokes.

However small may have been the fruits which the efforts of centuries produced for the drama, one trait is quite unmistakable in all its phases: namely, the zest and delight with which the people took part in it, either as authors, actors, or spectators, and the readiness with which the learned entered into the spirit of the people in their way of regarding the whole subject. But now even this last hold, the only one which could repay us for ploughing up a field so unproductive for art, was to disappear. In this, as in other kinds of poetry, the learned and the popular went side by side, but there was no field in which the injury done by the encroachments of the learned was so great as in this. In order to render the separation from the people complete, they wrote their poetry in Latin, the drama sank to a mere school exercise, and was used in the schools as a method to facilitate the learning of the languages of Antiquity. Sometimes indeed the pupils performed German pieces also, and occasionally Latin pieces were translated into German and played in that form, but that was not sufficient to prevent the German drama from sinking into obscurity and contempt. This abandonment of the field of real life which was the inevitable consequence of the exclusion of the cooperation of the people, was rendered still more complete by the composition and printing of dramas which were avowedly only intended to be read. By thus neglecting the stage, which is the indispensable mediator between the poet and the people, they really turned their back upon the latter, and condemned the popular drama to a miserable state of existence.[1]

The German Princes appear to have regarded the drama with no unfavorable eyes. They frequently assisted with the loan of costumes, armour, and properties of all sorts, and the scholars were often required to play their comedies at the courts. But a higher taste for dramatic art than that which found its gratification in these unartistic productions, is nowhere to be met with. People were satisfied with things as they were. Whilst music excited a lively interest, and was encouraged at the Courts by the establishment of permanent bands, the drama, on the other hand, was only admitted as an accessary, and rather tolerated for the sake of the players, than required as a necessity in itself. Whilst in England, France, and Italy, the patronage of Princes and persons of rank began at an early period to educate professional players out of dilettanti, the practice of dramatic art in Germany was left entirely in the hands of mechanics and school-boys, with whose crude performances the courts rested contented. Only the court fools and merry andrews enjoyed their protection, and these were sought for far and wide.[2] And yet we must allow that

by Andreas Hartmann, *Vom Zuestande im Himmel vnnd in der Hellen* was acted at Torgau before Christian i, Elector of Saxony. See Mor. Fürstenau, *Zur Geschichte der Musik und des Theaters am Hofe zu Dresden*. 8vo. Dresden 1861, p. 60.

[1] See Wilh. Wackernagel, *Geschichte* etc., p. 458—463.

[2] Floegel's *Geschichte der Hofnarren*. 'William der Geck von Burgundia.' See E. A. Hagen, *Geschichte* etc., p. 7.

as soon as improvements were once introduced they were gladly and warmly welcomed, for we shall see that after the state of the German theatre had been reformed through foreign influences, it received the most zealous support from the Princes. But the merit of having endeavoured to ennoble the drama of their own accord, and without any impulse from without, is one to which they have no claim.

Such was the state of the theatre in Germany at the commencement of the last decennium of the sixteenth century. Then it was that unexpected aid arrived from a country kindred alike to Germany by ties of blood and congeniality of spirit, — from England, where the educated classes were enjoying the almost over-ripe fruits of the dramatic muse. A weak ray from the sunlight of the Shakespearian drama fell on Germany, and was sufficient to bring new life and motion into the stagnating elements of the German stage.

From the earliest times the English people were preeminent above all the other nations of modern Europe for their peculiar aptitude for dramatic entertainments. The beginnings of dramatic art in England were not earlier than those in Germany,[1] perhaps not so early, but the religious plays even at a very early period are essentially distinguished from those French pieces, which were also adopted as models in Germany, by their greater

---

[1] J. P. Collier, *History of English Dramatic Poetry*, Vol. i, p. 1, says that no country in Europe, since the revival of letters, has been able to produce any notice of theatrical performances of so early a date as England, and in a note he adds that the plays of Hrotsvita have not been represented. This assertion, we believe, is altogether erroneous. Hundreds of details in the plays of Hrotsvita themselves show that they must have been written for representation. This does not exclude the fact that they were also intended for being read by the Nuns of Gandersheim in place of Terence's tragedies. Magnin, *Théâtre de Hrosvitha*, introd. p. vi says: "En effet *nous savons à n'en pas douter*, que c'est dans une illustre abbaye saxonne que furent représentés les drames de Hrosvitha, probablement en présence de l'évêque diocesan et de son clergé, devant plusieurs nobles dames de la maison ducale de Saxe et de quelques hauts dignitaires de la cour impériale etc." And Ph. Chasles, *Hrosvitha*, p. 247: "Mille details confirment cette assertion de M. Magnin." See also J. Bendixen, *Das älteste Drama* etc., p. 13: "And is it then actually the case, that between the Luneburg Heath and the Teutoburg Forest at the foot of the Brocken, while Wodan was following his wild chase on its summit, and Madam Holle haunted every bush, that the hand of a timid nun of the White Christ was not only among the first to lay her offerings on the altars of Thalia and Melpomene, but perhaps the very first to raise the curtain of their temple before the astonished eyes of the German World?" Mr. Édélestand Du Méril, *Origines latines du théâtre moderne*, 8vo. Paris 1849, p. 17 et seq. opposes Magnin's opinion, but the arguments which he brings forward for support of his theory are far from being conclusive. "Le manuscrit, qui est contemporain ... ne contient aucune instruction scénique, les personnages sont mal désignés, les actes et même les scènes n'y sont point marqués, et l'on y trouve des indications antipathiques à la nature du drame. La scène reste souvent vide et le lieu où elle se passe n'est jamais indiqué; les personnages viennent se mêler au dialogue sans préparation et se retirent sans raison." These are strange objections indeed! If they prove anything they speak more for than against Mr. Magnin. Most of the defects pointed out by Mr. Du Méril may be noticed even in English plays of the sixteenth century and we hope that he will not deny their having been composed for representation! "Il y a des changements de scène fréquents et de grand mouvements d'action qui demandent un temps considérable, et ne sont séparés que par quelques mots des autres scènes." All this might as well be said to prove that Shakespeare himself did not write his plays for representation! "Il eut fallu, dans le *Gallicanus*, qu'une armée defilât sur le théâtre." Why? Did not Shakespeare too introduce a handfull of soldiers as representatives of a whole army? "Le cadavre d'une jeune femme n'y est sauvé des derniers outrages que par une corruption prématurée." There is no necessity for representing a premature corruption on the stage; it may be fairly left to the imagination of the spectators.

unity of action, and by their striving after a dramatically effective representation of character, sometimes indeed rising to an individualisation of original figures, which lay far beyond the horizon of the art of the Middle Ages, and occasionally reminds us of the creations of Chaucer.[1] Here, as in Germany, notwithstanding the fact that the subjects were biblical, the comic element asserted itself at a very early period, but did not become, as sometimes in the latter country, the principal object of the whole piece. It was still further developed in the Interludes, which offered an excellent opportunity for interrupting the dull march of the Moralities by amusing Episodes, and it was in this way that the religious-moral play was transformed into the profane drama. It is to this peculiar prominence of the comic element in its national originality, that the early transplantation of English dramatic art to countries inhabited by kindred races is to be attributed. To the predecessors of the merry clown, and afterwards to the latter himself, that symbol of merry old England, are Germany and the Netherlands most probably indebted for their first acquaintance with the English drama.

As early as the year 1417 we meet with English actors on the continent, and indeed at Constance, where the English Bishops, who attended the great Council, had three plays performed, namely, 'The Birth of the Saviour,' 'The Arrival of the Saints,' and 'The Massacre of the Innocents'. Rehearsals had taken place before the Magistrates several days before the performance itself.[2] This remarkable incident in the history of the theatre appears to have stood in very intimate connection with the visit of the German Emperor, Sigismund, to England in the year 1416, the object of which was intended to bring about a peace between England and France. On this occasion Henry v and his guest Sigismund were present at a play which had the fate of St. George of Cappadocia for its subject.[3]

---

[1] Professor A. Ebert in his excellent essay: *Die Mysterien der Townley-Sammlung*, in *Jahrbuch für Romanische und Englische Litteratur*, Vol. i, Nos. 1 and 2, 8vo. Berlin 1858—59, was the first to point out these important advantages of the English Miracle-Plays. In the same essay he has refuted with great acumen and unanswerable evidence the opinion entertained by the historians of English Literature, that the English Mysteries were based on the French, and has proved, that their development was entirely spontaneous and national. Professor Ebert cites traits of a genuine German spirit, which never could have had their origin in France. He shews moreover with great critical discernment the specifically English character of precisely those points of difference which raise the English Mysteries, when judged according to their inward worth, so far above the French. This national element alone secured the English Mysteries a longer life than was allotted to such pieces in other countries; for we find them maintaining their ground in England by the side of the completely developed drama, down to the beginning of the seventeenth century.

[2] J. Lenfant, *Histoire du Concile de Constance*, 4to. Amsterdam 1714, p. 440. "Les Anglois se signalèrent entre les autres par un spectacle nouveau, ou au moins inusité en Allemagne. Ce fut une comédie sacrée que les evêques anglais firent représenter devant l'empereur le dimanche 31 de Janvier [1417] sur la Naissance du Sauveur, sur l'Arrivé des Mages et sur le Massacre des Innocents. Ils avoient déja fait représenter la même pièce quelques jours auparavant en présence des magistrats de Constance et de quantité de personnes de distinction, afin que les acteurs fussent mieux en état de faire bien leur rôle devant l'empereur." — The same narrative is to be found in Herm. von der Hardt's *Magnum Oecumenicum Constantiense Consilium*. 3 vol. fol. Francofurti et Lipsiae 1700.

[3] "The representation seems to have been divided into three parts and to have been accomplished by

The pleasure which this play afforded the Emperor must have been so great that the representation of similar things in Constance was intended as a peculiar attention, and it may be assumed that they were able to shew him something else, if not something better, than he could have become acquainted with from the German religious plays, which were also in full activity at that time.[1] Perhaps the Emperor saw at Constance the same players as those who had pleased him so well a year before in London. That they were able to display a greater degree of skill than their colleagues in Germany may be conjectured from the fact, that at that time acting was a regular profession in England, whereas in Germany the actors were still only amateurs. In the reign of Henry vi the profession of an actor had become completely naturalized, and companies of strolling actors were no longer anything uncommon.[2] Flag-bearers and trumpeters marched before them to announce the time and place of the performance. The Court and the nobility maintained their troops of actors, with which bands of music were always connected. Foreigners, and more especially Germans, were to be found among the latter at a very early period. Five Germans, Austrians and Bavarians, were in the service of Richard iii as Minstrels in the year 1483. In the month of March of the same year, two of them, Conred Smyth (Conrad Schmidt) and Peter Skeydell (Seydel?), obtained permission to return to the Duke of Bavaria, and again, in October, the three others, Henryke Hes, Hans Hes, and Mykell Yonger (Michael Jünger) received a similar permission to return to the Duke of Austria.[3] They probably made no secret in their native country, of the wonders of English dramatic art, as they had themselves witnessed it. In the same way we also find about the year 1516, several Germans among the eighteen foreign minstrels of Henry viii, whose names are mentioned in a MS. in the British Museum.[4] Somewhat later, the religious disputes which played rather too great a part on the stages of both countries, offered various points of connection. All John Bale's pieces were printed in German Switzerland, and when Luther hurled his pamphlets against Henry viii, and the question was discussed in Germany, "Whether the King

---

certain artificial contrivances, exhibiting first "the armyng of Saint George, and an Angel doying on his spores," secondly "Seint George ridyng and fightyng with the dragon, with his spere in his hand," and thirdly "a castel and Seint George and the Kynges daughter ledyng the lambe in at the castel gates." J. P. Collier, *History* etc. Vol. i, p. 20, from a chronicle in the Cottonian collection, British Museum, Cotton MSS. Calig. B. ii. See also (W. B. Rye) *The Emperor Sigismund at Windsor, A. D. 1416*. Retrospective Review, New Series, Vol. ii, 8vo. London 1854, p. 238.

[1] In the Records of the Grand-masters of the Teutonic Order at Marienburg a certain "Hannos, the blind speaker [Sprecher] of the New Roman Emperor" is mentioned between 1399 and 1410. This seems to indicate that the Emperor retained persons of a histrionic character at his court. E. H. Hagen, *Geschichte* etc., p. 7.

[2] J. P. Collier, *History of English Dramatic Poetry*. Vol. i, p. 23.

[3] Ibid. p. 34, from Harl. MSS. No. 433.

[4] MSS. Landsdowne, No. 2. See J. P. Collier, *History of the Engl. Dram. Poetry*. Vol. i, p. 83. The Minstrels named in the document are Italians, Germans, Frenchmen and Dutchmen. "Ihon de Bassani, Antony de Bassani, Jasper de Bassani, John Baptiste de Bassini, Marcus Antonius, Nicholas de Forrewell [probably Nicolas Wohlfahrt], Pellegryne Symon, Antony Symon, Nicholas Andria, Antony Maria, John de Savernake, Guyllam Guillam, John de Bovall, Nicholas Puvall, Hanse Hansvest, Haunce Hichhorne, Peter de Welder, 18 mynstrells."

of England or Luther were a liar,"¹ it will have been well known in Germany, that just this very King had greatly enjoyed a play, in which "the heretic Luther like a party friar in russet damaske and black taffeta", and Luther's wife, the honest Käte von Bora, "like a frow of Spyers in Allmayn in red sylke" were held up to ridicule.²

It was impossible therefore, but that the fame of the English stage penetrated to Germany at a very early period. Later, in the time of Queen Elisabeth, when the relations of England to the Continent had become more numerous, it became good *ton* among the German and Dutch Princes and Nobility to pay a visit to England, a privilege, which up to that time had only been enjoyed by the French and Italians. What a rich intellectual life here unfolded itself to their view, an intellectual life, such "that the world had never seen the like since the best days of Greece!"³ Here the theatres were at the height of prosperity, the great masterpieces, those imperishable ornaments of the human intellect, were revealed to the people through the medium of a thoroughly cultivated and artistic stage, and the whole dramatic art had arrived at a degree of development which it had hardly attained in other countries half a century later.

Of such travellers, as may safely be presumed not to have disregarded the English theatre, we will only mention a few. Count Frederick of Mömpelgard (born Aug. 19, 1557, died Jan. 29, 1608) who in August 1593 succeeded Duke Ludwig on the throne of Wirtemberg, left Mömpelgard on July 10, 1592, on a tour of pleasure to England. He went first to Cassel, to the Landgrave William of Hesse, who stood on a footing of great intimacy with Elisabeth of England, and obtained from him a letter of introduction to the Queen. He embarked at Embden on the 7th of August and after a stormy voyage landed on the 9th at Dover, from whence he continued his journey to London. His suite consisted originally of 1. Hans Georg von Brünighofen, Grand Steward, 2. Johan Docourt, Licentiate and Ducal Counsellor, 3. Franz Ludwig Zorn von Bulach, Gentleman of the bed-chamber, 4. Hans Jacob von Mülnheim, also Gentleman of the bed-chamber, 5. Captain Saige, 6. Johan Bautin, surgeon, 7. Jacob Rathgeb, Secretary, besides seven servants, coachmen and grooms. Hans Christoph, Hereditary Sewer of Rheinfelden, joined the party on the way; but the latter, and the two above-mentioned H. G. von Brünighofen and Johan Docourt, must have returned on the ground of ill-health, so only five of the suite besides the seven servants arrived in England with the Count. This party travelled by way of Canterbury, Rochester, and Gravesend, and reached London on the evening of the 10th of August. Here the French Ambassador, de Beauvois, shewed the Count many attentions. The first five days were occupied in seeing the sights of London, and on the 16th, the Count and his suite, at the invitation of Queen Elisabeth, proceeded to Reading, where Her Majesty was then staying. Here he

---

[1] (Th. Murner.) *Ob der Künig vsz engelland ein lügner sey oder der Luther.* 4to. Strafsburg 1522.

[2] *The revells holldyn the Xth day of Novembyr, the xix^{th} yer of our sovrayn lord kyng harry ye viij^{th}.* (1528). See J. P. Collier, *History* etc. Vol. i, p. 108. From Richard Gibson's account at the Chapterhouse, Westminster.

[3] Friedrich Bodenstedt, *Shakespeare's Zeitgenossen.* Band i. 8vo. Berlin 1858, p. 13.

was received with great honour by the Earl of Essex, who on the following day presented him to the Queen. A second audience followed on the 18th, and after it, a banquet given by the Count to the Earl of Essex and the other grandees of the court. On the 19th the Count accompanied the Queen to Windsor, where he remained till the 21st, and was present at several hunting parties and other amusements which were got up in his honour. Hampton Court was next visited, from whence he returned to London. From the 25th to the 29th was devoted to an inspection of Oxford and Cambridge, and on the 30th he returned to London, where the intervening days before his return, which took place on the 4th of September, were passed in amusements of various kinds. Captain Saige, one of the Count's suite, was left in London on account of illness. The route chosen for the journey home was by way of Holland, and on the 19th of October the Count was again in Mömpelgard.[1] It is to another companion of the Count's, his secretary, Jacob Rathgeb, that we are indebted for a description of the journey, which contains many interesting details respecting England as it was in the days of Elisabeth.[2] Unfortunately the worthy secretary has given us no information respecting the Count's visit to the theatres, but notwithstanding this omission, we may safely assume that the Count did not leave them unnoticed. The allusions to him in the "Merry Wives of Windsor" Act iv. sc. 3 & 5, to which we shall afterwards refer, would appear to imply that he had entered into some closer connection with the theatre. Altogether indeed, Rathgeb appears to have only noted what he had himself wit-

---

[1] The following is the passport which the Duke received for his journey back to the Continent, as printed in the work noticed below:

"Theras this nobleman Count Mombeliard is to passe ouer Contrye in England into the lowe Contryes, These Shalbe to wil and command you in heer Maj.te name for such, and is heer pleasure to see him fournissed with post horses in his trauail to the sea side, and ther to seeke up such shippinge as shalbe fit for his transportations, he pay nothing for the same, forwich this shalbe your sufficient warrant, so see that you faile not therof at your perilles. From Bifleete, the 2 of September 1592.

Your Friend.

C. Howard.
(Locus sigilli.)

To al Justices of peace, Maiors, Bayliffes, and al other her Ma.te officers, in especial to my owne officers of the admyraltye."

[2] *Kurtze vnd Warhaffte | Beschreibung der Badenfahrt: | Welche der | Dvrchleuchtig | Hochgeborn Fürst vnd Herr | Herr Friderich, Hertzog zu Württemberg | vnnd Teckh, Grave zu Mümppelgart, HErr zu | Heidenheim, Ritter der beeden Vhralten Königlichen | Orden, in Franckreich S. Michaels, vnnd Hosen- | bands in Engelland, etc. In negst abgeloffe- | nem 1592. Jahr, | Von Mümppelgart aufs, In das weitbe- | rümbte Königreich Engellandt, hernach im zu- | rück ziehen durch die Niderland, bifs widerumb | gehn Mümppelgart, ver- | richtet hat. | Aufs I. F. G. gnedigem Bevelch, von dero mit- | raisendem Cammer-Secretarien* [Jacob Rathgeb] *auffs kürtzist, von | tag zu tag verzeichnet.* 4to. Tübingen, bey Erhardo Cellio. Anno 1602. With a woodcut portrait of the Duke and other plates. — Reissued together with the Duke's Journey in Italy: *Warhaffte Beschreibung Zweyer Raisen* etc. 4to. Ibid., In der Cellischen Truckerey. Anno 1603. This edition contains a poem of 27 pages in praise of the Duke, by Erhard Cellius, which is not in the first edition. The Journey in Italy is written by Heinrich Schickhart. The portrait of the Duke in the second edition is different from that in the first; it is that which adorns the first edition of the Journey in Italy, Mümppelgart, Jacob Foillet, 1602. Another re-issue of the Journey in Italy bears the imprint: Zu Tübingen, bey Erhardo Cellio. Im Jahr, 1603.

nessed, and that he should have accompanied the Count to the theatre is hardly probable. For it must be presumed that the Count visited the theatre in the company of some initiated person, such as perhaps the French Ambassador, or the Earl of Essex, who attended the Count in London after his return from Windsor, and etiquette would hardly have allowed him to take with him a subaltern such as Rathgeb. That the Count was present at a representation in Windsor, as some persons have supposed, I do not believe. He only remained there two days, which must have been entirely taken up by the events recorded by Rathgeb; for, as is well known, in those times the representations were not given in the evening, but during the day.[1]

It appears that during this visit, Elisabeth promised the Count to confer upon him the honour of the Order of the Garter, whenever a vacancy should occur. In the beginning of 1595, the Duke, who had now been some time on the throne, remembered this promise, and sent Hans Jacob Breuningen von Buchenbach, a much travelled cavalier who was acquainted with many languages, to the Court of Elisabeth, to request her to keep her word. He had the first audience on the 6th of April, and was received in a very splendid and gracious manner,[2] but the investiture of the order was declined under various pretexts. This Hans Jacob B. von Buchenbach also appears to have been acquainted with Essex, at least he was sumptuously entertained by him, on which occasion a question of precedence arose between the Ambassador of the Duke, and Count Philip von Solms, the Ambassador of the Landgrave Maurice of Hesse, which was decided in favour of the former.[3]

On the accession of King James, Duke Frederick sent another ambassador to England, the counsellor von Buwinghausen, after which he at last received the ardently wished for order, the insignia of which were brought him in October 1603 by a very splendid embassy under the conduct of Sir Robert Spencer and Sir William Dethik.[4] Of the festivities which took place in Stuttgart on this occasion we shall have to speak hereafter, as there were both English musicians and actors in the suite of the Ambassadors.

The second traveller of princely rank, whom we have to mention, is Ludwig, Prince of Anhalt (born at Dessau, June 17, 1579, died Jan. 7, 1650), who had not quite completed his seventeenth year, when in May 1596 he started on his travels, impelled by the desire

---

[1] J. P. Collier, *History of English Dramatic Poetry*. Vol. iii, p. 376.

[2] In Christoph Friderich Sattler's *Geschichte des Herzogthums Würtenberg unter der Regierung der Herzogen*, Vol. v. 4to. Ulm 1772, Beilagen p. 107, will be found the speech of the ambassador addressed to the Queen, in Italian.

[3] Sattler ibid. Vol. v, p. 159 and p. 183—185. — In the year 1594, a certain Stammler, who had been sent to England by Duke Frederick to buy cloth, had given himself out for an Ambassador at the Court of Elisabeth. It appears that he succeeded in obtaining an audience of the Queen, and that he also reminded her of the Garter. He was afterwards sent out of England on account of his disorderly conduct. Sattler, ibid., p. 185.

[4] It is a singular fact, that on various medals, struck in 1593 and 1602, the Duke is already represented with the Garter. On the title of Rathgeb's Diary too he is called Knight of the Garter. It therefore would appear that the Order was granted in 1592 at the Duke's visit to England, and that Breuningen applied for the Insignia only, which however were not sent to the Duke before 1603. See Sattler, ibid., p. 256.

of seeing the world. His companions consisted of his brother Hans Ernst who was only a year older than himself, and who in 1601 joined in the campaign against the Turks under the Duke of Mercoeur, Albrecht von Wutenau his governor, and Bernhard von Krosigk a page, who resembled the prince both in tastes and education. We know with the greatest exactness, day by day, all the adventures of travels which lasted nearly four years, everything indeed which occupied the mind of an observant young Prince thirsting for information, in as much as fifty years later, Prince Ludwig composed a description of his travels in German rhyme from his carefully kept journal. Provided with letters of introduction from the Prince's reigning brother, Christian i, to the Earl of Essex, whom however they did not meet with, the travellers proceeded by the route through Lower Saxony, Bremen, Oldenburg, and Holland, whence they embarked for London. They arrived at the latter place on the 23rd of June, and remained there fourteen days. They then proceeded to Greenwich where the Princes were presented to Queen Elisabeth, thence to Nonsuch, Hampton Court, Windsor, Oxford, and Cambridge, from which place they returned to London on the 24th of July, to leave it again by way of Gravesend, Rochester and Canterbury, for Dover, where they embarked for Dieppe. That Prince Ludwig was present at some of the representations of Shakespeare's plays on the London stage, is almost certain. It is true, in the description of his journey he does not name the plays which he had seen, but he speaks of four theatres in London, and of the historical pieces which were performed in them. The passage in question in his account of his travels, is as follows.

. . . . Hier besieht man vier spielhäuser[1]
Darinnen man fürstelt die Fürsten, Könge, Keyser
  In rechter lebens gröfs', in schöner Kleider pracht,
  Es wird der thaten auch, wie sie geschehn, gedacht.

Es wird die Beeren hatz und Ochsen streit erhalten,
Das durch den müfsiggang die hunde nicht veralten,
  Die gar zu freudig seind, fein starck und untersetzt,
  Wodurch sich oftermals der Edelmann ergetzt.

Es wird der Hahnen Kampf auch oftmals angestellet,
Sie werden, wie man wil, im Hause gleich gesellet
  Auf einen runden tisch der gantz beschlagen ist
  Mit matten, hier gebraucht man tugend, keine list,

[1] The Prince notices four playhouses only, but it is a known fact that there were at least seven, and perhaps ten, Theatres in London in 1596, viz, the Theatre in Shoreditch, the Blackfriars, the Curtain, Paris Garden, the Globe, the Rose and Newington Butts, and perhaps the Whitefriars, the Rose, and the Swan. The author's speaking of four only is explained by the fact that not all the theatres were open at that time in summer, or perhaps the Prince had visited those theatres which were called "Public", and not those which were called "Private".

Wan jetzt das beissen folgt, und manche Stunde wehret,
Bis sich das rechte glück zum sieger hat gekehret,
    Das wetten wird gar hoch von vielen angesetzt,
    Und welcher Hahn gewint, dem wird sein Herr ergetzt.[1]

TRANSLATION.

. . . . There are four theatres to see here,
Where Princes too, and Kings, and Emperors appear,
    In the true size of life, in handsome robes arrayed,
    And mention of their deeds, as they befel, is made.

And baitings too of bears, and eke of bulls they hold,
That through a lazy life, the dogs may not grow old.
    Which full of spirit are, strong, handsome, and thick-set,
    By which the nobleman does oft amusement get:

And fights between two cocks are often got up there,
They're matched too in the house, as one may choose a pair.
    Upon a table round, that's covered over quite
    With mats, here one employs no art, but virtue's might.

The biting follows now, full many an hour to last,
Till that complete success hath to the victor passed.
    The bets are very high, which many men will lay,
    And he is then regaled whose cock has won the day.

The Prince's travels contain moreover other interesting notices of England in the time of Queen Elisabeth. Especial mention is made of the great number of Germans living in London.

A very interesting and exact description of Elisabethan England has been given by Paul Hentzner, who was tutor to Christoph von Rehdiger, a young Silesian nobleman, nephew of the celebrated Thomas von Rehdiger, the founder of the splendid library at Breslau which still bears his name. Hentzner accompanied his pupil on his travels in Germany, France, England, and Italy.[2] They commenced their wanderings in the year 1596 and

---

[1] The description of the Journey is to be found in Joh. Christ. Beckmann's *Accessiones historiae Anhaltinae*, fol., Zerbst 1716, p. 165—216. The above passage is at p. 172. — It is entitled: *Fürst Ludwigs zu Anhalt Köthen Reisebeschreibung von ihm selbst in Deutsche Verse gebracht. Erste Reise durchs Niederland und Engelland in Franckreich* (1596—97). In fine: Vollendet den 31. des Mertzen Anno 1649. Follows: "*Die Reise in Italien*" (1598—99) p. 216—292. A portrait of the Duke will be found in Beckmann's *Historie des Fürstenthums Anhalt* (to which the *Accessiones* form a supplement). fol. ib. Vol. V, p. 466. — On his Journey and his life in general see also: F. W. Barthold, *Geschichte der Fruchtbringenden Gesellschaft*. 8vo. Berlin 1848, p. 29 et seq.

[2] Paulus Hentzner, *Itinerarium Germaniae, Galliae, Angliae, Italiae*. Norimbergae, sumt. autoris, typ. A. Wagenmanni, 1612. 4to. At that time Hentzner was counsellor to the Duke of Munsterberg in Silesia. — Other editions are: Breslae 1617, 4to. — Norimbergae 1610, 8vo. — Ibid. 1629, 8vo. — Lipsiae 1661, 8vo. — English

continued them till 1600. Their stay in England was in the year 1598, when Hentzner's pupil was eighteen years old. Sir Horace Walpole says in his preface to the English edition of Hentzner's travels quoted below: "The author seems to have had that laborious and indiscriminate passion for *seeing* which is remarked in his countrymen." In reality, Hentzner's work is one of the best accounts of the sights, customs, and manners of England under Elisabeth. What he tells us about the theatre is unfortunately not much; but it is sufficient to shew that the stage had attracted the attention of the travellers.[1]

"Without the city are some theatres where English actors almost every day represent Tragedies and Comedies to very numerous audiences, these are concluded with excellent music, variety of dances, and the great applause of the audience.

Not far from one of these Theatres, which are built of wood, lies the Royal Barge close to the river &c. .... There is still another place built in the form of a Theatre, which serves for the baiting of Bears and Bulls, they are fastened behind, and then worried by great English bulldogs etc."[2]

The ambassadors of German Princes were repeatedly at the Court of Elisabeth, and there can be little doubt that their reports which lie buried among the State-papers contain

---

Translation: *A Journey into England by Paul Hentzner, in the year m.d.xc.viii.* (Edited by Sir Horace Walpole.) 8vo. Strawberry-Hill, 1757. — *Travels in England 1598, to which is now added Sir Robert Staunton's fragmenta regalia*. 8vo. London 1797. — *Journey into England 1598*. 4to. Reading. At the private press of T. E. Williams. 1807. (50 copies printed.) Reprinted in Dodsley's collection of fugitive pieces. — See also, Beckmann's *Litteratur der Reisebeschreibungen*, Band ii, p. 11 et seq., and, *Retrospective Review*, Vol. i, p. 16—20. Another edition is, we understand, in preparation by Mr. W. B. Rye of the British Museum, in conjunction with other foreign accounts of England at the time of Shakespeare.

[1] The year 1598 is a most important date in the history of the stage and the life of Shakespeare. In that year Ben Jonson's play "*Every Man in His Humour*" was performed at Blackfriar's Theatre, it is said at Shakespeare's interposition and suggestion, and Shakespeare occupies the head place in a list of the principal comedians, who represented the *dramatis personæ*. — In the same year appeared the first edition of *Love's Labour's Lost* with Shakespeare's name on the title-page, and *Richard ii* and *Richard iii* were reissued with the author's name, though Andrew Wise, the publisher who issued them, had only a short time previously published *Henry iv* without mentioning the author. — A third edition of *Lucrece* was published in the same year. In 1598 Francis Meres published his *Palladis Tamia*, the principal source for the chronology of Shakespeare's plays, and in the same year Richard Barnefield gave his *Poems in Divers Humours*, where we read

"And Shakespeare, thou whose honey-flowing veine
(Pleasing the world) thy praises doth obtaine,
Whose 'Venus' and whose 'Lucrece' (sweete and chaste)
Thy name in Fame's immortal book hath plac't,
Live ever you, at least, in Fame, live ever.
Well may the bodye dye; but Fame dies never."

[2] The Latin text runs as follows:

"Sunt porrò Londini extra urbem *Theatra* aliquot, in quibus histriones angli Comoedias et Tragoedias singulis ferè diebus, in magna hominum frequentia agunt, quas variis etiam saltationibus, suavissima adhibita musica, magno cum populi applausu finire solent.

Non longe ab uno horum theatrorum, quae omnia lignea sunt, ad Thamesum Navis est Regia etc. .... Est et alius postea locus theatri quoque formam habens, Ursorum et Taurorum venationibus destinatus, qui a postica parte alligati, à magnis illis canibus et molossis anglicis ... mire exagitantur" etc.

c

many notices of great interest for the history of English civilisation. We have already mentioned Count Philip von Solms, Ambassador of the Landgrave Maurice the first of Hesse, a highly cultivated Prince, who received the sobriquet of "the learned".[1] He is one of the first German Princes who maintained actors at their courts, among whom there were Englishmen, of which subject we shall speak hereafter. It is possible that Count Philip of Solms had something to do with it. Landgrave Maurice built a magnificent theatre in Cassel, which he called 'Ottonium' in honour of his son Otto. A Count Hans Ernst von Solms, probably a brother of the above, had a comedy performed in the year 1597 at the Court of the Landgrave Louis of Marburg.[2]

This Otto (born Dec. 25, 1594, — died Aug. 7, 1617) kept up for many years a very close correspondence with Henry Prince of Wales, the son of James the first, and of just the same age as himself, and from whom in 1611, he received an invitation to the English Court. Otto started on his journey with a considerable suite, among whom there were: Otto von Starschedel, Privy Counsellor, Caspar von Widemarkter, a colonel, who while in the service of Henry the fourth of France had already visited the Court of Queen Elisabeth, Dietrich von Falckenberg, Burkard Schetzel, and Hermann Thalmüller, the Prince's tutor. The Prince first visited Maurice of Orange at the Hague. On the 30th of June Otto had his first audience of James the first at Greenwich, which was succeeded by an instructive and amusing visit at the English Court which lasted almost two months. The description of this journey by an unknown hand is in the library at Cassel. Unfortunately I have not yet had an opportunity of seeing the manuscript, but to judge from the quotations of Rommel,[3] it does not contain anything about the stage. In spite of this, it must

---

[1] Landgrave Maurice was himself a dramatic author. He has composed a number of Comedies and Tragedies, mostly in Latin, which are all lost. A few titles only of Latin plays composed by him, have come down to us. See Christ. v. Rommel, *Geschichte von Hessen*. Band vi. 8vo. Cassel 1837, p. 400, a passage printed from an account by Joh. Combach in a work called *Mausoleum Mauritianum*, ii, p. 66, where the English stage is mentioned.

[2] Rommel, ibid. p. 401, note 120: "1597 schickt L. Ludwig zu Marburg dem L. Moriz die Harnische und Kleider zurück, welche ihm derselbe zu einer Comoedia geliehen, die Graf Hans Ernst von Solms mit seiner Gesellschaft dort aufgeführt." — It does not appear whether "Gesellschaft" here means a company of players. In the latter case, Count Solms would be the first German nobleman who entertained players as a part of his household.

[3] Rommel, ibid. p. 327, speaks only of visits to the churches, feasts of the orders of knighthood, banquets at Court and at the Lord Mayor's, running at the ring, games of ball at Richmond at Prince Henry's, a journey to Scotland, and costly presents at parting for Otto and his companions, among whom Starschedel and Widemarkter received the honour of knighthood. Otto received a jewel from the King with 120 diamonds, from Prince Henry four fine horses, from another English nobleman a crossbow for shooting deer, a buck (with the word 'Landgrave' engraved on its collar) which they set at liberty, and a "*Commemorant*" (Carmoran?) for fishing. The King, who conversed with Otto on the bad English pronunciation of Latin, and quoted some verses from Horace, went to church with him to celebrate the anniversary of the gunpowder plot, and afterwards touched several persons for the King's evil. Two hundred guards always marched by the side of his carriage, and cleared the way with their halberds. The attendant who handed him the wine-cup, performed this office kneeling; on being dubbed a knight, Starschedel answered the King in Latin, Widemarkter in French. Besides the Earl of Lincoln,

be assumed that Prince Otto was present at theatrical representations, for James as well as Prince Henry were great patrons of the stage. The theatrical life of 1611 was rich in incident. Two editions of 'Hamlet' (the fourth and fifth) appeared with Shakespeare's name, then a second edition of 'Titus Andronicus', without a name, and in the 'Accounts of the Revels at Court' we find two pieces of Shakespeare, 'The Tempest' and 'The Winter Nightes Tayle' represented at Whitehall by the King's players.

Duke John Frederick of Wirtemberg, the son and successor of that Frederick, of whose journey to England in the year 1592 we have spoken above, sent his eldest brother, Duke Louis Frederick to England in the year 1608 to endeavour to induce James the first to join the Protestant Union of the German Princes. Among his followers was that same Benjamin von Buwinghausen, whom Duke Frederick had already sent to England on the occasion of the accession of James the first. Two years later, in 1610, Duke Louis Frederick undertook a second journey to England for a similar purpose and one of his attendants, his secretary Jacob Wurmser von Vendenheym, has written an account of this journey in French. The original MS. is in the British Museum (Addit. MSS. No. 20001). It is a daily chronicle of the ambassador's stay at the Court, as also of the events at the Court of James and at other places. The Diary extends from March 16, 1610, to July 24 of the same year, and affords several interesting notices of the places visited by the Duke both in coming and returning. He embarked from Flushing, where an English garrison was stationed, on Tuesday the 12th of April, and arrived at Gravesend on the following day, when he was waited on by Sir Lewis Lewkenor, Master of the Ceremonies, and the next day conveyed in the Royal barges to London "au logis de l'Aigle noir". On the 16th, the Duke had his audience of the King, who was accompanied by the Queen, the Prince Henry, the Duke of York (afterwards Charles the first), the Princess (Madame Arabella Stuart) and a young Prince of Brunswick, at that time also on a visit to James. Several days were afterwards spent in receiving and paying visits, and on the 23d the feast of St. George was kept with the usual ceremonies.[1] Under the date of the 30th of April we find the following notice, which is not without interest for the history of the theatre: "S. E. alla au Globe, lieu ordinaire où l'on joue les commedies; y fut representé l'histoire du More de Venise."[2]

whom Elisabeth sent to Cassel to a christening in 1596, Otto met a Brandenburg ambassador, who presented the King during the chase with some living wild boars. Otto sat at the side of the Lord Mayor, who was waited on by pages, his sword hanging against the wall, and at whose banquet an excellent alto sang to the instruments. It is mentioned incidentally, that at that time a pound of tobacco cost in London 330 florins. On the 5th of September 1611, Widemarkter made his report to the Landgrave Maurice, of the journey and safe return of his son by way of Brussels.

[1] See Sir Frederick Madden's account of Wurmser's Manuscript in Mr. Staunton's edition of Shakespeare, Vol. i. 8vo. London 1858, p. 688, of which the above is an extract.

[2] According to this we must correct what Dr. William Bell, *Shakespeare's Puck and his Folkslore*. Vol. ii, p. 251 et seq. says respecting the journey of the Duke. The Author confounds Duke Louis Frederick with the Duke Frederick to whom Shakespeare alludes in the *Merry Wives of Windsor*. According to Dr. Bell, it was one and the same person who visited England in 1592 and in 1610. But Duke Frederick died on the 29th of Jan. 1608. Con-

The above few examples are sufficient to shew that the English Theatre in the days of its prime, could not remain quite unknown and disregarded in Germany. However meagre may have been the accounts which those travellers brought home with them, and however narrow the circle into which they may have penetrated, they were nevertheless sufficient to pave the way for the English actors, who towards the end of the sixteenth century formed the resolution of trying their fortune in Germany, and to bring the English drama within the German horizon.

Recourse has been had to the most extravagant conjectures to explain this fact, so remarkable in the German and English dramatic history, and so important in its results for the German stage. Sometimes we are told that these actors were not Englishmen at all, but young Germans connected with the Hansa company of merchants in Hamburg, or adventurers, who had brought translations of the most popular pieces to Germany. Sometimes they are said to be German amateurs who had gone to London, and had returned with a stock of plays and parts which they had studied there.[1] Another supposition is, that these English actors had come to Germany with the English auxiliary troops who were in the army of Gustavus Adolphus.[2]

sequently the conclusions which Dr. Bell draws from the supposed identity of the two travellers, respecting the date of the authentic version of *The Tempest*, likewise fall to the ground. — Mr. Staunton, in the introductory note to Sir Frederick Madden's account quoted above, falls into the same error of confounding the two Dukes. — The first journey of Duke Louis Frederick, who was the second son of Duke Frederick did not take place till the middle of the year. The "*Relation Benj. von Buwinckhausen wegen seiner Verrichtung in Engelland die Union der Evangel. Fürsten betreffend*" (Account of Benj. von Buwinckhausen of what he did in England concerning the Union of the Evangelical Princes) bears date Sept. 1, 1608. It is to be found in Sattler, *Geschichte des Herzogthums Würtemberg*. Vol. vi, *Beilagen* No. 5, p. 17—20. Respecting the journey, see ibid. Vol. vi, the work itself, p. 12.

It may not be superfluous to mention a Swiss traveller, Johann Rudolph Hess, (born in 1588, died in 1655, probably the same who was Director of the Arsenal and member of the Great Council) who must have visited London about 1614. He no doubt frequented the London theatres as may be concluded by the fact that, amongst the books which he has carried home with him to Zurich, there are six plays, viz. 1. Ben Jonson's *Volpone*, 1607. 2. *A pleasant conceited comedy, wherein a man may choose a good wife from a bad*, 1608. 3. *The insatiate contesse, a tragedie*, 1613. 4. *The first and second Part of the troublesome Reigne of Iohn King of England, written by W. Sh.*, 1611. 5. Shakespeare's *Hamlet*, 1611. 6. (Shakespeare's) *Romeo and Juliet*, 1609. All in 4to. One of his books bears the inscription: "Ex libris Joh. Rodolphi Hessii Tigurini. Constat Londini. 16.." (The last two figures are cut off.) — The books are now at the Municipal Library at Zurich. See Prof. Tycho Mommsen's edition of *Pericles Prince of Tyre, a novel by George Wilkins printed in 1608*. 8vo. Oldenburg 1857, p. iii.

[1] *Deutsches Theater, herausgegeben von* Ludewig Tieck. 8vo. Berlin 1817. 2 vol. Vol. i, p. xxiv. To Tieck belongs the merit of having first directed attention to the English Comedians, but his utterly ungrounded conjectures have introduced confusion into the question from the very beginning. The authority of his name occasioned others to repeat his assertions without giving them much consideration, for the above-mentioned conjectures are to be met with wherever the English Comedians are in question. Even Mr. William J. Thoms, who was the first person in England to direct attention to these English Comedians and the literary questions connected with them, accepts Tieck's speculations without qualification. Mr. Thoms' suggestive essay is to be found in the *New Monthly Magazine*, ed. by Theodore Hook, Jan. 1841, p. 19—29: *On the connection between the early English and early German drama, and on the probable origin of Shakespeare's Tempest, in a letter to Thomas Amyot Esq.*

[2] *Zeitung für die elegante Welt*. 4to. Leipzig 1827. No. 50.

Thus, at the very outset, worthless speculations have raised difficulties in the explanation of an event, which was the natural result of the simplest facts; and as nobody has taken the trouble to collect the materials necessary to fathom this important question, nobody down to the present day has really been able to explain, to what the transformation of the German theatre, which is unquestionably due to these strolling companies, is indebted for its origin and progress.

Since the powerful impulse which Shakespeare and his contemporaries had given to the English stage, the number of the theatres in London had increased very rapidly. A necessary consequence was a constant increase in the number of persons, who, urged either by natural inclination or by motives of gain, tried their fortune in these new resorts of art. This must have given rise to an overfilling of the profession, which considerably exceeded the real demand, and resulted in a diminution in the emoluments of the actors. The mediocre and subordinate actors must have suffered more especially from this cause. Inferior performers were constantly leaving London to seek a livelihood in the provinces, and when this resource also failed them, they again returned to the capital.[1] In addition to this, the unfavorable eye with which they were regarded offered obstacles of another kind in the provinces, which in London had long been overcome by the popularity which the theatres enjoyed.[2] At the same time it can have been no secret among these persons that English talent of every description was fully appreciated and well remunerated on the Continent. English musicians, fiddlers, flutists, trumpeters, to say nothing of English athletes and riders, had been objects of popular admiration in Germany and the Netherlands since the middle of the sixteenth century. From 1556 to 1584 the names of English musicians are constantly met with in the accounts of the Margravine Court in Prussia, to which popular artists of every description flocked in one uninterrupted succession.[3] They are also mentioned in other parts of Germany. At the Court of Vienna a Flemish actor and his company appear as early as 1560, and after 1569 we repeatedly meet with Italian comedians, and among them with a certain Taborino, who in 1570 was regularly engaged as

---

[1] J. P. Collier, *History of English Dram. Literature.* Vol. iii, p. 437.

[2] "It appears from Mr. Thompson's work on the history of Leicester that, early in the reign of Elisabeth, the corporation discountenanced popular amusements. In 1566 they stopped the fees that had usually been paid to the bearwards, who kept bears for the amusement of the people, and to the players who had frequently performed in the Guildhall. In the year 1582, they forbade any dramatic performances except they were authorized by the Queen or the Lords of the Privy Council, and then the acting was to be witnessed by the Mayor and his brethren only. This spirit was carried to so great an excess, that the Mayor in 1586 appears to have provided Lord Worcester's players with a dinner, as an inducement for them to proceed without playing" etc. *Shakespeare Society's Papers,* Vol. iv, p. 145. Art. xvii, *Dispute between the Earl of Worcester's players and the corporation of Leicester, from the Records of that city.* By J. O. Halliwell.

As late as 1597 an act, first passed in 1572, was renewed with additional force, by which the number of itinerant performers was limited; and in 1599 the Earl of Leicester's players could not venture to set out for the provinces, without obtaining a patent from Elisabeth by which they were enabled to perform "comedies, tragedies, interludes and stage-plays" in any part of the Kingdom.

[3] E. A. Hagen, *Geschichte des Theaters in Preußen,* p. 46.

Imperial comedian.¹ The London actors must also have remembered that Italian players had performed in London in 1577—78, and that Italians had also met with considerable success in France and Spain.² Why then should not English actors, who need not place less confidence in their art, also obtain similar successes abroad? In the year 1585, moreover, such motives received from without an additional impulse, which put in motion the wanderings of the actors towards the most kindred countries of the Continent. It was in this year that the Earl of Leicester went to the Netherlands at the head of the troops which Queen Elisabeth sent to the assistance of the United Provinces, then engaged in a rebellion against Philip the second. Whether the magnificent Earl, who had long maintained a company of actors at his own cost, hit himself upon the idea of theatrical performances as a means of enhancing the splendour, which he intended to display in Holland, or whether strolling players attached themselves to his vast retinue of their own accord, it is sufficient for us that we know from a letter sent to England by Sir Philip Sydney, and dated Utrecht, that at least one actor, namely "Will, the Lord of Leicester's jesting player" accompanied the Earl, and it is propable that others, of whom we know nothing, did the same.³

[1] Ed. Devrient, *Geschichte der deutschen Schauspielkunst*. Vol. i, p. 149.

[2] See Schlager, *Wiener Skizzen*. 8vo. Wien 1839, *Sitzungsberichte der Wiener Akademie* vi, p. 1. and Gervinus, *Geschichte der deutschen Dichtung*. Vol. iii, p. 104.

[3] See John Bruce's *Who was "Will, my Lord of Leicester's jesting player?"* in the *Shakespeare Society's Papers*. Vol. i, 1844, p. 94. — The grounds of our conjecture that Will was not the only player who accompanied the Earl are to be found in the above-mentioned paper. If, as Mr. Bruce endeavours to shew, we recognize in this "Will" the player William Kemp, there would be nothing extraordinary in his having attached himself to the Earl from the mere love of adventure, as we know of Kemp that he was a man of a roving spirit, who had also visited France and Italy. See ibid. p. 93, also J. P. Collier's *Shakespeare*, edit. of 1844, Vol. i, p. cxxix. That Kemp also visited Germany is evident from a passage in Sloane MS. 392, fol. 401, dated Sept. 2nd, 1601. See *Coventry Plays* ed. by Halliwell, p. 410. At the end of his paper Mr. Bruce propounds the question, whether Shakespeare may not possibly have accompanied the Earl of Leicester to the Netherlands. Dr. W. Bell, *Shakespeare's Puck and his Folks-lore*, 1862. Vol. ii, p. 235 assumes without any sufficient reason that this Will was no other than Shakespeare himself. A similar assertion is also made by Mr. W. J. Thoms in his paper, *Was Shakespeare ever a Soldier?* in *Notes and Queries*, 2nd Ser. Vol. vii, 1859, p. 330—351. See also Dr. Bell's article in the *Morgenblatt*, 4to, Stuttgart 1853, No. 50, *Was Shakespeare ever in Germany?* Dr. Bell answers this question in the affirmative, and assumes that Shakespeare did not return to England with Leicester's players, but joined one of the later companies, which went to Germany by way of Holland. We meet with "the Lord of Leycester's players" in 1587 in Stratford, where they received a present of 15*l* from the corporation. Until more powerful arguments are brought forward than those produced by Dr. Bell, we must regard this subject as an open question. It appears to follow moreover from a passage in Stowe's *Chronicle*, p. 717, which coincides exactly with the date of Sir Philip Sidney's letter, that the festivities in Utrecht were not so much dramas in the stricter sense, as spectacles of another character. "It is there said that the feast was succeeded by dancing, vaulting, tumbling, and an exhibition, probably of a pantomimical character, termed 'The Forces of Hercules', which gave great delight to the strangers, for they had not seen it before." Stowe had this description from Segar, the herald, who was present. See J. Bruce, ibid., p. 92. In a paper published in Wirtemberg, a writer has recently ventured the assertion that Shakespeare had made some stay at the Court of Stuttgart. I have not seen the paper in question, but suspect that some wag or other has amused himself with a mystification. In all probability the Embassy of James the first to the Court of Stuttgart in 1603, to which we have alluded at p. xiv, is brought into connection with this supposed visit. Imagine Shakespeare at the summit of his fame, in the same year in which Hamlet was brought upon the stage, contributing to the convivial pleasures of the Stuttgart Court as member of a second-rate company of players!

This appears to be established by an event of the highest importance in the history of the English Theatre, one which has been quite neglected hitherto, although Thomas Heywood referred to it as early as the year 1612. In his 'Apology for actors'[1] there is the following passage, which though often cited has never been properly investigated.

"At the entertainement of Cardinall Alphonsus and the Infant of Spain in the Low countryes, they were presented at Antwerpe with sundry pageants and plays: the King of Denmarke, father to him that now reigneth, entertained into his service a company of English comedians, commended unto him by the honourable the Earle of Leicester: the Duke of Brunswicke and the Landgrave of Hessen, retain in their courts certaine of ours of the same quality."

The King of Denmark "that now reigneth," i. e. in the year 1612, in which year the 'Apology for actors' first appeared, was Christian the fourth (1588—1648), and his father, in whose service the company of English comedians is stated to have been, was Frederick the second (1559—1588). Hence we arrive at the striking conclusion, that prior to the year 1588 English players must have taken their art to foreign countries, and the interest which this fact is calculated to excite, is considerably increased, when we prove that this event had already taken place in 1585, that the actors, (we do not know whether all or only some of them) who had been sent by Leicester to the King of Denmark, had gone to Germany as early as 1586, and that among them there were at least two, who subsequently attained a prominent position on the London stage and who not only were acquainted with Shakespeare but also stood on an intimate footing with him, and one of whom was probably the first to embody Shakespeare's clowns before an English audience — no others than Thomas Pope and George Bryan.

Whether the Danish King dismissed all those actors at once, or whether he only parted with some of them to Christian the first, the Elector of Saxony, at his request, is uncertain. However this may be, in October 1586 we meet with five Englishmen, who had quitted the Danish service, at the Saxon Court. It is true, in the documents now before us they are called "Instrumentalists"; and this was probably their original and principal profession. But that there were also actors among them, or that they themselves followed the profession of acting as well as that of music, is proved not only by the evidence of Heywood, who calls them comedians, but also by that of one of the documents themselves, and especially by that of the names of Thomas Pope and George Bryan.

The three following documents are preserved in the Royal Archives at Dresden. The first two are holographs of Christian the first, the first addressed to King Frederick the second of Denmark, the second to the Steward, Hans Thilo. The third is the Elector's decree respecting the appointment of the Englishmen.[2]

---

[1] Republished by the Shakespeare Society in 1841, 8vo, p. 40.

[2] See Moritz Fürstenau, *Zur Geschichte der Musik und des Theaters am Hofe der Kurfürsten von Sachsen.* 8vo. Dresden 1861, p. 69—72. — The two letters of the Elector have been printed before in *Anzeiger für Kunde der Deutschen Vorzeit.* 4to. Nürnberg 1859, No. 1.

"An Se. Königl. Majestät zu Danemark.

Ew. Königl. Majestät Einspänniger, welchen Sie den Englendischen Instrumentisten zugeordnet, hat Uns Ew. Königl. Maj. Schreiben zu seiner Ankunft bei Uns zurecht überantworten lassen. Dafs nun Ew. Königl. Majest. Uns auf Unser freundlich Bitten Uns nicht allein diese Instrumentisten freundlich haben zukommen lassen, sondern auch mit denselben zuvor vff eine gewisse Unterhaltung vorgleichen vnd ihrer Abfertigung halber so fleissige Vorsehung haben thun lassen, vnd also derohalben Sich so oft vnd vielmals Unserthalben bemühet, dessen thun Wir Uns gegen Ew. Königl. Majest. ganz dienstlich vnd freundlich bedanken.

Waidenhain, den 19. October 1586."

TRANSLATION.
To His Royal Majesty of Denmark.

Your Royal Majesty's one-horse carriage which you assigned to the English Instrumentalists has duly delivered to us on its arrival Your Royal Majesty's letter. That Your Royal Majesty at our friendly request have not only been so friendly as to allow these instrumentalists to come to us, but also have arranged with them beforehand for a certain maintenance, and have made such careful provisions for expediting them, and have therefore with respect to them so often taken trouble in our behalf, for this we offer our thanks to Your Royal Majesty most truly and friendly.

Waidenhain, the 19th of October 1586.

"An den Hausvoigt Hansen Thilo.

Lieber Getreuer: Unser gnädigster Befehlich ist, Du wollest vnsern Englendischen Instrumentisten von Unsertwegen auferlegen, sich alsbald nach Deiner Anmeldung mit ihren Instrumenten anhero bei Tags vnd Nachts zu Uns zu begeben, vnd die Trauerkleider, so Wir ihnen machen lassen, mitzubringen, damit sie allhier darinnen auffwarten können: vnd damit sie der Fuhre halber nicht gehindert werden, wollest Du ihnen Unserer Kutschen eine, so die Sachen pflegen zu fahren, welche unter denselben am besten fortkommen kann, verordnen, der sie bis gegen der Zosse [?] führe, bei Tags vnd Nachts, allda sie zu ihrer Ankunft Amtsfuhre bekommen werden, auch demselben Kutscher befehlen, dafs er nach ihrer Ankunft gegen der Zosse [?] folgenden Tags vollends ledig hereinfahren soll, vnd solches Alles dermafsen mit Fleifs bestellen, damit berührte Instrumentisten je eher, je besser allhier sein mögen.

Berlin, den 25. October anno 1586."

TRANSLATION.
To the Steward Hans Thilo.

Dear and trusty servant: Our gracious command is, you do on our behalf command our English Instrumentalists immediately after your announcement to repair hither to us with

their instruments by day and night, and bring with them the mourning clothes which we have had made for them, in order that they may wait upon us in them here; and that they may not meet with any impediment with regard to conveyance, will you appoint for them one of our carriages such as are used to convey things, and whichever of them can get on the best, which may bring them as far as to the Zosse [?] by day and night, where on their arrival they shall have an official carriage, also will you tell the coachman that on the following day after their arrival at the Zosse [?] he is to drive in here quite empty, and will you diligently arrange everything in such a way that the said Instrumentalists may be here as soon as possible.

Berlin, the 25th of October, 1586.

BESTALLUNGSDEKRET.

Von Gottes Gnaden, Wir Christian Herzogk zu Sachssen etc. Thuen khuendt kegen Jeder Mannigklich, Nachdeme Vnsere liebe getreuen, Tomas Konigk [Thomas King], Tomas Stephan [Thomas Stephen], George Beyzandt [George Bryan], Tomas Papst [Thomas Pope] vnd Rupert Persten [Pierst?] Aufs Engelandt, Geyger vnd Instrumentisten, eine Zeittlangk bei der Konigklichen Würde zür Dennemarken gewefsen die Vnfz Ire Kon. W. Zukommen lassenn, Das wir solche zu Dienst an Unsern Hoff besteldt vnd auffgenommen, Vndt thun solchs hiemit vnd in crafft des brieffes, Das sie Vnfz getreu vnd dienstgewertigk vnd schuldigk sein sollen, Sich an Unserm Hoffe wesentlich zu enthalten, Vnd do wir Raisen, Vns, Vf Vnseren beuehlich Jedesmahls folgen, Wan wir taffel haltten, Vnd sünsten so ofte Inen solchs angemeldet wirdt, mit Iren Geygen vnd zugehörigen Instrumenten, auffwarten vnd Musiciren, Vns auch mit Ihrer Springkunst vnd andern, was sie in Zirligkeit gelernett, lüst vnd ergetzlichkeit machen, Vnd sich sünst kegen Vns vorhalten, vnd bezeigen, was getreuen vleissigen Dienern zustehet, eignet vnd gebüret, Welches sie also versprochen vnd zügesagt, Vnfz auch darüber sämbtlich einen Reuerfz vbergeben habenn. Dakegen vnd Züergetzlichkeit solcher Irer Dienste, wollen wir Inen Järlich, so lange diese Vnsere Bestallung weret, Funfhundert taler, Zu den Vier quatember Zeitten von dem 16. Octobris negst Vorschienen anzurechnen, Aufz Vnser Renth Kammer, Defsgleichen Jedem Järlich ein Kleidt, Vnd Viertzigk Thaler zu Haüfz Zinfz, oder herbrigen Geldt vff sie alle Zugleich reichen, Vnd sie mit freien Tisch zu Hoffe, Auch wenn wir Raisen, freyen fhuer vorsehenn lassen.

TRANSLATION.
THE APPOINTMENT.

By the grace of God, We Christian Duke of Saxony &c. make known to all men: Whereas our beloved and trusty Thomas King, Thomas Stephen, George Bryan, Thomas Pope, and Rupert Persten [Pierst?] of England, fiddlers and instrumentalists, have been a long time with the Royal Dignity of Denmark, whom His Royal Majesty has allowed to come to us, that we have appointed and received the same into our service

at our Court, and do so hereby, and in virtue of this letter, that they may be trusty and obliging and dutiful, to demean themselves well at our Court, and when we travel to follow us always at our command, and when we hold a banquet to play as often as the same is ordered them, and attend with their fiddles and instruments belonging thereto, and play music, and amuse and entertain us also with their art in leaping and other graceful things that they have learnt, and in other respects so demean and behave themselves towards us as becomes, behoves, and beseems, true and zealous servants, which they accordingly have promised and declared, and have also all together given us their bond. On the other hand, and for the greater delight of such their services, we will pay to them yearly as long as this our appointment lasts, five hundred thalers at the four quarterly times from the 16th of October last [1586], out of our treasury, in like manner to each yearly one coat, and forty thalers for house-rent, or of lodging money, for all of them together, and have them provided with a free table at court, also, when we travel, with free conveyance.

A separate leaf annexed to the above document bears the signatures of the artists named in it, of which we give a Facsimile (see Plate i, No. 1). The German translations facing the English names have been added by another person. In another decree, which is of no importance for our object there stands, for instance, "Thomas Stephans von Lunden in Engellandt".[1] We need not be surprised that besides music, which at all events was the principal thing, mention is made here only of their "art in leaping and other graceful things that they have learnt," for under this expression the dramatic art was also understood in Germany at that time. The term 'Comedian' or 'Player' hardly occurs at all, just because actors by profession were still unknown. No one will doubt that we have to do here with the Comedians mentioned by Heywood. The connection with "certaine of ours of the same quality" at the Courts of Brunswick and Hesse, by which are meant actors who were staying at those courts at the time at which Heywood wrote, accordingly in the year 1612 or immediately before it, confirms the correctness of this conclusion. — Was then Thomas Pope really the later colleague of Shakespeare? This does not appear to us to admit of any doubt. No other actor of this name is known to us of that time, and he belongs to the few whose connection with the London stage can be traced back to a time prior to Shakespeare's connection with the Blackfriar's Theatre in 1589, for we know that before 1588 he had taken a part in Tarlton's play of 'The Second Part of the Seven Deadly Sins'.[2] The above-mentioned Englishmen are not met with again in the Dresden Archives after 1586, although other 'Jumpers and Dancers' are named at a later period, as for instance in 1588. It is probable therefore that the Englishmen quitted the Saxon service soon after 1586, and

---

[1] See M. Fürstenau, *Zur Geschichte* etc., p. 72.

[2] See J. P. Collier's *Memoirs of the Principal Actors in the Plays of Shakespeare,* printed for the Shakespeare Society, 8vo, London 1846, p. 120—128. To the Memoir of Pope I am indebted for all that follows above concerning him. — Thomas Pope is twice mentioned in Henslowe's *Diary,* ed. for the Shakespeare Soc. by J. P. Collier. 8vo. London 1845, p. 109 & 235.

returned to England. On the London stages Thomas Pope had played the parts of the 'rustic clowns', and there is nothing surprising therefore in the supposition, that at an earlier period of his life, he had condescended to still more subordinate histrionic arts.[1] It appears, that in the year 1593 he belonged to the same company as Edward Alleyn,[2] and in 1596 his name stands at the head of the eight Petitioners to the Privy Council for the repair of the Blackfriars theatre, among whom Shakespeare's name also appears. And again in 1599 he and John Heming represent the company of the Lord Chamberlain's servants, when they received 30*l*. for the performance of three plays at Court. In 1598 he had a part in Ben Jonson's 'Every Man in his Humour', and in 1599 another in 'Every Man out of his Humour' by the same author. He died in 1604. As to George Bryan, it is not quite clear what position he held amongst the actors of the Blackfriars Theatre, but he evidently belonged to it at the time when Shakespeare was a member of it. Also his connection with the London Theatres may be traced back to a period prior to 1588, as he also took a part in 'The Second Part of the Seven Deadly Sins'. Chalmers states that George Bryan "played the Earl of Warwick in 'Henry the Sixth', during 1592"[3] but he gives no authority for his statement. He probably confounded Shakespeare's plays of 'Henry vi' with the introduction of that King attended by the Earl of Warwick, and others, in Tarlton's 'Seven Deadly Sins'. Bryan did act the Earl of Warwick in that piece. Chalmers' assertion that Bryan was "certainly dead" in 1598 and that "he did not live long enough to represent any part in Ben Jonson's 'Every Man in his Humour'" is, according to Mr. J. P. Collier equally doubtful. "The truth is" says the latter "that we are ignorant when or where Bryan died; but there is good reason to believe that he was living in the spring of 1600, for we read the following entry in the register of baptisms at St. Andrew's Blackfriars, which most likely applies to our actor:

George, sonne to George Bryan. 17. Feb. 1599."

Of the other three members of the King of Denmark's Company we possess no further information. Neither have any particulars been preserved respecting the performances of this company in Dresden and Berlin. In the latter capital they have probably only performed as musicians, as they had to appear in mourning costumes. But it is sufficient for us, that we here meet with English actors, who before leaving England must have been already well-known members of the profession, practising their art in two Capitals of the German States. Can we suppose that all these circumstances remained un-

---

[1] See above p. XXII, note 3. Lord Leicester's players too did not decline to act in pantomimes, and if the company recommended to the King of Denmark by Leicester was connected with the Earl's visit to the Low-Countries, as we believe it was, Thomas Pope may have acted in the pantomime described by Stowe.

[2] See *Memoirs of Edw. Alleyn*, Founder of Dulwich College, ed. for the Shakespeare Soc. by J. P. Collier. 8vo. London 1841, p. 26.

[3] See a Memoir of him in Mr. Collier's work named above, p. 129—131. Chalmer's statement is to be found in *Suppl. Apology for the Believers in the Shakespeare papers*. 8vo. 1799, p. 160.

known to the members of the London stage? Most assuredly not; and there is nothing to prevent our assuming, that those actors who were anxious to improve their external position, hit upon the idea of practising their art in foreign countries, an idea which was still further nourished by the English love of roving. Fortunately, we are not obliged to content ourselves with these combinations to support our conjectures, but are able to establish their correctness. The following remarkable letter of Richard Jones, an actor, to Edward Alleyn, the founder of Dulwich College, is evidence of the truth of our assertion.

"Mr. Allen, — I commend my love and humble duty to you, geving you thankes for yor great bounty bestoed upon me in my sicknes, when I was in great want: god blese you for it. Sir, this it is, I am to go over beyond the seeas w^t Mr. Browne and the company, but not by his meanes, for he is put to half a shaer, and to stay hear, for they ar all against his going: now, good Sir, as you have ever byne my worthie frend, so helpe me nowe. I have a sute of clothes and a cloke at pane fo^r three pound, and if it shall pleas you to lend me so much to release them, I shall be bound to pray fo^r you so longe as I leve; for I go over, and have no clothes, I shall not be esteemed of; and by god's help, the first mony that I gett I will send it over unto you, for hear I get nothinge: some tymes I have a shillinge a day, and some tymes nothinge, so that I leve in great poverty hear, and so humbly take my leave, prainge to god, I and my wiffe, for yor health, and mistris Allene's which god continew. — Yo^r poor frend to command,

Richard Jones."[1]

Here we see an actor, and as we shall shew presently by no means the least important one of his times, forming the resolution "to go over beyond the seeas with Mr. Browne and the company" in order to escape from his embarrassed circumstances. But the letter bears no date. When was it written? Did he adhere to his intention, or, if the "company" really went "beyond the seeas", when did this happen, where did it go to, and of what persons did it consist? All these points and several others are cleared up in the following passport, which bears the signature of the same C. Howard, who a year later made out the passport for Duke Frederick of Wirtemberg on his return from England. (See p. xiii.)

"Messieurs, comme les présents porteurs, Robert Browne, Jehan Bradstriet, Thomas Saxfield, Richard Jones, ont deliberé de faire ung voyage en Allemagne, avec intention de passer par le païs de Zelande, Hollande et Frise, et allantz en leur dict voyage d'exercer leurs qualitez en faict de musique, agilitez et joeuz de commedies, tragedies et histoires, pour s'entretenir et fournir à leurs despenses en leur dict voyage. Cestes sont partant vous requerir monstrer et prester toute faveur en voz païs et jurisdictions, et leur octroyer en ma faveur vostre ample passeport soubz le seel des Estatz, afin que les Bourgmestres des villes estantz soubs voz jurisdictions, ne les empeschent en passant d'exercer leur dictes qualitez par tout. Eñquoy faisant, je vous en demeureray à tous obligé, et me treuverez,

---

[1] From the *Alleyn Papers* ed. by J. P. Collier for the Shakespeare Society, 1847, 8vo, p. 19.

très appareillé à me revencher de vostre courtoisie en plus grand cas. De ma chambre à la court d'Angleterre ce Xme jour de Febvrier, 1591.

Vostre tres affecsionné à vous

fayre plaisir et sarvis

C. Howard."[1]

TRANSLATION.

Gentlemen, as the present bearers, Robert Browne, John Bradstriet, Thomas Saxfield, [Sackville], and Richard Jones, have determined on making a journey in Germany, with the intention of passing through the countries of Zealand, Holland, and Friesland, and while going on their said journey, of practising their profession by performing of music, feats of agility, and games of comedies, tragedies, and histories for maintaining themselves and providing for their expenses on their said journey. These presents are therefore to request you to shew and afford them every favour in your countries and jurisdictions, and to grant them in my favour your full passport under the seal of the states, to the end that the Burgomasters of the towns being under your jurisdiction, do not hinder them in passing from practising their said profession everywhere. In your doing which I shall remain obliged to all, and you will find me very ready to return your courtesy in greater instances. Given from my chamber at the Court of England the tenth day of February, 1591.

Your very devoted to doing you pleasure and service

C. Howard.

These two documents put to silence all such conjectures as those mentioned above. We know now, that the 'English Comedians' were really Englishmen, and also what the motive was which induced them to leave their native country. There is another conjecture which has often been hazarded, but which now appears entirely without foundation. It has been supposed, that the Netherlands were always the original goal of the wanderings of these strolling players, that they there became connected with Flemish actors, and went with them to Germany. We now learn the reverse of all this. Holland, Zealand, and Friesland were only to be visited en passant, but Germany was to be the main object of their travels, and it was only as a means of getting there, and of obtaining the necessary funds for the journey, that they intended to practise their art in the Netherlands. This appears to me very strong evidence for the assumption that the company went to Germany in consequence of an invitation. If they expected to meet with encouragement for their art in the Netherlands, why should they from the very first have directed their attention to Germany? Besides, the circumstance that the passport is addressed only to the Flemish,

---

[1] The letter is addressed to the States-General of the Netherlands and has been discovered in the Archives of the Hague by Mr. J. A. de Zwaan Cz. — First published in Mr. L. Ph. C. van den Bergh's "'s Gravenhaagsche Bijzonderheden," Hague 1857, 12mo, p. 41. See also Albert Cohn, *English Actors in Germany*, in the *Athenaeum* No. 1652, June 25, 1859, and the same article republished by Mr. W. J. Thoms in *Notes and Queries* 1859, July 9. See also Dr. W. Bell, *Shakespeare's Puck*, etc. Vol. ii, p. 250.

and not to the German Authorities, appears to favour this view. It is most probable that upon their first leaving England, the actors were already provided with German credentials which promised them a safe conduct in Germany, and procured them attention from the municipal authorities. At a future page we shall find Robert Browne, the leader of the Company, appearing again a few years later in connection with the art-loving Landgrave Maurice, in Cassel. The knowledge which we obtain from Lord Howard's document, respecting the character of the intended representations is very accurate. Comedies, Tragedies, and Histories are to be performed, a designation, from which we may safely conclude, that the Company took with them the same pieces, which were known upon the London boards by the same names. The intention of increasing the attraction of their representations by "musique" and "agilitez" is also to be explained by the practice of that time upon the London stage.[1] But we can hardly suppose that all these performances for obtaining popularity were the province of the four above-mentioned actors themselves; we must rather assume that the Company took with them several subordinate persons, who at least undertook the "agilitez". They might calculate on finding musicians, even Englishmen, on the spot, for there were a great many of them at that time on the Continent.

Who then were the four friends who formed a party for a journey to Germany? Two of them at least were actors who must have already acquired a certain reputation in England. Robert Browne[2] and Richard Jones belonged to the company of the Earl of Worcester's players as early as 1586, as we learn from the following document taken from the Records of the City of Leicester.

"Willm Earle of Worcest^r hathe by his wrytinge, dated the 14 of January, A° 28° Eliz. Re. lycensed his s^{r}vaunts, vz. Robt. Browne, James Tunstall, Edward Allen, Wm. Harryson, Tho. Cooke, Richd. Johnes, Edward Browne, Ryc. Andrewes, to playe and goe abrode, using themselves orderly, &c. in these words, &c. These are therefore to require all suche her highness offycers to whom these p^{r}sents shall cm̄, quietly and frendly, within yor severall p^{r}sincts and corporacons, to p^{r}myt and suffer them to passe wth your furtherance, vsinge and demeanynge y^{r}selves honestly, and to give them (the rather for my sake) such entertaynment as other noble men's players have" &c.[3]

---

[1] Henry Chettle in his *Kind-hearts Dream,* 1592, makes coney-catchers complain, that the players "spoiled their trade" by singing jigs in which they were exposed. — Stephen Gosson in his *Plays Confuted in Five Actions,* talks of vaulting, tumbling, dancing of jigs, galliards etc. — With respect to Music performed between the acts Antony Munday in his *Two Italian Gentlemen* (about 1584) mentions the different kinds of music to be played after each act, whether 'a pleasant galliard,' 'a solemn dump,' or 'a pleasant allemaigne.' See J. P. Collier, *History* etc. Vol. iii, p. 380 and 448.

[2] This player and others of the same name seem to have been members of one family. In the Earl of Worcester's company we meet with an Edward Browne, and a William Browne is named as performer of one of the characters in Shakerley Marmion's *Hollands Leaguer, a comedy,* 1632, 4to. See J. P. Collier, *History* etc. Vol. ii, p. 21.

[3] *Dispute between the Earl of Worcester's players and the Corporation of Leicester in 1586.* Ed. by J. O. Halliwell. *Shakespeare Soc. Papers,* Vol. iv. p. 145.

Robert Browne is most probably the same person, who soon after 1570 married the widow of Edward Alleyn, the father of the founder of Dulwich College of the same name. He had already been an actor and a haberdasher at the same time. Edward Alleyn was the proprietor of an inn, and as the old practice of using inn-yards for theatrical representations was still in vogue at that time, the prospect of owning the inn may very likely have been one of the motives which induced Browne to marry Alleyn's widow. There can be little doubt that Mr. and Mrs. Browne lost no time in turning to advantage the histrionic talents of Edward Alleyn, the son, who afterwards became the celebrated actor, and who in 1599, in conjunction with Philip Henslowe, whose daughter he married, built the Fortune Theatre; and this again would explain the neglect of Alleyn's education, of which Fuller complains in his 'Worthies'. Moreover Fuller's statement that "Alleyn was bred a stage player" is in harmony with this supposition.[1] Richard Jones, the last mentioned actor in the above document, stood in very close connection with Robert Browne, indeed he appears to have been a partner in Browne's theatrical enterprises, for on the 3rd of January 1588—89, Edward Alleyn purchases for the sum of 37l. 10s. 6d., Richard Jones' share of "playing apparels, play-books, instruments, and other comodities" which had belonged to him and Browne, and the latter's step-sons, John and Edward Alleyn, in common.[2] In the year 1590 Browne must also have given up his theatrical connection with his two step-sons, for it was in that year that he undertook his first journey to the Netherlands. The two friends left the Theatrical Company of the Alleyns so very nearly at the same time, that we are justified in attributing this step to their having already resolved on their expedition to Holland. It would follow from this assumption that R. Jones was also one of the party, although we do not find him mentioned by name in the following entry in the town accounts of the city of Leyden. But there is no reason to be surprised at this, as only Robert Browne is mentioned as the leader, and his companions are briefly styled, "his fellows". It is also possible moreover that the undated letter of Jones to Alleyn refers to the first journey.

"Betaelt aen Robert Brone, Engelsman, ende zynde medehulpers, 'tsamen vyftien guldens over geliche somme hem toegevoucht voor't verthoonen ende spelen von verscheyden comedien ende historien mitsgaders 't doen van verscheyden sprongen by hems, zoo voor Burgermeestren alsvoor de gemeente diser state verthout, blijckende by de Ordonantie van dato vii. Octr., 1590. xv. gl."[3]

TRANSLATION.

Paid to Robert Browne, Englishman, and to his fellows, in all fifteen guilders, over and above the sum of the like amount, granted to him for having acted and played divers

---

[1] See Edward Alleyn's *Memoirs* ed. by J. P. Collier for the Shakespeare Society, p. 145.
[2] Ibid. p. 4.
[3] *Navorscher*. 4to. Amsterdam, Vol. viii (1858), p. 7.

comedies and histories, besides for having made divers leaps, by him performed as well in the presence of the burgomasters as before the community of this city, as appears by order of date, Oct. vii, 1590. xv. guilders.[1]

Robert Browne, and, if we accept the supposition that Richard Jones accompanied him, the latter also, must have returned to England from this visit to the Continent towards the end of 1590 or the beginning of 1591, in order to form the company intended for Germany. The meaning of the passage in Jones' letter to Alleyn: "but not by his meanes, for he is put to half a share, and to stay, hear, for they are all against his going," is not clear to us. The words immediately preceding, "I am to go over beyond the seeas w[h] Mr. Browne and the company" stand in direct contradiction with them, for according to them, Browne was the chief person in the enterprise, and how then could he remain at home, and why should he especially receive only half a share?[2]

In Henslowe's 'Diary' mention is twice made of a player Browne. Edward Browne whom we meet with in 1599[3] is certainly the same person as the Browne we found above among the Earl of Worcester's players. The second mention refers to the year 1596 "Lent unto them to feache Browne X[s]".[4] No Christian name is given here, and it is quite possible that we have our Robert Browne again before us, who appears to have been in England in 1596; in that year a Robert Browne joined the Embassy of the Earl of Lincoln, which Queen Elisabeth sent to the Court of Cassel to be present at the christening of the daughter of the Landgrave Maurice, who was named after the Queen. It is probable that Browne had acquired a knowledge of German, at that time undoubtedly a rare case in England, — and this must have made him appear to the Earl of Lincoln a very welcome companion on an Embassy to Germany. It is also not improbable that Browne on his first journey to Germany, which

---

[1] *Notes and Queries*, Sec. Series, Vol. vii, Jan. 8, 1859, p. 36. Translated from the *Navorscher*. Dr. Bell. *Shakespeare's Puck*, Vol. ii, p. 250 conjectures that the date appended to Lord Howard's passport ought to be 1590 instead of 1591 and that the Leyden document refers to the same journey and to the same company as the passport. I can see no plausible reason for the conjecture, and it is a fact that 1591 is the date of the original document. It is hardly credible that the date should be wrong in an official document, but where errors of date occur, the wrong year is generally the preceding one and not the next. At the beginning of a new year a hasty scribe may put down the date of the old one, but it would be quite inexplicable that in February 1590 a person in his senses should put down 1591!

[2] Malone knew this letter of Jones through a copy in his own possession, without, however, having the slightest idea of its importance for the history of the English stage. Mr. Collier also in his preliminary remarks to this letter in the *Alleyn Papers* regrets not having any clue to the date of the letter and to the identity of Mr. Browne. The missing clue to both will be found above. It is moreover rather surprising, that it never occured to Mr. Collier, who published the *Alleyn Papers* in 1843, that this Browne, and the Browne mentioned by himself in 1841 in the *Memoirs of Edward Alleyn*, might be one and the same person.

[3] *The Diary of Philippe Henslowe* ed. by J. P. Collier, for the Shakespeare Society, 1845, 8vo, p. 73.

[4] Ibid. p. 78. — It does not appear why Browne and another player 'Fleacher' [Fletcher?] mentioned in the same passage, were to be fetched.

[5] From the Hessen-Cassel State-Records. See Rommel, *Geschichte von Hessen*, Vol. vi, Cassel 1837, p. 390.

was his second to the Continent, had entered the service of the Landgrave Maurice (who reigned 1592—1627) as an actor, for that the Landgrave maintained English comedians at his court, is a fact which we shall prove presently. If we accept this conjecture, we may easily conceive that Browne, with his knowledge of the Court of Cassel, was able to render the Earl of Lincoln very valuable services. At all events Richard Jones had returned to England in 1594, if not earlier, as appears from Henslowe's 'Diary', p. 66. "Sowld Mr. Richard Jones, player, a manes gowne of peche coler, In grayne, the 2 of september 1594 to be payd by fyve shillinges a weeke imediatelye followinge &c." From 1594 to 1601 he is very often mentioned by Henslowe. In the year 1595 his name occurs in a list of players, which Mr. Collier believes to be that of the principal actors forming the company of the Earl of Nottingham. He undoubtedly belonged to the company connected with Henslowe and Edward Alleyn, and as this company for a period of two years, namely from June 1594 to July 1596, while the Globe Theatre was building, either played together with, or at least occupied the same theatre as, the company to which belonged Shakespeare, it is not improbable that Jones came into contact with Shakespeare, and assisted in the representation of his plays.

Thomas Sackville and John Breadstreat appear to have occupied a less prominent position among the members of the London stage. Neither of them is mentioned in Henslowe's Diary, nor have we been able to discover their names among the other orginal authorities respecting the London theatres of those times, which have appeared in print. On the other hand we have been so fortunate as to find both of them in Germany, and of Thomas Sackville at least we can state with certainty, that he entered the service of Duke Henry Julius of Brunswick, of whose connection with the English comedians we shall speak more at length presently.[1] In all probability the whole company mentioned in Jones' letter and Howard's passport, appeared on the stage of this Prince in Wolfenbüttel immediately after its arrival in Germany; and we must here refer once more to the conjectures we have expressed above, that these actors came to Germany in consequence of an express invitation. Unfortunately the exchequer-accounts of the years 1590—1601 are missing from the Brunswick Court Archives from which the following notices respecting Thomas Sackville have been taken;[2] and as Robert Browne, as shewn above, probably returned to England in 1596, and Richard Jones most certainly did so in 1594, the exchequer-accounts later than 1602 cannot give us any information respecting them. But, as will appear from the following entries in those accounts, Thomas Sackville remained in Germany at least till 1617, and we shall see indeed that he became completely domiciled at the Court of Wolfenbüttel. His name is spelt very differently at different places, but we may see from all of them that Sackville,

---

[1] This confirms the conjecture I have made in the article, *English Actors in Germany*, (see p. xxix, note), that the actors were connected with Duke Henry Julius.

[2] For the extracts following on the next page, which have never been published before, I am indebted to Mr. C. W. Sack of Brunswick, Registrar to the Duke of Brunswick.

and not Saxfield as in Lord Howard's passport, is the correct orthography.[1] In one document of the year 1597 of which we possess no further description, he is called "Thomas Sackefiel, Princely servant at Wolfenbüttel". In the same year, he and another English actor, who is named Edwardus Wakefiel [Wakefield] had a quarrel in a tavern in Brunswick. They had received a commission from a merchant in London "Wilhelm Thouwasen" (evidently a corruption) to draw on a woollendraper in Brunswick for 239 thalers. — The following are exact translations of extracts from the accounts of the Court of Brunswick, as far as they are still extant.

"1602. Aug. 30. At the verbal command of my most gracious Princess and Lady to Thomas Sacheviele, according as Her Princely Grace has graciously presented the English comedians, — 100 thalers.

Thomas Sacheviels at the verbal command of my Princely Grace and Lady to his bill for goods, on account, — 300 thalers.

1602. Oct. 1. Thomas Sacheviele on account for his purchases for the Princely kitchen, surgery, and wardrobe, — 375 thalers 14 gr.

1602. Oct. 2. At the gracious written order of His most Illustrious Highness, to the Court Tailor, Michael Wolframb, and to Thomas Sacheviele for the purchase of English and other black garments to the behoof of the funeral of the Princely widow, blessed be her memory, — 5000 thalers." (Wolframb and Sackville were sent to Leipsic for a similar purchase, and 3737 thalers were paid to them on the 31st of December.)

"1602. Decemb. 28. Edward Wakefield on account of Arnd von Wobersnow [?] having been accepted by the Princely Exchequer, — 160 thalers."

(From 1603 to 1607, the accounts are missing).

"1608. Feb. 2. At the command of His most Illustrious Highness, to the English Comedians as a gracious gratuity, — 100 thalers.

1608. Feb. 27. To the English Comedians as a gracious present, — 30 thalers.

To the English musicians, ditto, — 100 thalers.

To Thomas Sackefiel servant, given for three pieces of flesh-colour, and three pieces of blue silk ribbon, — 11 thalers."

(July 4, similar payments to Sackville.)

From this date to 1614, the accounts are missing; only in 1613, Thomas Sachuell is mentioned once in a payment of 180 florins.

"1615. May 8. To the English Comedians who have waited upon us for a time in our Princely Court, — 600 thalers."[2]

---

[1] Mr. W. J. Thoms, when he republished my letter to the *Athenæum* (see p. xxix, note) in *Notes and Queries*, at once conjectured that Saxfield would turn out to be Sackville. It is evident from the above extracts and from Sackville's own handwriting as given in a facsimile, that the conjecture was a happy one.

[2] The following names of artists are met with in the accounts of this year, but they were for the most part musicians under the celebrated Prætorius, who was leader of the band: Wessel Wessaliensis, Gregoris Hulvet, Jacob Mancino, Isaac Torall, Tonnies Bulgentern.

This proves that the English Comedians had left the Court, and had returned again for a time, a supposition which is confirmed by the entry of a payment of ten dollars, of the date of Sept. 10, 1614 to the 'Brandenburg Comedians'.

1616. Under Duke Frederick Ulric, Tonnies [sic] Sacheviel is met with in a list of payments, for 270 florins.

1617. In a list of payments of arrears of salary, Thomas Sachviel, with 2564 flor. 2 gr.[1]

The name does not appear again in the accounts after 1617; and it may be conjectured that Sackville joined the English Comedians who in 1617 entered the service of the Elector of Brandenburg. We shall have occasion to refer to them at a future page.

As far as regards John Breadstreet, I am able to state nothing more than that he must also have remained a long time in Germany. I owe the certainty with which I can affirm this fact, to a happy accident, which put in my hands a so-called 'Stammbuch' [Album amicorum] containing the autographs of Breadstreet and Sackville, the former with the date of Feb. 1, 1604, the latter with that of March 24, 1606. For the facsimile of these autographs see Plate i, No. 2 & 3. The place where they were written is unfortunately not given. John Breadstreet has germanised his name into 'Breidstrass', from which one is tempted to conclude that his real name was not Breadstreet, but Broadstreet. The orthography of proper names at that time was by no means fixed, and such an error as that in Lord Howard's passport was nothing uncommon. The owner of the album was a certain Johannes Cellarius, born in Nuremberg, Dec. 26, 1580, died in Genoa, April 17, 1619. He studied law, afterwards became steward to the Barons von Egg, whom, in 1610, he accompanied to Holland, France, England, and Italy. After his return he became Syndic of the city of Nuremberg. The album was commenced in the year 1599. The stamped leather binding bears the inscription "J. C. N. 1599". It contains a great number of autographs of celebrated scholars and nobles of the time, with their arms and other emblazonments, most of them dated from Altorf, Jena, Brunswick, and Nuremberg. The latest are those of the year 1606. Besides the two mentioned above, some names of other Englishmen[2] are also to be found among the autographs, only one of which deserves more especial mention here, as it leads to the conjecture that its author was also connected with our present subject. It is that of the celebrated English composer and lute-player, John Dowland, a contemporary of Shakespeare, whom the latter has immortalized in his 'Passionate Pilgrim.'

> If music and sweet poetry agree,
>   As they must needs (the sister and the brother)
> Then must the love be great 'twixt thee and me,
>   Because thou lov'st the one, and I the other.

---

[1] We find mentioned in the same list with him, Ludeke Eimens, Valentin Alslingk, Georg Hoffmeister. — But it does not appear whether they were actors, or to what profession they belonged.

[2] *e. g.* "Henricus Fitus de Bell Anglus, Jenae 26. Novemb. 1603."

> Dowland to thee is dear, whose heavenly touch
>   Upon the lute doth ravish human sense;
> Spenser to me, whose deep conceit is such,
>   As passing all conceit needs no defence.
> Thou lov'st to hear the sweet melodious sound,
>   That Phœbus' lute, the queen of music, makes;
> And I in deep delight am chiefly drown'd,
>   Whenas himself to singing he betakes.
> One god is god of both, as poets feign;
>   One knight loves both, and both in thee remain.

John Dowland must have visited Germany several times. In the year 1584 he travelled in France, and from thence went to Germany where he met with the most flattering reception at the courts of the Landgrave Maurice in Cassel, and of Duke Henry Julius of Brunswick in Wolfenbüttel. Perhaps Dowland is the lute-player whom Henry Julius sends to the Landgrave, in order that the latter may compare him with the other musicians. Maurice answers: the former can play good motets and madrigals, the latter is a better composer.[1] From Germany Dowland proceeded to Italy. In the year 1595 appeared in London his 'First booke of songs or ayres of foure parts, with tablature for the lute.' Shortly after this he repaired to the Danish Court. 'The second book of songs' is dated from Helsingör, the 1st of June 1600. As the autograph in the album cannot have been written before 1599, it may be safely assumed that Dowland visited Germany a second time: in 1603 he had returned to England. About this time appeared his work, 'Lachrimæ, or seven tears figured in seven passionate pavans', which became so popular, that from this time Dowland assumed the sobriquet of 'de Lachrimæ'.[2] The autograph in the album therefore must have been written after 1603. As it bears no date, it is possible that it owes its origin to the visit of Cellarius to England in the year 1610, but this is not probable, as the album contains no other inscription bearing a later date than 1606, and none which could have been written in England.

CHAPTER II.

Having now done our best endeavours to transmute the myth of the 'English Comedians' into palpable reality, it only remains for us to shew what influence they exercised upon German dramatic literature and the German theatre generally, both of which, as we have seen above, were still in their infancy. We may easily form some estimate of this influence from the fact, that the English comedians were the first professional actors who appeared

---

[1] Rommel, *Geschichte von Hessen*, Bd. vi, p. 417.

[2] The popularity of this work seems to have lasted a very long time, for in Thomas Middleton's comedy *No Wit no Help like a Woman's*, 1657, it is alluded to as follows:
"No, thou playest Dowland's Lachrimæ to thy master."

in Germany. If we only imagine the contrast between these practised members of the London stage and the journeyman-mechanics and schoolboys who composed the acting companies in Germany, we cannot be surprised that the appearance of the former put an end at once and for ever to the performances of the latter. Even if these did drag on a miserable existence in some parts of Germany, this was only owing to the circumstance that the foreign companies, which were at first only isolated phenomena, could not be immediately known throughout the whole country. But wherever they came, they undoubtedly bore off the victory. Independently of their services in driving away the old dramatic subjects, their skill and security on the stage, the greater experience with which they availed themselves of all their resources, their more correct calculation of effects, in short all the advantages which the professional artist has over the amateur, must have procured them a willing audience. Hitherto the performances were not intended for the sake of the spectators, the performers were themselves the primary object of the plays. With the English comedians the first and exclusive object was the gratification of the public.[2] The drama left its narrow local private sphere, and entered a public one, became an integral part of public life, while the public obtained their rights, and the theatre became a public interest. Now indeed an interest in the dramatic art may be observed among the German princes; they vie with one another in inviting the foreigners to their courts, and the first court theatres arise in Germany. The enormous advantages which accrued to dramatic literature as also to the public from this thorough revolution in all matters appertaining to the theatre, have either been entirely overlooked or very much underestimated by writers on the history of literature. In their blind zeal against the foreign element, which was thus introduced into the dramatic literature, they regret the loss in naiveté[2] with which the native dramatists up to that time had certainly treated the people very lavishly, but they forgot that by the reflection of this naiveté alone, which is always rather a lively element among the masses, the stage never could become those boards which represent the world. It is true that with these English comedians scenes of blood and horror became quite naturalized upon the German stage, that the coarse jokes of the clown must often have offended the ears of modest maidens, and that the English actors would have done well to take Hamlet's warning to heart; but what are all these drawbacks in comparison to the advantages which the dramatic life derived from this invasion of the theatre? And then for the tales and stories of Boccaccio, Fiorentini, and Straparola &c. the frivolous subjects of which had passed into the drama, were they not already in the hands of the people in numerous translations? And were the obscenities of the Shrovetide Plays, which surpassed everything that the English had accomplished in the same di-

---

[1] See Ed. Devrient, *Geschichte* etc. Vol. i, p. 166.

[2] *e. g.* Karl Goedeke, *Grundrifs* etc. Vol. i, p. 407, who has nothing else to say of the transformation of the German drama which is owing to the English Comedians, than that with it "the old strict decency was lost" ("die alte strenge Ehrbarkeit ging verloren").

rection, so very remote, that we are justified in laying the corruption of taste to the account of the latter? The real corruption took place at a later period, when the companies contained very few English, and the rude soldiery of the thirty year's war had poisoned the German morals. It is true, the refinement of the popular taste formed no part of the design of those foreign companies; their sole object was to please the public, and it may be assumed that to this end they are far more likely to have accommodated themselves to the state of things as they found it, than to have made any very arduous endeavours to introduce a new taste. For a number of years they travelled from one end of Germany to the other, and the great popularity which they everywhere enjoyed is an evidence of their having possessed some other hold on public favour than the coarse excitement of the masses. Even if Germany had gained nothing more through these innovators than an acquaintance with the subjects of Shakespeare and of the early English stage, in whatever form they were presented to the public, — this alone would have been an ample compensation for any loss in innocence and naiveté, for which some writers would like to make them answerable.

The first dramatic author of Germany in whom we can perceive the influence of the English comedians, is the above-mentioned Duke Henry Julius of Brunswick (born 1563, died 1613) who was the first to maintain a regular theatre at his court, the establishment of which was in all probability contemporaneous with the first appearance of the English actors in Germany. Henry Julius, like Maurice of Hesse, was one of the most distinguished princes of his time, who himself a scholar, paid great attention to all subjects of intellectual interest. As a child he had been a sort of prodigy, devoted to the arts and sciences from his earliest years, and the admiration of the learned, while still a tender stripling. At the age of ten years he argued with great brilliancy in a theological disputation. In the year 1576, when only thirteen years of age, he was appointed by the Emperor Maximilian as Rector of the University of Helmstedt, which had been just founded, and entered upon his office with a speech superabounding in learning. Soon after this he occupied the episcopal residence in the bishopric of Halberstadt. In the year 1589 he succeeded to the throne, and in 1590 married his second wife, Elisabeth, daughter of Frederick the second, King of Denmark.[1] Henry Julius entertained a very decided love for the theatre. We may safely presume that he possessed an intimate acquaintance with the works of Hans Sachs and Frischlin, as well as other dramatic writers of the time. During the journeys which he made to other German Courts a little before his accession to the throne, he probably became acquainted with their theatrical representations. The manner in which in 1590 he introduced himself to his betrothed is a characteristic trait of his love of theatricals.[2] He left his attendants behind him half a day's journey from Copenhagen, proceeded to the palace

---

[1] Herman Grim, *Das Theater des Herzogs Heinrich Julius zu Wolfenbüttel* in his *Essays*, Hannover 1859, p. 144, makes the Duke marry the *daughter* of Christian iv. But in 1590 Christian iv was only thirteen years old. The Princess Elisabeth, who became the wife of Henry Julius, was the *sister* of Christian iv.

[2] For the narrative following above we are also indebted to Mr. C. W. Sack of Brunswick.

of Kronenburg in the disguise of a foreign pedlar, and offered all sorts of jewelry for sale. When the Princess bride wished to pay for the things she had selected, the pedlar declared they were only to be sold at the price of a bridal night. The answer excited great indignation, and the pedlar was thrown into prison, which, to keep up the farce, he took very quietly. Upon the arrival of the Duke's suite, but not before, the comedy was brought to a very merry termination. As may easily be conceived, there were great festivities at the Danish Court, and as we have shewn above that English actors had already become quite domesticated there, it may safely be assumed that if any of them were still in Copenhagen in 1590, they were not idle on such an occasion. Frederick the second, the father of the Princess Elisabeth, the bride of Henry Julius, to whom Heywood's information refers, (see p. xxiii), and who in 1586 sent the English actors to the Elector of Saxony, died indeed as early as 1588. But Heywood probably only intended to say that Frederick had first invited the comedians, which does not exclude the supposition that they remained longer at that court. Under the reign of Frederick the second, and for a short time after his death, under the reign of the minor, Christian the fourth, a very lively intercourse was maintained between the Courts of Denmark and England. The Princess Anna, a younger daughter of Frederick the second, and afterwards therefore the sister in law of Duke Henry Julius, had been selected as the future bride of James the sixth of Scotland, afterwards James the first of England. Frederick sent an embassy to Edinburgh for the purpose of opening the negociations. This embassy must have passed through England and touched London on its route. Queen Elisabeth threw obstacles in the way of the intended union, as she was anxious for a marriage between James the sixth and Catharine of Navarre. In the mean time the marriage with the Danish Princess was arranged, and in 1589 James sent an embassy to Copenhagen to fetch the young bride. The ship which conveyed the Princess, was wrecked on the coast of Norway, and unfavorable winds obliged her to remain in Opslo, to which place James hurried to consummate his nuptials. In February 1590 James repaired to Copenhagen with his young wife, and was present at the marriage of Henry Julius, who had now become his brother in law. This very intimate connection between two princes, both possessing considerable literary culture, probably exercised some influence on the Wolfenbüttel stage at a later period, after James had ascended the English throne. Also the visit which Duke Frederick of Wirtemberg paid the English Court in 1592 may have had some connection with that stage, for Henry Julius stood on terms of friendly intercourse with that Prince also, on which point the accounts of the expences of the Court of Brunswick contain many notices.[1]

But whatever may have been the manner in which Henry Julius made the acquaintances of the English comedians, it is certain that he entertained several of them at his Court shortly after his return, and for no very short period, for we have seen from the Brunswick exchequer accounts that even after 1612, to which year Heywood's notice refers,

---

[1] Communicated by Mr. C. W. Sack.

English actors are still mentioned. After the return of the Duke with his young wife, his wedding was again celebrated in Wolfenbüttel, at that time the residence of the Dukes of Brunswick, on which occasion there was a display of splendour and magnificence such as had rarely been witnessed before. Banquets and representations of all kinds took place. Unfortunately we are not acquainted with any details of these nuptial festivities. Pastor Voelkerling, the only contemporary chronicler who mentions them, only remarks, that numerous fencers in great splendour tried their skill with foreign fencers, and that similar magnificence had never been witnessed before in Germany. Here we must again regret the loss of the Court Exchequer accounts of the years 1590—1601, as we should probably have ascertained from them whether foreign actors were present or not. The Duke himself was the author of ten plays, nine of which were printed in the years 1593—1594.[1] It is probable that some of them had been written at an earlier period, and there is every reason to conjecture that one of them, and indeed the most important, the 'Tragi-comedy of Susanna'[2] was acted in 1590 on the occasion of these nuptial festivities. Perhaps indeed it was composed for this occasion. From the terms with which the prologue commences, it is evident that a very numerous assemblage of all classes was present. It

---

[1] As far as has been ascertained as yet, all the poetical attempts of Henry Julius belong to the department of the drama. We have no other authorities for determining the time at which they were written, than the dates of the printed editions. According to these, all the ten pieces with which we are acquainted, were composed in the years 1593 and 1594, before Julius had attained his thirty first year. Their titles are as follows:

1. *Tragi-comoedia von der Susanna.* 1593. (*Tragi-comedy of Susanna.*) Another version also published in 1593.
2. *Tragoedia von einem Buler vnd Bulerin.* 1593. (*Tragedy of a lover and his mistress.*)
3. *Comoedia von einem Weibe.* 1593. (*Comedy of a woman.*)
4. *Comoedia von einem Wirthe.* 1593. (*Comedy of a landlord.*)
5. *Tragoedia von einem vngerathnen Sohn.* 1594. (*Tragedy of a profligate son.*)
6. *Tragoedia von einer Ehebrecherin.* 1594. (*Tragedy of an adulteress.*) There is a rhyming version of this play by Joh. Olorinus Variscus [Joh. Sommer]. 1605.
7. *Tragica comoedia von einem Wirthe oder Gastgeber.* 1594. (*Tragi-comedy of a host, or feast-giver.*)
8. *Comoedia von einem Edelmann.* 1594. (*Comedy of a nobleman.*)
9. *Comoedia von Vincentio Ladislao.* 1594. (*Comedy of Vincentio Ladislao.*) Of this piece there is a rhyming version by Elias Herlicius. 1601.
10. *Der Fleischhauer.* (*The Butcher.*) Published for the first time in Dr. Holland's edition, from the original manuscript.

A collected edition was published in 1855 for the Stuttgart Literary Society by Dr. W. L. Holland. It is entitled: *Die Schauspiele des Herzogs Heinrich Julius von Braunschweig nach alten Drucken und Handschriften, herausg. von Dr. Wilh. Ludw. Holland.* 8vo. Stuttgart 1855.

[2] *Tragica Comoedia Hibeldeha von der Susanna wie dieselbe von zweyen Alten, Ehebruchs halber, fälschlich beklaget, auch vnschüldig verurtheilet, aber entlich durch sonderliche Schickung Gottes des Almechtigen von Daniele errettet, vnd die beiden Alten zum Tode verdammet worden, mit 34. Personen. Gedruckt zu Wolffenbüttel, Anno nach Christi Geburt M. D. xciii.* 8vo. (*Tragi-comedy of Susanna, how she was wrongly accused of adultery by two old men and innocently condemned, but finally saved through the Grace of God by Daniel, and how the two old men were condemned to die.*) [The word 'Hibeldeha', which is to be found on the title-pages of all the Duke's plays, means: Henricus Iulius Brunsvicensis Et Luneburgensis Dux Episcopatus Halberstadensis Antistes.] In Dr. Holland's edition p. 1—169. A second edition "*aufs new kürtzer verfasset.*" Ibid. M. D. XCIII. 8vo. In Dr. Holland's edition p. 170—208.

begins by addressing the "Most Serene, High-born, Gracious Princes and Lords, also Princesses and Ladies," and then the "Noble Worships, honorable, learned, estimable and most gracious Lords and Squires, and dear friends." The first scene then contains extremely copious and lengthy admonitions how a young woman ought to behave herself towards her husband. It appears to have been composed for the particular occasion, and has only a very slight connection with the piece itself. This is all the more evident from the circumstance, that a second edition of the same piece, which also appeared in 1593, does not contain this scene, and that the prologue has received a very different form, through the omission of the longwinded address to the audience, as also of other passages which had evidently been intended only for the particular occasion. There is every probability therefore in favour of the supposition that the 'Susanna' was the first piece which the Duke wrote, and as it bears evident traces of English influence, we are justified in concluding that he had already become acquainted with the English comedians at the time he composed this piece.[1] The 'Susanna' is a subject which had been repeatedly treated in Germany by others before Henry Julius,[2] and also in England Thomas Garter's 'Commodye of the moste vertuous and godlye Susanna' had appeared in print in 1578, and had been entered in the books of the Stationer's Company as early as 1568—1569. The Duke's piece contains many features of the German and Latin versions but differs from them entirely in the dramatic arrangement. Perhaps these variations may manifest some approximation to the English play, with which I am not acquainted. It is sufficient to observe that the Tragi-comedy of the Duke's contains things which had never been introduced be-

---

[1] For much of what I have said on the 'Susanna' as well as for the remarks that follows on the position of the Duke as a dramatic author in general, I am indebted to Herman Grimm, *Das Theater des Herzogs Heinrich Julius von Braunschweig*, in his "*Essays*," 8vo. Hannover 1859. I must confine myself to this general mention of the work, as I should otherwise be obliged to refer to it perpetually. — The Memoir is by far the best that has ever been written on the Duke as a dramatic author, and it is to be regretted that the subject has not received a more comprehensive treatment at Mr. Grimm's hands. What he has given is more a sketch than an "Essay". The connection between the *Ehebrecherin* and the *Merry Wives of Windsor*, though alluded to by Dr. Holland, appears to have escaped Mr. Grimm.

[2] This subject had been brought upon the stage as early as the fifteenth century, as appears from a German piece of that time, the manuscript of which is at Vienna. See Goedike, *Grundrifs* etc., Vol. i, p. 93. In 1535 Paul Rebhun composed *Ein geistlich spiel võ der gotfürchtigen vñ keuschen Frawen Susanen*. 4to. Zwickaw 1536. 8vo. Wittemberg 1537. 8vo. Zwickaw 1544. (*A religious play of the god-fearing and chaste maid Susanna.*) 1559: Leonard Stöckel *Historia von Susanna in Tragoeden weise gestellet zu vbung der Jugent zu Bartfeld in Vngern*. 8vo. Wittenberg 1559. (*The history of Susanna, set forth in form of a tragedy for the practice of youth, at Bartfeld in Hungary.*) Joachim Leseberg wrote a 'Susanna' in the Low German dialect, 1609. Another 'Susanna' was acted in Bremen as early as 1563, and, as it seems, also in Low German dialect. See Duntze's *Geschichte der freien Stadt Bremen*, Vol. iv. 8vo. Bremen 1851. There is a 'Susanna' in Latin by Xystus Betulius (Sixtus Birk), 8vo. Augustæ Vindel. 1537, Coloniæ 1538, Tiguri 1538, Coloniæ 1539, Aug. Vindel. no date, and 1564 — and by Nicodemus Frischlin 1578. The latter was translated into German by Jacob Frischlin 1589, 8vo, and by Andreas Calagius, 8vo. Gœrlitz 1604. A 'Susanna' in the Danish language was also acted before Frederick the second, the father in law of Henry Julius, but probably a translation of the Latin of Xystus Betulius: *Susanna, Comico-tragedia i danske Rim*. 4to. Kjobnhaven 1578. The author is Peter Jensen Hegellund.

fore in any German play, and which evince a knowledge of theatrical requirements which the Duke could not have derived from any of his predecessors, or from the arrangements of the German stage of his own times. He has displayed great skill in the manner in which he has interwoven an underplot with the principal subject, a feat which had not been successfully accomplished by any of his predecessors or contemporaries, not even by Jacob Ayrer, who, as will be seen hereafter, wrote under the influence of the English comedians. In Ayrer's works, these episodes advance by the side of the principal action, without any inward connection with it, while, on the other hand, in Henry Julius, they are made subservient to the development of the whole piece. But an entirely new character in the 'Susanna' of the Duke's is the fool, John Clant, who also plays the principal part. Even the name is nothing more than a transformation of the English 'clown'. Merryandrews are also to be met with among the Duke's predecessors, but it was first on the Wolfenbüttel stage that an independent part was allotted to the clown. Before that time, it had not been prescribed to the fool, what he had to say; he was not involved in the action of the piece, but it was left entirely to him to amuse the public in any way he thought proper, just as in the case of the court-fools outside the theatre. The same liberties which the fool enjoyed in society were also allowed him on the stage; no part was written for him, — as representative of the life off the stage, he interrupted the action of the piece, and destroyed the illusion of the spectators. He is rarely mentioned among the 'dramatis personæ' of the old pieces. Sometimes he appears as speaker of the prologue, and sometimes we meet with a marginal note: 'here the fool says something.' But in Wolfenbüttel the fool belonged to the body of the performers; he no longer interferes in the action according to his own will and fancy, as a sort of mediator between stage and audience, but, like the other actors, has his own prescribed part to perform. This premeditated introduction of a comic figure is very striking; but what is far more so both in the 'Susanna' and the other pieces of the Duke's, is the dramatic progress of the dialogue, and the theatrical construction of the action. In these points he imitated no one, for no one before him understood how to adapt a work for the stage in such a careful and masterly manner. One thing proceeds naturally out of another, and carries the plot onwards; the scenes have their point, — the progress of the intrigue has its ever-increasing interest. This merit of the Wolfenbüttel pieces is so striking, that notwithstanding the fact that some of them are still extant in the Duke's own hand, notwithstanding the knowledge which he possessed, and the utter absence of any evidence to shew who besides himself could have written these pieces, it appears highly probable that some one of the actors must have assisted him in giving his compositions that theatrical finish which evinces a greater acquaintance with routine, than even Henry Julius, with all his talent, could ever have given them without a long practical experience of the requirements of the stage. As far as concerns the 'Susanna' of the Duke, we will only observe that a piece of the same name belonged to the Repertory of the English comedians, for in 1602 they performed in Ulm a piece 'Of the Prophet Daniel, the chaste Susanna, and the two judges in

Israel',[1] and in a poem printed in 1597, referring to the English comedians, which we shall give at a future page, the 'Susanna' is expressly mentioned. If now Henry Julius really received the aid and counsel of an actor in the composition of his piece, it cannot have been from a German, for up to that time, nowhere in Germany had there been the slightest appearance of any such knowledge of theatrical management as that which appears in the 'Susanna'. We have therefore good reason to assume the presence of English influence, and consequently of English actors in Wolfenbüttel at the time when the play was composed and performed; for we have no notices of other foreign actors in Germany at that time, and should hardly be justified in attributing to any others such an influence as that above-mentioned. If the wedding festivities in Wolfenbüttel took place in 1591, and not in 1590, on which point there is no certain information, our four wanderers under Robert Browne's management may have assisted in the performances. We have above seen one of them in the service of the Duke, and it is highly probable that the whole company on its first arrival in Germany immediately repaired to the court of Wolfenbüttel. That English actors had been there, long before 1597, (see p. xxxiv), may be safely concluded from a piece of the Duke himself. In the tragedy of 'An Adulteress' which appeared in print in 1594,[2] but may have been written several years previously, we meet with the following passage in Act II, sc. 3:

Gallichorœa. Ich hette es dir Teutsch genung gesagt, wenn du es sonst verstehen woltest.
Johan Bouset. Ick bin ein Englisch Mann, ick en son dat dudsch sprake niet wal verstahn.

[*Gallichorœa.* I should have told you in plain enough German, if you had been willing to understand it.
John Bouset. I am an English man, I do not well understand any one that speaks German.]

John Bouset, the clown, does not play here the part of an Englishman, but it is perfectly clear, the words have been put into his mouth only to excuse to the audience his unintelligible pronunciation. We have already called attention to the fact, that the jester in the Duke's pieces is a copy of the English Clown.[3] This becomes still more evident, when we consider that a large proportion of the English theatrical jokes turns upon

---

[1] v. Alvensleben, *Allgemeine Theaterchronik*, 1832, No. 158.

[2] *Tragedia Hibeldeha von einer Ehebrecherin, wie die jren Man drey Mal betreucht, aber zu letzt ein schrecklich Ende genommen habe. Mit acht Personen.* 8vo. Wolfenbüttel 1594. (*The tragedy of Hibeldeha, of an adulteress, how she betrayed her husband three times, but at last came to a dreadful end.*) In Dr. Holland's edition p. 401—444. A rhyming version has been given by Joh. Olorinus Variscus [Joh. Sommer]: *Tragoedie von geschwinder Weiberlist einer Ehebrecherin .... sehr kurtzweilig, bossierlich vnd lustig beschrieben, vnd vffm Braunschweigischen Fürstlichen Haufs vnd Festung Wolffenbüttel in Prosa agiret. Nun aber auff vieler Begehr in lustige anmuthige Reym mit Fleifs gesetzt.* 8vo. Magdeburg, Joh. Francke, s. a. Preface dated 1605. (*A tragedy of the quick female cunning of an adulteress .... very amusingly, comically, and pleasantly described, and publicly acted in prose, in the Brunswick Princely House and Castle of Wolfenbüttel. But now at the desire of many persons carefully done into pleasant rhymes.*) In Dr. Holland's edition p. 555—639.

[3] The various names assigned to him are: Johan Clant, Johan Bouset, Bousset and Bouschet. Is Bouset perhaps a corruption from "*bossed*"?

the distortion and misunderstanding of words, a species of artifice which was very largely employed in the jokes of the Wolfenbüttel clowns.

The connection of the Wolfenbüttel with the old English stage becomes still more manifest from the general colouring of the Duke's pieces, as, for instance, the 'Tragedy of a profligate son'.[1] It is an accumulation of brutal murders. A boy's body is cut open on the stage, the murderer drinks his blood, roasts his heart on a coal fire, and eats it. Then he drives a nail into his father's head, strangles his cousin, cuts his mother's throat, and then at a revel suddenly finds the heads of the murdered upon the dishes instead of viands. Who can help being reminded by this of Titus Andronicus in the first form of the piece, before Shakespeare had handled the subject, the leading features of which we probably have before us in the German piece which was played by the English comedians in Germany? — Afterwards the murdered persons appear as ghosts, drive the murderer mad, and carry him off. Is it possible to read this, without being reminded of Macbeth, Richard the second, and Cymbeline?

But the Duke's 'Comedy of Vincentius Ladislaus'[2] leads us still more directly to Shakespeare. It contains the rough prototype of Benedick in 'Much Ado about Nothing'. How very close the connection is between the two pieces will appear from the following passages.

MUCH ADO ABOUT NOTHING, ACT I, SC. 1.

Beatrice. I pray you is signior Montanto returned from the wars or no?
Mess. I know none of that name, lady: there was none such in the army of any sort.
Leon. What is he that you ask for, niece?
Herc. My cousin signior Benedick of Padua.
Mess. O! he is returned, and as pleasant as ever he was.
Beatr. He set up his bills here in Messina, and challenged Cupid at the flight; and my uncle's fool, reading the challenge, subscribed for Cupid, and challenged him at the bird-bolt. — I pray you how many has he killed and eaten in these wars? But how many hath he killed? for, indeed, I promised to eat all of his killing.
Leon. Faith, niece, you tax signior Benedick too much; but he'll be meet with you, I doubt it not.
Mess. He has done good service, lady, in these wars.

---

[1] *Tragoedia. Hiehabdel. Von einem vngeratenen Sohn, welcher vnmenschliche vnd vnerhörte Mordthaten begangen, auch endlich neben seinen Mit-Consorten ein erbaermlich schrecklich vnd grewlich Ende genommen hat. Mit 18. Personen. Gedruckt zu Wolfenbüttel Anno 1594.* 8vo. (*Tragedy of a profligate son, who committed inhuman and unheard of murders, and at last with his consorts came to a miserable, shocking, and cruel end. With 18 persons. Printed at Wolfenbüttel 1594.*) In Dr. Holland's edition p. 335—400.

[2] *Comoedia Hidbelepihal von Vincentio Ladislao Sacrapa (sic) von Mantua Kempfern zu Roſs vnd Fueſs, weiland des edlen vnd ehrnuesten, auch manhafften vnnd streitbaren Barbarossae Bellicosi von Mantua, Rittern zu Malta ehelichen nachgelassenen Sohn. Mit zwölf Personen.* 8vo. Wolfenbüttel M.D.XCIV. (*Comedy of Vincentius Ladislaus Satrap of Mantua, Combatant on horseback and on foot, lawful son of the noble and honourable and warlike Barbarossa Bellicosus of Mantua, Knight of Malta. With 12 Persons.*) In Dr. Holland's edition, p. 507—554. — Another edition 1599, ibid. 8vo. A rhyming edition is by Elias Herlicius Cicensis, 8vo. Wittemberg 1601. In Dr. Holland's edition, p. 641—734.

Beatr. You had musty victual, and he hath holp to eat it: he is a very valiant trencher-man; he hath an excellent stomach.

Mess. And a good soldier too, lady.

COMOEDIA VON VINCENTIO LADISLAO, ACTUS PRIMI, SCENA PRIMA.

Lakey. Es gehet mir jetzundt eben, als wie man im Sprichwort saget: Wer viel newe Herrn sucht, pfleget sich selten zuuerbessern, Sölches befinde ich jetzundt auch. Zuuor hatte ich einen guten vnd frommen Junckern, Jetzo aber bin ich bey einen gekommen, das ich schier nicht weis, wie ich mit jhme daranne bin. Er gibt wünderliche vnd seltzame anschlege für, In seinem sinn lest er sich bedüncken, es sey niemandts klüger als er. Mich soll doch gelüsten, was er hie suchen wil, Ich wuste ja nicht, was er hie zuschaffen haben möchte, Es wäre dann, das er sich hier ein zeitlang wolte für einen Narren äffen vnd vexieren lassen, Wie solches dann zu Herrn Hofe gemein ist. Er wil heute hier kommen, wird auch vielleicht nicht lange aus sein, Vnd hat mich vorher geschicket jhm die Herberge zubestellen etc.

SCENA SECUNDA.

Adrian. Wo wanderstu her Lackey? Wem stehest du zu?

Lackey. Ich stehe meinem Junckern zu. Vnd wolte jhm gerne Herberge bestellen.

Adrian. Wer ist dan dein Juncker?

Lackey. Es ist ein stadtlicher vom Adel, vnd ein Kempffer zu Rofs vnd Fues, Sein Name ist, Vincentius Ladislaus Satrapa von Mantua etc.

SCENA QUINTA.

Lackey. Ich weis nicht, was mein Juncker vor ein seltzamer Man ist. Dan damit ja jederman zum anfang hier erfahren möge, das er ein Narr sey, hat er seinen Namen auff einen Zettel schreiben lassen, Vnd mir befohlen, Denselben an die Thür zuschlagen. Nun bin ich sein Diener, Ich mus thun, was er mir beuehlt, Ich wils anschlagen, Was gehets mir die lenge an, Aber mit der weyse werde ich nicht alt bey jhme werden. (Der Lackey schlegt den Zettel an, darauff stehet geschrieben, wie volget: Vincentius Ladislaus Satrapa von Mantua, Kempffer zu Rofs vnd Fues, weilandt des Edlen, vnd Ehrnuesten, auch Manhafften vnd Streitbaren Barbarossæ Bellicosi von Mantua, Ritters zu Malta, Ehelicher nachgelassener Sohn, mit seinen bey sich habenden Dienern vnd Pferden.)

TRANSLATION.

COMEDY OF VINCENTIUS LADISLAUS. ACT I, SC. 1.

Servant. It is with me now, just as they say in the proverb: He who often seeks a new master, seldom betters himself. That is just what I find now. Formerly I had a kind gentle squire for a master, but now I am with such a one, that I can't conceive how I am ever to get on with him. He puts forth such strange and curious projects. In his own opinion he fancies there is no one cleverer than himself. I should like very much to know what he wants here. I can't imagine what he can have to do here unless he wanted to get himself laughed at and jeered at for a time as a fool, as is the common at princes' courts. He means to be here to-day, and perhaps will be here before long, and has sent me on before to secure him a lodging etc.

SCENE 2.

Adrian. Where are you going, servant? and whom do you belong to?

Servant. I belong to my master, and should be glad to engage a lodging for him.

Adrian. Who is your master then?

Servant. He is a citizen of quality, and a Combatant on horseback and on foot. His name is Vincentius Ladislaus, Satrap of Mantua, etc.

Scene 5.

Servant. I don't know what strange sort of man my master is. For that everybody may learn here at once that he is a fool, he has had his name written on a bill, and ordered me to fasten it up against the door. Now I am his servant. I must do what he orders me. I will fasten it up; what is it to me after all? But after this fashion, I shan't grow grey in his service. (The servant fastens up the bill, upon which there is written as follows: Vincentius Ladislaus, Satrap of Mantua, Combatant on horseback and on foot, lawful son of the noble and honorable and courageous, of the late warlike Barbarossa Bellicosus of Mantua, Knight of Malta, with the servants and horses that attend him.)

The passage in Beatrice's speech 'He set up his bills here in Messina' is happily illustrated by this scene. Now we know exactly what it was she meant to say. What Beatrice wanted to make Benedick appear, Vincentius is in reality: a boastful Bramarbas, whose cowardice is a match for his bragging, the butt of the jeers of all the world, and in all his adventures always the dupe, the typical 'Capitano' of the old Italian stage, a quintessence of the lying stories of all the quarters of the world, all of which however he outdoes in bombast.[1] Such a coincidence as that apparent in the above parallel cannot be purely accidental; and besides this, there is another point of resemblance between the two pieces. The real humour of the scenes between Benedick and Beatrice consists in each of them having been separately persuaded that the other is in love with him or her. There is a similar incident in Vincentius. The braggadocio is talked into the belief that the beautiful Angelica is in love with him. He of course falls into the snare, and the Duke promises that the consummation shall take place the same evening. A page in disguise represents the bride. The fool prepares the bed by stretching a sheet over a tub full of water. Vincentius mounts the bed, falls into the water, and is summarily dismissed with ignominy and disgrace. Slight as the connection may appear between all this and the charming love passages between Benedick and Beatrice, the gist of the intrigue in both cases is the trick played on a man possessing an exaggerated opinion of his own merits by making him believe that a girl is in love with him. The Vincentius Ladislaus was unquestionably written and performed long before 'Much Ado about Nothing' which first appeared in print in 1600, and is only to be met with in the books of the Stationer's Company in that year. May then Shakespeare have become acquainted with this piece of the Duke's through the actors on their return to England, and has he metamorphosed the clumsy braggart Vincentius into the amiable Benedick, whose apparent frivolity and conceit were not able to resist the promptings of his heart? Such an assumption could hardly be ventured without better evidence than that which we have adduced, and there is no other at present forthcoming. A far more pro-

---

[1] On the type of the 'Capitano' who under different forms appears on the stages of all the countries of Europe, see Herman Grimm, *Das Theater* etc. p. 164—169.

bable supposition is, that both authors took their matter either from an old English piece derived from an Italian source, or directly from an Italian source with which we are unacquainted. This common origin probably contains both the intrigues which in 'Much Ado about Nothing' are worked up together, and of which Henry Julius has taken the subordinate one, and made it his principal plot, while Jacob Ayrer, who probably took his 'Beautiful Phænicia'[1] from the same piece, has worked up both intrigues. When we come to the consideration of this piece, we shall treat more fully of the existing sources, and shall find that there must be some common origin hitherto unknown to us, whence Shakespeare, Henry Julius, and Ayrer derived their matter.

Still more intimately connected with Shakespeare is the Duke's already mentioned 'Tragedy of an Adulteress', the plot of which entirely agrees with that of the 'Merry Wives of Windsor'. A man 'Gallichoræa' [Hahnrei, i. e. a cuckold] employs a student to put his wife's virtue to the test, and endeavours to surprise her, but is always made a fool of through his wife's cunning, and obliged to beat an ignominious retreat. But he also has another mortification, for the student, who has no idea that the go-between is really the husband of his lady-love, always reports to him his successes with the fair one, and the tricks she has played her husband. For the better comprehension of this piece, and that the reader may be able to judge of the degree of resemblance between the two pieces, we annex a short sketch of the plot of the 'Tragedy of an Adulteress'.

Act. i, sc. 1. Enter Gallichoræa, the merchant. He complains that he has reason to doubt his wife's fidelity. He wishes for an opportunity to put it to the proof. Scene 2. Enter John Bousset, the servant, [the clown], Gallichoræa alludes to his wife's infidelity, and at last proposes to his servant that he should sleep with her. If he succeed with her, he is not to suffer any punishment, but, on the contrary, to receive a reward. John Bousset steadfastly declines this proposal. Act ii, sc. 1. Enter Pamphilus, a poor student. He complains of his poverty, and wished he could meet with some goodnatured man in this foreign town, who would assist him. Enter Gallichoræa, and John Bousset. The former enters into conversation with Pamphilus, and advises him to try his fortune with the women. Pamphilus agrees, and Gallichoræa proposes his own wife, but without informing Pamphilus that she is so. Pamphilus is to tell Gallichoræa the next morning, what success he has had. Then follows a conversation between Gallichoræa and John Bousset, which however does not advance the action of the piece. Sc. 4. Gallichoræa and John Bousset. Enter Scortum, the wife of the former. Her husband pretends that he must go into the country, and in all probability will not return that night. He then tells the fool that he will conceal himself in a house, and surprise his wife in the middle of the night. Sc. 4. Scortum says, that she is quite aware that her husband only wants to try her. She only hopes that some handsome young fellow may visit her, and when her husband comes home she will manage matters so that he knows nothing about it, for it is a trade in which she has

---

[1] See p. 77—112 of the present volume.

had plenty of practice. Sc. 6. Pamphilus comes before the house, entices the wife out with his music, and then begs for a night's lodging, which, in the next scene, is willingly granted him. Sc. 8. Enter Gallichoræa with the clown. The former demands admittance. After some words have been exchanged through the closed door, the wife opens it, and tells her husband she did not like to do so at first, lest it might be some stranger who wanted to deceive her. While they are going into the house, Pamphilus jumps out of the window, and having stated, that he had been appointed to come again the following evening, runs away. Act iii, sc. 1 and 2. John Bousset betrays the infidelity of the wife to neighbour Adrian, who had heard the noise in the night. Gallichoræa joins them, and persuades the neighbour not to believe the clown. Sc. 3. Pamphilus relates to Gallichoræa his adventure of the previous night, and how he had escaped when the husband arrived. The wife had shewn him a hiding-place under the window, and after her husband had searched the house for some time, she had led him up stairs, and then called out to him in a loud voice, 'Now sweetheart, go, it is time.' This had been the signal agreed upon for Pamphilus to escape unperceived. He then promises to give Gallichoræa an account of his next visit to the wife. In the next scene the fool derides the husband. Sc. 5. Gallichoræa tells Scortum that he is now going away again, and will not allow himself to be detained by strangers, as yesterday. His wife is very anxious about him, and charges John Bousset to look very attentively after his master. After they have both left her, she wishes that the young fellow of yesterday may soon return; she will contrive to outwit her husband, if he should come back again. Sc. 6. Pamphilus comes, and is admitted into the house. Act iv, sc. 1—3 Gallichoræa and the fool come before the house again, and demand admittance. A conversation follows, just as on the former occasion, and they are admitted. Some time after, the husband comes out again, and opens the shutter from the outside in order to discover the lover. The wife comes out to him, and says: "O Lord, my dear husband, what are you doing here? I do believe you think I have a lover in the house." Gallichoræa confesses, that he certainly does entertain that opinion, upon which his wife answers: "If I did not wish to be honest, I would blind you so, that you should know nothing about it, not even if you were already in the house." Gallich.: "How would you manage that?" Scortum: "I would manage it so. (She covers his eyes with his cloak.) Do you see that, my dove?" In the mean time, Pamphilus jumps out of the door, and runs away. Act v, sc. 1. Neighbour Adrian has heard the noise again the night before. Gallichoræa endeavours to bring him off the right road, but Adrian still believes that Scortum's infidelity is at the bottom of it. Sc. 2. Gallichoræa complains to the fool, that he is now worse off than before, in as much as formerly he still had his doubts whether his wife really did play him false, but now he knows that she is no better than she should be, and yet he must not say so, as he cannot convict her of it; besides, everybody would laugh at him, as he had himself sent the young fellow to her. The fool is of opinion, that the husband had himself made his wife a whore, which he denies, as she had been one before, and he had only wished to prove her. In the next scene, Pamphilus again

relates to Gallichoræa his adventures of the preceding night, and that he had an assignation with her for the same evening. Gallichoræa pretends to his wife, that he had received a message from his brother, calling him away from home in a great hurry, and adds, that he does not know when he will come home again. Scortum behaves just in the same manner as on the previous occasions, and determines to deceive her husband a third time. Pamphilus comes, and is admitted. Act vi. Gallichoræa is determined to set fire to the house with a torch, if Scortum does not deliver up her lover. As she is not able to appease her husband, she begs him at least to allow her to save her linen, that she may have something to clothe herself with. Gallichoræa helps her to carry out the cask full of clothes, and then enters the house again to continue his search. In the mean time Pamphilus jumps out of the cask, and runs away. Adrian comes to pacify Gallichoræa. The latter is very melancholy at not being able to find anything. Then follows a scene, in which Gallichoræa reproaches his wife. His melancholy increases. He then learns again from Pamphilus, how he had been fooled a third time. Pamphilus declares that he will not return to the wife again, and takes his leave. Neighbour Adrian learns the whole story from the fool. Gallichoræa takes his dishonour very much to heart, and goes raving mad. The fool and the neighbour at last succeed in putting him in chains, and lead him into the house. Scortum then is troubled with remorse at having driven her husband mad, and resolves to take her own life. Devils come, and strangle her. A moral epilogue concludes the piece.

We add here a few scenes from the sixth act, which place the connection of this piece with Shakespeare beyond all doubt.

Act VI, Scene 1.

Gallichoræa. Scortum. Johan Bouset (tregt zwey Fackeln). *Pamphilus. Adrian.*

Gallich. Johan kom fort, vnd gib mir die eine Fackel her, die ander aber behalt du.
Joh. Bous. Was wollt ihr mit der Fackel machen.
Gallich. Ich wil Huren vnd Buben zusammen im Hause verbrennen.
Joh. Bous. Seid ihr toll, was wollt ihr machen? Ihr werdet die ganze Stadt anstecken.
Gallich. Da ligt nichts an, kom du nur her. (Als sie vor das Haus kommen klopfet er mit Gewalt an vnd ruffet gar laut.) Holla, mach auff, du hast mich nun lang gnug bey der Nasen herumb geführt, ich wil dich nun einmal wider bezalen, lass sehen, hast du den Bulen noch einmal versteckt, was gilt's? Ich wil ihn finden, darumb gedenke, vnd gib ihn mir heraus, oder sihe ich wil dir das Haus oben dem Kopfe anstecken. (Die Frau kömt gar geschwinde heraus gelaufen.)
Scortum. Behüte Gott Man, Was wolt jhr nun anfangen? Wollet jhr mich dann nun gar zum Betler machen? Vnd diese gantze Stadt in Noth bringen.
Gall. Das hilfft nicht darzu, Ich wil kurtz rundt wissen, wo der Bule ist.
Scortum. Ich habe keinen Bulen im Hause, Vnd wollet jhr ja so toll sein, Vnd das Haus anstecken? So helfft mir doch erst meinen Leinen Zeug heraus tragen, Damit wir ja noch etwas behalten, das wir anziehen mögen, Werdet jhr alsdann einen Bulen im Hause finden, So bin ich zufrieden, Das jhr nicht allein das Haus anzündet, Sondern mir darzu den Hals entzwey schlaget.
Gall. Wo ist denn das Zeug?
Scort. Hier stehets im Hause im Faſs. Vnd ist darzu vngewaschen Zeug.

Gall. Den willen wil ich dir noch thun, Aber finde ich auch darnach jemandts im Hause, so nicht darin bescheiden ist, So wil ich mich dann auch gar nicht erbitten lassen.

Scort. Das bin ich dann auch wol zufrieden, Ich wil alsdann auch keine gnade begeren. (Sie gehen ein, vnd der Man hilfft der Frawen das Zeug hinaus tragen, als das geschehen, spricht er:)

Gall. Nun wil ich wieder hinein gehen, vnd Visitieren. (Gehet hinein, inmittelst springet Pamphilus aus dem Fafs heraus, in welchem er mit dem Zeuge bedecket gewesen, vnd laufft dauon. Adrian kompt inmittelst darzu gelauffen im Schlaffpelz, vnnd laufft gar geschwinde nach dem Hause, rüfft vnd spricht:)

Adrian. Was ist hie zuthun? Wollet jhr nun ewer eigen Haus anstecken, Vnd die Stadt in grundt verbrennen. (Gehet abe.)

Scene 6.

[*Gallichorœa* gehet gar trawrich vnd seufftzet, inmittelst kompt *Pamphilus* gegangen.]

Pamph. Gott grüsse euch guter Herr, Ich wolte euch vor alle beforderung dancken vnd meinen abscheit nehmen.

Gall. Wiltu dann nun so daruon.

Pamph. Auff difsmahl ist meines pleibens nicht lenger hier.

Gall. Gefellt es dir dann hier nicht mehr?

Pamph. Auff difsmahl nicht.

Gall. Bistu gestern wieder an dem ort gewesen?

Pamph. Ich bin freilich dar gewesen, Ich meinte der Man hette mir schier die Leuchte gebracht, als er ein kam.

Gall. Wie gieng denn das zu?

Pamph. Wie solt es zugehen, der tolle Narr wolte das Haus anstecken vnd sagt zur Frawen, sie solt jm den Bulen heraus langen. Die Fraw, wie sie solches hörte, Verbarg mich in ein Fafs, vnd warff darauff alt leinen gerethe, Lieff darnach geschwind zum Man vnd bath, Wann er ja das Haus anstecken wolte so möchte er doch jhres zeuges schonen, vnd jhr das helffen heraus tragen, Das that er, vnd trug mich also selber zum Hause heraus, Als er aber wieder hinein gieng vnd suchte, Sprang ich heraus vnd lieff dauon.

. . . .

Gall. O ich vnglückseliger Mensch, O das ich nie geboren were, Ach das ich nur Todt were, So dörfften die Leute meiner so nicht spotten, etc.

TRANSLATION.

Act I. Scene 1.

Gallichorœa. Scortum. John Bouset (bearing two torches). *Pamphilus. Adrian.*

Gallich. John, come here, and give me one of the torches. The other you may keep yourself.

John Bous. What are you going to do with the torch?

Gallich. Burn whores and rogues together in the house.

John Bous. Are you mad? What will you do? You'll set fire to the whole town.

Gallich. That does not signify. Only you come here. (When they have come before the house, he knocks violently at the door, and calls out very loud:) Holla! Open the door. You have been making a fool of me long enough. Now will I pay you out for it at last. Let us see; if you have got your lover hid there again, what does it matter? I will find him, therefore mind what I say, and give him up to me, or look here, I will set fire to the house above your head. (His wife comes running out of the house in a great hurry.)

Scortum. God forbid, husband! What do you want to do? Do you want to make a beggar of me then, and bring the whole town into trouble?

Gallich. That's all of no good. I am determined to know without any more pother, where your lover is.

Scortum. I have not got any lover in the house, and will you really be so mad as to burn the house down? At least help me to carry out my linen, that we may keep something to put on. If you then find a lover in the house, you have my leave not only to set the house on fire, but to break my neck into the bargain.

Gall. Where is your linen then?

Scort. Here it stands in the house, in a tub. And dirty linen it is too.

Gall. I will do you that one favour more; but if I then find anybody in the house who does not belong to it, I will not listen to any more entreaties.

Scort. I am quite satisfied with that. I will not ask then for any favour more. (They go into the house, and the husband helps his wife to carry out the linen. When this is done, he says:)

Gall. Now I will go in again, and have a search. (He goes in; in the mean time Pamphilus jumps out of the tub, and runs away. While this is taking place, Adrian rushes out of his house in his night-gown, runs up to the house, shouts out and says:)

Adrian. What is to be done? Will you set your own house on fire, and burn down the town? (Exit.)

SCENE 6.

[Enter *Gallichorœa* very melancholy, and sighing *Pamphilus* joins him.]

Pamph. Good morning, my dear sir. I wished to thank you for all the advancement you have procured me, and then take my leave.

Gall. Are you going away then?

Pamph. For the present I shall stay here no longer.

Gall. Don't you like the place then any more?

Pamph. Not for the present.

Gall. Were you at the same place again yesterday?

Pamph. O yes, certainly, I was there. I thought the husband meant to bring me the candles when he came.

Gall. How was that?

Pamph. How should it be? The mad fool wanted to set fire to the house, and told his wife she must give up her lover to him. When the wife heard this she hid me in a tub, and threw some old linen over me. Then she ran out to her husband, and begged, that if he was determined to set the house on fire, he would at least spare her linen, and help her carry it out. He did so, and so he carried me out of the house too. But as soon as he had gone in again, I ran away.

. . . .

Gall. O miserable man that I am! O that I had never been born! Alas, if I were only dead, the people could not laugh at me so, etc.

Compare with the above scenes 'The Merry Wives of Windsor', Act iii, sc. 3 and 5. Here we must greatly regret the uncertainty which prevails respecting the chronology of Shakespeare's plays. The 'Merry Wives of Windsor' appeared for the first time in print in 1602, and indeed in a very imperfect form, certainly not that in which it came from Shakespeare's hands. It is in Jan. 1601—1602, that the piece first appears in the 'Registers of

the Stationer's Company'. We first meet with it in its genuine form in the Folio of 1623. Johnson places it between 'Henry iv' Part 2 and 'Henry v', therefore about 1598—1599. Malone places it between Parts 1 and 2 of 'Henry iv', that is to say, about 1596—1597. Chalmers does the same. Halliwell contended for the assumption that the earliest form came from Shakespeare's pen, an opinion which he afterwards gave up. Collier rejects the first form as not genuine. The allusion in Shakespeare's piece to a German Duke, which we have already noticed, unquestionably refers to Frederick of Wirtemberg, who, we know, was in Windsor in 1592.[1] But this Prince as we have seen above, travelled under the name of Count Montbeliard. This was not an assumed name; the Duke was really Count Montbeliard until he ascended the throne, and was even called so in his native country. If therefore, as some persons have argued, the 'Merry Wives of Windsor' were written soon after 1592, why should Shakespeare have transformed the Count into a Duke, as the person alluded to was known to the audience as Count, and not as Duke?

It therefore appears no unjustifiable assumption that the Duke had already succeeded to that title, when Shakespeare wrote his piece. Soon after his return from his visit to England, Count Montbeliard succeeded to the Ducal throne. This event, affecting a prince now personally known at the English Court, was in all probability a subject of conversation there, and may have suggested to Shakespeare his allusion to the foreigner as Duke. Or this allusion may also have been occasioned by the Duke's application for the Order of the Garter in the year 1595. For these reason, we believe we shall be nearer the truth, if we place this play between the years 1593 and 1596. The 'Adulteress' of Duke Henry Julius was first printed in 1594. It may have been written and acted one or more years earlier; but however that may be, the date of its composition and representation are near those of Shakespeare's immortal comedy. Was Shakespeare acquainted with the Duke's play? Who would like to affirm that? But we may be allowed to observe, that the intrigue in the 'Merry Wives' is in many respects more similar to that of the 'Adulteress,' than the hitherto received source of that play, namely, the tale of the 'Two Lovers of Pisa' in Tarleton's 'Newes out of Purgatory' 1590, which again is a new version of the Tale of the Ring, in Gio. Fr. Straparola's 'Tredeci piacevoli notti'.[2] A very similar story is to be found in Giovanni Fiorentino's 'Il Pecorone', which has passed into an English Collection of tales, entitled 'The fortunate, the deceived, and unfortunate lovers', which Malone asserts already existed in print in Shakespeare's life, although no older edition than

---

[1] Pointed out for the first time by Mr. Charles Knight in his edition of Shakespeare.

[2] The Italian text with an English translation will be found in "*The first Sketch of Shakespeare's Merry Wives of Windsor*" ed. by J. O. Halliwell. London, printed for the Shakespeare Soc. 1842, p. 112—125, and Tarlton's English version, ibid., p. 125—135, and in J. P. Collier's *Shakespeare's Library*, as well as in Johnson-Steevens' edition of Shakespeare. — See also *Quellen des Shakespeare in Novellen, Märchen und Sagen*, herausgegeben von Th. Echtermayer, L. Henschel und Karl Simrock. 3 vol. Berlin. 1831. Vol. i, p. 231, and Charles Simrock's remarks, Vol. iii, p. 221. The latter translated into English, for the Shakespeare Soc. and ed. by Halliwell, 1850, p. 76.

that of 1632 in 4to is now extant.[1] The love-adventures of Falstaff are most undoubtedly to be referred to this source, but it admits of a question whether there may not be some intermediate link, which also originating from the same sources, has undergone the same changes as those which appear again in Shakespeare's deviations from the Italian tales, and which Henry Julius has also adopted. A very important deviation from the above-mentioned sources consists in this: that in the play of Henry Julius, the whole action of the piece originates with the husband, who entertains suspicions against his wife, and desires to put her virtue to the test. Similarly in Shakespeare's play, Ford endeavours to test his wife's fidelity by means of Falstaff's intrigues, which he encourages. That Falstaff had already laid his plans without Ford's intervention, is of very little importance here. This is managed differently in the two Italian stories. In neither of them is the husband's motive the wish to try his wife. In one story the husband only wishes to prove to the young man that his wife is more beautiful than the young man's mother, whom the son had described as quite incomparable in this respect, and in the other, the teacher gives his young pupil, who is ardently longing for some love adventure, the necessary instructions how such affairs are to be managed; that the pupil should commence his experiments with the wife of his teacher, is purely accidental, and not owing to the cooperation of the husband. Another point of coincidence between the 'Merry Wives' and the 'Adulteress', is this: that the two lovers, in the one case Pamphilus, and Falstaff in the other, are both influenced by mercenary as well as other motives in their love adventures. Falstaff says of Ford: "Hang him, poor cuckoldy knave! I know him not. Yet I wrong him to call him poor: they say, the jealous wittolly knave hath masses of money, for the which his wife seems to me well-favoured. I will use her as the key of the cuckoldy rogue's coffer, and there is my harvest-home." In the 'Adulteress', Pamphilus complains of his poverty, upon which Gallichorææ answers: "Why you are a fine, straight, well-made. young fellow, and seem to me as if you were sure to please the women. There are handsome young women in this town; do you only make acquaintance with them, and you are sure to get money and clothes enough." It is also to be observed in the 'Adulteress', that the duped husband is constantly abusing himself as a cuckold [in German 'Hahnrei'] and that in Shakespeare, Ford does the same. One character in the 'Adulteress', quite independent of the original sources, is that of Jan Bouset, the servant of Gallichorææ, which has at least great external similarity with Dr. Caius, as both speak in an unintelligible dialect.[2]

In the tale of Giovanni Fiorentino, the husband is taken in by his wife twice, in that of Straparola three times, as in Shakespeare and in Henry Julius. In Giovanni the lover is concealed the first time under a heap of linen, which the husband quietly passes by. After he is gone, the wife sups with the lover, who passes the night with her. The

---

[1] Fiorentino's Text with an English Translation in "*The first Sketch*" etc. p. 86—101 and the English version of 1632, ibid., p. 101—112. See also *Quellen* etc. Vol. i, p. 201 and Vol. iii, p. 221. Simrock's remarks in English, p. 76.

[2] In the Susanna the peasants use different dialects. The same thing also occurs in Plautus.

second time, the wife puts out the candle when her husband approaches, and in the very moment that he is about to enter the house, she pushes her lover out of the door. He thrusts his sword through the heap of linen, and as he finds nobody there, is well beaten by his wife's brothers, and treated as if he were mad. In Straparola, the first time, the young man is concealed in a bed, the curtains of which are drawn close, the second time in a trunk, and covered over with clothes. In this case also the husband passes by without any suspicion, and after he has left the house, the lover slips away. The third time he is concealed in a cupboard, and when the husband is preparing to set fire to the house, and the cupboard is also in danger of becoming a prey to the flames, the wife orders it to be removed to a place of safety, under the pretence that it contains papers appertaining to her dowry. We see by this how far both authors deviate from Shakespeare and Henry Julius. Only the concealment in some receptacle, which is also full of linen or clothes has passed into both pieces. The lesser details in these have more resemblance with each other than with the Italian tales. In Shakespeare, Ford, in order to fix the fool's cap more firmly on his head, must himself ask what is in the basket; in Henry Julius, Gallichorœa is even made to assist with his own hands in removing his wife's paramour to a place of safety. The tales do not contain a trace of anything resembling Falstaff's disguise as the witch of Brentford, neither is this episode to be found in Henry Julius; on the other hand, the second adventure in the 'Adulteress', the spreading out the cloak, that Pamphilus may escape behind it, has considerable resemblance to a disguise. As many of the above-mentioned deviations from the Italian in which Shakespeare and Henry Julius agree, are to be met with in a German story, I will give a brief sketch of its subject. It is entitled the Tale 'Of a Goldsmith and a poor Student' in Michael Lindner's 'Rastbüchlein', 1557 or 1558.[1]

A goldsmith in a far-famed city suspects his beautiful wife of infidelity, but has never been able to obtain any proofs of his suspicions. One day, as the goldsmith is standing in his shop, which is at a considerable distance from his private residence, a poor scholar or student begs an alms of him. The student is a handsome young fellow, and appears to the goldsmith a very likely person to put his wife's virtue to the proof. Pretending therefore not to have any money about him, he directs the student to go to a certain place, where he will have sweet dalliance with a beautiful woman, and receive plenty of money into the bargain, but he is on no account to mention the goldsmith's name. The student promises discretion, and is directed to the goldsmith's wife, who, while the goldsmith returns to his shop to work, sees the handsome youth, admits him, and has her own will

---

[1] *Rastbuchlein. Darinn schöne kurtzweilige, lecherliche vnd lustige Bossen vnd Fablen, wellithe Hystorien gleich sein, verfast vnd beschriben seind, den Feyrenden, oder sonst ruhenden, lieblich zulesen vnd anzuhören. S. l. e. a.* — Second edition, s. l. M.D.LVIII. — The tale alluded to is founded on the Italian Novels. For more details see Dr. Holland's edition of the Plays of Duke Henry Julius, p. 874. Henry Kurz p. 144 compares our play with Hans Sachs' *Kuplet Schwieger*. — The above narrative is to be found in Dr. Holland's edition of the Plays of Henry Julius.

with him. Presently the goldsmith comes home. His wife is terribly frightened, and places the student "outside the shop, on a board, on which nails, sticks, and other things are generally placed." The husband searches the house in vain, gives it up, and returns to his work. After this, the wife "finishes her business" with the student, refreshes both herself and him with sweetmeats, gives him some money, sends him away and begs he will soon come again. The student relates all this to the goldsmith, who persuades him to go there a second time. He does so, is received just in the same manner as the first time, and goes to bed with her. Before he has left her, the husband comes again, and searches for the student, whom the wife "has hung over a pole, and covered over with some old clothes." He returns to his shop. The student goes to him again, tells him what has happened, and is persuaded, though not without difficulty, to go to the wife for a third time. The wife receives him with greater kindness than ever. But just as "they have finished their business," the husband knocks at the door. The wife conceals the student in a great tub, and throws the "dirty linen" over him. The husband searches in vain, threatens to burn down the house, the wife begs him to help her first "to carry the dirty linen in the tub out of the house, that when all the things are burnt, we may have at least a shirt to put on." The husband and wife take the tub on their shoulders, carry it into the street, and return into the house again. The student jumps out, and runs away to the goldsmith's shop. The goldsmith "who was not very particularly in earnest about burning down his house" returns there too. The student tells him all that has happened. The goldsmith says: "My dear boy, the woman, with whom you have had to do, is my wife, and it is I who have been to the house three times, and asked after you. But even had I found you, I should not have done you any harm, for all that I have done was only to learn something about the goings on of my wife." He exhorts the student to silence, and to leave the town. The student follows his counsel.

The third adventure in Shakespeare's play, the charming scene at Herne's oak, cannot be referred to anything in the tales, nor in the Duke's piece, and yet the latter also offers here an external point of connection in the concluding scene, in which the devils punish the faithless wife with death and eternal damnation, just as Falstaff is thrown into agonies of terror by the improvised fairy scene as a punishment for his lecherous practices.

The connection of Shakespeare's glorious comedy with the tales as well as with the 'Adulteress' is, as we have seen above, of a purely external nature; but a purely external motive was sufficient for him to breathe a new life into the crude elements of the mere outward form, and to produce a poetic whole. Perhaps one of the English comedians on their return, may have communicated to him the plot of the Wolfenbüttel play. We have learnt above that in 1594 Richard Jones, and in 1596 Robert Browne, were again in England. To attempt to deny that Shakespeare made any use whatever of these sources, on the ground of the very different form which the subject assumed in his hands, appears to us a decided mistake. The number of coincidences in the external circumstances is far too great to justify such a supposition. On the other hand, to seek for models for the internal

construction of Shakespeare's dramas will always be time and trouble thrown away; and we are far more likely to find the real sources of his dramas if we direct our attention exclusively to their purely external incidents. And as we know so little of the process of his intellectual development, the comparison of what he has formed out of these rude traditional subjects with these subjects themselves, is the only possible method left us of watching him as it were in the workshop of his genius. The truth is, says Charles Knight somewhere, that no one can properly appreciate the extent as well as the subtlety of Shakespeare's invention, its absorbing and purifying power, who has not traced him to his sources.

We have here seen four of the ten of the Duke's plays in connection with the English Comedians and with Shakespeare. It may be further remarked, that also the 'Comedy of a Nobleman'[1] is probably founded on an old English subject[2] in the ballad from which Gottfried August Bürger took his subject for another ballad two hundred years afterwards.[3]

In all the ten pieces, with the exception of the 'Tragedy of a profligate Son', the clown plays a principal part, and generally speaking we may recognize in them a method of handling a subject which could only have been learnt from the English Comedians, the general plan not quite deficient in art, the characters various and real. Only one of all these pieces, the 'Susanna', is biblical, and even in this case it is only the subject which is biblical, for the method of treating it is altogether secular. It is expressly called a 'Mirror of the course of the world.' All of these pieces are written in prose, and indeed in a prose, which, as Gervinus remarks, is incomparably better than all the verses of that time. Even this prose form is due to the English influence, for before the appearance of the English actors, hardly any dramatic author had ventured to write otherwise than in rhyming verses,[4] and how difficult they found it to give them up, appears from the fact, that it was considered necessary to put several of the Wolfenbüttel pieces into that form, before they ventured to put them on the stage in other places. In comparison with the awkward management of the verse, prose naturally allowed a far freer movement, from which the theatrical element, the representation of these pieces, derived very great advantage. Thus we see the English influence operative from the first in the case of an author, who possessed more dramatic talent than all his predecessors, his contemporaries, and immediate successors. It was for this reason also that his contemporaries were less decided in their devotion to the new

---

[1] *Comoedia Hibaldeha von einem Edelman, welcher einem Abt drey Fragen aufgegeben. Mit fünff Personen. Wolffenbüttel 1594.* 8vo. (*Comedy of a nobleman who proposed three questions to an abbot. With five persons. Wolffenbüttel 1594.*) In Dr. Holland's edition p. 475—505. — Another edition: Magdeburg, Joh. Francke, s. a. (1599). 8vo.

[2] Wilh. Wackernagel, *Geschichte* etc., p. 463, note 7.

[3] The same story forms the plot of a German Shrove-tide play of the 15th century: *Ein spil von einem Keiser und eim Apt.* See A. Keller, *Fastnachtsspiele*, p. 199—210.

[4] Some few examples only are extant of plays written in prose, which cannot weaken our argument. Jacob Camerlander's *Hurenwirt*, about 1542, is a dramatic transformation of a dialogue in a dramatic form, written in prose. In 1583 a prose-play "*Vom Raube der Proserpina*" has been acted at Innsbruck. Prose translations of Terence cannot be considered as exceptions to the above statement. See ibid. p. 464, note 14.

school: while Henry Julius from the very commencement of his career as a dramatic writer entirely broke with the past once for all, we see Jacob Ayrer still yielding a partial allegiance to the time and style of Hans Sachs, and indeed with far less talent and skill than the latter. One lasting conquest, however, had been secured for the German stage: namely, that in the place of the biblical and polemical subjects popular ones were now introduced, such as were already rife among the people in the form of tales and stories, and this must have amply compensated them for their exclusion from the stage itself. For the new direction of the stage was by no means confined to Wolfenbüttel, but forced its way into other parts of Germany, although the transition to purely profane subjects did not become general till a later period, when numerous companies of strolling actors had been formed. As an instance of this, we will only mention here the 'History of the Merchant of Padua',[1] which, as it appears, was acted in Breslau in 1596. This piece has for its subject the narrative part of Shakespeare's Cymbeline, but we shall not give it any further consideration here, as it does not stand in any intimate connection with Shakespeare or the old English stage; on the contrary, its affinity to Cymbeline is entirely referable to the use made of the same common Italian sources.

There were English Comedians at the Court of the Landgrave Maurice of Hesse in Cassel, at the same time as at the Court of Wolfenbüttel. We have already had occasion to mention some circumstances respecting them. Considering the great intimacy between the two Princes, it is probable that the Wolfenbüttel Comedians may have been sent sometimes to Cassel; we have seen above that this was at least the case with the musicians.[2] Maurice, who was no less fond of splendour than Henry Julius, and also a man of great cultivation, endeavoured to make his Court a nursery for the refinement of manners. He appears to have directed his attention to theatrical representations at a very early period, and before he had had a permanent theatre built,[3] and maintained professional actors, the pupils of the Court- and Knight Academy received instruction to qualify them for acting. They

---

[1] *Eine Schöne Historia, Von einem frommen Gottfürchtigen Kauffmann von Padua, welcher zu Mantua in beysein anderer Kauffleute, wegen seines lieben frommen Weibes Ehr vnd frömigkeit, sein Hab vnd Gut verwettet, gestellet durch Zachariam Liebholdt von Solbergk. Gedruckt zu Brefslaw durch Georgium Bawman, Anno M.D.xcvi.* 8vo. (*A pretty history of a pious godly Merchant of Padua, who at Mantua in the company of other merchants lost all his property in a wager on his dear wife's honour and piety, set forth by Zachary Liebholdt of Solbergk.*)

[2] The Landgrave was himself a composer. Peacham, in his *Emblems*, p. 101, states, that he has seen eight or ten volumes of motets composed by the Landgrave himself. But when he proceeds to tell us that while Maurice was staying in London, he kept his own band there, there must be some mistake; for there is nowhere any evidence of the Landgrave ever having undertaken any journey to London at all. It is true, at the advice of Henry the fourth of France such a journey had been intended, and it was with this view that the Landgrave learnt English, and practised it with the Englishmen in his service; but the plan was frustrated by the death of Elisabeth. Rommel, p. 421—22. In some instructions which Maurice drew up for some pupils of the Knight's Academy whom he despatched on their travels, he remarks: "The Italian music is the finest, the English excellent, the French and Belgian but mediocre." Rommel, ibid.

[3] See ante p. xviii.

once performed a drama in six languages.¹ Long before the year 1595 there must have been regular companies of actors engaged at the Court of Cassel, for in 1595 the Landgrave Maurice writes to John Lucanus, his agent in Prague, that his comedians were then travelling with leave of absence, and that in case they wished to act at Prague he was to afford them any assistance in his power.² We must understand this as referring only to English comedians, as regular German companies of professional actors did not exist at that time. In 1597 Landgrave Maurice writes as follows to some unknown personage of princely rank: "At the request of Your Highness that we would send the arms, suits of mail, costumes, and whatever else we may have for the performance of the comedy of the Old Potentates, we have given orders that all such things as we may have at hand should be forwarded to Your Highness immediately, with the request that Your Highness will let the comedians so prepare themselves, that in case we should visit Your Highness we may also at once gratify our eyes with them."³ In the Archives of the Treasury at Cassel there is a list of the expences of the Court of the Landgrave Maurice during his residence in the neighbouring palaces in the years 1597 and 1598, in which we meet with the following entries respecting the Comedians.⁴

For boards for the stage for the comedy	5 thalers.
For six ells of white woollen cloth for the Englishmen for the comedy	2 thalers.
For white clothes for the clown	4 thalers.
A pair of shoes for the fool	4 thalers.
To an Englishman for his pay	20 thalers.
To the Treasurer, Heugel, to settle with the Englishmen	300 florins.
To the Italian Jan and his riders twice, together	150 thalers.

According to a manuscript chronicle of a certain Buch, as early as 1602, Maurice "tired of the dancing and jumping" got rid of the "confounded" (i. e. the expensive) Englishmen. This, however, cannot refer to the Comedians, or else there must have been several companies in succession in the service of the Court of Cassel, for we find English actors at the Court of the Landgrave till the year 1613. In 1607 his servant informs him that the Englishmen were dissatisfied with the smallness of their salaries, and had said that they would now perform their last comedy in Cassel, but he did not know whether this was meant in earnest or was only a joke. The servant speaks of the comedy to be performed as that "Of the two British Kings at war, of whom the one takes the son of the other, but the latter the daughter of the former, prisoner."⁵ Here we see that the English Histories also belonged to the stage library of our Comedians. How far their fame had extended

---

¹ Rommel, *Geschichte* etc., Vol. vi, p. 400.
² Id. ibid. p. 402.
³ Id. ibid. p. 402.
⁴ Id. ibid. p. 444—445.
⁵ Id. ibid. p. 401. — This was no doubt an English play. In the course of our observations we shall have occasion to revert to a drama, which may be identical with the above.

appears from the fact, that in the year 1609 John Sigismund, the Elector of Brandenburg, begged the Landgrave to send him the Comedians for four weeks, to practise their art at the festivities which he had arranged in honour of the nuptials of his brother, the Administrator of Strasburg. The request was of course most willingly complied with.[1] In 1611 they play in Darmstadt. In 1612 we find them in Nuremberg, where they performed with great success, as we learn from a contemporary Nuremberg Chronicle.[2]

Here then do we see two German Princes, both of whom were distinguished among their equals and contemporaries for their culture and their talents, vying with each other in a noble emulation to naturalize English dramatic art at their respective courts. But this remarkable and striking phenomenon could not of course remain confined to the two points at which it first appeared. At both of these courts, that of Cassel more especially, there was a very lively intercourse with foreigners, — scholars and artists of all kinds, nobles and princes feeling themselves attracted by the Landgrave Maurice, who, besides possessing great intellectual gifts, was extremely fond of splendour and magnificence. His Court was the scene of a constant succession of visitors consisting of the most eminent personages of the time. No wonder then that the fame of these actors, whose task it was to amuse the visitors with their art, soon spread through all Germany. Indeed we see that before the end of the century, the services of the comedians were no longer confined to the courts but met with a hearty recognition among the people. It is probable that the success of the Wolfenbüttel and Cassel companies soon allured others from England, at any rate we meet with them at other places.

About the year 1597[3] there must have been English Comedians at Frankfort on the Maine, to play during the fair, as we learn from a humorous poem printed in 1597. This production possesses all the greater importance for our present object, as it gives us some information respecting the outward appearance and doings of the Clown, who of course constituted the chief attraction. We accordingly annex the following extracts from it.

---

[1] Rommel, *Geschichte* etc., Vol. vi, p. 402.

[2] The Chronicle alluded to is written in the beginning of the seventeenth century. See Joh. Chr. Siebenkees, *Materialien zur Nürnbergischen Geschichte*. Vol. iii. 8vo. Nürnberg 1794, p. 52.

[3] In the same year English players were at Utrecht:
> "Schenkelwyn, July 31. Sekere Engelsche comedianten, voor hore speelen opten stadhuyse 8 q. Fransche wyns."
> (July 31. To certain English Comedians for their playing at the Town-hall, eight quarts of French wine.)

See *De Staads-Kameraars-Rekeningen dienstbaar gemaakt aan de Geschiedenis*, in Dodt's *Archief voor kerkelijke en wereldsche Geschiedenissen inzonderheid van Utrecht*. Deel iii, p. 271. — See also *Notes and Queries*, Vol. vii, 1853, p. 114.

These may have been the same players whom we meet at Frankfort, though it is not unlikely that the latter are identical with Landgrave Maurice's players, who as we have seen above, had obtained his permission to go abroad as early as the year 1595, and whom he sent, in the very same year of 1597, to some German Prince. They may have passed through Frankfort on their journey back to Cassel, in order to take advantage of the assemblage of persons who came from all sides to the Frankfort fair.

"Da war nun weiter mein Intent,
  Zu sehen das Englische Spiel,
    Davon ich hab gehört so viel.
Wie der Narr drinnen, Jan genennt,
  Mit Bossen war so excellent:
Welches ich auch bekenn fürwar,
  Daſs er damit ist Meister gar.
Verstellt also sein Angesicht,
  Daſs er keim Menschen gleich mehr sicht.
Auff tölpisch Bossen ist sehr gschickt,
  Hat Schuch, der keiner jhn nicht trückt.
In sein Hosen noch einer hett Platz,
  Hat dran ein vngehewren Latz.
Sein Juppen jhn zum Narren macht,
  Mit der Schlappen, die er nicht acht,
Wann er da fängt zu löffeln an,
  Vnd dünckt sich seyn ein fein Person.
Der Wursthänsel ist abgericht,
  Auch ziemlicher maſsen, wie man sicht:
Vertretten beyd jhr Stelle wol,
  Den Springer ich auch loben soll,
Wegen seines hohen Springen,
  Vnd auch noch anderer Dingen:
Höfflich ist in all' seinen Sitten,
  Im tantzen vnd all seinen Tritten.
Daſs solchs fürwar ein Lust zu sehen,
  Wie glatt die Hosen jhm anstehen.

. . . .

Ist sonst auch wol proportioniert,
  Sein langes Haar jhn auch was ziert.
Aber ein Kunst die fehlt jhm noch,
  Vnd spreng er noch einest so hoch,
Welch wol diente zu seinen Sachen:
  Wenn er sich könnt vnsichtbar machen,
Noch mehr Gelt er verdienen möcht,
  Dann nicht alle, versteht mich recht,
Hineyn zu diesem Spiele gehn,
  Die lustige Comedien zsehen.
Oder der Music vnd Saitenspil,
  Zu gefallen, sonder jhr viel
Wegen des Narren groben Bossen,
  Vnd des Springers glatten Hosen."[1]

Then it was further my intent,
  To see the English play,
    Of which I'd heard the people say
The fool, 'twas he named Jan they meant,
  Was with his jokes so excellent.
In which I too confess forsooth,
  He is a master in good truth;
For so distort his face he can,
  He looks no longer like a man.
And many a clownish trick he knows,
  Wears shoes that don't much pinch his toes.
His breeches would hold two or more,
  And have a monstrous flap before.
His jacket makes him look a fool
  With all the blows he takes so cool,
When he the gallant would play well,
  And clearly thinks himself a swell.
The clown is skilled as well as he,
  His equal quite, as one may see:
Both know full well to play their part.
  I must praise too the leaper's art,
Because so very high he springs,
  And also for some other things.
His manner is so full of graces
  In dancing, and in all his paces,
To see it's really a delight,
  And then his hose too sit so tight.

. . . .

He's well-proportioned too of limb,
  And his long hair looks well on him.
One art he lacks howe'er he try,
  And should he jump, oh e'er so high,
Which would improve his tricks, I ween,
  If he could make himself unseen.
Then far more money earn he might,
  For all men, understand me right,
Do not unto this play repair
  At merry comedies to stare,
Or for the music and the lute,
  But very many of them do't
To see the fool's coarse jokes and blows,
  And leaper's tightly-fitting hose.

---

[1] Marx Mangoldt, *Marckschiffs Nachen, darinn nachgeführet wirdt, was in dem nächst abgefahrenen Marckschiff aufsgeblieben*, etc. 4to. s. l. 1597, p. 12. — This is a continuation of the same author's *Marckschiff oder Marckschiffer Gespräch von der Franckfurter Meſs*. 4to. s. l. 1596.

In the course of the poem, as we have already stated above at p. xliii, the 'Susanna' is mentioned as having been performed by the Comedians.

In the year 1599, English actors and musicians played at Hildesheim, and indeed in the English language. They were probably the Comedians of Duke Henry Julius, who had come over from the neighbouring Wolfenbüttel.[1]

CHAPTER III.

It is hardly probable that the places mentioned in the preceding chapter were the only ones visited by the English Comedians. On the contrary, if we now direct our attention to the dramatic writer already mentioned, Jacob Ayrer, we may safely assume that among other places, Nuremberg had received them within its walls at a very early period. At all events what we have already stated is sufficient to shew that the English Comedians were quite at home in Germany when Jacob Ayrer composed the greater part of his dramas, and that either in Nuremberg or elsewhere he may easily have become acquainted with the pieces they performed as also with themselves.

Of the circumstances of Jacob Ayrer's life we know next to nothing. All that can be stated with certainty is, that on the 13th of October 1593 he received the freedom of the city of Nuremberg, and that he died there on the 26th of May 1605, as a notary and proctor to the Court.[2] He is supposed to have come to Nuremberg as a boy, without any means of subsistence, to have served in an iron-monger's shop, and afterwards to have commenced a similar business himself. When this did not prosper, he went to Bamberg, and devoted himself to the desk, where, compelled by poverty, he learnt so much

---

[1] "Im nämlichen Jahre [1599] im Monat September hatte man in Hildesheim Englische Schauspieler und Musikanten, die Vorstellungen in Englischer Sprache gaben." *Beiträge zur Hildesheimischen Geschichte.* Vol. iii. 8vo. Hildesheim 1830, p. 192. See also ibid. Vol. i, p. 331. — This information, which is the more important as it mentions expressly that the representations were given in English, was originally derived from a contemporary Mss. Chronicle at Hildesheim, by the late Mr. Zeppenfeldt, Curator of the Hildesheim Records (Archivarius) in *Sonntagsblatt* 1810, No. 35, 1811, No. 48 and in *Mittewochenblatt* 1819, No. 45 & 46. All my efforts to get at the literal wording in the original document, in which my learned friend, Senator Friedr. Culemann of Hannover, assisted me most energetically, remained unsuccessful. It seems that the Chronicle to which Mr. Zeppenfeldt was indebted for the information has disappeared at Hildesheim.

[2] Extracts from the Municipal Archives at Nuremberg:
"Jacobus Ayrer, Licentiat, wurde am 13. October 1593, zum Bürger in Nürnberg aufgenommen und zahlte 10 fl. Stadtwährung."
(Jacob Ayrer, licentiate, was admitted as a citizen of Nuremberg, Oct. 13, 1593, and paid 10 florins in Nuremberg currency.)
"26. Martii, 1605, starb der Ehrbar Jacob Ayrer der Elter, publicus notarius und der Gerichten Procurator ins Hengässlein."
(Died on the 26th of March 1605 the Honourable Jacob Ayrer the elder, Public Notary and Attorney to the Court of Justice, in Henlane.)
See Will. Bell, *Shakespeare's Puck*, Vol. ii, p. 287. G. A. Will's *Nürnberger Gelehrten-Lexicon*, Vol. i, 8vo. Nürnberg 1755, s. v. *Ayrer*, and Nopitsch's continuation, Vol. i, Altdorf 1802, p. 35.

through practice and study as to become a proctor to the Court and City tribunal of that place. His attachment to the Evangelical faith, however, induced him again to leave the Catholic Bamberg, and return to Nuremberg. Like Henry Julius, with whose pieces perhaps he was not unacquainted, he left the path of the religious drama, and addressed himself entirely to the people, but did not, like that writer, entirely break with the traditions of the past in respect of the form. He retained the old verse of Hans Sachs; but what constitutes his essential distinction from his Nuremberg predecessor, is the circumstance, that he wrote all his pieces for the sole object of representation, and in many of his tragedies and comedies displays a degree of skill in theatrical arrangements, and a knowledge of the requirements of the stage, which must place him far above Hans Sachs in this respect. The arrangements of his theatre must have been very similar to those of the old English stage. We shall have occasion to draw attention to this in several passages. His dramatic works were not published before 1618, long after his death, and although the 'Opus theatricum'[1] contains thirty tragedies and thirty-six Shrovetide-plays, we possess in them only a part of his dramas, as promise is made in the preface of forty other "fine merry comedies and tragedies, religious and profane," which were to follow soon after. They have never appeared, and only three unpublished pieces have been lately discovered in the Royal Library in Dresden, together with nineteen others which are printed in the 'Opus theatricum'. The manuscript is probably in Jacob Ayrer's own hand.[2] This dis-

[1] *Opus | Theatricum | Dreifsig | Aufsbündtige | schöne Comedien | vnd Tragedien von allerhand Denck- | würdigen alten Römischen Historien vnd anderen Politischen | geschichten vnd gedichten, Sampt noch andern Sechs vnd dreifsig | schönen lustigen vnd kurtzweiligen Fafsnacht | oder Possen Spilen, | Durch Weyland den Erbarn vnd wolgelährten Herrn Jacobum | Ayrer, Notarium Publicum, vnd Gerichts Procuratorn zu Nürmberg seeligen, Aufs | mancherley alten Poeten vnd Scribenten zu seiner weil vnd luft mit sonderm fleifs zusammen col- | ligirt, vnd in Teutsche Reimen Spilweifs verfaffet, das man alles Persönlich | Agirn kan, Sampt einem darzu gehörigen Register. | Gedruckt zu Nürmberg durch Balthasar Scherffen. | Anno* MDCXVIII. vi, 464 and 167 leaves. fol. (*Opus Theatricum. Thirty excellent beautiful Comedies and Tragedies of all sorts of memorable old Roman Histories and other Political stories and poems. Together with other six and thirty beautiful merry and amusing Shrovetide or Farce pieces. By the late honorable and learned Mr. Jacob Ayrer, Public Notary and Proctor to the Court at Nuremberg, collected out of various old Poets and writers with especial industry for his own amusement and gratification and composed in German rhymes for being acted &c. Together with an index appertaining thereto.*) — The first 464 leaves contain the "Comedien vnd Tragedien", the 167 following leaves are occupied by the "Fafsnacht oder Possen-Spile." At the end of the work stands "Gedruckt zu Nürnberg, durch Balthasar Scherff. Im Jahr MDCX." The Shrovetide Plays *may* have been printed in 1610, and the impression of the Comedies and Tragedies, for some reason, now unknown, may have been delayed until 1618; this however is very improbable. No mention of any such interruption of the impression is made in the long elaborate Preface, and the wrong date 1610 at the end is most probably nothing else than a printer's blunder. — Dr. Bell, *Shakespeare's Puck*, Vol. ii, p. 282 conjectures that MDCXVIII (1618) ought to be MDCVIII (1608), that the latter date indicates the beginning and the date (1610) at the end, the conclusion of the work. Nothing justifies this conjecture. Under the preface we read "*Datum Nürnberg, den 1. Januarii ... Im sechzehenhundert vnd achtzehenden Jahr*", and in the catalogues of the Leipzig Easter Fair ('Ostermefskatalog') the work does not appear before 1618. In the volume for 1618 we find it noticed in this way: "*Opus Theatricum* (both parts): *Nürnb. bey Michel Külfsn vnd Simon Halbm. 1618 in Fol.*" — A complete list of Ayrer's 69 pieces is to be found in K. Goedeke's *Grundrifs* etc. Vol. i, p. 412—415.

[2] See A. G. Helbig, *Zur Chronologie der Schauspiele des Jacob Ayrer*, in *Literarhistorisches Taschenbuch*, herausg. von R. E. Prutz, 1847, 8vo. Hannover, p. 441—444.

covery is especially valuable, as the date of its composition is attached to each piece, according to which the twenty two pieces of the manuscript were all written between the years 1595 and 1598. Two Singing plays (Singspiele) were each written in a single day.[1] It seems to us almost beyond the shadow of a doubt, that nearly all Ayrer's pieces were composed after 1593, the date of his return to Nuremberg. Some few, perhaps those which treat religious and purely epical subjects, may belong to an earlier period. In the preface to the 'Opus theatricum', the publisher says: "The late honorable ... Mr. Jacob Ayrer the elder, Imperial Notary, Citizen and sworn proctor to the Courts at Nuremberg, has during his life-time, in addition to his no small amount of business, partly private, partly that appertaining to his office, after diligent transaction of the same, in his hours of leisure and times of recreation been pleased to amuse and delight himself with the laudable composition of poetry, for the which he had an especially excellent genius and a *felix*, nay a *divinum ingenium*."[2] As mention is made here only of Ayrer's official duties in Nuremberg, we are justified in concluding, that at least at the time of the publisher, nothing whatever was known of any literary productions of his belonging to an earlier period, for we gather from a later passage in the preface that Ayrer's relations were still alive.

---

[1] This enables us to correct Koch's statement in his *Grundriſs* etc., that Ayrer's pieces were composed between the years 1570 and 1589, as also Tieck's conjecture (*Deutsches Theater*, Vol. i, p. xviii) that few of them were written before 1610, which is simply impossible, as Ayrer died in 1605. No less incorrect is Gottsched's statement in *Nöthiger Vorrath*, Vol. i, p. 121, that a German translation of Julius Redivivus by Frischlin, printed in 1585, is from Ayrer's pen. The title of the work alone is sufficient to shew that the translation is by Jacob Frischlin, the brother of Nicodemus Frischlin. This is one of Gottsched's numerous uncritical fancies, which was also adopted by Karl Schmitt in his *Jacob Ayrer. Ein Beitrag zur Geschichte des deutschen Dramas*. 8vo. Marburg 1851, p. 9. The same writer also draws conclusions respecting the year of Ayrer's birth, which are therefore incorrect. Also Dr. William Bell in his *Shakespeare's Puck* etc., Vol. ii, p. 278 et seq. draws conclusions from it respecting the time at which Ayrer's pieces were written, which are accordingly equally unfounded. See Karl Goedeke's *Grundriſs*, Vol. i, p. 323 and 411.

The above-mentioned conjecture of Tieck's is principally founded on a passage in the 'Julius Redivivus': "Das Trucken man erfunden hat Zu Maintz in der fürnemben Stadt Als nach Christi defs Herrn Geburt Vierzehen hundert Viertzig zehlt wurd Hans Guttenberg derselbig hiefs Der das erste Buch trucken liefs Vor Hundert vnd Siebentzig Jahrn," which may be roughly translated as follows: "The art of printing man invents In the famous town of Mentz, Fourteen hundred and forty years After Christ on earth appears. Hans Guttenberg the printer hight, Whose printed book first saw the light, Hundred and seventy years ago." This would certainly give the date of 1610, but as Ayrer died in 1605, the passage cannot be genuine, but must have been interpolated by some other hand. This solves Karl Goedeke's doubt as to whether the passage really was interpolated or not. (*Grundriſs*, Vol. i, p. 412.) A passage in Ayrer's Shrove-tide play '*Der Königin Podagra Tyranney*' referring to Hans Sachs shews the date of its composition to have been 1602. See ibid. p. 414.

[2] From this passage Dr. Bell has drawn the extraordinary conclusion that his dramas "were composed before he (Ayrer) was occupied by public affairs" — while the natural inference is precisely the reverse.

The German Text of the passage is as follows: "Weyland der Erbare ... Herr Jacob Ayrer der Elter, Kayserl. Notarius Burger vnd der Gerichten alhie zu Nürnberg geschworner Procurator ... hat in seinen lebzeiten, neben seinen nicht wenig obgelegenen, so wol Ampts als Privat gescheften, nach fleifsiger Expedirung derselben, zu seinen müssigen ruhstunden vnd erquickzeiten, jhme belieben lassen, in der Loeblichen Poeterey, darzu er dann sonderlich einen guten geist vnd Foelix ja Divinum ingenium gehabt, sich selbsten zu erlustiren vnd zu ergötzen."

When we consider that according to the notices in the Dresden manuscript Ayrer must have been a very rapid writer, there seems nothing improbable in the supposition that all his pieces were composed between the years 1593 and 1605. But however that may be, many of his dramas bear external and internal traces of English models, and it does not admit of a doubt, that all Ayrer's literary activity received its direction from his acquaintance with the English Comedians. Thus we find it remarked in the preface, that his comedies and tragedies were not alone graceful and pleasant to read, "but that everything was arranged after the life, and so managed, that just according to the new English manner, everything could be acted and played" ("sondern auch alles nach dem Leben angestellt und dahin gerichtet, das manns gleichsam auf die neue Englische manier und art, alles Persönlich Agirn und Spilen"). Hitherto this acquaintance with the English Comedians has been regarded as a proof, that those pieces which are known to have been produced under their influence must have been written after the year 1600, in as much as little or nothing was known of the English actors in Germany before that time. Should any doubt, however, still exist as to the incorrectness of this conclusion, in spite of the other evidence we have adduced, the Dresden Manuscript must remove it at once, for in some of the pieces it contains, the English models are expressly mentioned. Thus we find in the Singing pieces 'Of the three angry women', and 'The monk in the cheese-basket, to the same tune as they sing the English Rolant'; ('Von dreyen bösen Weibern', und 'Der Mönch im Kesskorb, Im Dhon wie man den Engeländischen Rolant singt') and in the 'Eulenspiegel, to the tune to which they sing the English play: Let us bide a while together, &c.' ('Im Dhon, wie man das Engellandische Spill: Lafst uns ein Weil bei einander pleyben &c. singt'). All these pieces were composed in 1598. In other dramas, which according to the Dresden Manuscript were composed before 1598, the Clown appears with a part written expressly for him, the surest sign of English influence. (See p. xlii.) We are therefore perfectly safe in assuming that Ayrer was acquainted with the English Comedians as early as 1595, and where this acquaintance is manifest in pieces, the date of which is unknown, we are not justified in concluding from it that any of his dramas must have been written later than 1600.

The first five pieces of the 'Opus theatricum' form a cycle of Roman histories which are partly called tragedies, partly comedies. This distinction is, with Ayrer, a purely external one: a piece in which deaths occur, is a tragedy, one in which there are none, a comedy, just as in Hans Sachs. In four of these comical histories, we already meet with the English Clown; and he is only wanting in the first of the five pieces. In the second piece, written in 1596, he is called 'Jahnn der Bott oder Engellendische Narr' (John the messenger, or the English Clown), in the third, also written in 1596, 'Jahnn der Bott', in the fourth, written in 1598, 'Jodel, der Lackey', and in the fifth, 'Jahnn Posset, der Bott'. In the 'Tragedy of the Emperor Otto the third'[1] he is called, 'Jahnn der Lackey'; in the

---

[1] *Opus theatricum*, i, fol. 85. Tragedia, *Von Keiser Otten des Dritten vnd seiner gemahlin sterben vnd end, aufs Manlio.* (*Tragedy of the death and end of the Emperor Otto the third and his consort, from Manlius.*)

'Tragedy of the Turkish Emperor Mahomet'[1] 'Jahn der Narr oder Possenreisser' (John the clown or merry andrew); in the 'Tragedy of the Greek Emperor at Constantinople'[2] 'Jahn der Narr oder Hencker' (John the Clown or Hangman); in the second part of the 'Comedy of Valentine and Urso'[3] 'Jahn der Engelländische Narr oder Prologus'; in the 'Comedy of Edward the third, King of England, and Elisa, Countess of Warwick'[4] 'Jahn Clam', similarly in the 'Comedy of the King of Cyprus';[5] in the 'Comedy of the beautiful Phænicia' 'Jahn der Kurtzweiler' (John the jester); in the 'Comedy of the two Syracusan brothers'[6] 'Jahn Panser'; in the 'Comedy of the Beautiful Sidea' (see p. 2) 'Jahn Molitor'; in the 'Comedy of the Old Gallant'[7] 'Jahn Grundo der närrische Knecht' (John Grundo, the foolish servant); and in the 'Comedy of the two Royal Counsellors'[8] 'John Türck der närrische

---

[1] *Opus theatricum*, i, fol. 147. *Schröckliche Tragedi. Vom Regiment vnnd schändlichen Sterben des Türckischen Keisers Machumetis des andern dis Namens, wie er Constantinopel eingenommen vnd gantz grausam tyrannisirt.* (Dreadful Tragedy of the government and disgraceful death of the Turkish Emperor Mahomet, the second of the name, how he took Constantinople, and tyrannized very cruelly.)

[2] Ibid. i, fol. 177. Reprinted in Tieck's *Altdeutsches Theater*, Vol. i, p. 200. *Tragedia, Von dem Griegischen Keyser zu Constantinopel, vnd seiner Tochter Pelimberia mit dem gehengten Horatio.* (Tragedy of the Greek Emperor at Constantinople, and his daughter Pelimperia with the hanged Horatio.)

[3] Ibid. i, fol. 272. *Comedia Ander Theil, Von Valentino vnd Vrso aufs der Beschreibung Wilhelmi Zilij von Beern in Vchtland.* (Comedy, Second Part. Of Valentine and Orson, from the account of William Zilius of Bern.)

[4] Ibid. i, fol. 384. *Comedia vom König Edwarto dem dritte difs Namens, König in Engelland, vnd Elipsa Herrn Wilhelm Montagy Gemahl, ein geborne Gräfin von Varucken* [Warwick]. (Comedy of King Edward the third of the name, King of England, and Elisa, wife of Lord William Montague, by birth Countess of Warwick.) — The same plot has been dramatised before in Germany: *Elisa. | Ein Newe vnd | lüstige Comoedia, Von | Edvardo dem Dritten | dieses Namens, Könige in Engel- | landt, Vnd Fraw Elisen | einer gebornen Gräffin von Warwitz, Gestellet | Durch | Philippum Waimern von | Dantzigk, B. R. D. | Summū crede nefas, animam p̄ferre pudori, | Et propter vitam, viuendi perdere causas. | Gedruckt zu Dantzigk, durch | Jacobum Rhodum. | 1591.* 12mo. (Elisa, a new and merry Comedy of Edward the third of the name, King of England, and Lady Elisa, a born Countess of Warwick, set forth by Philip Waimer of Danzig.) — This comedy has been represented at Danzig in 1591 by pupils of the Gymnasium, whose names are given on a separate leaf. In the preface the author mentions Bandello as his principal source. It is Novella 37 in Parte II of Bandello's novels. The comedy however deviates from the novel in many respects. Ayrer does not seem to have been acquainted with Waimer's play. Whether he knew the Old English 'Edward the third', ascribed to Shakespeare by some writers, is a question well worth investigation.

[5] Ibid. i, fol. 397. *Comedia Vom König in Cypern [Flavius] wie er die Königin in Franckreich [Clareta] bekriegen wolt, vnd zu der Ehe bekam.* (Comedy on the King of Cyprus how he wanted to make war against the Queen of France, and obtained her in marriage.)

[6] Ibid. i, fol. 424. *Comedia von zweyen Brüdern aufs Syracusa, die lang einander nicht gesehen hetten, vnnd aber von gestalt vnd Person einander so ehn(lich) wahren, das man allenthalben einen vor den andern ansahe.* (Comedy of the two brothers of Syracuse, who had not seen each other for a long time, and were so like each other in figure and person, that everywhere they were mistaken for each other.)

[7] Ibid. i, fol. 443. *Comedia von einem Alten Buler vnnd Wucherer, wie es jhme auff der Bulschafft ergangen, vnd wie er seines Weibs lieb probirt.* (Comedy of an old paramour and usurer, how he prospered in his loves, and how he put his wife's love to the proof.)

[8] Ibid. i, fol. 453. *Comedia von zweyen Fürstlichen Räthen die alle beede vmb eines gewettes willen vmb ein Weib Bulten, vnnd aber an derselben statt mit zweyen vnterschiedlichen Mägden betrogen worden.* (Comedy of two Princely counsellors, both of whom courted a woman for a wager, instead of whom they got two different maids.)

Knecht'. `Similar designations occur in the Shrove-tide plays, but in some of them the clown is not introduced. In 'The Tyranny of Queen Gout'[1] he is called 'Jahn Klan der Engellendisch Narr und ist ein Arzt' (John Clan the English Clown, a physician). Two of the Shrove-tide plays are entirely devoted to the Clown: the 'Carnival Play of the English John Posset (Bossed?) how he behaved in his service'[2], and the 'Shrove-tide Play of the lost English John Posset.'[3]

If these externals alone point imperatively to the Old English Theatre, the subjects themselves which were chosen by Ayrer offer still more irrefragable evidence of his intimate acquaintance with it. Thus in the 'Tragedy of the Greek Emperor at Constantinople and his daughter Pelimperia with the hanged Horatio' we have a new version of the 'Spanish Tragedy', following the original very closely, and indeed in all probability taken from the oldest form of this remarkable piece, which was afterwards remodelled by Thomas Kyd, and only appeared in print in 1602. But even Kyd's later form is supposed to have been played some years earlier on the London stages. Considering the great importance of the 'Spanish Tragedy' for the old English stage, it is a very interesting circumstance that for various reasons, which it is not necessary to mention here, Ayrer's 'Pelimperia' appears rather to have followed the first form of the piece which is entirely lost, and a translation of which is very much to be desired. In the present work we are obliged to reserve our space for pieces bearing more directly on our subject. In the 'Spanish Tragedy' as in the 'Pelimperia', a play is introduced within the play, just as in 'Hamlet', and as Gervinus has remarked, Ayrer's arrangement of the stage in this scene forcibly reminds us of the old English arrangement. In the next place, in the 'Comedy of the King of Cyprus', we meet with a subject probably taken at an earlier period by the English Dramatists from Bandello, which Lewis Machin, as it appears in connection with Gervase Markham, made use of in 1608, or shortly before, in his 'Dumb Knight'.[4] That Ayrer got this subject from the English Comedians appears to be established by the fact, that among the pieces which the latter played in Germany, and of which we shall have occasion to speak at a later page, there is one entitled: 'Ein lustig Pickelheringsspiel darinnen er mit einem Stein gar lustige Possen machet' (A merry play of the Clown, and of his merry tricks with a stone), which almost agrees with the comical episode in the 'King of Cyprus'. In the same manner also

---

[1] *Opus theatricum*, ii, fol. 38. *Comedischer Prozeſs, Action vnd Anklag wider der Königin Podagra Tyranney, mit angehenckter Defension, biſs zu Aufsgang des Proceſs.* (*Comedy suit, action, and accusation against the tyranny of Queen Gout, with defence annexed, to the end of the suit.*)

[2] Ibid. ii, fol. 110. Reprinted in Tieck's *Deutsches Theater*, Vol. i, p. 184—199. *Ein Faſsnachtsspill von dem Engelendischen Jann Posset wie er sich in seinen diensten verhalten, in deſs Rolandts Thon.* (*A Shrove-tide play of the English Jann Posset, how he behaved himself in his service, to Rolandt's tune.*)

[3] Ibid. ii, fol. 114. *Ein Faſsnachtspil der verlohren Engellendisch Jann Posset.* (*A Shrove-tide play of the lost English Jann Posset.*)

[4] *The Dumb Knight. An historical comedy, acted sundry times by the children of the Revels.* 4to. 1608; 4to. 1633. Entered on the Stationers' Registers, Octob. 6, 1608. Reprinted in Dodsley's *Collection of Old Plays*, Collier's edition, Vol. iv.

the two comedies 'Of an old paramour', and 'Of two princely Counsellors' have a great similarity with the farce 'Of the beautiful Maria and the old cuckold' in the 'English Comedies and Tragedies', of 1620;[1] and in the 'Comedy of King Edward the third' we meet with the quarrelling scenes between the clown and his wife, which are also to be found in the 'Comedy of Queen Esther and the proud Haman' in the same collection. Other pieces of Ayrer's, the subjects of which were also represented on the old English Theatres, but of which we cannot state with certainty that Ayrer derived them from that source, are as follows: 'A Tragedy of the reign and lamentable death of the Turkish Emperor Mahomet.' According to Henslowe's Diary, a play entitled 'Mahomet' was acted in August 1594, and George Peele has also composed one on the same subject, entitled, 'The Turkish Mahomet and Hiren the fair Greek.'[2] A play called, 'Valentine and Orson', by Anthony Munday and Richard Hathwaye, was performed in London in 1598. It is perhaps the same as that which is entered as an Interlude in the Books of the Stationer's Company as early as May 1595. We also find 'Valentine and Orson, a famous history' in their books in March 1600. The 'Comedy of the two brothers of Syracuse' agrees almost entirely with the 'Comedy of Errors', a subject which was familiar to the English stage long before Shakespeare, for in 1576 a 'Historie of Errors' was played in Hampton Court. But Ayrer may have written his piece after Plautus. A closer comparison might determine whether he took his subject from the latter or from an English source. It has been already observed that the Clown is introduced in this piece.

Of Ayrer's thirty-six Shrove-tide plays it is stated in the preface to the 'Opus theatricum', that "the invention is altogether new, and entirely his own." It must be confessed, that not one of these pieces can be traced to an English Original, but, on the other hand, Ayrer could only have taken the general character of them from the English Comedians, to whom the English jigs with singing and dancing must have come quite naturally, as they furnished them the best opportunity of amusing the public in spite of their foreign idiom.

---

[1] It may be observed here, that also Duke Henry Julius's *Comoedia von einem Weibe wie dasselbige jhre Hurerey für jhren Eheman verborgen, mit 6 Pers. Wolfenbüttel 1593*, in Dr. Holland's edition p. 261—295, (*Comedy of a woman, how she concealed her lechery from her husband. With six persons*) treats the same subject. The two pieces of Ayrer's appear to have been worked up later into one by some unnamed author: *Die Buhlerische Gesellschaft. Das ist: Zwey annehmliche erfreuende Comödien, die erste von einem alten Buhler, dem es auf seyner Freyerey seltsam ergangen ist; und die andere von zwey verbuhlten Rähten, so listiger Weise mit zweyen Mägden sind betrogen worden. Im jetzigen Jahr verneuert mit anweisenden Figuren. s. l. e. a. 8vo.* (*The amorous party. That is: two amusing agreeable comedies, the first of an old lover, who met with strange fortune in his wooing; and the second of two amorous counsellors, how they were cunningly deceived by two maids. Renewed in this present year, with explanatory figures.*) Gottsched's *Nöthiger Vorrath*, Vol. i, p. 182. Gottsched places this piece in the year 1623.

[2] Never published. It is alluded to in the *Merrie Conceited Jests of George Peele*, 1627, where it is termed a "famous play". Pistol's exclamation, "Have we not Hiren here?" is supposed to refer to it. One of the characters in Ayrer's play is "*Hircavena die schön Jungfrau*" and another "*Isidorus der Cardinal so die Histori beschrieben*" (*Isidorus the Cardinal who has described this History*). This latter character reminds that of Gower in Shakespeare's *Pericles*.

As we have already observed, the mere names of some of these farces of Ayrer's shew that he had derived his manner from the English actors, a fact which is also very evident from the part of the clown, who in Ayrer's pieces, as well in the tragedies and comedies as in the farces and singing pieces often appears with a whistle, just as the English Clown often does with a drum. Tieck conjectures that the Shrove-tide play, 'The vanquished Drummer' is an English farce. It may be so, but there is no known English piece from which Ayrer can have copied, though the manner certainly is altogether English.

Having thus given a general sketch of the relations of the whole of Ayrer's dramatic career to the old English stage, we now proceed to the consideration of two of his pieces which stand in direct connection with Shakespeare.

AYRER'S COMEDY OF THE BEAUTIFUL SIDEA.
(See p. 1—76.)

We give this piece complete in the German Original with an English translation annexed, not merely to promote the knowledge of Ayrer through one of his best pieces, but still more for the purpose of placing more easily within the students reach the only drama extant, which points to the origin of the plot of Shakespeare's 'Tempest'. Since Tieck directed attention to this piece in 1817, his conjecture that it is based upon an old English piece now lost, which Shakespeare also made use of in the 'Tempest', has been quoted by all the commentators, but according to all appearances none of them have become acquainted with the complete piece itself. English critics have probably been deterred by the difficulties of the old German style. The piece is now offered in an accessible form, and every one is able to judge for himself of the extent of its affinity to the 'Tempest'. That this affinity cannot be purely accidental, must be admitted at once by every attentive reader who is acquainted with the manner in which Shakespeare used the crude elements of his sources, but whether the common source of both authors is a drama, a legend, or a tale, will remain unsettled until the source itself has been discovered. Ayrer's piece has a thoroughly legendary character. The apparently historical personages are not to be met with in history. A Prince Ludolff of Lithuania has existed just as little as a Prince Leudegast of the Wiltau. The Wiltau is a fabulous name; the nearest approach to it is Wilna, but it does not appear that the latter has ever been so denominated. History has no record of any Polish Princess (Julia) who was engaged to be married to a son of a Prince of Wiltau (Engelbrecht). Ludolff says to Sidea 'May Jove &c.' and also in other passages the heathen gods are introduced. 'Heathen clothes' are expressly prescribed for Ludolff and Sidea, a direct proof that Ayrer placed the action in an ante-christian period. We thus find ourselves entirely on fabulous ground, while on the other hand, in the comic scenes, the tone and style of his contemporaries and a spirit of narrowminded localism are found to predominate, quite in the manner of the old German dramatists.

Ayrer is not the inventor of this subject; he has had either a legend or a play

before him. A proof of this is to be found in the first Act, where Leudegast says of Prince Ludolff:

Weil der zenkisch Herzog Leupold	Duke Leupold so loves strife and brawl,
Den Krieg und Zank hat also holt, &c.	That now he's challenged us to fall, &c.

No Duke Leupold appears throughout the whole piece, and the mention of one in this passage is a confusion of names which can only be explained by the supposition of a somewhat careless use of the original sources. It is true, in the introduction of humorous scenes and episodes this piece has many points of resemblance with the old English Theatre. But we have seen that all Ayrer's dramatic compositions after a certain date were under this influence, and this resemblance alone therefore is not sufficient to enable us to conclude, as Tieck has done, the existence of an old English Drama with the same subject. A circumstance of far greater importance is the fact, that the ideal arrangement as well as the single scenes and passages in both pieces display a most unmistakeable resemblance. Ayrer's removal of the action into the region of fable is a feature to which we have already alluded. In both pieces then we have two hostile princes, of whom the one (Prospero or Ludolff) practises the arts of magic to get the son of the other into his power, in both pieces this prince has a spirit in his service, through whose power the enemy's arms are rendered innocuous, and lastly, in both pieces an attachment is formed between the only daughter of the one prince, and the captive son of the other, which is eventually the means of bringing about a reconciliation between the hostile families. Both pieces are based on the idea of a retributory justice. If these points of resemblance in the fundamental structure of the two pieces are in themselves sufficient to exclude all possibility of an accidental coincidence, the numerous external points of agreement in the course of the two pieces must remove the last shadow of a doubt. In the one piece as in the other, the captive son of the prince is obliged to pile up logs of wood, and in both pieces this scene leads to the attachment of the lovers. In the 'Tempest', Act iii, sc. 1, Ferdinand says:

>My mistress, dearest,
>And I thus humble ever.

To which Miranda answers:

>My husband then?

Again in the 'Beautiful Sidea', Act iii, we find:

Engelbrecht.	*Engelbrecht.*
Ja dasselbe solt ihr trauen mir	Thou mayst place all thy trust in me,
Und ihr solt auch mein Gemahl sein.	And thou as consort soon be mine.
Sidea.	*Sidea.*
Bistu denn mein?	Art thou then mine?
Engelbrecht.	*Engelbrecht.*
Ja.	Yes.
Sidea.	*Sidea.*
So bleib ich dein.	Then I'm thine.

In the 'Tempest', Act i, sc. 2, Ferdinand says to Miranda:

> O! if a virgin,
> And your affection not gone forth, I'll make you
> The Queen of Naples.

and similarly in the 'Beautiful Sidea', Act iii:

Engelbrecht.	*Engelbrecht.*
Ja ich wolt mich eur Lieb ergeben	I would to thee my service give,
Zu dienst mit Leib vnd auch Leben	And ever love thee while I live;
Vnd euch zu einer Fürstin machen.	Thou shouldst a royal station grace.

Again we may compare the same scene in the 'Tempest', where Ferdinand draws his sword to defend himself against Prospero, and in which he "is charmed from moving" with the passage in the 'Beautiful Sidea' Act ii, in which Ludolff disarms Engelbrecht and his attendant by magic, and the latter is obliged to confess,

Mein Wehr kan ich nicht herauss bringen	My sword, sir, in its scabbard sticks;
Ich glaub das sie bezaubert sey.	I think it must enchanted be.

In the same manner, the scene in the fourth act of the 'Beautiful Sidea', in which the devils dance, reminds us forcibly of the 'Tempest', Act iii, sc. 3, in which the spirits with dance and mops and mowes carry out the table. — In Runzifall the devil, we have, in spite of all dissimilarities, the counterpart to Caliban, who indeed is not the evil one himself, but one of his progeny:

Prospero. Thou poisonous slave, got by the devil himself. Upon thy wicked dam, come forth! (Tempest, Act i, sc. 2.)

Just as Alonso institutes a search for Ferdinand in the 'Tempest', so does Prince Leudegast in the 'Beautiful Sidea' for his lost son, Engelbrecht.

We will, however, not anticipate any further, but will rather refer the reader to the piece itself for the numerous points of resemblance which we have not yet mentioned. "The origin of the plot of the 'Tempest' is for the present a Shakespearian mystery," are the words with which Mr. Hunter begins his dissertation upon that play. "That mystery I consider as solved" is Mr. W. J. Thoms'[1] assurance after having read Ayrer's 'Beautiful Sidea'. For our own part we cannot speak with so much confidence, for although in the Sidea, we possess the only link of connection between such source and the 'Tempest', we have not yet arrived at any certainty respecting the source itself. If we agree with most of the commentators that the 'Tempest' is one of Shakespeare's later works, there cannot be the slightest doubt that Ayrer's piece was written long before the 'Tempest'. In all those cases in which we are acquainted with the sources from which Ayrer derived his plots, we see that he almost always retains the original names for his principal persons; and as it is highly improbable that these, for the most part purely German, names should have occurred in an English drama of the sixteenth century, we cannot place much con-

---

[1] *On the connexion between the Early English and Early German Drama. New Monthly Mag.* 1841, January, p. 26.

fidence in the suggestion that any such work was the common source of the two plays in question. Ayrer appears rather to have worked after some German original, and this may have come to light in England in the form of some metamorphosis or other. Neither is it impossible, or even improbable, that Ayrer's piece itself may have come to Shakespeare's knowledge through the medium of comedians who had returned to England,[1] a conjecture which would only become utterly untenable, if an earlier English composition of the same or very similar contents should ever be discovered.

AYRER'S COMEDY OF THE BEAUTIFUL PHÆNICIA.
(See p. 77—112.)

At the first glance at this piece we see that it bears a very close resemblance to Shakespeare's 'Much Ado about Nothing', and that this resemblance is not confined to the serious portions of the two pieces, the principal features of which may be traced to Italian sources, but that also the humorous scenes between Beatrice and Benedick, the sources of which have hitherto been sought in vain, find their counterpart in the 'Beautiful Phænicia'.[2] Tieck, who again was the first to point out the connection of this piece with 'Much Ado about Nothing', has quite overlooked this circumstance, and yet is it precisely in these portions of the two pieces that the points of agreement are the most calculated to enable us to draw a conclusion respecting the source of Shakespeare's play. It is truly remarkable that just in these two pieces the connection between the comic episodes should have escaped Tieck's notice, while on the other hand he considers the comic scenes in the 'Sidea', which really have no connection whatever with anything in the 'Tempest', as a proof of some common dramatic original.

We have already (p. xliv) called attention to the relationship between Benedick and the Vincentius of Duke Henry Julius. The same elements are also to be met with in Ayrer's piece, although in an entirely different form; as that which in the former constitutes the principal action, is only an episode in the latter, the part of Vincentius being here assigned to the clown John. Externally indeed the two characters have nothing in common, but their dramatic significance is the same, and their adventures lead us to Benedick and Beatrice. The resemblance of Ayrer's episode with that of Shakespeare is apparently a very distant one, and yet again a very close one as soon as we disregard the persons and scenes, and only pay attention to the means employed by both authors for attaining the same

[1] Edward Cellius, among others, speaks of such English Comedians returning to England, in his description of the festivities which took place at the Court of Stuttgart in the year 1603, on the occasion of the already mentioned English Embassy. "Paucis ab hinc annis in Germaniam nostram Anglicani musici dictum ob finem expaciati, et in magnorum Principum aulis aliquandiu versati, tantum ex arte musica, histrionicaque; sibi favorem conciliarunt, ut largiter remunerati domum inde auro et argento onusti sint reversi." *Eques auratus Anglo-Wirtembergicus.* 4to. Tubingae 1605, p. 229.

[2] This has already been noticed by H. Grimm in his above-mentioned essay on the Theatre of Duke Henry Julius. For many of the observations respecting the connections between the 'Phænicia' and 'Much Ado about Nothing' that follow in the text, we are indebted to that work.

object. The gist of Shakespeare's intrigue consists in the joke of making Benedick believe that Beatrice is in love with him, and persuading Beatrice that Benedick is in the same case with regard to herself. Let us now compare this with John's first adventure in the 'Beautiful Phænicia'. He is in love with Anna Maria; his master offers to woo her for him in his name, and deceives him into the belief that she shares his affection. Hence arises the scene, in which the fool is made such a miserable dupe. Considered simply by itself, so distant a resemblance would not justify any conclusion respecting a common source. But here there is an additional circumstance, which decidedly favours such a conclusion. The foundation of Shakespeare's as well as Ayrer's piece is unquestionably Bandello's tale, 'Como il S. Timbreo di Cardona essendo col Re Piero d'Aragona in Messina s'innamora di Fenicia Lionato.'[1] This story contains nearly all the leading features of the principal action, the love affair between Claudio and Hero in Shakespeare, and that between Timbreo and Phænicia in Ayrer. Of the humorous underplots in both pieces, the tale does not contain the slightest trace.

Now we must remember that the two humorous couples of lovers stand in no relation whatever to the principal action in the two pieces. In Shakespeare indeed they are

---

[1] There is a French version of Bandello's tale by Belleforest. German imitations of it, of the sixteenth and seventeenth century, are mentioned below. Whether Ayrer knew the first two or not, is a matter of indifference, as No. 2, and probably No. 1, contains nothing which is not also in Bandello and Belleforest.

1. Mauritius Brand, *Phoenicia. Eine schöne, züchtige, liebliche vnd gedechtnifswürdige History was massen ein Arragonischer Graff de Colison sich in eine edle vnd tugentreiche sicilianische Jungfraw Phoenicia genannt, verliebt.* 4to. Danzig 1594. (*Phœnicia, a beautiful, chaste, delightful and memorable history, how an Arragonian Count of Colison fell in love with a noble and virtuous Sicilian virgin, named Phœnicia.*) — 2. *Phoenicia. Eine Liebliche vnd Gedechtniswirdige History, was massen ein Arragonischer Graffe de Colisan, sich in eine Edle vnd Tugentreiche Sicilianische Jungfraw Phoenicia genandt, verliebete. Vnd was denselben in Heyrath vnd Freysachen wiederfahren, welches billig ein Spiegel Weiblicher Ehr vnd Zucht mag genennet werden. Allen Züchtigen vnd Ehrliebenden Frawen vnd Jungfrewlein zum Newen Jahre beschrieben, durch Mauritium Brand.* 8vo. Magdeburgk bey Joh. Francken, s. a. [circa 1600]. (*Phœnicia. A delightful and memorable history &c. And what befel them in marriage and in courting which may rightly be called a mirror of maidenly virtue and honour. Written for all chaste and honorable ladies and virgins for the new year.*) — 3. *Lieb: Tugendt vnd Ehrn-Spiegel, Vermittels Herrn Timbrei von Cardona Lieb, gegen Phoeniciam Lionati, dero wunderbaren begegnussen vnd endlicher Ehevollstreckung, von Herrn Francisco Belleforest in Frantzösischer: vnd anjtzo aus derselben in Teutscher Sprach vorgestellet vnd ferner adorniret durch Wolfgangum Seidelum.* 12mo. Hof, Matth. Pfeilschmidt, 1624. (*Love, Virtue, and Honour's mirror .... set forth in French by Belleforest, and now done into German language by W. Seidel.*) — 4. The same version by W. Seidel, 12mo. Coburgk, in der Fürstlichen Druckerey, durch Joh. Forckel, in Verlegung Friederich Gruners, 1627. — I have not seen No. 1 and quote from Koch, *Grundrifs*, Vol. ii, p. 245, who again refers to *Catal. Bibl. Schwabianae*, Part ii, p. 269, and from K. Goedeke, *Grundrifs* etc., Vol. i, p. 413. I do not know therefore whether this original edition varies from No. 2, and whether it also contains the addition to the title "Mirror of maidenly virtue and honour". If so, then Ayrer has certainly taken his title from it; if not, then the addition to the title of No. 2 has been taken from Ayrer. — There is also a Latin version of the same subject, unless the title in Clessius, *Elenchus consummatissimus librorum* etc. Vol. ii, 4to. Francof. 1602, p. 241, is merely a translation of the German one No. 2. According to Clessius it is entitled: *Phoenicia: Historia de comite de Colisan ex Arragonia amatoria erga virginem ex Sicilia, nomine Phoenicia.* 8vo. Magdeburg 1600. — There is also a late dramatic version of the subject: Matthaei Kranich, *Comödia von einem Graven von Colisan mit 26 Personen zu agiren.* 8vo. Erffurdt, bey Joh. Bircknern (1620 or 1621). See Gottsched, *Schaubühne*, Vol. iv, p. 43.

interwoven with the external incidents in the most charming manner, but even with him they have no influence on the development of the principal action of the piece. In Ayrer, of course, anything like an internal connection with the main plot is quite out of the question. Is it possible then that two authors, when using the same tale, should add to it a new element so very similar in the two cases? We must confess, this appears to us quite inconceivable. In our opinion, either in Italy or in England a dramatic piece was founded on the novel, that Shakespeare, Henry Julius, and Ayrer were all acquainted with it, and that this piece contained a comic episode, which Shakespeare and Ayrer, each in his own way, interwove with the main plot, but which Henry Julius has detached, and worked up into a separate comedy by itself.[1] If this piece should ever come to light, we shall certainly find in it the origin of Shakespeare's allusion in Act i, sc. 1: "He set up his bills here in Messina, and challenged Cupid at the flight &c." Does not also the mention of Cupid and Vulcan at the opening of both pieces confirm this conjecture? In Shakespeare, Benedick says:

"Cupid is a good hare-finder, and Vulcan a rare carpenter";

and in Ayrer, Cupid says of himself,

| Mein Vatter der zornig Vulcanus | For Vulcan now my wrathful sire |
| Der hat mir etlich Pfeil geschmit. | Has a few arrows forged for me. |

In Shakespeare also, the connection of the fool with Cupid in Beatrice's speech: ... "and my uncle's fool, reading the challenge, subscribed for Cupid and challenged him at the bird-bolt" reminds us of the fool in Ayrer's piece, who is struck by Cupid's arrow. Then it must also be observed that the scenic arrangements in both pieces agree in the most remarkable manner. In both we have a dance, a serenade, and the scene at the coffin, but it must be confessed that the elements for it are to be found in the tale. But a careful comparison of the latter itself with our two pieces affords the most striking proof that there must have been some intermediate member between it and them. In the tale, Girando, in determining on the shameful act of treachery against Timbreo, is influenced entirely by a feeling of jealousy. In the same manner, in the episode in the fifth book of Ariosto's Orlando furioso, which Bandello has certainly made use of, and which also supplied the subject of 'The History of Ariodante and Geneuora', a drama acted in London as early as 1582, jealousy is the sole motive of the Duke of Albania. This is not the case either in Ayrer or in Shakespeare. In the former, Gerando meditates some rogue's trick against Tymborus, because he has become too powerful and influential. Afterwards he appears to put forward his admiration of Phænicia as a mere pretext for his revenge on Tymborus, for up to that time, there is no mention in the piece of any love affair between himself and Phænicia. Again in Shakespeare, the Bastard does not act from motives of jealousy, but only from a feeling of general discontent. This makes his depravity appear all the greater, and his treachery to Claudio all the blacker. Gerando in Ayrer stands in no

---

[1] See Herm. Grimm, *Das Theater* etc.

relations to Tymborus, just as in Shakespeare the Bastard has not the slightest connection with Claudio, who is most immediately affected by his treachery. In Ayrer Gerwalt, who invents the knavery, like Borachio in Shakespeare, is only the tool of another, to please whom, or in whose commission as it were, the trick is executed, this other being Gerando in Ayrer, and in Shakespeare the Bastard. In Bandello, on the other hand, the jealous Girondo is also the inventor of the plan by which Timbreo is deceived. Another very essential point in which the two plays diverge from the tale, is the following: In Bandello, the deceit is practised by means of a servant of Girondo, who is disguised to represent the pretended lover of Phænicia, and climbs into a room at a window which is left open day and night, and at which Phænicia is in the habit of appearing occasionally. This is sufficient to make Timbreo consider the suspicions which had been suggested to him, as well founded. The impostors do not appear at the window of the room, neither is there any conversation carried on between them. In Ayrer, the fool John is put into woman's clothes, and appears as Phænicia walking hand in hand with Gerwalt, her supposed lover, in her father's garden, and conversing with him. Timbreo sees them from his hiding-place, and hears their lover's talk. Similarly in Shakespeare, Margaret puts on Hero's clothes, and carries on a lover's conversation with Borachio, which Claudio hears from his hiding-place in the garden. Act iii, sc. 4 in Shakespeare's piece begins with a conversation between Hero and Margaret about the wedding-dress. Similarly, in Ayrer, the scene in which her intended marriage with Timbreo is broken off, is preceded by a conversation between Phænicia and her parents respecting her trousseau. The resemblance between the two pieces is very striking in the scenes, in which it is resolved to allow Hero and Phænicia to be considered as dead, in order to bring their innocence to light. In these scenes in Ayrer, the action advances in a somewhat compressed and dramatic style, while in Bandello he would have had a model which could only have encouraged his natural inclination to represent everything with great circumstantiality and numerous digressions. Bandello is extremely diffuse here, and makes Fenicia address a long-winded speech to the bystanders, who on their part also break out into very edifying lamentations. In these scenes, both in Shakespeare and Ayrer, the hope is distinctly expressed, that the pretended death of the slandered maiden may awaken the remorse of her lover, and eventually end in their happy union. This feature is altogether wanting in Bandello, and it is at the same time an important characteristic in the two dramatists, because in the principal catastrophe of the piece it points out the germ of the reconciliation, and softens the tragical character of the scene. The expectation of a reconciliation which is thus raised in the mind of the spectator justifies moreover the progress of the piece as a comedy. After the treachery, which has been practised against Phænicia, has been discovered, the prime movers in the criminal act, the Bastard in Shakespeare, and in Gerwalt Ayrer, disappear. This feature is also wanting in the tale.

'Much Ado about Nothing' appears to have been written either in, or about, the year 1600. Francis Meres does not mention it in 1598, but the first Quarto was published

in 1600. Ayrer's piece may have been written either earlier or later. As long as the chronology of his dramas is not established with greater certainty than has been hitherto the case, it is impossible to express any opinion respecting the priority of either author with regard to the two pieces in question.

It may be mentioned in conclusion, that Starter, a Dutch dramatist of the seventeenth century has also taken the same subject for one of his pieces.[1] But Mr. J. O. Halliwell is decidedly wrong in asserting that Starter copied Shakespeare,[2] as also Dr. W. Bell in his statement, that the Dutchman's piece was founded on Ayrer's.[3] The truth is, that in Starter's piece there are no traces either of 'Much Ado about Nothing' or the 'Beautiful Phænicia', and that there is every appearance of his having taken his subject directly from Bandello's tale or an early imitation of it. It is true, he also introduces comic personages who speak in the Frisian dialect, but they have nothing in common with the humorous episodes, either in Shakespeare or Ayrer.

CHAPTER IV.

In the course of our investigation up to this point, we have been able to distinguish three companies of English Comedians, who started from England on their travels as early as the sixteenth century. With the beginning of the seventeenth century these strolling companies become more and more numerous, and no longer confine themselves to the courts of princes, but extend their wanderings to every part of Germany in which they may expect to find a sufficient interest in their art.[4] It is true, some companies still continued to make the court of some art-loving prince their head-quarters, but even these led a migratory life, and it appears that they made the permission to do so, one of the conditions in their engagements. We have already observed something of the kind in the case of the Cassel Comedians. (See p. lix.) Besides the courts of Brunswick and Cassel, which, as we have already seen, entertained English actors till far into the seventeenth

---

[1] *I. I. Starters | Blyeyndich-Truyrspel, | van | Timbre de Cardone | ende | Fenicie van Messine, | Met een Vermaecklijck Sotte-Clucht van een | Advocaet ende een Boer op't plat Friesch. | Tot Leevwarden, | Voor Jan Jansen Starter, Boeckvercooper by de Brol, | in d'Engelsche Bybel. Anno, 1618.* 4to. 42 leaves. In rhyming verse. The Argument "Inhout des Spels" appears to be a condensed narrative of Bandello's novel.

[2] See *Athenæum*, April 21, 1862.

[3] See Dr. W. Bell, *Shakespeare's Puck* etc., Vol. ii, p. 285. Dr. Bell founds his argument on the identity of the *dramatis personae* in Ayrer's and Starter's plays, but he overlooks that the same names are given to those personages in Bandello's novel.

[4] This is confirmed by a curious passage in De Bry's *India orientalis*, Pars xii, fol., Francof. 1613, p. 137. "Vigesimo primo ejusdem mensis die rex iterum Anglorum navem petiit, magna stipatus mulierum caterva, quae omnes mimae erant, actrices comaediarum, et saltatrices. Solent autem hae mulieres agmine facto oberrare per provincias et oppida, acturae comaedias, *ut Angli ludiones per Germaniam et Galliam vaguntur*, vehentes secum omnis generis vestes et instrumenta histrionica, pro exigentia fabularum quas lusurae sunt, in quibus frequentissima sunt argumenta belli, amoris, et ejusmodi."

century, it was more especially the courts of Dresden and Berlin, which manifested the most active theatrical life.

The company to which Thomas Pope and George Bryan belonged, probably dissolved itself as early as 1587, for we meet with both of them in England before 1588. The taste for the English theatre had so completely established itself at the Saxon court, that it maintained its preponderance till far into the seventeenth century. Indeed, even after the influence of the French Theatre had obtained the mastery throughout Germany, the pieces which had been introduced by the English Comedians were not entirely banished from the Dresden stage, and we even meet with isolated cases of English actors long after the German companies had supplanted the English ones. In the course of our narrative we shall arrive at the astonishing fact, that the Germans became acquainted with the greatest masterpieces of Shakespeare through the medium of the stage, nearly a century and a half before any other nation except of course the English.

The Electress Dowager of Saxony, Sophia of Brandenburg, daughter of John George, Markgrave of Brandenburg, (born 1568, married to Christian I in 1582, a widow in 1591, died 1622) appears while still young, to have taken a peculiar interest in the English drama, and the English Comedians. In October 1600, several Englishmen, ["etzliche Engelender"] played a comedy before her and the young princes at the palace, for which they received the sum of 75 florins. In the same year there were also English Comedians at Memmingen, as appears from the following extract from a chronicle of that town: "1600, den 27. und 28. Hornung, hielten Engeländer Comedien allhier auff dem Saltz-Stadel, gab ein Person 4 kr."[1] (1600, Feb. 27 and 28, some Englishmen performed comedies here on the Saltz-Stadel, each person paid four kreuzers.) In June 1601, some Englishmen played again at the Court of Dresden, for which they received a hundred dollars gratuity ["Verehrung"] and $78\frac{1}{2}$ florins as payment.[2] They must therefore have come to Dresden as strangers, and were not in the Saxon service. Perhaps they were the same who had played at Memmingen; perhaps also they had come from Brunswick or Cassel on leave of absence. In 1602 some English Comedians performed at Ulm a play 'Of the Prophet Daniel, the chaste Susanna, and the two judges in Israel'. (See p. xlii). There must also have been some English actors in Amsterdam about this time, for an incident related by Heywood in the 'Apology',[3] of which we shall speak more at length at a future page, refers to them. Heywood expressly calls them "A well knowne company of our English comedians", a proof, that actors of reputation attached themselves to these companies. In September 1603, Lord Spenser and Sir William Dethick, Garter King-at-arms, were sent to Stuttgart by James the first, to bring Duke Frederick the Insignia of the Order of the Garter. (See p. xiv.) The Ambassadors displayed a great deal of splendour and magnificence, and among their suite they had some English musicians and actors, — "Four excellent Musicians with

---

[1] Christ. Shorer, *Memminger Chronik* etc. 4to. Ulm 1660, p. 115.
[2] Mor. Fürstenau, *Zur Geschichte* etc., p. 76.
[3] Ed. by the Shakespeare Society, p. 58.

ten other assistants."[1] A great banquet took place after the delivery of the Order to the Duke, and this was succeeded by representations given by the "Royal English Music, which the illustrious royal ambassadors had brought with them to enhance the magnificence of the embassy and the present ceremony, and who, though few in numbers, were eminently well skilled in the art. For" continues the chronicler of those festivities, "England produces many excellent musicians, comedians, and tragedians, most skilful in the histrionic art; certain companies of whom quitting their own abodes for a time, are in the habit of visiting countries at particular seasons, exhibiting and representing their art principally at the courts of princes. A few years ago, some English musicians coming over to our Germany with this view, remained for some time at the courts of great princes, their skill both in music and in the histrionic art having procured them such favour, that they returned home greatly rewarded, and loaded with gold and silver."[2] A dance followed the banquet, and then "the English players made their appearance, and represented the sacred history of 'Susanna' with so much art of histrionic action, and with such dexterity, that they obtained both praise and a most ample reward."[3]

The following year, [1604] we meet with a company of comedians in Holland, under the direction of a certain John Woods [Wood?].[4] The following extract from the Minutes of the Council of the city of Leyden [Gerechtsdag-boeken] refers to them.

Sept. 30, 1604. — "Die van de Gerechte opt voorschryven van Zijne Ex^e en versouc van Jan Woodtss, Engelsman, hebben toegelaten ende geconsenteert dat hy geduyrende deze aenstaende jaermarct met zijn behulp zal mogen speelen zeecker eerlick camerspel tot vermaeckinge van der gemeente, mits van yder persoen (comende om te bezien) nyet meer te mogen nemen nochte genyeten dan twaelf penn., ende vooral betaelen tot een gootspenning aen handen van Jacob van Noorde, bode metter roede, vier guld. om ten behouve van de armen verstrect te worden."

TRANSLATION.

The magistrates, at the command of his Excellency, and at the request of John Woodtss, an Englishman, have permitted and consented that he, with his company, during the approaching fair,

[1] A description of the festivities has been given by Erhard Cellius, entitled *Eques auratus Anglo-Wirtembergicus*. 4to. Tubingae 1605. The above passage is to be found at p. 120: "Quatuor excellentes musici, una cum decem ministris aliis."

[2] Id. ibid. p. 229. "Musica Anglicana Regiae, quam Regius illustris Legatus secum ad Legationis et actus huius magnificentiam adduxerat: non ita multos quidem sed excellenter in hac arte versatos. Profert enim multos et praestantes Anglia musicos, comoedos, tragoedos, histrionicae peritissimos, è quibus interdum aliquot consociati sedibus suis ad tempus relictis ad exteras nationes excurrere, artemq'; suam illis praesertim Principum aulis demonstrare, ostentareq'; consueverunt. Paucis ab hinc annis in Germaniam nostram Anglicani musici dictum ob finem expaciati, et in magnorum Principum aulis aliquandiu versati, tantum ex arte musica, histrionicaq'; sibi favorem conciliarunt, ut largiter remunerati domum inde auro et argento onusti sint reversi." See also *Notes and Queries*, Vol. iii, p. 21.

[3] Id. ibid. p. 244. "Histriones Anglicani mature prodibant; et sacrae Susannae historiam tanta actionis histrionicae arte, tanta dexteritate representabant, ut et laudem inde et praemium amplissimum reportarent."

[4] A John Wood, clerk, is mentioned in an arbitration-bond respecting certain disputes between Henslowe and a person named Abr. Wall. See *Alleyn papers* ed. by J. P. Collier for the Shakespeare Society, 1843, p. 49.

may play certain decent pieces for the amusement of the people, provided he take no more than twelve pennings from each person coming to see, and, above all, pay to Jacob van Noorde four guilders, to be applied to the use of the poor.[1]

Another company appears in Leyden in January 1605, provided with a letter of recommendation from the Elector of Brandenburg, dated the 10th of August 1604. We are not aware at what time this company had entered the service of the latter; but it is clear that it was under the direction of a certain John Spencer, for in the same year [1605] he is recommended by the Elector of Brandenburg to the Electress of Saxony. The identity of these companies is beyond all doubt. The following is an extract from the Leyden Minutes.

Jan. 6, 1605. — "Op't versouck aen die van de Gerechte gedaen by de Engelsche Comedyanten om te mogen spelen: staet geappostilleert. Die van de Gerechte deser stadt Leyden gesien in haer vergaderinge opt Raedthuys der voors. stede, de favorable brieven van Recommandatie ende testimoniael van den Forst van Brandenburch van de x Augustij des jaers XVIe vier, mitsgaders t consent by Zyne Ex^{ie} van Nassau verleent den xxij Decembris laest verleden, Es disponerende opt versouc int blanc van dezen, hebben voor zoo veel in hem is, de Engelsche Commedianten ende musicyns toonders in dezen, conform haer versouc toegelaten binnen deser stede te mogen spelen en haer consten doen ouffenen ende vertoonen ter gewoenlycke plaetse te weten opten groten hoff onder de bibliotecque, dewelcke hem toonders mits dezen ten eynde voorseyt, belast wert te werden ingeruymt, Ende dit al voor den tyt van veertien dagen eerstcomende, en mits, voor den jegenwoordige gracieuse toelatinge, gevende ten behouve van de gemeene huysarmen dezer stede een somme van twaelf gulden van xl groot tstuck. Aldus, gedaen opten vi January XVI^c eñ vyff. My jegenwoordich en is get. J. van Hout."

TRANSLATION.

On the request to the magistrates of the English comedians to be allowed to perform, was decided: The magistrates of this city of Leyden, having seen in their assembly in the Town-House of the aforesaid city, the favourable letters of recommendation and testimonial of the Prince of Brandenburg of the 10th Aug., 1604, as well as the consent granted by his Excellency of Nassau, the 22nd of Dec. last, have permitted the English comedians and musicians, according to their request, to perform and exercise and exhibit their arts in the accustomed place, namely, in the great court under the library; and this for the space of fourteen days, provided they, for this gracious permission, give twelve guilders of forty groats a-piece to the poor of this city. Done on the 6th Jan., 1605. Me present; and signed J. van Hout.[2]

We cannot ascertain when John Spencer came from England to Germany, but he must have been some time in the service of the Elector of Brandenburg when he received the letter of recommendation in August 1604. It is supposed that he had been obliged to leave his native country on account of his attachment to the Catholic Church.[3] He remained in Germany for a considerable number of years, and became one of the most celebrated managers of companies. In the course of our narrative we shall meet with him again at different places till as late as the year 1614.[4]

---

[1] See *Navorscher's Bijblad* 1853, p. xl, and *Notes and Queries*, Vol. vii, 1853, p. 360.

[2] To be found at the same place as the preceding one.

[3] See Hurter, *Ferdinand der Zweite*, Theil iii, p. 313.

[4] A Gabriel Spenser is mentioned in various places of Henslowe's *Diary*. In 1597 he belonged to the

In May 1605, the company proceeded from Leyden to the Hague, at least it is highly probable that it is the same company which we meet with at the latter place. It appears that several representations were given there during the fair. The States General were angry that this had taken place without their having been previously informed, summoned the actors to appear before them, who then alleged in their defence, that they possessed a licence from the Prince Stattholder, had obtained permission from the Magistracy to give representations for eight or ten days, and received three stivers as the price of admission; upon which they were prohibited from continuing their performances after the expiration of the week they had then entered upon. The following document, which is now published for the first time, refers to these circumstances.

Extract uit het Register der Resolutien van den Hove van Holland, van den 2ⁿ October 1602 tot den 28 Maart 1608. A. Duÿck, Griffier.

"10 May 1605. Wert verhaelt van de Engelse camerspeelders ende dat die fonder virlof van den Hove hier speelden ende wert den Procureur-Generael gelast te vernemen mit wiens last ofte consent sy speelen; hy refereert dat se acte van consent van syn Excellencie hebben ende toelatinge van den magistraet van den Haegen. Wert verstaen dat men se sal ontbieden in decleine camer ende selfshoiren, om daer de acte te fien. Sy gecommen wesende seggen acte te hebben, ende toelatinge voor 8 ofte 10 daegen van den magistraet te hebben, ende met heur consent te nemen van elck perfoin 3 stuvers; exhiberen naer de acte in forma, wert heur gevraecht waerom sy geen consent van den Hove en hebben versocht. Sy verclaeren fulex niet geweten te hebben van noode te wesen. Einteleyck wert verstaen dat se niet langer als dese weecke en fullen mogen speelen, ende her fulex aengeseit."

TRANSLATION.

Extract from the Register of the Resolutions of the Court of Holland, from the 2nd of October 1602 to the 28th of March 1608. A. Duÿck, Clerk to the Court.

10. May 1605. It is reported of the English actors, that they played without the permission of the Court, and the Procurator General is commissioned to inquire with whose authority or consent they play. They answer that they have acted with the consent of His Excellency and the permission of the Magistracy of the Hague. It is agreed that they shall be summoned to the little saloon, to hear them ourselves, and there to see them act. When they have come, they say that they have acted and have received permission from the Magistracy for eight or ten days, and with their consent to take from each person three stivers. After they have exhibited their acting in form, they are asked, why they had not endeavoured to obtain consent from the Court. They declare not to have known that it was necessary. Finally it is agreed that they shall not be allowed to play longer than this week, and that this shall be notified to them.

According to this, the company must have left Holland, and have returned to Prussia; for about September and October 1605, we meet them at Elbing and Kœnigsberg, where

---

Earl of Nottingham's players, and in 1598 he was killed by Ben Jonson in a duel in Hoxton Fields. See Henslowe's *Diary* p. 98. — In 1631, a certain John Spenser addressed an admonitory letter to an unnamed Lady who was present on the occasion of the performance of the 'Midsummer Night's Dream' on Sunday, Septemb. 27, 1631, in the house of John Williams, Bishop of Lincoln, in London. The letter is found amongst Bishop Laud's papers in the Library at Lambeth Palace. The Bishop of Lincoln and many persons of rank who were present at the play, were fined by Laud. See J. P. Collier, *History* etc. Vol. ii, p. 27—36. Has our catholic player turned Puritan?

they gave several representations before the Duchess Mary Eleanor, as appears from the following extracts from the Royal Archives in Kœnigsberg.

Elbing. Rathsrecess. Session vom 14. Sept. 1605.

"Ist beliebet den englischen Comödianten wegen dessen, daſs sie vorgestern einen Erb. Rath zu Gefallen agiret 20 Thlr. zur Verehrung zukommen zu lassen. Daneben aber auch ihnen zu untersagen, daſs sie nunmehr zu agiren aufhören sollen in Anmerkung sie gestern in der Comödie schandbare sachen fürgebracht."

Ausgabe-Register, fol. 127.

"75 Mark vff begehren Meiner gst. Fürstin vnd Frawen etc. der Herzogin in Preussen etzlichen Englischen Comedianten, welche vor Ihr fürstl. Gnd. agiret, zweimal getanzet vnd mit einer lieblichen Musica vfgewartet, gezahlt den 3. Octob." [1605].

TRANSLATION.
Elbing. Decree of the Council. Session of the 14th of Sept. 1605.

In consideration of what the English Comedians acted the day before yesterday for the pleasure of the Honorable Council, it is hereby resolved to award them a gratification of 20 thalers. Further, seeing that they yesterday represented disgraceful things in their comedy, it is decreed that they shall not act any more.

Register of Expences. Fol. 127.

75 Marks at the desire of my gracious Princess and Lady etc. Duchess of Prussia, to some English Comedians, who acted, danced twice, and performed delightful music before her Princely Grace, paid the 3rd of Oct. 1605.

Whether the company remained any longer in East Prussia or repaired for a short time to the Court of Berlin, is a question we are unable to decide. At all events it must have gone to Mecklenburg soon after, for it appears from a petition presented by it to the Council of the town of Rostock, which has been found in the town-archives and which is here annexed, that in March 1606, the company had already been there some time.

An E. E. Rath.

Ernuheste, Achtbare, Hoch vnd Wolgelerte, Hoch vnd Wolweise, E. E. vnd hw. sein vnsere gehorsame Dienste, mit besonderem fleiſse zuuor, groſsgunstige gepietende liebe Herrn,

Für E. E. vnd hw. vns biſs dahero bezeigte vberaus groſse vnd vilfeltige gunst vnd befoderung, in dem das wir nun allhie eine geraume Zeitt, von E. E. v. hw., groſsgunstiglich geduldett, vnd vnserm geringen vermugen vnd kunst nach, mit vnser Music auch geistlichenn vnd weltlichenn Historien, commedien vnd tragedienn, gemeiner Stadt, dienen mugen, vnd sonsten, Dafür sein wir gegen E. E. v. hw. nicht alleinn dienstliches hochstes fleisses danckbar, sondern wollen dasselbe auch umb E. E. vnd hw. mit vnserm geringen gebete, vnd Diensten, Zuuordienen vnd sonsten Zurühmen wissen,

Vnd ob wir also woll billig, E. E. vnd hw. vber gedachte bezeigte groſse vielfeltige gunst vnd befoderung, ferner womitt nicht beschwerenn solltenn, weil aber dennoch, vns hiebeuohr in andern Stettenn Da wir auch gewesen, vnsers vorhaltens halben allhie, E. E. vnd hw. vrkundt, in andern benachbartten Steten vnd sonstenn furzulegen habenn, Alſsbitten wir demnach auch dienstliches hochstes fleiſses, [weil wir vns ie ohne ruhm zumelden auch allhie still vnd eingezogenn vorhaltenn, auch nicht anders dan was lieblich vnd wol anzusehenn vnd zuhoren gewesen, agirt vnd musicirt] E. E. vnd hw. wollen vber vorige vns bezeigte grosse gunst vnnd befoderung, ferner auch noch in diesem so groſsgünstiglich erscheinen, vnd vnsers vorhaltenns halbenn, vns eine vrkundt vnter gemeiner Stadt insiegell groſsgünstiglich mittheilen vnd zukommen lassenn, vnd wir seinn es vmb E. E. vnd hw. mit vnsern

geringenn Dienstenn vnnd sonstenn wie vorgemeldett hinwider Zuuordieuenn Zum hochstenn gefliefsenn, Datum Rostogk denn 31. Martij 1606.

E. E. vnd hw.

gehorsame,
Marggrefen von Brandenborgk Diener
Engelsche Commedianten.[1]

TRANSLATION.

To the most honourable Town Council.

Right honourable, high and well learned, high and well-wise Gentlemen, to your honours and high mightinesses our most humble services, with particular esteem before. High-favouring, commanding, beloved Gentlemen, — As your honours and high worthies protected us until now with the greatest and most exceeding favour and advancement, considering also, that we were suffered here for a considerable length of time, to execute our music and religious and worldly histories, comedies and tragedies, as far as our art would permit, and serve this town, for which we are not only indebted and thankful with all our power to your honours and high worthies, but will also show our thankfulness by our humble prayer and services, and testify it elsewhere as we can; and though we should not further molest your high worthies, considering all that high favour and advancement; but as in other towns, where we performed before, we used to receive a certificate of our demeanour under the common town's seal, we beg most humbly and respectfully — [as we may say, without glorifying ourselves, that we used in this town, too, always to live quietly and retired, and to execute our music and plays only so as they may be looked at with pleasure and honesty], — your honours and high worthies may extend their favour, until now shown to us, as to give us a certificate of conduct under the common town's seal, and we are your honours' and high worthies' most humble servants, with the most profound respect. Datum Rostogk, 31 Martii, 1606. Your honours and high worthies' most obedient,

The Markgrave of Brandenburg's servants,
the English Comedians.

We must now return to Holland. On the 8th of June 1606, some English Comedians received permission from the Stattholder to play for a few days in the Hague. It is probable that they also performed in other towns of Holland, for as we meet with them again at the Hague in April 1607, we must assume that they also passed the intervening period in that country. We here subjoin the documents referring to this subject, which have not been published before, and which are taken from the 'Register of the Resolutions of the Court of Holland'.

"8. Juny 1606. Den Procureur Generael wert aengeseit dat de Engelsche commedianten eenige daegen sullen mogen speelen volgens 't consent van syn Excellencie.

23. April 1607. Wert den Procureur Generael belast de Engelsche commedianten te verbieden naer Woensdaege toecommende hier in den Haege niet langer te speelen, immers tot te kermisse toecommende. Den 26en is heur by apostille verboden meer te spelen en den Generael belast toe te sien.

27. April 1607. Wert den Procureur belast, enz Item dat hy zal spreecken met syn Excellencie, ten einde deselve aen de Engelse commedianten geen consent en verleene om te speelen tegen tverbot van den Raide heur op gisteren schriftelijck gedaen."

---

[1] See H. W. Baerensprung's *Geschichte des Theaters in Mecklenburg-Schwerin*. 8vo. Schwerin 1837, p. 11, and Albert Cohn, *Old English Actors in Germany*, Athenæum 1850, No. 1185, p. 738.

TRANSLATION.

8. June 1606. It is notified to the Procurator General, that the English Comedians shall be allowed to play some days according to the consent of His Excellency.

23. April 1607. The Procurator General is instructed to forbid the English actors to play any longer here in the Hague after next Wednesday until the next fair. On the 26th they are forbidden to play by a notice, and the Procurator General is instructed to see to it.

27. April 1607. The Procurator General is instructed etc. Item: that he shall speak with his Excellency to the end that he shall not give the English actors any permission to play against the prohibition served to them yesterday in writing by the Council.

We cannot easily believe that these are the Brandenburg Comedians again, for it appears to follow from the Rostock Petition that they had the intention of remaining some time longer in Mecklenburg. It is indeed possible that they were not very successful at the latter country, and therefore started soon afterwards on their way back to Holland, where they had met with great encouragement only a short time before. In the year 1608, the Authorities of the Hague issued a special proclamation prohibiting all representations, of whatsoever sort they might be, as scandalous and injurious to the community, so that there was an end to all theatrical performances at that place for some years.

There can be no doubt that it is the Brandenburg company which we meet with again in July 1607, offering their services in Elbing. But this time their application is refused, on the ground that it is "a tax upon the citizens", although a certain Brakel, residing in Elbing, probably an English merchant, interested himself in their behalf. At last they obtained permission to give private performances either in Brakel's house or elsewhere, a permission of which they no doubt availed themselves. This is the only instance of such performances in private houses, in connection with the English Comedians. We subjoin the document from the Kœnigsberg Archives.

Elbing. Session vom 16. Juli 1607.

"Engländische Comödianten halten heftig an, etiam intercedente Brakel deputato, ihnen zu gestatten ihre Spiele. Weil es aber eine Schatzung der Bürgerschaft ist und die jetzigen traurigen Läufte solches nicht zugeben wollen, hat ein Erb. Rath beschlossen, ihnen es abzuschlagen. Doch wofern der Herr Deputat, oder jemand anders ihres Spiels privatim begehren würde in seinem Hause, könne es gestattet werden."[1]

TRANSLATION.
Elbing. Session of the 16th of July, 1607.

The English Comedians urgently entreat that they may be permitted to perform their plays, deputy Brakel also interceding for them. But as this is a tax upon the citizens, and the present melancholy state of affairs will not permit it, the Honorable Council has resolved to refuse their request. Should however Mr. Deputy Brakel or anybody else wish them to perform privately in his house, they have permission to do so.

After this the English Comedians appear to have entirely deserted Prussia for some years. In the year 1609, the Elector finds himself obliged to request the Landgrave Maurice

---

[1] *Elbinger Anzeiger* 1827, No. 99. — E. A. Hagen, *Geschichte* etc. p. 53. All the preceding and following documents from the Royal Archives at Kœnigsberg are taken from Mr. Hagen's interesting and important work.

of Hessen to let him have his comedians for four weeks, that they might play at the festivities given in Berlin on the occasion of the marriage of his brother. (See p. lix.) It appears that the Prussian company had gone to Austria, for in the years 1607 and 1608, English Comedians under the management of John Spencer performed almost every day during the winter at the court of the Archduke at Gratz.[1] In November 1608 we meet with a certain W. Pedel in Holland, who is expressly mentioned as an Englishman in the minutes of the Council of Leyden. The document in question is as follows:

"Op te Requeste daerby den voorn. Willem Pedel, versochte aen die van de Gerechte der stadt Leyden omme te mogen speelen verscheyde fraeye ende eerlicke spelen mettet lichaem, sonder eenige woorden te gebruycken, stont geappostileert: Die van de Gerechte deser stadt Leyden hebben voor zoe veel in hem es, den thoonder toegelaten ende geconsenteert, laten toe ende consenteren mits desen binnen dezer stede inde Kercke vant Bagynhoff te mogen spelen voor de gemeente ende syne speelen verthoonen, mits dat hy hem daervan zalt onthouden geduyrende t'doen van de predicatien van Gods woorts, en dat de arme Weesen alhier zullen genieten de gerechte helfte van de incomende proffyten, en dat zulcx int geheel zullen werden ontfangen en gecollecteert by een persoon daertoe bij M^{ren} van de Arme Weesen te stellen ende committeeren. Aldus gedaen op ten xviij Nov. 1608."[2]

TRANSLATION.

On the request by which the aforesaid W. Pedel petitioned the authorities of the city of Leyden to allow him to exhibit various beautiful and chaste performances with his body, without using any words, was determined: The authorities of this city of Leyden have consented and allowed the exhibitor to perform in the church of the Bagynhoff within this city, provided he cease during the preaching of God's word, and that the poor orphans here have half the profits, and that they be received and collected by a person appointed by the masters of the poor orphans. Done on the 18th November, 1608.

In the year 1609 we find again a company of English Comedians at the Court of Dresden, where Christian the second orders that they should receive a payment of 500 florins. And again in the following year, [1610] 11 Englishmen, who had acted some comedies before the Electoral Lady, received 114 florins 6 groshen.[3] It is in all probability these eleven Englishmen who played from the 6th to the 10th of June 1610 at the festivities held in celebration of the marriage of the Princess Eva Christine with the Margrave John George of Brandenburg, as we learn from an unprinted description of that feast.[4]

"6. Juni .... Und nach dem Nachtessen [wurde] von Engellendern (so hievor auch zue Stuetgardt gespihlt) ein Comoedi aus dem Amadis agiret. — Den 9. Nachmittag ein andere Comedi von obgemelten Engellendern gespihlt. Sonntag den 10. nach dem Mittag-Imbifs im Schlofs-Hof ein Fecht-Schuel gleich darauf wider ein Comedi agirt."

---

[1] Karl Weifs, *Die Wiener Haupt- und Staatsaktionen.* 8vo. Wien 1854, p. 36.

[2] See *Navorscher*, Deel III, 1853, p. 17. *Notes and Queries*, Vol. VII, 1853, p. 114.

[3] Moritz Fürstenau, *Zur Geschichte* etc. p. 77.

[4] *Beschreibung der Vermählungs-Solennitäten Prinzessin Even Christinen mit Marggr. Joh. Georgen zu Brandenburg, in Jägerndorf An. 1610.* — See Friedr. Carl v. Mosen, *Kleine Schriften*, XI, p. 371—427.

TRANSLATION.

June 6 .... And after supper, a comedy from the Amadis was played by the Englishmen (who had also played before at Stuttgart). — June 9. In the afternoon another comedy was played by the above-mentioned Englishmen. Sunday the 10th. After dinner a fencing-match in the palace-court, immediately after which another comedy was acted.

Of the performances at Stuttgart, mentioned in the above passage, there is no record extant.

In the Autumn of the same year another company appears at the Hague. The above mentioned prohibition must have ceased to be in force, for by a resolution passed on the 24th of Sept. 1610, the Authorities of the town grant them permission to play on Monday, Tuesday, Wednesday, and Thursday, on the condition of their paying 20 florins to the use of the poor. On the 29th of the same month, this permission is extended for a further period of eight days.

"Extract uit het Register der Resolutien van den Hove van Holland, van den 17ⁿ April 1608 tot den 10ⁿ Mei 1617. A. Duyck, Griffier.

24. September 1610. Seeckere Engelse commedianten wert geconsenteert te spelen, manedach, dinxdach, woensdach ende donderdach mits betaelende aen de diaconen voor den armen 20 pond, sonder anders ofte langer te spelen op arbitrale correctie."

TRANSLATION.

Extract from the Register of the Resolutions of the Court of Holland of the 17th of April 1608 to the 10th of May 1617. A. Duyck, Clerk to the Court.

24. September 1610. Certain English actors receive permission to play Monday, Tuesday, Wednesday, and Thursday, paying 20 pounds to the guardian of the poor, but not to play otherwise or longer on pain of punishment.

In Kœnigsberg the English actors appeared again in the year 1611, at the court of Prince Albrecht Frederick. They are probably the same who entered the service of the Elector John Sigismund in 1611. Here we meet once more with John Spencer, who had gone back to England or to Holland, and indeed at the head of nineteen actors, and sixteen musicians.[1] They receive on the 30th of November 1611, according to the deed of their appointment, 720 Marks; and a suit of clothes is also made for them, consisting in part of a cloak of white English cloth, trimmed with black silk braid, and lined with red. On the 30th of August 1611, John Sigismund left Berlin for Kœnigsberg, for the purpose of receiving the investiture of the Duchy, which was to take place on the 15th of November. He stopped at the frontier until he proceeded on his journey to Warsaw. The actors accompanied the Elector to Ortelsburg, and their dresses were sent after them in a "baggage-waggon" (Rüstwagen). After the investiture had taken place, he made his public entry into Kœnigsberg on the 26th of November; and in the following year, a very grand representation, 'The Turkish Triumph-comedy' is given, "the Theatre in the old grand saloon" is covered with red lining-cloth, and the City of Constantinople is built for the comedians. All sorts of work are

---

[1] See C. M. Plümicke, *Entwurf einer Theatergeschichte von Berlin*. 8vo. Berlin 1781, p. 34, and E. A. Hagen, *Geschichte* etc. p. 48.

necessary for this purpose. For the preparation of a cloud "blue body-colour and black canvas and fringes" are required. David Rose, the court-painter, hands in a bill for 117 marks 42 shillings. The wardrobe is rich and costly. Blue, red, and white cloth, gold border, 70 ells of red silk, 50 ells of red cord, Monks' dresses, 18 large and 17 long plumes, a sword with a gilt hilt, and a wooden shield are purchased. Four death's heads, carved work and turned work, are delivered by the court-turner and two carvers. Fourteen instrumentalists have "assisted in the comedy of Constantinople". In addition to their regular salary the comedians received particular gratuities, and it happened more than once that they had to be ransomed out of the inns and taverns, John Spencer at the head of them. All these statements are founded on documents and accounts in the Royal Archives at Kœnigsberg. They are printed literally in E. A. Hagen's 'Geschichte' etc. p. 53—58. As Hagen's work was printed for private circulation, and is therefore comparatively little known, we subjoin those extracts which bear on our present subject, just as they stand in the originals:

"30 Mark den Englischen Commedianten welche für vnserm gnedigsten Fürsten vnd Herrn HEn. Albrecht Friederichen &c. eine Commediam agieret vnd getanzet, zur Verehrung gezahlt den 23ten Juli (1611.) — 720 Mark den Englischen Commedianten vf Rechnung der Bestallung an 400 Thlr. zu 36 Gr. den 30. Novemb. 1611. — 150 Mark den Englischen Commedianten als dieselbe nach Ortelsburg verreiset vf Rechnung den 7. Octob. 1611. — (Ist ihnen von Churfürstl. Gnaden erlassen. 1612.)"

TRANSLATION.

30 Marks as a gratuity to the English actors, who acted a comedy and danced before our most gracious Prince and Lord, Henry Albrecht Frederick &c., paid the 23rd of July 1611. — 720 Mark to the English actors to the account of their salary of 400 thalers at 36 groshen, paid the 30th of November 1611. — 150 Marks paid to the English actors on account, on occasion of their travelling to Ortelsburg, the 7th of October 1611. (This debt was remitted them by His Electoral Grace in 1612.)

Then follow the order of John Sigismund directing that dresses should be provided for the 19 English actors, and 16 instrumentalists, dated Ortelsburg, 16 Oct. 1611; the answer of the counsellors that this has been done, 24 Oct. 1611, the list of the cloths which had been purchased, as also their destination, and lastly a list of different sums expended for the actors, as well as for the various articles necessary for the performances. Among them are the following items:

"7 Mark 12 sh. Hans Tanapfel Bildschnützer hat 4 Todtenköpfe und ein Schild zur Commedia geschnützet.

Christian Salbert Messerschmidt hat für die Commedianten ein Schwerdt mit einem verguldeten Gefäfs gemacht. 7. Febr.

1080 Mark Johann Spencern Commedianten an 600 Thlr. zu 36 Gr. so ihm noch vf den von Ihr Churfürstl. Gnaden getroffenen Contract restiret, empfing er selbst 4. Febr.

124 Mark 47 sh. Vor Brennholz durch die Commedianten erkauft. 26. Mai.

6 Mark Zins von 18 grofse und 17 lange Federbüsche, so der Andreas Körner zu der türkischen Triumph-Commœdien geliehen. 17. Juny.

23 Mark 9 sh. vor allerlei Hölzer Drehwerk durch die Commedianten beim Hofdreher bestellt. 1. July.

81 Mark 33 sh. vor blaue Leibfarbe und schwarz Leimet [Leinwand] und franczſsen, Alles zur Wolken zu der Triumph-Commedia dem Meister Dietrich zahlt. 21. Aug.

87 Mark 39 sh. vor allerlei Schnitzwerk zu der Triumph-Commedia durch Alexander Crause Bildschnützer. 21. Aug.

111 Mark 15 sh. vor allerlei Tischlerarbeit zu der Triumph-Commedia durch Christoph Dosin gefertigt. 21. Aug.

117 Mark 42 sh. Dauid Rose Hofmaler für allerlei Arbeit, so er vf Churfürstl. Befehl den Commedianten gefertigt. 16. Oct.

26 Mark 9 sh. Auslösung Ihr Churfürstl. Gnaden Comediant Johann Spenser welcher vom 28. Oct. bis vf den 8. Novemb. 1612 bei Christoph Hertlein gelegen.

47 Mark 48 sh. Auslösung der Churfürstl. Comedianten etc. 23. Jan.

47 Mark 48 sh. Auslösung der Churfürstl. Comödianten welche Anno 1612 bei Hans Jacob gelegen etc. 13. März.

30 Ehlen (Futtertuch) zu Münchs-Kleider, noch 81 Ehlen rott futter Tuch das teatrum zu belegen im alten grofsen Saal.

25 Ehlen flechsen Leimbt [Leinwand] den Commödianten zur erbauung der Stadt Constantinopel — (und noch andere ähnliche Posten zu gleichem Zweck).

1613. 1229 Mark 24 sh. Johann Spenczern Commoedianten an Seiden-Waaren von Heinrich Klehe ausgenommen, an 683 Thaler à 36 Gr. welches ihm in Berlin an seiner Besoldung soll gekürzet werden."

TRANSLATION.

7 Marks 12 sh. Hans Tanapfel, carver, has carved four death's heads, and one shield for the comedy.

Christian Salbert, cuttler, has made a sword with a gilt hilt for the comedians, the 7th of Febr.

1080 Marks, being about 600 thalers at 36 gr. to John Spencer, comedian, balance which was still due to him on the contract made with his Electoral Grace, he received himself on the 4th of Febr.

124 Marks 47 sh. for firewood bought by the actors, May 26.

6 Marks for the hire of 18 large and 17 long plumes lent by Andrew Kœrner for the Turkish Triumph Comedy. June 17.

23 Marks 9 sh. for various articles turned in wood, ordered of the court-turner by the actors. July 1.

81 Marks 33 sh. for blue body-colour and black canvas and fringes, all for the cloud for the Triumph Comedy, paid to Master Dietrich, Aug. 21.

87 Marks 39 sh. for various carvings for the Triumph Comedy, made by Alexander Crause, carver. Aug. 21.

111 Marks 15 sh. for various articles of joiner's work for the Triumph Comedy, made by Christopher Dosin. Aug. 21.

117 Marks 42 sh. to David Rose, court-painter, for various works executed by him for the actors, at the command of the Elector. Oct. 16.

26 Marks 9 sh. as ransom of His Electoral Grace's comedian, John Spencer, who had lodged with Christopher Hertlein from the 28th of October to the 9th of November 1612.

47 Marks 48 sh. as ransom of the Electoral comedians etc. Jan. 23.

47 Marks 48 sh. as ransom of the Electoral comedians, who had lodged with Hans Jacob in the year 1612, etc. March 13.

30 Ells (lining-cloth) for monk's dresses, also 81 ells of red lining-cloth for covering the theatre in the old great saloon.

25 Ells of flax linen for the comedians for the building of the city of Constantinople — (and various other similar items for the same object).

1613. 1229 Marks 24 sh. to John Spencer, comedian, for silk goods received from Henry Klehe, part of 683 thalers at 36 grosh. which is to be deducted from his salary in Berlin.

In April 1613 the Englishmen were dismissed, and received a letter of recommendation from John Sigismund to the Elector of Saxony, dated Grünnig, 16 April, 1613. It is preserved in the Dresden Archives, and is as follows:

"Es hat sich gegenwärtiger Englischer Comödiant Johann Spenzer, eine Zeit her in unsern Diensten aufgehalten und sich in seiner unterthänigsten Aufwartung dergestalt erwiesen, daſs wir darob ein gnädiges Gefallen getragen. Wenn er aber nunmehr andere Oerter zu besuchen und unter andern auch seine Kunst und Comödien in Dresden ansehen zu lassen gemeint, haben wir ihm diese unsere Commendation mitgeben wollen. Ersuchen Ew. Lbd., Sie geruhen ihm nicht allein auf ein Wochen vier oder mehr, ein solches zu vergönnen, besonderem [sondern] ihm auch sonst alle Gnade zu erweisen." [1]

TRANSLATION.

Bearer of these, the English comedian John Spencer, has been a considerable time in our service, and in his humble waiting on us has so borne himself, that we have derived a gracious pleasure therefrom. But when he purposed to visit other places, and among the rest also to exhibit his art and his comedies in Dresden, we have wished to give him this our recommendation. We request Your Highness will be pleased not only to give him permission to do so for four weeks, or more, but also to shew him all favour in other respects.

The company cannot have remained long in Dresden, for we meet with it in Nuremberg as early as June 1613, on which subject a contemporary chronicle of Nuremberg gives some information.

"1613. Sontag den 27. Junj, vnd etliche Tage hernach aufs Eines Erbarn Raths grofsgünstigen erlaubnifs, haben defs Churfürsten zu Brandenburg Diener vnd Engelische Comoedianten schöne Comedien vnd tragödien von Philole vnd Mariane, Item von Celide vnd Sedea, Auch von Zerstörung der Stätte Troia vnd Constantinopel, vom Türcken vnd andere Historien mehr, neben zierlichen täntzen, lieblicher Musica, vnd anderer Lustbarkeit, im Halfsbrunner Hof allhie, in guter teutscher Sprach in köstlicher Mascarada vnd Kleidungen agirt vnd gehalten, hat erstlich ein Person 3 Creutzer, vnd letzlich 6 Creutzer zuzuschen geben muefsen, darumb sie ein grofs Volckh ihnen zugelauffen, vnd mit sich hinweg gebracht haben." [2]

TRANSLATION.

1613. On Sunday the 27th of June and a few days following thereon, with the gracious permission of the Honorable Council, the Elector of Brandenburg's servants and English Comedians have acted and held beautiful comedies and tragedies of Philole and Mariane, also of Celide and Sedea, also of the Destruction of the city of Troy, and city of Constantinople, of the Turk, and other such histories, besides graceful dancing, lovely music, and other entertainments, here in the Hailsbrunn Court,

---

[1] M. Fürstenau, *Zur Geschichte* etc. p. 76.

[2] From a Ms. chronicle of the city of Nuremberg by Stark. See Joh. Chr. Siebenkees, *Materialien zur Nürnbergischen Geschichte*, Vol. iii. 8vo. Nürnberg 1794, p. 52—54. In Lersner's *Chronica der Reichsstadt Frankfurt a. M.* Fol. Frankfurt 1706, this visit of the English Comedians is mentioned as having been paid to Frankfort, which is evidently a mistake, as there is no place called "Hailsbronner Hof" in that city.

in good German language, in rich masquerade and costumes. At first each person had to give three creutzers, and latterly six creutzers to see it, which caused a great crowd of people to run after them and to follow them.

As we learn from the same chronicle, English actors had already appeared in Nuremberg the year before; but this was the company of the Landgrave of Hesse, which had come over from Cassel. (See p. lix.)

From Nuremberg John Spencer proceeded with his company to Regensburg, and played before the Emperor and the assembled Diet.[1] In September 1614, we meet with the "Brandenburg Comedians" at Wolffenbüttel (see p. xxxv), and the same year an English actor obtained permission from the Town-Council to play in Brunswick. He played on two successive evenings, but on the third evening had no audience ("kein Volk", literally, no people) as the notice runs, and the Council granted him one thaler as compensation.[2] There can be no doubt that John Spencer was the actor in question.

It appears that the Elector John Sigismund could not get on very long without his English actors, for after he had dismissed one company in 1613, a new one is engaged in February [March] 1614, as we learn from a decree of appointment made out for the brothers William, Abraham, and Jacob Pedel, Robert Arzschar, [Archer?] Behrendt Holzhew, [Woodhew?] and August Pflugbeil. The first four received 100 florins each, besides their board at court gratis, and two suits; the two others received only 100 florins between them. The salaries were to be paid quarterly, and the suits to be made by the Court-tailor. The actors engage "to wait constantly and with all faithful diligence on the Elector on his travels, and at his court, and to shew themselves cheerful and willing, and allow themselves to be employed in their art according to the ability of each, respectively, in jumping, acting, and other amusements, whenever called upon to do so, and in the best way that they are able, so that His Electoral Highness may take a gracious pleasure therein."[3]

This engagement was not of long duration, for as early as Easter 1615, the brothers Pedel, Holzhew, and Pflugbeil were dismissed. But Arzschar remained at his post till the 16th of May 1616, but then he was also dismissed with a sum of 250 thalers as settlement of his claims. We have already met one of the brothers, William Pedel, in Holland in 1608. (See p. lxxxiii.)

There was a third company in Holland about the same time, for on the 9th of

---

[1] See Schlager, *Ueber das alte Wiener Hoftheater*, in *Wiener Skizzen*, Vol. iii. 8vo. Wien.

[2] Adolph Glaser, *Geschichte des Theaters zu Braunschweig*. 8vo. Braunschweig 1861, p. 13.

[3] C. M. Plümicke, *Entwurf einer Theatergeschichte von Berlin*. 8vo. Berlin 1781, p. 36—37. The German Text of the above quoted passage in the appointment runs as follows: "Den Churfürsten jedesmal bei Reisen oder im Hoflager treuen Fleisses zu warten, und sich in ihrer Kunst, nach eines jeden Geschicklichkeit mit Springen, Spielen und anderer Kurzweil, auf jederzeit Begehren, ufs Beste sie es immer zu Wege bringen können, unverdrofsen und willig zu erweisen und gebrauchen zu lafsen, alfo dafs S. C. D. darob ein gnediges Gefallen tragen könnten."

October 1612, some English actors obtained permission to play for fourteen days from the authorities at the Hague.[1]

To give a connected account of the wanderings of the different companies, and especially of that of our John Spencer, it was necessary to interrupt the chronological order in our narrative, and we must now revert to the year 1611, in order to mention a most remarkable incident which occured in that year. Unfortunately we are able to do little more than state the naked fact itself, as all our endeavours to obtain the document which establishes it have been unsuccessful. Landgrave Philip of Butzbach, Uncle of Landgrave George the second of Hesse-Darmstadt, made several journeys in North Germany in the year 1611, and among other places also visited Halle, where he was present at some splendid banquets at the Court of the Administrator of Magdeburg, with which theatrical representations were connected. In a letter which he wrote from this place, probably addressed to his nephew George the second, he states that he had seen a German Comedy 'The Jew of Venice' taken from the English. ("Teutsche Komedia der Jud von Venedig, aufs dem engeländischen.")[2] It is hardly necessary to observe that this refers to Shakespeare's 'Merchant of Venice', as Thomas Dekker's 'Jew of Venice' was not entered in the Register of the Stationer's Company till 1653, long after the death of the poet was never printed, and never acted during the poet's life; at least there is no allusion to its being acted or being known earlier than 1653. On the other hand Shakespeare's 'Merchant of Venice' was known by the title of 'The Jew of Venice'; for under the date of July 22, 1598, we find in the Register of the Stationer's Company the following entry: "James Robertes, A booke of the Marchaunt of Venyce or otherwise called the Jewe of Venyse."

Although, as we shall see presently, there is every probability that at least one piece of Shakespeare's, and that one, Hamlet, had been acted in Germany long before this, yet is the above the earliest authentic evidence that Shakespeare's masterpieces had been represented on a German stage during the poet's life-time, — certainly one of the most glorious incidents in the history of the German Theatre. Of the company which played at

---

[1] *Register der Resolution* etc. "9. October 1612. DEngelse commedianten wert geconsenteert 14 daechen te speelen, sonder schandael ende sonder consequentie."

[2] This remarkable fact was first mentioned by Mr. E. Pasqué in the '*Muse, Blätter für ernste und heitere Unterhaltung*,' herausgegeben von Dräxler-Manfred. Vol. I, p. 156. The author collected his valuable articles in this periodical, under the title: '*Geschichte der Musik und des Theaters am Hofe zu Darmstadt, aus Urkunden dargestellt von Ernst Pasqué. Erste Abtheilung, Periode von Georg I. bis Ludwig VI., 1567—1678*. 8vo. Darmstadt 1853. 64 pp. This work was printed for private circulation. Of the second part, there appeared only from p. 65 to 104. The continuation is to be found in the *Muse* 1854, Vol. iii p. 205—208, Vol. iv p. 629—726. I applied to Mr. E. Pasqué in the hopes of obtaining a copy of the letter of the Landgrave Philip of Butzbach which is in the Darmstadt Archives. But in spite of all the trouble which Mr. Pasqué kindly took in my behalf, it was impossible to obtain access to the letter, which unfortunately he had not copied on first discovering it, as the information it contained possessed only a secondary interest for him at that time. Since then the Darmstadt Archives have been arranged, and there are so many bundles of papers to be looked through to find the letter, that this has not been possible as yet. But the statements given above are perfectly authenticated, and the letter is undoubtedly extant in the Darmstadt Archives.

the Court at Halle, or any other circumstances connected with the theatre there, nothing whatever is known. Perhaps the papers referring to the Court of the Administrator of Magdeburg may be discovered in one of the Royal Prussian Archives. If the Exchequer accounts are still extant, we may feel quite certain that they will afford ample evidence that the English actors played there also. It is our firm conviction that they alone can have acted the 'Jew of Venice' in Halle.[1]

In the year 1612, or shortly before, there was a company of English actors in Brussels. They are alluded to by Heywood: "The cardinall at Bruxels hath at this time in pay a company of our English comedians."[2] These are perhaps the same players who, according to an entry in the 'Gerechts-dag-boeken' of the city of Leyden acted there in or about 1614.[3] English actors must have been known also in Amsterdam in the year 1615, as appears from the following passage in G. A. Brederode's drama, 'Moortje' Act iii, Sc. 4:

"Ick mach soo oock by geen reden-ryckers zijn:	To stay with rhetoricians I've no mind:
Want dit volckje wil steets met allen menschen gecken,	The fool they'll play with men of every kind,
En sy kunnen als d'aep haer afterst niet bedecken;	And, like the ape, exhibit what's behind
Sy seggen op haer les, soo stemmigh en soo stijf,	With gests so stiff their lesson they repeat,
Al waer gevoert, gevult met klap-hout al haer lijf!	You'd swear with staves their bodies were replete!
Waren't de Engelsche, of andere uytlandtsche	Heard you the English and other strangers sing?
Die men hoort singen, en soo lustigh siet dantse	Saw you their jolly dance, their lusty spring?
Dat sy suyse-bollen, en draeyen as een tol:	How like a top they spin, and twirl and turn?
Sy spreken 't uyt haer geest, dees leeren't uyt een rol."	And from the heart they speak — ours from a roll must learn . . . .[4]

A Frankfort versifier, in the year 1615, speaks of the English actors in a less flattering manner:

"Die Englische Comedianten	Folk like to see the English play,
Haben mehr Leuht den Predicanten	Far more than hear the parson pray;
Da lieber 4. stund stehn hören zu	Four hours rather stand and hear
Dan ein in die Kirch, da sie mit Ruh	The play, than one in church appear,
Flux einschlaffen auff ein hart banck,	Which seeming long, soon peaceful sleep
Dieweil ein stund in felt zu lang,	On oaken bench will o'er them creep.
Vnd Agieren doch so schlecht sachen	And yet these actors play such stuff,
Das sie der possn offt selbst lachen,	They must themselves oft laugh enough,

---

[1] The Prince who filled the office of Archbishop and Administrator of the Bishopric of Magdeburg was Christian William of Brandenburg, born 28 Aug. 1587, died 1 Jan. 1665. He occupied that place from 1598 to 1631. His wife was Dorothea of Brunswick, born 8 May 1596, daughter of Duke Henry Julius, the dramatic author. The marriage took place June 16, 1615. This indicates a friendly intercourse between Christian William and Henry Julius, which may have existed some time before the former married the latter's daughter. If so, the players who acted at Halle may have been those in the pay of the Duke. We have already seen that it was not uncommon for the Princes to send their players to each other.

[2] Heywood's *Apology for Actors*, ed. by the Shakespeare Society, p. 60.

[3] *Navorscher*, Deel iii, p. 17.

[4] *Navorscher* and *Notes and Queries*, Vol. vii, 1853, No. 180, April 9, p. 361.

Das siefs Gelt vonn den Leuten bringen	To think a man his money brings
Zu sich, vor so närrische dingen,	To them, to see such foolish things.
Der Narr macht lachen, doch ich weht	True, at the clown we laugh, and yet
Da ist Keinr so gutt wie Jan begehtt,	He's not half so good as John, I bet,
Vor dieser zeitt wol hatt gethan,	Whom we have seen here long ago;
Jestzt ist er ein reicher Handelfsman."[1]	He now is a rich John & Co.

We shall be justified in concluding from the above lines the presence of an English company in Frankfort-on-the-Maine in the year 1615. But we have a perfectly authentic account of a very numerous company of English actors in Cologne in that same year, in a manuscript in the British Museum (Harl. 3888.): "The Evangelic Fruict of the Seraphicall Franciscan Order. Centur. 5. Ab Anno Domini 1600 ad ann. 1628. Dublinij elucubravit. P. N. Archibold Capucinus aº 1628." It is an account, in the form of a chronicle, of all the conversions and castings out of the devil effected by the Capuchins, and other amusing stories, in which we certainly should not have expected to find any matter for our heretical investigations. And yet we must feel truly grateful to the pious Father Francis Nugent, that he allowed our Thespian friends to enjoy the good fortune of returning to the bosom of the only saving church, for it is to his zeal that we are indebted for the knowledge of a fact of considerable interest for our subject. The worthy Capuchin records under the date of 1615, as follows:

"Twentie fowre Stage players, arrive out of Ingland at Collen: all Inglish except one Germanian and one Dutchman. All Protestants. Betwixt those and father Francis Nugent disputation was begunne and protracted for the space of 7 or eight dayes consecutively; all of them meeting at one place together. The chiefs among them was one N. Spencer, a proper sufficient man. In fine, all and each of them beeing clearlie convinced, they yielded to the truth; but felt themselves so drie and roughharted that they know not how to pass from the bewitching Babylonian harlot to their true mother the Catholic church, that always pure and virginal sponse of the lamb" etc.

After this the narrative proceeds to state how Friar Nugent preached a sermon to them, and then follows the story of the "one Germanian", who dies as a good Catholic. We may conjecture from this, that the attempt to convert the Englishmen was unsuccessful after all.[2] We have here a second actor of the name of Spencer. John Spencer, it will be remembered, is alluded to as a confessor of the Catholic faith at a much earlier date.

In the following year, 1616, English actors again appear in Prussia, and this time in Danzig. The Counsel allows them to play eight comedies, but they are "not to repre-

---

[1] *Ein Discurfs von der Frankfurter Messe, vnd jhrer vnderschiedlichen Kauffleuten gut vnd böfs.* 4to. s. l. 1615, p. 8.

[2] Hunter, *New Illustrations of Shakespeare.* Vol. ii, p. 231, also relates this story, but incorrectly places it in the year 1613 instead of 1615. The Chronicle moreover is continued to the year 1645, apparently by the same hand, although 1628 stands on the title-page.

sent any unchaste pieces" and are only to take three groshen entrance-money for each person.[1]

In 1615, John Sigismund, the Elector of Brandenburg, had dismissed his second company of English actors, and about 1617 Squire Hans von Stockfisch (probably a theatrical nickname) a favourite of the Grand Chamberlain, Count Adam of Schwartzenberg received a commission from the Elector to procure a third company from England and the Netherlands.[2] Unfortunately we know no particulars about this company. We can only assert with safety that Squire Hans executed the commission which had been entrusted to him, for in the year 1620 he addressed a petition to Count Schwartzenberg, in which he begs for the payment of his yearly salary, as also of 1000 thalers in addition, which he asserts that he had spent in procuring the foreign actors. The Elector George William, who was the successor of John Sigismund, decrees in answer to this under the date of Koenigsberg, 4—14 March, 1620, that the arrears shall be paid, in case the petitioner can prove that he had really disbursed the thousand thalers in the affair of this company of comedians, "which had been last in Berlin;" but as he had been credibly informed that this was not the case, and that "the certificate given in his favour by the comedians, which he had presented, had been surreptitiously obtained", his claim must be dismissed. It clearly follows from this, that the actors were no longer in Berlin in March 1620. On the other hand we gather from a complaint addressed by George William to the Magistrates of Berlin, and from the answer of the Magistrates, that in 1623, "foreign actors" were again in Berlin,[3] but we do not know whether they were Englishmen; it is only certain that they were not in the service of the Court. George William was a pietist, and did not favour the theatre.

In 1618, at the command of the Elector, the English actors proceeded from Berlin to East Prussia. They played in Elbing, Balge, and Koenigsberg, were eighteen in number, and had Hans von Stockfisch at their head. In the accounts of the Electoral Court, we find the following entries connected with their stay there.

"19 Mark Sein vf gnedigen Befehl Ihr. Churfürstl. Gnaden einem Stockfischen welchen Ihr Churfürstl. G. nachm Elbing Comoedien (Comoedianten) von dannen anhero zu bringen abgefertigt haben an 50 Thalern zu 36 Gr. zahlt. 17. Maerz.

112 Mark 30 sh. haben Ihr Churfürstl. Dchl. den Englischen Comoedianten zu den vorhin empfangenen 50 Reichsthalern nochmals zur Verehrung zu geben gst. beuohlen, welche sie empfangen den 8ten November.

---

[1] Löschin, *Geschichte Danzigs*. 8vo. Danzig 1822. Vol. i, p. 388. It is also mentioned there, that in 1615 two "Brandenburg Comedians" were permitted to give seven comedies, provided they take not more than 2 gr. from each spectator; in 1623 the entrance fee is raised to 4 and in 1643 to 9 gr. — but we are not told whether these companies were English or German.

[2] C. M. Plümicke, *Entwurf* etc. p. 34. — K. Goedeke, *Grundrifs* etc., Vol. i, p. 408 wrongly assigns this event to the year 1607. Plümicke distinctly says "wenige Jahre vor des Churfürsten Tode" (a few years before the Elector's death) and as John Sigismund died December 23, 1619, the appointment cannot have taken place in 1607; besides, the Elector only succeeded to the throne in 1608.

[3] C. M. Plümicke, *Entwurf* etc. p. 41—43.

An die Oberräthe des Herzogthums Preufsen. Von Gottes Gnaden Johann Sigismund etc. Wir haben den Comoedianten, welche wie euch bewust, zu vnterschiedenen mahlen, vf vnser gnedigtes Begehren, in vnserm Gemache zu Königsberg vnd Balge agiret, fur ihre gehapte muhe, eins vor alles, zwei Hundert gulden Polnisch bewilliget, Befehlen euch demnach hiermit gnedigst, Ihr wollet ihnen solche 200 gulden, aus Vnser Renthkammer also vort entrichten lassen etc. Datum Elbing den 20. Juny 1619.

150 Mark. 18 Englischen Commedianten welche vor Ihr Churfürstl. Gnd. etzliche Commedien agiret, gezahlt den 22. Juny (1619)."

TRANSLATION.

19 Marks, at the gracious command of His Electoral Grace, being 50 thalers at 36 groshen, to a certain Stockfisch, whom His Electoral Grace sent to Elbing to bring from thence the English Comedians, paid March 17.

112 Marks 30 sh. which His Electoral Grace has graciously ordered to be given to the English Comedians as a second gratuity, in addition to the 50 rixthalers which they have previously received. Paid November 8.

To the High Counsellors of the Duchy of Prussia. We, John Sigismund, by the Grace of God, etc. have granted, once for all, two hundred Polish florins to the actors for their trouble, who, as is well known to you, have at different times at our gracious command, acted in our apartments at Koenigsberg and Balge, and hereby graciously order you accordingly to pay them the said 200 florins out of our treasury. Dated Elbing, June 20, 1619.

150 Marks to 18 English Comedians who acted several comedies before His Electoral Grace, paid June 22, 1619.

We have already seen one of our strolling companies in Danzig in the year 1616. After having been dismissed from that place, they appear to have proceeded to the neighbouring country of Poland, but before commencing this journey, they must have played at the Archducal Court at Gratz in Moravia. This is the second company we meet with there. From Poland they proceeded to Breslau, to the Court of the Archduke and Bishop Charles, with whom they had become acquainted at Gratz, to which place they again returned with a letter of recommendation from the Duke to the Stadtholder of Moravia, Cardinal von Dietrichstein. We gather all these circumstances respecting their movements from the letter itself:

"Dem hochwürdigen Fürsten vnserm freundlichen geliebten Herrn vnd gutten Freundt, Herrn Frantsen der Heiligen Röm. Khirchen des Titulo Sti. Silvestri Cardinalen von Dietrichstein, Bischoven zue Olmütz, Rom. Kay. May. geheimen Rath, auch deroselben Königreich vnnd Erbländern protectori.

Vnsere freundtliche willige Dienst, was wir sonsten mehr liebes vnd guethes vermögen zuevorn. Hochwürdiger Fürst, freundtlicher geliebter Herr vnnd guether Freund, Vnnfs haben an Euer Ldn. gegenwerttige Engelländische Comoedianten verschrifftlichen zue reccommandiren, vnd dahin zuebefördern gehorsambist angelanget, damit ihnen von E. L. verlaubet werden möchte, in dero Stätten Ihre geschickligkheit vnd Comicos actus zue exerciren;

Wan wir vns dan zueruckh wol eryndern können, dafs noch bei weilandt vnserer geliebsten Frawen Muetter hochehr- vnd Lobwürdigsten angedenckhens, lebens Zeiten, eben dieselbe Personen zue Grácz, ihre Comedien, gancz Erbar vnd zichtig, mit der Vnserigen allerseits genedigistenn gefallen vndt begnügen verrichtet. An Yezo aber aus Pohln, darin Sy dergleichen bei Ihrer Königl. vndt Ldn.

eczlich Monat Lang exhibiret mit Königlichen recommendationen vndt guetten Zeügnus, zue vns ankhommen, vndt sich gehorsambist angegeben habenn.

Diesemnach wir gedachten Comödianten, diese Ihnen zue ersprüfslichen genaden, gemeinte recommendation, an Euer Ldn. nicht wol verwiedern mögen, Ewer Ldn. hiemit freundtlichen ersuchende, dieselbte Ihnen, mehrbemelte Perschonenn, zue aller gewogenheit, vnd genaigtem willen von vnsertwegen wollten freundtlichen endffollen. sein lassen, damit Sy demüttigst verffüren möchtenn, das vnsern bei Euer Ldn. freundtliche Interuentionen, angenehmbe vnnd kräfftighe würgligkheit gefunden, vndt Sy sich Euer Ldn. hinwiederumb freundtlichen Zuerwiedern wier yeder Zeit gancz willig sein vnd verbleiben wollenn. Geben in vnser Stadt Neifs denn achtczehenden tag Martij im Sechczehendenhundert vndt Siebenczehenden Jahre,

Carl von Gottesgnaden Ertz Hertzog zu Oessterreich Hertzog zue Burgundi etc. Bischoffe zue Brixen vnnd Brefslaw Graffe zue Tirol.

Euer Ldn.   Guthwilliger vndt getreuer Freundt
                                                               Carl m. p."[1]

TRANSLATION.

To the Right Reverend Prince, our friendly and beloved Lord and good friend, Master Franz, of the Holy Romish Church, of the title of St. Silvester, Cardinal von Dietrichstein, Bishop of Olmütz, Privy-Counsellor of His Rom. Imp. Majesty, also Protector of the Kingdom and hereditary dominions of the same.

First (we offer) our friendly and willing service and whatever else of good and kind we may have in our power. Most Reverend Prince, friendly and beloved lord and good friend. English Comedians bearers of these presents, have respectfully requested us to give them a written recommendation to Your Highness, and to assist them to the behoof that it might be permitted to them by Your Highness to practise their skill and comic plays in Your Highness' residence.

When we remember that, during the life-time of our late most beloved lady mother of high and praiseworthy memory, just these same persons have performed their comedies at Gratz, quite honorably and decently, always with our most gracious pleasure and satisfaction, but that now they have come to us with royal recommendations and good testimonials from Poland, where they have some months long exhibited such comedies at their Royal Highnesses, and have respectfully announced themselves;

We may not well for the above reasons refuse them the desired recommendation to Your Highness for your salutary favour, kindly hereby requesting Your Highness will allow the same oftenmentioned persons to be recommended on our part to all favour and good will, to the end that they may humbly learn, that our friendly intervention with Your Highness may have found a powerful and agreeable realization, and Your Highness on the other hand may count on our being at all times willing to make a friendly return. Given in our town of Neiss, the 18th day of March in the year 1617.

Charles by the Grace of God Archduke of Austria, Duke of Burgundy etc., Bishop of Brixen and Breslaw, Count of Tirol.

Your Highness'
                                                   Well-inclined and faithful friend
                                                              Charles, m. p.

---

[1] The original letter is to be found at Brünn in the Archives of the States of Moravia, Boczek collection. No. 12265. See *Notizenblatt der histor.-statist. Sektion der K. K. Mährisch-Schlesischen Gesellschaft zur Beförderung des Ackerbaues, der Natur- und Landeskunde*, 1858, No. 3, a paper by Jul. Feifalik. See also Elwert, *Geschichte des Theaters in Mähren*, p. 26.

In the same year, some English actors, under the management of a certain John Green, played before the Emperor Ferdinand the second.[1] They were probably the same company, but we have not been able to ascertain any particulars respecting them.

In the summer of 1617 we again meet with a company of our friends at Dresden, where they must have already been engaged for a considerable time in the regular service of the Elector, John George the first, for on the 16th of August, 1617, Hans George von Osterhausen, the Marshal to the Court, reports to the Elector, that the actors have been very urgent in their entreaties for a leave of absence, which, in his opinion, it were as well now to grant them, "partly because they have themselves requested it, and partly because if they remain here longer, the expence of their maintenance and other things will be considerable." At the same time he asks for instructions as to how much he is to pay them by way of settlement. The Elector answers, under the date of Honstein, Aug. 17. "In as much as the ladies do not desire that they should play any longer before them," the Marshal "may institute a search in the Exchequer, how much in the year 1609 (see p. lxxxiii), and since then during our present reign at different times, has been given to such persons." The result is to be communicated to the Electress Dowager, and her opinion on the subject is to be heard, after which the Marshal is to make such a settlement with the actors "that they shall have no ground for complaint." The Marshal answers under the date of Dresden, August 19, that the Electress has fixed the sum at 300 thalers, which has accordingly been paid them. "Besides this, what they had consumed at their landlord's, before they had been supplied with their meals at Court, and whatever else they had required and used in the way of rooms, closets, and beds, amounted to 120 florins, which is also paid by the treasury."[2]

Thus the new dramatic art had made its way through the whole of Germany, and it is not surprising that now Germans also devoted themselves to the profession, entered into connection with the foreign actors, and formed independent strolling companies. The foreigners had now to support the competition of the natives; the latter had made themselves masters of the dramatic subjects which had been introduced by the former. Then there was the unspeakable misery occasioned by the war, then just commencing, which was destined to devastate all Germany for thirty long years. All these circumstances must have contributed to check the stream of emigrating English actors, and although we often meet with strolling companies under the name of "English Comedians," even till late in the century, we must assume that in many cases only a minority of the members, frequently indeed only the managers, were Englishmen, and in many others, that only the name was preserved as being an attractive advertisement. The question that has been often suggested, whether it is conceivable that plays were performed in Germany at that time in the English language, will engage our attention at a future page. It is sufficient to remark at present, that as we have already seen in the course of our narrative, Germans, and perhaps Dutch-

---

[1] See K. Weifs, *Die Wiener Haupt- und Staatsactionen.* 8vo. Wien 1854, p. 37.
[2] M. Fürstenau, *Zur Geschichte* etc. p. 77.

men also joined the English actors, that the latter only employed the English language, when they had found no native colleagues, and then only at first, for as many English actors remained a great many years in Germany, there is nothing extravagant in the assumption that they gradually made themselves acquainted with the German language.

The theatre had already begun to be felt as a general necessity, and although the interest in it had somewhat languished during the war, enough had been done to enable the actor's art to maintain its ground in spite of all storms. But it could not attain any fuller development. This could only have been accomplished by permanent stages, the erection of which was of course prevented by the fury of war; and dramatic art, in which the national element was only just beginning to manifest itself, might consider itself fortunate that its young blossoms were not entirely trodden to death. We will now give a brief summary of all that we further know respecting those companies which appeared under the denomination of English Comedians.

Two curious broadsides, the one of the year 1621, the other without a date have come into our hands, undoubtedly referring to a company of English Comedians which had been staying in the neighbourhood of Prague and replete with political allusions to the Bohemian troubles. We cannot arrive at any further conclusions from these obscure documents, a description of which we subjoin below.[1] The succeeding seven years form a gap in the annals of the English Comedians. Whether they actually disappeared from Germany, or whether it is purely accidental that we possess no information respecting their movements during this period, is a question which we cannot decide. It is certain, however, that even during these seven years, members of the London stage repaired to the Continent to escape from their painful situation at home. This is distinctly proved by a passage in a tract published in 1625, entitled, 'The Run-away's answer', in which some players and other persons defended themselves against the reproaches, which Thomas Dekker in his pamphlet, 'A Rod for Run-aways', had hurled against all those persons who had fled from London for fear of the plague. "We can be bankrupts (say the players) on this side and gentlemen of a company beyond the sea: we burst at London, and are pieced up at Rotterdam."[2] It may be conjectured therefore, that the actors who emigrated at that time, generally made Hol-

---

[1] 1) *Englischer Bickelhering, jetzo ein vornehmer Eysenhändeler | mit Axt, Beyl, Barten gen Prage jubilierende | Anno | Jetzt Jetzt zV haVen sJe seJne TaffeLn MIt BeIL VnD Barten. Phal. 47. §. 6.* (1621.) Begins: *In einem Buch auff einem Blat | Steht: Varietas delectat | Das heist soviel als: bleiben nicht | Was man gewesen macht lustig |* etc. Ends.: *Ade ich muss gehn' lauffen flugs | Ehe dann ich diese Mefs verseum | Glock drey mufs ich zu Prage seyn.* fol. With an engraving between the title and the text. I have seen another impression of the same broadside, with the initials "Schl." at the end. 2) *Engelandischer Bickelhäring, welcher jetzund als ein vor- | nemer Händler vnd Jubilirer, mit allerley Judenspiefsen nach Franckfort | in die Mefs zeucht.* | Begins: *Ejn alt Sprüchwort, besser verdorbn | Sey zehen mal, dann eins gestorbn |* etc. Ends: *Jhr seyt für mich, ich bin für euch | Jch hoff, ich woll bald werden reich. | Vnd euch die Spiefs nicht mehr zutragn, | Sondern auff einem starcken Wagn, | Euch Spiefs zuführn mit solcher meng, | Defs d' Welt mufs werden drob zu eng. |*
fol. With an engraving at the top.

[2] See J. P. Collier's *Memoirs of the principal actors in the plays of Shakespeare*. Printed for the Shakespeare Society. 8vo. London 1846, p. 142.

land the goal of their travels, and perhaps this choice was partly owing to the presence there of King Frederick of Bohemia, previously Frederick the fifth, Prince Palatine, who had fled to Holland in 1621. When the Prince Palatine married the Princess Elisabeth, the eldest daughter of James the first, he remained a considerable time in England, and at the nuptial festivities Prince Henry's players had often acted before him at Whitehall, on which occasion, among other pieces, Shakespeare's 'Much Ado about Nothing', 'The Tempest', 'The Winter's Tale', 'Othello', and 'Julius Cæsar' were performed. After the death of Prince Henry in 1612, his players entered the service of the Prince Palatine, a proof that he was in some way connected with the theatre.

In the years 1626—27, the theatre at the court of Dresden displayed an unusual amount of life and activity, and we know the pieces day by day which were performed by actors, who called themselves English Comedians. We shall return to these records in our next chapter. It will be sufficient to remark here, that the list of plays, which we probably possess quite complete, comprises almost exclusively wellknown English plays, and among them four of Shakespeare's tragedies. The actors accompanied the Elector to Torgau, where, on the 1st of April, 1627, the marriage was celebrated between the Princess Sophia and the Landgrave George of Hesse-Darmstadt. They were dismissed on the 6th of May. At Torgau the actors were lodged in private houses, and we learn their names from a list of their quarters, but unfortunately in most cases only their Christian names.

"Robertt: Pickelheringk mit zwei Jungen. (Pickelhering with two boys.) Jacob der Hesse. (James the Hessian.) Johann Eydtwartt. Aaron der Danzer. (Aaron the dancer.) Thomas die Jungfraw. (Thomas the maiden.) Johann. Wilhelm der Kleiderverwahrer. (William the keeper of the wardrobe.) Der Engelender. (The Englishman.) Der Rothkopff. (The red-haired.) Vier Jungen. (Four boys.)"

The Englishman was probably the manager of the company; all the others may have been Germans. Moreover a German company, one of the oldest, under the management of a certain Treu, who visited Berlin repeatedly in the years 1622—25, is stated to have played at Torgau on this occasion; and the first German opera, Daphne, composed by the celebrated Henry Schütz, was also performed.[1] The next notices respecting dramatic performances at the Saxon Court refer to the years 1630—36, but it does not appear whether English actors took any part in them. In the beginning of 1630, among other things, mention is made of a tragi-comedy, 'Isabella, Kœnigin von Klein-Britannien' ('Isabella, Queen of Little Britain.')[2]

The actors who were dismissed from Torgau in 1627 may perhaps have gone the

---

[1] M. Fürstenau, *Zur Geschichte* etc. p. 100. — Amongst the Musicians of the Elector there were several Englishmen, one of whom, John Price, deserves special notice. He was one of the most celebrated flute-players of his time. See Mersenne, *Harmonie universelle*. fol. Paris 1636. He was appointed Musician to the Elector on the 23d of April 1629, with a salary of 300 thalers a year. — A dancer, George Bentley, is mentioned at the same court in 1652, and an Instrumentalist, John Dixon, in 1663.

[2] M. Fürstenau, *Zur Geschichte* etc. p. 101.

following year to Nuremberg, where we meet with English Comedians in 1628. In April they acted a piece entitled 'Der Liebe Süfsigkeit verendert sich in Todes Bitterkeit' (Love's sweetness turned into Death's bitterness). We learn this from a very curious broadside, a sort of play-bill, which is preserved in the town-library of Nuremberg. As it is the only document of the kind with which we are acquainted, we give a facsimile of it. (See Plate ii.) We learn from it the manner in which the actors made known their arrival in foreign towns. What piece it is, that was designated by the above name, is more than we have been able to discover. The title would suit 'Romeo and Juliet' remarkably well.[1] The same or some other company of English Comedians appeared at Nuremberg in July 1628, and applied for permission to play for a few days. They wished to take three "batzen" the price of admission for each person, but on the second day the Council reduced it to six creutzers, of which they only received the half. They were allowed to play Tuesdays, Wednesdays, and Thursdays, for two weeks in succession, but not till after vespers on such days as might be feast-days. After the expiration of this time, they repeatedly begged for a prolongation of their licence, alleging that they had bought a great many things, and had spent all their money, but they were refused. Several German companies made a similar application before the end of the year, and with a similar result.[2]

In April 1629 we again meet with a company of English Comedians at the Hague. The Magistrates, as on the former occasion, grant them permission to play at the fair, for which they have to pay 30 florins to the Orphan Asylum. On the 23rd of May, and again on the 24th of December of the same year, the permission is renewed, and at the same time the "Tennis-court" in the present Hoflaan is assigned to their use.[3]

An interruption of ten years occurs here in our information respecting the English Comedians, and indeed it would appear that the war, which had now extended itself over all Germany, prevented the companies from visiting that country. The evidence of a contemporary is to this effect:

"Diesen Monsieur Pickelhaering haben die Engländischen erstmalen in Deutschland eingeführet, da es noch in guten Wohlstand war, und jedermann gerne mit Comoedien und anderen Aufzügen sich belustiget, welches nicht mehr viel geschehen wird."[4]

TRANSLATION.

This Monsieur Pickelhaering was first introduced into Germany by the English while it was still in a state of prosperity, and everybody liked to amuse himself with comedies and other representations, which is now no longer the case.

Towards the end of 1639, English Comedians are again mentioned in the Koenigs-

---

[1] The above mentioned Broadside has been first made known by Mr. F. E. Hysel, in his valuable work, *Das Theater in Nürnberg von 1612 bis 1863.* 8vo. Nürnberg 1864. Mr. Hysel kindly sent me the facsimile which accompanies the present work.

[2] F. L. v. Soden, *Kriegs- und Sittengeschichte der Reichsstadt Nürnberg vom Ende des 16ten Jahrhunderts bis zur Schlacht bei Breitenfeld, 7.—17. Sept. 1631.* Zweiter Theil. 8vo. Erlangen 1861.

[3] L. Ph. C. van der Bergh, *'S Gravenhaag'sche Byzonderheden,* p. 21.

[4] *Illuminirter Reichs vnd Welt-Spiegel.* 4to. s. l. 1631.

berg accounts, for a sum of 150 thalers. They and their trumpeters were conveyed by water in two boats to the Electoral Palace at Brandenburg.[1] In the year 1643, English Comedians were at Osnabrück, at the time of the Congress for the negociations between Austria and Sweden. On their leaving the place, the Town-Council gave them a testimonial to the effect that they had acted their Tragedies, Comedies, and Pastorals to the satisfaction of those who had witnessed them.[2]

From November 1644 till about February 1645, there was a company at the Hague. One of the documents in an action brought by a certain Vincent Wodroff, an English shoemaker ('Engelsch Schoenlapper') against the members of the company is still extant. It has never been published before, and though the greater part of it does not bear on our present subject, we subjoin it below.[3] Five of the company are mentioned in it by name: Jeremias Kite, William Coeck [Cook], Thomas Loffday [Loveday], Edward Schottuel [Scottwell], and Nathan Peet [Pate].

[1] E. A. Hagen, *Geschichte* etc. p. 60.
[2] Vehse, *Geschichte der geistlichen Höfe*. Vol. iii, p. 102.
[3] *Extract uit het Register der Dingtalen van den Hove van Holland, van den 30^{en} January 1645 tot den laatsten Maart daaraanvolgende. C. Rollant, Griffier.*

"Vincent Wodroff contra d'Engelsche Commedianten.

Op ten dach van huyden compareerde voor den Hove van Hollandt Maerten Deym, als procureur van Vincent Wodroff, Engels schoenlapper alhier in den Haghe, requirant, ende exhibeerde den voorseiden Hove zeeckere obligatie by Jeremias Kite, William Coeck, Thomas Loffday ende Eduart Schottuel, alle Engelsche commedianten, tsamen ende elcx int bijsonder onder behoorlijcke renunchiatie gerequireerden op den vi^{en} deser maent January voor Notaris ende getuygen gepasseert, versoeckende daerop condemnatie; waerop Gerrit Vinck als procureur van de gerequireerdens verclaerde volgende zyne speciale procuratie in de voorseide obligatie geexpresseert dat hy int voorseide versoeck consenteerde. Gehoort welck versoeck ende consent ende gesien dezelve obligatie alhier geinsereert.

Op huyden den vi^{en} dach der maent van Januario 1645, compareerden voor my Ferdinande Molckman openbaer notaris by den Hove van Hollant, geadmitteert, in 's Gravenhaghe residerende, ende voor de getuygen naergenoemt, Jeremias Kite, William Coeck, Thomas Lofday ende Eduard Schottuel, alle Engelsche commedianten, ende becenden tsamen ende elcx van hen int by sonder wel ende deuchdelyck schuldich te wesen aen Vincent Wodroff, Engelsch schoenlapper alhier en den Haghe woonachtich, de somme van drie hondert twee Karoli guldens drie stuyvers, spruytende ter zaecke van verteerde montcosten, camerhuur, ende andere nootelycke behoeften by hen commedianten, met henluyden medegesellen, als Nathan Peet met een jongen off zynen soon ende hen comparante daervoor zyluyden hen zyn sterck maeckende, daervan zyluyden d'een d'ander wel zullen weten te vinden, alle genooten binnen den tyt van thien off elff weecken lestleeden ende metten anderen finalyck affgerekent van alles tot nu toe, dewelcke voorseide somme van III^c II guldens III stuyvers zyluyden commedianten te zamen ende elcx van hen int bysonder aen den voorseiden Vincent Wodroff off den thoonder van desen zyn actie hebbende beloven te betalen altyt t'zynen vermanen, onder tverbant van hen evendieps toebehoorende commediants kleederen alles met den aenkleven van dien niet uytgesondert ende voorts generalyck hunnen persoonen en goederen, roerende en onroerende, hebbende ende vercrygende, geen van dien uytgesondert, subjecterende dezelve ende de keure vandien alle Heeren Hovenrechten ende Techteren, renunchierende ten desen eynde van 't beneficie van der divisien ordinis excussionis, den borgen tot voordeel verleent, ende van alle andere beneficien, zoe de rechten dicteren dat de generale renunchiatie van geender waerden en zyn ten zy saecke dat de speciale voorgaen. Ende tot meerder verseeckerheyt van tgeene voorseit is soo hebben zyluyden commedianten tsamen ende elcx van hen int bysonder onwederroepelyck geconstitueert Cornelis Pieck, Gerrit Vinck ende Maerten Deym, alle procureurs voor den voors. Hove van Hollant ende Hoogen Raede in Hollant te samen ende elcx van hen int bysonder, omme henluyden commedianten te samen ende elcx van hen int bysonder inne den in-

From the 14th to the 25th of July 1650, a company of 'Electoral Saxon Comedians' played some English comedies in the Town-hall at Zittau.[1]

On the 10th of November 1650, the Emperor Ferdinand the third published a letter of safe conduct for a company of English Comedians, to the following effect:

"Wir Ferdinand der Dritte, von Gottes Gnaden etc. bekennen öffentlich mit diesem Brieff und thuen kund allermänniglich: demnach Uns Fürweiser dieses, Wilhelmb Roe, Johann Waide, Gedeon Gellius [Giles?], Robert Casse sambt ihren Mitconsorten engelländische Comoedianten, unterthänigst zu vernehmen gegeben, wasmassen sie nunmehre eine ziembliche Zeit hero an unterschiedlicher hoher Potentaten Höfe, wie auch anderer Orten hin und wieder, allerley lustige Spiel vnd kurzweilige Comoedien öffentlich exhibirt und gespielt haben, unterthäniges bittend, daſs Wir ihnen solche allhie in Unserer Kaiserlichen Residenzstadt gleichfalls auf eine Zeit lang öffentlich zu agiren gnädigste Erlaubniſs ertheilen wöllten, und Wir uns darein (jedoch dass sie sich dabei aller Unehrbarkeiten, sowol in Worten als Actionen allerdings enthalten sollen) allergnädigst bewilliget: — als haben Uns sie darauf ferneres gehorsambst angezeigt, wie daſs sie nunmehr von dannen abzureisen, und besagte ihrer Profession unterschiedlichen anderen Orten, sowohl in dem heiligen Römischen Reich, als andern Unsern erblichen Königreichen, Fürstenthumben und Landen zu üben und zu treiben Willens wären, und derowegen Uns zu desto besserer und unverhinderlicherer Fortsetzung dieses ihres Vorhabens, umb Unser allergnädigste Hilf, Frei- und Sicherheit allerunterthänigst gebeten.

Wann Wir dann gnädigst angesehen, solch ihr diemüthig gehorsambste Bitt, besonderlich aber erwogen, daſs sie die Zeit über, so Wir ihnen alhier in unserer Stadt Wien und darüber auch in unseren Kaiserlichen Hof selbsten, ihre Comödien zu spielen gnädigst bewilliget, sich darinnen also verhalten dass Uns einige Klag wider Sie nicht vorkommen: als haben Wir mit wohlbedachtem Muth, gutem Rath und rechtem Wissen ihnen obgenannten Comödianten diese Kaiserliche Gnad gethan und Freiheit gegeben, daſs sie solche ihre vorhabende Profession aller Orten, sowohl in dem heil. Röm. Reich, als auch anderen Unseren Erbkönigreichen, Fürstenthumben und Landen unverhindert Männiglichs exerciren, treiben und sich derselben gebrauchen mögen; ihnen auch vor Niemands, wer er auch seye, Kein Eintrag, Irrung, oder Verhinderniſs zugefügt werden; jedoch daſs sie sich dabei aller Ehrbarkeit befleissen, auch aller unziemblicher Reden und Actionen gewiſslich enthalten sollen.

Gebieten hierauf allen und jedem Churfürsten, Fürsten, Geist- und Weltlichen, Prälaten, Grafen, Freyen, Herren, Rittern, Knechten, Landmarschallen, Landhauptleuten, Vicedomben, Burggrafen, Vögten, Pflegern, Verwesern, Amtboten, Schultheiſsen, Bürgermeistern, Richtern, Räthen, Bürgern, Gemeinden, und sonst allen andern Unsern und des Reichs, desgleichen Unserer Erbkönigreich, Fürstenthumben und Landen, Unterthanen und Getreuen, was Würden, Stands und Wesens sie seynd, ernstlich und festiglich mit diesem Brief, und wollen: daſs sie mehrbenannte engelländische Comödianten-Compagnia, sammt ihren Leuten, Pferden und Sachen nit allein aller Orten und Enden, zu Wasser und

houden van desen by den voorseiden Hove van Hollant ende Hoogen Raede in Hollant goetwillichlyk te laten condemneren ende betalen alle de costen, dewelcke hieromme zullen werden gedaen, gelyck te samen ende elcx van hen int bysonder nu en t'allen dagen van waerden te houden alle tgeene by heur voorseide Procureurs te zamen ende elcx van hen int bysonder hierinne gedaen ende gevordert zal werden, onder tverbant ende renunchiatie als hiervooren verhaelt, alles zonder bedroch. Aldus gedaen ende gepasseert ter presentie van Lambert Pieters van Outheusden, biersteecker ende Salomon de Paris, Engelscoopman, woonende alhier in den Haghe, als getuygen, die de minute van desen, beneffens de voorseide commedianten hebben ondertheyckent. Onder stont Quod attestor ende was ondertheyckent Ferd. Molckeman, Notaris publicus.

Heeft tvoorseide Hoff de voornoemde gerequireerdens gecondemneert ende condemneert henluyden mits desen omme de voorseide obligatie te volcomen ende achtervolgen naer hare forme ende inhouden. Actum den xi[en] January 1645. Present, Francken ende Kinschot."

[1] Pescheck, *Geschichte von Zittau*. 8vo. Vol. ii, p. 348.

zu Land frei, sicher und unverhindert durchkomben, passiren und repassiren, ihnen auch in allen Vorfallenheiten, wo es vonnöthen, geziembenden Vorschub leisten und allen geneigten befördersamben Willen erwaisen, sondern auch sie bei dieser Unserer ihnen ertheilten Gnad Freiheit und Verwilligung ruhig verbleiben, deren aller Orten frei und ungehindert geniessen, gebrauchen lassen, darwider mit beschweren, noch defs jemands Andern zu thun gestatteten in kein Weis noch weg, das meynen Wir ernstlich.

Mit Urkund dies Briefs besiegelt mit Unserem anhangenden Insiegel, der geben ist in Unserer Stadt Wien den zehenten Monatstag Novembris nach Christi .... Geburt im 1650sten, Unserer Reiche des Römischen im vierzehnten etc., des hungarischen im fünf und zwanzigsten, und des bohömischen im drei und zwanzigsten Jahre.

(gez.) Ferdinand.
(L. S.)[1]

TRANSLATION.

We Ferdinand the third, by the Grace of God etc. publicly declare and make known to all men by these presents: After the bearers of these, William Roe, John Waide, Gideon Gellius [Giles?], Robert Casse and their companions, being English Comedians, had most humbly given us to understand how that they for a considerable time past had publicly exhibited and acted all sorts of amusing plays and entertaining comedies at the Courts of various high potentates, as also at other places, humbly beseeching that we would likewise grant them our gracious permission publicly to act such things for a certain time in our Imperial residence, and we graciously granted them the said permission, (yet only so that they should entirely refrain thereby from all improprieties as well in their words as in their actions) whereas they have now further humbly announced to us, that they are desirous of leaving this place and of practising and exercising their said profession in various other places, as well in the holy Roman Empire as in our hereditary Kingdoms, Principalities, and countries, and to this behoof for the better and freer prosecution of this their intention, have humbly begged our aid, permission, and protection.

Graciously regarding this their humble and respectful petition, but more especially taking into consideration, that all the time in which we have graciously permitted them to act their comedies here in our city of Vienna, and yet more, in our Imperial Court itself, they have comported themselves in such manner that no complaints have been made against them; We, with due consideration, good counsel, and right knowledge, have shewn them this Imperial grace, and given them licence, that they may without hindrance publicly exercise, carry on, and use this their intended profession in all places, as well in the Holy Roman Empire as also in our hereditary Kingdoms, Principalities, and countries, and that they suffer no damage intended or otherwise or impediment, nevertheless so that they behave themselves quite honorably therein, and surely abstain from all unseemly speeches and words.

Hereupon we order all and every, the Electors, Princes, spiritual and secular, Prelates, Counts, Barons, Lords, Knights, Squires, Landmarshals, Captains general, Vicegerents, Burgraves, Prefects, Wardens, Administrators, Stewards, Bailiffs, Burgomasters, Judges, Counsellors, Citizens, Commonalties, and all other lieges and subjects of ourselves and of the Empire, as also of our hereditary Kingdom, Principalities and lands, of whatsoever dignity, rank, or character they may be, seriously and solemnly by this letter, and decree: that they not only allow the often-mentioned company of English Comedians, together with their people, horses, and effects to pass and repass at all places, by water

---

[1] As we do not possess a literal transcript of this document, we are obliged to print it from a text published by Mr. J. M. Schottky in *Unterhaltungen für das Theater-Publikum*, herausgegeben von Aug. Lewald. 8vo. München 1833, p. 135, where the orthography is modernised. See also *Der Freimüthige*. (A Periodical.) Berlin 1833, No. 144.

and by land, freely, safely, and without hindrance, and in all emergencies where it may be necessary, afford them all convenient aid, and render them all assistance and good will, but also allow them quietly to enjoy this grace, freedom, and permission granted to them and to use the same at all places freely and without hindrance, nor complain against the same, nor allow others to do so in any manner or wise: this is our serious will.

In Witness of this letter, sealed with our seal attached thereto, given in our City of Vienna the tenth day of the month of November in the sixteen-hundred and fiftieth year after the birth of Christ, in the year of our sovereignty, the fourteenth of the Roman Empire, the twenty-fifth of the Kingdom of Hungary, and the twenty-third of the Kingdom of Bohemia.

(signed) Ferdinand.
(L. S.)

This company was at Prague the following year, and, in a memorial addressed to the Royal Statholder and dated the 15th of December 1651, complained: "That at the lately issued gracious prohibition of your Most Noble Excellency and Grace they have ceased to act, and in as much as the maintenance of the company costs a great deal they have incurred no small expense, thus besides this, a great part of their clothes and property had been previously stolen and lost." In order to be able to bear these misfortunes more easily, the travelling artists beg to be allowed to play also the next four days of Advent, and declare in conclusion, that formerly at Vienna, they had "exercised their profession" even during Lent, before Cardinal von Dietrichstein and the Archduke Leopold of Austria. A few days later, after their request had been granted, they apply for permission to exhibit their performances and to act for three weeks longer after the next Christmas holidays, alleging their approaching departure for Vienna as a reason for their request, remarking by the way, "in consideration that two masters among our company are devoted to the Roman Catholic religion, and that we in other respects also use all decency both in words and actions."

On the 21st of July 1652, a certain John Bösslin or Gösslin of Basle advised that permission should be given to the English players "to act their comedies." The request was granted for fourteen days, but only on condition that they did not take more than two shillings for admission from each person. Upon this, on the 18th of August, the company offered in honour of their gracious masters "to hold a curious comedy, if they were only informed of the day and the time." The Council agreed, fixed the following day at three o'clock for the commencement of the play, left it to their chief officers to award such "gratuity" to the company of actors as they might deem proper, and further, granted the company permission to perform comedies for one week, but nothing objectionable.

Encouraged by these first performances in Basle, Joris Jolifus "English and Roman Imperial Comedian" sent an application from Strasburg to the Council of Basle in the beginning of 1654, with the tempting assurance "that with his well-practised company, not only by means of good instructive stories, but also with repeated changes of expensive costumes, and a theatre decorated in the Italian manner, with beautiful English music and

skilful ("rechten")¹ women" he would give universal satisfaction to the lovers of plays. In spite of all these fine promises, the request was refused.

The English actors could never obtain permission to perform in Zürich. The protocol of the Council says "they were simply refused permission". Texts from the Scriptures, passages from the Fathers and modern instances were cited against this love of playgoing, and it was proved that sometimes on days when plays had been performed, thunderstorms had arisen when the sky was clear and had destroyed both buildings and fruit, fires had broken out and could hardly be extinguished, and persons who had played the devil had never been happy afterwards. ²

The above-mentioned Joris Jolifus is undoubtedly the same person, who under the name of George Jeliphur, English comedian, received 15 florins in Vienna on the 15th of May 1653 "for acting a comedy with his colleagues before their Majesties". ³

At Windsheim on the Maine, on the 9th of March 1656, "the tragedy of Charles Stuart the English King, how he was taken prisoner by his parliament, condemned, and at last beheaded by the axe", was played "by English comedians". ⁴ In the course of the same year, some English Comedians came to Dordrecht in Holland. ⁵

In 1659, a certain Joseph Jori appears at Vienna, who calls himself an "English and Heidelberg comedian", and offers with his company to represent "such notable comedies and tragedies as that the like had never been seen in Germany before, or ever acted by others". The Council reports on his petition to the government, and is of opinion that "although one cannot derive any good from such comedies, but, as is well known, idleness and scandal of all sorts are only increased by them, moreover money, which any how is very scarce at present, is taken out of the country, we leave it to Your Grace's pleasure to decide whether Your Grace will advise His Imperial Majesty, that the petitioner may perhaps be allowed to practise his performances next year during the Carnival, or whether the same shall be dismissed altogether". ⁶

From the 11th of April 1660, the English comedians play again in Zittau, and indeed four times with the most clamorous applause. ⁷

As late as 1683, Grimmelshausen, the author of the celebrated 'Simplicissimus' makes mention of the English players in his 'Wonderful Birdsnest'. "At that time, a company of English actors had arrived in the town, who wanted to return home from thence, and were only waiting for a fair wind in order to sail. I obtained from them a terrible devil's mask etc." ⁸

---

¹ This is one of the earliest notices of women performing on the German stage.

² *Anzeiger für Kunde der deutschen Vorzeit.* 1855, p. 231. An article by Meyer von Knonau. From the Municipal Minutes of the city of Basle.

³ Karl Weifs, *Die Wiener Haupt- und Staatsactionen*, p. 36.

⁴ *Archiv für Geschichte und Alterthumskunde des Obermainkreises.* Vol. i, part 1. 8vo. Bayreuth 1831. From a Ms. chronicle of the city of Windsheim.

⁵ *Navorscher*, Deel iii, p. 17.

⁶ Schlager, *Wiener Skizzen aus dem Mittelalter.* Neue Folge. 8vo. Wien 1839, p. 252.

⁷ Pescheck, *Geschichte von Zittau.* Vol. ii, p. 348.

⁸ (H. J. Christ. v. Grimmelshausen), *Des wunderbarlichen ... Vogel-Nestes fernere Fortsetzung* [Anderer

Similar notices occur at this time and even later, but possess comparatively little interest for us, as the designation of the companies and the pieces they performed as English is only a reminiscence, and can no longer be referred with certainty to any real English origin. It is indeed, a remarkable fact, and a proof how deeply the English Theatre had taken root among the people, that in order to obtain from them a welcome reception, it was considered necessary to retain such designations at that period of deep humiliation for Germany after the Peace of Westphalia, when the French disregard of nature, which had corrupted German morals and manners, had also taken possession of the stage.

CHAPTER V.

We have not as yet been able to make more than a mere occasional mention of the acting stock of the English Comedians; it is now time however that we should speak more at length of the pieces by which the transformation of the German stage was effected. Hans Sachs had already adopted an English subject for one of his best pieces; at a later period Henry Julius and Jacob Ayrer wrote almost exclusively after English models, which had been brought them by the English players; and at the Courts of Cassel, Dresden and Berlin we have seen English taste exercising a preponderating influence, and subjects taken from English history represented on the stage. With the increasing number of English companies which occurred in the beginning of the seventeenth century, English subjects began to prevail upon the German stage, and a number of these pieces has been transmitted to us by means of a collection of 'English comedies and tragedies' printed in 1620, and professing to be the acting library of the English Comedians. But however important this collection may be as a speaking evidence of the influence of the English actors in effecting a transformation of the German stage, it cannot convey to us any conception of the dramatic art of the actors themselves. It is rather an evidence of the manner in which English subjects at that time were remodelled under German hands; and even in this respect its evidence is only of limited importance. For we have to do here with the adaptations of uneducated speculators, whose object was to spoil the market for the English, and to appropriate their subjects for the benefit of German companies, who had begun to compete with the English at an early period. It is impossible to imagine for a moment that the English actors themselves made this collection, as has often been asserted. This supposition is principally based on a false interpretation of the concluding passage of the preface, which is as follows:

"As then in our times the English Comedians, partly by their pretty inventions, partly by the gracefulness of their gestures, often also by their elegance in speaking, obtain great praise from persons both of high and low condition, and thus active clever minds take a delight in and a fancy for such inventions, to exercise themselves therein, therefore

---

Theil]. 8vo. s. l. Gedruckt Im Jahr 1683, p. 579. — See also the same work in A. v. Keller's edition of Grimmelshausen's *Simplicissimus*, Vol. iv. 8vo. Stuttgart 1862, p. 654.

have we been desirous to gratify them in this matter, and to print and publish these comedies and tragedies for their benefit; and as we shall perceive that they are agreeable and acceptable to them, more of the same shall soon follow them. In the mean time we hope they may be willing to make good and profitable use of these, and be contented with them."[1]

The sentence "therefore have we been desirous to gratify them &c" has been referred to the actors, but both this sentence and all that follows refer to the "minds" which take a delight in such "inventions," which, strictly considered, involves a confession of piracy. It is almost impossible that the foreigners should ever have thought of publishing these pieces to satisfy the curiosity of the public, when that very curiosity was precisely the most powerful feeling which attracted the public to their performances. There is moreover abundant internal evidence to shew that these pieces are not an authentic text, but have been merely taken down in a hurry from the mouths of actors. In many places the dialogue breaks off abruptly with an '&c.', without the sentence coming to an end, or its meaning being clear, — a striking proof that the writer either did not catch the conclusion, or did not understand it. Sometimes also there is a confusion among the characters, as for instance in 'Titus Andronicus', which is a strong argument in favour of our view. We possess therefore in this collection nothing but the subjects of the pieces which had been brought over by the English players, not the pieces themselves in the form in which they were played. So far from it indeed, the pieces had been corrupted by rude hands to such an extent, that hardly the mere skeleton was left, and it is not consistent therefore either with justice or sound criticism to attempt to draw any conclusions from these pieces respecting the theatrical merits of the English Comedians. If we allow that the English brought these pieces to Germany, as indeed we must, why should they have put them on the stage in such a cruelly mutilated state? Or are we perhaps to form such a very low estimate of the German spectators at the courts and elsewhere, as to assume that the actors were obliged to banish all poetry from their plays, in order to adopt them to the intellect of their audience? But even if we would place the intellectual level of the educated classes of those times so very low, — which we have no reason to do, — we should still have to seek elsewhere for an explanation of the manner in which these pieces have been treated; for the actors might always have felt quite sure of exciting a sufficient interest in their audience by the purely external incidents, by what we call plot and action, and need never have taken the trouble of recasting their pieces in another form. If, again,

---

[1] The German Text of the passage runs as follows: "Wann dann zu vnsern Zeiten die Englischen Comoedianten, theils wegen artiger Invention, theils wegen Anmuthigkeit jhrer Geberden, auch offters Zierligkeit im Reden bey hohen vnd Niederstands Personen mit grosses Lob erlangen, vnd dardurch viel hurtige vnd wackere Ingenia zu dergleichen inventionen lust vnd beliebung haben, sich darin zu üben, Also hat man jhnen hierinnen willfahren, vnd diese Comoedien vnd Tragedien jhnen zum besten in öffentlichen Druck geben wollen, da man nun vermercken wird, dafs sie jhnen lieb vnd angenehmb, sollen derselben bald mehr darauff folgen, vnter dessen wollen sie diese nützlich vnd wol gebrauchen, vnd jhnen gefallen lassen."

we assume that the collection altogether does not contain the pieces which the English Comedians had acted, and that the title and preface, which assert this, were only put out as a bait, the recasting of these English subjects would still only have been possible on the supposition that the editors had the printed English pieces before them, — and then this corruption and mutilation are quite inexplicable. There remains therefore no other alternative than that at which we have hinted above: illiterate scribes wrote down from memory what they had heard from the actors; the skeleton of the outward incidents which had remained in their memory was then filled up with a dialogue of their own composition, and in this manner pieces were fabricated, which contained nothing more of the originals than the mere outline.

A direct proof of the correctness of this view is to be found in the fact, that in almost all these pieces certain stereotype phrases are constantly recurring, indeed whole scenes have been transferred from one piece to another. Some of the jokes and tricks of the clown are repeated in the comic scenes of the different pieces. The clumsy hand of these workmen has moreover quite obliterated all traces of higher art in the dramatic treatment, in which the worst English pieces of that period far surpassed the best German ones, and has brought these pieces down to the level of the contemporary German productions. Their want of skill appears most strongly, in their utter ignorance of dramatic combination. There is no inward connection among the parts; we see a succession of moving incidents, adventures of all sorts, intended to excite the interest of the spectators, to gratify their curiosity and their love of spectacle, or to tickle their risible muscles, but all these incidents are merely placed side by side without any internal unity, and it is left to the spectator to form his own picture of what is going on in the minds of the persons concerned. The latter always appear in the climax of some affection, either joy or pain, anger or despair. The language has its ever-recurring stereotyped forms. The characters say: "Now will I do this," and afterwards "Now I have done that." The real dramatic action, even when brought with all its details before the eyes of the spectators, as for instance, the throat-cutting business in Titus Andronicus, must also be spoken of as having been done; — the drama could never entirely emancipate itself from the form of narrative.[1] It is impossible that the English actors, who must have been acquainted with the stage of their native country, could ever have acted in that way. But that illiterate Germans, such as the editors of the 'English Comedies and Tragedies', should have ignored all the deeper significance of these pieces, and should have attended only to the outward incidents, cannot be regarded as anything extraordinary, when we consider the productions of the German dramatic muse of that period. That the English actors offered something better than what was so highly lauded in those collections as their property, appears at once from the intellectual impulse which cultivated minds received from them. Valentin Andreae, who wrote between the years 1602 and 1620, composed two Latin plays, in order,

---

[1] See Ed. Devrient, *Geschichte* etc. Vol. i, p. 165.

as he himself says, to compete with the English Comedians.[1] A similar confession is made by John Rhenanus, a physician who had travelled in England, and who since 1610 had been in the service of the Landgrave Maurice of Cassel, to whom in 1613 he dedicated a comedy entitled 'The battle of the senses'. He says in his preface, that among the writers and performers of comedies of that time, the English maintained the first place as regards both composition and action; that they understood how to use prose and verse alternately, according to the nature of the subject, and that the actors were not ashamed to receive instructions from the poets &c; that they (the Germans) should endeavour to emulate them. He had now ventured to make this crude attempt, and begged Maurice's judgment of it, which had more weight with him than a thousand others.[2]

John Cam. Merck in the preface to his version of the Latin piece 'Beel', by Xystus Betulius, which he had put into verse, also speaks of the English players in terms of praise. He says that, to confess the truth, he was by no means dissatisfied with the manner of the English actors, but that in his new version he had been anxious to follow the old traditional custom rather than his own taste.[3] It is true, Gumpelsheimer, in his work published in Strassburg in 1612, in which he recommends the academicians to frequent the theatres on account of the very great advantage to be derived from them, does not mention the English players by name, but it is clearly the English whom he means when he says, that for invention and representation they surpass everything that had been seen in Germany, up to that time.[4] We should undoubtedly find a great many similar favourable judgments respecting the performances of our strollers, if we were to ransack the literature of the times for that purpose.

As the collection in question possesses great interest with reference to our subject, we shall now proceed to give a description of it.

Title: "Engelische Comedien vnd | Tragedien | Das ist: | Sehr Schöne, | herrliche vnd aufserlesene, | geist- vnd weltliche Comedi vnd | Tragedi Spiel, | Sampt dem | Pickelhering, welche wegen jhrer artigen | Jnventionen, kurtzweiligē auch theils | warhafftigen Geschicht halber, von den Engelländern | in Deutschland an Königlichen, Chur- vnd Fürst- lichen Höfen, auch in vornehmen Reichs- See- vnd | Handel Städten feynd agiret vnd gehalten | worden, vnd zuvor nie im Druck aufs- | gangen. | An jetzo, | Allen der Comedi vnd Tragedi lieb- |

---

[1] The two Latin plays alluded to are 'Esther' and 'Hyacinthus'. See *Joh. Val. Andreä Dichtungen.* 8vo. Leipzig 1786, introd. p. xxxii, and also his autobiography: *Selbstbiographie Joh. Val. Andreä,* herausgegeben von Seybold. 8vo. Winterthur 1799.

[2] The comedy has never been printed. The MS. is in the Electoral Library at Cassel. See Chr. v. Rommel. *Geschichte von Hessen,* Vol. vi, p. 497—98.

[3] *Beel. Eine Geistliche Comico-Tragoedia. Erstlich aus dem teutschen Exemplar Xysti Betuleii in die lateinische Sprach vertiert ... Nunmehr aber widerumb inn Teutsche Reimen vberlegt durch Joh. Cunr. Merckium.* 8vo. Ulm 1615.

[4] "Quantam plausibilem exactionem Germaniae nostrae imponant, usus testatur, monstrat experientia." Gumpelsheimer's *Gymnasma de exercitiis academicorum.* Argentorati 1612. See E. A. Hagen, *Geschichte* etc. p. 44.

habern, vnd Andern zu lieb vnd gefallen, der Gestalt | in offenen Druck gegeben, dafs fie gar leicht daraufs | Spielweifs widerumb angerichtet, vnd zur Ergetzligkeit vnd | Erquickung des Gemüths gehalten wer- | den können. | Gedruckt im Jahr M.DC.XX. | 384 leaves. 8vo. s. l.

(English Comedies and Tragedies, i. e. Very fine, beautiful and select, spiritual and worldly Comedy and Tragedy plays, with the clown, which on account of their fanciful inventions, entertaining and partly true histories, have been acted and given by the English in Germany at Royal, Electoral, and Princely courts, as well as in the principal Imperial- Sea- and Commercial towns, never before printed, but now published to please all lovers of Comedies and Tragedies, and others, and in such a manner as to be fit to be easily acted for the delight and recreation of the mind).

Contents: 1. "Comoedia Von der Königin Esther vnd hoffertigen Haman." — Comedy of Queen Esther and haughty Haman.

2. "Comedia. Von dem verlornen Sohn in welchen die Verzweiffelung vnd Hoffnung gar artig introducirt werden." — Comedy of the Prodigal Son in which Despair and Hope are cleverly introduced.

3. "Comoedia Von Fortunato vnd seinem Seckel vnd Wünschhütlein, Darinnen erstlich drey verstorbenen Seelen als Geister, darnach die Tugenden vnd Schande eingeführet werden." — Comedy of Fortunatus and his purse and wishing cap, in which appear first three dead souls as spirits, and afterwards the virtues and shame.

4. "Eine schöne luftige triumphirende Comoedia von eines Königes Sohn aufs Engellandt vnd des Königes Tochter aufs Schottlandt." — A beautiful, merry, triumphant Comedy of a King's son from England and the King's daughter from Scotland [Serule and Astrea].

5. "Eine Kurtzweilige lustige Comoedia von Sidonia vnd Theagene." — An entertaining, merry Comedy of Sidonia and Theagene.

6. "Eine schöne luftige Comoedia von Jemand vnd Niemandt." — A beautiful merry Comedy of Somebody and Nobody.

7. "Tragaedia. Von Julio vnd Hyppolita." — Tragedy of Julius and Hyppolita. (See p. 113 — 156 of the present work).

8. "Eine sehr klägliche Tragaedia von Tito Andronico etc." (See p. 157 — 236 of the present work).

9. "Ein luftig Pickelherings Spiel, von der schönen Maria vnd alten Hanrey." — A merry jest with the clowns, of the beautiful Mary and the old cuckold.

10. "Ein ander lustig Pickelherings Spiel, darinnen er mit einem Stein gar lustige Possen machet." — Another merry jest with the clown, in which he makes merry pastime with a stone.

"Nachfolgende Engelische Aufzüge, können nach Belieben zwischen den Comoedien agiret werden." — The following English interludes may be acted at pleasure between the Comedies (acts). All in verse, and most of them with musical notes. Five pieces without titles; the following are the persons represented in each of them:

11. Wife, Husband, Pickelhering, Boy, Soldier. — 12. Aliud. Pickelherring at Am-

sterdam, I have been. — 13. The Blanket-washer. Husband, Wife, Neighbour. — 14. Wife, Pickelherring, Servant-maid, Magister, Student. — 15. Nobleman, Pickelherring, Wife, Husband.

A second edition: "Zum Andern mal gedruckt vnd corrigirt. Gedruckt im Jahr M. DC. XXIV." 8vo. — Exactly the same contents.

No 1 of the first collection is a subject which had been very often treated on the old English stage. In 1561 there appeared 'A newe Enterlude drawen oute of the holy Scripture, of godly Queen Hester, very necessary, newly made and imprinted this present Yere 1561, at London by Wyllyam Pickerynge and Thomas Hacket.'[1] This piece is partly a biblical drama, partly a Morality; Vice is curiously enough represented by a jester, Hardydardy. Different from this, and probably with more resemblance to our pieces is a piece mentioned in Henslowe's Diary: 'Hester and Ahasuerus', which was acted by the Lord Chamberlain's players on the 3rd of June 1594. Of these, as is well known, Shakespeare was one. Again, an interlude was written in the seventeenth century, entitled 'Ahasuerus and Esther.' It is ascribed to Robert Cox, and is to be found in Kirkman's 'Wits or Sport upon Sport,' printed in 1672.

In the German piece, the clown is called Hans Knapkäse. He has the same contest with his wife for the mastery as Jann Posset in Ayrer's 'Edward III.' He is a carpenter, who builds the gallows for Haman, and hangs him upon it. "In this shadow" says Tieck we may always recognize the dramatic poet who has stage-effects at his command, so that the management and connection of the scenes betrays a very different spirit to the historical pieces of Hans Sachs, or those which Ayrer composed without any foreign model.[2]

No. 2 certainly has an English model, for, as Tieck justly observes, it is well put together and clearly executed. 'The Prodigal child' is a piece mentioned in 'Histriomastix' in 1610, and as early as 1568 a piece entitled 'Prodigality' was acted at Court, but this in all probability was a Morality.

The third piece in this collection, the 'Comedy of Fortunatus,' is interesting, because perhaps it enables us to conclude what was the original form in which this apparently very popular piece was played upon the old English stage. In Henslowe's Diary we find the piece continually mentioned between the years 1595 and 1599. "The 3 of February 1595, received at the first part of Fortunatus iij^{li}." It is probable that a second part appeared shortly after, for it is afterwards mentioned in Henslowe simply as "Fortunatus." But in November 1599, a new version of this piece was written by Thomas Dekker: "Received of Philipp Hinchlow, to pay Thomas Dekker, in earnest of a booke called the hole history of Fortunatus, xxxx^s." The piece was played at Court the same year, on which occasion Dekker was obliged to make an alteration, as appears from two other entries in

---

[1] See J. P. Collier *History* etc. Vol. ii, p. 253.

[2] *Deutsches Theater*, Vol. I, preface. — Hans Sachs wrote a play called 'Hester', and there is also an old Dutch play treating the same subject, and in which Haman is hanged. See Floegel, *Geschichte der komischen Litteratur*, Vol. iv, p. 339.

Henslowe. Dekker's version was printed in 1600. Tieck's conjecture, that the subject was known on the stage long before 1595, does not appear to have any foundation. But we may see from what has been already stated how popular this piece must have been from 1595 to 1600, and how natural it was that it should recommend itself to the notice of the English actors who came to Germany at that time. It is impossible however to determine with certainty whether it was played in Germany in its first form or in that of Dekker's version, for when we consider the coarse and arbitrary treatment of the German revisor, the absence from the German piece of certain touches which are found in Dekker, cannot be admitted as any evidence. The conclusion therefore, which Tieck would draw from the German form of the piece respecting that of the English one before Dekker's version, appears somewhat hazardous. Just as in Dekker, the scene lies partly in the Dominions of the Sultan, partly in England. When the scene is changed, Andalosia says "Now I am in London" ("Nun bin ich zu Lunden") It is worthy of remark that in this piece the clown (Pickelhering) has no regular written part, but whenever he enters we always find "Here the clown acts something", a certain proof that the editors of this volume were still in the old leaven.

The fourth piece seems to shew external traces of an English model, but we have not hitherto been able to discover what that model was. The English Prince is named 'Serule,' the Scotch Princess, 'Astrea'. England and Scotland are at war; during the battle the Prince becomes enamoured of the enemy's daughter, and takes advantage of a truce to obtain access to her in the disguise of a fool. One of the characters is named Runcifax, a master of the black art, which strongly reminds us of 'Runcifall the Devil,' in Ayrer's 'Beautiful Sidea'. Tieck says: "This comedy is one of the oldest." Upon what grounds this assertion is founded, does not appear, unless perhaps Tieck may have known the English prototype. The other persons represented are the King of England, the King of Scotland, and an attendant.

According to Tieck 'Sidonia and Theagene' is the weakest piece in the collection, and shews few traces of an English origin. In addition to the characters from which the piece takes its name, there are the following: Calarissis, Sidonia's father, Chrasilea her mother, Nausiclus, an old paramour, Cnemon, a peasant, a boy, and Alcke a maid. We may remark here, in passing, that a piece entitled 'Theagines and Chariclea' was played at the English Court as early as 1574.

The sixth play, observes Tieck, is one of the most remarkable, on account of the boldness with which it mixes up ancient English history with allegory. Arcial and Ellidor are alternately driven from the throne, during which changes the parasite always torments and scoffs at the fallen queen, while the honest Nobody is accused of all manner of vices, principally by the rascally Somebody, although he is really the most virtuous, unselfish, and generous character. The satire is very palpable, but is popular and well-sustained. Taken as a whole, the piece has its merits, notwithstanding the jargon in which it is written. Its English prototype is 'Nobody and Somebody, with the true Chronicle History

of Elydure, who was fortunately three several times crowned Kinge of England. Acted by the Queen's Servants.' 4to. s. l. (circa 1603). The principal characters of the German piece are: Marsianus and Carniel, two Counts, King Arcial and his Queen, King Ellidor and his Queen. Somebody (Jemandt), Nobody (Niemandt), Nothing, Nobody's servant, Nothing at all, Nobody's boy (Gar nichts, Niemandt Jung).[1]

The next two pieces of the collection are printed in the present work, together with an English translation:

THE TRAGEDY OF JULIUS AND HIPPOLYTA.
(See p. 113—156.)

At the first glance at this piece we recognize the strong resemblance which the story bears to the principal plot in Shakespeare's 'Two Gentlemen of Verona.' We are acquainted with the source of the underplot in Shakespeare's play, Julia's love to Proteus, in the Story of Felismena in the second book of Montemayor, but the source of the treachery of Proteus to his friend has not yet been discovered. Here now we have a drama based upon this conflict, and if we may trust the title of our collection, which is simply called 'English Comedies and Tragedies,' we must assume the existence of an English play from which the German has proceeded. Such a play has not yet been brought to light, and it appeared to us all the more necessary for that very reason to make our readers acquainted with the German piece in its entirety. The small amount of dramatic skill which this composition displays, is no ground for denying the existence of an English model, for of all the pieces in the collection, just this one has evidently been the most mutilated, as appears from the manner in which at many places the dialogue is abruptly broken off in the middle. Indeed there is every reason to conjecture that this piece is only a fragment constituting only an episode in a more comprehensive subject, as Tieck justly observes. If an English piece with a similar plot should ever be discovered, it will probably turn out to be a far more complicated composition; but we shall find in this, as in all other cases, that Shakespeare only borrowed from his sources the outward sketch of his sublime creation. For no inferior poet of his times could ever have conceived the beautiful contrast between Valentine's generous confidence, and Proteus's treacherous vacillation, and yet none but the work of an inferior poet could ever have passed into such utter oblivion. Our German piece has of course no trace of this beauty. Its subject is nothing more than the conflict of friendship with love, and the victory of passion over good faith. But in this it is the only dramatic counterpart to Shakespeare's play; and to this circumstance alone is it indebted for our attempt to rescue it from oblivion.

---

[1] A Dutch play *Yemant en Niemant* by Isaac de Vos. 4to. 1661 is probably an imitation from the German piece.

THE TRAGEDY OF TITUS ANDRONICUS.
(See p. 157—236.)

Titus Andronicus, though inferior in dramatic merit to all the other plays of Shakespeare, nevertheless betrays numerous traces of his genius. But apart from these it must always possess a peculiar value for the critical lovers of the great poet, as an evidence of the manner in which at the commencement of his splendid career, he accommodated himself to the then existing customs of the theatre, and the taste of the public as he found it at the time. It is well known that this piece passed through several forms before it assumed the one in which it appears in the folio of 1623. The Editors of the latter have added an entire scene which is wanting in the quarto editions, and the quartos do not present the piece in its original form. Whether Shakespeare found the piece already in existence and produced a new version of it, or whether he was the first to treat this subject at all, is a question which we cannot discuss here, and which probably will never be decided; but every circumstance is of considerable importance, which enables us to arrive at any conclusions respecting the original form of the piece. Now in our German 'Lamentable Tragedy' we have the play in all probability, in a form copied from the first design. But the coarse feeling, which was interested in the mere external action alone and not in the dramatic development, has prevailed in the treatment of this as well as almost all the other pieces in the collection, for the principal object has evidently been to reduce the piece to the smallest possible compass. Thus it is, that motives such as the feigned madness of Titus, who suggests to the Empress the idea of a disguise, are passed over in silence, an omission not at all extraordinary in such a version as this. We cannot make the original piece responsible for these absurdities, but if we disregard them, the original form of Shakespeare's tragedy, as Tieck has already observed, may still be distinctly seen to glimmer through. No notice has hitherto been taken of a circumstance in the German piece, which enables us to fix with tolerable certainty the date of the English one. In the year 1591, a piece entitled 'Titus and Vespasian' was performed on the London stage. It must have been very popular, for from the 11th of April 1591 to the 15th of January 1593, it is very frequently mentioned by Henslowe. In Shakespeare's 'Titus Andronicus' there is no Vespasian; no one therefore could ever imagine that the piece alluded to by Henslowe was the original form of the Shakespearian piece. A far more probable supposition is, that the subject must have been the destruction of Jerusalem, during the reign of the Emperor Vespasian, by his son Titus. But in our German Titus Andronicus, a Vespasian is one of the principal characters. It is a fictitious, and no historical personage. In the beginning of the piece he appears as the partizan of Titus Andronicus, for whom he claims the throne of Rome, but towards the end he is suddenly transformed into his son and avenger, who at the conclusion obtains the crown, — one of those instances of a confusion of characters to which we have already alluded, and which are strong evidence of the carelessness with which this German version of the piece was made. We may

safely assume that this Vespasian, like all the other characters of the German piece, was taken from the original 'Titus Andronicus,' and thus we should have to acknowledge that 'Titus and Vespasian' as the original on which Shakespeare's play was founded. In his first mention of it, under the date of April 11, 1591, Henslowe designates it on the margin with *ne*, which, with him, always signifies a piece given for the first time. This nearly agrees with what Ben Jonson says in the Introduction to his 'Bartholomew Fair,' first acted in 1614: "He that will swear 'Jeronimo' or 'Andronicus' are the best plays yet, shall pass unexpected at here, as a man whose judgment shows it is constant, and hath stood still these five-and-twenty or thirty years. Though it be an ignorance, it is a virtuous and staid ignorance; and next to truth a confirmed error does well." Ben Jonson's twenty-five years, which in 1614 had elapsed since the time when Titus Andronicus first came out, would give the date of 1589. He might easily have made an error of a couple of years, as it was not his object in the above passage to fix a date. On the 23rd of January 1593, the piece is first mentioned under the name of 'Titus Andronicus', and again with the addition *ne*; it is probably therefore the recast of the piece, as we have it in the folio of 1623. It was first published in 1600 without Shakespeare's name.[1]

All the succeeding pieces in the collection of the 'English Comedies and Tragedies' are undoubtedly of English origin, but when we consider the extremely arbitrary treatment that has been the lot of these farces, which are much further removed from their models than the greater pieces, we must despair of ever discovering the English originals, most of which are probably no longer extant. In the five "English Acts" we have at any rate genuine English Jigs, in rhyming verse, which were half sung half spoken, and, as in England, were performed between the acts, or at the end of the piece.

In the year 1630 a second collection, professedly of 'English Comedies and Tragedies'[2] was published, but it contains little English matter. 'Silvia and Aminta' is a new

---

[1] An old Dutch imitation of Shakespeare's 'Titus Andronicus' is: *Aran en Titus, of Wraak en Weerwraak: Trevrspel van Jan Vos*. 4to. t'Amstelredam 1641. Not less than eleven editions of it had been published by the year 1661, and even after that date it maintained its popularity on the Dutch stage. Salomon van Rusting gave a version of it in 1712, and Jacob Rosseau another in 1716. For a comparison of the Dutch and the English play see W. Bilderdijk, *Bydragen tot de Tooneelpoëzy*. 8vo. Leyden 1823, p. 13—90. — See also Albert Cohn, *Old English Actors in Germany*, Athenæum 1850, July 13, p. 738, and Id. *Shakespeare on the early German stage*, Athenæum 1851, Jan. 4, p. 21, where more particulars about Dutch imitations of the 'Titus Andronicus' are to be found.

[2] *Liebeskampff, oder Ander Theil der Engelischen Comödien vnd Tragödien, in welchen sehr schöne aufserlesene Comödien vnd Tragödien zu befinden vnd zuvor nie in Druck aufsgegangen. Gedruckt im Jahr 1630.* 8vo. l. c. (*Conflict of love, or the second part of the English Comedies and Tragedies, in which are found most excellent and select Comedies and Tragedies, never printed before.*)
    1. *Comoedia von Macht des kleinen Knaben Cupidinis.* (*Comedy of the little boy's Cupid power.*)
    2. *Comoedia von Aminta vnd Silvia.* — 3. *Comoedia von Prob getrewer Lieb.* (*Comedy of the trial of true love.*) — 4. *Comoedia von Koenig Mantalor's vnrechtmäfsigen Liebe vnd derselben Straff.* (*Comedy of King Mantalor's unlawful love and its punishment.*) — 5. *Singe Comoedie.* (*Singing Comedy.*) — 6. *Singe Comoedie.* — 7. *Tragi Comedia.* — 8. *Tragoedi vnzeitiger Vorwitz.* (*Tragedy of untimely curiosity.*)

version of the Aminta of Tasso, but it may possibly have been based on the English Pastoral of the same name by John Reynolds, which appeared in 1628. The last piece in the volume is founded on a tale of Cervantes 'El curioso impertinente', and, as Tieck observes, often follows the Spanish text with literal exactitude. The pieces of this collection have a very different general physiognomy from the old English pieces of the first; and even when the subjects may be of old English origin, the traces of the models are entirely effased, and can no longer be distinguished. The language is in the stilted style which was the fashion of the literature of the times, and displays the same coquetry with learning. The Clown has constantly scraps of Latin in his mouth, and grace of expression is sought for in the admixture of numerous foreign words. The Clown is introduced under various names: he is called 'Hans Worst', 'Schrämgen', 'Schampitache' [Jean Potage]. The compositions are flat, and to seek for dramatic effect in them, of which some of the pieces in the first collection are not quite destitute, is out of the question. A third collection in three volumes appeared in 1670. It is entitled 'The Scene of English and French Comedians' ('Schauplatz Englischer und Französischer Comoedianten'). All the English pieces it contains are taken from the first collection. It also contains a few pieces of the second collection, and the remainder of the work consists in French pieces after Molière and others.[1]

It would be an error to imagine that in the first of these three collections we possess the entire stage library of our English Comedians. Through the care of an officer of the Dresden Court, a catalogue has been preserved of the pieces which were acted there by the English Comedians in 1626.[2] The following is a literal transcript of it:

[1] *Schaubühne Englischer vnd Französ. Comödianten auff welcher werden vorgestellt die schönsten vnd neuesten Comödien, so vor wenig Jahren in Frankreich, Teutschland vnd anderen Orten .... seynd agirt vnd präsentirt worden.* 3 vols. 8vo. Frankfurt 1760. Vol. i. 1. *Amor der Arzt.* — 2. *Die Comödia ohne Comödia.* — 3. *Die köstliche Lächerlichkeit.* — 4. *Der Hahnrey in der Einbildung.* — 5. *Die Hahnreyinn nach der Einbildung.* — 6. *Die Eyfrende mit ihr selbst.* — 7. *Antiochus, eine Tragicomödia.* — 8. *Die buhlhaffte Mutter.* — 9. *Damons Triumphspiel.* — Vol. ii. 10. *Von Sidonia vnd Theagene.* — 11. *Der Verliebten Kunstgriffe.* — 12. *Lustiges Pickelhäringsspiel, darinn er mit einem Stein gar artige Possen macht.* — 13. *Von Fortunato seinem Wünschhütlein vnd Seckel.* — 14. *Der unbesonnene Liebhaber.* — 15. *Die grossmüthige Thaliklea.* — Vol. iii. 16. *Vom Könige Ahasvero vnd Esther vnd dem hoffartigen Haman.* — 17. *Vom verlohrenen Sohn in welchem die Verzweifelung vnd die Hoffnung gar artig introduciret worden.* — 18. *Von Königs Mantalors vnrechtmässiger Liebe.* — 19. *Der Geitzige.* — 20. *Von der Aminta und Sylvia.* — 21. *Macht des kleinen Knaben Kupidinis.* — 22. *George Dandin oder der verwirrte Ehmann.*

(*The stage of English and French Comedians on which are represented the most beautiful and newest comedies as they have been acted and represented a few years ago in France, Germany, and other places.* 3 vols. 8vo. Frankfurt 1670. Vol. i. 1. *Love the physician.* — 2. *The Comedy without comedy.* — 3. *The precious absurdity.* — 4. *The Cuckold in imagination.* — 5. *The Cuckoldess in imagination.* — 6. *The woman in a passion with herself.* — 7. *Antiochus, a tragi-comedy.* — 8. *The wanton mother.* — 9. *Damon's Triumph-play.* — Vol. ii. 10. *Sidonia and Theagene.* — 11. *Lover's tricks.* — 12. *A merry clown's play, in which he performs right merry tricks with a stone.* — 13. *Fortunatus' wishing cap and purse.* — 14. *The thoughtless lover.* — 15. *The generous Thaliclea.* — Vol. iii. 16. *King Ahasverus and Esther and the proud Haman.* — 17. *The reprobate son, in which despair and hope are prettily introduced.* — 18. *King Mantalor's unlawful love.* — 19. *The miser.* — 20. *Aminta and Silvia.* — 21. *The power of the little boy Cupid.* — 22. *George Dandin, or the puzzled husband.*)

[2] I am indebted for this valuable communication to Mr. Moritz Fürstenau of Dresden. The catalogue, which is written by the above-mentioned officer, is in an Almanac, published by Mag. Johannes Kretzschmer, 8vo.

SHAKESPEARE IN GERMANY.

"May 31. Dresten. Ist der Haupt Vogell abgeschossen vnd Landgraf Georg Koenig worden, auch haben die Engelender eine Comoedia von Hertzogk von Mantua vnd den Hertzogk von Verona gespielt auff den steinern sahl." (May 31. At Dresden. The great wooden bird has been shot down, and Landgrave George become King of the marksmen, and the English have represented a comedy of the Duke of Mantua and Duke of Verona in the Marble-hall.)

Junius 1. Dresten. Ist eine Comedia von der Christabella gespielt worden. (A comedy of Christabella acted.)
— 2. — Ist eine *Tragoedia von Romeo vnd Julietta* gespielt worden.
— 4. — Ist eine Comoedia von Amphitrione gespielt worden.
— 5. — Ist eine Tragicomoedia von Hertzogk von Florentz gespielt worden.
— 6. — Ist eine Comoedia vom König in Spanien vnd den Vice Roy in Portugall gespielt worden.
— 8. — Ist eine *Tragoedia von Julio Cesare* gespielt worden.
— 9. — Ist eine Comoedia von der Crysella gespielt worden.
— 11. — Ist eine Comoedia vom Hertzog von Ferrara gespielt worden.
— 20. — * Ist eine Tragicomedia von Jemandt vnd Niemandt gespielt worden. (Tragi-comedy of Somebody and Nobody)
— 21. — Ist eine Tragicomoedia von König in Dennemark vnd den König in Schweden gespielt worden.
— 24. — Ist eine *Tragoedia von Hamlet einen printzen in Dennemarck* gespielt worden.
— 25. — Ist eine Comoedia von Orlando Furioso gespielt worden.
— 27. — Ist eine Comoedia von den Koenig in Engelandt vnd den Koenig in Schottlandt gespielt worden.
— 28. — Ist eine Tragoedia von Hieronymo Marschall in Spanien gespielt worden.
Julius 3. — * Ist eine Tragicomoedia von dem Hamann vndt der Koenigin Ester gespielt worden.
— 5. — Ist eine Tragoedia von der Märtherin Dorothea gespielt worden.
— 7. — Ist eine Tragoedia von Dr. Faust gespielt worden.
— 9. — Ist eine Tragicomoedia von einem Königk in Arragona gespielt worden.
— 11. — * Ist eine Tragoedia von Fortunato gespielt worden.
— 13. — Ist eine Comoedia von Josepho Juden von Venedigk gespielt worden.

1626. Such almanacs were often used as diaries. It contains the memorandum: "*No. 2, 1626, der jungen Herrn,*" was probably therefore in the possession of the sons of John George the first, and the notes will therefore have been made by an officer of the court of the young princes. In the same volume there are also the almanacs for 1621 to 1625, 1627 to 1630, but with the exception of that for 1627, which contains the statements referring to this year, which will be found above, p. cxvii, we meet with no notes in them of any interest for our present subject. The handwriting is the same in both almanacs. — All these statements have been kindly communicated to me by Mr. Fürstenau.

Julius 22.	Dresten.	Ist eine Tragicomoedia von den behendigen Dieb gespielt worden. (Tragi-comedy of the dexterous thief) [worden.
— 23.	—	Ist eine Tragicomoedia von einem Hertzogk von Venedig gespielt
— 31.	—	Ist eine Tragoedia von Barrabas, Juden von Malta gespielt worden.
Augustus 2.	—	Ist eine Tragicomoedia von dem alten proculo gespielt worden.
— 29.	—	Ist eine Tragoedia von Barrabas, Juden von Malta gespielt worden. (See July 31.)
Sept. 4.	—	Ist eine Comoedia von Hertzogk von Mantua vnd den Hertzogk von Verona gespielt worden. (See May 31.)
— 6.	—	Ist eine Tragicomoedia von dem alten proculo gespielt worden. (See Aug. 2.)
— 15.	—	Ist eine Tragicomoedia von Hertzogk von Florentz gespielt worden. (See June 5.)
— 17.	—	Ist eine Tragicomoedia von den behendigen Dieb gespielt worden. (See July 22.)
— 19.	—	Ist eine Comoedia von König in Spanien vnd Vice Roy in Portugall gespielt worden. (See June 7.)
— 22.	—	Ist eine Tragicomoedia von den behendigen Dieb gespielt worden. (See July 22 and Sept. 17.)
— 24.	—	Ist eine Comoedia von Hertzogk von Ferrara gespielt worden. (See June 11.)
— 26.	—	Ist eine *Tragoedia von Lear, König in Engelandt* gespielt worden.
— 29.	—	Ist eine *Tragoedia von Romeo vnd Julietta* gespielt worden. (See June 2.)
Oct. 1.	—	Ist eine Tragoedia von der Märtherin Dorothea gespielt worden. (See July 5.)
— 4.	—	Ist eine Tragicomoedia von Gevatter gespielt worden. (Tragi-comedy of the God-father).
— 19.	—	✱ Ist eine Comoedia von verlohren Sohn gespielt worden.
— 22.	—	Ist eine Comoedia von den Koenig in Engelandt vnd den König in Schottlandt gespielt worden. (See June 27.)
— 29.	—	Ist eine Comoedia von den Graffen von Angiers gespielt worden.
Nov. 5.	—	Ist eine Comoedia von Josepho Juden von Venedigk gespielt worden. (See July 13.)
Decemb. 4.	—	Ist eine Tragoedia vom reichen Mann gespielt worden. (Tragedy of the rich man.)¹

---

¹ Another officer has still preserved some notices on these performances, without naming the performed pieces. His notices are found in a similar almanac entitled: *Alt vnd New Schreibcalender auff das Jahr* M. D. C. XXVI, *mit Fleifs gerechnet durch Simonem Partlicium von Spitzberg* etc. 8vo. Erffurdt, Martin Spangenburgk. (Old and new writing-almanac for the year 1626, purposely counted by Simon Partlicio von Spitzberg.) As his notices contain some additional information, we subjoin them here:

The following items refer to the year 1627:

Dresden. Febr. 2, 4, 8, 14, haben die Comoedianten gespielet. (The Comedians have acted.)

— — 15. Haben die Engeländer abermalſs agieret. (The English have acted again.)

In April 1627 the Court removed to Torgau on occasion of the wedding festivities to which we have already alluded, and the actors accompanied them.[1]

The * annexed to four of the above pieces denotes that they are to be found in the 'English Comedies and Tragedies'. Perhaps also the 'Comedy of the King of England' is identical with No. 4 in that collection, — perhaps it is the same piece which was played in Cassel in 1607, entitled, 'Two Kings of Britain at war'. (See p. lviii.) The 'Comedy of Amphytrion' was probably one based on Plautus. At a later period J. Dryden and L. Eckard treated the same subject. The Comedy of Orlando Furioso was probably Robert Greene's piece of that name. In the Tragedy of Hieronymo we have again the 'Spanish Tragedy', a subject which had also been handled by Ayrer.[2] The 'Tragedy of Doctor Faustus' is undoubtedly Christopher Marlowe's 'Tragicale Historie of Doctor Faustus'. The 'Comedy

---

Majus 29. Pfingstmontag. Zu Dreſsden Stillager. Haben die Englische Comedianten unter der Abendtmalzeit im Kirchsahl eine Comediam gespielet. (The English Comedians have represented a comedy at supper in the room near the chapel.)

Majus 31. Quatember. Zu Dreſsden Stillager. Hat der Rath alhier ein Vogelschieſsen gehalten. Auch haben die Englische Comedianten uffn steinern Sahl eine Comediam gespielet. (Quarters at Dresden. Shooting at a wooden bird. The English Comedians acted a comedy in the Marble-Saloon.)

Junius 1. Nicodemus. Zu Dreſsden Stillager. Haben die Comedianten abermahlſs agiret. (The Comedians acted again.)

Junius 2. Marcellus. ... Ist von den Englaendern ein Tragoedia gespielet worden. (A Tragedy acted by the Englishmen.)

Junius 4. Trinitatis. ... Haben die Comedianten agiret vnd Michael Molichs Sohn sambt ein Engelander getanzet. (The Comedians have acted, and Michael Molich's son and an Englishman have performed a dance.)

(June 5, 7, 8, 9, 11, 20, 21, 24, 25, 27, 28. The Englishmen acted again.)

Junius 29. ... Auch ist einer von den Englischen Comedianten heute frühe zu Dreſsden gestorben. (This morning one of the English Comedians died at Dresden.)

Julius 3. Spielten die Engländer wieder. (The Englishmen acted again.)

[1] The officer to whom we are indebted for the above catalogue of the pieces performed, has made the following notes of the performances in the Almanac of 1627.

5. Aprilis. Zu Torgau Stillager. Haben Ihre Churf. D.(urchlaucht) abermahls im Coburgischen zu Mittag taffel gehaltenn vndt hernacher den Comedianten zugehörtt. (In Torgau quarters. Their Electoral Highnesses have again dined in Coburg, and afterwards heard the comedians.)

6. Aprilis. Haben die Chur- vndt Fürstliche Personen abermahls den Comedianten zugehörtt. (The Electoral and Princely personages have again heard the comedians.)

8. 9. Aprilis. Spielten die Engländer wieder. (The English actors played again.)

13. Aprilis. Haben die Chur- vndt Fürstlichen Personen ein Bogenschieſsen gehalten vndt uffn Abendt der Musicalischen Comedien zugehörtt. (The Electoral and Princely personages have held a shooting match with the bow, and in the evening heard a musical comedy.) [Daphne, see Fürstenau.]

(April 24, 25, 28. The English actors played again.)

6. Majus. Haben die Comoedianten gespielet vndt darauff von Ihrer Churf. D. Ihre Abfertigung erlanget. (The comedians have played, and afterwards received their dismissal from their Electoral Highnesses.)

[2] The same play must have been very popular on the Dutch stage, as we know three editions of a Dutch version of it by Adrian van der Bergh: *Jeronimo Marschalck van Spanje, Treurspel.* 4to. 1621, 1638, and 1644.

of Josephus a Jew of Venice' is probably a piece, of which a MS., hitherto quite unknown, is in the Imperial Library at Vienna, and is entitled, 'A Comedy, called the wisely pronounced judgment of a female student, or the Jew of Venice', ('Comoedia genandt dass wohl gesprochen Urtheil eynes weiblichen Studenten, oder der Jud von Venedig'). It appears to be a mixture of Shakespeare's 'Merchant of Venice', and Marlowe's 'Jew of Malta'. The name of the Jew is Barrabas, as in Marlowe, but there are passages in the last act which coincide exactly with passages in Shakespeare's play, and the three lovers who woo Ancilla, the daughter of a counsellor, and her indecision, remind us of the story of the caskets.[1] It is also possible that this play is a version of Thomas Dekker's 'Jew of Venice', which appears to be irrecoverably lost. The following piece, the 'Tragedy of Barrabas, the Jew of Malta', is of course Marlowe's piece.[2] It is hardly necessary to observe that the pieces printed in Italics, are Shakespeare's Romeo and Juliet, Hamlet, King Lear, and perhaps Julius Cæsar.

It is worthy of remark that many of these plays maintained their ground for many years on the Dresden and other stages. In the years 1631 and 1632, 'Orlando Furioso', 'Julius Cæsar', and a 'Tragedy of Prince Serule and Hyppolita' (probably No. 4 in the collection of 'English Comedies and Tragedies') were performed again.[3] On the occasion of the marriage of Prince John George II. with Magdalene Sibylla of Brandenburg, an English Comedy was performed on the 5th of December 1638.[4] On the 11th of September 1646, we have again the 'Prodigal Son', and on the 12th, the 'Comedy of the proud youth, Eucasto', undoubtedly an echo of the English play 'Every Man', on the 15th of October, 'Romeo and Juliet', on the 17th of the same month, the 'Tragedy of the rich man and the poor Lazarus', unquestionably the same piece as that which stands last in our catalogue of 1626; on the 4th of November 1651, the 'Comedy of the Duke of Mantua, and the Duke of Verona'. On the 5th of December 1652, "the English Comedians acted a comedy of the Emperor Diocletian and Maximinus with the shoemaker." An English piece, entitled 'Dioclesian', had been played in the Rose Theatre as early as 1594. At a later period Beaumont and Fletcher wrote a play on the same subject, entitled 'The Prophetess' (licensed in May 1622, printed for the first time in 1647). On the 10th of December 1652, the same actors played a piece, 'Of the four royal brothers in England', and 'Somebody and Nobody'. The English Comedians are again mentioned in 1659. In March, they act the 'Farce of Pyramus and Thisbe', in June, 'King Lear and his two daughters', in November, a 'Comedy of the four resembling brothers, and the noble stranger', "as the Englishmen had translated them". On the 26th of February 1661 we have the

---

[1] I owe this information to Mr. Joseph Haupt of the Imperial Library, Vienna.

[2] An early Dutch version of Marlowe's piece is: *Joodt van Malta, ofte Wraeck door Moordt, Treur-Spel. Gerymt door Gysbert de Sille.* 4to. Tot Leyden, 1645.

[3] Mor. Fürstenau, *Zur Geschichte* etc. p. 102.

[4] See Ant. Weck, *Der ... Residentz- und Haupt-Vestung Drefsden Beschreibung und Vorstellung.* fol. Nürnberg 1680, p. 370.

'Tragi-comedy of the Moor of Venice', which is of course Shakespeare's Othello. The Comedies of 'Amphitrione' and 'The old Proculus' were again produced in 1663, as also in June 1664 'Orlando Furioso', and in February 1665 'Ahasuerus, Esther and Haman'. In the year 1671 we meet again in Dresden with two Englishmen, whom we have already met with above in 1650: Gideon Gellius [Giles], and John Bapt Waydt, of whom the former is here entitled Master of the exercises, the latter, Comedian. In the year 1672 the Electoral Family made some stay in Torgau, and the comedies of 'Christabella', and 'Chrysella' were again revived. In February of the same year, 'Peter Squenz, a comedy' was again performed in Dresden. In 1674, we meet with 'Josephus, the Jew of Venice', in 1676, 'King Lear of England', in 1678 'Christabella' again, also 'Amphitrion', 'Romeo and Juliet', the 'Old Proculus', and a piece which had not been mentioned before, the 'Comedy of the angry Catharine', a version of Shakespeare's 'Taming of the Shrew', to which we shall have occasion to refer at a later page.

The representation of these plays was by no means confined to the Dresden stage; on the contrary it is an ascertained fact that they became the property of all the companies throughout Germany. We know for instance the acting library of a company, which soon after 1650 addressed a petition to Duke Gustavus Adolphus of Mecklenburg Schwerin, who resided at Güstrow, that they might be allowed to wait on him 'with some actions in the English manner'. They had already performed several times in the town. Among the pieces which they had with them, we find 'Of the proud Haman, and the humble Esther', 'The quarrel between England and Scotland', 'The beheading of the King of England', probably the same piece we have already met with in Windsheim,[1] 1656, 'Diocletian', 'Julius Cæsar', the 'Martyr Dorothea', and others.[2] In this manner we find that these English dramatic stories had made the round of all Germany, and we are justified in asserting that they were in complete possession of the German stage of the seventeenth century. Besides these new versions with which we have become acquainted through the first part of the 'English Comedies and Tragedies', some others have also been preserved, two of which we present the reader in a complete form, and with an English translation annexed: an old German 'Hamlet', and a 'Romeo and Juliet'.

[1] Andreas Gryphius wrote a Tragedy: "*Ermordete Majestät oder Carolus Stuardus König von Großbritannien*", which must have been a different piece, as it was only composed in 1663.

[2] H. W. Bärensprung, *Versuch* etc. p. 26—27. All the members of the Company were Germans. At the head of it stood "Caspar Stiller mit seiner fraw, als meister, aus Hamburg" (C. S. with his wife, as manager, from Hamburg).

FRATRICIDE PUNISHED, OR PRINCE HAMLET OF DENMARK.
(See p. 237—304.)

There can be no doubt that there existed a far older German version of this piece than the one with which we are acquainted; and the latter is probably only a weak copy of the former, which will have stood in the same relation to the original form of the German piece, as the pieces of the 'English Comedies and Tragedies' to the form in which they were originally acted in Germany. About the year 1665, this piece was performed by the Veltheim company, but it is of a much older date than this, for we find it in the Dresden stage-library in 1626, and even then it was no new piece, as there is every reason to believe that it had been brought to Germany by the English players as early as 1603. The piece approaches most nearly to that form of Shakespeare's Hamlet which we find in the Quarto of 1603. As in the latter, so also here Polonius is called Corambus; and notwithstanding the very modernized form of the prologue, it bears so completely the stamp of the old English stage, that as Mr. Will. Bernhardy observes "we are tempted to assume that Hamlet must have appeared on the English stage in an earlier form than that of the Quarto of 1603, and that the German piece is a weak copy of the earlier form, little as the genius of the great poet appears in it, even in this later version.[1] But what is most particularly striking is the contrast between the prologue and the matter of the play itself. Almost all poetice motion has disappeared from the latter, which presents us with nothing more than a mere dry skeleton of the Shakespearian piece, while the prologue, in spite of all its coarseness, has many curious poetical touches and expressions, which curiously enough, remind us strongly of the modes of expression in Shakespeare and his contemporaries. It is notorious that the older English pieces often had prologues in the form of dialogue, and that the introductory words were not always spoken by one person alone, as in the old German Theatre. These prologues have often been lost because it was not considered worth while to have them printed; but often also, especially at a later period of the English stage, no prologue was written, because the practice was considered pedantic, and even Shakespeare had already spoken against it in his 'Romeo and Juliet'. The persons of the prologue were generally allegorical and mythological characters, but were sometimes also taken from everyday life, or from history. Thus in the 'Spanish Tragedy', Revenge and the Spirit of Andrea appear as prologue, but at the same time they are spectators and speaking characters throughout the whole of the piece. In Marston's 'Antonio and Malcida', a very remarkable piece, evidently written in imitation of Hamlet, the persons of the prologue are the characters in

---

[1] This opinion was first expressed by Mr. William Bernhardy in an essay well deserving perusal, and entitled: "*Shakespeare's Hamlet. Ein literar-historisch kritischer Versuch.*" We follow him in the argument given above for the establishment of this conjecture. Mr. Bernhardy's essay is to be found in *Hamburger literarisch-kritische Blätter* 1857, No. 49—103. At the conclusion, Mr. Bernhardy promises a thorough critical investigation of this interesting subject, which however he has not yet given us. It is to be hoped that he may still fulfil this promise.

the piece itself, and its subject is the distribution and description of the different parts. In that excellent old comedy, 'Wily beguiled', the persons of the prologue consist of an actor and a conjurer. In 'Locrine', Ate is the prologue, and in 'Pericles', the poet Gower. The prologue, moreover, of the old German Hamlet contains mystical and allegorical personages, and this circumstance as well as some turns of expression, which forcibly remind us of English poets, and some harsh un-German constructions appear to establish the foreign origin of the piece, and that it is a translation. Thus the expression "Queen of silence" (Königin der Stille) reminds us of a passage in 'Lust's Dominion', Act i:

> spotless night
> Empress of silence, and the queen of sleep.

Not less striking is the similarity of the address "Woman of ill fortune" (Unglücksfrau) to the lines in 'Macbeth' Act iii, sc. 5,

> And I the mistress of your charms,
> The close contriver of all harms.

and we cannot but remember that also Shakespeare in 'Macbeth' Act ii, sc. 5 speaks of "black Hecate's summons". Also the turn of expression in the prologue "in order that those who swim in the sea of murder", ("damit diejenigen, welche in der Mordsee schwimmen") and the words of Night, "I soar above" ("Ich fahre auf") may be compared with Henry vi Part I, Act iv, Sc. 7, "And in that sea of blood my boy did drench", and Macbeth, Act iii, Sc. 5, "I am for the air". Single passages in the German piece shew that an edition of the original must have been used which contained passages that are in the folio, but not in the first quarto, while other passages prove incontrovertibly, that precisely this quarto must have been the source employed by the translator. Thus, for instance, the Ghost says to Hamlet, "Mark me, Hamlet, for the time draws near when I must return to whence I came" and concludes his speech with the words "Thus was I robbed of kingdom, wife and life by this foul tyrant". The former is evidently taken from the words which the Ghost uses in our accepted text of Hamlet:

> My hour is almost come,
> When I to sulphurous and tormenting flames
> Must render up myself.

while the latter passage corresponds exactly to the order in which the Ghost mentions the same things in the original,

> Thus was I sleeping by a brother's hand
> Of Crowne, of Queene, of life, of dignitie
> At once deprived etc.

As the reader has the entire piece before him in this volume, it will not be necessary to call attention to the numerous passages, which, in spite of its dilution by unskilful hands, place its early origin beyond all doubt. In other places we can distinctly perceive the hand of the remodeller, who kept in view the circumstances of the theatre of his own time, and which have given the tone to many passages. His utter want of skill is suffi-

ciently proved by his introduction of the comic characters, the peasant Jens and Phantasmo, the fool, both of whom are altogether out of place in the piece. The manner in which the scenes taken from Shakespeare's tragedy have been vulgarized, the coarse humour which has been mixed up with the serious incidents, the box on the ears which the ghost gives the sentinel, and other absurdities, must of course be laid to the account of the revisor, just as in the case of the 'English Comedies and Tragedies', and not to that of the actors who first brought the piece to Germany. A remarkable reminiscence, which enables us to form a conclusion respecting the age of the piece, is Hamlet's relation of an incident connected with the players in Act ii, Sc. 7. There can be no doubt that this is the incident which, whether fact or fiction, is introduced in the tragedy entitled 'A Warning for fair women', written a little before 1590. In that piece as in this, the advantage of theatrical representations is intended to be proved. The passage is at the end of the piece:

> "A woman that had made away her husband,
> And sitting to behold a tragedy
> At Linne, a town in Norfolk,
> Acted by players travelling that way,
> Wherein a woman that had murdered hers,
> Was ever haunted with her husband's ghost,
> The passion written by a feeling pen,
> And acted by a good tragedian,
> She was so moved with the sight thereof,
> As she cried out, the play was made by her,
> And openly confessed her husband's murder."[1]

In Hamlet, Act ii, Sc. 2, Shakespeare alludes to a similar incident, perhaps the same.

> I have heard
> That guilty creatures, sitting at a play
> Have by the very cunning of the scene
> Been struck so to the soul, that presently
> They have proclaim'd their malefactions;
> For murder, though it have no tongue, will speak
> With most miraculous organ.

Heywood, in his 'Apology for actors', relates the same story, and adds that it had occurred "at Lin, in Norfolke" at the performance of the 'History of Fryer Francis' by the players of the Earl of Sussex. But then he relates a similar incident which is stated to have happened at the performance of the 'Four sons of Aymon' by English comedians at Amsterdam.[2]

"Another of the like wonder happened at Amsterdam in Holland. A company of our English comedians (well knowne) travelling those countryes, as they were before the burgers and other the chiefe inhabitants, acting the last part of the four Sons of Aymon, towards the last Act of the history,

---

[1] See J. P. Collier, *History* etc. Vol. ii, p. 438.
[2] See the Shakespeare Society's reprint, p. 58.

where penitent Rinaldo, like a common labourer, lived in disguise, vowing as his last pennance to labour and carry burdens to the structure of a goodly church there to be erected; whose diligence the labourers envying, since by reason of his stature and strength, hee did usually more work in a day than a dozen of the best (hee working for his conscience, they for their lucres) whereupon by reason his industry had so much disparaged their living, conspired among themselves to kill him, waiting some opportunity to finde him asleepe, which they might easily doe, since the sorest labourers are the soundest sleepers, and industry is the best preparative to rest. Having spy'd their opportunity, they drave a naile into his temples, of which wound immediately he dyed. As the actors handled this, the audience might on a sodaine understand an outcry, and loud shrike in a remote gallery, and pressing about the place, they might perceive a woman of great gravity strangely amazed, who with a distracted and troubled braine oft sighed out these words: "Oh my husband, my husband!" The play without further interruption proceeded: the woman was to her owne house conducted, without any apparant suspition; every one conjecturing as their fancies led them. In this agony she some few days languished, and on a time, as certaine of her well disposed neighbours came to comfort her, one amongst the rest being churchwarden: to him the sexton posts, to tell him of a strange thing happening to him in the ripping up of a grave: See here (quoth he) what I have found; and showes them a fair skull, with a great nayle pierst quite to the brain-pan: But we cannot conjecture to whom it could belong, nor how long it has laine in the earth the grave being confused, and the flesh consumed. At the report of this accident, the woman, out of the trouble of her afflicted conscience, discovered a former murder; for 12 yeares ago, by driving that nayle into that skull, being the head of her husband, she had treacherously slaine him. This being publickly confest, she was arraigned, condemned, adjudged and burned. But I draw my subject to greater length than I purposed: these therefore out of other infinites I have collected, both for their familiarnesse and latenesse."

It is not a little characteristic of the stage at that time, that the actors who first performed the German Hamlet did not rest satisfied with the mere allusion as they found it in Shakespeare, but related the incident itself. Whether the passage refers to the incident in Norfolk or to that in Amsterdam, it is a striking evidence that Hamlet was transplanted to the German stage at a very early period. The later revisor transferred the scene to Strasburg, as being nearer to his audience. It is probable that the company for which this new version was adopted, had come from Strasburg, where we have already seen English players in 1654. (See p. cii). We are inclined to believe that the first form of the version of the piece now before us was made about that time, but that the form in which it is here presented to the reader, and in which it has experienced many alterations and dilutions, is to be ascribed to a more modern hand.

TRAGEDY OF ROMEO AND JULIET.
(See p. 305—406).

We have no evidence to shew that this piece was ever performed in Germany earlier than 1626, and the version now before us is probably to be attributed to a somewhat earlier date. The employment of Alexandrines is a proof that it cannot have been made before the introduction of that species of verse by the Silesian poets. The places mentioned

at p. 375 of the present impression give no clue as to the place where the play was first produced, but dialect and orthography point to South Germany or Austria. Neither have we here the authentic text of the piece as it was played by the English Comedians, but a version calculated for the requirements of the stage at a later period, in which the English element was but very slightly represented in the companies, perhaps indeed was little more than a reminiscence. The reader will perceive at once that this piece did not proceed from any of the numerous sources on which the Shakespearian tragedy is based. On the contrary, it is Shakespeare's play, almost scene for scene; many passages indeed are literal translations. Though certainly against the intention of the editor, there are even instances in which really poetical passages have slipped in from the original unobserved, the poetry of which, however, can only be discerned after they have been divested of the jargon in which he has clothed them. But the reader will easily perceive how he has compensated himself for such mistakes, by the omission of all the finer motives of this magnificent tragedy, as also by the insertion of comic scenes which are utterly devoid of taste, and by their disgusting coarseness obliterate even the very small amount of tragic feeling of which this author is capable. But the treasure of poetic thought contained in this sublime fiction is so inexhaustible, that notwithstanding the mutilated form in which it is presented to us, we can still imagine that it must have excited immense interest in a German audience of the seventeenth century.[1]

The third piece of the English stage library of the Dresden company of actors that has come down to us, is at the same time the earliest impression of a German version of an entire Shakespearian piece, and is dated 1672. It is an imitation of the 'Taming of the Shrew,' under the title of "Art above all arts, the taming of a shrew &c."[2]. The German Public however had become acquainted with Shakespeare's comedy at a much earlier date. A piece called: "The surprising marriage of Petruvio with the wicked Catharine" was

---

[1] A Dutch piece must be mentioned here which most probably is in close connection with the German one: *I. Struys | Romeo | en | Ivliette. | Op de Reghel: | Naer een te hooghen vaert, en vlucht te seer verbolghen, | Plach dickmael in't ghemeen een haeste vàlte volghen. | Ghespeelt op de Amsterdamsche Camer, op Kermis, A° 1634. | t'Amsterdam, | Voor Dirck Cornelifz Houthaeck, Boeckvercooper op de | Nieuwe-zijds Kolck, in't Bourgoens Cruys. Anno 1634. | 4to. Black letter.*

[2] *Kunst über alle | Künste | Ein bös Weib gut zu machen. | Vormahls | Von einem Italiänischen | Cavalier practiciret: | Jetzo aber | Von einem Teutschen Edel-man glücklich nachgeahnet, | und | In einem sehr lustigen Possen- | vollem Freuden-Spiele | fürgestellet. | Samt | Angehencktem singenden | Possen-Spiele | Worinn | Die unnötige Eyfersucht ei- | nes Mannes artig betro- | gen wird. | Rapperschweyl | Bey Henning Lieblern 1672. | 12mo.* (Art above all arts, the Taming of the Shrew, formerly practised by an Italian Cavalier, but now happily imitated by a German Nobleman, and represented in a right merry Droll. Annexed is a Singing-Droll, in which the unnecessary jealousy of a husband is prettily deceived.) 238 pp., the last unpaged contains a poem: *Erklärung des Kupfer-Tittels.* Pages 231—237 are wrongly paged 331—337. The printed title is preceded by an engraved one: *Kunst über alle Kunst. Ein böf weib | guth Zu machen.* | Infra an engraving representing a Cavalier shutting the mouth of a snake-haired fury with a fox-tail. The '*Kunst über alle Künste*' ends on p. 217. At the foot of the same page

represented by students of the Gymnasium at Zittau in March 1658 and may have been brought to Germany by the English Comedians, long before that date. The piece has not come down to us,[1] but from the very title of it we may guess that it followed Shakespeare more closely than the version of 1672, in which the names of the characters are altered according to the own taste of the author, whereas in the older version the names of the principal, and perhaps of all the other, characters of Shakespeare's piece are preserved in their original form. The author of the 'Art above all Arts', in an address to the reader, alludes to frequent representations of the piece on the stage, before he undertook his own version of it:

"Kind reader. I can say of this comedy that it belongs to another, and yet is also mine. It belongs to another, because it has not only been often represented by comedians on the stage, but also because the plot, the old names and phrases shew him who has seen it and heard it before, that it is of Italian origin. I can call it mine, because I have

---

begins the Singing-Droll: *Singendes | Possenspiel | Die doppelt betrogene | Eyfersucht vor- | stellend.* (Dom Johannes, Dessen Frau, Mons. Pickelhering, Seine Liebste, Don Jean von Brabarey, Cavalier.)

This is the description of the copy belonging to the Imperial Library at Vienna, which most kindly was sent to me at Berlin at my request. — Another copy, formerly in the possession of Gottsched, is at the Grand-ducal Library at Weimar. It wants the lower part of the title-page with the place of printing and the date, which Gottsched, and Goedeke after him, fancied to be *Rappersdorf 1652*. No one had seen the Vienna copy. When Dr. Reinhold Koehler, Librarian to the Grand-ducal Library at Weimar, told me, that he intended to publish a reprint of the 'Kunst über alle Künste' from the Weimar copy, considered to be unique, I drew his attention to the Vienna copy, and from him I learn that they vary in many points. Dr. Koehler's reprint, with the corresponding scenes of Shakespeare's comedy and many notes, will be soon before the public. Judging from Dr. Koehler's former publications, we have reason to expect a most careful and valuable work, to which I beg to refer the reader who wishes for more particulars respecting the 'Kunst über alle Künste'.

[1] The earliest and indeed the only source to which it can be traced is Gottsched, *Nöthiger Verrath* etc. Vol. I, p. 210, where it is mentioned, under the date of 1658, in conjunction with three other pieces. "*Vier Schauspiele. 1. Androfilo oder göttliche Wunderliebe. — 2. Sylvia oder wunderthätige Liebe. — 3. Der klägliche Bezwang. — 4. Die wunderbare Heurath Petruvio mit der bösen Catharine, den 5. 6. 7. Martii auf dem Zittauischen Schauplatze vorgestellet.* Gott gIb DeIner CrIstenheIt FrIeDen hIer, Dort SeLIgkeIt. M. C. K. R. S. P." Gottsched it appears, took it for granted that the four pieces were printed and that Christian Keimann, at the time Rector of the Gymnasium at Zittau, is the author of them. He is mistaken in both conjectures. It is almost certain that 'The surprising marriage' has never been printed. After I had ascertained that none of the principal libraries of Germany is in possession of it, I addressed myself to Dr. A. Tobias, the librarian to the Municipal Library at Zittau, who not only informed me that no such piece is extant in the library, which moreover has received Keimann's and his son's collections of books, but at the same time kindly mentioned the circumstances which evidently have misled Gottsched in his conjecture. The four pieces have undoubtedly been represented at Zittau by the students of the College, and it was a custom on such occasions to print programs of the performances, containing the "argument" of the pieces, which by way of invitation were sent to the Municipal authorities. Such a program of the performances of the 5th, 6th and 7th March 1658 may have come under Gottsched's notice, and as Keimann, the author of it and the superintendent of the performances, had put his initials to it, Gottsched took him for the author of the plays themselves — a mistake which is the more pardonable, as Keimann was indeed a dramatic author, of whom several pieces are preserved. None of the four pieces however, ascribed to him by Gottsched, is his. A list of his works is to be found in H. J. Kämmel, *Christian Keimann. Ein Beitrag zur Geschichte des Zittauer Gymnasiums.* 4to. Zittau 1856.

composed it for its clever style, and have altered it as it pleased me out of my own head, and have added to it, just as the rapid fancies suggested to me, without much puzzling my head about it."[1]

We learn from this address that in or immediately before 1672 the piece was still given by the Comedians with the original names of the characters, and as we have the author's own confession, that he altered it "as it pleased him out of his own head", we may fairly assume that it was brought before the Public in its genuine Shakespearian shape. Even in its altered form, in which it is before us, it follows Shakespeare almost scene by scene, and also the dialogue may, in a great many instances, be retranslated into Shakespeare's text without many deviations from the language of the German imitator. The manner in which the latter has acquitted himself of his task, places him far above those of his predecessors with whom we have had to deal in the preceding pages, and though under his hands too, nearly all the more delicate charms of the Shakespearian muse have disappeared, it must be admitted that he possesses a certain amount of dramatic power. The following list of Dramatis Personae in, and extracts from the German piece will convey an idea of the spirit in which it has been composed and the abilities which are at the command of its author:

Personen dieses Freuden-Spiels.

Der geduldige Hiob in des frommen Socratis Hosen, Vorredner.
Herr Theobald von Grifflingen . . . . [*Baptista*.
Jungfer Catharina Hurleputz } dessen beyde Töchter . . . . [*Catharina*.
Jungfer Sabina Süpmäulchen } [*Bianca*.
Veit Schnitzer, Diener.
Sibilla Flöhpeltz, Cammermagd.
Herr Hartman Dollfeder, Erbsas zum Würbelwind, Jungfer Catharinen Freyer [*Petruchio*.
Ludolf Wurmbrand, Diener . . . . [*Grumio*.
Herr Sebastian von Unvermögen . . . . [*Gremio* } Edelleute und Mitbuhler
Herr Alfons von Nestlingen, ein zeitlang ein verkleideter Musicus . . . . [*Hortensio* } bey Jungfer Sabinen.

---

[1] "Gunstgeneigter Leser. Von diesem Freudenspiele kann ich sagen, dafs es eines andern und doch auch mein seye. Eines andern ist es, weil es nicht allein schon offt von Comoedianten auff dem Schauplatz für gestellet worden, sondern auch die Erfindung, alte Nahmen, und Redensarten, deme, so es zuvor angesehen und gehöret, zeigen, dafs es von Italiänischem Ursprunge: Mein kann ich es nennen, dieweil ich solchs, wegen seiner artigen Manier, gefasset, und aufs meinem Kopffe, wie es mir gefallen, geändert, und hingeschrieben, nach dem es die geschwinden Einfälle, ohne Kopff brechen gegeben." — Eschenburg, the celebrated translator of Shakespeare — (See *William Shakespeare's Schauspiele. Neue Ausgabe. Von Joh. Joach. Eschenburg.* Vol. iv. 8vo. Zürich 1775, p. 398), who pointed out the first the connection of the German piece with Shakespeare's comedy, is puzzled by the words "that it is of Italian origin" and doubts whether there may be an old Italian piece extant from which both authors may have copied. Such a position however cannot be maintained for a moment. The evident conclusion from the above passage is this: that the piece had been given to the author by the Comedians, and as the English origin of it was unknown to him, he concluded the Italian origin from the Italian names of the characters. Eschenburg himself has felt the weakness of his argument, for he points out phrases and expressions which can only have been translated from the English.

Herr Adrian von Liebenthal, der ältere . . . . [*Vincentio.*
Herr Hilarius von Liebenthal, der Jünger, Jungfer Sabinen Freyer, und der
    verkleidete Herr Johannes . . . . [*Lucentio.*
Felix Vielwind, Cammerdiener, und verstellete Jüngere von Liebenthal . . . [*Tranio.*
Fabian Affenschwantz, Diener . . . . [*Biondello.*
Frau Eulalia von Hohunk Wittib, Herr Alfons Vertraute . . . . [*Widow.*
Mag. Blasius Nasenweis, Rector paganus, der verstellete Aeltere von Liebenthal [*Magister.*
Meister Fritz Fingerhut vom Kratzenberg, kunstreicher Schneider und Kleider-
    macher . . . . [*Tailor.*
Matz Trümper, wohlbestellter Ofenschürer und Feuerverwahrer . . . . . . [*Curtis.*
Faulwamst, Immernaſs, Schlingenstrick. Drei Diener so nur ein Wort reden.

Act II.
(See Shakespeare's 'Taming of the Shrew'. Act II, sc. 1.)

Cath. Bekenne mir hier also bald und rund heraus, welchen du unter deinen Buhlern am liebsten habest, und spare mir ja die Wahrheit nicht: Oder ich will deines Fells nicht schonen.

Sab. Glaube mir, als wie der Wahrheit selbst, daſs unter allen Manns-Personen, so mir zu Gesichte gekommen, noch keiner in mein Hertz genommen (ist).

Cath. Auff eine Lüge gehöret eine Maulschelle (schlägt sie). Du lose Katze hast du dich nicht an Alfons vergaffet?

Sab. Ich gedencke meine Schwester du liebst ihn, wann dieses ist, sey nur zufrieden. Ich will dir ihn herzlich gern überlassen.

Cath. O ich sehe nun wohl, dein Ehrgeitz und leichter Sinn trachtet nach Reichthum . . .

Sab. Du thust mir groſs unrecht, wie in vielen Dingen. Wann es um seinet Willen ist, daſs du mir so feind bist, kanstu deinen Sinn wohl ändern. (Cath. bindet ihr die Hände.) Aber was fangst du doch für Kurtzweil mit mir an.

Cath. Ich sehe wohl, die Jungfer will gekurtzweilet seyn. Wart, (schlägt sie) wann dieses dann Kurtzweil ist, so ist alles andere Kurtzweil gewesen.

Theob. Wie nun, du rasendes Thier? Was ist hier zu thun? Was ist dies für ein boshaffter Muthwill; wer hat dir die Macht gegeben über dies arme Kind wütherisch zu herrschen? Ich glaube du wilst gar zu einem Henker an ihr werden, du boshaffter Schinder. Gehe hinein mein Kind, und bleibe von diesem Lindwurm. (Sab. weint.) . . . .

Cath. Wollet ihr mich noch aufhalten, mich an ihr zu rechen? Ich sehe nun, daſs ich gantz bey auch aufsgethan bin, diese untüchtige aber euer Augapfel ist, den man nicht anrühren darf. . . . Doch nein sie muſs einen Mann haben, der ihr auffwartet: . . . darmit ich ihr zu Ehren auff der Hochzeit barfuſs tantzen möge.

TRANSLATION.

Cath. Confess then to me openly and at once, which of your suitors dost thou love the best, and be not sparing with the truth, or I shall not spare thy hide.

Sab. Believe me as the truth itself, that of all the men I ever set eyes on, not one has yet been taken into my heart.

Cath. To a lie belongs a box on the ears. (Striking her.) Thou loose cat, hast thou not got foolish about Alfonso?

Sab. I think, sister, thou lovest him. If this be so, be quite at ease. I will most gladly leave him to thee.

Cath. Oh, I see now, thy ambition and trivial mind aim at riches . . .

Sab. Thou art very unjust to me in this as in many things. If it is on his account that thou art so angry with me, thou canst change thy mind. (Cath. binds her hands). But what jest is this that thou wilt play with me?

Cath. I see indeed, the maiden will be jested with. (Beating her). If this then is jest, then has all the rest been jest.

Theob. How now, thou mad animal! What is to be done now? What malicious insolence is this? Who has given thee the power to domineer so fiercely over this poor child? I believe thou really wishest to be her executioner, thou malicious hangman. Go in my child, and keep away from this dragon. (Sabine cries). . . . .

Cath. Will you prevent me from having my revenge on her? I see now that I am quite put aside by you, but this good-for-nothing is the apple of your eye, whom one must not touch ... but no, she must have a husband to wait on her ... that I may dance barefoot at her wedding in her honour.

Act II.
(See Shakespeare's 'Taming of the Shrew'. Act I, sc. 5.)

Hartm. Wann mir recht ist, so ist diese Herrn Alfons Behausung. Du, schlag einmal an.

Wurmb. Was schlag? Wann, was soll ich schlagen? Sehe ich doch niemand. Hat euch ja auch niemand leid gethan, den ich schlagen müſste.

Hartm. Schelm ich sage schlag an, und schlag nur stark an.

Wurmb. Dieses ist abermahl eine Ursach, pro more, vom Jauer, meinen Buckel auf schlägen zu beschweren. Soll ich euch schlagen? Da behüte mich St. Niclas für.

Hart. Narr ich sage dir, da schlag mir an, und stark genug, oder ich will dir deinen schelmischen Kopf zerschlagen.

Wurmb. Ich gedachte wohl, das Lied würde in solchem Thon aushalten. Mein Herr hat gewiſs einmal Lerm in seinem Kopffe, und haben jhm die Hornüssen das Gehirn zerwühlet. Ich soll jhn schlagen? der Teuffel schlagen jhn. Ja, wann es nicht über mich aufsgienge.

Hartm. Ich sehe wohl die Glocke will nicht läuten, ich ziehe denn den Schwengel. Ich wil dir die Ohren recken, und sehen ob du kanst fa, sol, la, singen. (Er ziehet jhn bey den Ohren hin und her.)

Wurmb. Mordio, Mordio, Lerm in allen Gassen. Helfio, Helfio! Mein Herr ist dem Verstand entlauffen, und wil sich bey mir aufhalten.

Hartm. Leichtfertiger Vogel, willtu nun singen?

TRANSLATION.

Hartm. If I am not mistaken, this is Signor Alfonso's house. Just knock once.

Wurmb. Knock what? When, what shall I knock? I do not see anybody. Nobody has done you any injury that I must knock him.

Hartm. Rogue, I tell you, knock, and knock hard.

Wurmb. This is another cause according to the custom of Jauer, to get a load of blows upon my back. Shall I knock you? St. Nicholas forbid!

Hartm. Fool I tell thee, knock there for me, and hard enough, or I will knock that roguish head of yours to pieces.

Wurmb. I thought that would be the end of the song. My master has certainly got a noise in his head, and the hornets have been rummaging in his brain. I beat him! The devil may give him a beating, if it do not pass over me.

Hartm. I see that the bell will not ring, until I pull the clapper. I will stretch your ears for you, and see whether you can sing fa, sol, la. (Pulls him backwards and forwards by the ears.)

Wurmb. Murder! murder! an alarm in all the streets! Help, help! My master has run away from his senses, and wants to lodge with me.

Hartm. You mad bird, will you sing now?

Act IV.
(See Shakespeare's 'Taming of the Shrew.' Act. IV, sc. 5.)

Hartm. Nun wollen wir den alten Herrn Theobald wacker überfallen. Wie scheinet der Mond so hell, wir haben gewiſs Vollmond.

Cath. Der Mond? Ei Schatz, es ist ja die Sonne.

Hartm. Was Sonne, soll ich wieder nicht recht sehen, Wurmbrand die Pferde aus dem Wirthshause. Wir müssen bei diesem Mondesschein wiedrum zurücke, welcher so gewiſs scheinet, als meines Vatters Sohn in meinen Hosen steckt.

Alf. Sagt doch wie er will. Jhr wiſst ja seinen Sinn.

Cath. Nun so bleibe doch bei diesem Mondesschein hier.

Hartm. Ich sage es noch einmal, es ist der Mond.

Cath. Ich sehe es nun selbst, daſs es nicht anders ist.

Hartm. Nun irrest du dich doch, es ist ja die gesegnete Sonne.

Cath. Gott lasse es dann die Sonne sein. Ich bin wohl zufrieden, lasset es ein Wachslicht, Stern, Fackel, oder was ihr wollet sein.

Alf. Der Bruder kann nun gemächlich die Waffen niederlegen das Feld ist schon erhalten.

TRANSLATION.

Hartm. Now will we come in upon the old Sir Theobald. How bright the moon shines! It must surely be full moon.

Cath. The moon! Why, love, it is the sun.

Hartm. What, the sun! So again I cannot see right! Wurmbrand, bring the horses out from the inn. We must turn round and go home again by this moonlight, which is shining now as surely as that my father's son is in my breeches.

Alf. Say as he wishes. You know his humour well enough.

Cath. Well then, remain here by this moonshine.

Hartm. I repeat it once more, it is the moon.

Cath. I now say myself, that it is nothing else.

Hartm. Now you are wrong though; it is the blessed sun.

Cath. God let it be the sun then; I am content, let it be a waxlight, star, torch, or what you will.

Alf. My brother may now quietly lay down his arms. The field is already won.

Many of the phrases and turns of expression bear on the face of them evident traces of having been translated from the English; and these passages are so numerous, and for the most part are such a literal translation of Shakespeare's text, that it may be safely asserted, that a German version of Shakespeare's 'Taming of the Shrew' in its original form had been placed in the author's hands.[1] The deviations from the original in the piece before us are, as we have seen, his own work, and not that of the players. The piece offers many points of connection with others from the library of the English Comedians.

---

[1] Simrock's conjecture, that the 'Surprising marriage of Petruvio' etc. was the original from which the author altered his piece, is plausible enough. See *Quellen des Shakespeare* etc. Vol. iii, p. 241.

Thus, for instance, the "Sword dance" ("Schwerd Tantz") is mentioned (p. 38) which is also introduced at the conclusion of 'Julius and Hippolyta.' At p. 126 we find the same play on the words "rapier" and "warm beer" ("Rappier" and "Warmbier") as in the German 'Hamlet' (p. 299). Also English expressions, such as "Ruffian" at p. 80 have been retained. Several passages seem to point to a South-German origin: p. 83, "But as my affair has so far gone on well, I must go to Frankfort" ("Aber weil nun meine Sache so weit richtig, muss ich nach Franckfort"). Hartman-Petruchio is a native of Worms. But then Hanover is also mentioned (p. 57): "It is also fair-time at Hanover" ("zu Hannover ist es auch Markt"). Scraps of French and Latin are of frequent recurrence. We have seen above from the passage at the conclusion, that the piece has been often acted, and there cannot exist a doubt that the 'Comedy of the angry Catharine' which was performed in Dresden in 1672, is identical with the piece before us.

At a later period, Christian Weise also chose the same subject for his 'Comedy of the angry Catharine' ("Die böse Catharina"), which was performed in Zittau in 1705.[1] Everything in this piece is so flat and common-place, that it is hardly possible to recognize a trace of Shakespeare in it. Incidents which are not found in Shakespeare's comedy have been added, and the dialogue has no connection with Shakespeare's text. We should have been inclined to imagine that Weise was entirely unacquainted with Shakespeare's play, if the names of his characters, Baptista, Cathárine, and Bianca, had not corresponded with those in the 'Taming of the Shrew.' He could not have taken them from Straparola's tale in the 'Piacevoli Notti,' as the names in it are different. It may be taken for granted therefore that Weise had seen the piece acted somewhere in Germany, and perhaps at his native town Zittau, in its first form, and then wrote his comedy from it, which is of far inferior merit to the 'Art above all arts.' The late date at which it was composed renders it unnecessary for us to consider Weise's piece more at length.

The Comedy of the clowns in Shakespeare's 'Midsummer Night's Dream' must have come to Germany before 1636, as the 'Absurda Comica, or Mr. Peter Squenz'[2] of Andreas

---

[1] Two Ms. copies of it are at the Municipal Library at Zittau, one of which was kindly sent me by Dr. A. Tobias. The piece has never been printed.

[2] *Absurda Comica. Oder Herr Peter Squentz, Schimpff Spiel.* 8vo. s. l. e. a. (circa 1660). Two editions probably printed in the same year. Reprinted in the collective edition of Gryphius's works, 8vo. Breslau 1698, in Tieck's *Deutsches Theater,* Vol. ii, and in G. Bredow's edition 8vo. Breslau 1823. — There has been a good deal of dispute about the first invention of the story on which the Interlude of the Clowns in the 'Midsummer Nights Dream' is founded. Henry Schmid (*Nekrolog der deutschen Dichter,* Vol. i. 8vo. Berlin 1785, p. 122) maintains that it is of French origin, but he has not brought forward the proof which he promised. Bredow (in the work mentioned above, p. 103), Wachler (*Vorlesungen über Deutsche Literatur,* 8vo. Frankfurt 1818, Vol. ii, p. 60) and H. L. Voss (*Shakespeare's Dramatische Werke,* Vol. i, p. 505) contend that the older play from which Gryphius copied was composed in imitation of a German farce. The extracts given above will clearly shew that Gryphius's piece is derived directly from Shakespeare. According to Bredow, Peter Squenz was from an early period a current designation of a clown. — A parody of Gryphius's piece is Christian Weise's *Neue Parodie eines Neuen Peter Squenzes von lauter Absurdis comicis,* in *Zittauisches Theatrum,* 8vo. Zittau 1683.

Gryphius' (born 1616, the year of Shakespeare's death, died 1664, a hundred years after Shakespeare's birth) is an imitation of it, which the author confessed to have taken from a version by Daniel Schwenter, who died in 1636. His piece, which appears to be lost, must have been very popular, as may be concluded from Gryphius's 'Address to the reader' which is as follows:

"Kind and honoured reader. Mr. Peter Squenz, now no longer unknown in Germany, and in his own opinion greatly celebrated, is here presented to you. Although his ideas may not all have quite so much point as he vainly imagines to himself, they have nevertheless till now been accepted and laughed at in different theatres, not without the special favour and amusement of the spectators. For which reason then, persons have been found here and there, who have had neither shame nor scruple to give themselves out for his father. ... But that he may no longer have to thank strangers for his origin, know that Daniel Schwenter, who has deserved well of all Germany, and is well practised in all sorts of languages and mathematical sciences, first brought him upon the stage in Altdorf, from which place he wandered further and further, till at last he met my dearest friend, who equipped him better, added to him some new characters, and had him represented together with one of his tragedies, to the eyes and judgment of all. But as he was afterwards quite forgotten by him, more important affairs engrossing his attention, I have been so bold as to demand him from the library of my said friend, to have him printed, and sent to you, my gentle and most honoured reader."

Tieck's conjecture that Schwenter wrote his Peter Squenz after the interlude of "Bottom the Weaver," is altogether false, as Bottom the Weaver was not printed till 1660, and certainly not played much before that time. Nothing can be more probable than that Shakespeare's piece was brought to Germany by the English Comedians. Such a farce must have been especially suitable for their object. That the whole of the 'Midsummer Night's Dream' belonged to the acting stock of the Comedians, is very unlikely. On the contrary, they probably only took from it the comedy of the clowns, as may also have been done occasionally in England. That Gryphius's piece is derived directly from Shakespeare must be evident to everybody at the first glance. It is almost the same arrangement, scene for scene, and hardly one of Shakespeare's jokes has been omitted. The few following passages may serve as a specimen:

Act I.

Pickelhäring. ... Aber saget Herr Peter Squenz. Hat der Löwe auch viel zu reden?
Peter Squenz. Nein, der Löwe muſs nur brüllen.
Pickelhäring. Ey so wil ich der Löwe seyn, denn ich lerne nicht gerne viel auswendig.
Peter Squenz. Ey nein! Mons. Pickelhäring muſs ein Hauptperson agiren.

. . . .

Kricks. Ja mich dünket aber, es solte zu schrecklich lauten, wenn ein grimmiger Löwe hereingesprungen käme, und gar kein Wort sagte, das Frauenzimmer würde sich zu heftig entsetzen.

Klotz George. Ich halte es auch dafür. Sonderlich wäre rathsam wegen schwangerer Weiber, daſs ihr nur bald anfänglich sagtet, ihr wäret kein rechter Löwe, sondern nur Meister Klipperl, der Schreiner. . . . .

Kricks. Kümmert euch nicht darum lieber Schwager, Herr Peter Squentz ist ein gescheidener Mann, er wird dem Löwen wol zu reden machen.

Klipperl. Kümmert euch nicht, kümmert euch nicht, ich wil so lieblich brüllen, daſs der König und die Königin sagen sollen, mein liebes Löwichen brülle noch einmal.

Peter Squenz. Lasset euch unterdessen die Nägel fein lang wachsen, und den Bart nicht abscheren, so sehet ihr einem Löwen desto ähnlicher. .... Der Kirchen-Lehrer Ovidius schreibet, daſs der Monden geschienen habe, nun wissen wir nicht ob der Monde auch scheinen werde, wenn wir das Spiel tragiren werden.

Kricks. Dem ist leicht zu helfen, wir müssen im Calender sehen, ob der Mond denselben Tag scheinen wird.

Klotz George. Ja, wenn wir nur einen hätten.

Meister Lollinger. Hier habe ich einen, den habe ich von meines Groſs-Vatern Muhme ererbet &c. . . . .

Kricks. Hört, was mir eingefallen ist, ich wil mir einen Pusch um den Leib binden, und ein Licht in einer Laterne tragen, und den Monden tragiren, was düncket euch zu der Sachen?
. . . .

Peter Squenz. ... Wie werden wir es mit der Wand machen? ... Piramus und Thisbe müssen mit einander durch das Loch in der Wand reden.

Klipperl. Mich düncket, es wäre am besten, man beschmierte einen um und um mit Leimwellern, und steckte ihn auf die Bühne, er müste sagen daſs er die Wand wäre, wenn nun Piramus reden soll, müste er ihme zum Maule, das ist zum Loch, hineinreden. Wenn nun Thisbe was sagen wolte, müste er das Maul nach der Thisbe kehren.

TRANSLATION.

Clown. ... But tell us Master Peter Squenz, has the lion much to speak?

Peter Squenz. No, he has only to roar.

Pickelhäring. Well, then let me be the lion; for I don't like having to learn much by heart.

Peter Squenz. Oh no, M. Pickelhäring must act a principal part.
. . . .

Kricks. Yes, but I rather think it would sound too awful for a furious lion to come in bounding upon the stage, without saying anything; the ladies would be too much frightened.

Klotz George. I think so too. On account of the pregnant women particularly, it would be advisable, to say at the beginning that you are no lion at all, but only Master Klipperl, the joiner.
. . . .

Kricks. Don't be afraid of that my dear brother in law, Master Peter Squenz is a clever man, he is sure to make the lion speak.

Klipperl. Don't be afraid of that; I will roar so charmingly that the King and Queen shall say: My sweet lion, pray roar again.

Peter Squenz. Let your nails meanwhile grow nice and long, and do not have your beard shaved, and you will resemble the lion all the more. ... Ovidius, the Ecclesiastic, says, the moon did shine, but we don't know whether the moon will shine when we shall act the play.

Kricks. That is easily managed, we must refer to the Calendar, and see if the moon will shine on that day.

Klotz George. Yes, if we only had got one.

Master Lollinger. Here I have one; it is a legacy from my grandfather's aunt.

. . . .

Kricks. Listen to what has occurred to me! I will tie a plush round my body and carry a light in a lantern, and thus represent the moon; what do you think of that?

. . . .

Peter Squenz. How shall we do for a wall? ... Pyramus and Thisbe must talk together through the chink in the wall.

Klipperl. I think it would be best to paint one of you with lime-water and to put him on the stage. He would have to say, he was the wall; and when Pyramus is to speak into his mouth, he must speak into the chink, and if Thisbe should want to say anything he would have to turn his mouth to Thisbe.

Compare with the above scene, Shakespeare's Midsummernight's Dream, Act I, sc. 2, and Act III, sc. 1.

Towards the end of the century, Michael Kongehl, a German Poet, (born 1646, died 1710) directed his attention to Shakespearian subjects. We have from his pen the 'Phœnicia awakened from death'[1] and 'The innocence of the innocently accused Innocentia.'[2] The former handles the plot of 'Much Ado about nothing', the latter, that of 'Cymbeline'. Kongehl has probably not known Shakespeare, and yet there are many passages differing from the tales, from which we should feel inclined to conclude that he did not derive his subject directly from Bandello or Boccaccio, but that there were some dramatic intermediate links from which he copied. Perhaps he may have seen similar pieces acted by the companies of actors.[3] His 'Phœnicia' agrees with Ayrer's piece as far as to the courtship of Tymbor, but the characteristic comic scenes as also the characters of Venus and Cupid are omitted. In the place of Venus we have here Tisiphone "a Fury from Hell" (see the old German 'Hamlet'), who makes Gerando her tool for the destruction of Phœnicia. In other respects the progress of the two pieces is very nearly the same, only that Kongehl is nearer than Ayrer to Bandello. Similarly in Kongehl's 'Innocentia' there is nearly everything which we find in Boccaccio's tale, on which Shakespeare's 'Cymbeline' is based, and yet there are deviations also here which, like the whole management of the piece, would lead us to suppose he had some dramatic model.

We may here remark that the Imperial Library at Vienna contains a number of MS. dramas of the seventeenth century, several of which are new versions of English pieces, which we must also reckon as having belonged to the acting library of the English players. To one of these MSS. we have already had occasion to refer (p. cxvii). Another without a

---

[1] *Die vom Tode erweckte Phönicia. Eine anmuthige Sicilianische Geschicht in einem Mischspiel (Tragico Comoedia) auf die Schaubühne gebracht.* 8vo. Königsberg s. a.

[2] *Der unschuldig beschuldigten Innocentien Unschuld. Eine nachdenkliche Genuesische Geschicht in einem Mischspiel (Tragico Comoedia) auf die Schaubühne geführt.* 8vo. Ibid. s. a. — Gottsched, *Nöthiger Vorrath*, Vol. i, p. 243—244, and after him K. Goedeke, *Grundrifs* Vol. ii, p. 519, mention the year 1680 as the date of the impression of both pieces, which however cannot have been printed before 1682 as Kongehl calls himself on the title-pages "Churfürstl. Brandenb. Secretarius", a dignity which he acquired only in 1682.

[3] The old German play of 'The Merchant of Padua' (see p. lvii) may have been known to Kongehl.

title, (MS. Suppl. 1136) treats the subject which forms the second part of Shakespeare's Winter's Tale. Dinas, the son of Damon, the shepherd, plays here the part of Autolycus. Then we have a 'Merchant of London,' undoubtedly John Ford's 'London Merchant,' and the 'Honest Mistress', which is of course Thomas Dekker's 'Honest Whore', and was first printed in 1664. In addition to these there is a copy of the date of 1755, of a probably much older piece, 'Phaeton,' perhaps a late imitation of Dekker's lost drama of this name. I have not seen these manuscripts,[1] as I did not hear of them till the present work was nearly through the press.

A Fragment of some English verses, falsely described as part of a Moral Play, which first came to light in Germany a few years ago, and consists of a single leaf in folio, printed, as it appears, from a block, has also been brought into connection with the English Comedians.[2] There is no other argument for this assumption than the circumstance that this fragment appears to have been printed on the Continent. We quite agree with the following remarks of Mr. Henry Bradshaw[3]: "The fragment cannot be considered part of a moral play, or any such production. If any one will glance at the various lists of John Lydgate's works, he will see enough to show him that this is a set of stanzas on the seven theological virtues, written most probably for scrolls to be put above or beneath figures representing these virtues on the wall of a room, or in some such position as many of Lydgate's verses are known to have been". The Fragment also belongs to a period, (the reign of Henry VIII or Mary) when there were no strolling companies of English actors on the Continent of which we have any knowledge.

In conclusion, we have to make a few observations as to how these English players performed. Various surmises have been made concerning the language in which they delivered themselves before the German public, and till very recently writers of note have considered it doubtful whether the English language was used in those performances on the German stage. It will be remembered that even the nationality of the English Comedians has been considered till lately an open question; but we trust that the facts alleged in the preceding pages have definitely set at rest all misgivings on this point, and if the contemporary evidence we have brought to light should have still left any doubt respecting the language employed, a document which we are enabled to adduce will conclusively settle that point also. We find the following entry in Röchell's Chronicle of the city of Münster (edited by Joh. Janssen, Münster 1852):

"Den 26. Novembris (1599) sindt alhir angekommen elven Engellender, so alle jungi und rasche Gesellen waren, ausgenommen einer, so tzemlichen althers war, der alle dinge regerede. Dieselben

On the 26th of November 1599 there arrived here eleven Englishmen, all young and lively fellows, with the exception of one, a rather elderly man, who had everything under his management. They

---

[1] I am indebted for a descriptive list of them to Mr. Joseph Haupt of the Imperial Library. Vienna.
[2] See *Athenæum*, 1856, Sept. 6, No. 1506. Dr. W. Bell, *Shakespeare's Puck* etc. Vol. ii, p. 268.
[3] See *Le Bibliophile illustré*. 1. Decemb. 1863, p. 141.

SHAKESPEARE IN GERMANY.

agerden vif Tage uf den rädthuse achter-einandern vif verscheiden comedien in ihrer engelscher Sprache. Sie hetten bi sich vielle verschieden instrumente, dar sie uf speleten, als luten, zitteren, fiolen, pipen und dergelichen; sie dantzeden vielle neuwe und frömmede dentze (so hier zu lande nicht geprucchlich) in anfang und Ende der comedien. Sie hetten bei sich einen schalkes naren, so in duescher sprache vielle bötze und geckerie machede under den ageren, wann sie einen neuen actum wollten anfangen und sich umbkledden, darmidt ehr das volck lachent machede. Sie waren von den rade vergeliedet nich lenger als ses taghe. Do die umb waren, mosten sie wedder wichen. Sie kregen in den vif taghen von den, so es hören und sehen wolten, vielle geldes; dan ein jeder moste ihnen geben zu jeder reise einen schillinck."

acted on five successive days five different comedies in their own English tongue. They carried with them various musical intruments, such as lutes, cithern, fiddles, fifes, and such like; they danced many new and foreign dances (not usual in this country) at the beginning and at the end of their comedies. They were accompanied by a clown, who, when a new act had to commence and when they had to change their costume, made many antics and pranks in German during the performance, by which he amused the audience. They were licensed by the Town-Council for six days only, after which time they had to depart. During those five days they took a great deal of money from those who wished to hear and see them, for every person had to give a [Bremen?] shilling to each of them at their departure.

This may have been the same company which had performed in the English language at Hildesheim in 1599 (see p. lxi.). It is probable that all these English players soon acquired a familiarity with the German language, or that they associated themselves with Germans and then merely undertook the managing part of the performances. As early as 1600, Landgrave Maurice of Hesse, in an agreement with his English players, stipulated that at his demand they should arrange such comedies, tragedies and histories as he or they might wish to be acted on the stage.[1] Thus we also find at a much later period, in 1659, that the English Comedians at the Dresden Court had to provide German translations of the plays which they intended to act (see p. cxviii). That those who settled in Germany acquired a perfect mastery of the German language, may be concluded from the facsimiles of the autographs of Thomas Sackville and John Breadstreet, to be found in the present work. The above extract shows moreover that the German language was not altogether excluded from performances enacted in English. It is most likely that the part of the clown was usually given by a German, who frequently availed himself of his privilege to interpret to the German audience the foreign idiom of his fellow-players. We learn further from the passage in Röchell's chronicle that the performances were opened and concluded by music and dancing. The intervals between the acts were not always filled up by the jests of the clown, but more frequently by music, as we are told by Michael Prætorius,[2] one of the principal writers on music at that time:

.... "Und gleich wie in comedien jedem Actu eine feine liebliche Musica Instrumentalis, mit cornetten, Violen oder andern dergleichen Instrumenten umbwechselnde, bisweilen auch mit Vocal-

.... So it is also done in comedies, where a sweet and lovely Musica instrumentalis is performed between the acts, with cornets, fiddles, and other similar instruments, varying sometimes with

---

[1] See Rommel, *Geschichte von Hessen*, Vol. VI, pag. 401.
[2] Michael Praetorius, *Syntagma Musicum*. 4to. Wittenbergae 1615, pars III, p. 110.

Stimmen angeordnet und von den Italis *Intermedio* genennet wird; Damit unterdessen die personatae personae sich anders vmbkleiden und zu folgendem Actu praepariren, auch etwas respiriren und sich erholen können" etc.	vocal music, called *Intermedio* by the Italians, in order that the personatae personae might be enabled to change their costume, to prepare themselves for the next acts and to recreate themselves.

The variety and brilliancy of the theatrical costume of the English Comedians has been noticed by another well-known writer of the period, John Sommer, commonly called Johannes Olorinus Variscus, who in his work "Geldtklage"[1] thus reflects on the luxury of his contemporaries:

"Da müssen die Kragen mit Perlen besetzet werden, vnnd wird ein solcher Pracht gesehen, dass sie einher gehen, wie die Englischen Comödienspieler in Theatro."	Their collars must be set with pearls, and such a display of finery is indulged in, that they strut along like the English Comedians in the theatre.

These were the actors, who, as the earliest representatives of the English stage abroad, initiated the Germans into dramatic art and, when Shakespeare was still living, transferred his works on German ground; but nearly a century elapsed after the English Comedians had disappeared, until Shakespeare's name appeared in Germany. The Gallomania which infected the nation, exhausted by the thirty years' war, and corrupted its morals, gradually destroyed the effect of English influence and interrupted for a long time that development of free dramatic art, so auspiciously begun under an early impulse, received from the representatives of the old English stage. — It was only in an indirect manner and most probably without any acquaintance with Shakespeare himself, that Andreas Gryphius, the only German dramatist of note in the seventeenth century, became indebted to English models for the vast superiority which he attained over his contemporaries. — Shakespeare's name occurs for the first time in Germany in Morhoff's "Unterricht von der deutschen Sprache und Poesie", 1682, but the author at the same time confesses himself perfectly unacquainted with his works. We next meet with Shakespeare's name in Barthold Feind's "Gedanken von der Opera" preceding a collection of his poems, 1708; but all that he has to say of Shakespeare is, that according to "M. le chevalier Temple" some persons, on hearing a reading of the tragedies of "the famous English tragedian Shakespeare", could not help sobbing loudly and shedding floods of tears. As late as 1740 the name of Shakespeare could appear in the works of the learned Bodmer in the guise of "Saspar" — the best proof that he knew Shakespeare only from hearsay. The first who was favoured with the gift of appreciating Shakespeare to a certain extent was a Baron von Borck, Prussian ambassador in London, who in 1741, translated 'Julius Cæsar' into German Alexandrines, a very creditable performance for that time, which however was tabooed by Gottsched and his school. But what must have been the mortification of the latter, when he saw his disciple John Elias Schlegel, the dramatist, so much appreciating Shake-

---

[1] Joh. Olorinus Variscus, *Ethnographia mundi, pars IV, Geldtklage.* 8vo. Magdeburgk (1614) p. 472.

speare as to admit his superiority over Gryphius; and this he really did in a periodical founded by Gottsched himself, the blind worshipper of French taste. A few other faint voices made themselves heard in praise of Shakespeare; the boldest of these belongs to a writer in a periodical "Der Englische Zuschauer" 1742, who had the courage to confess that he would much rather read any play of Shakespeare, however "irregular", than any of the most "regular" productions of the leading school. A few persons only, however, could boast of so intimate an acquaintance with Shakespeare, and for a series of years the latter continued to remain almost unknown in Germany. In Zedler's large Cyclopædia, 1743, Shakespeare is mentioned as having achieved great skill in poetry, "although he was no great scholar", and as having had "some subtle controversies with Ben Jonson, to the advantage of neither of them"; and even in 1751 the learnd Jöcher, in his "Gelehrten-Lexicon" copied this luminous dictum with the only addition: "He had a humourous turn of mind, but sometimes could be also very grave and excelled in Tragedies."

It was reserved for Lessing, the great regenerator of the German drama, to impress his countrymen with the genius of Shakespeare and with the conviction that a conscientious study of his works was the only means of rescuing the drama from total decline. The enthusiasm with which the Germans responded to this call of their greatest critic, and the results since obtained by them in the field of Shakespearean literature, are sufficiently well known; and it cannot be denied that no other nation has ever made a foreign poet so completely its own, as the Germans have done in the case of Shakespeare.

ADDENDA.

Pag. lix. The Company of English Comedians whom we meet at Frankfort in 1597 appears to have visited Stuttgart in the same year. Pfaff, *Geschichte der Stadt Stuttgart*, I, p. 116 relates: "A regular company of actors came to Stuttgart for the first time in May 1597; they were Englishmen, who performed during seven days before the court, and in recompense received from Duke Frederick I 300 florins, besides having their expenses defrayed." Duke Frederick I, it will be remembered, had visited England in 1592.

Pag. xcvii. According to the *Beschreibung des Stadt- und Direktionsbezirkes Stuttgart, herausgeg. von dem K. Statist. Topogr. Bureau.* 8vo. 1856, p. 417 there was a company of six English Comedians at the Court of Stuttgart in 1625, who held a permanent appointment. One of them was John Price who is spoken of as early as 1609, and who received a salary of 270 florins, besides his expenses at court, clothing, and other emoluments. Other names given are John and David Morell, and John Dixon. — We have met with one John Price, a celebrated musician, at the Dresden court. See p. xcvii, note. The company to which he belonged in 1609 must have been the one which performed at Dresden in the same year, and which in June 1610 performed at the festivities mentioned at p. lxxxiii. A company of Englishmen "who had also played before at Stuttgart" is expressly mentioned in the quotation from an unpublished MS. given at p. lxxxiii.

Pag. cvii. Another acknowledgement of the superiority of the English Comedians by a contemporary author will be found in Daniel von Wensin's *Oratio contra Britanniam*, delivered at Tübingen in 1613: "Nec diu est cum plerique artifices in Anglia peregrini et exteri et aurifabri Londini pene omnes fuerunt Germani: Anglis interea gulae voluptatibus .... et rebus nihili, atque adeo histrionae jugiter operam dantibus; *in qua sic profecerunt, ut jam apud nos Angli histriones omnium maxime delectant etc.* — (Nor is it long since that the majority of artisans in England were aliens and foreigners, and the goldsmiths in London were nearly all Germans. Meanwhile the English have given their constant attention to culinary pleasures and to trifles, but also constantly to the histrionic art, in which they have attained to such perfection that the English players delight us the most of all etc.) See Fr. Achillis Ducis Würtemberg. *Consultatio de principatu inter provincias Europae habita Tubingae in illustri collegio.* 4to. Tubing. 1613.

For these addenda I am indebted to Mr. W. B. Rye of the British Museum, who is in the possession of valuable materials respecting Foreign travellers in England under Queen Elizabeth and the subsequent reign.

PART II:

TEXTS.

COMEDY OF THE BEAUTIFUL SIDEA

BY JACOB AYRER OF NUREMBERG.

(CIRCA 1595.)

In Jacob Ayrer's *Opus theatricum*, Nuremberg 1618, in-fol., the Beautiful Sidea occupies folio 433 recto, col. 2, to folio 442. It is entitled:

Comedia
Von der schönen
Sidea, wie es jhr biß zu jrer
Verheüratung ergangen, Mit
16. Perſonen, Vnd hat
5. Actus.

(COMEDY OF THE BEAUTIFUL SIDEA, AND WHAT BEFEL HER TILL THE TIME THAT SHE GOT MARRIED. WITH 16 PERSONS AND IN 5 ACTS.)

The play has been reprinted in: *Deutsches Theater*. Herausgegeben von Ludewig Tieck. Erster Band. Berlin 1817, in-8vo, where it occupies pages 323 to 365.

A considerable want of care is perceptible in Tieck's edition which, in many places, deviates from the original impression. Nearly all the deviations are printer's blunders, no editorial alterations. Grammar and Orthography have been equally disregarded, syllables and words and indeed in one instance a whole line, have been omitted.

In the present impression of the German text the original has been strictly followed, even in its irregularities and punctuation.

COMEDIA
VON DER SCHÖNEN SIDEA.

Folgen die Personen in difs Spil. [1]

LUDOLFF der Fürst in Littau	1
SIDEA sein Tochter	2
LEUDEGAST der Fürst in der Wiltau	3
FRANCISCUS } seine zwen Rähte	4
ELEMAUS }	5
ENGELBRECHT defz Fürsten Sohn	6
FAMULUS sein Jung	7
JULIA defz Fürsten in der Wiltē fremde Jungkfrau	8
JAHN MOLITOR der Müller	9
ROLLUS der Bauer	10
DIETERICH der Schuster	11
FINELIA sein Weib	12
AGNES defz Schusters Tochter	13
ELA defz Baurn Tochter	14
RUPRECHT der Postbott	15
RUNCIFALL der Teuffel	16

ACTUS PRIMUS. [3]

RUPRECHT DER POSTPOTT *geht ein, tregt ein Brieff in einer kluppen vnd S.* [4]

Schweigt still vnd hört mir ein weng zu
Ein absag Brieff ich bringen thu
Von Leudegast dem grofsmechtigen Fürsten
Der wil Ludolffen den gedürsten
Vberziehen mit grosem Heer
Sehen das er sein hochmuth wehr
Vnd will auch nicht ehr lassen ab
Bifs er jhn gar vertrieben hab
Weil jhm so übel ist mit fridt
Helt kein Vertrag vnd Bündnufs nit
Darumb will ich euch allen rathen
Wo jhr nicht kommen wolt zu schaden
So seh ein jeder zu dem sein
Sie zihen schon vom Berg herein

COMEDY
OF THE BEAUTIFUL SIDEA.

Persons represented:

LUDOLFF, Prince of Lithuania.
SIDEA, his daughter.
LEUDEGAST, Prince of the Wiltau.
FRANCISCUS, } his two counsellors.
ELEMAUS, }
ENGELBRECHT, the Prince's son.
FAMULUS, his boy.
JULIA, the Prince in the Wiltau's foreign lady. [2]
JOHN MOLITOR, the miller.
ROLLUS, the peasant.
DIETRICH, the shoemaker.
FINELIA, his wife.
AGNES, the shoemaker's daughter.
ELA, the peasant's daughter.
RUPRECHT, the postman.
RUNCIFALL, the devil.

ACT I.

Enter RUPRECHT, THE POSTMAN, *bringing a letter in a clip.*

Be silent all and list to me:
I bear high words of enmity
From Leudegast, the mighty king,
Who means an armed host to bring.
Attack Ludolff, that man of greed,
See how pride stands him in his need.
Nor leave him till the recreant yield,
And vanquished fly the battle field.
For peace with him is nought but ill;
He neither pact nor treaty will.
If therefore you would grief eschew,
This counsel I would give to you:
Let each unto his own look well.
E'en now they rush from hill and fell.

---

[1] In the 'Opus theatricum' all the lists of *Persons represented* are placed at the end of each play.
[2] A Princess of Poland.
[3] All the designations of acts are placed at the end of each act throughout the 'Opus theatricum'.
[4] vnd S. — i. e. und sagt, *and says.* The same note, or the letter S only, is appended to all the characters' names in the 'Opus theatricum'.

COMEDY OF THE BEAUTIFUL SIDEA.

Darumb muſs ich eylendt Postirn
Vnd disen Brieff balt Praesentirn
[*Er geht ab.*

Kompt ROLLUS DER BAUR *schlegt in die hend*
Ja der Dieb hat zu vil gemützt
Ich hab das Meel gekneten jetzt
Es gehn mir ja schir zwen Läib ab
So weng ich lang nicht bachen hab
Vnd wenn ich jetzt den Dieb ergriff
Ich jhn mit Fäusten alsbalt anlieff
Wolt jhm das Meel vom Halſs rab schlagen

JAHN MOLITOR *geht ein in gestallt eines Müllners*
Sich Rolle mein, ich muſs dich fragen
Wer ist der dort so eylend Reit
Vnd sag mir auch was es bedeut
Er führt ein Brieff in einer kluppen
    ROLLUS
Du Dieb das dich ankumb die schnuppen
Was hab ich nach dem Reuter zu fragen
Hör Müller thu mir das vor sagen
Warumb stahlstu mir von mein Meel
    JAHN MOLITOR
Ich habs nit than bey meiner Seel
    ROLLUS
So hats aber dein Weib than die Hur
    JAHN MOLITOR *sagt gar ernstlich*
Ey nein mein Metz die nim ich nur
Auſs deinem Sack von deinem Korn
Vnd was das selbig mehr ist worn
Aber vom Meel nim ich kein staub
    ROLLUS
Ja dasselb ich auch gar wol glaub
Stihlstu vil Korn auſs dem Sack rauſs
So wird dest weniger Meel darauſs
Deſs ich bin heut wol worn innen
Hab kaum zehen Läib bachen künnen
Der jhr doch solten zwölff worden sein
    JAHN MOLITOR
Hör wann du die Läib machest klein
So kanstu jhr wol achtzehen bachen
    ROLLUS
Kom her vnd lern mich Haufsläib machen
Vnd spott mich noch wol auſs darzu
Ein rechter arger Dieb bistu
Von dem kombt niemand vnbetrogen
    JAHN MOLITOR
Ey das ist auff mein Seel erlogen
Ich bin nicht alzeit in der Mühl
Wie könt ich dann stehts nemen zu vil

And therefore must I post away,
This letter to present to-day.
[*Exit.*

Enter ROLLUS, THE PEASANT, *clasping his hands together.*
Yes, the thief has cribbed too much;
I have the meal just kneaded, such
Should give at least two good loaves more.
So little I ne'er baked before.
And if I now could catch the thief,
My fists should bring him soon to grief
Till from his neck the flour ran.

Enter JOHN MOLITOR *in the form of a miller.*
Tell me, my Rolly, if you can,
Who's riding there so fast away?
And what it means, I prythee, say,
He bears a letter in a clip.
    ROLLUS.
You thief! Pox take you! What's the rip.
And rider too indeed, to me?
Hark, Miller, tell me honestly,
Why of my meal so much you stole?
    JOHN MOLITOR.
I? not a jot! Upon my soul.
    ROLLUS.
Your wife has done it then, the whore.
    JOHN MOLITOR, *very earnestly.*
Oh no, my measure, never more,
From out your sack of corn I take,
And just whatever more it make.
But of the meal, — no jot, no jot.
    ROLLUS.
Aye, as for that, I doubt it not.
For if the corn you freely steal,
The less remains to grind to meal.
I'm up to that, my man, to-day.
Could scarcely bake ten loaves, I say!
Though twelve there should have been in all.
    JOHN MOLITOR.
Why, if you would but have them small,
Eighteen at least you well might make.
    ROLLUS.
Hallo! You'd teach me how to bake,
And cut your jokes upon me too!
A regular vile thief are you,
Who never fail to pluck your bird.
    JOHN MOLITOR.
Now that's a lie, upon my word.
I am not always in the mill;
How can I then the flour pill?

COMEDY OF THE BEAUTIFUL SIDEA.

So hab ich lauter gar from Knecht
Die thun den Bauren nit vnrecht
Zu mahl wann sie jhn was verehrn
Drumb mag ich dir nit mehr zuhörn
Es möcht sich zu weit reissen ein
          [*Jetzt drommet man.*

ROLLUS
Hör hör frembt Leut im Lande sein
Ich wil gehn zu den meinen sehen
Das mir kein schaden thu geschehen
          [*Sie gehn ab.*

LUDOLFF *geht ein mit* SIDEA *seiner Tochter in Heidnischen kleidern mit zweyen Trabanten, setzt sich vnd sagt zornig.*

Sidea liebe Tochter mein
Jetzund wir Bottschaft gwertig sein
Was der Fürst in Littau wird sagen
Dem wir sein Gsanden habn erschlagen
Dem vnser gmüth nit gfelt gar wol
Dann vnser hertz steckt zorens vol
Vnd so balt wir es können fügen
So wöll wir jhn mit gwalt bekriegen
Vnd treiben von sein Leut vnd Landen

SIDEA
Herr Vatter nichts guts thut mich anden
Wir haben vns wol für zuschauen
Dann keinem Feind ist nicht zutrauen
Darzu ist vnser Feind auch starck
Ist darzu sehr listig vnd arck
Dörfft vns mit gegen wehr begegen
Dar zu alles vnglück anlegen
So hett wir den schimpff allezeit
Von wegen der vermessenheit
Die wir bißher haben begangen
Doch mag eur Lieb auch raht empfangen
Von jhren wol verstendigen Rähten
Die solch sach baß erfahren theten
Als ich arme junge Jungfrau

LUDOLFF
Trabant balt zu der Pforten schau
Seind Leut drauß die für vns begern
Laß sie nur rein das wir sie hörn

Ein Trabant geht hin thut auff, so kompt RUPRECHT DER POST BOTT *tregt ein Brief in einer kluppen, neigt sich vor dem Fürsten*

RUPRECHT
Durchleuchtigster Fürst ich bin ein Bott
Gefreyt vor aller gfahr vnd noht
Gleich wol so bitt ich vmb genad
Hertzog Leudegast mich her gschickt hat

My men are in the pious way,
Won't cheat a peasant, no, not they;
Especially if tipp'd before;
And therefore I will hear no more.
The thing might get beyond a joke.
          [*Drumming without.*

ROLLUS.
Hark! hark! I fear that's foreign folk.
I'll go and mind my chattels all;
Lest any damage me befall.
          [*Exeunt.*

Enter LUDOLFF *with* SIDEA, *his daughter, in heathen costume, with two attendants.* LUDOLFF *sits down, and says angrily:*

Oh daughter sweet, my own Sidea,
The answer now must soon be here,
What will the prince in Littau say,
That we his envoy dared to slay.
Our spirit liketh him not well,
For anger doth our bosom swell.
As soon as we can war prepare,
He'll taste our mettle then and there.
We'll drive him from his land, we will.

SIDEA.
My heart forebodes, sir, nought but ill.
We for ourselves may well take heed;
For who would trust a foe indeed?
Besides our enemy is strong,
And cunning in devising wrong,
Perhaps may offer opposition,
And lead us on to our perdition.
And thus, my father, would our name
Be covered with undying shame
For those presumptuous acts of thine.
Oh, rather may thy heart incline
To those, who can with counsel aid
Far better than a simple maid,
Men, whose experience is great.

LUDOLFF.
Attendant, look thou to the gate,
Admit all who an audience seek;
We'll hear them, let them freely speak.

The attendant opens the door. Enter RUPRECHT, THE POSTMAN, *carrying a letter in a clip, and makes obeisance to the Prince.*

RUPRECHT.
Most noble Prince, I come to thee,
As envoy from all danger free,
But still your grace I'd humbly crave.
Duke Leudegast the missive gave,

COMEDY OF THE BEAUTIFUL SIDEA.

Im zorn mit diesem absag Brieff
Was der inhalt gibt sein begrieff

FÜRST LUDOLFF *nimbt den Brieff mit zorn aufs der kluppen, liest den vnd sagt zornig*

Dein Fürst der ist vns leiden gut
Sag wenn er hab eins Helden muth
Vnd will vns lernen kennen bafs
Thu er was er sich glüsten lafs
Wir wölln alhie seiner warten
In der mafs schlagen auff die schwarten
Das er sol sein hochmuth verstehn
Vnd du magst deins wegs wol fort gehn
Oder wir wölln dir füfs machen

Ruprecht der Bott neigt sich vnd geht ab, der Fürst sagt weiter.

Nun müfs wir auch thun zu den sachen
Vnd ein gewaltigs Heer bestelln
Dem Fürstn sein hochmuth dempffn wölln

SIDEA *sagt kleglich*

Ach jhr Götter last euch erbarmen
Es ist zu thun nur vmb mich armen
Ach thuts nicht lieber Herr Vatter mein

LUDOLFF

Halt nur das maul es mufs doch sein
[*Abgang jhr aller.*

Kompt LEUDEGAST DER FÜRST IN DER WILTAU *mit* FRANCISCO *vnd* ELEMAUS *sein zweyen Rähten gerüst*

LEUDEGAST

Weil der zenckisch Hertzog Leupolt
Den Krieg vnd zanck hat also holt
Das er vns fordert in sein Land
So seit nur behertzt allesand
Last vns erlangen Gut vnd Ehr
Kein Fried treff wir mit jhm nicht mehr
So lang wir vnd er thut leben
Wir haben vns darein ergeben
Das die Feindschafft so lang soll bleiben
Bifs einer den andern thu vertreiben
Von seinem Fürstenthumb vnd Land

FRANCISCUS

Darzu sind wir gerüst alsand
Vnd haben vns schon drein ergeben
Daran zu setzen Leib vnd Leben
Vnd alles was von nöten thut

ELEMAUS

Ja das Lebn, den Leib, auch das Gut
Vnd alles das so wir vermügen
Wenden wir als an zu bekriegen
Dem stoltzen Fürsten in Littau

In wrathful mood. This hostile letter
Informs thee of the import better.

PRINCE LUDOLFF, *frowning, takes the letter out of the clip, reads it, and then says angrily:*

Thy prince doth please us passing well;
And if a hero's courage dwell
Within his bosom, which he still
Would prove, why let him do his will.
We will his coming here abide,
And leave such marks upon his hide,
That he his insolence shall learn.
The way you came, you may return,
Or we will teach you expedition.

Exit Ruprecht, *the postman, making obeisance. The Prince continues:*

We now must look to our position.
A mighty army too provide,
To tame this haughty prince's pride.

SIDEA, *in a melancholy voice.*

Ye Gods! that this should e'er befall
Through wretched me, the cause of all!
Do it not, father mine! oh no!

LUDOLFF.

Girl, hold thy tongue; it must be so.
[*Exeunt.*

Enter LEUDEGAST, THE PRINCE OF WILTAU, *with his two counsellors*, FRANCISCO *and* ELEMAUS, *all armed.*

LEUDEGAST.

Duke Leupold so loves strife and brawl,
That now he's challenged us to fall
Upon his land, and fight it out.
Let's meet him then with hearts as stout.
Honour and wealth will we obtain,
And ne'er make peace with him again,
As long as both of us shall live.
Ourselves unto the cause we give,
Our enmity will never smother,
Till one of us shall drive the other
From principality and land.

FRANCISCUS.

'Tis for that end in arms we stand,
Devote ourselves unto the strife,
Though it may cost us limb and life,
And all that man has dear to him.

ELEMAUS.

Aye land, and goods, and life, and limb,
All, all we'll venture, all we can
We'll do, to conquer that proud man,
Who now in Littau holds the sway.

COMEDY OF THE BEAUTIFUL SIDEA.

FRANCISCUS
Wenn einer sicht von ferrn gar gnau
So geht im Feld dort auff ein staub
Das ist der Feind wie ich gelaub
Drumb hab acht es wird kappen geben
LEUDEGAST
Ja wir sehen die Fähnlein schweben
Darumb seit keck vnd auch bereit
Es wird geben ein kampff vnd streit
Die Feind greiffen vns hinden an
Drumb wehret euch nur dran, dran, dran

Lauffen Hertzog LUDOLFFS gesind ein, kempffen lang mit einander vnd werden LUDOLFFS Leut alle erschlagen,
LUDOLFF *fellt zu fufs*

LUDOLFF
Ach vnglück ist auff meiner seiten
Allein kan ich kein Heer bestreiten
Drumb bitt ich vmb genad vnd hult

HERTZOG LEUDEGAST
Das vnglück ist allein dein schuld
Vnd ich hett gut vrsach vnd recht
Das ich dich also balt vmbrecht
Mit eim grausamen bösen todt
Doch wil ich dich zu schand vnd spot
Lebendig jagen aufs dem Land
Balt glöb vnd schwer mit Mund und Hand
Das du vns das Land raumen wolst
Vnd darein nicht mehr kommen solst
Allein so viel sey dir vergünt
Was du vnd auch dein Tochter künd
Beide mit euch von hinnen tragen
Vngeführt auff Karn vnd Wagen
Dasselbig mügt behalten jhr
Wiltu das thun so glob es mir

LUDOLFF DER HERTZOG *sagt kleglich*
Als ich hab mir zu vil vertraut
Zu sehr auff meinen gwalt gebaut
Drumb die Grub die ich graben hab
Darin fall den halfs ich selbst ab
  [*Er globt an vnd geht traurig ab*

HERTZOG LEUDEGAST
Jr lieben Kriegsleut kompt herein
Last vns die Stadt auch nemen ein
Nun hab wir gwunnen Ehr vnd Gut
Zerstört des Fürsten vbermuht
Darfür thun wir euch vil dancks sagen
Das jhr thet leib vnd leben wagen
Vnd wölln vnter euch jetzunder
Aufs theiln in der Stadt den blunder
  [*Sie gehn alle ab*

FRANCISCUS.
I think if you would look this way,
You'll see a-field a cloud of dust;
It is the enemy I trust;
Take heed, for there are helmets there.
LEUDEGAST.
And standards floating in the air.
Therefore prepare ye for the fight,
Your courage, as your weapons, bright.
The foe attacks us from the rear;
But at them! at them! Never fear!

Duke LUDOLFF's people rush in and fight for some time. At last they are all killed. LUDOLFF *falls at Duke LEUDEGAST's feet.*

LUDOLFF.
Ill fortune to my side hath flown!
I cannot fight a host alone;
Therefore for quarter humbly sue.

LEUDEGAST.
Ill fortune is but thy just due;
And rightful cause would fail me not.
If I would kill thee on the spot,
With torture, yet I deem it best
To let thee live the scorn and jest
Of men, and chase thee from the land.
But swear to me with mouth and hand,
To cede the whole of thy domain
To us, nor e'er return again.
But then thus much I thee allow:
Of all thy goods, whatever thou
And daughter too together can
Convey by waggon, cart, or van,
The same to keep. If thou agree
To these conditions, swear to me.

LUDOLFF, *piteously.*
Alas! alas! I see at length,
I built too much upon my strength;
And therefore while I dug a pit
For others, fell myself in it.
  [*He takes the oath. Exit sorrowfully.*

LEUDEGAST.
The town is ours, enter here
And occupy it, comrades dear.
For wealth and honour you have gained,
The prince's arrogance restrained,
Great services with peril rendered,
For which our thanks to you are tendered.
So on to town, among you there
The plunder we will freely share.
  [*Exeunt.*

Kompt LUDOLFF *mit* SIDEA, *tregt einen weisen Silbern Stab in der hand.*

LUDOLFF

Ach wie thut mir die spot vnd schand
Vber die mafs so weh vnd and
Es möcht mir wol mein hertz zerbrechen
Das ich mich difsmal nit kan rechen
Hab verloren mein Fürstenthum
Mein Reichtum Wolfahrt Ehr vnd Ruhm
Vnd ob ich schon kein Land mehr hab
Will ich jedoch nit lasen ab
Gebrauchen alle renck vnd tück
Bifs mir widerumb scheint das glück
Vnd ich sey an meim Feind gerochen

SIDEA

Herr Vatter ich hab die gantze Wochen
In meinem hertzen gehabt grofs pein
Hab kein stund künnen frölich sein
Dann es hat wol mein hertz geand
Ach weh des jammers spot vnd schand
Kein wunder wer das mir vor schmertz
In tausent stücken zerspreng mein hertz
Vor lebt ich in Fürstlichem Stand
Jetzt hab ich weder Leut noch Land
Vor nennt man mich Fürstlichs Fräulein
Jetzund mufs ich ein Bettlerin sein
Vor hett ich als vol auff vngemessen
Jetzt wers noht das ich grafs thet essen
Vor hett ich viel die vmb mich worben
Jetzt mufs es sein einsam gestorben
Vnd weifs nicht wie es nimbt ein end

LUDOLFF *ist zornig, zuckt den stab.*

Halts maul das dich Jupiter schend
Vnd hab ein zeit gedult mit mir
Jetzt will ich bringen mein Geist herfür
Der mufs mir sagen wies vns auff Erd
Bifs zu dem todt ergehn noch werd

[*Er macht ein kreifs mit dem stab vnnd etliche Caracteres darein*

SIDEA

Ach wolt jhr den Geist thun beschwern
Last mich zuvor von hinnen kehrn
Dann er ist gar zu forchtsam mir

LUDOLFF

Schweig still er ist vnschedlich dir.

[*Er macht den Kreifs aufs, vnd klopfft mit dem Stäblein auff das loch, so springt der* TEUFFEL *herauſs, speit Feur aufs, geht in Kreifs vnd sagt zornig:*

Enter LUDOLFF *with* SIDEA, *carrying a white silver wand in his hand.*

LUDOLFF.

Alas! What torture 'tis to face
Indignity and foul disgrace!
My heart indeed is like to break
That now I can no vengeance take.
I've lost my kingdom, lost my name,
My wealth, my honour, and my fame!
And though no more of land possess'd,
Yet not a moment will I rest,
But use all stratagem and wile,
Till once more fortune on me smile,
And vengeance on my foe I wreak.

SIDEA.

Alas, my father! all this week
Such trouble doth my heart oppress,
I've known no moment's happiness.
Too truly did my heart forebode
Of foul disgrace this weary load.
It is no wonder, then, the smart
In thousand pieces burst my heart.
In princely state I lived before;
Now suite and laud are mine no more.
And princely rank belonged to me;
But now a beggar I must be.
Before I ne'er knew stint nor need;
But now on herbage I may feed.
Before would lovers round me sigh;
But now unwedded must I die,
Nor know I what the end will be.

LUDOLFF *angrily, twitching at his wand:*

Silence! May Jove dishonour thee!
Have patience with me while I call
My spirit, he shall tell me all
Will happen to us here below
Till death, for I'm resolved to know.

[*He draws a circle with his wand, and describes certain characters in it.*

SIDEA.

Ah, if the spirit thou would'st raise,
I pray thee let me go my ways.
The thought doth fill me with alarm.

LUDOLFF.

Silence! he will not do thee harm.

[*He opens the circles, and strikes the opening with his wand. The* DEVIL *springs out of it, spits out fire, walks round in the circle, and says angrily:*

Ludolff du bist ein böser Mann
Vor dir ich nirgent bleiben kan
So balt dir nur was schlechts fellt ein
Meinstu ich muſs schlechts bey dir sein
Nun magstu wissen vnd das ich
Noch mehr beschwerer hab als dich
Vnd kan dir nicht so gschwind auffhupffen
Obs dir schon thut ind nasen schnupffen
Drumb sag mir balt was wiltu mein

Ludolff

Du Schelm wann du so stoltz wilt sein
So sag mich ledig meiner glüeb
Oder mir alsbalt antwort gib
Warumb ich dich jetzund thu fragen

Runcifal der Teuffel

Was wiltu dann so thu mir sagen
Wiltus nit sagen so ziech ich hin
Meins wegs wo ich herkommen bin
Du hörsts das ich muſs weiters fort

Ludolff

So sag mir balt mit einem wort
Ob ich mich kan an meim Feind rechen

Runcifal

In warheit thu ich dir versprechen
Es wird geschehen nicht nach langen
Wirstu deins Feindes Sohne fangen
Vnd der wird dir lang Dienstbar sein
Vnd nach lang auſsgestandner pein
Wird er von dir ledig durchauſs
Kompt wider seim Vatter zu Hauſs
Als dann wirstu wider zu ehrn
Vnd wider guts glück zu dir kehrn
Ein mehrers kan ich dir nicht sagen
[Runcifal der Teuffel fehrt ab

Ludolff

So du im Walt hörst jemand Jagen
So zeig mirs an als balt will ich
Auff das best wol fürsehen mich
Das ich auch etwas thu erlangen
Könd ich den Jungen Fürsten fangen
Vnd das ich mich könd an jhm rechen
So will ich dir hiemit versprechen
Das er muſs bleiben mein Leib eygen
Wolt jhm auch alles böſs erzeigen
Wie vns sein Vatter hat gethan
Nun laſs vns in die Hütten gahn
Weil wirs doch jetzt nit besser han
[Abgang.

Ludolff, thou art a wicked man;
For thee I nowhere tarry can.
Whene'er thou mischief meditate,
Thou thinkst I must be with thee straight.
Now know, I serve not thee alone,
But others too for masters own,
And can't hop up at such a pace,
E'en though thou pull'st so long a face;
Say quickly what thou wouldst with me?

Ludolff.

Thou rogue! if thou so proud wilt be,
Either release me from my vow,
Or give immediate answer now,
Whatever I may ask of thee.

Runcifal.

What is it then? Come tell it me;
If not, why then the way is clear
For my return, which I came here.
For I must forth, as thou hast heard.

Ludolff.

Then tell me quickly in a word,
Can I revenge me on my foe?

Runcifal.

Thus much 'tis given thee to know:
Not many days will lapse, I wis,
Before his son thy prisoner is.
And he will serve thee long, at last
When that his term of trial's past,
He will from thee his freedom earn,
And to his father's house return.
Thy honours then will be restored,
And fortune too be thy reward.
But more I'm not allowed to say.
[Exit Runcifal, the devil.

Ludolff.

Shouldst thou hear huntsmen pass this way,
Inform me quickly, then will I
Arrange my plans so craftily,
That I may also something take:
Could I the prince my prisoner make,
And wreak my vengeance on him too,
Why then I promise this to you:
That he as slave remain behind,
And such ill-treatment shall he find,
As we must from his father bear.
Now let us to the hut repair,
As there is nothing better there.
[Exeunt.

ACTUS SECUNDUS.

Kompt JAHN MOLITOR *ist sehr staubig von Meel, lacht*

Ein Mühl die da Wassers gnug hat
Das es kan treiben nur drey Raht
Kan sich des nutzens nicht erwehrn
Vnd wol ein fauIln Müller ernehrn
Beydes mit Weib vnd auch mit Kind
Vnd mit all seinem Haufsgesind
Dann kein Ampt ist auff diser Erd
Wers vbel braucht ist Henckens wehrt
Vnd weil die Müller mützen gern
Den Baurn die Seck zu gar weit lern
So müssen sie jhr Dieb auch sein
Das klingt vor den Leuten nicht fein
Aber was ist daran gelegen
Man thut doch als nur von Gelts wegen
Vnd wenn des Menschen lust nicht wehr
O die Welt stünd jetzt nimmermehr
Daher wird einer ein ankleger
Der ander wird ein Hundts schleger
Der dritt ein Stattknecht oder Büttel
Der viert ein Baur in seinem Küttel
Der fünfft wird ein Schalck vnd Verräther
Der sechst ein Mörder vnd Vblthäter
Der sibend ein Wucherer werden thut
Der acht hat ein leichtfertigen mut
Der neund purgiret die privet
Der zehend mit bösen schäden vmbgeht
Der eylfft Peinlich sach exequirt
Der zwölfft desselben lehrknecht wirdt
Vnd also fort durch alle Ständt
So viel der tadelhafftig send
Vnd die man scheulich acht darneben
Dennoch thut man sich drein ergeben
Das schafft allein die Lieb vnd lust
Ich wer kein Müller worden sunst
Wenn ich nit so wol hett gewist
Was groser Nutz beym Mühlwerck ist
Ich mest all Jar etliche Schwein
Kauffen von mir die Metzger ein
Fragen nit wo ichs hab genummen
Guts Dreits gnug kan ich vberkummen
Das ich nit als verzehren kan
Ein gmesten Ochsen ich drinn han
Den schlag ich mir jetzt in mein Haufs
Ich mach Kefs vnd rühr auch Schmaltz anfs
Vnd hab mein bares Gelt dar zu
Allein das bringt mir grofs vnruh
Das ich Heur hab mein Weib verlohrn

ACT II.

Enter JOHN MOLITOR, *covered with flour, and laughing.*

A mill, which only has indeed
Water enough three wheels to feed,
Brings cash enough at least for that,
To keep a lazy miller fat,
His children too, and eke his spouse,
And all the servants in his house.
Each trade must its own pickings bring,
But not for that should tradesmen swing.
And as the millers like their snack,
Dig somewhat deep in peasant's sack,
Why truly they are thieves, but then
The word sounds ill to other men.
Yet who for that need take offence?
It's only done for sake of pence.
If man's desires lost their power,
The world could never last an hour.
One man informs against his brother;
As dog-killer too lives another.
The third as beadle may be seen;
The fourth a clown in gabardine.
The fifth, a rogue, betrays his friends;
The sixth cuts throats to gain his ends.
The seventh takes his cent per cent;
The eighth's on idle pleasure bent.
The ninth cleans privies out for pay;
The tenth malicious plots will lay.
Th'elev'nth for debt doth chattels seize;
The twelfth — his prentice if you please.
Thus through all trades it is the same;
There's always much deserves our blame.
And though they may detest the thing,
Yet use doth resignation bring.
The only joy is cash to win;
For I no miller should have been,
Had I not known the way a mill
May well be made one's purse to fill.
Each year I fatten swine, you see,
And these the butchers buy of me.
They don't ask how I fill the trongh.
With three good pigs I come well off.
For I can never eat them all.
A fatten'd ox have I in stall,
Which I shall slaughter in my yard;
Besides, I make both cheese and lard.
Of ready cash I have a store:
But one thing troubles me full sore;
This year hath ta'en my wife from me,

Wer sunst lieber ein Müller worn
Als der best Doctor in der Statt
ROLLUS DER BAUR *geht mit* ELA *seiner Tochter ein, die
tregt ein eingewickelts Kindt.*
ROLLUS
Sie da El dort steht der vnflat
Dem wölln wir dein Kindt heim tragen
Vnd, das er dich bhalt, zu jhm sagen
Thut ers nit so verklag ich jhn
ELA
O laſs vns nur balt zu jhm hin
    [*Sie gehn zu Jahn Molitor*
ROLLUS
Ey Müller da find wir euch recht
Weil jhr mir habt mein Tochter gschwecht
Die mit euch hat tragen ein Kindt
So müst jhr euch erkleren gschwindt
Ob jhrs wolt wider zu ehrn bringen
JAHN MOLITOR *kratzt sich im kopff*
Jr sagt mir von seltzamen dingen
Ich sol eur Tochter bringen zu ehrn
Dergleichen Kunst thet ich nie lehrn
Dann an ehrn mir selbst mangeln thut
Ist eur Tochter gut so bleibs gut
Ich bin des Kindes Vatter nicht
ROLLUS
Ja du Schelm du hast jhrs zugricht
Wil ich bei meinem Eid erhalten
JAHN MOLITOR *lacht, deut auff den Baurn*
Schau einer den leichtfertigen Altn
Der schwert da für die Tochter sein
Vnd glaubt was sie jhm bildet ein
Vnd er hats weder ghört noch gsehen
ELA
Nein es ist dennoch also gschehen
Vnd du laugnest so hart darfür
Das Kind hab ich allein von dir
Schaus nur es ist ein schöns Söhnlein
JAHN MOLITOR
Ists schön so solts ein Maidlein sein
So gried es seiner Mutter nach
Gebt mir ein bedacht heint den tag
Als dann so will ich mich erklern
ROLLUS
Ey gut das wöll wir thun gar gern
    [*Sie gehn ein wenig auff die Seiten, reden zusammen
in die Ohren, Jahn lacht, so kompt* DIETRICH
mit AGNES, *seiner Tochter, die tregt auch ein
Kind,* DIETRICH *geht zu jhm, vnd sagt zornig.*
Find ich dich hie du ehrlicher Mann

Else I would rather miller be
Than the best doctor in the town!
Enter ROLLUS, THE PEASANT, *with* ELA, *his daughter,
carrying a baby in swaddling clothes.*
ROLLUS.
Look, Ela, look! There stands the clown.
We'll tell him that thy child thou'st brought.
That he must both of you support:
If not, I'll prosecute the loon.
ELA.
O father, let us at him soon.
    [*They walk up to John Molitor.*
ROLLUS.
How lucky, miller, thou art there!
For thou to me must now declare.
As thou my daughter hast defiled,
And she hath borne to thee a child.
If thou'lt restore her honest name.
JOHN MOLITOR, *scratching his head.*
That's a queer notion, — is that same;
I should her honesty restore,
Yet never had the thing before!
My stock of it is nearly drained.
If honest once, she's so remained.
I'm not the father of her child.
ROLLUS.
Thou rogue! I know thou'st her beguiled.
Can take my solemn oath, I can!
JOHN MOLITOR *laughing, and pointing at the peasant.*
Now look at that old hasty man!
For daughter there he'll swear away.
Believe whate'er the wench may say!
He neither saw nor heard the act.
ELA.
Nevertheless, the thing's a fact.
And yet indeed thou wilt not own
I had the child by thee alone!
As pretty a boy as one may see.
JOHN MOLITOR.
If pretty, it a girl should be, —
Take after its own mother more.
Give me to-night to think it o'er,
And then I'll tell you my intent.
ROLLUS.
Aye, aye, — to that we will consent.
    [*They walk a little on one side, and whisper
together. John laughs.*
Enter DIETRICH *with* AGNES, *his daughter, carrying a baby.
He walks up to the miller, and says angrily:*
Thou honest man! I find thee here?

COMEDY OF THE BEAUTIFUL SIDEA.

JAHN *erschrickt, kratzt sich im kopff*
Ja was hab ich dann dir gethan
DIETRICH
Mein Tochter hast mir zschanden gmacht
Da hab wir dir das Kind gebracht
Das wird dir zu ziehen gebürn
Auch so mustu gen Kirchen führn
Mein Tochter bhalten zu der Eh
JAHN MOLITOR
Deiner Tochter ich keins Kinds gsteh
So hab ich sie auch nit genommen
DIETRICH
Lestus für die Obrigkeit kommen
So wirst wol sehen was du gwinst
Du must ins gfengknus auffs aller minst
Vnd dennoch bhalten die Tochter mein
Ich will dir ein guter Schwer sein
Vnd hundert gulten geben darzu
JOHAN[1] MOLITOR
Hundert gultn vnd wolt mir flicken die Schu
Das ich euch nichts darff lohnen darfür
Ein Weib ist not zu nemen mir
Dann ichs mit meinen Mäid vnd Knechten
Nicht als kan erstreiten vnd fechten
Aber verziecht ein weil hierinnen
Ich muſs mich vor darauff besinnen
[*Er geht abwärts, wo der Rollus mit seiner Tochter steht*
JAHN
Hört was wolt jhr mir geben dar zu
Wann ich eur Tochter nemen thu
Zu eim ehrlichen Heürat Gut
ROLLUS
Wann jhr mein Tochter nemen thut
Gib ich euch hundert gulten mit jhr
JAHN *deut auff den Schuster*
O der beut hundert Thaler mir
Vnd hat mir noch verheissen darzu
Vmb sunst zu flicken all mein Schu
Vnd ist sein Tochter schöner als die
ROLLUS
Wiltu zu Kirchen führen sie
So gib ich dir ein guten zahler
Zu jhr anderthalb hundert Tahler
Vnd führ dir vmb sunst aus dein mist
JAHN *schmutzt*
Das alles dennoch gut mit ist
Verziecht ich muſs nur etwas fragen
Ich will euch balt gut antwort sagen

[1] *Sic* in the original impression.

JOHN *frightened, and scratching his head.*
What have I done to thee? Oh dear!
DIETRICH.
What? Why my daughter thou'st defiled;
And now we've brought to thee the child,
Which it's thy duty to maintain.
And after that, of course 'tis plain,
Thou must in church my daughter wed.
JOHN MOLITOR.
Through me she ne'er was brought to bed,
Ne'er did I treat her in that sort.
DIETRICH.
Then let us go before the court,
And thou wilt see what thou wilt gain:
At least in prison to remain,
And wed my daughter none the less.
As father, I'll the marriage bless
With hundred florins if you choose.
JOHN MOLITOR.
A' hundred down, and mend my shoes,
And nothing for it have to pay?
I want a wife too any way.
For with my maid and servants too,
I cannot all the work get through.
Excuse me while I step aside,
And think before I choose my bride.
[*Aside to Rollus who is standing near his daughter.*
JOHN.
Now tell me, how much wilt thou give,
If I thy daughter take to live
With me, I mean in wedlock fast.
ROLLUS.
If thou my daughter take at last,
I will a hundred florins say.
JOHN, *pointing to the shoemaker.*
T'other will hundred dollars pay,
And promises he'll not refuse
To mend for nothing all my shoes.
His daughter's handsomer than she.
ROLLUS.
If thou to marry her agree,
I'll pay of dollars without fail
Hundred and fifty on the nail,
Thy dung besides for nothing cart.
JOHN, *chuckling.*
That is worth something too, as part.
Your pardon, — I'd a word to say
To him; — I'll answer you to-day.

JAHN *lacht*	**JOHN**, *laughing.*
Wann sie nicht wölln höcher nauff	If they their highest bid have made,
So wird aufs dem gebot kein kauff	We shan't do business I'm afraid.
[*Er geht zu dem Schuster*	[*Walking up to the shoemaker.*
Hört jhr mein Meister Dietrich	Now master Dietrich, do you see,
Für war eur Tochter ist nicht für mich	Your daughter's not the girl for me.
Ihr gebt jhr zu weng Heürat Gut	You will not dower give enough.
Der Rollus mir anbieten thut	'Tis Rollus offers me the stuff.
Zwey hundert Thaler, das jhrs wist	Two hundred dollars will he pay,
Vnd will mir aufs führn all mein mist	And all my dung will cart away,
So lang ich vnd er thut leben	As long as both of us shall live.
DIETRICH *verwundert sich*	**DIETRICH**, *much surprised.*
Zwey hundert Gultn wil ich dir geben	Two hundred florins will I give;
Ich meint ich thet der sach genug	If that won't do, the deuce is in it.
JAHN MOLITOR	**JOHN MOLITOR.**
So habt noch ein kleinen verzug	Be kind enough to wait a minute,
Ich wils gehn dem Rollus abschlagen	While I shew Rollus to the door.
[*Die zwey der Schuster vnd sein Tochter stosen die köpff zusammen, er geht zum Rollo.*	[*The shoemaker and his daughter put their heads together, while John walks up to Rollus.*
(**JAHN**)	**JOHN.**
Hört mit eim wort wil ichs euch sagen	I wish to say just one word more:
Er will zwey hundert Thaler geben	He will two hundred dollars give,
Vnd mein Schu flicken weil wir leben	And mend my shoes while both do live.
Nun ist sein Tochtr ein Burgers Kind	His girl, as burgher's daughter, too
Die ehrlicher als die Baurn sind	Ranks higher than the peasants do.
Darumb wil ich dieselben nemen	And therefore she shall bear my name.
ROLLUS	**ROLLUS.**
Ey, ich wolt mich in mein hertz schemen	'Twould be for me a downright shame,
Das ich nit so gut als er wer	Were I not quite as good as he.
Vil mag dir wol verheisen er	Though much indeed he promise thee
Nicht weifs ich wie er zahln wür	I don't know how he'll ever pay.
Jedoch so will ich geben dir	But yet two hundred will I say
Zwey hundert Thaler wie vor gemelt	Before the wedding, come now, — come!
JAHN	**JOHN.**
Zwey hundert Thaler ist vil gelt	Two hundred is a good round sum.
Nun hab ich zu bedencken frey	I'll take my leisure to reflect,
Welche mir die nutzlichste sey	From which I may most help expect.
[*Er geht wegk vnd eh er zum Schuster kompt sagt er*	[*He goes aside, but before he turns to the shoemaker, continues:*
Ich mag ebn der Hurn keine nit	I don't like either wench, — not I,
Jetzt wil ich machen ein vnfrid	So to get up a brawl will try.
Das die zwen sollen vneins wern	That they from words may come to blows,
Vnd weil sie aneinander bern	Exchange black eyes for bloody nose;
Die weil so treh ich mich davon	Then in the midst I'll take my leave.
[*Er geht zum Dietrich*	[*Walking up to Dietrich.*
Was sol ich mit deiner Tochter than	Thy daughter I can ne'er receive.
Rollus sagt vnverholn vnd frey	For Rollus says quite openly,
Das sie doch nur dein Hurnkind sey	No honest woman's child is she.
Vnd du seist auch nit Ehlich geborn	And thou thyself a bastard born.

COMEDY OF THE BEAUTIFUL SIDEA.

DIETRICH *sagt zornig*
Das sey dem schelm ein Eyd geschworn
Wolt er solchs ding von vns aufs geben
Es müst jhn kosten leib vnd leben
Ich will jhm sein Leib Himlblau schlagen
JAHN
Verzeich ich wil jhn vor recht fragen
[*Er geht zum Rollus*
Rollus dein Tochter ich nit mag
Geh hör was Dietrich von dir sag
Du seist ein schelm solst gedencken
Man thet dir dein Vatter erhencken
Auch hab man dir ein Bruder gricht

ROLLUS *laufft zum Schuster*
Du leugst wie ein schelm vnd böfswicht
Ey schweig ich wil dich lernen lügen
DIETRICH
Komb her du solst deins Manns wol kriegen
[*Sie schlagen einander, Jahn lacht, schlegt die hend zusammen vnd laufft ab, sie schlagen auch einander ab.*
LEUDEGAST DER FÜRST IN DER WILTAU *mit* FRANCISCO *vnnd* ELEMAO *seinen zweyen Rähten vnd seinem Sohn* ENGELBRECHT *sein auser defs Fürsten, wie Jäger staffirt, geht ein.*
LEUDEGAST
Weil jhr je naufs wolt auff das Jagen
So wil ichs euch mit treuen sagen
Das jhr gebt auff einander acht
Jr wist das der Feind stettigs wacht
Solt der euch Wehrlofs im Walt finden
Oder mit Waffen über winden
So leget er euch an grofs leidt
Darumb brauchet bescheidenheit
Vnd halt zusammen alle sander
ENGELBRECHT
Wir lassen gar nicht von einander
Hett sich einer verriten schon
So kan er durch der hörner thon
Leichtlich aus der jrr werden bracht
FRANCISCUS
Defs Ludolffs gwalt ich wenig acht
Der hat kein Leut vnd Land nicht mehr
Das man auff jhn darff sehen sehr
Zu dem wer weifs wo er vmb zeucht
Vor vns in fleder Meufs winkl kreucht
Er setzt sich gwifslich daher nicht
ELEMAUS
Er kompt vns nimmermehr zu gsicht
Seinthalb hat es kein mangel nit

DIETRICH, *angrily.*
On that the rascal shall be sworn.
If such things are maintained by him,
The lie shall cost him life and limb.
I'll beat him till his body burst.
JOHN.
Pardon, — I'll ask about it first.
[*Going up to Rollus.*
Rollus, thy daughter will not suit;
For Dietrich says, that by repute,
Thou art a rascal, and should rather
Remember that they hanged thy father,
And brother too, as far as that.

ROLLUS, *rushing up to the shoemaker.*
Thou liest, thou rogue, I tell thee flat!
Silence! I'll teach thee lies to hatch!
DIETRICH.
Come on! come on then! I'm your match!
[*They fight. John laughs and clasps his hands together. The others beat each other off the stage.*
Enter LEUDEGAST, THE PRINCE OF THE WILTAU, *with his two counsellors,* FRANCISCUS *and* ELEMAUS, *and his son* ENGELBRECHT. *All, except the prince, in huntsman's costume.*
LEUDEGAST.
As you've resolved to hunt to-day,
I'll a few words of counsel say.
Each of you keep the rest in view;
Be sure the foe is watchful too.
If he surprise you in the wood
Unarmed, or if by force he should
Subdue you, he'll do you a harm.
So stand prepared at each alarm,
Nor separate, — lest ill befall.
ENGELBRECHT.
We will not separate at all;
If one of us should ride astray,
By sounding of our horns, we may
Easily guide the truant right.
FRANCISCUS.
I don't think much of Ludolff's might.
He has nor land nor people more,
That we should heed him as before.
Besides, who knows where he may prowl,
Hiding perhaps like bat or owl?
You may be sure he is not here.
ELEMAUS.
Nor will again to us appear;
We may for him be quite at ease.

COMEDY OF THE BEAUTIFUL SIDEA.

LEUDEGAST DER FÜRST
Nun wol so ziehet hin in frid
Der Hirsch ist jetzund in der feist
Secht das jhr jhn abbruch beweist
[*Sie gehn alle ab.*
Kompt LUDOLFF *mit* SIDEA, *hat ein jedes ein weissen stab.*
LUDOLFF
Mein geist thet mir heint offenbarn
Das in dem Walt auffs gejäid wöll fahrn
Defs Hertzogen Sohn Engelbrecht
Der soll mir kommen eben recht
Den wil ich in dem Walt aufsspürn
Fangen vnd der mafs tribulirn
Der gleichen keim zuvor ist gschehen
SIDEA
Fürwar das wolt ich gern sehen
Wann wir den Vogl kriegen theten
Als dann wir gut hoffnung hetten
Wider zu bringen in die hend
Das gantz Fürstliche Regiment
Vnd woltn jhn weidlich Rancionirn
Vnd wolt er das leben nicht verliern
Müst er vns wider setzen ein
LUDOLFF
Schweig nur es soll sich schicken fein
Dann ich wil mich kurtz an jhm rechen
Oder mich vnd dich selbst erstechen
[*Er laufft mit der Tochter gantz traurig ab.*

Kompt ENGELBRECHT *mit seinen Famulo, schreien erstlich im eingang: holla, holla, holla, alsdann sie aufziehen, sagt*
ENGELBRECHT
Wir sind weit kommen von der Strassen
Wir schreyen oder die Hörner blasen
So gibt man vns doch kein antwort
Schau, schau, was gehn für Leut nur dort
Sie lauffen warlich auff vns zu
Darumb dich wol fürsehen thu
Sie greiffen zu den Rappirn, kompt LUDOLFF DER FÜRST *mit der* SIDEA, *hat in der ein hand ein blose Wehr, in der andern ein weisen stab*
LUDOLFF
Du Junger Fürst balt gib dich gfangen
ENGELBRECHT
Den Raub wirstu heüt nicht erlangen
Famule stofs durch jhn die Klingen
Sie wollen von Leder ziehen, LUDOLFF *schlegt mit den stab auff die Wehr,* FAMULUS
Mein Wehr kan ich nicht herafs bringen
Ich glaub das sie bezaubert sey

LEUDEGAST.
'Tis good, my friends, then go in peace.
The stag just now is gaining fat;
See how you put a stop to that.
[*Exeunt.*
Enter LUDOLFF *with* SIDEA, *each bearing a white wand.*
LUDOLFF.
Last night, the spirit did declare,
That Engelbrecht, the Prince's heir.
Will in the forest hunt to-day.
To me he's welcome any way.
For I will follow on his track,
Catch him, and plague him, that, good lack!
The like was never heard before!
SIDEA.
Nothing indeed would please me more.
If we could only catch this bird,
Our hope might not be long deferred.
To get once more into our hands
Our princely government and lands.
And then hard blows should be so rife,
That if he would not lose his life,
He must us quickly reinstate.
LUDOLFF.
Cunning's the thing, so hold your prate.
For vengeance take on him I will,
Or me, and eke thyself, will kill.
[*Exeunt, very sorrowfully.*

Enter ENGELBRECHT *with his squire. They first shout as they enter: holla! holla! holla! and then advance to the front.*
ENGELBRECHT.
From the right way we've wandered out,
And when we blow the horn or shout,
No answer's borne upon the air.
Look! look! what people are they there?
Indeed they're making straight this way!
Therefore be on your guard, I pray.
They lay their hands upon their swords. Enter PRINCE LUDOLFF *with* SIDEA, *carrying a drawn sword in one hand, and in the other a white wand.*
LUDOLFF.
Young Prince, I thee my prisoner make.
ENGELBRECHT.
To-day thou no such prize shalt take.
Boy, draw your sword, and him transfix.
They try to draw. LUDOLFF *strikes their sword with his wand.*
THE SQUIRE.
My sword, sir, in its scabbard sticks;
I think it must enchanted be.

ENGELBRECHT
Ja es ist lauter Zauberey
Ich bin erlembt an beyden henden
Kan mich nicht wol rucken vnd wenden
Derhalb weils nit kan anderst sein
So muſs ich sein der gfangen dein
Vnd diſsmals deines willens geleben
LUDOLFF
So thu mir deſs dein treu balt geben
Du lecker aber balt troll dich wegk
Oder ich tritt dich in den dreck
Vnd hau dir alle viere ab
Das ich vor dir zu bleiben hab
Vnd das dich fressen Krahen vnd Raben
FAMULUS
Ach weh ein böse Jagt wir haben
Gnediger Fürst in grosen Leid
Ich zu demmal von euch abscheid
[*Famulus geht ab.*
LUDOLFF
Jetzt bistu mein Leib eygner Knecht
Wie mich dein Vatter wider recht
Hat getrieben von Leut vnd Land
Vnd auffgethan groſs schmach vnd schand
Also solstu geschieden seyn
Von jhm vnd gantzer Landschafft dein
Solst meiner Tochter Holtz tragen
Vnd alles was sie dir thut sagen
Solstu verrichten vnd volbringen
Darzu solls dich mit schlegen zwingen
Vnd wo sie klags weis bringt für mich
Das du wolst etwas weigern dich
Als balt wil dich erschlagen ich
[*Er stöſt jhm zum abgang, schlegt jhn mit dem stab auff die Lend, also auch die Tochter, vnd gehn alle ab.*

ACTUS TERTIUS.

Kommen DIETERICH *vnd* ROLLUS *mit eim grosen geschrey geloffen,*
ROLLUS
Nun hör auff wenns anderst ist gnug
Kein Mensch mich mein tag also schlug
Vnd ich hab dir kein leid gethan
DIETRICH
Bin ich ein Hurn Kind so zeig an
Vnd von wem du es hast vernommen
ROLLUS
Es ist mir aufs meim maul nie kommen

ENGELBRECHT.
Yes, it is nought but sorcery.
That from my lamed limbs I learn,
For I can neither move nor turn;
And therefore, as no choice I see,
Thy prisoner I acknowledge me,
Will after thy good pleasure live.
LUDOLFF.
Of this at once thy promise give.
As for you, jackanapes, pack quick,
Or I'll thee in the kennel kick,
Thy limbs from off thy body hack,
That I on thee must turn my back,
And crows and ravens feed on thee.
SQUIRE.
Alas! what a sad hunt have we!
O gracious Prince, I sorely grieve,
That thus I from you take my leave.
[*Exit.*
LUDOLFF.
Now art thou verily my slave!
And as before thy father drave
Me most unjustly from my place,
And heaped upon me foul disgrace,
In the same way thou partest here
From father, country, all that's dear,
Shalt for my daughter carry wood,
Whatever else too she think good
To order, see thou dost it well,
Or heavy blows shall thee compel.
And should she e'er complain to me,
Thou shew'st thyself refractory,
Upon the spot I'll murder thee.
[*He beats him off, strikes him on the leg with his wand. Sidea does the same. Exeunt.*

ACT III.

Enter hastily DIETRICH *and* ROLLUS *with a great deal of noise.*
ROLLUS.
Hold! hold! enough, enough! Oh! oh!
No mortal man e'er beat me so!
And I to thee no wrong have done.
DIETRICH.
Tell me, am I a strumpets son,
From whom too thou the lie hast heard?
ROLLUS.
My mouth ne'er uttered such a word;

Der Müller aber sagen thet
Ein Schelmen jhr mich gschmehet hett
Vnd man hett mein Vatter ghangen
Also wers auch meim Bruder gangen
Das selbig wolt aufsführen ich
Dietrich
Ich hab kein schelm gscholten dich
So ist mir auch nie ingedencken
Von deins Vatters vnd Bruders hencken
Wie ich dann kein Wort weifs davon
Rollus
So hat vns also ghetzet an
Der Müller, dem wöll wirs nit schencken
Den schelm selber lasen hencken
Wir wollen jhn vor dem Schultheifs verklagen
Vnd nicht mehr dencken an das schlagen [1]
Weil wir darzu seind worden ghetzt
Es soll an jhm aufs gehn zuletzt
[Sie lauffen ab, kommen zur andern seiten wider rein
Dietrich
Der schelm hat sich gedrehet aufs
Rollus
Ja er ist je nit in seim Haufs
Jedoch so lafs ich gar nit ab
Bis ich den Hudler gfunden hab
Kompt Jahn, *hat sich wie ein alt Weib verkleid, geht an einem Krücklein,*
Dietrich
Mein liebe alte thu mir verjehen
Hastu nit den Jahn Müller gsehen

Jahn Molitor *in einer alten Frauengstalt, sagt klein*
Jahn Müller was soll ich jhn gsehn han
Was Teuffls hab ich mit jhm zu than
Fragt ander Leut die wissen drum
Rollus
Ey liebe alte Mutter kum
Ich kenn ein wol den wil ich fragen
Was gelts er wirdts vns gar balt sagen
Jahn *in gestalt der alten Frauen*
Ja wenn er das kan so ists viel
Derhalb ich auch mit euch gehn wil
[Sie gehn alle ab
Kompt Leudegast der Fürst *mit* Francisco *vnd* Elemaus, *setzt sich*
Leudegast
Es kombt mir zwar gar seltzam für
Das allein zuhaufs kommet jhr

---

[1] This line is omitted in Tieck's edition.

The miller though declared before,
Thou said'st I was a rogue, and more,
That father dangled in a noose,
And brother died too in his shoes;
That was the debt I wished to pay.
Dietrich.
I never called thee rogue, I say
Nor came it e'er into my head,
But what thy friends had died in bed.
I know no word about the matter.
Rollus.
The miller by his lies and chatter
Hath set us on, but we'll be quit;
The rogue himself shall hang for it.
Before the mayor we'll him arraign,
But won't try fisticuffs again.
And if he set us on before,
'Tis he at last shall pay the score.
[They run off at one side, and return on the other.
Dietrich.
Hulloa! the rogue has bolted clean!
Rollus.
At home he's never to be seen.
But hang me, if I leave the lout,
Until I've found the fellow out.
Enter John, *disguised as an old woman, and walking with a crutch.*
Dietrich.
Pardon old lady; hast thou seen
If John, the miller, here has been?

John, *speaking in a weak voice, like an old woman.*
The miller? What the deuce should he,
A miller, have to do with me?
Ask other people, who may know.
Rollus.
Come then, old lady, let us go.
I'll ask a man, whom I know well,
I'll lay a wager, he can tell.
John, *still imitating an old woman.*
That is no trifle, if he can;
And therefore I'll go too, young man.
[Exeunt.
Enter Prince Leudegast *with* Franciscus *and* Elemaus.
The Prince sits down.
Leudegast.
It seems to me most strange, I own,
That you should now come home alone,

COMEDY OF THE BEAUTIFUL SIDEA.

Vnd last mir aufs mein lieben Sohn
Den ich euch hoch befohlen han
Dann jhr ja sollet bey ihm bleiben
Last vns an alle örtter schreiben
Das ich erforsch wo er hin kum
Dann jhr brecht mich sunst mit jhm vmb
Das wer mir ein traurigs gejäid

FRANCISCUS

Es ist vns gar ein treulichs Leid
Das er so von vns kommen söll
Ein Hirschen hett wir im gestell
Den wolt der junge Fürst selbst bürschen
Vnd wird verlorn mit sambt dem Hirschen
Dem macht wir nach ein Jäger gschrey
Bliesen vnser Hörner dabey
Vermeinten er solt wider kehrn
So kond wir jhn nicht sehen noch hörn
Doch seind wir nicht verzaget gar
Weil wir wusten das bey jhm war
Sein Leib Jung, der geht da herein

FAMULUS *geht ein.*

FÜRST

Wo lestu dann den Sohne mein?
Wie hats euch auff der Jagt ergangen

FAMULUS

Ach weh der jung Herr ist gefangen
Als er nach Jaget einem Hirschen
Den er wolt aus seim gschofs erbürschen
Hat sich derselbig Hirsch verlorn
Vnd sind wir in dem Walt jrr worn
Weder Hund noch Jäger hörn kunden
Als wir gleich in gedancken stunden
Stiefs vns ein Weib auf vnd ein Mann
Der selbig grieff vns kecklich an
Wolt wir solten vns gfangen geben
Vnd betroht vns gar hart darneben
Wir aber grieffen zu den Wehrn
Wolten jhn von vns mit abkehrn
So hett er in der hand ein stab
Ein klein streich auf die Wehr vns gab
Da kond wir keine ziehen aufs
Vnd kam vns an ein solcher graufs
Das wir vns musten geben gfangen
Vnd als er vns hart troht nach langen
Hat er mich meins wegs heisen gahn
Vnd hat bhalten eur Gnaden Sohn
Also hat sich all sach zu tragen

LEUDEGAST

Ach du böfs vnglückliches Jagen

And leave my own dear son and heir,
Whom I entrusted to your care,
Most faithfully on him to tend.
Now everywhere I'll letters send,
To find out where the prince may be.
If lost, with him you've murdered me.
That were a sorry hunt indeed!

FRANCISCUS.

Oh Prince! our hearts within us bleed,
That we your son have not brought back:
We found a deer, were on the track,
The prince himself would shoot the same,
And thus we lost both prince and game.
We shouted loud, as huntsmen do,
And also on our horns we blew;
We thought he'd soon again appear.
But nought of him could see or hear.
Yet this did no alarm inspire,
Because we knew his faithful squire
Was with him, — he who enters here.

Enter THE SQUIRE.

THE PRINCE.

Where hast thou left my son so dear?
What of the hunt, I prythee, say?

THE SQUIRE.

The Prince is taken, — woe the day!
As eager in the hot pursuit,
He would himself the quarry shoot,
He lost it, — then we missed the way,
And in the forest went astray.
Nor hound nor huntsman succour brought;
When as we stood, absorbed in thought,
A woman came, and then a man,
Who straight a fierce attack began,
Demanded we should yield, and let
His rage appear in many a threat.
However, we clapped hand on sword,
Hoping the base attack to ward,
When he, who bore a wand, just laid
The lightest touch upon the blade,
And then we found we could not draw,
But were so struck with dread and awe,
That we submitted us in fear;
And after many a threat severe,
At last he bade me go my way,
But forced your Highness' son to stay.
And this is how the thing befell.

LEUDEGAST.

Oh wretched hunt, how sad to tell!

Wie übel kombstu mir zu Haufs
Vnd wenn ich wer gezogen naufs
So wer es mir auch also gangen
Wie sol ich nun mein sach anfangen
Das ich mein Sohn wider erlöfs
Ludolff der meints gegen vns gar böfs
Ist ers der mein Sohn hat bekommen
So wird jhm gwifs das leben gnommen
Darumb so dörff wir feyern nicht

ELEMAUS
Es ist ein seltzame geschicht
Davon nicht gut ist vil zusagen
Vnd doch hochnötig zu Rathschlagen
Wie man alle sach fang klüglich an

LEUDEGAST
So kombt last vns reden davon
Lang daher stehn ist wenig nutz
Meim Sohn dem müfs wir suchen schutz
[*Sie gehn alle ab.*

Kompt LUDOLFF DER FÜRST *mit seinem stab*
Jetzt hat sich das glück wider gwend
Vnd ich hab mein Feind in der hend
Dem will ich jetzund hart gnug sein
Schau was kompt da für gsind herein

Kommen DIETRICH *vnd* ROLLUS *mit* JAHN MOLITOR *in Weibskleidern,*

DIETERICH DER SCHUSTER
Gnediger Herr wir bede hetten
Mit euch etwas heimlichs zu reden
Weil wirs nicht können erfahren sunst
So helfft vns mit eur Zauber kunst
Wir wölln euch gern reichlich lohnen
Ein Müller thut naht bey vns wohnen
Der hat vns zugfügt grose schmach
Zu dem wir haben schwere klag
So lest er sich daheim nit finnen
Vnd dunckt vns in vnser sinnen
Die alte Frau wifs wo er sey

JAHN MOLITOR *in gestalt eines alten Weibs*
Nein ich weifs nit bey meiner treu
So weifs ich auch nicht wer er ist

LUDOLFF DER FÜRST *schüttelt den Kopff, legt jhr den stab auff den Kopff*
Ein recht lose Hur du bist
Ich kenn dich wol du loser dropff
Thu mir den stauchen von dem kopff
So wöll wir balt den Müller finnen

How fatal to my house thou art!
And had I also taken part,
I might have been a prisoner too.
Now must I try what I can do,
My son to rescue from his fate.
Ludolff doth bear us bitter hate,
And if my son is in his power,
His life is hardly worth an hour;
Therefore we may not idle be.

ELEMAUS.
It is a curious history;
And though there's not much hope indeed.
Of counsel there is utmost need,
What course were wisest to pursue.

LEUDEGAST.
Come, let us talk the matter through.
For idling here's a useless thing,
If we my son would succour bring.
[*Exeunt omnes.*

Enter PRINCE LUDOLFF *with his wand.*
Once more hath fortune changed, and I
Have in my hands mine enemy.
Hard measure shall he have: but see!
Who can these common people be?

Enter DIETRICH *and* ROLLUS *with* JOHN MOLITOR *in woman's clothes.*

DIETRICH THE SHOEMAKER.
There is a secret, which we two,
Most gracious sir, would learn of you.
What otherwise we cannot know,
Oh lend thy magic art to shew,
And for thy pains we'll pay thee well.
Near us there doth a miller dwell,
Who both of us hath put to shame,
And 'gainst him we would now reclaim.
But he won't let himself be caught
At home, and somehow we have thought
This old one, where he hides, could shew.

JOHN MOLITOR, *as an old woman.*
Now by my faith it is'nt so,
Nor know I who he is, I vow.

PRINCE LUDOLFF, *shakes his head, and lays his wand upon John's head.*
A regular loose wench art thou!
I know thee well, thou slipp'ry chap!
Old lady, just take off that cap,
The miller then will soon appear.

Er schlecht jhm den stauchen mit den stab vom kopff, so ists der Jahn Molitor,

DIETRICH
Nun kombst nit lebendig von hinnen
Wir wölln dich straffn nach vnsern sinn
Das durch dich nicht werd, als vorhin
Ein guter Mann bracht in vnrath

JAHN MOLITOR
O Herr Zaubrer ich bitt vmb gnad
Eur Kunst ist besser als die mein

LUDOLFF
Was begert jhr denn für ein pein
Das ich sol jhm anlegen fluchfs

ROLLUS
Herr Zaubrer macht jhn zu eim Fuchfs
Das er fort nicht sey so vermessen

JAHN MOLITOR
So wolt ich dir dein Hüner fressen
Vnd noch mehr vbls als jetzo than

DIETERICH
Herr Zauberer wenns der Herr kann
So mach der Herr ein Esel aufs jhm

JOHAN MOLITOR
Mein Närrischer Schuster, so vernim
Wenn du zum Esel machest mich
So wolt ich gar verderben dich
Das in dem Land Küh, Pfert, vnd Schwein
Müsten lauter Esel werffen allein
Der Heut zeucht man nur auff die Drummen
Wo wolstu Narr Leder bekummen
Was gelts ich wolt dirs Esels geben

DIETERICH
Ey so last jhn ein Menschen leben
Vnd straffet jhn nach eurem sinn

LUDOLFF DER FÜRST
Defs selben ich schon willens bin
Im Walt soll er hie bey mir bleiben
Vnd das keine löffley nit treiben
Mein Tochter vnd der Engelbrecht
Soll er auff sie acht haben schlecht
Vnd mir dasselbig zeigen an
Glob mirs balt an dastus wilt than

[*Er globt an, vnd sie gehn alle ab.*

SIDEA *bringt den Jungen Fürsten* ENGELBRECHT *gar übel bekleid, der tregt etliche klötz holtz vnd ein holtz hacken, legt sie nider* SIDEA *throt jhm mit dem stab*

SIDEA
Balt keil du mir das Holtz zu scheiten
Wiltu anderst die streich nit leiden
Du bist ein rechter fauler Hund

He strikes the cap off his head, and it appears to be John Molitor.

DIETRICH.
Never alive go'st thou from here.
We'll punish thee in our own way,
That no good man be led astray
By thee again to his perdition.

JOHN MOLITOR.
I sue for pardon, great magician;
Thy art is better far than mine.

LUDOLFF.
What punishment do you incline
To choose for him, say what's your whim?

ROLLUS.
Magician, make a fox of him,
And so take down his impudence.

JOHN MOLITOR.
Then I will eat your cocks and hens,
And do more harm than now, my man.

DIETRICH.
Mr. Magician, if you can,
Pray let him then a donkey be.

JOHN MOLITOR.
My foolish cobbler, dost thou see,
If thou wilt make an ass of me,
I'll thus contrive to ruin thee.
All thro' the land, cow, pig, and mare.
Shall nought but little asses bear,
Whose hide is only good for drums.
Tell me, whence then thy leather comes?
That thou the donkey art, is plain.

DIETRICH.
Why let him then a man remain.
And punish him as you deem fit.

PRINCE LUDOLFF.
Already I'd determined it.
He shall remain then with me here.
And lest the prince and my Sidea
Some passages of love should try,
He shall on both keep watchful eye,
And tell me all that happens there;
But first he shall obedience swear.

[*He swears. Exeunt omnes.*

Enter SIDEA *with the young Prince* ENGELBRECHT, *very meanly attired. He carries some logs of wood and an axe, and lays them down.* SIDEA *threatens him with her wand.*

SIDEA.
Now cut those logs, and do it quick,
Unless thou wish to feel the stick!
A lazy idle dog thou art!

ENGELBRECHT *fellt jhr zu fuſs, hebt die hend auff*
ENGELBRECHT

Ach ich bin kranck von hertzen grund
Vnd weis mir nicht weiter zu gehn
Noch einiger Arbeit vorzustehn
Dann ich bin aufsgemergelt matt
Mein gantzer Leib kein krafft mehr hat
Besser ists ich werd erschlagen
Dann täglich solchen last zu tragen
Vnd solche schwere arbeit zu than
Ich bitt so hoch ich bitten kan
Erschlaget mich folgents zu todt

SIDEA *sagt zum Leuten*

Wie wol in groſs vnglück vnd noth
Sein Vatter bringt den Vatter mein
Vnd mich sein Fürstlichs Fräuelein
Das wir hetten vrsach zur Rach
Doch wenn ich denck den sachen nach
So ist er auch Fürstlich geborn
Vnd an vns gar nicht schuldig worn
Darumb er, die warheit zu melden
Seins Vatters nit hat zu entgelten
So ist er ein solche Person
Dem ich schön halb nicht feind sein kan
Vnd wenn ich gleich solcher gestalt
Lang bleiben müst in disen Walt
Was hett ich lust vnd freud dabey
Wenn er mir wolt erweisen treu
Vnd mich behalten zu der Eh
Wolt ich jhm helffen aufs noth vnd weh
Ich wils jhm heimlich zeigen an
                 [*Sie geht zu ihm.*
Mein Engelbrecht was wolstu than
Wenn ich dir deiner Dienstbarkeit
Zu wegen brecht jetzt ein freyheit
Vnd dich als dann nem zu der Eh

ENGELBRECHT *fellt nider zu fuſs*

Ach schweigt, verstürtzt ich gar vergeh
All lebendig Götter diser Erden
Können nicht machen das war mög werden
Wenn aber das war werden künd
Mein sach zum aller besten stünd
Ja ich wolt mich eur Lieb ergeben
Zu dienst mit Leib vnd auch Leben
Vnd euch zu einer Fürstin machen

SIDEA

Dörfft ich dir trauen in den sachen

ENGELBRECHT *falls at her feet, and raises his hands.*
ENGELBRECHT.

Alas! I am so sick at heart,
Can hardly drag along my feet,
My task appointed to complete.
For I am tired out at length,
Nor has my body any strength.
'Twere better far I murder'd were,
Than every day such burdens bear,
And such hard work do evermore.
Most earnestly I thee implore,
That thou at once wilt strike me dead!

SIDEA, *ad spectatores.*

Although his father mine hath led
Into sore trouble and distress,
And me his daughter, a princess,
That he our vengeance might expect,
Yet when I on the thing reflect,
He also is a prince's son,
And to ourselves no ill hath done,
And should not therefore, truth to say,
Be forced his father's debt to pay.
And then such beauty too hath he,
I could not be his enemy;
And if I long such life must lead
Here in the forest, why indeed,
What happiness and joy to me,
If he would true and faithful be,
And take me as his wedded wife!
I'd help him out of all this strife.
My thought I'll tell him secretly.-
                 [*She walks up to him.*
My Engelbrecht, how would it be
If I, thy service to reward,
To thee thy freedom would accord,
And then thee for my husband take?

ENGELBRECHT, *falls at her feet.*

Oh speak not, or my heart will break,
For all the gods that rule below,
Could never make it happen so;
But could it really so befall,
My fortunes then stood best of all;
I would to thee my service give,
And ever love thee while I live;
Thou shouldst a royal station grace.

SIDEA.

If I my trust in thee may place,

Vnd du wilt dem so kommen nach
Mir mit der Hand vnd Mund zusag
So will ich ferners reden mit dir
ENGELBRECHT
Ja dasselb solt jhr trauen mir
Vnd jhr solt auch mein Gemahl sein
> [*Sie geben die hend aneinander*

SIDEA
Bistu denn mein
ENGELBRECHT
Ja
SIDEA
So bleib ich dein
Die Götter bleiben mit vns beyden
Nun soll vns nichts als der todt scheiden
Vnd das du meinen ernst auch spürst
Zih ich mit dir wo du mich hinführst

Sie trucken einander, kompt RUNCIFALL DER TEUFFEL

Sidea disen deinen anschlag
Ich deinem Vatter strachs ansag
Dann es will sich gar nicht gebürn
Das du dich lest von hinnen führn

SIDEA *nimbt jhrn stab schlegt jhn mit auffs maul, der deuter könn nicht reden, vnd geht traurig ab, alsdan spricht sie*

Also kan vns der Geist zu schaden
Bey meinem Vatter nicht verrahten
So können wir all bede sand
Die weil kommen aufs disem Land
> [*Sie gehn ab*

Kompt LUDOLFF DER FÜRST *mit* JAHN MOLITOR, *ist gar zornig schlegt den Jahnnen mit dem stab auff den kopff*

Wo ist Sidea sag mir balt
JAHN MOLITOR
Ich weis nit ist sie nit im Walt
So ist sie bey dem Engelbrecht
LUDOLFF
Bistu nicht mein Leibeigner Knecht
Der achtung auff sie haben sol
JAHN MOLITOR
Ja, ja, dasselbig weis ich wol
Aber Gnediger Herr jhr sein zwen
Vnd sagn mir nicht wo sie hin gehn
Drumb weis ich gar nit wu sie sein
LUDOLFF
Das sol dir kosten das leben dein
Drumb zih hin vnd such wo sie sind

And thou wilt aid in my intent,
And with both hand and mouth consent,
I will hold further talk with thee.
ENGELBRECHT.
Thou mayst place all thy trust in me,
And thou as consort soon be mine.
> [*They give their hands to each other.*

SIDEA.
Art thou then mine?
ENGELBRECHT.
Yes.
SIDEA.
Then I'm thine.
O may the gods desert us never!
Hence nought but death shall us dissever!
To prove that 'tis my will indeed,
I'll follow thee where'er thou lead.

They embrace each other. Enter RUNCIFALL THE DEVIL.

Sidea, to thy father straight
I go, and this thy plan relate.
For most unseemly 't will appear,
If thou art led away from here.

SIDEA *takes her wand, strikes him with it on the mouth. He makes signs that he cannot speak, and walks away melancholy.*

Now can he us to our dismay
No longer to my sire betray;
But we together, hand in hand,
May for the present leave the land.
> [*Exeunt.*

Enter LUDOLFF THE PRINCE, *with* JOHN MOLITOR. *He is very angry, and strikes John on the head with his staff.*

Now tell me quickly, where's Sidea.
JOHN MOLITOR.
I know not, but if she's not here,
She's sure with Engelbrecht to be.
LUDOLFF.
Now art thou not a slave to me,
Who had to keep them both in view?
JOHN MOLITOR.
Oh yes, I know, that's very true:
But then, my Lord, they're two, you see,
And where they go, they tell not me.
Therefore I know not where they be.
LUDOLFF.
That, rogue, shall cost thy life to thee.
But go at once, seek far and wide,

Vnd wirstu sie nit bringen gschwind
So schlag ich dir ab deinen grint
  [*Jahn Molitor kratzt sich im kopff vnd gehn ab.*

ACTUS QUARTUS.

Kommen ENGELBRECHT *vnd* SIDEA
  (SIDEA)
Ich hoff wir solln den Vatter mein
Nunmehr meinsts theils entrunnen sein
Jedoch bin ich so müd von gehn
Wenn ich michs gleich wolt vnterstehn
Vnd leg mir leib vnd leben dran
Jedoch nit weiters ich gehn kan
Ach weh wer ich daheimen blieben
Die brinnet Lieb hat mich getrieben
Das ich mich gab in solch gefehr
  ENGELBRECHT
Ach last euch sein die sach nit schwer
Wann jhr nicht weiters künd zu fufs
Man euch zu Kutschen führen mufs
Wart mein alhie bifs ich zurück
Euch wider ein Kutschen raufs schick
Mit Knechten die sollen euch holn
  SIDEA
Von meim Vatter hab ich mich gstoln
Meint jhr vnd das er es vnderlafs
Mir nicht nach forsch auff alle strafs
Vnd wenn er mich hie finden thet
Ich euch das letzt mal gsehen hett
Vnd müst sterben vor seim angsicht
  ENGELBRECHT
Ey das wölln ja die Götter nicht
Das euch eur Vatter nicht mehr find
Jr auff den Baum nauff sitzen künd
Darunder laufft er sechsmal für
Eh vnd wann er euch da aufs spür
Darzu bleibt jhr alhie nit lang
  SIDEA
Ach wie ist mir so angst vnd bang
Dann ich fürcht jhr vergesset mein
  ENGELBRECHT
Ach hertz Lieb last das sorgen sein
Ich verheifs euch mein treu vnd ehr
Die vergifs ich mein tag nit mehr
    [*Er hebt sie auff den Baum, sie sagt*
  (SIDEA)
Ich hoff ich will da sicher sein
Doch bitt ich euch vergest nit mein

If soon I hear not where they bide,
I'll lay my stick about thy hide.
  [*John Molitor scratches his head. Exeunt.*

ACT IV.

Enter ENGELBRECHT *and* SIDEA.
  SIDEA.
I hope that now all danger's past,
And father we've escaped at last.
For if I the attempt would make,
And life and limb thereon would stake,
So weary am I, that I know,
I could not one step further go.
Oh, that I had remained at home!
But burning love forced me to roam,
And this fatigue and danger share.
  ENGELBRECHT.
Oh yield not thou to such despair!
For if to walk thou art too weak,
Why then I must a carriage seek;
Till I return, wait here for me,
And I'll a carriage send to thee,
And what attendants thou require.
  SIDEA.
'Twas secretly I left my sire;
Dost think he ever will forbear
To have me searched for everywhere?
And if perchance he find me here,
I ne'er again should see thee, dear;
His presence would prove death to me.
  ENGELBRECHT.
Be sure, that's not the god's decree.
But that his search may fruitless be,
Perhaps you'd better climb this tree.
Six times he may run round, and more,
Ere he thy hiding-place explore.
Besides, thou needst not long remain.
  SIDEA.
My fears I can no more restrain,
Lest thou forget that I am there.
  ENGELBRECHT.
Oh dearest lay aside thy care.
My word of honor will I give,
I'll not forget thee while I live.
        [*He assists her to climb the tree.*
  SIDEA.
I hope in safety I shall be,
But do entreat, forget not me.

COMEDY OF THE BEAUTIFUL SIDEA.

ENGELBRECHT
Ey was sol das vergessens vil
Als balt ich euch da holen wil
        [Er geht ab.
Die Jungfrau sitzt auff den Baum, vnd sagt kleglich
Ach solt mich der Fürst setzen an
Dem ich hab so vil guts gethan
So wolt ich jetzt vnd all mein tag
Vber jhn schreyen straff vnd rach
Kompt FINELIA, *des Schusters Weib, will wasser holn*
      tregt ein Krug
Alhie in dieser armen Stadt
Es kein guten trinck Brunnen hat
Müssen das trinck wasser weit holn
Mein Mann mir daheim hat befohln
Ich solt eillend ein wasser bringen
Wasser macht weder Tantzen noch springen
Darumb ich bath vnd haben wolt
Das er ein Bier doch kauffen solt
So ist der Narr so karck vnd gnau
    [Sie geht zum Brunnen als woll sie eins schöpffen
Ey, ey, jetzund ich mich beschau
Aufs dem schatten in dem Brunnen
    [Sie wirfft den Krug nider, schwantzt auff der
        Brucken rumb
Meins gleichen nicht allhie wird gfunnen
Ein aufsbündig schön Creatur
Was hab ich mich geziehen nur
Das ich hab gnommen den Pechpatzen
Den hefslichen vngschaffnen Fratzen
Nun will ich bey jhm nicht mehr leben
Sonder mich strachs gen Hof begeben
        [Sie geht ab.
ELA *die Bauern Magd geht ein mit einem geschirr Wasser*
zuholen, kommt zum Brunnen will einschöpffen sieht den
        schatten
Nicht gnug kan ich verwundern mich
Jetzt so ich meinen schatten sich
Befind ich wie ich so schön bin
Ey ey wo hab ich nur dacht hin
Das ich vermeint den Müller zu nemen
Ich wolt michs in mein hertz nein schemen
Ob ich schon hab ein Eyssen abgrendt
Jedoch vil Leut in der Welt sendt
Die es nicht wissen oder schmecken
Vnd ich solt mich zu jhm verstecken
O nein ich mag den Müller nimmer
Ich will gehn Hof ins Frauenzimmer
    [Sie wirfft jhr Gefäfs auch hin, vnd geht gar
        stoltz ab.

ENGELBRECHT.
Why say so much about forget?
Ere long, we shall again have met.
        [Exit.
The maiden sits down in the tree, and says in a melancholy tone:
Ah if the prince should me betray,
And thus my services repay,
Then would I now, and evermore.
Dire vengeance on his head implore.
Enter FINELIA, *the shoemakers wife, carrying a pitcher*
      to fetch water.
In all this town the water's bad;
None fit for drinking to be had;
We fetch it from a distant spring.
I now must for my husband bring
Some in a hurry, water can
Excite to dance no mortal man,
And therefore I did beg and pray
The fool would buy some beer to-day;
But no, — he loves too well his pelf.
        [She goes to the spring to draw water.
Aye! Now that I behold myself
There in my image, all around
My like is nowhere to be found.
    [She throws down the pitcher, and walks coquettishly
        about the platform round the well.
A creature most exceeding fair!
Oh what a blunder made I there,
When I took up that cobbler wight,
An awful, awkward, ugly, fright!
I'll live with him no more, I swear,
But straight unto the court repair.
        [Exit.
Enter ELA, *the peasant's daughter, with a pitcher to fetch*
water. She goes to the well, and is about to draw some,
        when she sees the image.
My wonder's more than I can tell!
For now I view my image well,
I see that I am fair indeed;
Ah, what could ever me mislead
To think I could the miller take?
My heart for very shame doth ache.
Although I out of jail have got,
Yet many men, who know it not,
Are in the world, — that were a whim,
To hide myself with such as him!
Oh no, he'll never do for me;
A grand court-lady will I be.
    [She also throws down her pitcher, and walks
        haughtily away.

COMEDY OF THE BEAUTIFUL SIDEA.

JAHN MOLITOR *geht ein*
Mein Herr thut grausam schwermen vnd fluchen
Ich soll sein Tochter wider suchen
Weil ich nicht recht auff sie thet sehen
Thet mich lestern schenden vnd schmehen
Ja er thet mirs vnters gsicht sagen
Find ichs nicht, wolt er mich erschlagen
Ich bin den gantzen Walt durchloffen
Hab nichts gefressen noch gesoffen
Vnd brennd so mechtig heiſs die Sunnen
Schau da vnten hats ein schön Brunnen
Da will ich mich ein wenig laben,
　　[*Er geht zum Brunnen sicht nein, steht wider auff,*
　　　　sicht auff den Baum.
Vor dem schatten bin ich erschrocken
Wie tregt der Baum die schönsten Docken
Ach wie der aller glücklichst Brunnen
Weil ich da hab die Jungkfrau gfunnen
Nun will ich gehn sagen meim Herrn
Der wird sie gar bald holn wern
　　　　　　　　　　[*Jahn geht ab.*
SIDEA *sagt auff dem Baumen kleglich*
Ach wehe wo soll ich nun hinauſs
Mein hertzliebster bleibt zu lang aufs
Vnd ich bin durch deſs Wassers schatten
Dem Jahn Molitor schon verrahten
Vnd er wirds sagen dem Vatter mein
Ach web des jammers vnd der pein
Nun steh ich hie in neuer gfahr
Engelbrecht hat mein vergessen gar
Ach jammer weh wo soll ich hin
Das aller elendst Mensch ich bin
Das nicht auff dieser Welt kan leben
Ach wie thu ich in hertzleid schweben
O jammer weh ich hör schon Leut
DIETERICH DER SCHUSTER *geht ein vnd spricht*
Ich weiſs nicht was es doch bedeut
Meiner Frauen hab ich befohln
Das sie mir soll ein Wasser holn,
So kompt sie heimb so vnbesunnen
Sagt sie hab gsehen in den Brunnen
Wo sie sey so ein schönes Weib
Darumb sie nicht mehr bey mir bleib,
Sonder will kommen ins Frauenzimmer
So kan ich den durst leiden nimmer
Denn will ich nicht vor durst versincken
Muſs ich mir selbst holen zu Trincken
Darneben will ich auch beschauen
Was so närrisch hab gmacht mein Frauen
　　[*Er geht zum Brunnen schöpfft Wasser.*

Enter JOHN MOLITOR.
My master kicks up such a rout,
Swears I must find his daughter out;
'Cause I don't watch her like her nurse.
He must forsooth, storm, swear, and curse.
Indeed he to my face hath said,
If she's not found, he'll strike me dead.
I the whole forest through have beat,
And nothing had to drink or eat.
And 'tis so hot in such a sun;
Down there I see some water run.
I will refresh me with a draught.
　　[*He goes to the spring, looks into it, gets up again*
　　　　and looks up into the tree.
The shadow almost frightened me!
A pretty head-dress for a tree!
Most fortunate of springs art thou!
Through thee I've found the maiden now.
I'll go at once, my master tell,
And he'll soon fetch her from the well.
　　　　　　　　　　[*Exit.*
SIDEA *in the tree, says in a melancholy tone:*
Alas! Shall I now fly or stay?
Too long my love remains away!
The image that the water made,
Me to the miller has betrayed.
To tell my father would he go;
Alas! oh misery and woe!
Now am I in new danger here,
Forgotten by my love so dear:
Alas! Oh whither shall I hie?
Most wretched of all mortals I!
But death must soon my troubles cure,
Such bitter anguish I endure!
Oh misery! I hear them near!
　　Enter DIETRICH, THE SHOEMAKER.
What it all means, I've no idea!
To-day I told my wife to bring
Some water for me from the spring;
And ever since she has returned,
She's lost her wits, and says she's learned,
Through her fair image in the well,
She's far too beautiful to dwell
With me, but will to court repair.
This thirst I can no longer bear;
And as for thirst I would not sink,
Some water I will fetch to drink:
And also look into the pool,
To see what's made her such a fool.
　　　　[*Goes to the well to draw water.*

4

Der Brunnen giebt von sich ein schein
Ein schönes Weibsbild mufs da sein
Vnd hie über den Brunnen sitzen
       [*Er siecht sich umb, ersicht die Sidea*
Ja ich habs schon ersehen jetzen
Ach zarte Jungfrau saget mir
Was machet auff dem Baumen jhr
Wem steht jhr zu wo kompt jhr her,

      SIDEA *hebt die Händ auff*

Ach guter Freund ich bitt euch sehr
Jhr wollet mir doch helffen wider
Das ich komb von dem Baum hernider
Vnd beherbrigt mich nur zwen tag
Das ich ein weng aufsruhen mag
Vnd entgeh meim Feind aufs den henden
Helfft jhr mir das vnglück abwenden
Ich will euch geben reichen lohn,

DIETERICH DER SCHUSTER *hebt sie von dem Baumen*

Ey ja das will ich gerne thon
Jedoch es geht bey mir schlecht zu,

        SIDEA

Drinnen ich euch als sagen thu,
Wie ich bin leider kommen her
Dann ich fürcht mich sehr das ich wer
Gefangen wenn ich lang hie stehe
So kem ich in jammer vnd wehe
       [*Sie gehn mit einander ab.*

    Kompt LUDOLFF DER FÜRST

Allhie wart ich auff meinen Geist
Wenn mir der nicht mein Tochter weist
So ists mit dem Müllner verlorn
Vnd sey jhm dann ein Eyd geschworn
Er mufs sterben von meiner hand

Jetzt macht LUDOLFF *mit seinem Stab ein kreifs, so springt* RUNCIFALL *heraufs,*

      LUDOLFF

Runcifall mach du mir bekannt
Wo ist mein Tochter kommen hin
Auff dich ich hart erzörnet bin
Das du sie hast glassen davon
Vnd mir solches nicht zeiget an
  [*Runcifall deut er hab kein schuld daran, er künne nicht reden,*
      LUDOLFF
Wie stellst du dich, bald red mit mir,
      [*Runcifall deut er könns nicht*

The water does a form reflect;
A handsome woman, I expect,
Is sitting somewhere up on high.
       [*He looks round and sees Sidea.*
Yes, — I already her espy.
Ah, gentle lady, say to me,
What you are doing in the tree?
Whom you belong to, whence you came?

      SIDEA *raising her hands.*

Oh friend, your kindness would I claim,
And beg that you your aid will lend,
To help me from the tree descend,
For two days yield me an asyle,
Where I myself may rest awhile,
And also may escape my foe.
If thus you help avert the blow,
A rich reward I'll give to you.

DIETRICH, THE SHOEMAKER, *helps her down from the tree.*

Oh yes, all that I'll gladly do;
My house though is a wretched place.
        SIDEA.
When there, I'll tell you all my case,
How I unhappily came here;
For if I tarry long, I fear,
I may be taken, which to me
Would bring much grief and misery.
       [*Exeunt together.*

    Enter PRINCE LUDOLFF.

My spirit I'm expecting here.
Should he not shew me my Sidea,
The miller's a lost man, for now
I've sworn to him a solemn vow,
That he by my own hand shall die.

LUDOLFF *makes a circle with his wand.* RUNCIFALL *springs out of it.*

      LUDOLFF.

Now Runcifall, resolved am I
To learn where my Sidea may be.
And know I'm very wrath with thee,
That thou hast let her run away,
And not a word to me didst say.
  [*Runcifall intimates by signs that that is not his fault, as he cannot speak.*
      LUDOLFF.
What mean those gestures? Speak to me.
      [*Runcifall makes signs that he cannot speak.*

COMEDY OF THE BEAUTIFUL SIDEA.

LUDOLFF
Er ist verzaubert das merck ich schir,
 [*Er schlegt den Teuffel mit dem stab auffs maul.*
RUNCIFALL
Dein Tochter hat den Fürsten gnommen
Vnd ich bin eben darzu kommen
Vnd hab dir dasselb wöllen sagen
So hat sie mich auffs maul geschlagen
Das mir mein Zung verstummen thet
Vnd hab seither kein Wort mehr gredt.
Wie hab ich dirs dann sagen können
Alsdann theten sie dir endrinnen
Vnd ziehen zu seim Vatter hin,
 LUDOLFF *sagt kleglich*
Nun ich erst gar verdorben bin
Find sie mein Jahn Molitor nit
So hat mein hertz nimmer kein frid

In dem gehet JAHN MOLITOR *ein, hat ein Drümmelein vnd Pfeiffen, er pfeifft, der Teuffel hebt an zu Tantzen,*

LUDOLFFUS
Jahn weil du Pfeiffst vnd lustig bist
So sag mir wo mein Tochter ist
 JAHN
Eur Tochter,
 [*Er Pfeifft wider vnd Drummelt*
LUDOLFF
Ja meine Tochter wo ist sie
 JAHN MOLITOR
Ich hab gar wol gesehen die
 [*Jahn Pfeifft vnd Drummelt wider, so tantzt allweg der Teuffel,*
LUDOLFF
Wo hastu sie gsehen zeig an
 JAHN MOLITOR
Ich sah sie
 [*Er Pfeifft wieder, dann sagt er*
auff eim Baumen stahn
 LUDOLFF *sagt zornig*
Hör auff deins Pfeiffens, sag darfür
Von meiner lieben Tochter mir
 [*Jahn Pfeifft vnnd Drummelt, der Teuffel Tantzt, lauffen etliche Teuffel raufs, die alle Tantzen, endtlich hört Jahn Molitor auff,*
LUDOLFF
Ich glaub du seyst gar töricht worn
Dafs du thust so grausam rumorn
Jhr Geister ziecht eurs wegs bald fort
Vnd du sag mir bald mit eim wort
Wo du mein Tochter gsehen hast

LUDOLFF.
He is enchanted, that I see.
 [*He strikes the devil on the mouth with his wand.*
RUNCIFALL.
Thy daughter with the prince would fly.
Just at that minute, up popped I.
And as I wished to let thee know,
She gave me on the mouth a blow,
Which made me dumb, nor any word
Since then hath from my mouth been heard.
How could I then tell thee indeed?
On which they fled with utmost speed,
And hurried towards his father's seat.
 LUDOLFF, *says piteously.*
Oh now my ruin is complete!
And should the miller's search prove vain,
My heart will ne'er know peace again.

Enter JOHN MOLITOR *with a little drum and a whistle. He whistles, and the devil begins to dance.*

LUDOLFF.
John, as you whistle and are gay.
Where is my daughter, prythee say?
 JOHN MOLITOR.
Your daughter, —
 [*he whistles and drums again.*
LUDOLFF.
 Yes, pray tell me, do.
 JOHN MOLITOR.
That I have seen her is most true.
 [*John whistles and drums again, and the devil continues to dance.*
LUDOLFF.
Where have you seen her? — tell it me.
 JOHN MOLITOR.
I saw her —
 [*whistling again*
 standing on a tree.
 LUDOLFF, *angrily.*
Now cease that whistling! Do you hear?
And tell me of my daughter dear.
 [*John whistles and drums. The devil dances. Other devils appear, who all dance too. At last John leaves off.*
LUDOLFF.
You must have lost your wits, 'tis clear,
To kick up such a shindy here.
Ye spirits, take yourselves away.
But, you sir, in a word, I pray,
Where did you see my daughter now?

<table>
<tr><td>

JAHN MOLITOR

Sie sitzt dort auff eins Baumens ast
Zu allernechsten bey dem Brunnen
Vnd weil ich sie hab wider gfunnen
Bin ich erfreuet worden hoch
Kompt her wir wollens finden noch
Ich zwar hett sie gesehen nit
Der schattn im Brunnen sie verrieht
Als ich eben da trincken wolt

LUDOLFF

Ach das ichs wider kriegen solt
Drumb geh bald fort thu dich nicht bsinnen
Hilff mir wider mein Tochter finnen

[*Sie gehn ab.*

Kompt DIETERICH DER SCHUSTER *mit seiner Frauen,*

DIETERICH

Finelia mein sag doch mir
Was hastu eingebildet dir
Das du mir kein gut mehr wilt than

FINELIA

Mich reuts das ich dich gnommen han
Vnd darzu das ich bey dir bleib
Ich bin ein herrlichs schönes Weib
Dergleich keine ist in der Statt

DIETERICH

Sag wer dir solchs gesaget hat
Der hat dich übel überredt

FINELIA

Der widerschein mirs sagen thet
Welchen ich durch den schein der Sunnen
Hab aufs dem Wasser in dem Brunnen
Besser gesehen als zuvor nie

DIETERICH

So komb mit mir zum Brunnen, vnd sih
Ob du nicht selbst betrogen worn

FINELIA *geht mit jhm zum Brunnen, sicht hinein*

Mein vorige gstalt hab ich verlorn
Also wie ich jetzunder sich
Kan ich gar nicht verwechfsln mich
Vnd ich bin dir kaum gut genug
Aber da ich zerwarff den Krug
Da wart ich also zart vnd schön
Wie die Jungkfrauen zu Hof hergehn
Defsmal daucht ich mich dir zu gut

DIETERICH

Mein Finelia sey gemuht
Schau dorten dritt ein Jungkfrau rein
Die gab in Brunnen diesen schein

</td><td>

JOHN MOLITOR.

Sitting aloft there on a bough.
The tree is very near the water,
And just because I found your daughter,
I'm now in such a merry cue;
You'll find her still, if you come too.
It's true, I have not seen the maid;
She through her image was betrayed,
As I my thirst prepared to quench.

LUDOLFF.

Oh, that I could but catch the wench!
So go at once, in thinking waste
No time, till we've my daughter traced.

[*Exeunt.*

Enter DIETRICH, THE SHOEMAKER, *with his wife.*

DIETRICH.

Finelia mine, explain to me,
What fancy has come over thee,
That thou no service do me more?

FINELIA.

That I e'er took thee, I deplore,
And also that I live with thee;
I am so beautiful to see,
My like's not in the town, I know.

DIETRICH.

Tell me, who was it told thee so?
His counsel was n't very good.

FINELIA.

'Twas the reflection. Where I stood,
The sunbeams on the water fell,
And shewed my image in the well.
I'd never seen it so before.

DIETRICH.

Then come with me, and see once more
Whether it was not a delusion.

FINELIA *goes to the well, and looks into it.*

My beauty's gone, to my confusion!
And now I see myself so plain.
I can't mistake myself again.
For thee I'm hardly good enough;
But when the pitcher, in a huff,
I threw away, I was, methought,
As fair as ladies of the Court.
And so I seem'd for thee too good.

DIETRICH.

Finelia mine, now if you would
Look there, a maiden's coming here,
Who caused the image to appear;

</td></tr>
</table>

COMEDY OF THE BEAUTIFUL SIDEA.

Die ich fand sitzen auff dem Baum
Dein schön war ein erdichter traum
Dann dein schön taug zu der gar nit
    SIDEA *geht ein*
Mein Meister Schuster es ist mein bitt
Jhr wolt euch willig lassen finnen
Mir eurs Weibs kleider vergünnen
Das ichs anleg auff der Strassen
Vnd wolt sie mit mir gehn lassen
Das sie trag meine kleider mir
Reichlich will ichs belohnen jhr
Dann ich je nicht weiter beger
Als das ans Fürsten Hof ich wer
Ich will sie balt schicken zurück
    DIETERICH
Das als soll sein, darzu mit glück
Wölln euch die Götter beleiten
Vnd das wir mit bessern freüden
Balt wider zammen kommen mügen
Das wöllen alle Götter füegen
                [*Sie gehn alle ab.*

Kompt LUDOLFF DER FÜRST *mit* JAHN MOLITOR
    JAHN
Auff diesem Baum ob diesen Brunnen
Hab ich eur Gnaden Tochter gfunnen
Sie ist aber jetzt nicht mehr do.
    LUDOLFF DER FÜRST
Deins findensts bin ich so nicht fro
Such sie wo sie wird sein hinkommen
Du solst sie haben mit dir gnommen
Vnd sie mit dir heim haben bracht
    JAHN MOLITOR
Vor freud hab ich daran nicht dacht
Vermeint wenn eur Gnad selbst kemen
Vnd die Jungkfraw vom Baum nemen
So wer es vil ein grössre freud

    LUDOLFF *schlegt jhn mit den stab*
Was ists aber jetzt für ein Leit
Du vnbesunner grober knopff
Du bist ein einfeltiger tropff
Vnd gar ein einfeltiges Kalb
Was du solst thun thustu nicht halb
Das mustu zahlen mit der häut

    RUNCIFALL DER TEUFFEL *laufft ein*
Es ist vergebens was jhr streit
Ich bin jhr allenthalb nach zogen
Wir sind durch list von jhr betrogen

I found her sitting on the tree.
Thy beauty was all fantasy;
It can't at all with hers compare.
    Enter SIDEA.
Oh Mister cobbler, might I dare
Ask your permission to propose,
Your wife should lend me all her clothes,
To wear them on the public way,
And also that she with me stay
To bear my clothes for me, which aid
Shall liberally be repaid.
For nothing I desire indeed
More than to reach the court with speed;
I soon will send her back to you.
    DIETRICH.
It shall be so. With fortune too
May all the gods thy steps attend,
And may they grant that in the end,
We meet once more, and days enjoy
Of happiness without alloy!
                [*Exeunt omnes.*

Enter PRINCE LUDOLFF *with* JOHN MOLITOR.
    JOHN MOLITOR.
Upon this tree, above the water
It was, I found your Grace's daughter.
But she's no longer there, I see.
    PRINCE LUDOLFF.
Your finding's not much gain to me.
Learn where she's gone to, if you can;
You should have ta'en her with you, man,
And home unto her father led.
    JOHN MOLITOR.
That never came into my head
For joy; I thought that if should be,
Your Grace should fetch her from the tree.
It would be a much greater pleasure.

    LUDOLFF, *striking him with his wand.*
But now a trouble without measure,
Thou thoughtless stupid blockhead, thou!
Thou art a simpleton, I vow,
Oh silliest of silly calves!
What thou must do, ne'er do by halves;
For that thou payest with thy hide.

    RUNCIFALL THE DEVIL *runs in.*
It's useless now to storm and chide.
For everywhere I've sought thy child;
We all by her have been beguiled.

Sie zicht zum Fürsten von Wiltau
Da wird sie defs Engelbrechts Frau
Darumb last eur nachfolgen bleiben

LUDOLFF

Mein vnglück ist nicht zu beschreiben
Jetzt komb ich in mehr leids vnd schaden
Ich bin verkaufft vnd auch verrahten
Weis nicht wie ich mein sach anfang
Darumb last vns nicht warten lang
Sondern hinein gehn in mein höln
Allda wir still abreden wölln
Wie ich mög meine sach anstelln

[*Abgang jhr aller.*

ACTUS QUINTUS.

Kompt LEUDEGAST DER FÜRST INN DER WILTAU *mit* FRANCISCO *vnd* ELEMAO *vnd sagt kleglich*
(LEUDEGAST)

Ach wie soll ich meim hertzleid thon
Das Engelbrecht mein einiger Sohn
In seiner schrecklichen Gefengknufs
So lang auffgehalten werden mufs
Wir haben vil nach jhm aufsgsand
Aber es findet jhn niemand
Das ich besorg er sey schon gstorben
Nun hab ich jhm ein Weib erworben
Nemlich defs Königs Tochter aufs Poln
Die wir schon haben her lassen holn
Die wartet seiner mit verlangen
Vnd als sie hört das er ist gfangen
Will sie sich nimmer trösten lahn
Sie auch nicht mehr erhalten kan
Sie will morgen wider heimb fahrn

FRANCISCUS

Wir sollen keinen fleifs nicht sparn
Sonder dran wenden was wir künnen
Bifs wir den Jungen Fürsten finnen
Auch soll man bey nacht vnd bey tag
Mit Kriegsmacht Ludolff folgen nach
Vnd jhn erschlagen wie ein Hund
Dann er feirt doch zu keiner stund
Vns vnd dem Land schaden zu thon

ELEMAUS

Wöll wir eur Fürstlich Gnaden Sohn
Bringen aufs defs Ludolffen Henden
Müfs wir ein groses Heer aufssenden
Vnd jhm den mit gwalt tringen ab

To Wiltau's prince thy daughter sped,
There with young Engelbrecht to wed;
To cease pursuit were therefore well.

LUDOLFF.

My fate is worse than words can tell!
On me new trials now are laid.
I've been deceived! I've been betrayed!
I do not know what course to choose!
'Tis better then no time to lose,
But to my cave at once repair,
And we can then determine there,
How best to manage the affair.

[*Exeunt omnes.*

ACT V.

Enter LEUDEGAST, PRINCE OF WILTAU, *with* FRANCISCUS *and* ELEMAUS.

LEUDEGAST, *in a piteous tone.*

What words can all my anguish say,
That Engelbrecht remains away!
My only son, — so long remains,
And wears a wretched captive's chains!
We've sent to search the country round,
But yet he's nowhere to be found,
That I'm afraid he must have died.
Now I have found for him a bride:
The daughter she of Poland's king,
Whom messengers I sent to bring.
With longing waits she his return;
And when she does his story learn,
No consolation will accept,
Nor let herself be longer kept.
To-morrow will she homewards wend.

FRANCISCUS.

Now all our efforts will we spend,
Nor any trouble will we spare,
Until again the Prince is there.
By day and night we will pursue
This Ludolff, with our forces too,
And like a dog, this prince we'll kill.
For if he can but do us ill,
He knows no rest until it's done.

ELEMAUS.

We'll get your Princely Grace's son
Out of this Ludolff's hands, although
A mighty host must strike the blow,
And carry him by force away.

COMEDY OF THE BEAUTIFUL SIDEA.

Mich dunckt wie ich vernommen hab
Das sich Leut finden vor der Thür
            LEUDEGAST
Was draussen ist das lafs als für
Vielleicht kompt vns ein Bottschaft her
Von meinem Sohn ohn als gefehr

ELEMAUS *thut auff, so gehet* ENGELBRECHT *gar übel zerrissen ein,* LEUDEGAST DER FÜRST *stehet auff, gehet jhm entgegen,*

           (LEUDEGAST)
Ach secht ach weh was soll wir thon
Ach sey vns willkomm lieber Sohn
Ach solstu sein ein Fürst geborn
Vnd so gar übl sein ghalten worn
Ach wo bistu blieben die zeit
Geht eylend vnd bringt jhm ein Kleid
Neu Schu vnd auch ein Finger Ring
Vnd seyt mit mir all guter ding
Du aber sag wie ist dirs gangen
           ENGELBRECHT
Ludolff der Fürst hat mich gefangen
Durch den kam ich in grofs vnruh
Must jhm holtz genug tragen zu
Vnd auch dasselb schneiden vnd spalten
Vnd thet mich auch gar übel halten
Vnd seiner Tochter übergeben
Die mir balt gnommen hett das leben
Dann thet sie sich über mich armen
Halb todt krancken Menschen erbarmen
Thet mir forthin nicht mehr so wehe
Die hat mich gnommen zu der Ehe
Ist mit mir zogen bifs nahend her
Als sie kund nicht fort kommen mehr
Hab ich sie abwegs von der Strassen
Auff einen Baumen steigen lassen
Auff einer Kutschen her zuholn
Drumb Herr Vatter es werd befohln
Das man Sidea führt hie her

[*Jetzt kommen die Räht bringen jhm kleider legen jhn an,*

           LEUDEGAST
Mein lieber Sohn was fehlt dir mehr
Dann alles was du thust begern
Das woll wir dich gnedig gewern
Auch theten wir dir vmbschauen
Nach der aller schönsten Jungkfrauen
Die solstu nemen zu eim Weib
Derhalb mein Sohn fort bey vns bleib
Vnd gib dich nicht wie vor in gfehr
Jhr Herrn bringt doch die Jungkfrau her

Unless my ear deceives me, they
Are persons at the door I hear.
           LEUDEGAST.
Whoe'er they be, they may appear.
Perhaps they bring the news to me,
My son's regained his liberty.

ELEMAUS *opens the door, and* ENGELBRECHT *enters very shabbily dressed.* PRINCE LEUDEGAST *rises, and goes to meet him.*

           LEUDEGAST.
Oh see! alas! What must be done?
Oh! welcome home beloved son!
Alas, that thou a prince by right
Should e'er return in such a plight!
Where didst thou of thy time dispose?
Go quick, and fetch him other clothes,
New shoes, and eke a ring. Ye may
Rejoice with me my friends to-day.
But tell me, how's it gone with thee?
           ENGELBRECHT.
Ludolff, the Prince, has taken me.
Through him I came to grief and care.
And logs enough too had to bear,
Must cut and split them at his will.
He treated me extremely ill,
And gave me over to Sidea.
At first I for my life did fear;
But soon she did commiserate
My wretched and half-dying state;
No longer would she give me pain;
As husband would she me have ta'en:
Has walked with me, until to-day,
Not far from here, her strength gave way.
I led her from the road aside,
And helped her up a tree to hide,
Until a carriage could be got.
And therefore, Sire, deny me not,
But orders give to fetch her here.

[*The counsellors return with clothes which they put on Engelbrecht.*

           LEUDEGAST.
Wouldst thou aught else, o son, most dear?
For all thy wish, whate'er it be,
We graciously will grant to thee.
We've also look'd around to find
The fairest of all womankind,
Whom thou, my son, as wife shalt take,
And stay with us for her dear sake,
And keep thyself from danger clear.
But now, sirs, bring the lady here,

COMEDY OF THE BEAUTIFUL SIDEA.

Die hie schon lang gewartet dein
Die wird auch hoch erfreuet sein

Elemaus geht ab, tregt die Kleider ab, kompt wider bringt Juliam die Jungkfrau

(ELEMAUS)
Gnediger Fürst ich bring die Jungkfrau
Das sie eur Gnaden Sohn anschau
Dem wir mit freuden theten sehen

JULIA *die Jungkfrau*
Den Göttern wöll wir lob verjehen
Die eur lieb zu Land gholffen han

ENGELBRECHT
Mein freud ich nicht aufssprechen kan
Das ich die stund hab eine gnommen
Vnd das vnglück daraufs ich kommen
Kan mir kein Mensch glauben auff Erden
Doch hoff ich es soll besser werden
Nach Regen kompt der Sonnenschein

LEUDEGAST DER FÜRST
Hertzlieber Sohn so komb herein
So wöll wir reden von den Sachen
Wie wir auffs ehest ein Hochzeit machen
Vnd als auffs köstlichst richten zu
Das es an nichten mangeln thu

[*Sie gehn alle ab*

ENGELBRECHT *führet die Jungkfrau*, LUDOLFF DER HERTZOG *geht ein mit seinem* JAHNEN

Jahn Molitor nun sein wir verdorben
Es mufs sein gwunnen oder gstorben
Mein Tochter will ich wider han
Oder mein leben setzen dran
Will der Jung Fürst Sidea bhalten
Mufs er mich beim Vatter dem alten
Wider zu hult vnd gnaden bringen
Weil du bist schuldig an den dingen
Das Sidea ist zogen davon
So wirstu wissen das best zuthon
Oder zu zahlen mit der häut

JAHN MOLITOR *ziecht ab*,
Ein kluger Mann ward ich allzeit
Drumb wenn eur Gnad mir folgen wolt
Mein Kleider jhr anziehen solt
So wolt ich eure ziehen an
Vnd darinn auch gen Hof mit gahn
So vil practict suchen vnd finden
Wie wir wider wegk führen künden
Die Sideam oder den Jungen
Dardurch wird der alt Fürst bezwungen

Who long has waited his return,
Which she will be rejoiced to learn.

Exit ELEMAUS, *taking Engelbrechts former clothes with him. He returns again, leading the lady* JULIA.

ELEMAUS.
Oh Gracious Prince, I bring to thee
The maid, your Grace's son to see,
Whom we so joyfully did greet.

JULIA.
We'll thank the gods with praises meet,
Who helped thee to thy happiness.

ENGELBRECHT.
I cannot all my joy express,
That such an hour was granted me.
The misery, from which I flee,
None can believe me when I tell;
But now I hope that all is well;
The sun will after rain appear.

LEUDEGAST.
My dearest son, just enter here,
And we'll discuss the whole affair,
How best a wedding to prepare,
And all on such a costly scale,
That nought of pomp or splendour fail.

[*Exeunt.*

ENGELBRECHT, *leading in the lady. Enter* DUKE LUDOLFF *with his* JOHN.

John Molitor, our day's gone by,
And we must either win or die.
My daughter I will have again,
Or stake my life upon the main.
If the young Prince will keep Sidea,
Then his old father, that is clear,
Must me his former favour shew.
And as it is your fault, you know,
That my Sidea has run away,
Why manage it, as best you may,
Or with your back you'll pay for it.

JOHN MOLITOR, *pulling off his coat.*
I never wanted much for wit;
So if your Grace my counsel take,
To wear my clothes a shift would make,
I then your Grace's clothes would wear,
And to the court we'd both repair;
And there such cunning plans we'd lay,
How we again could bring away
Either Sidea or the Prince,
As soon his father would convince,

Das er zu fürkommung den schaden
Eür Fürstlich Gnad auch thet begnaden
Vnd machet mit euch einen Fridt
        LUDOLFFUS DER FÜRST
Ja wol versuchen schadt doch nit
Wir wolln versuchen vnser Heil
Guts glück wöll sein auff vnserm theil
                [*Sie gehn ab*
   Kompt JULIA *vnd sagt traurig*
Ach ich bin in erfahrung kommen
Fürst Engelbrecht hab vorhin gnommen
Sideam die allrschönst Jungkfrau
Defs Fürsten Tochter in Littau
Ach weh vnd wann das war soll sein
So würd sie sich auch lassen ein
Mein Verliebnufs zu disputirn
So müst ich als die letzt verliern
Darzu bestehn in spot vnd schand
Vor Reich vnd Armen in dem Land
Ach wenn ich das solt haben gwist
Es hett mich keines Menschen list
In das Land nimmermehr gebracht
Der Fürst mir die sach wol gut macht
Verheist mir Silber Hügel vnd Berg
Geht mir derhalb nichts über zwerg
Möcht ich villeicht noch wol bestehn
Ich will jetzt in mein Gmach nein gehn
                [*Abgang.*
Kompt SIDEA, *hat über jhre schöne Kleider eine schlechte Schauben an, eine stauchen auff, die sie bald von jhr werffen kan, tregt ein Scheurn voll Getrancks*
        (SIDEA)
Nun bin ich wol gen Hof her kommen
Aber sehr böse mehr vernommen
Nemlich das der Fürst Englbrecht
Hab nun mehr gar vergessen schlecht
Mein wohlthat die ich jhm gethan
Auch leib vnd leben gwaget dran
Aller dings aufs den augen gsetzt
Vnd ein andere gnommen zu letzt
Mit der er heint helt sein Hochzeit
So hab ich jhm ein Trunck bereit
Mit dem ich schleich nein zu den Gästen
Vnd wenn sie sind bereit am besten
So beut ich jhm den trunck zu Trincken
Den ersten tropffen den er will schlincken
Der macht das er mich mufs erkennen
Mich ebrn vnd mit Namen nennen
Vnd denken was er mir versprach
Mich zu Kirchen führen darnach

That he, his losses to replace,
To favour must restore your Grace,
And then a peace conclude with you.
        LUDOLFF.
'Tis well; th'attempt no harm can do.
Once more then shall our luck be tried;
Oh fortune favour thou our side!
                [*Exeunt.*
  Enter JULIA, *and says sorrowfully.*
Alas! already, as I hear,
The Prince was plighted to Sidea,
Most beautiful all men have thought her.
In Littau she the Prince's daughter.
Oh woe is me! for if it's true,
There's one thing she'll not fail to do.
My claim to Engelbrecht refuse,
And I, as last, must surely lose,
The mark of jest and scorn to stand
To rich and poor throughout the land.
Ah! had I known all that before,
The arts of man had nevermore
Persuaded me to venture here.
The Prince doth generous appear.
Promises silver, hill, and vale;
For that indeed I need not fail,
Perhaps I still might hold my own.
But now I'll to my room alone.
                [*Exit.*
Enter SIDEA *with a shabby cloak over her fine clothes, and a hood on, all of which she can throw off. She bears a goblet full of some beverage.*
        SIDEA.
'Tis true, I now have reached the court.
But with it sad experience bought.
For young Prince Engelbrecht, I hear.
Hath now alas! forgotten sheer
The services I rendered him,
At peril too of life and limb;
Hath cast me, wretched maid, aside.
To take another for his bride!
To-night he means to wed the fair.
So I have got a potion rare,
With which I too will be a guest;
And when the moment seems the best,
Will ask him just to take a sip,
And when a drop hath touched his lip.
He'll know me, — will me honour do, —
And by my name will call me too,
Will recollect his plighted troth,
To wed me then be nothing loth.

Damit vnser traurigkeit anfang
Gewinn ein frölichen aufsgang
　　　　　　　　　　[*Sie geht ab*

Kompt LEUDEGAST DER FÜRST *mit seinen Rähten* FRAN-
CISCO *vnd* ELEMAO, JULIA *vnnd* ENGELBRECHT *seinem Sohn,
setzt sich,*
(LEUDEGAST)

Nun weil heut ist der Hochzeit tag
So legt von euch als leit vnd klag
Es samblen sich die Fürsten vnd Herrn
Von allem Landen weit vnd ferrn
Die begeren vns difs Fest zu zirn
Darumb so wil vns auch gebürn
Das wir jhn erzeigen als guts
Darumb seit alle gutes muts
Balt wöll wir nach altem Exempl
Gehn in Jovis des grosen Templ
Euch darinn lassen Copulirn
Essen Trincken vnd Musicirn
Rennen, Stechen, Streiten vnd Kempffen
Mit kurtzweil alles trauren dempffen
Darumb empfangt die frembten Gäst
Vnd ehret sie auffs aller best

Sie neigen sich alle, Kompt SIDEA, *wie vor gemelt, ver-
kleidet, tregt jhre Scheurn in henden, gibt jnen die hend,
sagt darnach zum Breutigam*
(SIDEA)

Herr Breutigam ich bin ein gsande
Villeicht euch gar ein vnbekante
Doch von grossen Leuten hergschickt
Das jhr euch jetzt stattlich erquickt
Vnd heut erfahrt das jhr nicht west
So trinckt den Wein, der ist der best
Den wil ich euch verehren heut
Auff euer Fürstliche Hochzeit

ENGELBRECHT *nimbt die Scheurn sicht sie an trinckt legt
die hend zusammen*
(ENGELBRECHT)

Ach weh ich bin je gwest vermessen
Das ich hab so schendlich vergessen
Sidea der hertzliebsten mein
O weh weh jammer angst vnd pein
Weh hertzenleid seufftzen vnd schmertzen
　　　　　　　　　　[*Er zuckt den Dolchen*
Ich will meinem betrübten hertzen
Hiemit helffen aufs langer pein
Vnd mir selbsten ein Richter sein
Das ich meiner liebsten vergessen
　　　[*Sidea fellt in Dolchen, sie lauffen alle zu,*

And thus what hath begun in sorrow,
May end in joy upon the morrow.
　　　　　　　　　　　　　[*Exit.*

Enter PRINCE LEUDEGAST, *with his counsellors* FRANCISCUS
and ELEMAUS, *his son* ENGELBRECHT *and* JULIA.
LEUDEGAST *sits down.*
LEUDEGAST.

As we've a wedding here to-day,
I pray you, put all care away.
The lords and princes, far and wide,
Are thronging in from every side.
They wish to honour this our feast,
A hearty welcome then at least
Is due to them, and all of you
Should wear a cheery visage too.
We soon, old custom to obey,
To great Jove's temple wend our way,
In wedlock join the youthful pair,
With feasting and with music there,
We'll race, we'll tilt in mimic fight,
With mirth all sorrow put to flight.
Therefore receive the stranger guest
And honour him, as you may best.

They all bow. Enter SIDEA, *disguised as already described.
She bears a goblet in her hands. She gives them her hand,
and then turns to the bridegroom.*
SIDEA.

Sir Bridegroom, I am sent to you.
Perhaps a stranger, it is true,
But sent by those of high repute
That you your strength might now recruit,
And learn, what else you'd ne'er have guessed.
Drink then this wine, it is the best.
This offering at your feet I lay,
As present on your wedding-day.

ENGELBRECHT *takes the goblet, looks at it, drinks, and
clasps his hands together.*
ENGELBRECHT.

Alas! how heartless! was it not?
That I so shamefully forgot
Sidea, the loved one of my heart!
Oh woe and anguish! pain and smart!
Alas! oh misery, and grief!
　　　　　　　　[*He lays his hand on his dagger.*
This burdened heart I'll bring relief,
From longer torture will I free,
And to myself my judge will be,
That I forgot my dearest — best!
　[*Sidea snatches at his dagger, and the others run up.*

COMEDY OF THE BEAUTIFUL SIDEA.

SIDEA
Mit was thorheit seit jhr besessen
Seit getrost all sach wird noch gut
Drumb fast euch selbst ein kecken mut
Ob jhr schon auff der wilten Strafsen
Sideam auff dem Baum verlassen
So lebt sie doch noch frisch vnd gsund
Vnd jhr solt sie sehen jetzund.

SIDEA *wirfft die schauben vnd stauchen von sich,* ENGELBRECHT *fellt dem Vatter zu fufs*

(ENGELBRECHT)
Ach Herr Vatter erbarmt euch mein
Secht das Mensch das da kompt herein
Ist ein Tochter Fürsten Ludolffs
Defs gmüt war böser denn eins Wolffs
Der hat mich jhr zu eygen geben
Die hat mich erhalten beim leben
Vnd hett die Jungkfrau nicht gethan
Wehr ich vor lengst erfaulet schon
Der versprach ich Ehliche pflicht
Vnd als sie fort konnt kommen nicht
Stellt ichs auff einem Baum im Walt
Verhiefs sie her zu holen balt
Wie ich euch zeigt Herr Vatter an
Darnach ich es vergessen han
Vnd mich mit Julia verlobt
Derhalb mein gwissen also tobt
Das ichs nicht kan zu Kirchen führn
Will eh mein leben drob verliehrn

Zu der Julia sagt er
Drumb bitt ich Fürstlichs Fräuelein
Last euch erbarmen meiner pein
Vnd gebt mich meiner Ehpflicht lofs

JULIA
Es ist daran nicht glegen grofs
Wann jhr sie vor mir habt genommen
Solt ich billich nicht her sein kommen
Dann das erst gelübt gehet doch vor
Also mufs ich nun armer thor
Von jederman grofs schimpff einnemen
Doch habt jhrs euch noch mehr zu schemen
Als ich die ich nichts darumb west

LEUDEGAST DER FÜRST
Ach last bey euch bestehn das best
Ist es gschehen vnwissent doch
Das euch kein schimpff so grofs vnd hoch
Wie jhr vermelt draufs kan entstehn
Thut mit vns in die Kirchen gehn
Wir wöllen euch mit seines gleichen
Ein Gfürsten Sohn schönen vnd reichen

SIDEA.
What madness now hath thee possessed?
Take comfort! all is well at last.
Be of good cheer, the danger's past,
Although upon the road, so drear,
Thou in a tree hast left Sidea,
She's still alive, and fresh and healthy,
As thy own eyes shall shortly tell thee.

SIDEA *throws off her cloak and hood.* ENGELBRECHT *falls at his father's feet.*

ENGELBRECHT.
Take pity on me, Father dear!
Seest thou that person coming here?
The daughter of Prince Ludolff she,
And fiercer than a wolf is he.
He gave me to her for her own.
I owe my life to her alone.
Had she not helped me in my need,
I'd perished long ere this indeed.
I vowed to marry her, and so,
Until she could no further go,
We fled, and then upon a tree
She sat, and was to wait for me.
All this I did to you explain,
But soon forgot it all again;
My troth to Julia did I vow,
For which my conscience stings me now.
She cannot therefore be my wife,
And should it even cost my life.

Turning to Julia, he continues
Oh Lady! I would thee implore,
Take pity on my trouble sore,
And give me back my plighted troth!

JULIA.
To do so I am nothing loth.
If thou before hast ta'en Sidea,
'Twere better I had ne'er come here.
The prior vow is here the rule,
And therefore I alas! poor fool
Am now exposed to scorn and blame,
And yet thou hast more cause for shame
Than I, who nought about it knew.

LEUDEGAST.
Bear us no grudge, whate'er thou do;
'Twas but an error after all.
That no dishonour thee befall,
So great as thou hast pictured, thou
Hadst better grace the wedding now.
I promise thee, ere we have done,
We'll wed thee to a prince's son,

COMEDY OF THE BEAUTIFUL SIDEA.

Eh jhr wegk kompt noch wol begaben
Auch solt jhr von vns abtrag haben
Alles eurs schadens grofs vnd klein
   [*Er geht zu der Sidea gibt jhr die hend*
Ach solt ihr denn mein Schnur fort sein
Eur Vatter ist mein ergster Feindt
So wolt ich das er auch köm heint
Wir wolten vns beede vertragen
Vnd forthin bey all vnsern tagen
Kein vnfried haben nimmermehr
Auch habet danck der treu vnd ehr
Die jhr habt meinem Sohn gethan
   [*Man klopfft,*

DER FÜRST
Lieber sich wer klopffet an

Man thut auff, geht LUDOLFFUS DER FÜRST *mit* JAHN
MOLITOR *ein, stellt sich in ein ecken,*

HERTZOG LEUDEGAST
Wer seint die Leut die herein gehn
Zwar gar ungleicher Gsellen zwen

SIDEA *sicht vmb erkennt als balt jhrn Vatter*
Ach weh es ist der Vatter mein
Wie waget er sich da herein
  Zu jhrem Vatter sagt sie
Ach Herr Vatter was macht jhr hie
Für euch bin ich erschrocken je
Das jhr euch daher wagen thut

LUDOLFF
Ach solstu sein mein fleisch vnd blut
Vnd mich so jämmerlich verrahten
   [*Er geht zu Leudegast*
Ich bitt eur Lieb wöll mich begnaden
Weil sich die sach so hat begeben
So will ich fort bey meinem leben
Nimmermehr thun wider eur Liebt

LEUDEGAST DER FÜRST *gibt jhm die hend*
Weil sich all ding also begibt
Das wir nun sollen gut Freund sein
Gib ich euch eur Land wider ein
Vnd mach mit euch ein stetten Fried
Das keiner mehr den breche nit
Sonder es stets dabey soll bleiben
So wöll wir den fleissig beschreiben
Nach dem wir vns werden bereden
Vnd Sigln mit vnsern Secreten
So balt die Hochzeit hat ein end

Handsome and rich too shall he be,
And recompense we'll give to thee
For all thy losses great and small.
   [*He goes to Sidea, and gives her his hand.*
Henceforth I thee my daughter call.
Thy father is my bitter foe.
Would he were here to-night, that so
We might at once here end our strife,
And live as neighbours all our life,
Nor cause again for quarrel find!
My thanks for all the service kind
That thou hast shewn my son before.
   [*Knocking without.*

LEUDEGAST.
See there, who's knocking at the door.

The door is opened. Enter PRINCE LUDOLFF *with* JOHN
MOLITOR, *and stands in a corner.*

LEUDEGAST.
Who are those persons that I see?
They're most unequal company.

SIDEA *looks round, and immediately recognizes her father.*
Alas! it is my father's face!
How could he venture to this place?
  Turning to her father she continues,
O father say, what brings thee here?
I must for thy dear safety fear,
That thou so great a risk should run.

LUDOLFF.
My flesh and blood! Oh thou art none,
Myself so vilely to betray!
   [*Turning to Leudegast*
Your Grace's pardon I would pray.
As that's the turn which the affair
Has taken, by my life I swear,
Your Grace I'll ne'er again offend.

LEUDEGAST, *giving him his hand.*
As all things seem that way to tend,
That we henceforth good friends should be,
I will restore thy lands to thee.
A lasting peace too will I make,
Which neither of us e'er shall break,
But always faithfully maintain.
The terms set down in language plain
After due consultation, we'll
Affix our signature and seal,
Soon as the wedding's taken place.

LUDOLFF

Aller vnfried soll sein verwend
In lauter Lieb vnd gut Freundschafft
Das auch fort derselbig hat krafft
Vnd fang balt an zu dieser stund
Versprich ich euch mit Hand vnd Mund

LUDOLFF *gibt jhm die Hand, vnd sagt zu seinem Eyden,*

Nun wünsch ich euch vil glücks vnd heil
Wiewol ich euch hart hielt zum theil
Ist es doch abgangen ohn schaden
Vnd noch alles zum besten grahten

LUDOLFF *sagt zum* JAHNEN

Seh hin, hab dein Kleider wider
Leg mir dargegen meine nider

Er legt sich Hochzeitlich an, LEUDEGAST *nimbt* JULIAM *bey der hand.*

(LEUDEGAST)

Weil sich dann das glück zu vns wend
Vnd alle feindschafft hat ein end
So kompt allsampt mit vns herein
Last vns lustig vnd frölich sein
Vnd die Hochzeit anfangen schan
Euch Julia gebn wir zum Mann
Vnsern Fürsten Herrn Franciscum
Mit einem zimlichen Reichthum
Auff das dest grösser werd die Freüd

[*Er führt sie zum Fürsten* FRANCISCO *giebt sie zusammen*

So gebn wir euch zusammen beyd
So geht die Hochzeit in eim hin

FRANCISCUS

Es ist kein schad es bringt ein gwin
Hertz allerliebste nun seit getröst
Aus allem leidt seit jhr erlöst
Die Heurath soll euch nicht gereuhen

JULIA

Wenns eur Lieb meint gen mir in treuen
Ich mit eur Lieb zu frieden bin
Vnd ist mir alles trauren hin
Will auch als thun was euch gefellt

LEUDEGAST DER FÜRST

Weil dann alle ding ist bestellt
Vnd die zeit ist vorhanden schon
Das man die Hochzeit fange an

LUDOLFF.

My love and friendship for your Grace
Shall terminate our difference.
And that the same at once commence,
Aye from this very moment too,
With hand and mouth I promise you.

LUDOLFF *gives him his hand, and says to* ENGELBRECHT:

I wish thee joy for many a year;
And though thy treatment was severe,
There's no great harm now all is past,
For it has turned out well at last.

Turning to JOHN MOLITOR.

Just take these clothes, for they are thine;
And then I'll beg thee, put off mine.

LUDOLFF *puts on a wedding garment, and* LEUDEGAST *takes* JULIA *by the hand.*

LEUDEGAST.

As fortune now to us doth wend,
And all our discord's at an end,
Let's all together step in here,
Be joyful and of merry cheer.
The wedding shall at once proceed,
And Prince Franciscus, he shall lead
Thee Julia to the altar, who
Shalt have with him a fortune too.
This will enhance our great delight.

[*He leads* JULIA *to* FRANCISCUS, *and joins their hands.*

Thus then do we you two unite,
And both the weddings join in one.

FRANCISCUS.

Our gain is great, our loss is none.
Oh dearest heart, have comfort thou,
Released from all thy troubles now!
This marriage thou shalt ne'er repent.

JULIA.

If in good faith thy love is meant,
I with thy love am satisfied,
Henceforth will lay all care aside,
And all thy pleasure try to do.

LEUDEGAST.

As every thing's prepared for you,
And now the time has come indeed,
In which the nuptials should proceed,

So folget vns allsampt hernach
Vnd leget von euch alle klag
Heut ist eur aller Freuden tag
　　　　[*Sie gehn alle in einer Ordnung ab.*

　　JAHN MOLITOR *bleibt herauſs vnd beschleust*
Diese History zeiget an
Böſs sey dem sterckern stand zuthan
Derhalben wo es sich zutregt
Das man zu zoren wird bewegt
Das man sich darinn moderir
Bedenck wenn man die sach verlier
Was schads vnd nachtheyl drauſs entstehe
Wol sagt man aygner schad thut wehe
Jedoch soll man den sterckern reichen
Viel lieber schweigen oder weichen
Als sich mit jhm in zanck begeben
Dann der sterckst thut gmeincklich ob schwebē
Vnd ob schon der gering hernach
Erfind ein vortheil zu der rach
Soll er sich doch deſs nicht anmassen
Vermeints glück nicht verführn lassen
Dieweil es sich offt thut begeben
Das heut ein theil thut oben schweben
Das er doch kürtzlich wider fellt
Dann girigkeit Gott nicht gefellt:
Sonder wie die Schrifft thut melten
Wöll er das böſs selbst vergelten
Drumb thu man ein wenig gemach
Vnd handel also in der sach
Das sichs zu beyden theilen leit
Vnd auſs vorigen zanck vnd streit
Werde ein ewig einigkeit.
　　　　　　　　[*Abgang.*

ENDE.

Follow me all of you, I pray,
And put all care from you away,
That all of us rejoice to-day.
　　　　[*Exeunt omnes in procession.*

　　JOHN MOLITOR *remains, and says in conclusion:*
Of this our story, hear the gist!
'Tis ill the stronger to resist.
Wherever therefore it may prove,
That stronger men our anger move,
'Tis best our anger to allay,
Remember, if we lose the day
What damage may to us be done:
Wise proverb: 'Look to number one.'
Tow'rds those who rich and stronger are,
Quiet submission's better far
Than eagerly the thing contest;
For stronger mostly comes off best.
Though afterwards indeed the weak
Devise how they may vengeance wreak,
They should not think themselves too sure.—
Let fancied fortune them allure.
For often doth it chance, I say,
That he, who's uppermost to-day,
To-morrow must endure a fall:
God loves not arrogance at all.
For in the Scripture there's a line:
"All vengeance," saith the Lord, "is mine!"
Be gentle therefore to thy foe,
And bear thee in thy quarrel so,
That each may due forbearance shew,
And out of former strife and woe,
Eternal amity may grow.
　　　　　　　　[*Exit.*

THE END.

COMEDY OF THE BEAUTIFUL PHAENICIA

BY JACOB AYRER OF NUREMBERG.

(CIRCA 1595.)

In JACOB AYRER's *Opus theatricum,* Nuremberg 1618, in-fol., the COMEDY OF THE BEAUTIFUL PHAENICIA occupies folio 408 recto, col. 2, to folio 433 recto, col. 1. It is entitled:

Spiegel Weiblicher zucht vnd Ehr.

Comedia

Von der schönen

Phaenicia vnd Graf Tym-

bri von Golison aufs Arragonien,

wie es jhnen in jhrer Ehrlichen Lieb gangen,

bifs fie Ehelich zufammen komen, Mit

17. Perfonen, vnd hat

6. Actus.

(MIRROR OF MAIDENLY VIRTUE AND HONOUR. COMEDY OF THE BEAUTIFUL PHAENICIA AND COUNT TYMBRI OF GOLISON FROM ARRAGON, AND HOW THEY FARED IN THEIR HONORABLE LOVE UNTIL THEY GOT MARRIED. WITH 17 PERSONS AND IN 6 ACTS.)

Reprinted in: *Deutsches Theater.* Herausgegeben von LUDEWIG TIECK. Erster Band, Berlin 1817, in-8vo, where it occupies pages 252 to 321.

COMEDIA
VON DER SCHÖNEN PHAENICIA.

Die Personen in dise Comedi.

PETRUS der Koenig in Arragonien	1
TYMBORUS der Graf von Golison sein Kriegs Rath	2
REINHART } seine beede Räth	3
DIETERICH }	4
LIONITO VON TONETEN, der Alte Edelmann	5
VERACUNDIA sein Gemahl	6
PHAENICIA sein Tochter	7
BELLEFLURA Phaenicia Schwester	8
VENUS die Göttin der Lieb	9
CUPIDO jhr Kindt mit sein Pfeil vnd Bogen	10
PHILLIS der Phaenicia Kammer Frau	11
LIONATUS ein Alter vom Adel, zu Messina	12
GERANDO ein Ritter, OLERIUS VALERIAN genandt	13
ANNA MARIA ein Kammer Jungfrau	14
JAHN der kurtzweiler	15
MALCHUS der pracher od. betriger	16
GERWALT der betriegerisch Edelmā	17

ACTUS PRIMUS.

VENUS *die Göttin geht ein, mit blosen halfs vnd armen, hat ein fliegents gewand, vnd ist gar Göttisch gekleit ist zornig vnd S.*

Ich wolt hie gern klagen mein not
Das mich vnd mein Sohn macht zu spot
Tymborius der Graf von Golison
An Königs Hof zu Arragon
Der helt sich Mannlich starck vnd vest
Hat im nechsten Krieg than das best
Da Prochyte angfangen hat
In Sicilien das grofs blutbad

Cupido hat vil Pfeil verschossen
Nach jhm send all gangen in windt
Vulcanus ist zornig vnd geschwindt
Vnd will jhm keine Pfeil mehr schmiden
Wird offt mit mir drob zu vnfrieden

COMEDY
OF THE BEAUTIFUL PHAENICIA.

Persons represented:

PETER, King of Arragon.
TYMBORUS, Count of Golison, his counsellor of war.
REINHART, } his two counsellors.
DIETERICH, }
LIONITO OF TONETE, the old nobleman.
VERACUNDIA, his wife.
PHAENICIA, his daughter.
BELLEFLURA, Phaenicia's sister.
VENUS, the goddess of love.
CUPID, her child with his arrow and bow.
PHILLIS, Phaenicia's attendant.
LIONATUS, an old nobleman of Messina.
GERANDO, a Knight, called OLERIUS VALERIAN.
ANNA MARIA, a maid of honour.
JOHN, the clown.
MALCHUS, the swaggerer or impostor.
GERWALT, the false nobleman.

ACT I.

Enter VENUS *with bare neck and arms wearing a loose robe. She has the attire of a goddess, and says angrily:*

I would complain, my son and I
Have now become the mockery
Of Tymbor, Count of Golison,
Of the King's Court of Arragon.
He bears him manly, stout, and true;
In the last war the most did do,
When Prochyte the slaughter great
In Sicily did perpetrate.

[She relates further, that she had caused many a hero to desert the profession of arms for the love of women; but that the Count offered the most obstinate resistance, and did not care for women at all.]

Cupid has many arrows shot
At him, which all in air are spent.
Vulcan is wrath and violent,
Will no more arrows for him make,
And at me too offence doth take.

COMEDY OF THE BEAUTIFUL PHAENICIA.

Darumb so mufs ich mich bedencken
Wie ich den Ritter möcht ablencken
Das er auch Weiber lieb möcht han.

Therefore I must devise a way,
How I the knight inveigle may,
That he may love the ladies too.

[She then proceeds to state, that the beautiful Phaenicia was to appear at the tournament which Peter, King of Arragon, intended to hold at Messina; the Count was to fall in love with her there, and then she, (Venus) would soon tame him.]

CUPIDO *geht ein, wie er gemalt wird, mit verbunden augen, hat ein Pfeil auff sein bogen.*

Frau Mutter habt fort kein verdrufs
Mein Vatter der zornig Vulcanus
Der hat mir etlich Pfeil geschmit
Vnd sagt ich könn mit fehlen nit
Sonder treff was ich treffen sol.

Enter CUPID, *as he is painted, with his eyes bound, and an arrow in his bow.*

Dear mother lay aside thine ire,
For Vulcan now, my wrathful sire,
Has a few arrows forged for me,
And says that they unerring be,
And hit whatever I may wish.

[At this Venus is very much delighted, and promises Cupid a new tunic, if he hits Tymborus well. Exeunt Venus and Cupid. Upon this John enters, wounded by Cupid's arrow, which is still sticking in his back. He exclaims that he is suffering violent pains in his heart through love for Anna Maria, without whom he cannot live. He then abuses Cupid, and draws the arrow out of the wound. His master Gerando enters, attracted by the noise. John complains to him of his miserable condition, and Gerando promises to assist him, and to plead his cause with Anna Maria. Exeunt John and Gerando. — Enter the King and two Counsellors. The tournament is to take place. 'In the mean time all the ladies ascend the battlements, and look down from them.'[1] Tymborus beats all his adversaries, (Lionito, Lionatus, and Gerando) in single combat. The King closes the tournament; his guests follow him to join in the dance.]

GERANDO *geht allein ein.*

Tymbor der Graf von Golison
Legt vns hie allen grofs schandt an
Der thut gar hoch herprechen sich
Weil er im Franckreichischen Krieg
Durch verrehterey angericht hat
Vberaufs ein sehr groses blutbadt
Das man Sicilisch Vesper heist
Vnd jhn der König so gar hoch preist
Des helt er sich dest steüff vnd strenger
Vnd ander gegen jhm vil wenger
Sein Künheit wechst von tag zu tagen
Der hats im Turnir als wegk gschlagen
Vnd ist beim Königlichen Abent essen
Zu nechst oben bey dem König gesessen
Bey jhm das Königlich Frauen zimmer
Das ich es kan zusehen nimmer
Sonder bin gleich gangen davon
Weil ich schir safs zu vnderst an
Vnd will der sachen dencken nach

GERANDO, *returns alone.*

Tymbor, the Count of Golison,
Most dire disgrace is laying on
Us all, pretensions doth advance,
Because that in the war with France
He a most treach'rous plan had laid,
A dreadful massacre had made,
Sicilian Vespers called, a thing
For which he's lauded by the king.
He holds himself so stiff and high,
Treats others so disdainfully,
He bolder grows from day to day,
In tourney bears each prize away,
And at the royal supper, he
Was seated next his Majesty.
I saw the royal lady there
Sit next him, which I could not bear,
But soon determined me to go,
Because I sat far down below;
And now some stratagem I'll seek,

---

[1] This stage direction possesses a peculiar interest, as giving us some insight into the arrangement of the German stage at that time. It appears to have been similar to that of the English stage. The whole space was divided into two parts, separated from each other by a curtain. The battlements from which the ladies look down, were a raised gallery at the back of the stage. The change of the locality was effected by the drawing or closing of the curtain in the back-ground.

Wie ich mich an jhm rechen mag	How I on him may vengeance wreak.
Nun ists mit Kempffen gar vergebens	'Tis vain with arms to wage the strife,
Mir schad der schimpff die zeit meins lebens	It brings dishonor for my life.
Er ist zu Khün, lüstig vnd scharff	He is too bold, too strong of limb.
An jhn ich mich nicht richten darff	I should have no success with him;
Sonder mufs mich nur dahin schicken	Must therefore some sly plan devise,
Das ich mit falschem Practicken	By which with cunning and with lies,
Ihm etwa schand vnd schimpff beweifs	Dishonor on his name may rest.
Ich will ankehren allen fleifs	I'll spare no pains, but do my best
Vnd will mich an dem Grafen rechen	Against the Count for vengeance' sake.
Mir wöll dann Gott das leben brechen.	Then God be pleased my life to take.
[*Er geht zornig ab.*	[*Exit angrily.*

[Venus and Cupid return, and place themselves in ambush. Trumpets are heard. Enter the King and his Counsellors.¹ All sorts of side-play. Then Tymborus with Phaenicia and all the rest in couples, begin the dance. Cupid shoots his arrow at the Count. The latter is hit, and immediately struck by Phaenicia's beauty. The King breaks off the dance, and leads the guests to supper. Venus and Cupid remain behind alone. Venus says she will urge the Count to woo Phaenicia in dishonorable love, but that she shall only become his in lawful wedlock.]

ACT II.

[Enter Gerando. He repeats his complaints of the arrogance of Tymborus, whom the King's favour has made proud. Anna Maria joins him. Gerando informs her of the passion which his servant John entertains for her. Anna Maria is highly exasperated, and Gerando finds her very ready to agree to his plan for deceiving John. The latter enters, and to his delight learns from his master that Anna Maria is burning with love for him, and has appointed to give him a meeting that night. The clown praises his own cleverness, and then walks away with his master. Enter Tymborus. He complains of the pains of love, and considers how he may win the beautiful Phaenicia. At first he thinks of writing her a letter, but afterward determines to serenade her. Exit. — Enter Gerando. He goes to Anna Maria's house to wait for John at the place of rendezvous, and then to cool his burning love by throwing a pail of water over his head. The poor fool appears and makes his presence known. Gerando answers in a feigned voice, and the above-mentioned cooling-process follows. John runs away, forswearing all love for the future. Then follows Tymborus's serenade before Phaenicia's house. He appears with his musicians. After they have given a specimen of their art, a singer endeavours to allure the fair one with a love song of six verses. The lover is not listened to, and withdraws with his musicians.

Enter Lionito, Phaenicia's father, and Veracundia, her mother, — soon afterwards Phaenicia, who on being asked, whether she knew who had serenaded her, replies, that it must have been Tymborus, as he had given signs of his passion for her during the dance. After some advice from her mother, they all withdraw. An interview follows between Tymborus and Phaenicia, which gives him no more grounds for hope than his serenade had done before.]

ACT III.

[The first scene forms an episode, which like John's courtship of Anna Maria, stands in no

---

¹ At the end of the last scene, the procession had certainly left the front part of the stage by passing through the opened curtain. It now returns, and the front of the stage represents the royal saloon.

connection with the principal action. 'Malchus, the cheat,' pretends to be the ghost of John's mother, and swindles John out of all the ready cash he had inherited from her.[1]

Tymborus has now written a letter to Phaenicia, which has been delivered by Phillis, the lady's maid, who endeavours to promote the interests of Tymborus with her mistress. In the next scene, in spite of all Phillis's persuasion, Phaenicia declares angrily that she does not wish to receive any more letters.[2] Tymborus is very much disheartened at this answer.

'Therefore have I put all my misery and pain into this song,'
which Phillis is to bring her mistress. Tymborus declares that he wishes to die, if Phaenicia will not listen to his suit. Hitherto he had only endeavoured to obtain her love, not her hand, as she, a poor though noble lady, was not of equal birth with himself, a rich Count. But now he determines to sue for her hand, as he cannot possess her on any other terms. Lionatus 'the old nobleman,' is to convey his proposals to her parents.[3] In the following scene, Phillis sings Tymborus's song, which is also six verses, to her mistress. The latter confesses that she had never heard a more beautiful song. After this, her father and mother inform Phaenicia of the offer of Tymborus. Phaenicia gives her consent.]

ACT IV.

[In the first scene of this act, John recovers the stolen money from Malchus.

Gerando appears, and declares his great vexation that Tymborus was affianced to Phaenicia, as she had also won his own heart. He confides his unhappiness to John, and orders him to bring Gerwalt, as he wishes to ask his counsel. The latter is then also informed of Gerando's unhappy love.]

GERWALT
So geh ich zu dem Grafen hin
Phänicia auffs höchst verklag
Wie das man vnehr von jhr sag
Mit jungen Gesellen in jhren Garten
Will jhn darinnen lassen warten
Zu nachts wol bey den Moneschein
Steigen mit eurn Knecht allein
In Weibers kleidern, mit den wil ich
Gar freundlichen besprechen mich
Als ob er Phänicia wer
Ihn führn in Garten hin vnd her
Endlichen mich in einer ecken
Mit jhn verlirn vnd verstecken
Das vns der Graf nicht mehr kan sehen
So meint er, es sey mit jhr geschehen
Wird jhr die Heürat wider auff sagen

GERANDO
Was ich hab will ich als dran wagen

GERWALT.
I'll go unto the Count at once,
Phaenicia gravely will defame,
Assert she's lost her own good name
In her own garden with young men,
To which he shall have entrance then
At night, by moonshine, where too we,
Your servant and myself, will be;
He in girl's clothes. With him I'll walk,
And in a friendly manner talk,
As if that he Phaenicia were,
And lead him round the garden there;
Then with your man I'll step aside,
And somewhere in a corner hide,
Where both of us are out of sight.
Then thinks the Count, she's ruined quite,
Will therefore his engagement break.

GERANDO.
All that I have, for that I'd stake.

---

[1] These episodes shew that the Clown had become a want on the German stage, which it was absolutely necessary to satisfy, probably to please the 'groundlings' in the pit.
[2] This scene reminds one very forcibly of the scene between Julia and Lucetta in the 'Two Gentlemen of Verona.'
[3] In Bandello, this mediator is called 'the Messenian nobleman.'

COMEDY OF THE BEAUTIFUL PHAENICIA.

Geht nur hin, richt die sach wol aufs
Ich will wider schleichen zuhaufs
  [*Sie gehn mit einander ab, schwatzen gemechlich mit ein ander.*
  Dann kompt TYMBOR DER GRAF
Heut ist der aller glücklichst tag
Weil mir ist geschehen die zusag
Das Phänicia mein soll sein
Verschwunden ist all schmertz vnd pein
All mein anfechtung ist vergangen
Zu jhr steht mir all mein verlangen
Dann ich hab warlich recht gethan
Das ich mehr hab gesehen an
Jhr Tugent, zucht, dann zeitlichs gut
Nun bin ich frölich, vnd wolgemuth
Gott helff vns beiden glücklich zammen
Vnd lafs vns auch lang leben beysammen
Der Graf spacirt hin vnd wider, ficht mit den henden, in dem geht GERWALT *der Edelman ein.*
  (GERWALT)
Gnediger Herr verzeihet mir
Was haben euer Gnaden für
Das sie also melancolirn
  TYMBOR
Nein zwar ich geh sonst hie spacirn
In lieblichen süssen gedancken
Vor hett ich schmertzen wie die krancken
Die send mir Gott lob all verschwunden
Das bin ich fro, wie andere gsunden
Alles leid hab ich gelegt ab
Dieweil ich nun bekommen hab
Phänicia die aller schönst Jungfrauen
  GERWALT
Gnediger Herr thut mit zuschauen
Das jhr nit werd betrogen mit
Ich wolts eur Gnaden gönnen nit
Phäniciam kennt jhr nicht recht
  TYMBOR
Last jhr mir mein Braut vngeschmecht
Wolt jhr mit mir bleiben zufrid
  GERWALT
Gnediger Herr ich schmech sie nit
Sonder sag eur Gnad soll zuschauen
Vnd jhr so vil guts nicht vertrauen
Als eur Gnad jhr möcht bilten ein
  TYMBOR
Soll dann das nicht geschmehet sein
Nun solt jhr nicht kommen von mir
Jhr sagt dann was jhr wist von jhr
Oder ich werd eins mit euch wagen

Go, put thy project well in train;
I'll quietly slip home again.
  [*Exeunt conversing together in a friendly manner.*
  Enter COUNT TYMBORUS.
To-day's the happiest of all
I've known, it gives me right to call
My own Phaenicia mine alone.
All pain and trouble now have flown,
All opposition now is past,
All my desire's on her cast.
For I in this have rightly done,
That I by virtue have been won,
And not by riches or by greed.
Now am I happy, blest indeed!
May God to both his favour shew,
And length of days on us bestow!
The Count walks up and down, and throws his arms about. In the mean time, enter GERWALT *the nobleman.*
  GERWALT.
My gracious Lord, pray pardon me.
What may your Grace's reason be.
That you so very sad appear?
  TYMBORUS.
No, faith! — I'm only walking here,
In pleasant thought, although before
A sick man's pains indeed I bore.
But now, thank God! all that is past,
Like healthy men, I'm blest at last.
All grief and care I've laid aside,
Since I have won her for my bride,
Phaenicia, — fairest of the fair!
  GERWALT.
O gracious Lord, I pray take care,
Lest you in her should be deceived;
For I should be most truly grieved;
Should you not judge the maid aright.
  TYMBORUS.
Against my bride no word of slight,
Or all our friendship is forgot.
  GERWALT.
O gracious Lord, I slight her not,
But say, your Grace yourself should see,
Nor trust that so much good there be
In her, as to you seemeth now.
  TYMBORUS.
Are not those slighting words? I vow,
Ere from this spot I let you stir,
You tell me what you know of her,
Or we'll decide it with the sword.

Gerwalt

Gnediger Herr ich wils nicht sagen
Sonder heut die nacht solt jhr sehen
Was thu in jhren Garten gschehen
In einer stunden bey dem Monschein

Tymbor

Ja wie solt ich kommen hinein
Dieweil die Pforten ist verspert

Gerwalt

Ein gute Lättern darzu gehört
Da kriecht jhr in die Haselstauden
Halt euch drin ohn regen vnd schnauden
Da werd jhr kennen vnd hörn mich
Was mit jhr werd fürbringen ich
Das jhr, jhr werd nicht mehr vertrauen

Tymbor

Ich glaub es nicht von der Jungfrauen
Doch was des Menschen Aug selbst sicht
Das kan das hertz betrigen nicht
Ziecht hin die nacht bricht schon herein
Ich will balt in dem Garten sein
    [*Tymbor geht ab.*

Gerwalt

So geh ich recht zum Jahnnen zu
Das ich den Grafen betrigen thu
    [*Er geht auch ab.*

Gerwalt.

I will not say a word, my Lord;
This night though will I shew to you,
What in her garden she will do
By moonlight, — in another hour.

Tymborus.

To get there is not in my power;
Ere then, they've always locked the door.

Gerwalt.

I'll have a ladder there before.
You'll creep in near the hazel-trees,
But must not either move or sneeze,
And then you'll hear and see me too,
And mark what I with her shall do,
Nor longer in the maid confide.

Tymborus.

I cannot think it of my bride.
By what the eye of man can see,
His heart can ne'er deluded be.
But hence; the day is breaking, so
I soon will to the garden go.
    [*Exit.*

Gerwalt.

Now I at once to John will hie,
That I the Count may mystify.
    [*Exit.*

[A short scene follows between Veracundia and Phaenicia, in which the latter expresses her gratitude to her parents.]

Jetzund wird ein Lättern aufsen des eingangs angeleint, daran steigt Tymbor *herunder, als wenn er vber ein Maurn stieg, vnd dann so sagt er.*

Alhie so bin ich in dem Garten
Vnd will der Abentheur erwarten
Die mir Gerwalt thet offenbarn
Die warheit dardurch zu erfahrn
    [*Er steckt sich in ein ecken,*
Alda kan ich bey dem Monschein
Sehen wer hie geht aufs vnd ein

Es steigt Gerwalt, *vnd dann der verkleidt* Jahn, *in Weiberkleidern auch herab, Gerwalt führt Jahnnen bey der hand, Jahn brangt wie ein Weib,*

Gerwalt

Ach Phänicia hertzliebste mein
Jetzt send wir abermahl allein
Vnser Bulwerck hie zuverbringen

Jahn

Ey schweigt nur gar still zu den dingen
Das es mein Vatter nicht erfahr
    [*Sie gehn im Garten hin vnd wider, setzen sich zusammen*

A ladder is placed against the wall outside the entrance. Tymborus *comes down by it, as if he had climbed over the wall.*

Here in the garden will I bide,
Till the adventure should betide,
Which Gerwalt did to me declare,
And learn the truth of the affair.
    [*Conceals himself in a corner.*
The moonshine here will plainly shew
Whoever in or out may go.

Gerwalt *also comes down the ladder, and then* John, *disguised in woman's clothes. Gerwalt leads John by the hand, who makes a little parade to shew himself off, like a woman.*

Gerwalt.

Phaenicia! Ah, my love, my own!
Now are we once again alone,
And can enjoy our dalliance sweet.

John.

Speak not so loud, I do entreat,
Lest that my father hear thee too.
    [*They walk up and down the garden, and then sit down together.*

COMEDY OF THE BEAUTIFUL PHAENICIA.

TYMBOR DER GRAF
O ho vnd ist das gleichwol wahr
Das hett ich nicht glaubt mufs ich jehen
Hett ichs nicht ghört vnd zum theil gsehen
Nun pack dich hin zum Teuffel wegk
Du leichtfertiger loser schandfleck
Ich meint du werst in dein geberten
Die aller züchtigst auff der Erden
So bistu ein loser hurnsack
An liechten galgen dich wegk pack
Ich will gehn Lionito sagen
Jhr die Heürat wider abzuschlagen
[*Er ist gar zornig vnd geht ab.*
GERWALT *sagt zu Jahnnen*
So komb wir wöllen auch zuhaufs
JAHN
Was hab wir hie gerichtet aufs
Nichts, dann ich hab je kein Menschen gsehen
GERWALT
Du erfehrst wol, was ist geschehen
[*Sie steigen wider vber die Lätter ab.*

TYMBORUS.
O ho! And is it really true!
I never had believed it — no,
Had I not heard and seen it so.
Oh, may the devil take thee now!
A loose and shameless wanton thou!
Oh! when I thought upon thy worth,
'Twas as the chastest maid on earth.
But thou'rt a wanton whore, I see.
So get thee to the gallow's tree!
To Lionito I'll explain,
The marriage must be off again.
[*Exit very angry.*
GERWALT, *to John.*
Come let us homewards wend our way.
JOHN.
But what have we done here, I pray?
Nothing, — for people I've seen none.
GERWALT.
Oh, you'll soon learn what we have done.
[*They climb over the wall again by means of the ladder.*

[The preparations are now made for the wedding, but are interrupted by a message from Tymborus.]

LIONATUS DER EDELMAN *geht ein beut jhn allen die hand sie empfangen jhn gar freundlich*
LIONATUS
Hertz lieber Vatter es ist mein bitt
Jhr wolt mirs alles verargen nit
Ich bring euch ein Bottschafft zu haufs
LIONITO DER ALT
Mein Vetter was ists sagts nur raufs
Es soll euch sein ohn allen schaden
LIONATUS
Es schicken mich her jhr Genaden
Vnd künden euch die Heürat ab
Die ich jhm neulich geworben hab
Vnd lest euch anzeigen dabey
Eur Tochter nicht frum von Ehrn sey
Drumb wöll seim stand nicht gebürn
Ein solche dirn zu Kirchen zuführn
Was er jhr geschenckt das mag sie bhalten
PHÄNICIA *geht herfür*
Ach dafs sein ewig Gott mufs walten
Wer hat das zeigt dem Grafen an
Das ich hett wider Ehr gethan
Der thut mir grofs gwalt vnd vnrecht
All Vppigkeit hab ich verschmecht
Auch mir mein tag nie für genommen
Das mir jetzt von euch ist fürkommen

Enter LIONATUS THE NOBLEMAN. *He offers the hand to all the others. They receive him in a very friendly manner.*
LIONATUS.
My Lord, I have to you a suit,
That you 'no blame to me impute,
About a message that I bear.
LIONITO.
What is it, cousin? Quick, declare;
You shall not suffer, — never fear.
LIONATUS.
The Count hath pleased to send me here,
To say that now his mind is changed
About the marriage just arranged,
And add, your daughter, shame upon her,
Hath altogether lost her honour.
With such a wench his rank allows
No interchange of marriage-bows.
His presents though she may retain.
PHAENICIA, *advancing.*
To think that God doth o'er us reign!
Who to the Count has me accused
Of ever having been abused?
He wrongs me, — has misjudged me quite,
I've scorned whate'er seems loose or light,
And never planned in all my days
Such things as to my charge he lays.

Das ruff ich Gott zu zeigen an
Das heiſs eysen auch tragen kan
Zu bewehrung meiner vnschult
Ach Gott solt ich dann deine hult
In vnehrlicher lieb verlirn
Mich Böse begirt lassen verführn
Das sey jmmermehr weit von mir
O Herr Gott ich befelch mich dir
Vor angst muſs ich mein geist auff geben
    [*Sie singt darnider, sie halten sie,*

LIONITO
Ach sol mein Tochter kommen vmbs leben
Ehe sie jhr vnschult thut purgirn
So will ichs nach jhrem todt aufsführn
Dann ich weiſs das jhr vnrecht gschicht

LIONATUS
Herr Vatter habt mirs frübel nicht
Ich kan meins theils davon nit sagen
Wers also hat in Grafen tragen
Doch kan mans noch wol werden innen
    [*Er geht ab*

VERACUNDIA
Philis in meinen Kestlein drinnen
Hab ich ein köstliches Aquavit
Vnd bringt auch ander labung mit
    Zu Phänicia sagt sie
Hertz liebe Tochter laſs dich erweichen
Lebstu noch, so gib mir ein zeichen

LIONITO
Was sol sie geben sie ist schon todt
Jhr woll gnaden der liebe Gott
Sie lest von sich fallen alle glieder
    [*Phillis kombt mit dem wasser vnd labung, man streicht sie an,*

VERACUNDIA
Jhr krefft kommen ein wenig wider
Sie hat jetzund ein Athem gholt

LIONITO
Ich bitt sie balt abtragen wolt
Kombpt sie wider zu jhrer Krafft
Soll der sach schon raht werden gschafft

Sie gehn mit jhr vmb, auff die letzt sagt PHÄNICIA
Ach Gott, ach wie ist mir geschehen
Wie so vil schönes ding hab ich gesehen
Das ich gwiefs mercken muſs dabey
Das ich im Himel gwesen sey
Ach führet mich ein wenig ab
Dann mein krafft ich verlorn hab
    [*Die Weibs Personen fürn sie ab,*

I call on God to shew to you,
That I can bear hot iron too,
My innocence to certify.
Oh God! and is it like that I
Would lose thy grace in love impure. —
Let foul desires me allure?
Such things be ever far from me!
O God, I place my trust in thee.
For anguish I must yield my breath.
    [*She sinks down, the others support her.*

LIONITO.
Ah! should it prove my daughter's death,
Before her innocence is clear,
I'll make it afterwards appear;
For I am sure she injured is.

LIONATUS.
O Cousin, take it not amiss.
I cannot, for my part, declare,
Who told the Count of the affair.
Perhaps though we the source may trace.
    [*Exit.*

VERACUNDIA.
You'll find within the house a case
Of precious cordials, Phillis dear;
And also bring refreshments here.
    Turning to Phaenicia:
O daughter dear, if thou dost live,
I beg of thee some token give!

LIONITO.
What should she give? She is quite dead.
May God shed blessings on her head!
You see her members lifeless sink.
    [*Phillis returns with water and refreshments. They endeavour to restore her.*

VERACUNDIA.
Her strength is coming back, I think,
For she just now has fetched a sigh.

LIONITO.
Bear her away immediately.
And when she has again come to,
We'll think what course we should pursue.

They walk about with her, at last PHAENICIA *says:*
Oh God! Oh what does it all mean?
How have I so much beauty seen,
That I must certainly believe,
'Twas Heaven did my soul receive?
Oh, lead me hence some rest to seek,
For still I feel extremely weak.
    [*The women lead her away.*

COMEDY OF THE BEAUTIFUL PHAENICIA.

LIONITO
Auff das es ein weil bleib dabey
Das Phänicia gestorben sey
So wollen wirs in kleidern beklagen
Ein toden Sarg gen Kirchen tragen
Denselben an jhrer statt begraben
Villeicht möcht der Graf ein reuhen haben
Was er hat an jhr begangen
Vnd möcht ein bessern bericht empfangen
Das sie die schand nicht hab gethan
Sich wider vmb sie nemen an
Dann ich weifs das jhr vnrecht gschicht
So lests auch Gott geschehen nicht
Das die Wahrheit verdrucket werd
Villeicht sich dann der Graf vmbkehrt
Vnd seiner Braut auffs neu begert,
[*Abgang.*

LIONITO.
In order that it may be said
Phaenicia is already dead,
We will funereal garments wear,
To church an empty coffin bear,
And bury it without a corse.
Perhaps the Count may feel remorse.
That he hath done her such great wrong,
The truth discover too ere long,
That she ne'er merited disgrace,
And then restore her to her place.
That she's been wronged, I surely know.
Nor will God leave the matter so,
That truth at last should be suppressed.
Perhaps the Count then will not rest,
Till of his bride again possessed.
[*Exeunt.*

ACT V.

[Servants in mourning bring in a coffin upon which is written: To the Memory of the innocent, noble and virtuous Phaenicia of the Lionitos. Exeunt. Enter John, reads the inscription on the coffin, is surprised at Phaenicia's death, remembers having played Phaenicia in the garden, and goes to his master to bring him the news of her death.

The Count now appears, and soon afterwards Gerando, both in mourning, and lament the death of the beautiful Phaenicia. Gerando expresses his great sorrow that he has been the cause of her death. The Count asks the meaning of these remarks. Gerando begs him to follow him to the church, where he will then confess every thing. They both withdraw, but soon appear again, and the scene in the church is left to the spectator's imagination. The agony of remorse completely overcomes the Count, and he is about to take his own life. Gerando however prevents him, throws his sword at his feet, kneels down before him, confesses the treachery which Gerwalt had practised against the Count, and begs the latter to take vengeance on himself. The Count is touched by this honest confession, and forgives the great wrong that has been done him on condition that he will beg for pardon of the parents and their deceased daughter. They then kneel at the coffin in prayer, rise, and clasp each others' hands. John, who had been sent after Gerwalt, now returns with the intelligence that he had decamped. The Count vows revenge, and then goes with Gerando to seek Phaenicia's parents.

Enter Lionito and Veracundia. The former informs his wife of the great grief of Tymborus for Phaenicia.]

Es geht GRAF TYMBOR *ein, mit* GERANDO DEM RITTER,
tragen alle beede leidt.
LIONITO DER ALT EDELMAN *empfengt sie, desgleichen auch geben sie allen die hend,*
TYMBOR
Herr Schwehr mir ist leid eur vnmuth
Der mich nicht wenig krencken thut
Als ob der wer selbst eigen mein

Enter COUNT TYMBORUS *and* GERANDO THE KNIGHT, *both in mourning.* LIONITO, THE OLD NOBLEMAN, *receives them. They all shake hands.*

TYMBORUS.
Father, your sorrow grieves me sore.
Indeed, it could not grieve me more,
Had I alone to bear the same.

LIONITO

Wehe denen die dran schultig sein
Das ich bin vmb mein liebs Kind kommen
Jedoch weil sie Gott hat genommen
Zu jhm aufs diesem armen leben
So kan ers auch wol wider geben
Wenn es ist sein Göttlicher will

TYMBOR *fellt zu fufs*

Ach Gott ich bin dran schultig vil
Wolt Gott das ichs könd widerbringen

GERANDO *fellt auch zu fufs,*

Ich bin die gröst vrsach der dingen
Die seind erfolgt aufs bösem raht
Aber ich bitt durch Gott vmb gnad
Vnd wollt jhrs nicht verzeihen mir
So stosset in mich mein Rappir
Als ich es wol verschultet hab

TYMBOR

Ach Gott, die gröst vrsach ich hab
Das ich die Heürat hab auff kündt
Ich hab begangen ein grose sündt
Die mir nicht wol kan werden vergeben
Dann ich bracht sie damit vmbs leben
Ach Herr Schwehr wenn es sein kan
So nembt mich wider zu gnaden an
Ich weifs wol das ich hab vnrecht
Vnd eur Tochter vnschultig gschmecht
Vnd das ich hab geglaubt zu balt
Ich ergieb mich in euren gwalt
Schafft mit mir was euch selbst gefelt

LIONITO

Gnediger Herr vnd Strenger helt
Eur Gnaden haben glaubt zugeschwind
Vnd mich gebracht vmb mein frombs Kindt
Das ich in Tugent hab erzogen
Das hab ich offt hertzlich erwogen
Vnd bringet mir auch grosen schmertzen

TYMBOR

Ich trag die gröst pein vnd schmertzen
Erstlich das ich hab glaubt so gern
Vnd das ich jhr nun mufs entpern
Aber was soll ich armer than
Niemand dann Gott mir helffen kan
Vnd meinen schmertzen mir abladen
Ich bitt Herr Vatter thut mich begnaden
Last mich gleichwol euren Sohn sein
Ich will die zeit des lebens mein
Euch in keinem punct wider streben

LIONITO.

Woe, woe to those who are to blame
That I my own dear child should lose!
But as God to himself did choose
To take her from this life of pain,
He can too give her back again,
If it should be his holy will.

TYMBORUS, *falling at his feet.*

Ah God! In this have I done ill!
Oh that I could her life restore!

GERANDO, *also falling at his feet.*

For this I am to blame far more,
As the result of counsels base.
But in God's name I sue for grace!
And should it be refused by you,
Then with my rapier run me through,
As I deserve most thoroughly.

TYMBORUS.

Ah God! the chiefest cause was I!
That I the marriage did decline,
I must confess great sin was mine,
Which you indeed can ne'er forgive;
For otherwise she still might live.
O father, if it still might be,
Your favour shew again to me!
I know indeed the wrong I wrought her,
That I ill used your blameless daughter,
Believed on evidence too slender.
Myself I therefore now surrender:
Do with me what seems good to you.

LIONITO.

My gracious Lord, it is most true,
Your Grace too lightly has believed,
And of my daughter me bereaved,
Whom I in virtue's paths had led.
This often to my heart I've said;
Great pain too has it given me.

TYMBORUS.

Mine is the greatest misery:
First that I have so soon believed,
And now that I'm of her bereaved.
But what can I, most wretched, do?
'Tis God alone can help me through,
Relieve me of my present pain.
O father, take me back again
To favour! treat me as thy son!
And while my course of life doth run,
I will in nought oppose thy will.

LIONITO

Eur Gnaden sey es als vergeben
So fern mir eur Gnad saget zu
Wenn sich die verheürathen thu
Das sie Heürathen mit meim Raht
Ich hoff zu Gott, es gescheh ohn schad
Dann ich jhr nichts böfs rahten will

TYMBOR

Defs erbietten ist vil zu vil
Ich hets euch nicht dörffen anmuten
Darumb so nemb ichs auff in guten
Vnd glob euch das an Eydsstat an
Ohn eur wissen nichts mehr zu than
Bey den alten find man gut raht

GERANDO

So bitt ich gleicher weifs vmb gnad
Ob ich schon thöricht ghandelt hab
So bitt ichs eur Lieb wider ab
Wie auch Phänicia ich hab than

LIONITO

Es ist leider geschehen schon
Doch ist es mir ein groser schad
Das jhr so eim Närrischen raht
So vnbesunnen habt nachgsetzt
Mich vnd mein gantzes gschlecht verletzt
Jhr solts auch bey mir nicht endgelten
Jedoch thut nichts mehr davon melten
Wie jhr mein Tochter habt vmbbracht
Das mir mein leid nicht werd neu gmacht
Kombt rein vnd Est mit mir zunacht
    [*Sie gehn alle ab.*

LIONITO.

Your Grace has my forgiveness; still,
Only in case it's understood,
That when to marry you think good,
You'll marry as I may advise.
God grant no harm may thence arise,
For my advice shall not mislead.

TYMBORUS.

The offer's generous indeed!
To your forgiveness I'd no claim,
So gratefully accept the same.
In place of oath, I promise you,
Without your knowledge nought to do;
The aged ever are discreet.

GERANDO.

I too forgiveness would entreat.
Although I acted foolishly,
I pray your love to pardon me,
As I Phaenicia too implore.

LIONITO.

Alas! it can't be undone more.
But great the loss to me, that you
Such foolish counsel did pursue,
So thoughtlessly have injured me
Alas! and all my family!
I from all vengeance shall abstain;
But do not speak of it again,
How 'twas that you my daughter slew,
Lest that my grief break out anew.
I go to supper. Pray come too.
    [*Exeunt.*

ACT VI.

[Enter John and his master Gerando. John informs the latter, that he does not wish to serve him any longer. Lionito then explains to his wife, that he only wished to carry out his plan respecting the union of Phaenicia with the Count. They are joined by the Count and Gerando.]

LIONITO

Jhr lieben Herrn gebt euch zufrieden
Vergest der alt geschehen Dingen
Die man je nicht kan wieder bringen
Doch solche schwermuth abzuladen
So west ich erstlich eur Gnaden
Ein aufs pündig schöne Jungfrauen
Vnd eur Gnad soll mir das vertrauen

LIONITO.

My Lords, I pray ye, be content!
Forget the things of long ago!
You cannot bring them back, you know.
Your Grace's spirits though to raise,
I know a maid whose beauty's praise
Must rank her fairest of the fair.
Your Grace may also trust me there,

COMEDY OF THE BEAUTIFUL PHAENICIA.

Sie ist Edel doch nicht gar reich
In dem der Phänicien gleich
Auch ist sie, wol so schön als sie
Vnd ist kein Maler gewesen nie
Der sie gleicher abmahlen könd
Ja wenn sie lebendig selbst da stündt
Künt man finden kein vnderscheid
Defs gleich in zucht vnd höflichkeit
Ist sie gleich der Phänicia
Vnd würd genand Lucilia
Wolt ich eur Gnad zum Gemahl geben

Tymbor

Wie wol ich hab begert zu leben
Einig hinfürter ohn ein Weib
Jedoch ich auch bestendig bleib
In dem was ich eur Lieb verhiefs
Das ich derselben wolt folgen gewiefs
Das will ich halten weil ich thu leben
Vnd wenn jhr mir ein Weib wolt geben
So felt sie mir zuhabn nit schwer
Wenns nur eines Baurn Tochter wer
Wenn michs eur Lieb kan lassen sehen

Lionito

Eur Gnad kumb mit mir es soll gschehen
Doch hab ich sie nicht in meim haufs
Sonder auff meinen Schlosse draufs
Dahin wöll wir zu Gast vns laden
Ich hoff es soll vns sein ohn schaden

[*Sie gehn alle ab.*

Though poor, she is of noble race,
May by Phaenicia take her place;
And beautiful indeed as she.
No painter too, whoe'er he be,
Could make a likeness to compare.
And were my daughter standing there
Alive, no difference you'd see.
In manners and in courtesy
She is just like Phaenicia,
Her name though is Lucilia
Her would I give your Grace as wife.

Tymborus.

Although I wished to pass my life
Henceforth as single and unwed,
Yet I adhere to what I said,
When I your Lordship gave my word,
My choice to you should be referred.
I'll keep this promise while I live;
And if to me a wife you'd give,
I'll make no difficulty there,
Though she a peasant's daughter were.
Might I perhaps the lady see?

Lionito.

With pleasure, if you'll come with me.
We cannot here the lady meet,
Because she's at my country seat.
We will as guests ourselves invite,
And then I hope 'twill all come right.

[*Exeunt omnes.*

[A short conversation ensues between Phaenicia and Belleflura. The scene must be imagined as taking place at the palace, whither Lionito had ordered his daughter to be brought. The sound of the trumpets is heard, which announce the arrival of Lionito and the two suitors. The ladies withdraw. The persons thus announced now enter. Lionito bids them welcome to his palace.]

Lionito

Gnediger Herr ist euch zu Sinn
Wie ich vor mit euch redet drinn
Das jhr die Jungfrau haben wolt
Jr sie zu sehen kriegen solt

Tymbor

Was ich vor einmal hab geredt
Das beger ich zu halten stet
Das sollen mir eur Lieb zutrauen

Lionito *sagt zu Gerando.*

Vnd jhr solt auch ein Jungfrau schauen

Lionito.

Do you, my Lord, still recollect,
How we agreed to the effect,
That you should take the maid to be
Your wife, and that you her should see?

Tymborus.

Whatever I may once decide,
By that I always will abide;
I beg, dear Sir, place trust in me.

Lionito, *to Gerando.*

And you shall too a maiden see

Die euch auch möcht werden zu theil
Jedoch bitt ich euch keine feil
Warumb das aber thut geschehen
Das werd jhr noch wol hörn vnd sehen
Ich meins mit euch alln beeden gut

GERANDO
Was eur Lieb will ist, dasselb thut,
Dann wir beede eur Diener sein

LIONITO
Kammer Frau heist die Jungfrau rein

Sie Trincken, in diesen kompt PHÄNICIA *vnd* BELLEFLURA *vnd geht jhn die Kammer Frau nach, gar schön geputzt, in groser Zucht vnnd Demut, geben erstlich den Frembden Herren, darnach auch jhren Eltern die Hand, nemen als dann die Collation, tragens vmb, vnd schencken ein, Tymbor sicht die Phänicia an, führt Gerando auff die seiten.*

(TYMBOR)
Ach Gerando nun glaub ich frey
Das der Phänicien Seele sey
Leibhafftig in das Mensch gefahrn
Sie kan gleich eben wie sie gebarn
Sie kan jhr sitten vnd gepreng
Hat auch jhr alter vnd jhr leng
Das ich jhr gar nicht feind sein kan

GERANDO
Ach weh, ach Gott was hab ich than
All mein hertzleid wird mir verneut
Das ich sie hab so vervntreut
Defs mufs ich in mein hertz mich schemen

TYMBOR
Ey solt ich dises Mensch nicht nemen
Ich nembs, wenn ich schon Keiser wehr

GERANDO
Ach Gott erst wird mein leid mir schwer
Doch weil hie seind der Jungfrau zwu
Villeicht ghört mir die ander zu
 [*Sie gehn wider mit groser Reverentz zu den andern Gästen,*

LIONITO *sagt zu Phänicia.*
Lucilia ist dir zu muth
Mein gnedign Herrn den Grafn zu nemen

Who wishes to be yours, but still
I only mean, if 'tis your will.
But how this is, shall soon appear,
That presently you'll see and hear.
For what I do is kindly meant.

GERANDO.
Whate'er you do, we are content;
As servants to your will we bow.

LIONITO.
Woman, call in your mistress now.

They drink. In the mean time enter PHAENICIA *and* BELLEFLURA, *followed by the waiting-woman. They are handsomely attired, bear themselves with great modesty and decorum, first offer their hands to the strangers, and then to their parents. After this they hand round the refreshments, and pour out the wine. Tymbor looks at Phaenicia, and then leads Gerando aside.*

TYMBORUS.
Gerando, I must freely own,
I think Phaenicia's soul alone
Can animate that maiden's frame.
For all her gestures are the same;
She has her style and manners quite,
Her age she has, and also height;
That she my liking too hath won.

GERANDO.
Alas! Oh God, what have I done!
Now all my grief breaks out anew
That I such treach'rous acts could do!
To my heart's core I feel my shame.

TYMBORUS.
Aye, shall I not the maiden claim?
I'd take her, though a crown I wore!

GERANDO.
I ne'er felt all my grief before!
But as two maidens here I see,
Perhaps the other falls to me.
 [*They return to the other guests, making low obeisance.*

LIONITO, *to Phaenicia:*
Lucilia, do you feel inclined
My gracious Lord, the Count, to take?

COMEDY OF THE BEAUTIFUL PHAENICIA.

PHÄNICIA *neigt sich gegen dem Vatter vnd dem Grafen,*
Wenn sich jr Gnaden mein nit wol schemen
Vnd das nicht halten für ein Tatel
Dieweil ich allein bin vom Adel
Nicht hohs herkommen wie sein Gnad
Zu Lionito.
Vnd eur Lieb befind das im Rath
So folg ich eur Lieb allezeit

TYMBOR
Ach diser Red zufriden seit
Die Tugent Edel machen kan
Das Weib kriegt den stand durch den Mann
Wie er ist, also ist auch sie
Dieweil er lebet je vnd je
Seit jhr schon nur Edel geborn
Seit jhr doch heut zur Gräfin worn
Dann euch will ich vnd keine mehr

LIONITO *gibt sie zusammen,*
So geb ich euch zu Gottes Ehr
Beide Ehelichen zusammen
Gott geb euch glück,

TYMBOR *vnd sein Bruder sagen*
Amen, Amen.
[*Er zeicht ein Ring von der handt vnd ein Ketten von halſs henckt jhrs an, steckt jhr den Ring an, vnd trucket sie, helt sie bey der hand.*

PHÄNICIA
Ach Edler Gemahl saget mir
Ward vormals auch verheürat jhr
Ehe vnd wann eur Gnad mich namb

TYMBOR *schlegt an sein Brust*
Ach schrecklicher red mir nie für kam
Ach diese frag bringt mir groſs schmertzen
Vnd gehet mir so tieff zum hertzen
Das sie mich gleich gar will vmbbringen
Thut mich ein Mann zu weinen zwingen
O Phänicia was hab ich thon
Ich wolt ich wer gestorben schon
Für dich, wie schweb ich in vnmuth

PHÄNICIA
Gnediger Herr habt mirs zu gut
Ich hab in allen guten gfragt

PHAENICIA *bows to her father, and then turns to the Count.*
If you should no objection make,
My Lord, or hold it cause of shame,
I only bear a noble name,
Not so illustrious as your Grace,
To Lionito:
You find it too, my sire, in place,
I'll follow you for evermore.

TYMBORUS.
No more of this, I do implore.
Virtue a noble's rank affords;
The wife's rank's settled by her lord's.
For she who bears a noble's name,
Must, while he lives, be just the same.
If only noble, as you say,
A countess you become to-day;
I'll have no other all my life.

LIONITO, *joining their hands.*
I join ye thus as man and wife
Together, to God's honour, then.
God grant you happiness!

TYMBORUS *and* GERANDO.
Amen!
[*He takes a ring from his hand and a chain from his neck, hangs the chain upon her, and puts the ring on her finger. He embraces her, and holds her by the hand.*

PHAENICIA.
Ah, noble husband, tell me now,
Have you been bound by marriage vow
Before your Grace hath taken me?

TYMBORUS, *beating his breast.*
A sadder question could not be.
Your words occasion me great pain,
And pierce me to the heart again.
Strike at my life, and strike so deep,
That I, a man indeed, must weep.
What have I done, my sainted bride!
Would that I had already died
For thee! What misery is this!

PHAENICIA.
My Lord, pray, take it not amiss!
My question was but meant in love.

Tymbor

Ach das sey Gott im Himel klagt
Mein voriges Lieb thut todt liegen
Für die ich in die Höll wehr gstiegen
Wie auch Orpheus hat gethan
Solt ich all verdambt Seel bestahn
Wie Hercules, vnd sie erquicken
Wolt ich mich alsbalt dar zu schicken
Aber es kan doch je nicht sein
Defs ist desto gröser mein pein
Die kein Mensch auff Erd kan ermessen

Lionito

Ey schweigt thut diser klag vergessen
Lang gnug ich euch auffzogen han
Secht eur vertraute doch recht an
Wie wenn sie eur Phänicia wehr

Tymbor *sicht sie an*

Auff der Welt sehe ichs nimmermehr
Werd jhrs aber, wers mir dest lieber
Vnd ich wolt als erleyden drüber
Vnd mein halbe Grafschafft drumb geben

Lionito

Hie steht sie, vnd thut warhafft leben
Wiewol wir meinten sie wer todt
Hat sie doch wider erquicket Gott
Welcher gewifslich haben wolt
Das sie eur Gemahl werden solt
Die hab ich euch an die hand geben

Tymbor *sicht sie an, verwundert sich*

Ach Phänicia thustu noch leben
So solst mir desto lieber sein

[*Er fellt jhr vmb den halfs*

Ach Phänicia die allerliebste mein
Nun sey Gott gelobt vnd geehrt
Der mir dich auch hat wider bschert
Du bist mein auffenthalt vnd freud

Phänicia

Der sey globt vnd gebenedeyt
Der vns nach solch grosen Trübsal
Hat gnediglich gholffen ein mal
Der geb vns Segen, Heil vnd glück.

Tymborus.

My plaint was meant for God above!
My former bride, now dead and cold,
For her, as Orpheus did of old,
To hell I'd go, — though there to see
All the damned souls in misery,
As Hercules, — and her awake
To life — would straight the journey take.
But that can never be, I know;
And all the greater is my woe.
How great indeed, can none conceive.

Lionito.

Hush, hush, from henceforth cease to grieve.
My jest has long enough been tried;
I pray look closer at your bride.
What, should it your Phaenicia be?

Tymborus, *looking at her.*

O ne'er shall I that maiden see!
But were it she, how glad were I!
I'd suffer all most cheerfully,
And half my earldom would I give.

Lionito.

Here stands she, and doth really live.
Though God we thought the maid had ta'en,
Yet hath he quickened her again;
And it most surely was his will,
That she should be your consort still;
'Twas she whom I your Grace would give.

Tymborus, *looking at her in astonishment.*

Phaenicia, dost thou really live?
Thus art thou dearer than before!

[*Embracing her.*

Phaenicia, loved for evermore,
Praise be to God, and honour too,
Through whom again, I'm blessed in you!
You are my joy, my hope, my stay!

Phaenicia.

Praise be to him alone, alway,
Who after such great grief and pain,
Hath helped us graciously again.
O may he grant us happiness!

[Gerando now receives Belleflura as his bride, and Lionito announces that the double nuptials, to which Peter, King of Arragon, is to be invited, will be solemnized on the following day. The

piece now concludes with a moral song of eleven verses, called 'The Maiden's Mirror,' in which the virtues of the Maiden are celebrated. The following are three of the eleven verses, viz. the two first and the last.]

1.

Ihr zarten Jungfraun hört mir zu
Von aller Jungfrau Spiegel,
Vnd merckt was ich euch singen thu
Von der zucht wahren Spiegel,
Gottes forcht wist
Der anfang ist
Vnd weg zu der Weifsheite,
Wer den Weg geht
Gar wol besteht, ja wol besteht,
Vnd liebt auch Gott allzeite.

2.

Dann wer Gott fürcht, der liebt auch jhn
Vnd helt ob seinen worten,
Vnd wandelt fleissiglich darinn,
Helt die an allen orten,
Das vierdt Gebott
Hat geben Gott,
Das man sol Eltern ehren,
Wer dasselb thut
Der hat es gut, ja hat es gut,
Gott wird jhn vil bescheren.

11.

Schliefslich so ist mein fleissig bitt
An all zarten Jungfrauen,
Jr wolt es doch vergessen nit
In den Spiegel offt schauen,
Der weiset gleich
Was fehlet euch,
Thut eure Mängel kehren,
Wenn jhr das thut
So habt jhrs gut, so habt jhrs gut,
Kompt hie vnd dort zu Ehren.

ENDE.

1.

Ye tender virgins, list to me,
What is the virgin's mirror;
And mark what I shall sing to ye,
Of chastity's true mirror.
God's fear, I wist,
The first thing is't,
And way to Wisdom's door;
Who that way go
Shall stand, ye know, stand firm, ye know,
And love God evermore.

2.

For who fears God, he loves him too,
Doth make his word his care,
His way therein with zeal pursue,
And keep it everywhere.
Commandment named
The fourth, proclaimed
By God, is, parents honour,
What maid doth so
Doth thrive, ye know, yes thrive, ye know,
God showers his blessings on her.

11.

To end my song, one prayer I raise
To all ye virgins soft,
That ye will not forget to gaze
Into the mirror oft.
It makes appear
Your failings clear,
Your faults will drive away too,
If ye do so,
Ye'll thrive, ye know, ye'll thrive, ye know,
To honours come some day too.

THE END.

TRAGEDY OF JULIUS AND HYPPOLITA

ACTED IN GERMANY, ABOUT THE YEAR 1600, BY ENGLISH PLAYERS.

The Tragedy of Julius and Hyppolita forms part of the first volume of "*Englische Comedien vnd Tragedien*" 1620, 12mo, reprinted 1624, 12mo. In the edition of 1620, from which the present impression has been taken, it occupies folio K k, 7 verso to folio N n, 4 recto. It is entitled:

VII.

Tragædia.

𝔙𝔬𝔫 Julio 𝔲𝔫𝔡 Hyppolita.

(TRAGEDY OF JULIUS AND HYPPOLITA.)

TRAGÆDIA
VON JULIO VND HYPPOLITA.

Personæ.

Fürst.
Hyppolita Fürstliches Fräwlein.
Romulus }
Julius } zweene Römer.
Grobianus Pickelhering oder Julij Diener.
Romuli Diener.

ACTUS PRIMUS.

Jetzt kompt der Fürst, Romulus, Julius *vnd* Hyppolita *herauſs, der Fürst steigt hinauf, Julius stehet gar melancholisch auff der Seiten.*

Fürst.

Edeler Römer, ein Monat habt jhr nun gewartet, nach dem jhr mich angesprochen, daſs ich euch meine Tochter zum Gemahl geben solt. Sagt mir nun liebt jhr sie von Hertzen?

Romulus.

Von Grund meines Hertzen thue ich sie lieben.

Fürst.

Liebe Tochter sag an, hastu Romulum lieb?

Hyppolita.

Ja hertzlieber Vater vnnd dafern es ewer Will, hab ich jhn vor mein Gemahl auſserkoren.

Fürst.

So habe ich genug, als wünsche ich euch hierzu ein langes Leben, vnnd gebe euch meine junge Tochter, mein einige Hoffnung vnd Trost auff Erden.

Romulus.

Gnädiger Herr dieses schöne Fräwlein ewer geliebte Tochter, thue ich höher achten, denn Silber vnd alles Goldt, vnd thu mich vor dieses Kleinodt höchlich bedancken.

[*Hat sie bey der Handt.*

TRAGEDY
OF JULIUS AND HYPPOLITA.

Persons represented:

The Prince.
Hyppolita, the princess.
Romulus }
Julius } two Romans.
Grobianus Pickelhering (the Clown), servant to Julius.
Servant to Romulus.

ACT I.

Enter the Prince, Romulus, Julius, *and* Hyppolita. *The Prince comes forward. Julius stands a little apart from the others, very melancholy.*

Prince.

Noble Roman, you have now waited one month, since you urged your suit for my dear daughter's hand. Tell me now truly, do you love her with all your heart?

Romulus.

I love her from the bottom of my heart.

Prince.

Dear daughter, say, dost thou love Romulus?

Hyppolita.

Yes, dear father, and an it be your will I have chosen him for my husband.

Prince.

Enough, enough. I wish you a long life, and give you my young daughter, my only hope and comfort upon earth.

Romulus.

My lord, I esteem this beautiful lady, your beloved daughter, more highly than silver and gold, and render you my hearty thanks for this your Jewel.

[*Holds her by the hand.*

TRAGEDY OF JULIUS AND HYPPOLITA.

FÜRST.
Wann gefelt euch dann Hochzeit zu halten.

ROMULUS.
O Gnädiger Herr, lieber heut denn morgen, aber es wil mir erstlich gebühren, dafs ich nach Rom ziehe, vnd es meinen Eltern ansagen, dann wann sie gar nichts von meiner Heyrath wissen solten, würde es jnen vbel gefallen, hoffe in kurtzer Zeit wieder allhier zuseyn. Derhalben begehre ich von ewer Gnaden, vnnd von meiner hertz allerliebsten Vrlaub.

FÜRST.
Edler Römer, kan diese Reise keinen Anstandt haben, bifs nach Vollendung der Hochzeit. Ich bitte bedencket euch, sehet zu dz jhr verreist, Hochzeit haltet.

ROMULUS.
Gnädiger Herr, solches hab ich zuvor bey mir bedacht, aber es kan nicht sein, denn sein Eltern mufs man hierin nicht gantz vnd gar hinden setzen. Bitte derwegen vmb Vrlaub.

FÜRST.
Mufs es denn so seyn, so gebe ich meinen Willen drein, hoff jhr werdet euch nicht lassen auffhalten.

HYPPOLITA.
Ach mein hertz allerliebster, kans müglich seyn, so verharret, warumb wollet jhr doch so vnbarmhertzig seyn, vnd von mir ziehen.

ROMULUS.
Mein getrewes Lieb, wie Vngern ich von euch scheide, könt jhr nicht gleuben, aber es kan nicht anders seyn, dennoch habt dieses zum Troste, meinen getrewen Freund vnd Bruder Julium, wil ich euch befehlen, dafs er euch in meiner Absentz mit lieblichen discursen ergetze vnd also die Zeit verkürtzere. Da steht er, wir wollen zu jhm gehen. Getrewester Freundt vnd Bruder Juli wie so melancholisch.

JULIUS.
Getrewer vnd liebster Bruder, ich bin nicht melancholisch.

ROMULUS.
O Bruder sag mir die Vrsach deiner Betrübnüfs, du woltest dich hart halten, aber kontest nicht, kan ichs mit meinem Blut wenden, wil ichs nicht lassen.

JULIUS.
Die Warheit zu sagen liebster Bruder, so machet mich deine Reise betrübt, denn du weist wie sehr ich dich liebe, ja mein leben vor dich hin zugeben, ich gering achtete. O vnmüglich solt ich nicht trawrig seyn.

ROMULUS.
Es ist war. Von Jugend auff seyn wir vns getrew

PRINCE.
When is it then your pleasure to celebrate your nuptials?

ROMULUS.
My lord, I should prefer to-day to-morrow. But it is my duty first to go to Rome to announce my intended marriage to my parents, lest, if they hear nothing of it, they should take offence. I trust shortly to be here again, and therefore I beg your Grace and my best beloved, to grant me leave to go.

PRINCE.
Noble Roman, cannot this journey be postponed till after the solemnization of the marriage. Pray bethink you, and celebrate your nuptials, ere you undertake this journey.

ROMULUS.
My lord, I have considered the thing well; but it cannot be, for in such a matter we must not quite neglect our parents. I pray you therefore, grant me leave to go.

PRINCE.
Since it must be so, I give my consent. But do not suffer yourself to be detained.

HYPPOLITA.
Sweet my love, an it be possible, remain; — why will ye be so unmerciful as to go from me?

ROMULUS.
Mine own dear love, you know not how loath I am to go from you; but it must be so. And take comfort for I commit you to the loving care of my faithful friend and brother Julius, who in my absence will delight you with pleasant speech and thus while the hours away. There he stands, let's go to him. Most faithful friend and brother Julius, why so melancholy?

JULIUS.
Gentle and beloved brother, I am not melancholy.

ROMULUS.
O brother, disclose to me the cause of thy sadness! thou would'st fain shut it up within thyself, but canst not. I would shed my blood to turn it from thee.

JULIUS.
In truth, dear brother, thy journey makes me sad. Thou know'st what love I bear thee, and that I account my life as naught to serve thee. O how can I be otherwise than sad?

ROMULUS.
'Tis true. From childhood have we been faithful

gewesen, aber liebster Bruder, wormit sol ich solches recompensiren, sage hierin abe den Weiblichen Hertze, vnnd betrübe dich nicht meines hinweg reifsens, denn es kan nicht anders seyn, darumb mein getrewer Freundt, vnd Bruder, befehle ich dir mein schön Hyppolitam mein allerliebste, ich bitte tractire sie mir freundlich in meiner absentia. Vnd schöne Hyppolita betrübet euch nicht, denn ich hoffe in gar kurtzen, ewer hell Christall Augen wieder anzuschawen mit Mercurii Flügeln wil ich eilen wieder zu euch zu kommen, darzu so bald ich zu Rom angelange, wil ich euch mit Schrifften visitiren.

FÜRST

Last vns jetzt hinein gehen, vnd Juli kömpt mit vns, dafs wir Romulo das Geleit geben.

[*Sie gehen hinein Julius betrübt.*

JULIUS.

Wie Vngern, sehe ich dich von hinnen ziehen:

[*Felt auff die Knie.*

O ich wolte dafs du nimmer widerkemest, alsdenn wer ich der glückseligste Mensch, vnd mach mir schon etc.[1]

ROMULUS. *Kömpt wieder.*

Warumb folgestu nicht lieber Bruder? Was bedeutet, dafs du auff den Knieen sitzet?

JULIUS.

Hertzlieber Bruder ich ruffe die Götter an, dafs sie dir wollen favorabiles seyn, vnd in kurtzen wieder anhero verfügen.

ROMULUS.

O du bist mir ein getrewer Freundt, deines gleichen an Trewheit, hab ich noch nie in der Welt funden. Derhalben befehle ich dir noch eines, ergetze mein allerliebste, in meiner absentia mit lieblichen discursen vnnd tractire sie mir wol, denn ich weifs du bist mir der getreweste, darumb ich sie auch nur dir allein befehle.

JULIUS.

O mich getrew. [*Fellet auff die Knie.*] Ich schwere bey der Sonnen, Monden vnd Sternen etc.

ROMULUS.

Stehe auff getrewester Freundt vnd Bruder, kein Eydt begehre ich von dir zu haben, meynestu dafs ich dir ohne das nicht gleuben thue. Nun ade, ade, mein getrewer Freundt, wie Vngern ich von dir scheide, kanstu nicht gleuben, Ade ade, je lenger hie je lenger dort.

[*Gehet hinein.*

to each other. But, gentle brother, how can I recompense thee? — Here say adieu to thy woman's heart, and grieve not for my journey, for so it must be. Wherefore, my faithful friend and brother, I do commend to thee my fair Hyppolita, my sweet love, and beg thee to entreat her kindly in my absence. And fair Hyppolita, do not afflict yourself, for I trust ere long, again to behold your clear crystal eyes. I'll hasten back to you on the wings of Mercury, and as soon as I have arrived in Rome I will visit you with letters.

PRINCE.

Now let us go in, and Julius comes with us, that we may see Romulus on his way.

[*Exeunt the Prince, Romulus and Hyppolita. Julius is sad.*

JULIUS.

How loath am I to see thee depart!

[*Falls on his knees.*

O that thou never would'st return! Then should I be happiest of mortals, and even now I make me etc.[1]

Re-enter ROMULUS.

Wherefore didst thou not follow us, dear brother? What means this kneeling?

JULIUS.

Gentle brother, I am calling upon the gods to be favourable to thee, and to bring thee soon back again.

ROMULUS.

O thou art a true friend to me. Thy like for faithfulness have I nowhere found in all the world. Wherefore once more I pray thee, delight my love in my absence with sweet discourses, and entreat her well for the love thou bear'st me. And for as much as I know thou art of all the most faithful to me, I commend her to thee alone.

JULIUS.

O me, faithful! [*Falls on his knees.*] I swear by the sun, moon, and stars etc.

ROMULUS.

Rise up, most faithful friend and brother! I crave no oath of thee; think'st thou I cannot trust thee without one? Now farewell, — thou canst not know how loath I am to part from thee. Adieu, adieu, the longer here, the longer there.

[*Exit.*

---

[1] These unfinished passages, which occur frequently not only in this, but in all the other pieces of the collection of "*Englische Comedien vnd Tragedien*," prove that the texts have been hastily got up for the press and that the writers themselves could not have had any share in the publication.

JULIUS.

Ziehe dafs du mögst den Halfs brechen, vnd nicht wieder kommen. Jetzt mufs ich auff Prakticken dencken, Romule Romule getrewer Freundt bistu wol, aber jetzt mufs ich dir vntrewe Brüderschafft beweisen. O schön Hyppolita was kan dein schön Gestalt, nicht zu wegen bringen, O was solte Liebes Brunst nicht aufrichten. O Hyppolita du Wunder unter allen Weibespersonen, du must mein seyn, oder ich mufs nicht leben, nun mufs ich gedencken wie ichs wolle anfahen, man sagt, practica est multiplex, nun ich mufs auch eins darvon versuchē.

[*Gehet ab.*

JULIUS.

Ay, go, — and so that thou break thy neck and never return. Now must I contrive my plan. Romulus, Romulus! a faithful friend art thou to me, 'tis true; but now must I prove to thee what faithless brotherhood is. O! lovely Hyppolita, what cannot thy fair form effect. O! what cannot love accomplish. O! Hyppolita, thou wonder amongst women, thou must be mine, else I cannot live. Now I must bethink me how to set about it. Men say 'practica est multiplex'; — now 'tis for me to try one.

[*Exit.*

ACTUS SECUNDUS.

JULIO.

Juli bedencke dich nun wol, was du bey Romulo thust. Hie habe ich Brieffe von Rom bekommen, die sol ich der schön Hyppolita seiner allerliebsten vbergeben, aber es kan nicht seyn, dieselbigen mufs ich vnterschlagen, vnd an dessen Statt habe ich andere geschrieben. Bedencke dich nun wol Juli es ist ein Römer den du betreugst, sie suchen Rache vber ihre Feinde, vnd triumphiren stets vber alle ander, in der gantzen Welt. Aber wenn du auch der streitbahrste Römer werest, wolte vnnd könte ich nicht vnterlassen, dir jetzt vntrew zu werden, mein Vorhaben mufs ich nun fortsetzen, denn was thut Liebe, nicht vmb dero willen, ich jetzt mein Leben in die eufserste Gefahr setze, wolan es mufs so seyn. Holla mein Diener Grobiane kom heraufs.

GROBIANUS *kömpt heraufs, der Herr pfeiffet. Stehet still.*

GROBIANUS.

Mein Herr mufs ja meynen, dafs er einen Hundt vor sich habe.

[*Julius pfeiffet noch einmal.*

GROBIANUS.

Pfeiff du jmmer hin, ich bin dein Hundt nicht.

JULIUS.

Jung hastu nicht gehöret, dafs ich dich geruffen, wornach siehestu dann?

GROBIANUS.

Nein Gnädiger Herr, ich hab kein ruffen gehört, sondern pfeiffen, vnd gemeinet jhr Gn. hetten den Hundt zu sich gepfiffen.

JULIUS.

Kom hier Grobiane vnd observire mein Wörter

ACT II.

JULIUS.

Julius, consider well how thou dost act by Romulus. Here have I letters to deliver to fair Hyppolita, his sweet love; but it must not be, — I must keep them back, and in their stead I have writ others. Pause and weigh well, Julius — 'tis to a Roman thou play'st the knave, and they seek vengeance on their foes and triumph over all others in the world. Ay, an wert thou the most contentious of all Romans, I would not, could not refrain from being faithless to thee in this matter. I must fulfil my purpose now; — for what will not love do, for whose sweet sake I place my life in jeopardy? Well, it must be so. Ho! my servant Grobianus, ho!

Enter GROBIANUS, *his master whistles. He stands still.*

GROBIANUS.

May-be my master thinks he has a dog before him.

[*Julius whistles again.*

GROBIANUS.

Whistle away, I am not thy dog.

JULIUS.

Boy, hast thou not heard me call? Wherefore dost thou stand so?

GROBIANUS.

My lord, I heard no calling, but whistling, and thought your worship was whistling to his dog.

JULIUS.

Come hither, knave, and mark ye well my words.

wol, diese Brieffe soltu tragen zu der schönen Hyppolita, dich anthun, gleich einen Postboten vnd zu jr sagen, dafs dich Romulus von Rom zu jhr gesant, mit diesen Brieffen. Sieh hie hastu Geldt, verrichte es trewlich hernach soltu mehr von meinen Händen empfangen.

GROBIANUS.

Gnädiger Herr, was solte ich vmbs Geldt nicht aufsrichten? Wenn ich könte Geldt darfür bekommen, so wolt ich meine Mutter eine Hur vnd meinen Vater einen Schelm heissen, ewern Befehl wil ich trewlich aufsrichten.

JULIUS.

So mache dich bald fertig, vnd übergieb jhr die Brieffe.

GROBIANUS.

Es sol geschehen.

[*Gehet weg.*

JULIUS.

Also hoffe ich die schöne Hyppolitam vor mein eigen Gemahl zubekommen, Juli fast ein Hertz, ja ein eyssern Hertz, denn ein hohes hastu angefangen, dasselbe mustu aufsführen.

Stehet allein in tieffen Gedancken. Kömpt herauſs der
FÜRST. HYPPOLITA *ist betrübet, geht sitzen.*

FÜRST.

Es ist vmb das Weibesvolck ein seltzam Manier, vornemlich gar wunderlich, wenn sie verliebet seynd, denn schreyen, heulen, vnd weinen, ist jhr täglich Speise, so jhr liebster nicht bey jhnen ist. Wie zum Krankheit Tochter bistu so närrisch? wirdt doch dein Romulus wieder kommen, warumb betrübstu dich dann.

HYPPOLITA.

O Vater ich habe Vrsache zu weinen, weil ich nicht weifs, ob mein liebster ist gsundt nach Rom kommen denn die Zeit ist nun verflossen, in der er gelobet vō der zuschreiben. Da sehe ich Jul. in tieffen gedancken stehen, liebr Vater wollen wir nicht zu jhm gehen, vnnd fragen ob er nichts von Rom bekommen.

[*Gehen zu jhm.*

FÜRST TOCHTER.

Einen guten Morgen Juli.

JULIUS.

Ich sage jhr Gn. auch schönen Fräwlein höchlich danck.

FÜRST.

Juli wisset jr nicht was jhm zu thun sey, denn meine Tochter gar verzweifeln wil, weil jhr liebster ein wenig von jhr gewesen?

JULIUS.

O Gnädiger Herr, darfür wird man bey keinen

Bear these letters to fair Hyppolita, dress thee as a postboy, and say that Romulus charged thee with these letters from Rome. Here is money, perform thy errand faithfully, and by and by my hands shall be more liberal.

GROBIANUS.

My lord, what would I not do for money! An I could get money for't, I'd throw whore at my mother and call my father rogue. A trusty messenger I'll prove to do your bidding.

JULIUS.

'Tis well — prepare thee quickly, and go deliver the letters.

GROBIANUS.

On the instant.

[*Exit.*

JULIUS.

So may I hope to possess fair Hyppolita as my own wife. Julius, take heart, ay an iron heart. Thou play'st a high game and must not faint in the midst of it.

[*Stands apart in deep thought.*
Enter the PRINCE. HYPPOLITA *is sad and sits down.*

PRINCE.

How strange are women's ways, how passing strange! When they are in love, crying, weeping, roaring is their food, an their sweetheart is not with them. Daughter, thy folly will cause thee to fall sick, thy Romulus will surely come to thee again; wherefore then grievest thou?

HYPPOLITA.

O father, I have cause to weep, for I know not whether my sweet love hath reached Rome in safety, as the time is past in which he swore to write from thence. There I see Julius standing in deep thought. Dear father, let's go to him, and learn whether he has received aught from Rome.

[*They approach Julius.*

HYPPOLITA.

A good morning, Julius.

JULIUS.

Have thanks your worship, and you too, fair lady.

PRINCE.

Julius, can you not advise me? My daughter is quite desperate because her love hath left her for a short time.

JULIUS.

My lord, no doctor hath a remedy for that, for

Doctore einig Mittel finden, denn es vns Menschen von Natur angebohren, vnd wircket solches die inbrünstige Liebe.

HYPPOLITA.
Guter Freundt habt jhr nicht Schreiben von Rom bekommen.

JULIUS.
Nein schönes Fräwlein gar keine.

HYPPOLITA.
O die Zeit ist gleich schon verflossen, in der er mir bey seiner getrew Lieb geschworen zuschreiben.

JULIUS.
Schönes Fräwlein traget gar keinen zweifel, ich weifs vnd kenne sein Hertz, dafs was er zusaget, gewifslich helt, vnd kan seyn dafs der Bote, welchen er gesand, nicht eile.

Kömpt GROBIAN.

GROBIANUS.
Glück vnd all Heil schönes Fräwlein.

HYPPOLITA.
Ich dancke dir Bote von Hertzen, O sage mir bald kömpstu nicht von Rom.

GROBIANUS.
Ihr habt es errathen von Rom kom ich, vnd bin von Romulo zu euch gesandt.

HYPPOLITA.
O glückselige Stunde, O glückseliger Bote, zeig mir bald den Brieff von Romulo meinen Hertzallerliebsten.

GROBIANUS.
Verziehet ein wenig, ihr musset erstlich den Boten sein penunse geben.

HYPPOLITA.
Sieh da hastu, thu bald den Brieff her, wornach ich ein grofs verlangen gehabt.

GROBIANUS.
Da seyn die Brieffe, so mir mein Herr Romulus gegeben.
[*Sie küsset den Brieff.*

HYPPOLITA.
O sey mir willkommen. Hier seyn noch zwey Brieffe, einer an Julium, der ander an euch hertzlieber Vater.

FÜRST.
An vns auch Tochter? das ist sehr gut. Weine nun auch Tochter, ich weifs wol, dafs der gute Romulus zuschreiben nicht vnterlassen würde.
[*Lesen, sie verwundern sich sämptlich, kratzen sich bey den Haaren.*

we mortals are born with it, and ardent love effects it.

HYPPOLITA.
Good friend, have you received no writing from Rome?

JULIUS.
Fair lady, none whatever.

HYPPOLITA.
O the time is already past, in which he swore by his true love to write to me.

JULIUS.
Fair lady, do not torment yourself with doubts, for full well I know his heart, that what he has surely promised he will as surely hold. It may be that the messenger whom he has despatched tarries on the way.

Enter GROBIANUS.

GROBIANUS.
All happiness and peace to you, fair lady!

HYPPOLITA.
I thank thee, messenger, most heartily! O tell me quick, dost thou come from Rome?

GROBIANUS.
You have hit it; from Rome I come, and am sent to you by Romulus.

HYPPOLITA.
O blessed hour! O blessed messenger! show me quick the letter from Romulus, my heart's treasure!

GROBIANUS.
Wait a little. First you must remember the messenger.

HYPPOLITA.
Take this; — produce the letter speedily for which I have so yearned.

GROBIANUS.
There be the letters, as delivered to me by my master Romulus.
[*She kisses the letter.*

HYPPOLITA.
Welcome, o welcome! here are two other letters, one to Julius, and one to you, dear father.

PRINCE.
For us too, daughter? that is well, — very well. Weep now too, daughter, I knew that good Romulus would not fail to write.
[*They read, are one and all astonished, and scratch their heads.*

TRAGEDY OF JULIUS AND HYPPOLITA.

HYPPOLITA.

O weh O weh Eva im Paradiese, wie schändlich würdestu betrogen?

FÜRST.

O Stadt Troja, durch list wordestu gewonnen.

[*Sie lesen noch besser.*

JULIUS.

O du betrieglichster Mensch vnter allen Mannspersonen, du Eckel vnd Schandfleck vnter allen, wie hastu dieses können vber dein Hertz bringen.

HYPPOLITA.

O Angst, O Todes Angst, grösser schmertzen hab ich niemaln auff Erden empfunden. O verfluchet seystu Romule, verflucht sey die Stunde, worin ich dich zum ersten ansichtig worden. O warumb haben die Götter euch Mannsbilder ordiniret vnd erschaffen, daſs jhr vnsere arme Jungfräwliche Hertzen so peinigen vn ängstigen müsset. O jhr Poeten warumb schreibet jhr die Weibespersonen seyn wanckelmütig? O nein jhr thut vns vnrecht, jhr Mannespersonen seyd voller Wanckelmütigkeit, die vngetrewesten, vnbarmhertzigsten Creaturen auff Erden, jhr seyd gleich wie der Wind wehet. O verfluchter vntrewer Romule, ist daſs die trewe Liebe, so du mir zugesagt vnd geschworen, hey jhr vnsterblichen Götter, verkürtzet mir doch mein Leben, auff daſs mein Hertzleid ein ende nehme.

FÜRST.

Liebe Tochter, stell dich zu frieden, denn dein Wehklagen dir nichts nutzen wird. Pfui du verfluchter Romule, wie bistu so voller Vntrew worden?

JULIUS.

Ja wol voller Vntrew vnd Schande, schad ists, daſs er ein Römer gebohren. Pfui du verfluchter vntrewer Mensche, nun sol dir all dein Freundschafft abgesaget seyn, dargegen aber wil ich dich mit Haſs vnd Feindschafft verfolgen thun, weil du so vntrew vnd vnbarmhertzig an der jenigen thust, welche jhr Leben vor dich hette geben, dir sol alle Freundschafft auffgesagt seyn, vnd gleub gewiſs, daſs ich solches rechnen wil. darumb schöne Princessin seyd nicht betrübet, denn ich alles solches rechnen wil. Erfrewet euch vnter dessen, daſs jhr solch ein vngetrewen Menschen nicht seyd theilhafftig worden.

FÜRST.

Lieber Juli, sagt vns was euch doch der verrätherische Bösewicht geschrieben.

JULIUS.

Gnädiger Herr, es ist einerley Meynung, aufsgenommen hier hat er vnter geschrieben. Grüſse mir den alten Narren, Hyppolitae Vater den alten Scheisser,

HYPPOLITA.

Alas! alas! Eve in Paradise how shamefully wert thou deceived!

PRINCE.

O! Troy thou wert taken by stratagem.

[*They read on.*

JULIUS.

O thou most deceitful amongst men, thou abomination and disgrace, how couldst thou find it in thy heart!

HYPPOLITA.

O anguish! O mortal anguish! never have I experienced such sore pain on earth. O! cursed be thou Romulus, cursed be the hour when first I set my eyes on thee! O wherefore have the Gods made and created you men to wring with anguish our poor virgin hearts! O, ye poets! wherefore do you write that women are fickle! O no! you do us wrong, you men, 'tis you who are full of fickleness, the most perfidious, the most unmerciful creatures on earth, who change with every wind. O accursed, o false Romulus, is that the constant love you promised and swore to me? Ho! ye immortal gods shorten my days, that the troubles of my heart may cease!

PRINCE.

Dear daughter, be calm, for thy lamentations can avail thee nothing. Fie, thou accursed Romulus! How couldst thou be so false?

JULIUS.

Ay, full of perfidy and shame! Pity is it that he is born a Roman. Fie, thou accursed treacherous man! Henceforth do I renounce thy friendship, nay more, I will pursue thee with my hate and enmity, that thou hast acted so perfidiously, so mercilessly towards her, who would have given her life for thine. All friendship be henceforth withdrawn from thee, and, trust me, I will call him to account. Therefore, fair Princess, grieve no more, for I will surely call him to account for this. Meanwhile rejoice that you have not become the consort of so vile a man.

PRINCE.

Dear Julius, pray tell us what this treacherous villain has writ to you.

JULIUS.

My lord, it is all to the same effect, save the postscript here: 'greet that old fool, that simpleton, Hyppolita's father of whom I have made a laughing-stock. You

mit dem ich ja wol den Narren getrieben. Sie meynen last es was sachte angehen, hem, hem, hem, meynen sachte.

FÜRST.

Hem, was der Teuffel schilt er mich vor einen alten Narren vnd Scheisser, der Teuffel danck dirs. Aber was schreibt der lose Kerl mehr?

JULIUS.

Da lese es Jhr Gn. selber.

[*List, schüttelt den Kopff.*

FÜRST.

Aber wie zum Element sol ich dieses verstehen? So meynen laſs es was sachte etc.

JULIUS.

Ich kans nicht errathen, ich wil aber wol gläuben, daſs Jhr Gn. solches wird vor ein gewönliche Rede gehabt haben.

FÜRST.

Ja es ist recht nun befinde ich mich. Wenn der lose Kerl bey meiner Tochter zu sitzen, vnd sie zu hertzen pflegte, hatte ich vor eine gewonheit also zu redent. Nun spottet er vnser noch zu vnsern Schaden. Ist diſs das Deo gratias vor alle Wolthat? Der Teuffel muſs mir ja den losen Kerl zu erst zugeführet haben. Nun sehe ich wenn er sich so freundlich vnd demütig gegen mir gestellet, hat er den Geck mit mir getrieben, hole der Teuffel solche Gäste, ich begehre dein nicht.

GROBIANUS.

Schönes Fräwlein, was vor Antwort sol ich Romulo bringen.

HYPPOLITA.

[*Reisset den Brieff entzwey, vnd wirfft jhn auff die Erden.*

Also, also bring ich dieses zur Antwort.

FÜRST.

[*Reisset seinen auch entzwey.*

Vnd also bring ich von mir Antwort.

GROBIANUS.

Gnädiger Herr was vor Antwort sol ich von Jhr Gn. haben.

JULIUS.

Bescheidt haben? O sag den Grewel vnd Vnzier vnter allen Mannespersonen, den verfluchten vntrewen Romulo, daſs ich sein ärgster Feind seyn wil, zu vnser beyder Tagen ihn solches nimmer zuvergessen, vnd so vnd so

[*reist entzwey.*

wil ich jhn antworten.

think I should go to work gently, hm, hm, hm, gently I say'.

PRINCE.

Hm! Why the devil does he call me an old fool and a simpleton? — the devil thank him for it! But what more does the varlet write?

JULIUS.

Perhaps you had better read it yourself.

[*He reads, and shakes his head.*

PRINCE.

But how, by all the elements, am I to understand this? Think I should go to work gently, etc.

JULIUS.

I cannot guess, but should be inclined to think that perchance my lord has been accustomed to employ this manner of speech.

PRINCE.

Ay, ay, now I understand it. When the varlet used to sit by my daughter and embrace her, it was my custom so to speak; and now he scoffs at us to our hurt! Is this the Deo gratias for all our benefits? It must have been the devil himself that sent the rascal to us. Now I know that while he was pretending such kindness and humility, he was only making a fool of me. Devil take such guests, I'll none of them.

GROBIANUS.

Fair lady, what answer shall I take to Romulus?

HYPPOLITA.

[*Tears the letter and throws it on the ground.*

That, that is my answer.

PRINCE.

[*Tears his also.*

That is my answer too.

GROBIANUS.

My lord, what answer from your lordship?

JULIUS.

What answer? O tell this monster, this abomination of men, this accursed perfidious Romulus, that I am his bitterest enemy, and never to the end of my life will forget it, and so and so

[*tearing the letter*

do I answer him.

GROBIANUS.

Ich wils wol gläuben, dafs Jhr Gn. sein ärgester Feind ist vnd bleiben wird. Also ade von hinnen ich mich mache.

[*Geht weg.*

JULIUS.

Schönes Fräwlein, achtet jhr wol wirdig vmb des verfluchten vntrewen Romuli wegen betrübt zu seyn.

HYPPOLITA.

Ja ich bin betrübet, vnd das betrübste Weibesbild auff der Welt.

JULIUS.

Ich bitte verbannet jhn aufs ewern Sinn vnd Gedancken, so seyd jhr mit Fröligkeit wider ernewert.

FÜRST.

Solches ist auch mein Rath, liebe Tochter, dafs du jhn gar aufs deinen Hertzen verbannest, vnd nimmer an jhn gedenckest, sonsten wird das winseln, wehklagen kein Ende haben, lasset vns hinein kehren, vnd nicht mehr an jhn gedencken, denn ich habe Vrsache, solche Schmach aber werde ich mein Tage nicht vergessen.

ACTUS TERTIUS.

JULIUS.

Holla, holla Diener Grobiane kom heraufs.

GROBIANUS.

Hie bin ich gnädiger Herr.

JULIUS.

Hör Diener, dir ich am meisten vertrawe, wie du auch selbst weist, dafs ich dir vertrawt, welches ich sonst leichtlich keinen gethan hette, fahr also fort, es sol dein Schade nimmer seyn.

GROBIANUS.

Gnädiger Herr, ich bin bereit Jhr Gn. in allen zu folgen vnd zu gehorsamen, auch die Sachen also zu verrichten, dafs es Jhr Gn. nicht besser begehren sol.

JULIUS.

Du bist mein getrewester Diener, darumb ich dich auch allein zu meinen geheimen Sachen brauch. Nim hin diesen Brieff, trag jhn alsobald zur schönen Hyppolita, vermelde jhr darneben mein freundlichen Grufs vnd Dienste, sag vnd machs jhr grofs vor, wie hefftig ich in jhr verliebt, wie jämmerlich ich mich gebehre, dafs ich weder esse noch trincke, auch keine Ruhe haben kan, sondern stets seufftze: In Summa mache

GROBIANUS.

I fully believe, my lord, that you are, and will remain, his bitterest foe. Farewell, I hie me hence.

[*Exit.*

JULIUS.

Fair lady, do you hold it worth your while to be sad for that accursed false Romulus?

HYPPOLITA.

Ay, I am sad, and the saddest woman on earth.

JULIUS.

Pray banish him from your thoughts and heart, and let joy restore you.

PRINCE.

Such is my counsel too, dear daughter. Banish him quite out of thy heart and never think of him more; else will there be no end of tears and lamentations. Let us go in and never mention him again, for indeed I have reason. But never to the end of my life shall I forget such outrage and dishonour.

ACT III.

JULIUS.

What ho! Grobianus come here!

GROBIANUS.

Here I am, my lord.

JULIUS.

Listen, knave. In thee have I placed most confidence. Thou knowest I have trusted thee, a thing I do but rarely; go on as thou hast begun, thou shalt never rue it.

GROBIANUS.

My lord, I am ready to follow and obey your lordship and to manage everything so, that your Lordship shall not wish to have it better.

JULIUS.

Thou art my trusty knave, therefore I use thee in my secret matters. Here, take this letter, bear it without delay to fair Hyppolita, convey to her my sweet greeting and humble service, unfold to her in many words how sick I am for love, how pitiably I bear myself, that I can neither eat nor drink nor rest, but am always sighing. In fine, make the devil big and ten times bigger than he is. I promise thee, knave, thy suit

den Teuffel grofs vnd zehenmal mehr, denn es ist, fürwar Diener wirstu etwas mit deinen procuriren erhalten, Goldt, Silber, vnd grofs Gnad sol dein recompension seyn, mach dich nun auff, zur Stunde, vnd brauch ja wol deine Zunge.

GROBIANUS.

Gnädiger Herr, Jhr Gn. gleuben mir, dafs ich mit höchstem Fleifs die Sache wil anbringen.

[*Nimpt den Brieff, gehen hinein.*

HYPPOLITA.

Weil Trew vnd Glaube ist worden klein, werd ich nun bleiben gar allein. In Betrübnifs Jammer vnd Elend wil ich nun mein gantzes Leben zubringen, stets seufftzen vnd Thränen mussen meine Speise seyn. So bald des Tages Liecht anbricht, werde ich eingedenck seyn wie ein Mensch voller Vntrew stetigs pflag zu mir zu kommen. All getrew Lieb thu ich verfluchen. Mit Standthafftigkeit hab ich getrewe Lieb zu halten mir angelegen seyn lassen, aber es ist mir vbel belohnet worden, was mag von mir haben wollen, der so eilends zu mir kömpt.

[*Kömpt Grobianus.*

Mich deucht ich nie ein grewlichern Kerl gesehen hab.

GROBIANUS.

Schönes Fräwlein, meines jetzigen Handwercks ich ein Briefftträger bin, hie hab ich einen an Jhr Gn. mit demütiger Bitte, denselben zu vberlesen. Mein Herr Julius lest Jhr Gn. zu 1000. malen grüssen, von welchen ich auch diesen Brieff habe.

HYPPOLITA.

O das tausendtmal grüssen thönet noch stets vor meinen Ohren. Es kömpt mir aber dieses gar seltzam vor vom Julio, sintemal ich zuvor nur eins von jhm zu empfahen pflag. Hie steht: Schönest auff Erden, die inbrünstig grosse Liebe, so ich zu euch trage zwinget mich nunmehro mit aller Macht euch solches zu offenbaren. Weil ich aber also in ewren Stricken gefangen liege, habe ich nimmer keine Ruhe, all Witz vnd Verstandt thut mir schier vergehen. Ich kan mit Warheit wol klagen, dafs ich der vnglückseligste Mensch auff Erden sey. Werde ich aber von diesen Banden auffgelöset, schätz ich mich vor den Glückseligsten. Darumb schönest Hyppolita, die jhr mein Leben in ewren Händen, vnd gefangen habt, beweist mir Liebe, weil ich gegen euch mit solcher inbrünstigen liebe vmbgeben, weil es Venus vnd Cupido in jhren choro also beschlossen. O reist abe die Bande, thut mich nicht länger kräncken, sondern glückselig machen. Dieser Brieff ist vergeblich geschrieben. Liebe, Liebe, ich bin

shall bring thee recompense in gold, silver and great favour. Be gone this instant, and use thy tongue well.

GROBIANUS.

My lord, your lordship may rely on me to speed your cause with all diligence.

[*He takes the letter. Exeunt.*

HYPPOLITA.

Since faith and trust are gone, I'll spend my virgin days alone. In sadness, wretchedness, and misery, must I pass my whole life; sighs and tears must be my daily food. As soon as day dawns, I shall remember how a man, false and perfidious, used to come to me. I'll execrate all true love. It has been my heart's desire to love with constancy, but my love has met with but a poor return. — What can this man want of me, who is coming in such haste.

[*Enter Grobianus.*

Methinks I have never seen a more detestable fellow.

GROBIANUS.

By trade, fair lady, I'm a letter-bearer, and bear one for you, which I humbly entreat you to peruse. My master Julius sends a thousand greetings to you, lady, and this letter.

HYPPOLITA.

O how the thousand greetings still resound in mine ears! Yet still, from Julius methinks 'tis strange, seeing one greeting was his wont before. Thus he writes: 'Fairest on earth, the great and fiery love I bear you compels me now with irresistible power to reveal it to you. My wits and understanding are clean gone, and I know no rest, because I am a captive to your charms. I can with truth complain that I am the most wretched man on earth. But were I once liberated from these bonds, I were the happiest. Wherefore, fairest Hyppolita, who doth hold my life in her hands, show me a little love, seeing that I bear you such great and fiery love, and that Venus and Cupid have decreed it in their choir. O burst these bonds, afflict me no longer, but make me happy.' — This letter is writ in vain. Love, love, I have had my fill of thee! I have loved enough, and thereby the matter is at rest for ever. Shall I love again? Nevermore! Ye false men, ye are born but to make fools of us women, with your whining words. Hear

deiner satt, genug habe ich geliebet, vnd darbey sol es gäntzlich beschlossen seyn. Solt ich nun wiederumb lieben? Nimmermehr: Jhr betrieglichen Mannespersonen seyd nur gebohren, mit kläglichen Worten die Jungfrawen ins Narrenseil zu führen. Höre Diener sage deinem Herrn, dafs ich den Brieff empfangen, Antwort darauff, achte ich vnnötig.

GROBIANUS.

Schönes Fräwlein, dofern ich kein andere Antwort von Jhr Gn. erlange, so hengt er sich vor allen Element auff, dann schönes Fräwlein, jhr können nicht gläuben, wie voller Pfeilen er geschossen. Fürwar er klaget sehr vmb E. Gn. sie sey dessen allein ein Vrsache, ich verleih ein gut Wort vor meinen Herrn, denn er mich sehr darumb gebeten, ich sol es höher vor Jhr Gn. anbringen, als es jmmer ist, er isset vnd trincket nicht, er hat auch keine Ruhe, so hefftig ist er gegen Jhr Gn. verliebet, vnd wenn er noch schläfft, seufftzet er, redet im Schlaffe: Hyppolita,:, darumb gnädiges Fräwlein, Jhr Gn. machen ein grofs Vnruh, dafern sie dieses nicht wendet.

HYPPOLITA.

Meinethalben kan er wol zu frieden seyn, mache dich nur von hinnen, vnd bringe deinen Herrn zur Antwort, dafs ich den Brieff empfangen.

GROBIANUS.

So werde ich meinem Herrn ein vnangenehmer Bote seyn, Botenlohn, Goldt, Silber vnd grofs Gnade, welches mir mein Herr zugesagt, werde ich nun müssig gehen. Damit ich dennoch etwas darvor habe, bitte ich Jhr Gn. mir ein Zehrpfennig mitzutheilen.

HYPPOLITA.

Begehrestu nur das? Sieh da hastu einen Ducaten, damit mache dich von hinnen.

[*Nimpt.*

GROBIANUS.

Höchlich Jhr Gn. ich dancken thu, allerschönest, allertugendtreichstes Fräwlein, dessen lobwirdig Nahme erschallet in alle Welt, die Warheit auch zu sagen, jhr Gn. ist die Allerschönest auff Erden, ich hette es nie gläuben wollen, wenn ichs nicht gesehen. An Schönheit thu ich Jhr Gn. vergleichen der Göttin Veneri. An Tugenden der Göttin Dianae. Ich kan nicht Wörter finden zu preisen, wie wol billich.

HYPPOLITA.

Nach solchen Lob ich auch wenig fragen thu, hette ich dir keinen Ducaten geben, so were ich auch nicht in dein Lob gerathen, mach dich alsobald aufs meiner praesentz, weil ich deiner nicht länger allhie begehre.

[*Gehen hinein.*

me, knave, tell thy master I have received his letter, further answer is unnecessary.

GROBIANUS.

Fair lady, if so be I get no other answer from your ladyship, he'll go hang himself in face of all the elements, for, sweet lady, you cannot imagine how full of darts he is. In sooth he suffers much; and you lady are the sole cause. I would put in a good word for my master, because he entreated me to do so, and tell to you, gracious lady, how he can neither eat nor drink nor yet find rest, so violently is he in love with your ladyship, and when he sleeps he sighs, and exclaims, 'Hyppolita!' Wherefore, gracious lady, you will cause him much disquietude, if so be you are not minded to avert it.

HYPPOLITA.

He may be happy for aught it concerns me. Be gone, and take this answer to your master — I have received his letter.

GROBIANUS.

Thus I shall be an unwelcome messenger to my master, and I must lack the recompense, the gold, the silver, and the great favour, my master promised me. But that I may have somewhat for my pains, I beg a bounty of you, gracious lady.

HYPPOLITA.

Desirest thou naught but that? Hold, take this ducat and be gone with thee.

[*He takes it.*

GROBIANUS.

I give you my best thanks, most virtuous and most beauteous lady, whose matchless name resounds throughout the world. To speak the simple truth, your ladyship is the most beautiful lady on earth. I could never have believed it, had I not seen it. In beauty I compare you Madam to the goddess Venus, in virtue to the goddess Diana. I have no words to praise you as 'tis meet.

HYPPOLITA.

I care but little for such praise; had I given no ducat I had received no praise; wherefore begone from my presence, as I have no longer any need of you.

[*Exeunt.*

TRAGEDY OF JULIUS AND HYPPOLITA.

Kömpt der Fürst *vnd* Julius.
Fürst.
Juli sonder gůter Freund, wol hab ich euch observiret vnd angehöret bitten vmb meiner Tochter Hyppolitam. Es ist euch nun bewust, wie Romulus sich mit jhr verbunden vnd verlobet, vnd wie das vntrewe Mensch sie verlassen, was Schimpff vnd Spott mir, so wol meiner Tochter dardurch kommen. Derhalben ich nichts liebers sehe, daſs sie nur in diesem Gewäsch möge vermählet werden. Ich euch zu jhr wol tüchtig erkenne, darumb gebe ich meinen Willen darein, daſs sie euch möge vermählet werden, dennoch in meinen Willen es nicht allein, sondern auch in jhren stehet, darumb ist mein Rath, daſs jhr sie selber anredet, vnd ewer Liebe jhr an praesentiret.

Julius.
Wie hoch ich erfrewet kan Jhr Gn. nicht gläuben, ich bitte Jhr Gn. vnterthänig, daſs er sie zu sich wolle kommen lassen, auch Jhr Gn. wolle helffen sie darzu bereden.

Fürst.
Gar wol, ich hoff es sol alles gut werden. Holla Hyppolita kom eilends zu mir.

[*Kömpt.*

Hyppolita.
Gnädiger Herr Vater.
Fürst.
Liebe Tochter, dieser junge Cavallier Julius mit dir etwas zu reden hat, hör jhn wol zu, vnd thue jhn guten Bescheidt geben.

Hyppolita.
Gnädiger Herr Vater, guten Bescheidt jhr jhn wol geben könnet, mich deucht ich sein Anbringen zuvor wissen soll.

Fürst.
Zuvor wissen, so mustu ein Prophetin seyn.
Julius.
Schönest Creatur, so du jemaln den Erdboden betreten, die inbrünstig lieb, so ich zu euch trage, zwinget mich mit Macht es euch zuoffenbaren. Seynd mich der blinde Cupido geschossen, bin ich ein ander Mensch worden, da ich war zuvor frölich, bin ich nun trawrig, vnd nach dem ich noch nicht occasion habe gehabt mit euch allein Gespräch zuhalten, vnd mein Anliegen zu offenbaren, bin ich stets in Betrübniſs gewesen. Weil ich denn jetzt so gar in ewer Macht vnd Gewalt, so komme ich demütig bittend, O Vrsache habe ich zu bitten, Jhr Lieb wol mir dieses wenden, vnd von der Last erlediget, O schönes Fräwlein meiner Hoffnung nicht mehr ich wünschen wolt, denn daſs Jhr Lieb in

Enter the Prince *and* Julius.
Prince.
Julius, my rare good friend, I have observed you closely and heard your suit for my daughter Hyppolita. It is known to you how Romulus was bound and betrothed to her, and how the perfidious wretch abandoned her, and with what infamy and ridicule he covered both me and my daughter. For this reason I desire nothing better, than that she should be married, and get clear of all this gossip. And as I acknowledge you to be quite worthy of her, I give my consent to the marriage. Nevertheless, as the matter does not lie in my will alone, but also in hers, my counsel is, that you address yourself to her and disclose your love.

Julius.
Your grace cannot conceive how rejoiced I am to hear it. I humbly entreat your grace to call her hither, that so your grace may lend your powers of persuasion.

Prince.
I hope thy suit will prosper. Ho! Hyppolita, come here directly!

Enter Hyppolita.
My gracious lord and father.
Prince.
Dear daughter, this young cavalier Julius hath somewhat to say to thee; listen to him and give him a favourable answer.

Hyppolita.
My gracious lord and father, you may give answer for me. Methinks his petition is foreknown to me.

Prince.
Foreknown! then must thou be a prophetess.
Julius.
Most fair and lovely creature that ever trod the earth, the fervid love I bear you compels me with irresistible power to disclose it to you. Since blind Cupid has shot at me I am become another man; whereas formerly I was joyous, I am now sad, and since I lacked opportunity to hold discourse with you alone, to lay my petition before you, I have been in constant sorrow. As then I am so wholly in your might and power, I come to you with a humble entreaty. Oh I have cause to pray that your love may avert this from me, and relieve me of my burden. O lovely lady of my hope, I could wish nothing better than that you might look into my heart as through a window, and behold its temper, and know

mein Hertz gleich durch ein Fenster sehen könte, wie es jetzt beschaffen, wie es im Fewr lieget vnd brennet, O könte ich wünschen, das zugleich auff mein Hertz geschrieben stünde, wie es mit jhn beschaffen, getrewen Liebhaber würde man mich nennen, darumb schönest mein tausendt vnd aufserwehlten Schatz mein hertzallerliebste nehmet dieses zu Hertzen, machet mich glückselig, erzeiget mir recompension, vnd beweiset mir liebe.

HYPPOLITA.

Lieben vnd liebhaben ist nicht zu reden, solt ich noch lieben? O nein, denn lieben ist gewifs betrüben, es liebe mich einer getrewlich oder nicht, so thue ich doch alles in den Wind schlagen. Freund Juli warumb bittet jhr, vmb solches welches jhr zuvor wisset, dafs es nicht seyn kan, es ist euch bewust, wie ich geliebet, vnnd wie ich bezahlet, derhalben schwere ich im Tempel, vor der Göttin Diana allein zu dienen, darbey auch ein keusches, reines vnd Jungfräwliches leben zu führen. Zwar Juli euch ich nicht verachten thue, denn jhr meiner wol wirdig, aber dieses kan nicht seyn, vnnd alle ewer lieb, die jhr bey euch traget, were mein Rath, dafs jhr es gar in der Lufft vertreibet, last abe, last abe von lieben, jhr liebet vmbsonst vnd vergebens, vnd machet euch nur zum Narren.

JULIUS.

Zum Narren, zum Narren, ich wils fürwar wol gleuben schönst Hyppolita, E. L. beweiset mir jetzund die gröste Vnbarmhertzigkeit. Jetzt wird eines verrätherlichen Mannes Vbelthat allen Mannspersonen zugerechnet, allerschönest Hyppolita, Jhr L. bedencke dieses, dafs bei Romulo vngetrew vnd falsche liebe war, in mir aber ist getrewe, standthafftige vnd inbrünstige liebe.

Ad spectatores.

O nicht inbrünstige liebe, warumb ward ich meinem Getrewesten auff Erden vngetrew? O schönes Fräwlein, seyd nicht so gar vnbarmhertzig, last erweichen ewr hart vnd kaltstälern Hertz, O löset auff den der so schwer in ewer Gewalt gefangen lieget, beweiset mir liebe, sonst komme ich in höchste Noth vnd Jammer.

HYPPOLITA.

Fürwar Juli ich bedencke solches, wie Romulus ein vngetrewe liebe, vnd jhr ein getrewe liebe führet. Ich weifs mich noch zuentsinnen, dafs Romulus eben wie jhr sein getrew mir vorzusagen wuste. Nein, nein, ich begehre mit keinen getrewen Hertzen vmbzugehen, last ab :,: füget euch zu einer andern Madon mit ewern getrewen Hertzen, es ist vergebens, ja gar vergebens.

how it is consumed with a burning fire. O could you read what is written on my heart, you would call me a true lover. Therefore, most fair, most exquisite and rarest treasure, my best beloved, take this to thy heart; make me blessed, and return my love!

HYPPOLITA.

It is easy to prate of love and loving — can I still love? O no, for to love were but to bring sorrow. Whether I am loved faithfully or no, I cast love to the winds. Friend Julius, wherefore do you wish for that, which you know before I cannot give. You are not ignorant how I have loved, how I have been repaid. Therefore, in the temple, before the goddess Diana I swear to serve no one but her, and to lead a chaste, pure and virgin life. 'Tis true, Julius, I despise you not, and you are worthy of me; but this cannot be. Be advised, scatter to the winds all the love you bear within you. Cease, cease from loving, you love in vain, you love hopelessly, and only play the fool.

JULIUS.

Ha! Play the fool, play the fool, fair Hyppolita, in sooth I fear it! Dear lady, how cruel do you show yourself in this! You impute one false man's misdeed to all men. Fairest and most beautiful Hyppolita, weigh this: though Romulus' love was false and treacherous, mine is faithful, constant and most fervent love.

Ad spectatores.

O not fervent love, wherefore was I false to the truest on earth? — O sweet lady, be not so very unmerciful, — suffer your hard and flinty heart to be softened! O liberate him who lies so heavily fettered by your power, and show me some love, else I perish in deepest wretchedness and woe!

HYPPOLITA.

In truth Julius I do believe that Romulus bore me a false love, and you a true. I well remember, that Romulus, like yourself could discourse fluently of love. No, no, I desire to ensnare no faithful heart, — desist: get you to another Madonna with your faithful heart; it is in vain, — altogether in vain.

TRAGEDY OF JULIUS AND HYPPOLITA.

JULIUS.

O Vnbarmhertzigkeit bistu doch eben so mächtig, wie der Donner vnter den Himmel, gleich eine Donnerkeil schlegstu jetzt durch mein junges Hertz, vnd thust es noch häfftiger vorsehren vnd verderben, O warumb lieb ich, du grimmiger Todt, warumb wilstu meiner nicht begehren, ich vnglückseeligster Mensch. Mein Vorhaben gehet den Krebsgang.

Ad spectatores.

Was ist mir nun gelüstet, mein Vntrew, so ich an meinen getrewesten Freunde auff Erden, der sein Leben vor mich gelassen, vollnbracht. Juli Juli. Worein hastu dich geführet?

[*Steht betrübt.*

FÜRST.

Juli warumb so betrübt? Sagt mir vnnd was jhr guts erhalten bey meiner Tochter?

JULIUS.

Gnädiger Herr, die Vrsach meines Betrübnüfs ist diese, dafs ich nichts erhalten mag, jhr Gn. Tochter wil gar nichts hören, von der trewen Lieb, die ich zu jhr trage, sie gedenck dafs die Vntrew Romuli, so tieff in jhren Hertzen stecke, auff dafs auch jemaln ein man so glückseelig seyn sol, jhrer theilhafftig zu werden. Denn sie auch bey der Göttin Diana geschworen, Jhre Tag in Jungfräwlichen Leben zu vollnbringen. O wann nun jhr Gn. mein procurator seyn wolten, so gebe ich mich ein wenig zufrieden.

FÜRST.

Wolan gebt euch zufrieden, ich wil mein Fleifs thun, dafs sie euch liebe. Hyppolita. Liebste vnd eigne Tochter, du weist wie ich dich von Jugend auff hefftig geliebet, gleich einen Vater mag gebühren. Nun bistu zu deinen Jahren kommen, derowegen mir dich zuversehen gebühren wil, alfs habe ich diesen jungen Printz Julio dich jhm zu eigen zugesaget, drumb lafs dirs gefallen, weil er dein an gebürth Tugenden vnd Reichthumb wol wirdig ist.

HYPPOLITA.

Liebster Herr vnd Vater mein, Julius der junge Printz, ist meiner liebe wol wirdig, aber jhr liebde bedenck zuvor die grosse Vntrew, so Romulus an mir bewiesen, welches mir so sehr eingetrieben, dafs ich mirs gäntzlich vorgenommen, mich nimmermehr zuverheyrahten.

FÜRST.

Liebe vnd einige Tochter du thust gar weit jrren, die vberflüssigen Gedancken thun dir deinen verstandt gar benehmen, bedencke dieses hinwieder Romulus ist mit falscher vnd vntrewer Liebe dir gewogen gewesen,

JULIUS.

O cruelty, thou art as mighty as the thunder from heaven! like a thunderbolt dost thou fall now into my young heart, searing and withering it up! O wherefore do I love, thou grim fierce death, wherefore dost thou not desire me, most miserable of men! My design goes backwards.

Ad spectatores.

What boots the perfidy I've practised on my most faithful friend on earth, who would have given his life for mine. Julius, Julius, what hast thou brought thyself to!

[*Stands melancholy.*

PRINCE.

Julius, wherefore so sad? Tell me, what favours from my daughter?

JULIUS.

My lord, the cause of my sadness is this, that I have had none. Your daughter will listen to naught of the true love I bear to her. She fancies that the faithless Romulus so holds her heart, that another can never be blessed by possessing her. Moreover she has sworn by the goddess Diana to spend her days in virginity. O! if your grace would sue for me, I could be somewhat more at ease.

PRINCE.

Well now, compose yourself, I will do my utmost for that she may love you. Hyppolita, my dear and only daughter, thou know'st how fervently I've loved thee from thy youth as a father may. Now hast thou come to that age, when it is fitting that I should endow thee; for which purpose I have promised thee to this young Prince Julius. Be content therefore, seeing he is equal to thee in birth, virtues, and riches.

HYPPOLITA.

Dearest sir and father mine, Julius, the young Prince, is well worthy of my love; but consider first the great unfaithfulness, which Romulus has practised towards me, and which has struck so deep, that I have quite determined never to wed.

PRINCE.

Dear and only daughter, thou goest far astray; thy too luxuriant fancies deprive thee of thy wits. Weigh this again. Romulus with his false and treacherous love was dear to thee; but this Julius, as I do well observe,

dieser Julius aber liebet dich von Hertzen, wie ich von allen Vmbständen mercken kan, also dafs ich fast mein Tage keinen Menschen gehöret, d' höher were verliebet gewesen, fürwar Tochter du magst gar kein Vnterscheidt zwischen guten vn̄ bösen, du bist mein einig Erbe des Fürstenthumbs, vnd soltestu nicht vermählet werden, so würden wir die frölichsten Tage erlebet haben, vnd das landt würde dardurch in frembde possession gerahten, nicht also liebe Tochter, thue demselben, der falsch vnd vntrew mit dir gehandelt, nicht die liebe an, dafs du soltest besitzen bleiben. Wirstu mich lieben, so wirstu mir auch folgen.

Julius.

O schöne Hyppolita was ist auff der Welt, da man wahre liebe kan an den Tag geben, vnd mehr in Warheit bekräfftigen, denn durch einen Eydt, welchen ich denn jetzt auff meinen Knieen ablege, vor jhr liebten. So thue ich nun schweren vor allen vnsterblichen Göttern, dafs die Liebe, so ich schönes Fräwlein zu euch trage, vnverfälschet sey, sondern getrew, standthafftig, ja dafs sich mein Hertz nimmer zur Ruhe geben wird, ich bin denn zuvor ewer Liebte theilhafftig worden, die brennend vnd trewe Liebe lest nimmer nach, sie macht offt den trawrigsten Menschen, auch offt den frölichsten von derer beyden eins, ich werde ersettiget werden. O schönest Fräwlein, wen ich nicht mit recompensiren bezahlet werde, so mufs ich ohn Zweifel sterben, wenn denn ein solches geschehe, man sprechen möchte, dafs jhr an meinem Tode ein Vrsach, vnd dessen hernach kleiner Ehre hettet. Vnd fürwar ich gleub, wenn E. L. ein solches bedächten, das Gewissen sich betrüben würde, dafs sie ein solch Vnbarmhertzigkeit an mir gethan hette, vnd zu sich selbsten sprechen werde, O weh O weh, was grosses vbel ich begangen, dafs ich mich nicht vber Julium den getrewesten Liebhaber erbarmet habe? O weh mir jmmer, dafs ich jhn so jämmerlich mit meiner Vnbarmhertzigkeit getödt habe: Solch Wehklagen vnnd Gedancken weren doch alle verlohren, vnd weren nur Vrsache die Vnruhe zuvermehren. Vnd damit E. L. nicht zu solchen komme, lafs sie doch jhr steinern Hertz erweichen, vnd mich Gnade empfahen, ehe denn ich den Todt leide.

Fürst.

Liebste Tochter, du hast ja nun genugsam angehöret, mit was inbrünstiger liebe dieser junge Printz Julius kegen dir vmbgeben, drumb lafs doch abe von deinen Vorsatz, vnd dafern du mich jemaln geehret, so lafs dir Julium gefallen, vnd gib jhn dein Hertz, gleich wie er dir gethan hat.

loves thee in his heart, so that, as I can perceive from all the circumstances, I have hardly ever known a man more deeply in love than he. In sooth, daughter, thou mak'st no difference between good and bad; thou art the sole heir of my princedom and shouldst thou not wed, our happiest days would be at an end, and my lands would fall into stranger's hands. Wherefore do not, dear daughter, do not remain unwed for love to one who has repaid thee with falsehood and perfidy. If thou dost love me, do my will.

Julius.

O fair and lovely Hyppolita, what else is there in the world to prove and confirm true love more than a solemn oath, which here upon my knees I swear before you, dear lady. Before the immortal Gods I swear, the love I bear you, fair lady, is no feigned love, but true and constant, nay that my heart will never know peace till it becomes a sharer in your love. True and fiery love never ceases, it often makes the saddest men, and often too the gayest, and one of these I must surely be. O fairest lady, if you do not reward me, doubtless I must die; and should this happen, they will say you are the cause of my death, and you will reap little honour by it. And verily, I do believe, my lady, if you will consider this, your conscience would be sad and sore at such hideous cruelty, and would thus discourse: Alas! alas! how great a sin have I committed, in not taking pity on Julius, the most true and faithful of lovers. Woe is me, that I have murdered him miserably with my hideous cruelty! Such bitter thoughts and regrets would be all in vain, and would only add to your remorse. That you be not, my lady, reduced to such sad state, pray suffer your hard heart to be softened, and show me grace, ere I endure this death!

Prince.

Dearest daughter, thou hast surely listened to the fill to this fiery tale of love from Prince Julius. Wherefore desist from thy resolve, and if ever thou hast honoured me, admit Julius to thy favour, and bestow on him thy heart as he has his on thee.

HYPPOLITA.

Hertzliebster Vater, weil es dann ewer hertzlicher Wille, das ich mit Julio sol vermählet werden, vnd er mir getrewe liebe zugeschworen, ich auch nichts mehr von jhn fordern kan, so laſs ich es mir alles wolgefallen, vnd nach ewren Willen zu leben, bin ich pflichtschuldig.

FÜRST.

Hertzliebe Tochter, du thust mich jetzt höchlich erfrewen.

JULIUS.

Aber mich 1000 mal mehr, glückseelig sey die Stunde, in welcher mir die lieblichen Wörter zu Ohren kommen.

FÜRST.

Wolan Juli. Hie empfänget mein Tochter, lebet lang mit jhr in Friede vnd Frewde.

JULIUS.

Die Götter all in gemein seynd jetzt gepreiset daſs sie mich diesen Tag erleben lassen. Vnd Gnädiger Fürst demütig thue ich mich bedancken, daſs mir jhr Gn. gewirdiget vnd seine einig Tochter geben, was in Menschlichen Kräfften stehet zuwieder gelten, mit liebe, Frewde, vnd wie es jmmer seyn möge, daran jhr Gn. Frewde vnd Trost an vns haben möge, sol nur mein stetes nachtrachten seyn.

FÜRST.

Ich zweifel nicht, jhr werdet mir ein Trost in meinem Alter seyn, aber hiervon darnach weiter, jetzt last vns hienein kehren, vnd bedencken wie ehest das Beylager in allen Frewden möge gehalten werden.

ACTUS QUARTUS.

ROMULUS.

O lieber Gott was hab ich gehöret, daſs mein vngetrewer Gesell Julius, mir meine hertz allerliebste Braut entfreyet, nun ich komme vnd gedencke mit jhr meine Frewde zu haben, so ist es durch Falschheit vnd Betrug alles vorgebauet. O kein Wort kan ich bald vor schrecken mehr reden. O du vngetrewer verrähterlicher Bösewicht, verflucht seystu, vnd deiner Seelen müsse nimmer Rath werden

Zum Diener.

Aber du mein getrewer Freundt, ich bitte sag niemand ein Wort darvon, daſs du mich hie gesehen hest.

HYPPOLITA.

Dearly beloved father, as it is your hearty will that I should wed Julius, and he has sworn to love me truly, I can demand no more and must submit, as it is my bounden duty to obey your will.

PRINCE.

Beloved daughter, now dost thou rejoice me much.

JULIUS.

And me a thousand times more; blessed be the hour, that brought the sweet words to my ear!

PRINCE.

Well Julius, here receive my daughter, live long with her in peace and happiness.

JULIUS.

Be all the gods together praised for this day! And, gracious Prince, be humbly thanked that you have held me worthy of your only daughter! Whatever is in mortal power, to recompense with love, and joy, whatever may yield your grace comfort and delight in us, shall be my sole and constant aim.

PRINCE.

Doubtless you will prove a comfort to me in my old age. But more of this anon. Now let us go in and confer on the festivities which shall soon be held in great joy and mirth.

ACT IV.

ROMULUS.

O Heavens, what have I heard! that my perfidious fellow Julius hath robbed me of my sweet bride and wedded her, now that I am come expecting to find my joy in her! All, all is lost through his perfidy and falsehood. I scarce can utter a word for horror. O thou perfidious, treacherous villain, my curses light upon thee, and may thy soul never know peace!

To the servant:

But thou, my faithful friend, say no word to anybody that thou hast seen me here.

TRAGEDY OF JULIUS AND HYPPOLITA.

SERVANT.

My lord, I'll do your bidding, and not say a word of your return to any one.

[*Exit servant. Romulus paces up and down in great dejection, and meanwhile finds the false letter which the Prince's daughter in her rage had torn in two pieces.*

ROMULUS.

Here I find a letter. Methinks I ought to know this hand. O wonder see, it is my perfidious brother Julius' handwriting! It runs thus:

[*Reads the letter.*

Fair lady, I hereby make known to you, that you can never be mine, for I am already wedded here at Rome to one much fairer and richer than yourself.

[*Drops the letter and speaks:*

O woe to the treacherous deed! What is this world? Naught but the dregs of infamy and lies. O that such an infamous deed had never been! O now to live longer were a torment of hell. O would that pale death might triumph o'er my heart! But let me think of justice, for who would then revenge me on my foes? Nay, nay, this very day my hand shall bathe in thy blood. Revenge and to the rescue will I shout out after thee. Nay, nevermore is her proud body destined for thy arms; for in the evening when thy mirth is greatest, I'll take thy life miserably in the dance, that henceforth thou mayest nevermore deceive, as thou at present hast done by me. But see, there comes the false wretched man out of the church triumphantly in great state and splendour. I know what I will do: I will retire, disguise myself as a servant, and help thee dance the bridal dance, but such a tragedy I will act with thee, that never shalt thou deceive and sadden any one more.

JULIUS.

[*Enters with his bride from the church. Romulus stands at a distance looking on, goes away after a time and disguises himself. They begin to dance. Julius speaks to Hyppolita:*

Pray, tell me, my rare treasure, how did you like the musicians and comedians that acted the tragedy yesterday?

TRAGEDY OF JULIUS AND HYPPOLITA.

HYPPOLITA.
Schönes Lieb die Musicanten gefallen mir nicht vbel, die Comœdianten aber gefielen mir aufs dermassen wol, denn ein jeglicher agirte seine Person wol vnd prächtig.

FÜRST.
Sieh da sieh da, was macht jhr beyde, lieber last vns nun lustig vnd frölich, diese Hochzeit verbringen, junger Printz wie stehet jhr so stille, wollet jhr mit ewrer Braut nicht zu tantze.

JULIUS.
Gnädiger Herr vnnd Vater, jetzt wollen wir zu tantzen anfahen, holla jhr Musicanten seyd lustig vnd last euch hören.

[*Jetzt fänget man an zutantzen, da der vollnbracht kömpt Romulus sampt ander vermummet, vnd præsentiret sich vor einen Mittäntzer, wie jhn Julius siehet spricht er.*

Sieh sieh wer ist der, es mag wol keine geringe Person vnd vns zu ehren anhero kommen seyn. Geht zu jhm, willkommen willkommen, mein Freundt, wollet jhr vns zu Ehren ein Täntzlein mit vollnbringen?

[*Romulus schweiget still, wil nicht reden, machet tieffe Reverentz.*

DIENER.
Gnädigster Printz, ich vernehme es wird ein Student von Padua seyn, so also vermummet E. F. G. Beylager hat wollen condecoriren helffen, denn dieselben solches wol in Gebrauch zu haben pflegen.

JULIUS.
Nun so thue ich mich kegen euch, jhr seyd wer jhr wollet gnädig bedancken, vnd thue euch meine allerliebste hiemit ein Frantzösisch Täntzlein zu vollnbringen, vbergeben.

ROMULUS *acceptiret sie, machet hohe Reverentz so wol kegen dem Breutgam, als Braut, wie er aufsgetantzet, præsentiret er sie den Breutgam wieder, vnd spricht zu Julio.*

Gnädigster Printz, E. F. G. wolle nun mit seiner liebsten Princessin, auch ein Täntzlein verrichten E. F. G. lasse jhr doch wie es dero nicht zu wieder, den Tragœdien Tantz auffmachen.

JULIUS.
Warumb dafs mein Freundt? Warumb nicht ein andern lustigen Tantz.

DIENER.
O gnediger Fürst vnd Herr es ist ein prave Tantz, gehet sehr schön vnd lieblich, vnd gezimet wol solchen Personen, als E. F. G. zu tantzen.

HYPPOLITA.
Dear love, the musicians were not amiss; but the comedians pleased me mightily, for each acted his part splendidly.

PRINCE.
What, what, ho! what are you two about? Come, let us be mirthful at this wedding. Young Prince, how is it you're so still? Lead your bride out to the dance!

JULIUS.
My gracious lord and father, we will now begin. Ho! musicians, strike up, give us a merry measure.

[*The dancing begins. When it is finished, Romulus and others enter masked; he presents himself to a partner, Julius remarks him and speaks:*

Ha! see, who is he? It is most surely no low person, who comes hither to do us honour. Let us go to him. Welcome, welcome, my friend! we pray you, do us the honour of joining in the dance!

[*Romulus remains silent, he will not speak, bows low.*

SERVANT.
Most gracious prince, I have learned that this mask may be a student from Padua, come to grace your princely festivities, as is their custom.

JULIUS.
Be ye who ye may, I thank you graciously for your presence and give you my sweetheart as partner in a French dance.

ROMULUS *accepts her, bows profoundly to the bridegroom as also to the bride. The dance finished, he presents her to the bridegroom and speaks to Julius:*

Most gracious prince, I pray your grace to try a dance with your sweet princess, the tragedy dance, if your grace has no dislike to it.

JULIUS.
Wherefore that, my friend? Why not some other merry dance?

SERVANT.
My gracious lord and prince, it is a brave dance, goes very sweetly and beautifully, and it becometh well such persons as your grace, to dance it.

JULIUS.

So machet auff jhr Musicanten, machet auff den Tragædien Tantz.

[*Die Musicanten machen auff, Julius tantzet mit der Braut, vnter dessen giebt sich Romulus zuerkennen, zeucht die Kappen ab, vnd mit blossen Dolch spricht er zu Julio.*

ROMULUS.

Sieh du vntrewer verrähterlicher Mensch kennestu mich noch wol. Siehe hie diese Tragædiam hastu getantzet.

[*Ersticht jhn mit den Dolchen vnd wirfft jhn hernach auff die Erden, der Fürst vnd seine Tochter erzittern für schrecken, Romulus spricht zu jhr.*

Vnd du vntreweste Creatur, warumb bistu mir so vntrew worden, ist die recompens meiner getrewen beständigen Liebe? O Hyppolita, Hyppolita, ist deine Liebe so gering kegen mir gewesen, vnd hast dich von mir deinen getrewen Liebhaber zu dem Schandtfleck aller Manspersonen, den vngetrewen Julio gewandt.

HYPPOLITA.

[*Ist noch in der Meynung, dz Romulus die Brieffe geschrieben.*

O weh, O weh, wie angst ist meinen jungen betrübten Hertzen, O weh, O weh, sol dann nun vmb meinet willen vngestrafft, ein solcher Mordt geschehen, Nein nein das mufs nicht seyn, sondern hiemit wil ichs büssen.

[*Nimpt den Dolch von der Erden auff, vnd ersticht sich.*

FÜRST.

O du Mörder, eines schrecklichen Todes mustu sterben.

ROMULUS.

Ja frewlich, ja ja das wil ich auch thun, aber dafs ich den Schaum vnd Vnflat, aller bösen Menschen, den vngetrewen Verrähter erstochen, habe ich grosse Vrsach, vnd wenn ichs nicht gethan, wolt ich es noch thun. Von grosser Qual vnnd Hellen Angst meines Hertzens, kan mein Mundt kein Wort mehr reden. Dennoch solt jhr wissen, dafs ich die Brieffe nicht geschrieben, sondern dieser verfluchte vntrewe Mensch, hat es aufs lauter Falschheit Vntrew vnd Abgunst in meinen Namen verfertiget, vnd diese jämmerliche Tragædien angerichtet. Aber diese Princessin, die arme Creatur hat sich erbarmlich, vnd vnschuldig vmb jhr Leben gebracht. Nun nun wil ich jhr in der Vnschuldt vnnd Tode, gleicher Gesellschafft leisten. O Fortuna,

JULIUS.

Ho! musicians, strike up then, strike up the tragedy dance.

[*The musicians strike up, Julius dances with his bride, meanwhile Romulus discovers himself, draws off his cap and speaks to Julius with a naked dagger in his hand.*

ROMULUS.

Look, perfidious treacherous wretch, dost thou recognize me? See here this is the tragedy thou hast danced.

[*He stabs him with the dagger and then throws him to the ground. The prince and his daughter tremble with terror. Romulus speaks to her:*

And thou, most faithless creature, wherefore wert thou false to me? Is that the recompense of my true and constant love? O Hyppolita, Hyppolita! was then thy love for me so slight that thou could'st turn from me, thy true and faithful lover, to that plaguespot amongst mankind, that false Julius?

HYPPOLITA.

[*Still believing that Romulus had written the letters.*

Woe, woe is me! What anguish for my sad young heart! alack and well-a-day, shall such a foul murder, committed for my sake, pass unrevenged? Nay, nay, that must not be, thus shall I expiate it.

[*Raises the dagger from the ground and stabs herself.*

PRINCE.

O thou murderer! thou must die a dreadful death.

ROMULUS.

Ay verily, ay, ay, I will do that too, but for stabbing that false traitor, that scum and dregs of mankind, I had great cause; and were't not done I'd do it still. The torments and anguish of the hell within me prevent my utterance. Nevertheless be it known to you, that it was not I who wrote the letters, but this false accursed man, out of falsehood, perfidy, and spite, devised them in my name and brought about this miserable tragedy. But this princess, poor creature, has miserably and innocently taken away her own life. Well, I will bear her company in innocence and death alike. O Fortuna, Fortuna, seeing thou hast so sorely deprived us of thy favours, I will sacrifice myself in defiance of thee and the whole world. Ho! take example by me ye deceitful hearts, ho!

TRAGEDY OF JULIUS AND HYPPOLITA.

Fortuna, diewil du vns deine Gaben so sehr entzogen, wil ich dir vnnd der gantzen Welt zu Trotz mein Leben dahin opffern, huy nempt ein Exempel jhr betrüglichen Hertzen, huy nempt ein Exempel jhr getrewen Hertzen, nempt ein Exempel jhr Liebhaber, nehmt ein Exempel jhr Liebhaberin, vertrawet keinem als ewern eigen Hertzen. Ade ade.

[*Ersticht sich.*

FÜRST.

Ach weh vnnd vber weh, dafs ich solch elend ja erbärmliche Tragædien, habe mit meinen betrübten Augen ansehen müssen. Nun nun schwere ich bey allen Göttern, dafs ich die Tage meines Lebens in keines Menschen Angesicht hinfuro mehr kommen wil, sondern wil alfsbald in einen finstern vnnd wilden Waldt gehen, vnnd ein Einsiedels Leben führen, mit meinen Fingern wil ich eine Höle in die Erden graben, vnnd darin mein stetiges Lager haben. Neun Stunden lang wil ich mein Andlitz täglich zur Erden legen, vnnd vmb meiner Tochter todt schreyen vnnd weinen, die Wurtzeln sollen meine Speise, vnnd dafs Brunnwasser mein Getränck seyn, ich wil nicht auffhören mit schreyen vnnd jämmerlichen Wehklagen, bifs der grimmig Todt sein gifftig Pfeil durch mein zermalmtes vnnd betrübtes Hertz schiessen wird. Nun ade Ade du böse Welt, ein einsam Leben mir jetzt gefelt. Ich gehe jetzt hin mein Strassen thue dich gäntzlich verlassen, Ade Ade.

take example by me ye faithful hearts, take example ye lovers, take example ye fair ladies, trust to no heart but to your own. Farewell, farewell.

[*Stabs himself.*

PRINCE.

Ah! woe and thrice woe, that my sad eyes have beheld such pitiful distressful tragedies! Now, now I swear by all the gods, that henceforth I will no longer live in the sight of man, but go into a dark savage wood and lead a hermit's life, with my fingers will I dig a hole in the earth, and there will I make my nightly couch. Every day will I lie for nine hours with my face to the earth, and cry and weep for my daughter's death. Roots shall be my food, and water from the well my drink. I will not cease my cries and pitiable lamentations, till grim death has shot his poisoned arrow into my bruised, afflicted heart. Now farewell, farewell thou wicked world, a solitary life is now my sole desire. I go from hence and quit for ever thy frequented paths. Adieu, adieu!

FINIS.

THE END.

TRAGEDY OF TITUS ANDRONICUS

ACTED IN GERMANY, ABOUT THE YEAR 1600, BY ENGLISH PLAYERS.

The Tragedy of Titus Andronicus forms part of the first volume of "*Englische Comedien vnd Tragedien*", 1620, 12mo, reprinted in 1624, 12mo. Republished by Ludewig Tieck, in *Deutsches Theater*, Band I, Berlin 1817, in-8vo, pag. 367—407.

In the present impression the first edition of 1620 has been strictly followed. In the latter the play occupies folio Nn, 4 verso to folio Ss, 4 recto, and is entitled:

VIII.

Eine sehr klägliche Tragædia von
Tito Andronico vnd der hoffertigen
Kayserin, darinnen denckwürdige
actiones zubefinden.

(A MOST LAMENTABLE TRAGEDY OF TITUS ANDRONICUS AND THE HAUGHTY EMPRESS, WHEREIN ARE FOUND MEMORABLE EVENTS.)

TRAGÆDIA
VON TITO ANDRONICO.

Personæ.

VESPASIANUS.
RÖMISCHE KÄYSER.
TITUS ANDRONICUS.
ANDRONICA.
ÆTIOPISSA Königin aufs Mohrenland. Käyserin.
MORIAN.
HELICATES Königin aufs Mohren, erster Sohn.
SAPHONUS Königin aufs Mohren, ander Sohn.
ANDRONICÆ GEMAHL.
VICTORIADES.
BOTE.
WEISE WÄCHTER.

ACTUS PRIMUS.

Jetzt kömpt heraufs Vespasianus vnd hat die Römische Krone in der Hand. Titus Andronicus hat ein Lorbeer Krantz auff seinem Häupte, auch kömpt der Keyser, aber damalen war er noch nicht Römischer Keyser. Auch die Königin aufs Morenlandt, welche schön vnd weifs, sampt jhren zween Söhnen; vnd der Morian, welcher schwartz vnd geringe Gewandt vber seine prechtige Kleider gezogen, vnd welcher der Königinnen Diener, vnd heimlich mit jhr buhlet. Diese viere aber hat Titus Andronicus gefangen genommen. Auch ist da die Andronica.

VESPASIANUS.

Jhr edelen Römer wisset euch zu entsinnen, wie dafs vnser Kayserthumb jetzt leer vnd verstorben ist, derhalben wil sich gebühren, dafs man bey Zeite darzu sehe, dafs ein Kayser wiederumb erwelet werde, damit man die grosse Vneinigkeit vnd Zanck des gemeinen Mannes müge zuvor kommen. Weil ich dann nun keinen andern wüste, dem es solte zuerkandt werden, als diesem Titum Andronicum, weil er jetzt der vornembste vnd neheste darzu ist, auch niemandt in dieser Stadt Rom, der sich besser vmb sie verdienet, mit blutigen gefehrlichen Kriegeswesen, als er, vnd auch ein jeglich

TRAGEDY
OF TITUS ANDRONICUS.

Persons represented:

VESPASIAN.
THE ROMAN EMPEROR.
TITUS ANDRONICUS.
ANDRONICA.
ÆTIOPISSA, Queen of Ethiopia, Empress.
MORIAN.
HELICATES, eldest son of Ætiopissa.
SAPHONUS, second son of Ætiopissa.
CONSORT OF ANDRONICA.
VICTORIADES.
MESSENGER.
WHITE GUARDS.

ACT I.

Enter Vespasian with the Roman Crown in his hand; Titus Andronicus with a laurel-crown on his head; the Emperor of Rome that was to be. The Queen of Ethiopia, lovely and of fair complexion, together with her two sons; Morian, the Queen's attendant and paramour, with a plain black mantle over his handsome dress. The four last are captives of Titus Andronicus. Andronica.

VESPASIAN.

Noble Romans, it is well known to you, how that our Empire is now vacant and demised, wherefore it is meet to look to it in time that an Emperor is elected, that we may ward off discord and strife in the commonalty. And as I know no other fitting candidate than this Titus Andronicus, in as much as he is the most exalted and the best entitled; and as there is no man in this city of Rome whose deserts to her in bloody and perilous battles were greater than his; and as every body loudly says that the Roman crown is due to him by right, so let us all wish him joy, place

Mann schreyet, daſs jhm von Rechtes wegen die Römische Krone gebühret zutragen. So last vns sämptlich jhn darzu Glück wünschen, die Krone auff sein Häupt setzen, vnd jhn allezeit für vnsern gnädigsten Keyser halten vnd ehren.

Keyser.

Was? solte nun Titus Andronicus die Krone für mich auff sein Häupt setzen, nein, nimmermehr muſs das geschehen, dann ich der neheste bin, vnd sie mir von Rechteswegen gebühret zutragen. Derhalben jhr Römer bedencket euch wol vnd weiſslich was jhr thut, damit in dieser edelen Stadt Rom sich kein Auffruhr vnter vns errege, vnd sie nicht in Noth vnd Gefahr komme.

Titus Andronicus.

Ihr Römer solt wissen, daſs mir doch nichtes vmb dieses Keyserthumb zu thunde ist, dann ich nun ein alter betagter Mann, vnd die Zeit meines Lebens in steten vnd gefährlichsten Kriegen mich habe gebrauchen lassen. Ob nun wol alle Stimmen auff mich gehen, vnd ein jeglich Mann mir das Keyserthumb zueignet. So sollet jhr dennoch sehen, daſs ich vmb Friedes willen gerne einem andern vbergeben wil, daſs durch concordiam vnd Eintracht zwischen dem Keyser vnd dem Rathe, auch dem gemeinem Manne ist Rom das Häupt der gantzen Welt geworden, solte denn nun in der Mawren an despenation vnd Zweytracht sich erheben, so würde es mussen zu grunde gehen. Derhalben wil ich die Hoffart an die Seite werffen, vnd mich vielmehr der Demuth befleissigen: So kompt jetzt alle heran, vnd lasset vns den Keyser krönen, wünschet jhm alle mit lauter Stimme Glück vnd Heil.

[*Titus Andronicus setzet jhm die Krone auff sein Häupt, vnd sagen alle mit lauter Stimme:*

Langes Leben, viel Glück vnd Heil, wünsche ich dem vnüberwindlichsten vnd Groſsmächtigsten Römischen Keyser.

Keyser.

Nun meine liebe Getrewen, weil jhr mich dann für eweren Keyser erwehlet, vnnd haltet, so verpflichte ich mich auch widerumb euch mit sonderlichen Freyheiten zu privilegiren, Leib vnd Blut mit euch, für vnser Vaterlandt, wagen, vnd allzeit mit trewen meynen. Vnd Titus Andronicus die jhr mir dieses Keyserthumb gerne vnd willig vmb der gemeinen Nutz vnd Friedes willen, vbergeben, bin ich sonderlich mit grosse liebe vnd Trewe gewogen, begehre derhalben ewre schöne Tochter Andronica für meine Keyserin, vnd sol heute, wie eine Keyserin gekrönet, vnd mir vermählet werden, so jhr ein Gefallen dran habet.

the crown on his head, and consider and honour him as our most gracious Emperor.

Emperor.

What! shall Titus Andronicus place the crown on his head instead of me? No, that shall never happen, for I am the next heir and it belongs to me by right. Therefore Romans, consider well and wisely what it is ye do, that there may be no insurrection in our noble city which might place it in great peril.

Titus Andronicus.

Romans! you shall know, that I care nought for Imperial rule, for I am now far advanced in years, and have been engaged all the days of my life in long and perilous wars. Although all voices are for me, and everybody bestows the Imperial title upon me, you shall see, that for the sake of peace I will make way for him; for it is by concord and unison between the Emperor, the Senate, and the commonalty, that Rome has become the head of the whole world. Should dissension now arise within her walls, it would infallibly work her ruin. Therefore I will now give up all pride, and will practise humility: So come and let us crown the Emperor, let us salute him with uplifted voices.

[*He places the crown on the Emperor's head, and all cry:*

Long life and great happiness to the invincible and most powerful Roman Emperor!

Emperor.

Well then beloved citizens, as you elect and consider me your Emperor, I bind myself in return to grant you privileges and special liberties, to stake with you my life and blood for our beloved country, and ever to act in good faith. And to you Andronicus, who for the common weal and the sake of peace willingly gave up the Imperial crown to me, I am beholden in love and fidelity, and therefore solicit your fair daughter Andronica as my Empress, and she shall be crowned to-day and be wedded to me, an it please you.

TITUS ANDRON:

Grofsmächtigster vnd vnüberwindlichster Keyser, ich lafs mir solches sonderlich wol gefallen, dafs er meine hertzliebe Tochter Andronicam zur Keyserin begehret, damit desto mehr Friede vnd Freundschafft vnter vns losiren, so vbergebe ich euch hiermit meine Tochter, vnd wünsche euch beyde ein friedsames, langes vnd glückseliges leben.

[*Vbergibt jhm seine Tochter, der Keyser nimpt sie bey der Hand.*

KEYSER.

In grossen Ehren vnd Würden sol sie von mir gehalten werden, aber ich bitte, saget mir, was seyn das für welche, die da hinter euch stehen.

TITUS ANDRONICUS.

Grofsmächtigst Keyser, dieses Weibesbild ist die Königin aufs Morenlandt, die zweene seyn jhre Söhne, der Schwartze aber ist jhr Diener, welche ich alle gefänglich mit mir aufs Ætiopia mithero gebracht.

KEYSER.

Sie thun mir sonderlich wolgefallen, fürnemblich das Weibliche Creatur, vnd wolte wünschen, dafs sie meine möchten seyn.

TITUS ANDRONICUS.

Grofsmächtigst Keyser, so sie Ewer May: gefallen, wil ich sie jhm wol verehret haben.

[*Nimpt die Königin, vnd führt sie für den Keyser.*

Also Königin aufs Mohrenlandt, spreche ich euch jetzt von mir frey vnd lofs, vnd schencke euch hie meinem gnädigen Herrn Keysern.

KÖNIGIN AUSS MOHRENLANDT.

Grofs vnd mächtig Keyser von Rom, ich bin jetzt sampt meinem Sohne vnd Diener E. May: Gefangene, vbergeben vnd offeriren vns selbst Ewer May: für seine geringste Diener, er mache es mit vns was sein Wille ist.

KEYSER.

Schöne Königin aufs Morenlandt, ich bin euch günstig, vnd in grossen Gnaden sampt den ewrigen gewogen: Derhalben seyd nicht melancholisch vnd betrübet, sondern fasset ein frölich Gemüthe, denn zu grossen Dingen wil ich euch erheben, vnd solt bey ewrem vorigen Stande gleich einer Hochgebornen Königinnen gehalten werden.

ÆTIOPIS.

Allergnädigster vnd Grofsmächtigster Keyser, für diese grosse Gnade, thue ich mich gegen E. May: in Vnterthänigkeit bedancken.

TITUS ANDRONICUS.

Most mighty and invincible Emperor I am right well pleased that you solicit my most beloved daughter for your Empress, that there may reign more peace and friendship between us. I hereby give you my daughter, and wish you both a peaceful long and happy life.

[*Presents him his daughter. The Emperor takes her hand.*

EMPEROR.

She shall be held by me in high respect and honour. But pray tell me who are those who stand behind you?

TITUS ANDRONICUS.

High and mighty Emperor, this woman is Queen of Ethiopia, those two are her sons, the black man is her attendant, all of whom I brought away with me as captives from Ethiopia.

EMPEROR.

They please me right well, and the woman in particular. I could wish they were mine.

TITUS ANDRONICUS.

High and mighty Emperor, an they please your Majesty, accept them as presents from me.

[*Presenting the Queen to the Emperor.*

And thus Queen of Ethiopia do I release you, and present you to my gracious Lord and Emperor.

ÆTIOPISSA.

High and mighty Emperor of Rome, I am now together with my sons and servants your Majesty's captives. We surrender and offer ourselves to your Majesty, as your most humble servants; dispose of us at will.

EMPEROR.

Beautiful Queen of Ethiopia, I am favourably disposed to you and yours. Therefore grieve and repine not, but be of good cheer; for I will raise you to high position, and you shall be maintained in your former station as a high born Queen.

ÆTIOPISSA.

Most gracious and high and mighty Emperor, I thank your Majesty most humbly for this great favour.

TRAGEDY OF TITUS ANDRONICUS.

KEYSER.

Nun die Zeit ist verflossen, so last vns jetzt nur sämptlich hinein kehren.

[*Gehen hinein, der Morian bleibet.*

MORIAN.

Laſs mich auch nu diese alte Lumpen ablegen, weil ich sehe, daſs meine heimliche Bulinne Gunst vnd Gnad beym Keyser hat.

[*Ziehet den alten Rock abe.*

Denn ich hoffe sie wird noch vielmehr grösser Gnad vnd gratia bey jhm erlangen, vnd mit jhrem schmeichel vnd liebkosen zu wege bringen, daſs er sie lieb gewinne, vnd Keyserin in Rom werde, wenn dann das also keme, so mache ich den Keyser warlich zum Hanrey, vnd treib vielmehr meine Lust vnd Frewde mit jhr, denn der Keyser. Aber ein jeglicher meynte, ich were nur der Königinnen Diener, nein warlich, ich bin allzeit jhr heimlicher Buhle gewest, vnd vielmehr bey jhr geschlaffen, denn der König auſs Morenlandt jhr Gemahl, daſs er auch zuletzt Vnrath an mir vnd der Königinnen vermercket, liefs derhalben grosse acht auff mich haben, daſs ich nicht zu jhr kommen köndte, worüber dann die Königin auff jhrem Gemahl sehr vngedüldig war, daſs ich nicht, weil er mich so sehre bewachen liefs, in vierzehen Tagen nicht kundte zu jhr kommen, dann der Keyser kundte jhr nicht halb so wol die Lauten schlagen, denn ich. Nam derhalben veniam, vnd vergab jhme damit in ein Becher Weins, jhren König, daſs ich also meinen freyen Paſs wieder zu jhr hette: Ja viele, die meine Bulinne vnd mich nicht gerne da sahen, habe ich heimlich in jhre Schlaffkammer bey Nachte ermordet, tausendt vnd tausendt Schelmerey vnnd Rauberey hab ich vollenbracht, vnd düncket mir gleichwol, daſs ich noch nicht genung Schelmerey gethan habe, ja der König selbst, vnd ein jeglich Mann, hatten eine grosse Furcht für mir, wegen meinen grosse Ritterlichen Thaten vnd Kriegesmacht, dann ich allewege in Schlacht Ordnungen, auch gefehrlichen Kriegen vmb mich geschlagen, gleich wie ein grimmiger Löwe, auch nicht wie ein Mensche, sondern wie ein lebendiger Teuffel, daſs ich nun zu letzt durch alle Welt, durch meine grosse, vnmenschliche Mannliche Thaten bin bekandt worden, vnd mir der Name gegeben, der Blitz vnd Donner auſs Moren Land: Dieses mein Geschrey kam auch zuletzt für die Römer, die sich dann mit gewaltiger Hand auffmacheten, vnd zu vns in Ætiopia kamen, verhereten vnd verderbeten das Land so grawsam, wie niemalen mag erhöret seyn. Ich aber machete mich da gegen sie auff, mit meinem Heere, in Meynung, sie solten mich nicht viele Wesens machen, vnd

EMPEROR.

Time is growing short, so let us now all go in.

[*Exeunt. Morian remains.*

MORIAN.

Let me now put off these old rags, as I see that my secret mistress has the good favour of the Emperor.

[*Takes off the old mantle.*

For I hope, that she will obtain higher favours of him, and so manage him with flattery and caresses, that he will become so fond of her, as to make her Empress of Rome. And if that really comes to pass, I vow I will make a cuckold of the Emperor, and will enjoy her more than the Emperor. Everybody thought that I was merely the Queen's servant; no indeed I have always been her paramour, and slept oftener with her, than the King of Ethiopia her husband, so that he at last grew suspicious of me and the Queen. He therefore had me watched that I could not come to her, wherefore the Queen became very impatient of her husband and I, having been watched closely, could not see her for a whole fortnight, for the Emperor could not satisfy her half as well as I. She therefore took the liberty to poison him with a cup of wine, so that I had again free access to her. Indeed many who disliked me and my concubine have been killed by me in their sleeping chamber at night. Thousands and thousands of villainies and robberies have I committed, and yet it appears to me that I have not had enough of them. The King himself and everybody feared me much on account of my valorous deeds and my prowess; for in all battles and perilous wars I fought like a fierce lion, not like a man but like a furious devil, so that I became renowned all over the world by my great superhuman deeds, and obtained the name: The Lightning and Thunder of Ethiopia. This fame at last also reached the Romans, who thereupon set out upon an armed expedition for Ethiopia, desolating and devastating the land with an atrocity such as has not been heard of within the memory of man. So I set out against them with my army, thinking to make short work with them and to drive them back in such a manner that none should return to Rome alive. But when the battle began, I saw how dreadfully old Titus Andronicus met my blows, that he was my superior and ten times more daring than I. Nor have I seen in all the days of my life more warlike and better tried troops than those Romans. I was quite dismayed at this, for I saw that my battle array was thrown into

wolte sie also zu rücke treiben, daſs keiner wiederumb lebendig nach Rom kommen solte. Da sich aber der Streit erhub sahe ich wie grewlich der alte Titus Andronicus dagegen schlagete, mein Vbermann ward, vnd zehenmal töller denn ich war. Ich auch die Tage meines Lebens kein streitbarer oder versucheter Kriegesvolck gesehen, als eben die Römer. Worüber ich dann gar verschrocken ward, weil ich sahe, daſs meine Ordnung gar zertrennet ward, vnd die meinen dahin geschlagen wurden, gleich wie die Hunde. Nicht lange darnach kam der alte Titus zu mir mit eil rennen, vnd stosset mich mit sein Glene so grawsam von meinem Pferde (welches noch niemalen kein Mensche gethan) daſs ich auch von mir selbst nichtes wuste, ob ich lebendig oder todt war, vnd zerschlugen darnach allesampt, das kein einiger mehr darvon kam. Nahmen darnach ein groſs Geldt, sampt mir, die Königin, vnd jhren Herren Sohnen, vnd brachten nach Rom, jetzt aber wil ich hingehen, vnd hören was weiter wird vorfallen.

[*Gehet weg.*

ACTUS SECUNDUS.

Jetzt kömpt herauſs der Keyser, Königin, sampt jhren zweyen Söhnen vnd Morian.

KEYSER.

Schöne Königin, zehenmal grösser lust vnd Begierden habe ich zu euch dann zu des Titi Andronici Tochter, welche ich jhm wieder gesandt, vnd sagen lassen, daſs sie mir nicht gefelt, auch nicht Keyserin zu Rom wird werden, derhalben sollet jhr nun hinfuhro nicht mehr gefangene Königin genennet werden, sondern Keyserin von Rom, so setze ich euch jetzt auff ewer Häupt die Crone, vnd sollet meine getrewe Gemahlin seyn, denn Göttin Venus hat mich so sehr gegen euch verwundet, daſs ich auch keine Ruhe habe, ehe daſs ich ewres stoltzen Leibs theilhafftig werde.

[*Setzet jhr die Krone auff.*

KEYSERIN.

Groſsmächtig Keyser diese grosse Ehre vnd digniteten, so mir von Ewer Majestät wieder verehret, bin ich vnwirdig. Ob mich aber auch wol Göttin Venus sehr vnd hefftig gegen Ewer Majestät auſs Blödigkeit nicht dürffen offenbaren.

KEYSER.

So last vns nun, meine schöne Keyserin, hinein gehen, vnd vnser Zeit in frewden vertreiben.

[*Nimpt sie bey der Hand, vnd gehen hinein, Morian folget ein, die zween Söhne bleiben.*

disorder, and my men beaten like dogs. Presently old Titus ran up to me and so cruelly threw me from my horse with his lance (which no man ever did to me before) that I did not know whether I were alive or dead. They then cut down every man, that none escaped. Whereupon they took rich treasures, together with me, the Queen and her sons, and brought us to Rome. Now I will go and watch the coming events.

[*Exit.*

ACT II.

Enter the Emperor, the Queen with her two sons, and Morian.

EMPEROR.

Lovely Queen, my love and passion for you is ten times greater than for the daughter of Titus Andronicus, whom I have sent back to him with the message that I liked her not; nor is she to become Empress of Rome. Wherefore, from henceforth, you shall not be called a captive Queen, but Empress of Rome. I now place the crown on your head, and you shall be my trusty consort; for Goddess Venus has so possessed me in your favour, that I shall have no rest until I enjoy your stately person.

[*He places the crown on her head.*

EMPRESS.

Most mighty Emperor, I feel unworthy of the great honor and dignity which your Majesty bestows on me. And although the Goddess Venus has inflamed me with a violent desire for your Majesty, I was too timid to show it.

EMPEROR.

So let us then, my beautiful Empress, go in and pass our time in pleasure.

[*He takes her hand. Exeunt. Morian follows, the two sons remain.*

TRAGEDY OF TITUS ANDRONICUS.

HELICATES.

Hertzlieber Bruder, last vns nun in Frewde vnd Wonne leben, denn diese vnsere Gefengnifs ist vns nicht zum Schaden vnd Nachtheil, sondern gereichet vielmehr zu grossen Ehren, ich frage hertzlieber Bruder, wo wolte vnsere Fraw Mutter doch zu grösseren vnd höheren Ehren gekommen seyn, denn allhie, weil sie Römische Keyserin worden ist.

SAPHONUS.

Ja hertzlieber Bruder, für grosser Frewde meines Hertzens kan ich nicht genug drüber jubiliren, denn im Morenlandt weren wir doch nimmermehr so hoch erhoben worden, als hie, von wegen vnser Fraw Mutter, vnter diesen edlen Römern, die da vber der gantzen Welt beschreyet seyn, derhalben wolte ich auch wol mit frölich seyn, aber einerley peiniget vnd kräncket mein Hertz sehr.

HELICATES.

Hertzlieber Bruder, solche Betrübnifs des Hertzens möchte ich gerne wissen.

SAPHONUS.

O hertzlieber Bruder, du solt wissen, dafs ich gegen die schöne Andronica so hefftig sehre mit Liebes Brunst vmbfangen, dafs ich auch nicht weifs was ich bald anfangen sol. Aber dieses betrübet mich zum meisten, dafs sie schon einen hat mit welchem sie vermählet worden.

HELICAT.

Lieber Bruder an demselben liege ich jetzt auch schwerlich kranck, vnd wil nicht gleuben, dafs du so hefftig gegen sie solt verliebet seyn, als ich, derhalben lafs ab von solchen Gedancken denn ich bin der Elteste, vnd wil jhren Leib theilhafftig werden, derhalben mufs ich auff Mittel vnd Wege dencken, vnd mit vnser Fraw Mutter Diener darumb consuliren, wie man jhrem Gemahle sein Leben heimlich nehme.

SAPHO:

Wie Bruder, ob du wol elter bist denn ich, so solt du mir dennoch keinen Abtrag hierinnen thun, ich hoffe habe eben so viele was einem Manne gebühret dann du, vnd wenn es solte eine Wette gelten, wer sich zum meisten in den Venus Kampff brauchen köndte, weifs ich warlich ich wolte dir abgewinnen. Derhalben lieber Bruder, lafs mir dieses allein, vnd suche dir ein andere, denn von dieser wil ich nimmermehr lassen, vnd sol kein ander darzu kommen, denn nur allein ich.

HELICAT.

O du armer Narre, was woltu doch breit einem Weibe zu schaffen geben, nein warlich du bist nicht tüchtig darzu, lafs abe, lafs abe Bruder, sie mufs meine

HELICATES.

Dearest brother, let us now live in joy and pleasure, for this captivity is not to our disadvantage, but rather to our great honour. I ask you, beloved brother, where would our mother come to greater honours than here as she has now become a Roman Empress.

SAPHONUS.

Yes, dear brother; my heart is so elated that I cannot sufficiently express my joy; for in the East we should never have been raised so high as here on account of our mother, among these Romans who are so renowned all over the world. Therefore I would also gladly rejoice with you, but one thing pains and tortures my heart.

HELICATES.

Dearest brother I would wish to know what ails your heart.

SAPHONUS.

O dearest brother, you must know that I am so violently taken with love's desire for this fair Andronica, that I know not what to do. But it grieves me most to know that she is already married with another.

HELICATES.

Dear brother, I deeply suffer from the same illness, and cannot believe that you are so much in love with her as I; therefore give up this idea, for I am the eldest and will possess her body. I must therefore consult with my mother's servant, and find means to take away her husband's life.

SAPHONUS.

Being my brother, although you are the eldest, you ought not to thwart me. I hope that I have as much of a man in me as you; and if we were to lay a wager as to who would be the better champion of Venus, I am confident, I should get the victory. Therefore, dear brother, stand not in my way and seek another mistress; for I shall never give this one up, and no other shall possess her but myself.

HELICATES.

O you poor fool, how can you think of meddling with women? No in truth you are not fit for it. Give it up, brother, give it up; she must be mine. You are too

TRAGEDY OF TITUS ANDRONICUS.

werden, vnd bist gar geringe darzu, dafs du mir darvon solt abdringen, oder aber wir werden vns darumb schlagen, dafs die Hunde das Blut lecken.

SAPHO.

Bruder ich sag dafs kein grösser Narr in der Welt ist dann du, dafs ich aber von jhr solte ablassen, vnd du sie haben woltest, sol dir nimmermehr angehen, vnd ist war, dafs sie nur einen haben kan, derhalben so ziehe vom Leder, vnd wollen Ritterlich darumb kempffen, denn ehe sie einen andern für mir bekommen solte, wil ich viellieber mein Leben darfür lassen.

HELICATES.

Ja Bruder gerne, denn einer von vns beyde mufs weggereumet werden, vnd sage eben so, ehe du sie für mir solt theilhafftig werden, wil ich mein Leben auch dafür lassen, derhalben lafs vns an einander gehen, vnd nichts schonen, hawe nun fort.

[*Hawen schon gegen einander, mittler weile kömpt der Morian, vnd rennet darzwischen.*

MORIAN.

Nicht, nicht jhr Herren, was wolt jhr nun zu tausendt Teuffel anfahen, wolt jhr zween Brüder euch dann so feindlich einander nach dem Leben setzen, nein das sol kurtzumb nicht geschehen, weil ich noch bey euch bin, vnd gebet euch zu frieden, oder ich schlag auff euch beyde, dafs jhr die Elemente krieget dann jhr wisset, so ich auch anfahe, bin ich erger denn der Teuffel: Aber saget mir, was ist die Vrsache, dafs jhr euch so sehre gehessig seyd.

HELICATES.

Mein lieber Morian, jhr sollet wissen, dafs ich hefftig verliebet gegen die Andronica, mein Bruder saget auch dafs er sehre gegen sie verliebet, derhalben haben wir vns darumb gezancket, ich wil sie haben, vnd er wil sie auch haben, hat mich derhalben den Kampff angeboten, weil sie nur einen kan haben.

MORIAN.

Mufs ich nun nicht lachen, dafs sich jhre zwey vmb eine Jungfrawe schlagen, die bereits einen Mann hat, aber höret mich Saphonus, mich dünckt es were besser, dafs jhr ewren Bruder, der da elter ist, die Andronica allein liesset, vnnd jhr euch eine alleine aufssuchet, dann es seyn mehr schöne Römische Frawen, denn Andronica.

SAPHONUS.

Nein mein lieber Morian, das kan nicht seyn, denn in die Andronica bin ich gar zu sehr verliebet, vnd wil nimmermehr von jhr lassen, derhalben last vns kempffen.

[*Saphonus wil wieder zu jhm an, Morian gehet dazwischen.*

unworthy to make me yield, or we shall fight it out that the dogs shall lick our blood.

SAPHONUS.

Brother, I tell you there is no greater fool in the world than you; you shall never succeed in making me give her up to you. In truth she can only have one of us, therefore unsheath your sword and let us fight for her like true men; for rather than permit her to have another, I will stake my life.

HELICATES.

Yes brother, willingly; for one of us must be put out of the way. And I also say, rather than you shall share her with me, I will give up my life. Therefore let us have at each other and shew no mercy. Strike!

[*They fight. Morian rushes in and interposes.*

MORIAN.

Not so, my lords! What the devil are you at? Will two brothers thus beset each other in deadly strife? No, that shall never be, I vow, as long as I am with you. Peace! or I beat you black and blue. For you know when I once begin I am worse than the devil himself. But tell me the cause of your animosity.

HELICATES.

My dear Morian, you must know that I am violently in love with Andronica. My brother says that he also loves her deeply. This is the cause of our quarrel. I wish to have her, and he also wishes to have her, and so he challenged me to combat, because she can only have one of us.

MORIAN.

Must I not laugh to think that you would fight for a dame who has a husband already! But listen to me, Saphonus. It seems to me that you had better leave Andronica to your brother who is your elder, and seek one for yourself, as there are other handsome Roman ladies besides Andronica.

SAPHONUS.

No, no my dear Morian, this cannot be; for I am too fond of Andronica to give her up. Therefore let us fight.

[*He makes another attack, Morian interposes.*

MORIAN.
Nein nicht also, höret mich weiter, was düncket euch, dann Helicates verlasset jhr die Andronica, vnd suchet euch ein andere vnd beste in gantz Rom aufs, ich wil euch darzu behülfflich seyn vnd sie verschaffen.

HELICATES.
Nein ich kan von sie nicht lassen, denn zu hefftig sehre bin ich in sie verliebet, derwegen wollen wir vns beyde darumb schlagen, vnd nicht auffhören, bifs einer darvon beliegen bleibet.

[*Wollen wiederumb zusammen, der Morian stosset sie mit gewalt von einander.*

MORIAN.
Was dem Teuffel, wollet jhr dann nun gantz vnd gar wiederumb zusammen, ich rathe euch noch einmal, seyd zufrieden, oder ich schlage warlich darzwischen, dz jhr beyde zeter schreyt. Vnd höret mich nun weiter, was ich euch sagen wil, vnd seyd jhr dann da nicht mit zu frieden, so weifs ich euch nichts mehr zu thunde. Weil dann nun keiner von sie lassen wil, sollet jhr derhalben ewer leben nicht nehmen, sondern ich wil euch darzu behülfflich seyn, dafs jhr Gemahl sol vmbs leben kommen, vnd nehmet sie denn alle beyde, vnd brauchet sie genugsam.

HELICAT.
Mein lieber Morian, ich bin damit gar wol zufrieden, seyd vns behülfflich darzu.

SAPHON.
Ich bin dar auch wol mit content.

MORIAN.
So folget mich nun jhr Herren, vnd last vns weiter bedencken, wie wir die Sache anfahen sollen.

ACTUS TERTIUS.

Jetzt kömpt herauſs der Keyser mit der Keyserin, auch Titus Andronicus.

TITUS ANDRON:
Grofs vnd mächtiger Keyser, ich habe Jhr May: sampt dero vielgeliebten Keyserin, zu ehren eine schöne Hirschgejaget auff den morgenden Tag anstellen lassen, vnd bitte Ewer May: auch die schöne Käyserin vnterthänig, sie wollen sich in der Frühe auff der Jaget finden lassen, vnnd die Zeit in Frewd vnnd lust vertreiben.

KÄYSER.
Lieber Titus Andronicus in der Morgenstunde, wil ich mich mit meiner schönen Käyserin auffmachen, vnd auff der Jaget erscheinen, aber saget mir, werden viele Römer mit reiten.

MORIAN.
No, not so! listen to what I have to suggest. Suppose, Helicates, you were to give up Andronica, and seek another lady for your love, the best in Rome; I will assist you in this.

HELICATES.
No, I cannot give her up, for I am too deeply in love with her. So let us rather fight for it, and not desist until one of us be killed.

[*They close, Morian separates them.*

MORIAN.
What, the devil! Are you determined to be at each other's throats then? Once more I advise you to keep the peace, or else I shall join in, till I make you both howl again. And listen further to what I have to say, and if you are not pleased then, I know not what to do. You shall not kill one another for being unwilling to give her up; but I will assist you to kill her husband, and then you can take her, and use her at your will.

HELICATES.
My dear Morian, I am well pleased with this proposal; lend us your assistance.

SAPHONUS.
I am likewise contented.

MORIAN.
So follow me, sirs, and let us further consider how to go about the matter.

ACT III.

Enter the Emperor with the Empress, also Titus Andronicus.

TITUS ANDRONICUS.
High and mighty Emperor, in honor of your Majesty and your well beloved Empress I have ordered a stag hunt for to-morrow, and most humbly beseech your Majesty and the fair Empress to be present at an early hour and to pass the time in joy and pleasure.

EMPEROR.
Beloved Titus I will set out early in the morning with my lovely Empress to be present at the hunt. But tell me shall we be joined by many Romans?

TRAGEDY OF TITUS ANDRONICUS.

TITUS.
Ja Grofsmächtigster Käyser, zimlich viel werden allda erscheinen, mein Bruder Victoriades Brutinen vnd mein Tochter Androva Gemahl.

KÄYSER.
So, es ist gut mein lieber Titus Andronicus, wir wollen vns nun darzu præpariren.
[*Gehen ein.*
Nun ist die Morgenstunde heran gekommen, vnd man jaget die Jägerhörne vnd Trumpeten werden geblasen.
Titus Andronicus kömpt heraufs.

TITUS ANDRON:
O wie lieblich vnd freundlich singen jetzt die Vogel in den Lufften, ein jeglich suchet jetzt seine Nahrung, vnd die Jaget ist auch schon angefangen, in Frewde vnd Herrligkeit. Aber mein Hertz ist mir dennoch beängstiget vnd beschweret denn ich diese vergangen Nacht, solch ein schrecklichen Traum gehabt, vnd nicht weifs was er mir bedeuten wirdt. Nun mufs ich wiederumb zum Käyser reiten, der persönlich bey der Jagt vorhanden.
[*Gehet weg etc.*
Jetzt kömpt heraufs Andronica, hat jhr Gemahl bey der Handt, die Käyserin kömpt jhm entgegen, die Jäger blasen.

ANDRONICA.
Hertzliebes Gemahl, schöner vnnd lustiger Jaget habe ich mein Tage nicht gesehen.

GEMAHL.
Ich auch mein schöne Gemählin kan mit Warheit sagen, dafs ich auff vielen Jagten gewest, aber nimmermehr lustiger vnnd frewdiger gesehen. Was aber sehe ich jetzt für ein Wunder die Käyserin die da gar alleine eilents zu vns spatzieret.
[*Käyserin kömpt zu jhnen.*

KÄYSERIN.
Sieh welch grofs Wunder nimpt mir doch diese Andronica, wie gehestu mit deinem Gemahl so gar allein. Hastu nicht ein tausent Reuter vnnd Fufsvolck hinter dich, die da auff euch warten.

ANDRONICA.
Schöne Käyserin ich frage euch wieder, wie kömpts dafs jhr alleine gehet, vnnd auch nicht ein Hauffen Diener auff euch bestellet haben, Aber ewren Spott den jhr jetzt an vns treibet, thue ich doch weniger denn nichtes achten, von jhne auch leichtlich vertragen. Verhoffe auch wann es würde von nöthen seyn, wolte ich eben so wol ein tausent Reuter vnnd Fufsvolck können auffbringen dann jhr.

KÄYSERIN.
Andronica dafs du jetzt so frech vnnd mit spitz-

TITUS ANDRONICUS.
Yes truly, most high and mighty Emperor, a goodly number will attend; also my brother Victoriades and the husband of my daughter Andronica.

EMPEROR.
Very well, my dear Titus Andronicus, we shall hold ourselves ready.
[*Exeunt.*
The morning hour is now arrived, they hunt; blowing of horns and trumpets.

Enter TITUS ANDRONICUS.
O how sweetly and pleasantly do the birds sing in the air! each seeking its food; and the hunt has likewise commenced in joy and splendour. But yet my heart is oppressed and uneasy, for that I had last night a most dreadful dream, and know not what it portends. I must now again join the Emperor who is present at the hunt in person.
[*Exit.*

Enter the husband of Andronica leading her by the hand; the Empress advances to meet him; the huntsmen blow their horns.

ANDRONICA.
My most beloved husband, a finer and more entertaining hunt I never saw in all my life.

HUSBAND.
I also my fair wife, can truly say that I have been at many hunts, but never did I see a gayer and merrier one. But what wonder do I see? The Empress is coming hurriedly towards us!

EMPRESS, *coming up.*
How greatly do I feel surprised at this Andronica! How comes it that you and your husband are quite alone? Have you not a thousand followers on horseback and on foot to attend you?

ANDRONICA.
My fine Empress, I ask you in return, how comes it that you walk alone and have not a host of servants waiting upon you? But I scorn your railery, and can easily bear it. I hope that I could as easily as yourself raise a thousand followers on horse and foot, if it were necessary.

EMPRESS.
Andronica, as you ask me so pertly and insolently

finnigen Worten wiederumb fragest, warumb ich auch alleine gehe, soltu wissen, dafs es mir also gefelt. Aber ich frage wie kömpts doch, dafs du mir so frech vnd trotziglich darffest antworten. Bin ich nicht deine Käyserin, vnnd solst nicht wissen, wie hoch du mich ehren soltest, gedenck nun aber nicht, dafs ichs also darbey wil bleiben lassen.

ANDRONICA.

Ja Käyserin, wie man ins Holtz ruffet, also krieget man ein Wiederschall, denn wie jhr mich aufs hoffertigen Gemüth fraget, so antworte ich euch. Ob jhr aber wol Käyserin seyd, wil ich euch drumb nicht vnter den Füssen liegen, denn bedencket dieses, waret jhr nicht erstlich meines Herren Vater Gefangen, vnnd nun weil jhr Käyserin worden seyd, wisset nicht wie jhr euch für Hoffart lassen wollet. Derhalben könnet jhr wol jmmer hinfahren in ewer Hoffart, vnd mich bleiben lassen wer ich bin. Ich frage, was hat diese Stadt Rom für Nutz von euch vnnd den ewren gehabt, was hat sie aber für Nutz von den meinigen, vnd mein Herr Vater, ja warlich wenn der es nicht gethan, vnd mit seinen Ritterlichen Händen erhalten, dafs Käyserthumb vnnd gantz Rom würde vorlangst zu Boden gangen seyn, thut aber so viele böses an mir, was jhr nicht lassen könnet.

KÄYSERIN.

O mein Hertz wil mir im Leibe zerspringen, gehe mir aufs meine Augen du verfluchete Creatur, wann ich dann dein Hochmuth nicht straffen könte, so wolte ich mich selbest tödten. Sieh ich thu schweren bey allen Göttern, dz ich zuvor nicht essen oder trincken, auch nunmehr mein Häupt sanffte legen wil, bifs ich mein Muth sats vnd genugsam an dich gekület, vnd mit Frewden vber dir triumphiret.

[*Gehet ein Schritt sex fort, da kommen jhre zween Söhne zu jhr, die Andronica redet vnter dessen in geheim mit jhrem Gemahl.*

HELICATES.

Gnädige Fraw Mutter, es nimpt vns grofs Wunder, dafs jhr so gar allein, vnnd von allen spatzieren gangen. Aber vielmehr thun wir vns verwunderen, warumb jhr so sehre betrübet, vnnd in schwermütigen Gedancken gehet.

MUTTER.

O mein liebe Söhne, offenet ewre Ohren, vnd observiret meine Wörter wol, jhr sollet wissen, dafs ich nit weit von hie einem Orte spatzierte, da die Andronica sampt jhrem Gemahl ist, welche mich also erfasset vnd mit spöttischen vnnd hönischen Worten, wer vber mich bald toll vnd vnsinnig worden, derhalben

why I am also walking alone, you must know that it is my pleasure to do so. But I ask how comes it that you dare answer me so insolently and defiantly? Am I not your Empress, and do you not know that you ought to treat me respectfully? But do not imagine, that I shall not resent it.

ANDRONICA.

Well, Empress, it is only a Rowland for an Oliver; for if you question me haughtily, I answer you in the same manner. Although you are Empress, I will not lie at your feet; for you must consider that you were at first my father's captive, and now that you are Empress, your pride knows no bounds. You may keep up your pride, but let me also be as I am. What is the benefit, I ask you, that this city of Rome has derived from you and your kinsmen, to what she has reaped from mine? Forsooth my father had not preserved her with his chivalrous arms, the Empire and all Rome would have perished long ere this; but you may do me as much harm as you like.

EMPRESS.

O my heart will burst! Get out of my sight, you accursed creature! If I could not punish your insolence I would kill myself. I swear by all the Gods that I will neither eat nor drink nor lay me down to rest, until I have taken my fill of revenge on you, and have triumphed over you.

[*She walks a little further and meets her two sons; meanwhile Andronica speaks softly to her husband.*

HELICATES.

My gracious mother, we are much surprised, that you walked away quite alone; but much more are we lost in wonder as to what may be the cause of your grief and melancholy.

EMPRESS.

O my dear sons, give ear to my words, and mark them well; you must know, that I was walking not far from here to a spot where I found Andronica and her husband, whereupon she assailed me with jeering and scornful words in a manner to drive me mad; therefore come and take signal revenge on her, treat her cruelly

kömpst nur vn̄ rechnet euch mächtiglich wieder an sie, vnd gehet erbärmlich mit jr vmb, vn̄ erstecht jr alfsbald jren Gemahl an d' Seiten, davorn jr mich lieb habet, so jhrs aber nicht thut, so wil ich euch verfluchen vnnd nicht für meine Söhne halten.

SÖHNE.
Gnädige Fraw Mutter, wir seynd willich euch zu gehorsamen. Kömpt nu mit vnd zeiget vns an welchen Orte sie seyn, so wil ich jhm alfsbald sein Leben nehmen.

MUTTER.
Nun so folget mir vnd habt keine Erbarmnifs mit sie.

[*Gehen zu jhm.*
Helicates ziehet sein Schwerdt.

HELICATES.
Sich finden wir euch hie, du hast nun gar zu lange gelebet.

[*Ersticht jhn.*

O mordio mordio.

ANDRONICA.
Ach wehe, ach wehe, ist dar denn kein wehe vnd zeter dieser mordtliche Todt.

[*Gehet für den todten Cörper auff die Erde sitzen.*

KÄYSERIN.
Sieh nun du hoffertiges Weib, wie gefelt dir difs, was dūncket dir, hab ich den Eydt nicht gehalten, welchen ich geschworen; Ja dieses sol noch gar nichts seyn, sondern so wil ich dich zämen, dafs du mir vnter meinen Fufssolen solt liegen, vnd ich vber deinem Leichnam trete, dein gantz Geschlechte, mit sampt deinem Väteren vnd Brüder wil ich gar aufsrotten, vnnd bey meinem Gnädigsten Herrn Käyser mit List vnd Practicken zu wege bringen, dafs sie alle eines jämmerlichen Todes sterben sollen, aber ich bin dir hoffertige Mensche so spinne feindt, dan mir vnmüglich ist, lenger lebendig für meine Augen zusehen. Derohalben mein lieber Sohn, thue mir jetzt dein Schwerdt, damit wil ich jhr selbst jämmerlich jhr Leben nehmen.

[*Wil jhm das Schwerdt nehmen.*

SAPHO:
Hertzliebe Fraw Mutter, dasselbige kan ich thuen, derhalben bedenckt euch erstlich recht.

ANDRONICA.
O du aller vnbarmhertzigste Weibesbildt, ist dann kein Füncklein Erbärmnifs in dir, ja wann mein Herr Vater wissen solte, sie würden nicht wissen wie grimmiglich, sie sich wiederumb an euch rechnen, solte, keinen Stein würden sie auff dem andern liegen lassen,

and, if you love me, kill her husband by her side; but if you do it not I will curse you, and henceforth nevermore regard you as sons of mine.

HELICATES and SAPHONUS.
Gracious mother, we are willing to obey you. Only come with us and show us where they are, and we will forthwith take away his life.

EMPRESS.
Well then follow me, and have no mercy upon them.

[*They go up to them.*

HELICATES, *drawing his sword.*
Ah, do we find you here? you have now lived much too long. [*Runs him through with his sword.*
(HUSBAND.)
O murder, murder!

ANDRONICA.
O misery! Is there no one to proclaim this horrible murder!

[*She sits down by the corpse.*

EMPRESS.
Look you now, you haughty woman. How like you this? What think you, have I not kept my vow? But this is only the merest trifle. I will so tame you that you shall lie under my feet, I will tread on your corpse, I will exterminate your whole kindred with your parents and brothers, and by my cunning and crafty designs will prevail upon the Emperor to let them die a miserable death. But you, proud woman, are so hateful to me, that I can no longer bear to see you alive. Therefore, my dear son, give me your sword, that I may take away her life myself.

[*She wishes to take his sword.*

SAPHONUS.
Dearest mother, I can do that; therefore first bethink yourself.

ANDRONICA.
O you most merciless woman, is there not a spark of compassion in you! Ah, if my father could but know this, he would think no revenge cruel enough; he would not leave one stone in its place, but would would rip up the very earth on which you stand. Oh, haughty Empress,

sondern die Erde, worauff jhr stehet gar vmbreissen. O weh du hoffertige Käyserin erbarm dich vber mich, vnd nim mir auch jetzt mein Leben, denn lenger ist mir vnmüglich, vnnd bringet mir Hellen Angst.

KÄYSERIN.

Ja ich gleube es wol, wanns dein Vater vnd Bruder wüsten, die da nicht streiten wie Menschen, sondern ärger wie der Teufel, so solten sie wol bald derhalben gantz Rom mit der Käyserlichen Pallast zu Grunde reissen, vnnd wie die vngestümme Löwen rumoren, aber demselben muſs ich zuvor kommen, vnd darauff bedacht seyn, daſs sie es nimmermehr zu wissen bekommen. Weil ich dann aber höre, daſs dir lenger zu leben Hellen Angst wer, ich auch das ärgeste nicht erdencken kan, wormit ich dich quele, so wil ich dich noch eine zeitlang leben lassen: Vnd jhr meine liebe Söhne, ich weiſs daſs jhr grosse Lust zur Bulerey habet, vnd voll Venus Safft seyd, derhalben vbergebe ich sie euch, gehet mit jhr an den grawsamesten Orten dieses Waldes, vnnd brauchet beyde ewer Lust genugsam an sie, vnd richtet sie also zu, daſs sie keines Menschen gleich ist, werdet jhr aber ein Erbarmen mit jhr haben, so gedencke daſs mein Zorn weit vber euch ergrimmen, vnd nicht viele gutes bedeuten wirdt.

SOHN.

Gnädige fraw Mutter, wir sein ewren Befehl gehorsam.

[*Gehen zu Andronica, wollen sie auffheben vnd mit jhr davon gehen.*

ANDRONICA.

O ist das denn keine Hülffe, O ist da kein Erbarmniſs, ich bitte last mich bleiben, vnd nehmet mir mein Leben.

KÄYSERIN.

Nein ich wil durchauſs die geringste Erbarmniſs nicht mit dir haben. Nun Söhne nehmet sie alſsbald hinweg für meinen Augen.

[*Nehmen sie hinweg, gehen mit jr ins Holtz, alſsbald kömpt der Morian.*

MORIAN.

Sieh wunder vnd vber wunder, was zum Teufel bedeutet vns dieses Käyserin, daſs jhr hie so gar im Walde allein gehet, jetzt hat mir der Käyser befohlen euch zu suchen.

KÄYSERIN.

Mein getrewer Bule, laſs dich nicht wunder nehmen, vnd sey nicht so zornich, denn ich hette lust alleine zu spatzieren, wil aber alſsbald mit dir zum Käyser gehen. Aber mein hertzlieber Bule, wir seyn jetzt gar

have mercy on me, and take away my life also! for it is impossible for me to live any longer; it would be the torture of hell.

EMPRESS.

I believe it indeed, if your father and your brother knew this, they who fight not like men but more fiercely than devils, they would forthwith pull down all Rome together with the Imperial palace, and would rage like lions; but I must prevent this, and take care that they shall never know it. And as I hear that life is hell's torture to you, and as I cannot now think upon a greater torment for you, I will let you live a little longer. And as I know, my dear sons, that you have a great desire for love's pleasures, I give her up to you. Go with her to the wildest parts of this forest and satisfy your desires fully; and treat her so that she shall no longer resemble a human being; but if you have pity on her, remember that my anger will be roused against you, and portend you little good.

HELICATES and SAPHONUS.

Gracious mother, we will obey your order.

[*They go up to Andronica, attempt to raise her, and carry her off.*

ANDRONICA.

O is there no help? Is there no pity? I implore you let me remain here, and take away my life!

EMPRESS.

No, I will have no pity on you. Well, sons, take her out of my sight.

[*They carry her off into the forest. Presently enter Morian.*

MORIAN.

Behold this wonder of all wonders! What the devil does this signify, Empress, that you are walking alone in the forest? The Emperor ordered me to look for you.

EMPRESS.

My faithful lover, be not surprised; neither be so angry, that I had a wish to walk alone. I will now go with you to the Emperor. But, my sweet lover, we are now quite alone in this fine and delightful wood, and I

alleine in diesem schönen lustigen Waldt, vnd ich ein grofs appetit gekriegen zum Spiele der Göttin Venere, derhalben lafs mir von dir ergetzet werden, vnd mache mir Frewde.

MORIAN.

Nein schöne Käyserin, ob euch jetzt wol die Göttin Venus gewaltig thut reitzen zu jhren Spiele, so regieret, vnd hat mich doch wiederumb eingenommen Gott Mars. Kan derhalben jetzt nicht seyn, vnd werdet auff difsmal meinen Leib nicht theilhafftig werden so last vns jetzt gehen zum Käyser, der da lange nach euch gewartet hat: [*Gehet hienein.*

ACTUS QUARTUS.

Jetzt kömpt herauſs Titus Andronicus, Vespasianus, Victoriades stehen betrübt.

TITUS ANDRON:

O hertzlieber wie sehre ist mir mein Hertz beängstiget, drumb dafs der Käyser meine zween Söhne in Gefängnifs eingezogen, weifs aber im geringesten nicht was die Vrsache ist, ich habe an den Käyser geschrieben, er wolle mir die Vrsache vermelden, warumb meine Söhne so schleunig seyn gefangen genommen, der mir dann wiederumb geschrieben, dafs meine Söhne der Käyserin gefangen weren, vnd sie gröblich wieder jhr mifsgethan, sich mit Calumnien vnd schmehen Worten an sie vergriffen, derhalben müssen sie eines eiligen Todes sterben, solte ich dann mein eigen Fleisch vnd Blut dahin richten sehen, würde mir grofs Schmertz vnd Peine bringen: Aber wem sehe ich da zu mir kommen, der Käyserinnen Morian.

Jetzt kömpt Morian zu Andronicus.

MORIAN.

Glück zu alte Titus Andronicus. Seyd nun guter Dinge vnd frölich, dann gute Botschafft bring ich euch.

TITUS ANDRON:

Danck habet Morian, saget an was bringet jhr für Zeitung.

MORIAN.

Jhr solt wissen dafs mich die Käyserin zu euch gesandt, lest euch sagen, daferne jhr ewere Söhne lieb habt, vnnd sie vom Tode erretten wollet, sollet jhr ewre rechte Handt abhawen, vnd sie durch mich vberschikken, so sollen sie euch alfsbald wiederumb zugestellet werden.

TITUS ANDRON:

O mein lieber Morian, wie frölich Botschafft bringestu mir. Ja wenn die Käyserin auch alle beyde

have a great longing for the pastime of the goddess Venus, so let us disport and enjoy ourselves.

MORIAN.

My lovely Empress, if you are under the influence of the goddess Venus, I am ruled and mastered by god Mars. Therefore it cannot be now; but let us go to the Emperor, who has been long waiting for you.

[*Exeunt.*

ACT IV.

Enter Titus Andronicus, Vespasian, Victoriades sorrowfully.

TITUS ANDRONICUS.

O my beloved, how oppressed is my heart, that the Emperor has put my two sons into prison! I have not the slightest knowledge of the cause of it, and wrote to ask him to let me know why he so suddenly imprisoned my sons. To this he replied, that my sons were imprisoned on account of the Empress whom they had grossly insulted and offended with slanderous and scornful words. For this reason they are to be put to death speedily. Were I to see my own flesh and blood executed it would cause me great pain. But who is approaching yonder? It is Morian, the attendant of the Empress.

MORIAN, *approaches.*

I give you joy, old Titus Andronicus! Be of good cheer, for I bring you a welcome message.

TITUS ANDRON.

Thanks, Morian, say what news you bring.

MORIAN.

You must know that the Empress sends me to you to tell you, that if you love your sons and wish to save them from death, you must cut off your right hand and send it through me. They shall then be sent back to you immediately.

TITUS ANDRONICUS.

Oh, my dear Morian, what a joyful message you bring me! Nay even if the Empress desired both my

Hände begehrete, wolte ich sie gerne abhawen, aber jetzt wil ich meine Handt abhawen, vnd sie dir vbergeben. etc.

VICTORIADES.
Hertzlieber ich bitte, last mir meine Handt abhawen, denn solt jhr ewer Ritterliche Handt abhawen, were zuerbarmen.

VESPASIANUS.
O hertzlieber Vater ich bitte lasset zu, daſs ich meine Handt abhawe, denn es seyn meine hertzliebe Brüder.

TITUS ANDRON:
Nein mein hertzlieber Bruder, auch mein lieber, ewre Handt sollet jhr nicht darfür geben, sondern mir wils gebühren.

[Fallen für jhm auff die Knie.

VICTORIADES.
Hertzlieber Bruder wir thun einen Fuſsfall vnnd bitten zum höchsten, daſs jhr wollet ewre Handt vnbeschädiget lassen, vnnd daſs ich nur meine Handt abhawe.

TITUS ANDRON:
Stehet auff vnd kniet nicht für mir, weil jhr dann also ernsthafftig drein dringet, muſs ichs wieder meinen willen nachgeben, vertraget euch nun beyde drumb, wer seine Handt verlieren soll.

VICTORIADES.
Ja hertzlieber Bruder, wir wollen darumb losen, jetzt aber wollen wir hinein gehen, vnd ein Beil holen, dem es aber trifft, sol alſsbald für jedermänniglichen seine Handt abhawen.

[Victoria. Vespasianus gehen hinein.

TITUS ANDRON:
Ich wil euch gleichwol nun beyde vexiren, denn vnter dessen jhr loset vnd das Beil holet wil ich meine Handt abhawen.

[Gehet ein.

MORIAN.
Muſs dann nun das vexieren heissen, so pfleget der Teufel seine Muttel vexieren, aber du alte Titus Andronicus, ob ich wol ein vnharmhertziges Hertz habe, so tawret mir dennoch deiner den die Käyserin vexiret dir jetzt deine Handt abe, damit du nicht dermal eins Rom möchtest vmbkehren, wann du aber meynest, wirst deine Söhne bekommen, so wirstu nur allein die Häupter dafür zusehen kriegen.

Jetzt kömpt Titus hat seine Handt abgehawen Victoriades, Vespasianus komen auch.

VESPASIANUS.
Gnädiger Herr Vater, ich habe gewunnen, daſs ich hands, I would willingly cut them off. But now I will cut off my hand and give it to you.

VICTORIADES.
Dearest brother, I implore you let me have mine cut off, for it were a pity indeed to cut off your chivalrous hand.

VESPASIAN.
O beloved father, I implore you let me cut off my own hand, as it is for my dear brothers.

TITUS ANDRONICUS.
No, my dearest brother, no, dearest son, you shall not give your hands, for that part belongs to myself alone.

[They kneel down before him.

VICTORIADES.
Dearest brother, we implore you on our knees, to preserve your hand unhurt, and to let me cut off mine.

TITUS ANDRONICUS.
Rise, and kneel not before me. As you insist upon it so earnestly, I must yield against my will, therefore agree between you, which is to lose his hand.

VICTORIADES.
Yes, dear brother, let us cast lots for it. Now let us go fetch an axe, and he on whom the lot falls shall forthwith cut off his own hand instead of the other.

[Exeunt Victoriades and Vespasian.

TITUS ANDRONICUS.
Nevertheless I only wish to deceive you both; for while you are casting lots and fetching the axe, I will cut off my own hand.

[Exit.

MORIAN.
If that be called deceit, the devil also deceives his mother; but although I have a pitiless heart, I feel for you, old Titus Andronicus, for the Empress tricks you out of your hand that you may not some day overturn Rome; but when you hope to have your sons again, you will only get their heads instead.

Enter Titus with his hand cut off, also Victoriades and Vespasian.

VESPASIAN.
Father, I have won. I may now — O woeful sight!

sol jetzt: O wehe O wehe, warumb habt jhr doch ewer Handt abgehawen, dieses ist ja warlich zu erbarmen, hertzlieber Vater.

TITUS ANDRONICUS.

Ich bitte sagt nun nichtes mehr davon, denn es ist all geschehen, sehet hie Morian, bringet diese meine Handt der Käyserinnen vnd führet alſsbald meine liebe Söhne wiederumb zu mir.

MORIAN.

Nun ade, ich werde auch ja etwas davon bringen.
[Gehen zusammen hinein.

Jetzt kömpt herauſs Helicates vnd Saphonus, welche zuvor mit der Andronica in den Walde gangen, jhre Wollust mit sie gebrauchet, vnd sie jämmerlich zugerichtet, beyde Hände haben sie jhr abgehawen, vnd die Zunge auſs dem Munde gerissen, haben sie zwischen sich.

HELICATES.

Also muſs man es machen, wenn man bey schönen Frawen geschlaffen, daſs sie es nicht können nachsagen, die Zungen muſs man jhr aufsschneiden, damit sie es nicht sagen, auch jhre beyde Hände abhawen, daſs sie es auch nicht schreiben, gleich wie es hier mit dieser gemachet, aber was sol man nun weiter mit jhr anfahen, wir müssen sie hie im wilden Walde gehen lassen, daſs sie nur zu letzt doch den wilden Thieren zu Theil werden. So kom lieber Bruder laſs vns gehen. Nun ade ade Andronica.
[Gehen weg.

Andronica bleibet alleine seufftzen siehet kläglich kegen Himmel: Nicht lange darnach kömpt jhr Vater Victoriades, vnd siehet sie, da sie jhn aber siehet leuffet sie ins Holtz.

VICTORIADES.

Ach wehe, ach wehe, was für ein groſs Vnglück finde ich hie, die Andronica die da nicht eines Menschen gleich ist. O verberge dich nicht für mir.
[Leufft hinein, holet sie wiederumb herauſs.

O du armes Creatur, wer hat dich so erbärmlich vnd vnmenschlich zugerichtet, ach wehe deine Zunge ist dir aufsgerichtet, deine beyde Hände sein dir abgehawen, O wehe dieses mögt einem Stein erbarmen, O kom mit mir, du solt hie nicht bleiben.
[Gehet hinein.

Nun kömpt herauſs Titus Andronicus, Vespasianus, alsbald kömpt der Morian bringet die beyden Häupter vnd die Handt.

MORIAN.

Sehet hie alter Titus, ich habe ein Erbarmniſs mit euch, daſs ewre edle vnd streitbare Hand also ist ab-

Why have you cut off your hand, dearest father? This is a piteous sight!

TITUS ANDRONICUS.

I entreat you, say no more about it, for it is already done. Look here, Morian, take this hand to the Empress and bring me back my dear sons quickly.

MORIAN.

Well adieu, I will indeed bring back something of them.
[Exeunt.

Enter Helicates and Saphonus, who had gone into the forest with Andronica upon whom they satisfied their lust. Having also barbarously mutilated her, cut off both her hands, and torn out her tongue, they now bring them with them.

HELICATES.

Thus must a man act when he has slept with a handsome woman, so that she may not divulge it. He must cut off her tongue, that she may not tell it, and cut off both her hands, that she may not write it, as we have done to this one. But what shall we do with her now? We must leave her in this dismal forest, that she may be devoured by wild beasts. Come, dear brother, let us go. Farewell now, Andronica.
[Exeunt.

Andronica alone, sighing and looking up weepingly to heaven. Presently enter her uncle Victoriades. He perceives her; but on seeing him she runs into the wood.

VICTORIADES.

Woe is me! What great misfortune do I find here! Andronica no longer in the resemblance of a human being! O hide not yourself from me.
[He runs out to bring her back.

O you poor creature who has so cruelly and foully maimed you? Alas! your tongue is torn out, both your hands are cut off. O this is enough to melt a stone! Come with me; you shall not remain here.
[Exit.

Enter Titus Andronicus, Vespasian, and soon after Morian, carrying two heads and hands.

MORIAN.

Behold Titus, I feel pity for you, that your noble and chivalrous hand has been cut off thus. The Em-

gevexiret worden. Hie schicket sie euch die Keyserin wieder, vnd dieses seyn ewre beyde Sohnes Häupter.

[Morian leget sie für jhm. Titus vnd Vespasianus können kein Wort mehr für Angst reden, stehen gleich als todte Menschen.

Nun ich gehe weiter von hinnen, wirstu aber dieses also darbey bleiben lassen, so wird dich die Keyserin sampt deinem Geschlechte, mit Betrübniſs vnd Verrätherey aufstilgen, vnd euch also weg reumen.

[Gehen weg.

TITUS ANDRON:

Ach, ach, ach zeter vnd mordio, vber dich Blutgierige, betriegliche Weibesbild, wor ist wol jemals ein betrieglichers, hoffertigers vnd Blutdürstigers Weib gewesen, denn diese verfluchete Keyserin, O selber mag ich mich anspeyen, daſs ich sie habe leben lassen, vnd nicht die Gurgel abgestochen, da sie mein Gefangene war, O du vnbarmhertzigste vnd vndanckbareste Weibesbild, wie kan doch müglich seyn, daſs die Sternen am Himmel dir nicht sollen feind seyn, ja die vnvernünfftigen Creatur werden mit mir weinen vnd betrübet seyn. O jhr himlischen Götter werdet solche Vbelthat nicht dulden können, ach verleihet mir Witz vnd Verstandt, daſs ich möge weiſslich bedencken, wie ich mich an die hoffertige Keyserin möge doppelfeltig rechnen. O du verfluchte Creatur, wie hastu mich doch so betrieglich vmb meine Hand gebracht.

[Nimpt die Hand auff von der Erden.

Ja du edele Hand, wie bistu so bezahlet für deine trewe Dienste, O du vndanckbare Rom, diese Hand hat dich offte vnd vielmal von deinen grawsamen Feinden errettet. Ja wann die es nicht gethan, würdestu vorlängst zerschleiffet seyn, von keinem Römer wüste man mehr zu sagen, O wie offte hastu edele Hand gegen tausendt Hände streiten müssen, vnd die gefährlichsten blutigsten Kriege hastu mit victoria vberwunden, ach meine liebe Söhne, welche Angst vnd Pein bringet es mir, daſs ich ewre Häupter also muſs für mir liegen sehen, O nimmermehr solt jhr weg gesetzet werden, ehe ich dann meines Feindes Häupter dabey habe, Ach wehe, ach wehe, Ritterlich vnd Männlich habet jhr für Rom gestritten, auch ein streitbar Hertze von mir geerbet, aber du vndanckbare Rom, wie hastu es jhnen bezahlet, O vndanckbare Rom, wie eilestu zu nach deinem Vnglücke.

VESPASIANUS.

O hertzlieber Vater, solche Tyranney vnd Teuffels Vndanckbarkeit ist nicht erhöret, so lang die Welt gestanden, so ichs aber nicht solte rechnen, were ich nicht werth, daſs ich den Erdboden betreten solte, der-

press sends them back to you, and here are the heads of your two sons.

[He puts them down before him. Titus and Vespasian stand speechless and almost lifeless with horror.

I am going now, but if you rest (not?) satisfied with this the Empress will exterminate you and your stock by affliction and treachery, and thus put you out of the way.

[Exit.

TITUS ANDRONICUS.

O bloody treacherous woman! Was there ever a more perfidious haughty and bloodthirsty woman than this accursed Empress! O I could spit at myself, that I allowed her to live instead of cutting her throat when she was my captive. O you most pitiless and ungrateful woman, how is it possible that the stars in heavens are not your enemies! Even brute creation will weep and wail with me: Ye gods in heaven! you will not tolerate such iniquity! Oh grant me sense to bethink myself wisely, how to be doubly revenged upon this haughty Empress. Accursed creature, how treacherously have you robbed me of my hand!

[Takes up the hand.

Noble hand, how have your faithful services been requited! O ungrateful Rome, this hand often saved you from your cruel enemies. Had it not done so, you would ere this have been torn to pieces, — there would be no trace of Rome now. How often, noble hand, had you to do battle against a thousand hands! the most perilous and sanguinary wars have been victoriously fought by you. Ah me, my dear sons, what anguish and pain do I suffer to see your heads before me! O you shall not be put aside, until I also have the heads of my enemies. Alas, alas! you fought bravely and nobly for Rome, and you had inherited a brave heart from myself. But ungrateful Rome, how have you repaid it! O ungrateful Rome, how quickly do you hasten towards your downfall!

VESPASIAN.

O beloved father! such savagery and diabolical ingratitude has not been heard off since the beginning of the world. But I should not be worthy to tread this earth if I did not avenge it. Therefore I can no

halben kan ich mich nicht länger enthalten, vnd bitte, leget mich an Wehr vnd Waffen, vnd gebet mir in beyde Hände ein lang streitbares Schwerdt, damit ich gehe zum Pallast, vnd alles was mir ankömpt, wil ich darnieder hawen, auch nicht streiten wie ein Mensche, sondern wie ein rasender Teuffel, keine Eiserne Thüre sol mir so starck seyn, sondern wil es zermalmen vnd zerbrechen, vnnd wann ich dann den Keyser mit der Keyserinnen habe darnieder geleget, wil ich noch in die vndanckbaren Römer hawen, so lang ich jmmer kan vnd mag, mich auch darnach gerne wil nieder schlagen lassen, dann ich mein Leben nichtes mehr achte.

TITUS ANDRONICUS.

Ach nein hertzlieber Sohn, solches ist dir vnmüglich, du würdest doch nicht lebendig in den Pallast kommen, du bist nun mein einiger hertzlieber Sohn, wir mussen vns nun recht bedencken, wie wir vns an sie rechnen, ob ich aber wol eine Hand, so wil ich dennoch genugsam damit verletzen vnd beschädigen, du aber hertzlieber Sohn must das beste thun.

Jetzt kömpt Victoriades, bringet die Andronica.

VICTORIADES.

O hertzlieber Bruder, das grewlichste spectacul, so jemalen für ewren Augen kommen, sehet jhr nun. Hie ist ewre Tochter Andronica, welche ich also im Walde gefunden, jhre Zunge ist jhr aufsgerissen, vnd beyde Hände abgehawen.

[*Titus verschrecket sich grawsamlich, zittert vnd bebet, treibet grofs Elende.*

VESPASIANUS.

O wehe, o wehe.

[*Fellet in Ohnmacht nieder zur Erden, Victoriades gehet zu den Häupten, weinet bitterlich Titus geht auff die Knie sitzen.*

TITUS ANDRON:

Ach, ach du grosses Vnglück, wie vberfelstu mich so schleunig, auch wunder dafs mein Hertz nicht zu stücken springet. Ach mordio ach mordio, diese vnmenschliche Vbelthaten, ach wehe, ach wehe, dir Stein thu ichs klagen, vnd ob du mir wol nicht helffen kanst, so gibstu mir dennoch kein Widerwort, vnd liegest stille, hie wil ich liegen, vnd mit bitterlichen weinen nicht auffhören, bifs so lang das eine grosse Fluth von meinen Thränen von mir fliesset, bey Winterzeiten wil ich den Schnee vnd Frost mit meinen Thränen weg schmeltzen, Ach wehe, ach wehe, dieser grawsame vnd tyrannische Rath ist gar zu erbärmlich.

[*Stehet auff, gehet zur Tochter.*

Ach du mein hertzliebe Tochter, wer hat dir deine

longer restrain myself. Pray give me my armour, and put a long and warlike sword in my hands, that I may go to the palace and cut down everything, that comes in my way. I shall not fight like a man, but like a furious devil. No iron door shall be too strong to be forced and shattered; and when I have laid low the Emperor and the Empress, I will also cut down the ungrateful Romans as long as I have strength and will left me, and until I am struck down myself; for I no longer value my life.

TITUS ANDRONICUS.

Oh my dear son, that is impossible; you would not get into the palace alive. You are now my only beloved son. We must now consider well how we may best revenge ourselves; and although I have only one hand, I will do harm and injury enough with it. But you, dearest son, must do your best.

Enter Victoriades with Andronica.

VICTORIADES.

Oh my beloved brother, behold the most horrible sight that ever met your eyes! Here is your daughter Andronica, whom I found in the forest, her tongue torn out and both her hands cut off.

[*Titus is horror-struck and violently agitated.*

VESPASIAN.

O woeful, woeful spectacle!

[*He sinks down in a swoon; Victoriades approaches the heads and weeps bitterly. Titus falls on his knees.*

TITUS ANDRONICUS.

Alas, alas! how rapidly and suddenly do misfortunes fall upon me! It is wonderful that my heart does not break. Oh murder, murder! These inhuman misdeeds! Ah woe is me! woe is me! I tell my sorrows to thee, o stone, and although thou canst not help me, thou answerest not and remainest silent. Here will I lie and not leave off crying until I have flooded the earth with my tears; in winter they shall melt away the snow and frost. Alas, alas! this cruel and tyrannical Senate is too contemptible.

[*He rises, and goes towards his daughter.*

Ah my dearly beloved daughter, who is it that has

Zunge aufsgerissen, ich kan wol erachten, daſs du deiner Keuſchheit beraubet bist, vnd dir derhalben deine Zunge aufsgerissen, damit du den Thäter nicht aufssagest, dennoch haben sie dir auch deine schneeweisse Hand abhawen, wormit du es nicht Schrifftlich soltest offenbaren, ist es so nicht hertzliebe Tochter, Ach wehe, ach wehe, du kanst es nicht sagen.

[*Seufftzet sehr, wincket mit dem Häupte.*

Du must ja vielleicht mit dem wincken anzeigen, daſs es also ist.

[*Wincket mit dem Häupte noch einmal.*

Aber hertzliebe Tochter, allhie seyn deine beyden Brüder Häupte, welche die hoffertige Keyserinne hat abhawen lassen.

[*Sie verschricket sich sehr, siehet vnd seufftzet gegen Himmel, gehet zu den Häuptern, vnd küsset sie.*

VICTORIADES.

O vber dieses grosse Elende mögen sich die Steine erbarmen, aber was hilffts vns, daſs wir hier stehen vnd weheklagen, last vns nun sämptlichen hinein gehen, vnd bedencken, wie wir dieselben, welche sie also zugerichtet, erfahren.

TITUS ANDRON:
Ja hertzlieber Bruder, es ist der beste Rath, wir wollen hinein gehen, auch keine Ruhe haben, biſs wir sie erfahren.

[*Gehen hinein.*

torn out your tongue? I may well guess that you are robbed of your chastity, and that your tongue has been torn out that you may not betray the evil-doer; but they have also cut off your snow white hand, that you may not reveal it by writing. Is it not so dearest daughter? Alas, alas! you cannot tell me.

[*She sighs and nods.*

You must perhaps tell me with signs that it is so.

[*She nods again.*

But dearest daughter, here are the heads of your two brothers, which the Empress has caused to be cut off.

[*She stands appalled, looks up to heaven and sighs, then goes to the heads and kisses them.*

VICTORIADES.
Oh, this great misery is enough to soften a stone. But what avails our standing and wailing here? Let us all go in and deliberate how to detect those who thus martyred her.

TITUS ANDRONICUS.
Well counselled, dear brother. We will go in, and know no rest until we have found them out.

[*Exeunt.*

ACTUS QUINTUS.

ANDRONICUS, ANDRONICA, VICTORIADES.

TITUS ANDRON:
Ach wehe, ach wehe, hertzliebe Tochter, mein altes Hertz wil mir im Leibe zerspringen, daſs ich dich so vnmenschlich für meinen Augen sehe, wie lieb vnd werth habe ich dich die Tage meines Lebens gehalten, mit wie viel grosser Mühe vnd Sorge habe ich dich aufferzogen, ja wenn ich mit Triumph pflag wiederumb nach Rom zu kommen, vnd mein Leichnam vom Feinde sehr verwundet war, ich auch grawsame schmertze hatte, wenn ich aber dich gegen mir so frölich lauffende kommen sahe, mit deiner Lauten, mir für Frewde zuempfahen, vertriebestu du mir damit meine wundliche Schmertzen, auch durch deine liebliche Rede, erfrischetest du offte mein altes Hertze. Aber wormit wiltu

ACT V.

ANDRONICUS, ANDRONICA, VICTORIADES.

TITUS ANDRONICUS.
Alas, my most beloved daughter, my old heart almost breaks to see you in this pitiful state. How dear to my heart have you always been! With how much trouble and care have I brought you up! When I used to return in triumph to Rome, suffering much pain from the wounds received from the enemy, and saw you joyfully hastening to meet me with your lute, you made me forget my pain, and refreshed my old heart with your pretty innocent talk. But wherewith will you now play the lute to gladden me, and wherewith will you speak? You are robbed of all this. Shame, shame upon the cruelty done to you! Ah, if I only knew who did it — who has mutilated you thus inhumanly, I should

nun die Lauten schlagen, wormit du mich erfrewest, auch wormit wiltu reden, solches alles ist dir beraubet, Ach, ach, der grawsamen an dir begangenen That, ach wehe wann ich nur wüste, wer dir es gethan, vnd so vnmenschlich zugerichtet hette, wolte ich mir ein wenig zufrieden geben, aber es ist vnmüglich, daſs du es kanst offenbaren, sieh da kömpt dein Bruder, sage mir, was ist das, welches du bringest?

[*Vespasian: hat ein Korb mit Sand, vnd ein Stecken.*

VESPASIANUS.

Hertzlieber Vater, ich hab hierinnen Sand, vnd meine hertzliebe Schwester Andronica solte versuchen, ob sie mit diesem Stecken offenbaren vnd schreiben köndte, welcher sie so erbärmlich zugerichtet.

TITUS ANDRON.

O hertzlieber Sohn, wann sie es damit könte an den Tag geben, wolte ich ein wenig ruhe finden, für mein altes kranckes Hertz. Aber giefs nun den Sand aufs auff die Erden, vnd thue jhr den Stecken.

[*Er giesset den Sand an die Erden Titus Andron: thut der Tochter den Stock zwischen den beyden Stummelen.*

Sieh da hertzliebe Tochter, vnd schreib damit auffs Sand, dieselben Namen, welche dir deine Zung vnd Hände beraubt.

[*Sie nimpt den Stecken, vnd schreibt damit.*

Ach hertzliebe Tochter, nun hab ich genug, da stehet Helicates vnd auch Jagd. O hertzliebe Tochter, ist es nicht also, daſs dich Helicates vnd Saphonus in der nehesten Jagd also zugerichtet.

[*Andronica wincket mit dem Häupte niederwerts.*

Zeige mir auch hertzliebe Tochter, hat die Keyserin auch schuldt dran.

[*Neiget das Häupt.*

O verfluchet sey die Jagd, vnd der Tag, worin sie ist gehalten worden, ich meynte die solte in Frewden vollendet werden, vnd ich dadurch desto mehr Gnade beym Keyser erlangen wolte, aber nun sehe ich, daſs mein allergrösseste Vnglücke dadurch entstanden ist. O der schreckliche Trawm, der mir die vorige Nacht für der Jagd fürkam, hat mir dieses Vnglücke bedeutet. Nun kom, derhalben wirstu mussen zu grunde gehen, so höret mir nun zu, hertzlieber Bruder, auch hertzlieber Sohn, vnd observiret meine Wörter wol, wir mussen vns nun præpariren zu einem gefährlichen blu-

be somewhat consoled. But it is impossible for you to disclose it. Here comes my brother; tell me what it is you bring?

[*Enter Vespasian with a basket of sand and a staff.*

VESPASIAN.

Dear father, I have brought sand here, that my sister Andronica may try whether she could not write with this staff and make known the man who hath brought her to this pitiful state.

TITUS ANDRONICUS.

O dear son, if she could bring this deed to the light of day I should find some rest for my sick old heart. Spread the sand on the floor and give her the staff.

[*Vespasian spreads the sand on the floor. Titus Andr. puts the staff between her stumps.*

Take this, my dear daughter, and write in the sand the names of those who deprived you of your tongue and hands.

[*She takes the staff and writes.*

Ah dear daughter, now I know enough, I read here Helicates and hunt. Dear daughter, is it not that Helicates and Saphonus have thus misused you during the late hunt?

[*Andronica nods.*

Show me also whether the Empress shares the guilt.

[*She nods.*

Oh accursed be the hunt and the day it was held! I hoped it would end in joy, and that I should endear myself still more to the Emperor; but now I see that it has been the cause of my greatest misfortunes. Alas! the awful dream I had in the night before the hunt, betokened this misfortune. Come then, if we are doomed to perish, listen to me, dearest brother, and you too, dearest son, and mark my words well. We must now make preparation for a perilous and bloody war, and enlist a host of soldiers wherewithal to overthrow Rome. We must make such havoc of her as has never been

tigen Kriege, vnd eine grosse mänge Soldaten werben, damit wir Rom rund vmbkehren, vnd wollen also mit jhn hausiren vnd vmbgehen, wie niemalſs erhöret, auch daſs kein Stein vber den andern sol liegen bleiben, derhalben wollen wir vns hie sämptlich verknüpffen, vnd zu vnsern Göttern schweren, nicht auffzuhören mit blutigen gefährlichen Kriegen, biſs das Rom zu grunde gerissen, den Keyser vnd die mörderliche Keyserin, sampt jhren zween verfluchten Söhnen in vnser Gewalt haben, daſs wir auch nimmermehr mit jhn ein Vertrag wollen machen, auch nicht die geringste Erbarmniſs haben, sondern daſs wir zum grawsamsten vnd schrecklichsten mit jhnen handeln wollen, auffs ärgeste es einer erdencken kan.

heard of before. Not one stone shall lie upon another. Therefore let us all combine and swear to the Gods, not to stay our bloody warfare until Rome be overthrown, and until we have the Emperor and the murderous Empress with her cursed sons in our power, never to come to terms with them nor have pity on them, but to treat them with the most refined and dreadful cruelty.

VICTORIADES.

Hertzlieber Bruder, ich thue schweren bey allen himlischen Göttern, daſs ich nicht zu rechnen wil auffhören, so lang ich lebe, biſs wir die Keyserin sampt jhren Söhnen in vnser Gewalt haben, all mein Güter wil ich verkauffen, vnd dafür streitbare Männer werben lassen.

VICTORIADES.

Dear brother, I swear by all the Gods in heaven not to stay my vengeance as long as I live until we have the Empress with her sons in our power. I will sell all my property to enlist warlike men.

TITUS ANDRONICUS.

O hertzlieber vnd vertrawter Bruder, wie hoch erfrewet mich, daſs jhr mir so grosse vnd mächtige Hülffe verheisset. Nun wil ich jetzt anfahen zu schweren, nit auffzuhören zu rechnen, biſs so lange ich lebe, erstlich wil ich schweren bey meiner gewesenen streitbarn Hand, darnach bey meines Sohnes Häupten, darnach vber meine Tochter.

TITUS ANDRONICUS.

O my most beloved and trusty brother, how glad I am that you promise me such great and powerful assistance. I will now swear never to stay my vengeance as long as I live. Firstly I will swear by the warlike hand that once was mine, then by the heads of my sons, and then by my daughter.

Jetzt gehet Titus Andron: auff die Knie sitzen, vnd fangen an ein Klagelied zu spielen, die andern alle gehen vmbher, sitzen da die Häupter liegen. Titus nimpt seine Hand, helt sie vnd siehet gen Himmel, seufftzet, schweret heimlich, schläget sich für die Brust, leget nach vollendung des Eides die Hand weg, darnach nimpt er das eine Häupt, darnach auch das ander, schweret bey einem jeglichen besondern, zu letzt gehet er zu der Andronicam auch, die da auff die Knie sitzet, schweret bey derselben auch, wie er zuvor bey den andern, darnach stehen sie sämptlich wieder auff.

Titus kneels down and begins to sing a dirge; the others sit down by the heads. Titus takes up his hand, raises it and looks up to heaven, sighs, mutters vows, strikes his breast, and puts down the hand after having sworn. Thereupon he takes up the heads and swears by each of them singly; finally he approaches the kneeling Andronica and swears by her as before. This done, they all rise again.

Nun den Eid hab ich abgelegt, vnd geschworen, alle meine Haabe vnd Güter wil ich verkauffen, vnd mein Sohn sol die streitbaresten vnd tapffersten Männer dafür werben. Höre hertzlieber Sohn, nim alles grosse Gut auſs meiner Schatzkammer, mach dich damit bald von hinnen, vnd werb ein grosse mänge Volckes, so viele du jmmer bekommen kanst.

I have now taken my oath, and vowed to sell all my property, that my son may enlist the most warlike and the bravest men. Hark my son, take all my great wealth from my treasury; depart hence, and enlist as many warriors as you can get.

VESPASIANUS.

Hertzlieber Vater, darzu hab ich ein groſs Be-

VESPASIANUS.

Dearest father, I am most anxious to do so, and

gierde, so thue dennoch erstlich schweren bey dem Gott Mars, das ich nicht zu toben vnd wüten wil auffhören, bifs so lange der bleiche Todt vber mein Hertz triumphiret. Nun ade O hertz vnd trauter Vater, ich ziehe von hinnen, streitbar Volck zu werben, nicht lange, so sollet jhr hören die Trommeten blasen, vnd dafs ich ein grawsam Volck bringe, die da sollen rauben, brennen vnd tödten, gleich wie der Gott Mars selbst. Also Ade, ade.

[*Gehet davon.*

Titus Andron:
Hertzlieber Sohn, die Götter wollen dir günstig seyn, ob ich wol meine Hand verlohren, so hoffe ich doch, mein hertzlieber Sohn wird desto besser streiten, denn ich jhn in der nehesten Schlacht mit den Morianern fechten sahe, gleich wie ein grimmig Tigerthier, an dir habe ich noch alle meine Hoffnung, vnd so ich mein altes Leben hierüber müste enden, weifs ich, du wirst gleichwol dich an den Feinden mächtiglich zu rechnen wissen. Nun aber wil ich dem Keyser ein ewigen Vnfried von mir ansagen lassen. Hollah Bote kom herauſs.

[*Kömpt herauſs.*

Bote.
Hie bin ich, gnädiger Herr, habt jhr mir etwas zu befehlen?

Titus Andron:
Höre vnd observire meine Wörter wol, was ich dir sage, du solt hingehen zum Keyser, vnd vbergeben jhm dieses Schwerdt, mit diesen Worten, dafs ich wil sein ewiger Feind seyn vnd bleiben, vnd meine grösseste Kriegesmacht vber jhn aufsgiessen wil, auch nimmer auffhören wil, bifs ich jhn sampt der Keyserin, vnd seine zweene Söhne in meiner Macht vnd Gewalt habe, gehe nur hin, vnd verrichte dieses verständig.

Bote.
Gnädiger Herr, es sol von mir zum besten verrichtet werden.

[*Nimpt das Schwerdt.*

Titus Andron:
Aber höre weiter, wann du dann dieses gesaget hast, so vbergib jhm diesen Brieff, mit dem was drinnen ist.

[*Nimpt den Brieff.*

Red jhn gar trotziglich an, gleich wie einen Vnfriedes Boten gebühret.

Bote.
Wolan gnädiger Herr, ich wil jhm alles vbergeben.

therefore swear by the God Mars not to check my rage and fury until pale death triumph over my heart. Farewell now beloved and trusty father, I depart hence to enlist warlike men. Before long you shall hear the trumpets blow, and know that I am bringing with me a ruthless host, that shall plunder, burn, and kill, like the God Mars himself. Farewell!

[*Exit.*

Titus Andronicus.
May the Gods favour you my son! I have lost my hand indeed, but I hope that my dear son will fight all the better; for in the last battle with the Moors I saw him fight like a fierce tiger. You are all my hope, and even if I had to end my old days in this attempt, I know that you will take signal revenge on our enemies. I will now send a declaration of eternal enmity to the Emperor. Holla messenger, come in!

Enter Messenger.
Here I am, my lord, have you any orders for me?

Titus Andronicus.
Hear and mark my words well. Go to the Emperor and deliver him this sword with the message, that I am and remain his eternal enemy, that I shall let loose all my forces against him, and shall not rest until I have him together with the Empress and her two sons in my power. Go and deliver this rightly.

Messenger.
My lord, it shall be done to the best of my power.

[*He takes the sword.*

Titus Andronicus.
But hear me further; when you have delivered this message, hand him also this letter and what is enclosed therein.

[*Messenger takes the letter.*

Address him in a defiant tone as befits a messenger of war.

Messenger.
Very well my lord, I will deliver it all.

[*Exeunt.*

Gehen hinein. Jetzt kömpt heraufs der Keyser vnd die Keyserin.

KÄYSER.

Schöne Keyserin, ich mufs mich vber ewre List verwundern, da jhr des Titi Andronici Söhne die Häupter liesset weg schlagen, die da gröblich wider euch gesündiget hetten, wie jhr saget, damit wir aber nicht derhalben von jhm angefasset werden, habt jr jm seine rechte Hand abvexiret, wormit er dann die Tage seines Lebens ein grawsam Blut vergossen.

KEYSERIN.

Ja gnädiger Herr vnd Keyser, mufs also das Vnglücke zu wider kommen, sonsten wann ich die Hand nicht bekommen, weifs ich warlich, er solte den Keyserlichen Pallast damit zu grunde gerissen haben. Nun aber wollen wir seine Macht nicht grofs achten, vnd derselben wol widerstehen, wiewol er gleichwol nicht wird ruhen, vnd mit vns ein Streit anfahen.

KEYSER.

Es ist war, schöne Keyserin, Titus sol nimmer keine grosse Zeichen mehr thun, dennoch fürchte ich mich für seinem Sohne Vespasianum, wie man von jhm saget, dafs er dem Vater im streiten sol gleich seyn.

KEYSERIN.

Ja gnädiger Herr vnd Keyser, ich mufs bekennen, dafs er in Ætiopia, da mir sein Vater gefänglich annam, also beschreyet wurde, dafs er gleich grawsam dem Vater gestritten hette, aber gnädiger Herr vnd Keyser, traget nun für demselben gar keine Sorge, denn ich da mufs mit List vnd Practicken darzu verdacht seyn, dafs man demselben aufs dem Wege reume. Was aber mag vns das newes bedeuten, dafs der so eilends zu vns kömpt.

BOTE.

Du grofsmächtiger Keyser von Rom, ich bin ein Bote an dir gesand von Tito Andronico, derselbe thut ein Schwerdt, welches bedeuten sol ein ewigen Krieg, zwischen dir vnd jhm, vbersenden. Er wil allzeit dein Recher vnd eusserster Feind, vnd wil auch nimmermehr auffhören, bifs er dich, sampt der Keyserinnen, vnd jhren zween Söhnen in seiner Macht vnd Gewalt hat.

KEYSER.

Wie nun Bote, du verrichtest deine Botschafft noch trotzig genug. Wil dann nun Titus Andron: einen Blutigen Krieg mit mir anfahen, solches hette ich wol nimmermehr gemeynet. So gib her das Schwerdt.

[*Nimpt es.*

Vnd sage jhm wieder, weil er ja zu Vnfriede lust,

Enter the Emperor with the Empress.

EMPEROR.

Lovely Empress, I admire the stratagem, by which you had the heads of the sons of Titus Andronicus cut off, for having so grossly offended you as you said; and by which you prevented him from harming us by tricking him out of his right hand, with which he has caused so much cruel bloodshed all his life time.

EMPRESS.

Yes, my lord and Emperor, it is thus that we must avert misfortune. If I had not got his hand, he would assuredly have destroyed the Imperial palace with it. Now we may despise his power and resist it; though he will not rest before he can wage war against us.

EMPEROR.

Indeed, lovely Empress, Titus will never again do great wonders. But I fear his son Vespasian; they say that he equals his father in battle.

EMPRESS.

Yes, my lord and Emperor, I must avow that in Ethiopia, where his father made me his captive, he was reputed to equal his father in fierce bravery. But my lord and Emperor, be not uneasy on his account, for I will devise stratagems to put him out of the way. But what tidings can that man bring, that he comes with such haste?

MESSENGER.

High and mighty Emperor, I come as a messenger from Titus Andronicus, who sends you a sword which is to signify eternal war between you and him. He will always wreak revenge upon you, and be your mortal enemy, and will never rest until he has yourself, and the Empress with her two sons in his power.

EMPEROR.

Messenger, you deliver your message defiantly enough. That Titus Andronicus means to wage bloody war against me is what I should never have thought. Give me the sword then.

[*He takes it.*

Tell him, since he is bent upon war, I boldly ac-

wil ich Feindes genug seyn, vnd dafs ich jetzt seine geringe Macht leichtlich widerstehen wil, vnd nichtes achten thue.

BOTE.

O grofsmächtiger Keyser, ein grofs Vnglück ist dir sampt den deinen bereitet, vnd ob er wol seine Hand nicht mehr hat, so wird doch sein streitbarer Sohn desto besser toben, vnd grawsamlicher gegen dir wüten, welche dann jetzt in vielen Königreichen herumb ziehen, vnd ein grofs vnd mächtig streitbares vnd aufserlesenes Volck thut werben. Derhalben weifs ich gewifs es wird nicht lange weren, so wird er den Pallast mit gewaltiger Hand angreiffen, vnd rund vmb belägeren, auch nicht auffhören, bifs ers rund vmb gekehret, vnd dich sampt den deinen in seine Gewalt hat, hier aber habe ich noch einen Brieff, welchen du verlesen solt.

[*Keyser nimpt den Brieff.*

KEYSER.

Du vnverschambter Bote, wie darffstu mir so kühn vnd frech thun anreden, so thue ich schweren bey alle Götter, für dein trotzigten Worten solt du nimmermehr von hinnen kommen, vnd wil dich genugsamlich dafür straffen.

[*Machet den Brieff auff.*

Aber was finde ich hier in diesem Brieffe, ein blosses Schermesser, nun nimmermehr sollen mir die Götter helffen, sondern ich wil diesen grossen Frevel vnd Trotz rechen. Aber du Bote, solt alfsbald an den Galgen gehencket werden. Diener nim jhn alfsbald von hinnen, vnd vberantworte dem Hencker, dafs er jhn von Stunden an weg henge.

BOTE.

Gnädiger Herr Käyser, ich hoffe nicht, dafs mir hie wird Gewalt wiederfahren, vnnd den Hencker vberantwortet werden, dann solches were wieder allen Kriegsgebruch, ich habe ja nichtes mehr gethan, sondern die Botschafft meines Herrn also aufsgerichtet, wie er sie mir befohlen hat.

KEYSER.

Es hilffet nichtes dazu, dein Leben mufs dir genommen werden, hörstu nicht Diener nim jhn alfsfort für meinen Augen weg. etc.

cept the challenge, that I can now easily resist his weak force, and that I care nought.

MESSENGER.

O high and mighty Emperor, a great disaster awaits you and yours; and though he is deprived of his hand, his warlike son, who is now wandering through many kingdoms to collect a large and mighty army, will all the more furiously make you feel his rage. For that I am certain he will ere long attack the palace with a powerful force, and beleaguer it; nor will he desist until he has turned it inside out, and has you and yours in his power; I have also a letter here for your perusal.

EMPEROR, *taking the letter.*

Insolent messenger, how darest thou address me so audaciously and impertinently! I swear by all the Gods not to let thee depart hence, but to punish thee cruelly for thy insolence.

[*He opens the letter.*

What do I find in this letter! Nothing but a razor? May the Gods never help me if I do not avenge this daring outrage! Come sirrah, you must be hanged presently. Attendants take him hence and deliver him up to the hangman, that he may hang him immediately.

MESSENGER.

Gracious Emperor, I hope they will not lay violent hands on me and give me up to the hangman, for that would be contrary to all the usages of war. I have done no more than deliver my lord's message as I was bid.

EMPEROR.

That will not avail you; I must have your life. Do you not hear, attendant? Take him instantly out of my sight.

ACTUS SEXTUS.

Jetzt kömpt heraufs die weise Muhme, hat ein junges schwartzes Kindt im Arm, welches der Morian mit der Käyserinnen gezeuget.

WEISE MUTTER.

Ich suche jetzt allenthalben den Morian, welchem ich dieses Kindt sol vberantworten, dafs ers sol heimlich weg bringen, dann diese Nacht hat es die Käyserin zur Welt gebohren, vns es mit dem Morian welcher jhre heimliche Bule gezeuget, jetzt aber kan ich jhn an keinem Orte finden, weifs nicht wo ich mit dem Kinde hin soll. Aber dar kommen der Käyserinnen Söhne, die hievon nichtes wissen sollen, ach wehe, ich weifs nicht was ich nun machen soll.

HELICATES.

Last mich sehen weifs Mutter, was du allda bey dir trägest, hertzlieber Bruder kom vnd siehe dieses grofs Wunder, ein junger schwartzer Teufel ist hie verhanden.

SAPHONUS.

Ich kan mir nicht genugsam drüber verwunderen, aber hörstu weise Mutter, die Warheit soltu vns' bekennen, so ferne du wilt lebendig von hie gehen, wer das Kindes Mutter ist, vnd bey welcher vnser Morian geschlaffen, denn ich sehe dafs er der Vater ist.

WEISE MUTTER.

Gnädiger Herr, ich wolt es euch wol offenbahren, wanns jhr wolt in geheim vnd still bey euch behalten, denn es ist keiner der darvon weifs denn ich, vnd wann es dieselbe erführe, dafs es were von mir aufskommen, würde ich eines elenden Todes sterben müssen.

SAPHONUS.

Nein weise Mutter nimmermehr sol es von vns aufskommen, sondern wollens stille bey vns behalten, bekenne vnd sage vns nun die Warheit. So du vns aber etwas vorbringest, vnd wir hernach in der Warheit anders erfahren, so soltu nichts gewissers von vns zuerwarten haben, denn einen grawsamen Todt.

WEISE MUTTER.

Nun so wil ich euch die Warheit sagen, jhr sollet wissen, dafs der schwartze Morian welcher ewer Fraw Mutter heimlicher Bule, hat dieses Kindt von jhme gezeuget, vnd weil sie dann nun sahe, dafs das Kindt schwartz war, verschrack sie sich sehre vnnd befahl mir alfsbald, das ich heimlich solte zum Morian gehen,

ACT VI.

Enter the midwife with a black child in her arms, which has been begotten of the Empress by the Moor.

MIDWIFE.

I am now looking everywhere for Morian to whom I am to deliver this child, that he may secretly put it out of the way. The Empress brought it into the world last night; it is the progeny of Morian her paramour. But I cannot find him anywhere, nor do I know whither to go with the child. But here come the Empress's sons who are not to know anything about it. Oh dear, I know not what to do!

HELICATES.

Let me see, midwife, what you are carrying there. Sweet brother, come and look at this great wonder; here is a young black devil.

SAPHONUS.

I am quite amazed at it! but hark ye, midwife, as you love your life, confess the truth. Who is the mother of this child that slept with Morian, since I see that he is the father?

MIDWIFE.

My lord, I will readily tell it you if you will keep it secret, for there is nobody knows about it but myself; and if she happened to hear that I had divulged it, I should have to die a miserable death.

SAPHONUS.

Not so. It shall never be known through us; we will keep it secret. Confess now, and tell us the truth. But if you tell us anything that turns out to be untrue, you may rely upon it, that a cruel death awaits you at our hands.

MIDWIFE.

Well then I will tell you the truth. Know then that this child has been begotten by Morian, who is the secret lover of your mother. But when she saw that the child was quite black she was frightened, and ordered me to go secretly to Morian and to take this child to him, that he may have it secretly brought up.

vnd jhme dieses Kindt bringen, dafs ers heimlich solte lassen aufferziehen, damit kein Mensche davon etwas erfahren möchte, nun aber etwas suche ich vnd kan jhn nirgents finden.

[*Sie stehen, sein vber jhrer Rede gar erschrocken.*

SAPHONUS.

Ach wehe diese grosse Schande, verfluchet sey der ehrvergessen Bösewicht, der Morian der vns vnsere Mutter zu Schanden gebracht hat, worüber wir dann ein ewig Spott vnd Hon davon haben müssen, aber hertzlieber Bruder, lafs vns den ehrvergessen Schelm nicht lenger leiden noch dulden, sondern in der ersten vnser Ansichtigkeit, wollen wir jhme jämmerlich erschlagen.

HELICATES.

O hertzlieber Bruder, mein Hertz ist mir betrübet. Das ich nicht weifs, was ich anfahen soll, drumb dafs vns der morderliche vnd ehrvergessen Schelm, in solche grosse Schande gebracht, wer derhalben wol werth, dafs man jhme in heissen Oele sieden liesse. Aber was wollen wir mit dem vbergeben Schelme anfahen, denn würden wir zu streiten mit jhm anfahen, so würden wir doch nicht lebendig von seinen Händen entrinnen können.

SAPHONUS.

So weifs ich doch warlich nicht, was man anfahen sol, bleibet dz Kindt lebendig, so kömpts doch entlich aufs, vnd wir kommen dadurch zu Schanden, derhalben, so thue es mir jetzt her, das ichs alsbald vmbbringe.

Nimpt das Kindt von jhr, ziehet das Schwerdt aufs, wil es vmbbringen, vnter dessen kömpt der Morian siehet dz er das Kindt wil vmbbringen, leuffet eilents zu jhm, reisset jhm es aufs den Händen.

MORIAN.

Nicht, nicht lafs bleiben, vnd bring es mir nicht vmbs Leben, denn ich mercke es ist mein Kindt, oder ich schlage dich zwischen die Ohren, dafs du nimmer vonn hinnen kömpst.

SAPHONUS.

O du ehrvorgessen Schelm, wie hastu vns sampt vnser Mutter in solche grosse Schande gebracht, wie hastu dürffen so kühne seyn, mit meiner Mutter die Wollust zupflegen, hastu nicht gedacht, dafs du dein Leben drumb verlieren müssest.

MORIAN.

Wo nun jhr Herren, seyd nur halb so zürnich, dann es ist vnnöhtig, wollet jhr aber zürnich auff mich

so that nobody should know anything about it. I am now looking for him, but cannot find him anywhere.

[*They stand in dismay at her words.*

SAPHONUS.

Oh what a burning shame! A curse upon this infamous knave Morian, who has dishonoured our mother and brought us into ridicule and contempt! Sweet brother, let us no longer tolerate this miscreant, but put him to a miserable death as soon as we set eyes upon him.

HELICATES.

O sweet brother, my heart is sore oppressed. I know not what to do. As for this bloodthirsty and infamous villain, who has so greatly dishonoured us, he deserves to be boiled in hot oil. But what are we to do with the villain? If we were to quarrel with him, we should not escape with our lives.

SAPHONUS.

I know not indeed what to do. If this child remains alive, the matter will be known and we shall be disgraced. Therefore give it me here, that I may kill it at once.

He takes the child, draws his sword, and is on the point of killing it; meanwhile Morian comes in, and on seeing that the other is going to kill the child, rushes up and snatches it out of his hand.

MORIAN.

Leave that child alone and don't kill it, for I perceive it is mine, or else I will knock you on the head so that you will never again stir from this place.

SAPHONUS.

O you villainous scoundrel, how have you dishonoured us and our mother! How dared you satisfy your lust with her? Did you not fear to atone for it with your life?

MORIAN.

How now Sirs! why are you so incensed against me? There is no occasion for it. But if you will fall

14

sein, so sollet jhr wissen, daſs jhr euch einen argen Teufel auff den Halſs ladet, vnnd den Göttern thun dancken, daſs jhr mir wiederumb zu Freunde habet, das ich aber mit ewer Mutter Bulerey getrieben, vnd sie diesen Sohne von mir gezeuget, frage ich erstlich, ob ich nit jhr Diener gewesen, vnd alles was sie hat von mir haben wollen, ich alles pflichtschuldig zuverrichten mir gebühren wolte. So sollet jhr wissen: daſs sie mich zur Bulerey getrieben vnd gezwungen, weil jhr ewern Vater die Lauten nicht so wol hat schlagen können, auch dieser jetzige Käyser als ich. Derhalben jhr Herren gebet euch zufrieden, vnd seyn mit mir content, denn ich bin ewer Stieffvater, vnd dieser mein Sohn ist ewer Stieffbruder, wie kömpts dann daſs jhr wollet auff ewren Vater vnnd Bruder zornich seyn.

SAPHONUS.

O du ehrvorgessen Schelm, magst des Teufels Vater seyn vnd nicht vnser, ich rate, der die trotzigen Wörter jnne hielte, oder es wird dir vbel bekommen, es ist genug, daſs du vns bereits in solche Schmach vnd Schande gebracht.

MORIAN.

Was jhr Herren wollet jhr noch zürniger seyn, ich thue schweren bey alle Götter, werdet jhr mir nicht bald auſs meinen Augen gehen, ich, wil kegen euch beyde schlagen, daſs man darnach die Stücken sol zusammen raffen vnnd suchen.

[Morian fänget an zu reden mit der weise Mutter, sie schütteln jhre Köpffe, seyn zornich vnd gehen davon.

Aber höre du weise Mutter, wie ist es mit der Käyserinnen, ist sie auch frölich Mutter worden, vnnd wor wiltu mit dem Kinde hingehen.

WEISE MUTTER.

Ja Gnädiger Herr, sie ist noch wol vnd frisch auff, vnd eine fröliche Mutter worden, sie hat mir aber befohlen, das ich euch suchen solte, vnd das Kindt vberantworten, auch dabey vermelden, daſs jhrs solt heimlich auff den Berg Thaurin tragen, da ewr Vater wohnet, vnd es jhm zu aufferziehen geben, vnnd daſs es ja nimmer aufskeme, daſs es von der Käyserinnen gebohren were.

MORIAN.

Es ist gut, ich wils also machen aber hör mich weiter vnd sage, weiſs auch ein einich Mensche vmb dieses Kindt, daſs es der Käyserinnen zugehöret, vnd erzehle mir auch, was für welche seyn dabey gewest, da das Kindlein von der Mutter empfangen ist.

out with me I wish you to know, that you will have the devil to pay, and will thank the Gods if I make friends with you again. That I should have had connexion with your mother, and begotten this son, what of that? I ask you first, have I not been her attendant, and was it not my bounden duty to do all she desired? You shall know that it was she who tempted and compelled me to commit adultery, for neither your father nor the present Emperor could satisfy her so well as I. Therefore, Sirs, moderate yourselves and be not displeased with me, for I am your step-father, and this son of mine is your half-brother. How can you be angry with your father and brother?

SAPHONUS.

O you villainous scoundrel, you may be the devil's father, not ours. I advise you to check your impertinence lest you come to grief. It is enough that you have dishonoured us.

MORIAN.

Why Sirs, persist in your ill-temper? I vow by all the Gods that if you do not get out of my sight, I will cut you into a thousand pieces.

[He talks to the midwife; the brothers shake their heads and go away.

But hark, midwife! How is the Empress? Was she glad to become a mother, and where art thou taking the child to?

MIDWIFE.

Yes my lord, she is right well again and a happy mother, but she ordered me to find you and to deliver the child to you. She also bids me tell you to take the child secretly to Mount Thaurin where your father resides, that he may bring it up. Nor does she wish it to be known as the son of the Empress.

MORIAN.

Very well, it shall be done. But tell me further, does any body else know this child belongs to the Empress? tell me also what people were present at the child's birth?

TRAGEDY OF TITUS ANDRONICUS.

WEISE MUTTER.

Gnädiger Herr es weifs kein lebendiger Mensche davon, dafs es der Käyserin zugehöret, dann mir allein, ich vnd der Käyserinnen Söhne, welche da ich suchete, sie mir entkegen kommen, fragten vnd peinigten mich alle, das ich müste die Warheit bekennen, wenn es recht zugehörete, sonsten hetten sie mich getödtet. Da aber das Kindt entfangen wurdt, sollet jhr wissen das keiner bey der Käyserinnen war dann ich allein.

MORIAN.

Es erfrewet mich aber zwar zehenmal mehr, das keiner dabey gewesen, dann nur alleine du, aber derhalben mustu hie dein Leben verlieren.

[*Ziehet das Schwerdt aufs, ersticht sie.*

WEISE MUTTER.

O wehe, O wehe.

[*Felt todt zur Erden.*

MORIAN.

Sich so liege nun da, ich weifs es wird nun von dir nicht aufskommen, denn mit deinem Tode bin ich derhalben versichert, wann dar aber weren mehr gewest, die drumb gewust, solten sie für meinen Händen sterben, es weifs ja nun niemandt, denn der Käyserinnen Söhne, verhoffe auch die werden wol still schweigen, vnd jhre eigen Mutter Schande nicht offenbahren, sondern sie vielemehr helffen bemandelen.

[*Stehet still, siehet seinen Sohn dafs Kindt welches er in dem Arme träget schlaffen.*

Du aber mein hertzlieber vnd newgebohrner Sohn, wolten dich deine Brüder vmbbringen, Nein das müsten sie nicht anfahen, oder sie würden mit sterben müssen, du hast eine Gestalt an dir gleich wie ich, aufsgenommen eine spitze Nase vnd Kin gleich wie die Mutter hat, aber man pfleget zusagen, dar sitzet der Teufel ein, du bist gleich nun Fleisch von meinem Fleische vnd Beine von meinem Beine, ich mufs nun aber dazu bedacht seyn, wie ich dich aufferziehe, dafs du dermal eins gleich deinem Vater kanst nachthun, Hundemilch Käse vnd Wasser sol deine Nahrung seyn, bifs so lange du gehen kanst, so wil ich dich in allen Sachen vben, damit du solst hart lernen, vnd dermal eins ritterlich streiten vnd kempffen, auch Harnisch für deinen Händen entzwey reissen, gleich wie ich. In aller Schelmerey vnd Mörderey wil ich dich abrichten, damit du keinen Teufel achtest, vnd bey grossen vnd hohen Weibsbildern ein solch gratia vnnd Gnade erlangest, gleich wie ich, dz sie sich auch entlich selbst für dir

MIDWIFE.

My lord, there is not a living soul knows that it belongs to the Empress, except myself, and the Empress's sons who met me as I was looking for you, and extorted the truth from me as to whom it belonged; had I not told them, they would have killed me. But when the child came into the world, nobody was with the Empress but myself.

MORIAN.

I am indeed all the better pleased that nobody but yourself was present, but on that account you must now die.

[*He draws his swords and kills her.*

MIDWIFE.

O me!

[*She falls down dead.*

MORIAN.

So now you are down, and I know the matter will not get abroad through you, for your death is my security; had there been other persons who knew it, they should have died by my hands. Now no one knows it, for the Empress's sons will keep the secret I hope, and not proclaim their mother's shame, but rather help to cloak it.

[*He pauses, and looks at the sleeping child in his arms.*

My sweet and new-born son, thy brothers wished to kill thee. No, they must not attempt that, or they would have to die also. Thou hast looks like mine own except a sharp nose and chin like thy mother; but they say that therein lurks the devil. Thou art indeed flesh of my flesh and bone of my bone; I must now consider how to bring thee up, that thou may one day emulate thy father. Cheese of dog's milk with water shall be thy food, till thou canst walk. I will put thee to all kinds of exercises, that thou mayst become hardy, and learn how to fight bravely and to tear up a coat of mail with thy hands like myself. I will tutor thee in villainies and bloody deeds of all kinds, that thou needst not care for any devil, and, like myself, shalt obtain such favours of great and high-born ladies as will even make them fear thee. I will now take my child to my father, who is just such another black devil as myself and lives on Mount Thaurin, that he may bring it up, and say that it is his own,

14*

fürchten müssen. Nun so gehe von hinnen, vnd dieses mein Kindt wil ich bringen zu meinem Vater, der dann auch solch ein schwartzer Teufel ist dann ich, vnd auff dem Berge Thaurin wohnet, dafs ers mir sol aufferziehen, vnnd sagen dafs es sein eigen ist, damit keiner erfahre wem es zugehöret, die Käyserin mag nun auff ein frisches dencken auffs folgende Jahr.

so that no one may know to whom it belongs; the Empress may now turn her thoughts to a fresh one next year.

ACTUS SEPTIMUS.

Jetzt werden die Heertrommel geschlagen, vnd die Trompeten blasen auff, vnd ist die Zeit, dafs Vespasianus sein Kriegesheer welches er geworben kegen Rome bringet, hat grawsam gewütet, alle Stäte so den Römern zugehöret, rund vmb gekehret. Kömpt herauſs.

VESPASIANUS.

Mit einen grossen tapperen vnd aufserlesenen versuchten Kriegesvolcke bin ich jetzund kegen Rome kommen, sechtzig tausent Räuter hab ich in vollem Kürifs, vnd hundert tausent man zu Fufs, damit ich jetzt durch gantz Italiam gezogen, vnd alle Stäte worein wir gekommen gar zerschleiffet, dafs kein Stein mehr auff den andern lieget, auch gantz Italien haben wir so verschrocken, dafs sie allenthalben herumb lauffen, gleich wie die Feldtflüchtigen vnnd nirgents Hülffe haben, ein grawsam vnd vnzehlig Volck haben wir bereits dahin geschlachtet, dafs ach vnd wehe schreyet man allenthalben wo wir kommen, aber solches ist noch gar nichts zu achten, sondern nun sol es noch erstlich 10. mal grawsamer angehen, auch thue ich nochmalen bey alle Götter schweren, nimmermehr mit meinem Kriegesheere abzuziehen, bifs ich den Käyser, die hoffertige Käyserin sampt jhren zween Söhnen in meiner Gewalt habe, aber was sehe ich jetzt für ein Wunder zu mir kommen.

Jetzt kömpt ein Soldat, hat den Morian sampt dem Kinde gefangen.

SOLDAT.

Gnädiger Fürst vnd Herr, ich thue E. F. G. diesen Morian welchen ich für dem Berge Thaurin gefangen, in Vnterthänigkeit für seinen Gefangnen vbergeben.

VESPASIANUS.

Du mein lieber vnnd getrewer Soldate vber diesen Gefangen bin ich hoch erfrewet, denn es ist einer von vnsern eussersten Feinden der Käyserinnen Diener, welchen ich gar wol kenne, hörstu schwartzer Teufel ein

ACT VII.

Beat of drums and flourish of trumpets. Vespasian approaches Rome with his army, having made great havoc, and desolated all the cities of the Romans.

VESPASIAN.

With a large and brave army of picked and experienced troops do I now march against Rome. I have sixty thousand horsemen in full armour and a hundred thousand men on foot; I have marched through the length and breadth of Italy, and have razed all the cities through which we passed, that not one stone lies upon another. I have struck such terror into all Italy, that the people wander about in all directions like deserters, and know not where to look for help. We cruelly have massacred such a number of people, that we hear cries of anguish everywhere on our march. But this is nothing, — tenfold more cruel work shall now begin; and I once more swear to all the Gods not to withdraw with my army until I have the Emperor, and the haughty Empress with her two sons in my power. But what wonder do I see here!

Enter a soldier with Morian and the child as captives.

SOLDIER.

My prince and general, I humbly deliver up to your Highness this Morian, whom I made prisoner of war on Mount Thaurin.

VESPASIAN.

My dear and faithful soldier, I am highly rejoiced at this prisoner, for he is one of our greatest enemies; he is the Empress's servant whom I well know. Hark ye, black devil, you are a welcome guest to me!

TRAGEDY OF TITUS ANDRONICUS.

angenehmer Gast bistu mir, aber sag mir was woltu auff dem Berge Thaurin machen, vnd was ist das für ein schwartzer Teufel, dem du in deinem Arme trägest.

MORIAN.

Hat mich dann niemalen ein einiger Kerl so schandtlofs gefangen genommen, weil ich gelebet, dann dieser. Ich mag wol sagen dafs jhr vnd ewer Anhang die Teufel selber seyn mit streiten vnd kempffen. Ich bin so toll vnd rasendlich dafs ich nicht weifs was ich anfahen soll, ich mag mich selbest verfluchen, ewer Gefangner bin ich jetzt, wollet jhr mir mein Leben schencken vnnd Gnade beweisen, so wil ich ewre Ohren erfüllen mit grofs Wunder vnd Admiration, was die Käyserin mit jhren zween Söhnen an ewre Schwester Andronica gethan, auch wie ewre Brüder sein vmbs Leben kommen, auch so wil ich euch trewlich dienen, vnd wieder den Käyser streiten helffen, wollet jhr aber mir nicht Gnade beweisen, so wil ich euch im geringsten nichts offenbahren, denn hie bin ich, vnd habe mich all vbergeben, kan nun eins Todts sterben.

VESPASIA:

Ob du schon gefangen, bistu dennoch trotzich genug, erzehle mir aber alle Sachen vnd sage mir die Warheit, wer, an welchem Orte, vnd zu welcher Zeit, vnd vmb welcher Vrsache meine Schwester Andronica jhre Hände vnd Zunge so jämmerlich beraubet. Auch wie meine Brüder sein gefangen genommen, vnnd vmb welche Vrsache sie seyn dem Tode vberantwortet worden, wann ich dann nun dasselbige angehöret soltu dein Leben behalten.

MORIAN.

So eröffnet nun ewre Ohren, vnd höret mir wol zu. Jhr sollet wissen dafs ich der Käyserinnen allezeit heimlicher Bule gewest, aber so wol wie sie noch Königin in Mohrenlandt war, wie auch hie vnd weil sie dann allzeit ein hoffertiges vnd vberaufs hoffertiges Gemühte gehabt, dafs sie auch keinen neben sich hat leiden wollen, vnnd weil sie dann sahe, dafs jhr vnd die ewren in solchem grossen vnd hohen Ruhm waret, auch so mächtig vnd reich, dafs jhr dem Käyser gleich waret, könte sie solches in jhrem hoffertigem Gemühte nicht dulden noch leiden, sondern hat euch je vnd allewege auffs eusserste, verfolget, es weren aber auch der Käyserinnen Söhne beyde kegen ewre Schwester Andronica mit Liebe entbrant, hielten mich derwegen dazu, dafs ich jrem Gemahl solte auff den Dienst warten vnnd vmbbringen, dafs sie darnach jhre Wollust mit sie treiben könten, ich aber wartete mit allem Fleifs auff jhn, dafs ich jhn wolte vmbbringen, hatte aber niemalen Gelegenheit dazu, könte jhn auch nicht antreffen vmbzu-

But what was your business on Mount Thaurin, and who is the black devil you carry in your arms?

MORIAN.

Never in all my life did a fellow singlehanded, so ignominiously make me his prisoner as he did. I make bold to say that you and your party are the veriest devils for fighting. I am so madly enraged, that I know not what to do. I could curse myself. I am now your prisoner, and if you will give me quarter and spare my life, I will fill your ears with wonder and amazement at what the Empress and her sons have done to your sister Andronica, and in what manner your brothers have lost their lives. I will also serve you faithfully against the Emperor; but if you will not give me quarter, I will not disclose anything, since having once surrendered I can only die once.

VESPASIAN.

You assume a defiant tone for a prisoner, at any rate. But tell me all the circumstances and the real truth, as to who was the perpetrator, the whereabouts, at what time and for what cause my sister Andronica lost her hands and tongue so pitifully; also the way my brothers were imprisoned, and the cause for which they were deprived of their lives. When I have learnt all this, you shall be allowed to live.

MORIAN.

Then open your ears and mark me well. You must know that I always was the paramour of the Empress, both when she was still Queen of Ethiopia, and here. But being of so overweening a disposition that she could not bear a rival, and seeing that you and your family stood in such high renown, and that you were so powerful and rich as to be the Emperor's equal, she could not endure this in the pride of her heart, but seized every opportunity to persecute you to the utmost. But the Empress's sons fell violently in love with your sister Andronica, and desired me to watch and to kill her husband, that they might afterwards gratify their lust with her. So I watched him anxiously with intent to kill him, but never had an opportunity of doing so. Now at the time when your father Titus Andronicus had the great stag-hunt, at which the Emperor, the Empress with her two sons, and likewise your sister with her husband were present, it happened that the Empress was walking alone in the forest to look for me. She

bringen. Da nun aber die Zeit war, dafs ewer Vater Titus Andronicus die grosse Hirschjagt hielt, worauff dann war der Käyser die Käyserin sampt jhren zween Söhnen auch ewre Schwester Andronica sampt jhrem Gemahl, begibt sich dafs die Käyserin nach mich gar alleine im Walde suchet, die Wollust mit jhr zutreiben, könte mich aber nicht finden, kömpt aber an die Andronica vnd jhren Gemahl, die da beyde alleine seyn, redet sie mit gar hoffertigen Worten an, die Andronica giebt jhr nicht viele nach, sondern antwortet jhr trotziglich. Worüber dann die Käyserin aufs bofshafftigen Gemühte von hinnen rennet, vorschweret sich so hoch, dafs sie noch essen oder trincken wil, ehe dann sie jhren Muth an jhr gekühlet, so kommen jhr vngefähr jhre Söhne entkegen, dieselben vermahnet sie dafs sie sich sollen an der Andronica rechnen, vnnd jhren Gemahl an der Seiten erstechen, oder sie wil sie nicht für jhre Söhne achten, sie aber seyn willig gehen mit jhr an den Ort da Andronica ist, da erstechen sie jhren Gemahl an der Seiten, darnach befehlet sie jhnen, dafs sie die Andronica nehmen sollen, vnd brauchen jhre Wollust beyde an sie, vnnd solten sie darnach also zurichten, dafs sie keines Menschen gleich were, also nehmen sie sie weg, hawen jhr darnach beyde Hände abe, reissen sie jhr die Zunge aufs, so hette nun die Käyserin weiter im Sinne, ewer gantze Geschlechte aufszurotten, liefs derhalben ewren zween Brüderen, durch mich vnnd durch Angebung meines Rechtes gefangen nehmen, vmb gar nichtiger Vrsachen willen, vnnd liefs sie also enthäuptgen. Damit sie sich aber künfftiglich von ewrem Vater keines Vnglücks zugewarten hette, liefs sie jhm sagen, dafs seine Söhne gröblich wieder jhr gesündiget hetten, vnnd müssen derhalben sterben. So er sie aber lieb hette, solte er seine Handt für sie geben, alfsdann solten sie jhm lebendig wieder zugestellet werden, vexiret jhn also dazu seine streitbahre Handt abe, schicket sie jhm wieder mit den Häuptern, also habt jhr jetzt nun den gantzen Handel von mir erstanden, auch sollet jhr zu letzte wissen, dafs die Käyserin dieses Kindt vonn mir gezeuget, welches ich wolte auff den Berg Thaurin bringen.

VESPASIANUS.

Ja mit wunder vnd vber wunder sein mir jetzt meine Ohren vber deine Wörter erfüllet, O wehe nimmer werde dir wol du hoffertige Käyserin, mit sampt deinem Sohne, nun so bin ich dennoch so viele frölicher, weil ich nun alles weifs, wie es zugangen, wornach ich mich wieder richten kan, denn in allen sols dir so wieder vnd zehen mal ärger gehen. Aber ich habe es jetzt auch nicht nöhtig, dafs ich dir dasselbige

could not find me but met Andronica and her husband, who were there alone. She addressed them in haughty terms; Andronica was not behindhand with her, but replied sharply. Hereupon the Empress runs off, solemnly vowing not to eat or drink until she had taken revenge. It so happened that just at that moment she met her sons. She immediately called on them to revenge her on Andronica by stabbing her husband at her side, declaring that if they did not, she would not own them as her sons. They complied, went with her to the spot where Andronica was, and stabbed her husband at her side. She then ordered them to take Andronica with them and violate her, and afterwards mutilate her in such a manner, that she should no longer resemble a human being. They accordingly carried her off, cut off both her hands, and tore out her tongue. The Empress further resolved to exterminate your whole family, and so upon my advice she caused your two brothers to be imprisoned upon some trivial pretence and to be beheaded. But in order to secure herself against being harmed by your father she sent him word, to say that his sons had outrageously offended her, and that they must die on that account. But if he loved them, he was to give up his hand for them after which they should be returned to him alive. In this manner she tricked him out of his warlike hand, and sent it back together with the heads. You have now got out of me the whole affair, and shall know in conclusion that the Empress has been delivered of this child, which was begotten by me, and which I was going to take to Mount Thaurin.

VESPASIAN.

Indeed your words fill my ears with wonder and amazement! O! haughty Empress, I shall never pardon you and your sons. But I am now much more resigned since I know how it all came about. I know now how to act, for you shall pay for this tenfold over. Nor am I bound to keep my promise to you, since the accursed Empress, who had demanded my old father's warlike hand, promising to restore his sons

halte, welches ich verheissen, sintemal die verfluchte Käyserin von meinem alten Herr Vater seine streitbare Handt abfodert, verheiſs jhm darvor seine Herren Söhne lebendig, aber es ward nicht gehalten, derhalben Morian mustu sterben ohne alle Gnade vnd Barmhertzigkeit. Diener nimb jhn von hinnen. Vberantwort jhn alsobald dem Hencker, daſs er jhn alſsbald erhencke mit seinen Kindern.

MORIAN.
Wo nun dem Teufel, sol ich dann nun hangen, daſs wird mir vbel vnd vngewonet ankommen, ist dann gar keine Barmhertzigkeit, ich bitte schencket mir mein Leben.

VESPASIANUS.
Nein dein Leben sol dir nicht geschencket seyn, vnd nicht die geringeste Gnade haben, derhalben nimb jhn von hinnen, daſs er alſsbald wird erhencket, vnd das Kind mit jhm.

MORIAN.
Wo nun, harre ein wenig, sol ich Hangelbeeren fressen, kom ich heute noch zeitig genug, kan es dann nicht anders seyn, daſs ich sterben muſs, so bin ich willig, weil ichs gar wol vnd vorlängst verdienet. Aber ich bitte euch, erbarmet euch meines Kindes, vnd last es nicht mit mir sterben, denn es hat noch nichtes böses gethan, lasset es aber zur Kriegesrüstung aufferziehen, so weiſs ich fürwar, es sol ein tapffer vnd streitbarer Heldt werden.

VESPASIANUS.
Deines Kindes wil ich mich erbarmen, vnd es zu streiten vnd kempffen aufferziehen lassen, aber du mache dich bald von hinnen.
[Gehet fort.

MORIAN.
Hette ich doch all mein Tage nicht gedacht, daſs ich noch solte auffs letzte erhencket werden, nun so gehe fort vnd erhencke mich geschwinde weg, ehe ich noch mehr dran gedencke.
[Gehen weg.

Jetzt kömpt der Käyser herauſs.
KÄYSER.
Solch groſs Blutvergiessen vnd gefährlicher Krieg mag nicht erhöret seyn, auch daſs Rom in solche grosse Angst vnd Gefahr gestanden, denn nun so hefftig der Vespasianus der Stadt zusetzet, so grawsam hat er die vmbliegende Städte verderbet, daſs es mag zu erbarmen seyn, 4. Feldschlachten haben wir mit jhm gehalten, aber er hat sie vns alle abgewonnen, vnd ein grawsam mänge Volcks dahin geschlachtet, streitet auch so

alive, did not keep her promise. Therefore Morian you must now die without mercy. Attendant, lead him away. Deliver him up to the hangman immediately, that he may hang him together with his child.

MORIAN.
If the devil will have it that I am to be hanged, I don't think it will agree with me, for I am not used to it. Is there no mercy? Pray spare my life.

VESPASIAN.
No, I shall neither spare your life nor have the least mercy on you. Therefore take him away to be hanged immediately together with his child.

MORIAN.
Just tarry a little, if I must eat gallows pears the day is long enough for it. So if perforce I must die, I am ready, for I have deserved it well long ago. But pray have pity on my child — take not away its life also, for it is still quite innocent! Only let him be brought up as a warrior and I am certain that he will become a brave and warlike hero.

VESPASIAN.
I will have pity on your child and bring him up as a warrior, but as for you, take yourself off instantly.
[*Exit.*

MORIAN.
Indeed, I should never have thought, that I was destined to be hanged. Well then come away and hang me quickly before I have time to think about it.
[*Exeunt.*

Enter EMPEROR.
Such dreadful bloodshed, — so dangerous a war are things unheard of till now. Never has Rome been in such trouble and peril before! But the great hardships which Vespasian inflicts upon Rome are quite equalled by his cruel devastation of the surrounding cities. It is piteous, piteous! Four battles have we fought against him and lost. He has slaughtered such numbers, and he fights so fiercely that nobody dares to come near him

grawsam, dafs keiner darff in der Schlacht an jhm nahen, sondern fliehen alle für jhm. Mein Keyserlichen Pallast hat er gestriges Tages mir zu trotze voller Flenten geschlossen, ja alle meine Kriegsleute seyn schon zaghafftig, dürffen sich nicht zu jhm hinaufs nahen, sagen, dafs sie nun in die tägliche Erfahrung kommen, dafs alle welche zum Feinde hinaufs ziehen, gewifs nicht wieder kommen, worüber denn nun mein Hertz so beängstiget, dafs ich nicht weifs, was ich anfahen sol, denn meine Macht wird von Tage zu Tage kleiner, vnd der Feind nimpt jmmer noch mächtiger zu, derhalben wir seiner Macht nicht mehr können oder werden Widerstand thun, wo man jhm nicht mit List oder Betrug einen Schaden thut, vnd meine Keyserinne, die sich jetzt mit jhren Söhnen vermumschantzet, jhn nicht betrieget, jetzt aber ist sie hingangen, die Götter wollen jhn darzu favorales seyn, vnd Gnade verleihen, ich wil hinein gehen, vnd erwarte stets mit grossen Begierden, was sie werden aufsrichten vnd zu wege bringen können.

in battle, but all fly from him. He invested my Imperial palace yesterday in defiance of me, — nay all my soldiers begin to flinch; they venture not to sally forth to engage him. They say it is their daily experience, that all who march out to meet the enemy are sure never to return. My heart is so oppressed that I know not what to do, for my forces are daily reduced, and those of the enemy are on the increase. We shall not be able to oppose them unless we ruin him by cunning and treachery, and unless he is deceived by my Empress who is now disguising herself with her sons. She is now gone; may the Gods favour her! I will go in and anxiously await the result.

[*Exit.*

Gehet hinein, die Keyserin kömpt herauſs, sampt jhren zween Söhnen, haben sich vermumschantzet.

KÄYSERIN.

Hertzliebe Söhne, jetzt kennet vns niemandt, denn wir vns gnug vermumschantzet, hört mir aber, was ewer Thun allda beym Tito Andronico seyn sol, jhr sollet nun genawe achtung haben, was er für listige Krieges Practicken sich wider den Keyser fürnimpt, dafs wir vns alfsbald zu wissen thun, damit wir vns dafür zu hüten wissen, so jhr werdet sehen, dafs sein toben vnd wüten sol länger wehren, vnd dieses grawsam Blutvergiessen an die vnserigen nicht auffhöret, so sehet zu, dafs jhr jhn, sampt seinen streitbaren Sohn Vespasianum heimlich ermordet, also wird dann dieser gefehrlich Krieg ein Ende gewinnen, folget mir nun nach, wir wollen gleich zu seinen Pallast gehen.

Enter the Empress with her two sons, all in disguise.

EMPRESS.

My sweet sons, nobody will know us now in this perfect disguise; but now listen to me. This shall be your business with Titus Andronicus. You shall closely watch the cunning strategems of war which he plans against the Emperor, that we may give information to each other and be on our guard. And if you see that he goes on devastating the land and ruthlessly shedding our blood, then contrive to assassinate him and his warlike son Vespasian and thus put an end to this desolating war. Follow me now to his palace immediately.

[*Gehen hin zu dem Pallast, ruffet den alten Titum.*

Holla, holla guter Freund Titus Andronicus, kom ein wenig zu mir herunter.

[*Titus siehet von oben hinunter.*

TITUS ANDRON:

Was seyd jhr für welche, dafs jhr so vber mich ruffet?

KEYSERIN.

Alter Titus Andronicus, wir sind deine guten Freunde, vnd die Götter haben mich mit diesen zu dir gesand, dafs ich dir diese beyde sol vbergeben, denn sie von den Göttern geordiniret, in dem Krieges Wesen mit gutem Rathe behülfflich zuseyn, damit man seinen Feinden in kurtzen vberwindet.

[*They go to the palace, and she calls old Titus.*

Holla! my good friend Titus Andronicus, just come down for a minute.

TITUS ANDRONICUS, *looking down.*

Who calls me there?

EMPRESS.

Old Titus Andronicus, we are your good friends, and the Gods have sent me to you with these men, that I may deliver them both to you. They are appointed by the Gods to assist in the war by their good advice, so that we may soon conquer the enemy.

TITUS ANDRON.

O dieselben sollen mir gar angeneme seyn, vnd in grossen Ehren von mir gehalten werden, aber jetzt kom ich zu euch hinunter, mit Frewden zu empfahen.

[*Gehet hinunter.*

KÄYSERIN.

Nun mein Lieber, ich habe jhn euch an præsentiret, vnnd gehabt euch wol, ich gehe von hinnen.

Gehet weg, nun kömpt Titus Andronicus herausser.

TITUS ANDRON:

Sagt mir, wo ist der Dritte geblieben?

HELICATES.

Sie ist wiederumb von hinnen gangen, da sie vns jhn an præsentiret hat.

TITUS ANDRON:

Ja warlich jhr sollet mir solche willkommene Gäste seyn, wie ich nimmermehr gehabt, Holla Soldaten, kommet eilends herausser.

[*Kommen jhrer zween herausser.*

Kompt hie, vnd haltet mir diese beyde steiff vnd feste. Nun jhr ehrvergessene vnd mörderliche Schelme, meynt jhr daſs ich so gar von sinnen kommen bin, daſs ich euch nicht kennen solte.

[*Ziehet jhn die Kappe vom Angesichte.*

Seyd jhr nicht der Keyserinnen Söhne, vnd meynet mich verrätherlich vmb mein Leben zu bringen. Aber jetzt habe ich, woran ich mich rechnen kan, bringt mir da alſsbald ewer ein, ein scharffes Scheermesser vnd ein Schlacht Tuch herausser. Ja jetzt hab ich ein heimlichen Rath bey mir erdacht, worin ich alle meine Feinde fangen wil, vnd meinen Muth wiederumb genugsam an sie kühlen.

Jetzt kömpt einer, bringet jhm ein scharffes Scheermesser vnd Schlacht Tuch, er macht das Tuch vmb, gleich als wenn er schlachten will.

Gehe auch geschwinde hin, vnd hole ein Gefäſs.

[*Gehet hin.*

Vnd du kom mit demselben Mörder, den du hast, hieher vnd halte jhm seine Gurgel herüber, daſs ich sie kan abschneiden.

[*Bringt Gefäſs.*

Vnd kom du hie mit deinem Gefäſs, halt es jhme vnter die Gurgel, vnd fange alles Blut darein.

Der elteste Bruder wird erstlich herüber gehalten, er wil reden, aber sie halten jhm das Maul zu.
Titus schneidet jhm die Gurgel halb abe.
Das Blut rennet in das Gefäſs, legen jhn da das Blut auſsgerennet, todt an die Erden.

TITUS ANDRONICUS.

O they shall be most welcome, and held by me in great honour. I will come down directly, and give them a joyful reception.

[*Goes down.*

EMPRESS.

My sweet sons, now I have introduced you to him, farewell I depart.

[*Exit.*

Enter TITUS ANDRONICUS.

Tell me, where is the third person gone?

HELICATES.

She went away, as soon as she had introduced us to you.

TITUS ANDRONICUS.

Yes indeed, you shall be such welcome guests to me as I have never had before. Holla soldiers! come here quick!

[*Enter two soldiers.*

Come here and hold these two fellows fast. Now you infamous murderous villains! do you think that I have so entirely lost my senses not to know you?

[*He unmasks them.*

Are you not the sons of the Empress, and do you not treacherously seek my life? But now I can take my revenge. Bring me, one of you a sharp razor and a butcher's apron. I have devised a snare wherein I will catch all my enemies to satiate my revenge on them.

[*A sharp razor and an apron are brought. He puts on the apron, and makes preparations to slaughter them.*

Now go and fetch a basin quickly.

[*Exit soldier.*

And you come hither with the murderer you watch, and hold his throat that I may cut it.

[*A basin is brought.*

And you come here with the basin and hold it under his throat to gather all the blood.

[*The eldest brother is first held down, he wishes to speak, but they stop his mouth. Titus half cuts his throat. The blood runs into the basin. After it is all run out, they lay him down dead on the floor.*

15

Nun kom du ander auch heran.

Helt jhn eben so die Gurgel herüber. Er weigert sich hefftig zum Tode, wil reden, aber sie halten jhm das Maul zu.
Titus schneidet jhm in die Gurgel, das Blut wird auffgefangen, darnach todt an die Erden gelegt.

Nun habe ich jhnen die Gurgel beyde halb abgeschnitten, was ich aber nun geschlachtet, darüber wil ich selber Koch seyn, die Häupter wil ich gar klein zuhacken, vnd sie in Pasteten backen, worauff ich denn den Keyser sampt jhrer Mutter zu gaste bitten wil, vnd alfsbald ein Friedes Boten nach dem Keyser schicken, jhr aber nempt alfsbald die Cörper, vnd bringet sie mir in die Küchen.

[*Gehet hinein.*
Bringen die Cörper weg.

ACTUS OCTAVUS.

Jetzt kömpt herauſs der Keyser, auch die Keyserin.

KÄYSER.

Schöne Keyserin, ich bitte erzehlet mir, waren dem Tito Andronico ewer Söhne auch lieb, die jhr jhm anpræsentiretet, gleich als weñ sie jhm Götter schicketen.

KEYSERIN.

Gnädiger Herr vnd Keyser, der alte Titus war sehr froh drüber, kam alfsbald zu jhnen herunter, vnter dessen gieng ich wieder weg, verhoff meine Söhne werden in grossen Ehren bey jhm erhalten werden, vnd alles was sie jhm rathen, wird er folgen, aber da kömpt jetzt ein Bote, was mag der vns gutes bringen?

Der Bote geht fürm Keyser.

BOTE.

Glück, Heil vnd alle Wolfahrt warten auff E. Käys: May: Groſsmächtigster vnd vnuberwindlichster Keyser von Rom, ich bin ein Bote, vnd gesand von meinem gnädigen Herrn Tito Andronico zu Ewer Keyserlichen May: lest ewer May: durch mich vermelden Fried vnd Einigkeit, vnd daſs er nimmermehr keine Wehr noch Waffen wider Ewer May: führen wil sondern ein ewig Verbündniſs vnd Friede mit E. May: machen, last vns darneben bitten, E. May: wolln mit seine schöne Keyserin zu jhm auff ein Panckct kommen, daſs also desto mehr Friede vnd Einigkeit möchte gemacht werden.

Now come here too, you other.

[*Holds his throat in the same way. He resists violently and wishes to speak, but they stop his mouth. Titus cuts his throat, the blood is collected, after which they lay him down dead.*

I have now cut their throats, and what I have slaughtered I will cook myself. I will hash up these heads and bake them in pasties; then I will invite the Emperor and their mother. The messenger of peace shall be sent off at once to the Emperor. But you make haste, take these dead bodies and carry them into the kitchen.

[*Exeunt with the dead bodies.*

ACT VIII.

Enter the Emperor and the Empress.

EMPEROR.

My lovely Empress, pray tell me whether Titus Andronicus was pleased with your sons whom you introduced as being sent to him by the Gods.

EMPRESS.

My lord and Emperor, old Titus was highly pleased, and came down immediately. Meanwhile I came away, hoping that my sons will be held in great honour by him, and that he will follow their advice in everything. But here comes a messenger, what good tidings may he bring us?

MESSENGER.

All hail to your Imperial Majesty, high and mighty and invincible Emperor of Rome. I am a messenger sent by my noble lord Titus Andronicus to your Imperial Majesty. He bids me offer you peace and amity, he will never again wage war against your Majesty but wishes to enter into an eternal bond and alliance with your Majesty. I am further to entreat that your may be pleased to come with your lovely Empress to a banquet, so that peace and unity may be all the better established.

TRAGEDY OF TITUS ANDRONICUS.

KÄYSER.

Diese deine angetragene Botschafft, machet mir grosse Frewde vnd Wonne meines Hertzens, daſs weil der alte Titus Andronicus Friede vnd Einigkeit mit mir machen wil, sage jhm aber wiederumb von mir, daſs ich mich drüber sehre erfrewet, vnd alſsbald Persönlich bey jhm mit meiner Keyserin erscheinen wil.

BOTE.

Groſsmächtiger Keyser, ich wil diese Relation weiſslich verrichten.

[*Gehet weg.*

KEYSERIN.

Dieses ist wol gewiſs, gnädiger Herr vnd Keyser, daſs meine zween Söhne zu diesem Friede geredet, welchen denn der alte Titus folge geleistet.

KÄYSER.

Haben sie mir dieses zu wegen gebracht, so verheiſs ich jhnen warlich dafür, daſs sie derhalben von mir zu hohen Dingen sollen befordert werden. Aber schöne Keyserin, wir wollen nicht länger seumen, sondern vns alſsbald zu dem Tito Andronico verfügen.

Gehen hinein zu Titum, sie fangen an zu spielen, vnter dessen wird die Taffel zugerichtet, vnd die Pasteten auffgetragen. Nicht lang darnach kömpt Titus Andronicus herauſs, hat das Tuch, so mit Blut besprenget, noch vmb, vnd ein Messer in der Hand, der Keyser vnd die Keyserin gehen hinter jhm, dar folget die Andronica vnd Vespasianus vnd Victoriades.

TITUS ANDRON:

Groſsmächtiger Keyser vnd schöne Keyserin ich thue mich höchlich bedancken, daſs jhr auff meine Bitte erschienen seyd. Ich bitte aber Ewer Majestät wolle sich mit seiner Keyserinne setzen, vnd dieses mein geringe tractament vorlieb auff vnd annehmen.

KÄYSER.

Guter Freund Titus Andronicus, höchlich bin ich drob erfrewet, daſs dieser blutiger gefährlicher Krieg ein ende genommen, vnd wir zu Fried vnd Eintracht seyn gerathen.

[*Gehet oben an die Taffel sitzen, die Keyserin bey jhm.*

Aber sagt mir, warumb gehet jhr mit der Schürtzen?

[*Victoriades gehet sitzen.*

TITUS ANDRON:

Groſsmächtiger Keyser, ich bin selber Koch geworden, vnd die Pasteten für E. May: zugerichtet.

KÄYSER.

Nun es ist alles gut, ich bitte Titus, kompt mit ewrem Sohne bey vns sitzen.

EMPEROR.

Your message, that old Titus Andronicus wishes to make peace with me, rejoices and delights my heart. Tell him therefore on my part, that I am highly pleased, and that I will immediately come in person with my Empress.

MESSENGER.

High and mighty Emperor, I will duly deliver this message.

[*Exit.*

EMPRESS.

It is quite certain, my lord and Emperor, that my sons have brought about this tender of peace from old Titus.

EMPEROR.

If so be that they have brought this about, I promise them high promotion. So lovely Empress, let us not tarry longer, but betake ourselves forthwith to old Titus Andronicus.

They go to Titus; hautboys sound, while the table is being dressed and the pies served. Presently enter Titus Andronicus still wearing the blood-stained apron, and with a knife in his hand. The Emperor and Empress follow him, then Andronica, Vespasian and Victoriades.

TITUS ANDRONICUS.

Mighty Emperor and lovely Empress, I most humbly thank you for responding to my invitation. I pray your Majesty and the Empress to be seated and kindly to partake of my humble repast.

EMPEROR.

My good friend Titus Andronicus, I am highly rejoiced that this bloody and desolating war is come to an end, and that we are joined in peace and amity.

[*He sits down at the upper end of the table; the Empress sits at his side.*

But tell me, why wear you this apron?

[*Victoriades sits down.*

TITUS ANDRONICUS.

Mighty Emperor, I have become cook myself, and have made pasties for your Majesty.

EMPEROR.

I am right pleased, but pray Titus, come with your son and sit at our side.

TITUS ANDRON:
Nein großmächtiger Keyser, ich werde jetzt nicht sitzen gehen, sondern wil E. May: dienen, du aber hertzlieber Sohn Vespasianus, gehe sitzen, vnd leiste dem Keyser Freundschafft.

VESPASIANUS.
Ja hertzlieber Vater, ewerm Befehl bin ich jederzeit willig nachzukommen.
[*Gehet sitzen.*

KÄYSERIN.
Lieber Titus Andronicus, ich bitte lasset ewre Tochter Andronica auch sitzen.

TITUS.
Nein schöne Keyserin, daß kan nicht seyn, sie muß für euch stehen vnd dienen. Ich bitte aber E. May: wollen essen vnd frölich seyn.

Gehet hin zu den Pasteten, schneidet dem Keyser, auch der Keyserin davon für, Vespasianus aber isset nichts, der alte Titus gehet fürm Tische betrübet spatzieren.

KÄYSERIN.
Warlich die Tage meines Lebens hab ich nicht bessers von Pasteten gegessen, alß jetzt, kan aber nicht wissen, worvon es möge zugerichtet seyn, oder was dasselbige ist, so drein gebacket.

TITUS ANDRON:
O schöne Keyserin, ich bitte, esset besser davon, weil er euch so wol thut schmecken, worvon er aber gemachet, wil ich der Keyserinnen darnach erzehlen.

Schneidet noch ein Stücklein davon, legts der Keyserinnen für.

KÄYSERIN.
Aber mein lieber Titus Andronicus, saget warumb seyd jhr so melancholisch, vnd esset nit.

TITUS ANDRON:
O schöne Keyserin, esset jhr nun wol davon, ich aber bin voll grosser Betrübniß, ja der Betrübste in der gantzen Welt, daß ich auch nicht weiß, was ich vor Angst sol thun oder anfahen.

KÄYSERIN.
Aber ich bitte euch, saget mir warumb seyd jhr so betrübet, vnd was hat euch betrübt gemacht?

Titus geht für die Andronica.

TITUS ANDRON:
Keyserin, durch dieses elende Mensche, meine hertzliebe Tochter, bin ich so vnmenschlich sehre betrübet. Nun aber ist mir länger vnmüglich, dich also elendig-

TITUS ANDRONICUS.
My gracious Emperor, I will not sit down now, but will wait upon you, but you my dear son Vespasian, go and bear the Emperor company.

VESPASIAN.
Yes my beloved father, I am ever ready to obey your orders.
[*He sits down.*

EMPRESS.
My dear Titus Andronicus, pray bid your daughter sit also.

TITUS ANDRONICUS.
No my lovely Empress, that cannot be; she must stand and wait upon you. But I entreat your Majesty to eat and be cheerful.

[*He goes up to the pies, carves them, and places portions of them before the Emperor and the Empress. Vespasian eats nothing; Titus walks sorrowfully up and down.*

EMPRESS.
I have never eaten a better pie than this in all my life, but I cannot imagine what they are made of.

TITUS ANDRONICUS.
O my lovely Empress, pray take some more as you relish it so much; and I will tell my Empress afterwards what they were made of.

[*He cuts off another piece, and places it before her.*

EMPRESS.
But my dear Titus Andronicus, tell me why you are so melancholy, and why you do not eat.

TITUS ANDRONICUS.
O my lovely Empress, please you eat heartily. As to myself I am filled with grief, indeed the most afflicted man in the world, and know not what to do in my affliction.

EMPRESS.
But pray tell me why are you so sorrowful, and what has caused you this grief?

TITUS ANDRONICUS, *going up to Andronica.*
My Empress, it is on account of this unhappy damsel, my beloved daughter, that I am so deeply afflicted. But it is no longer possible for me to see you so

lich für meinen Augen zusehen, vnd für Vngedult wil mir mein Hertz im Leibe zerplatzen, sieh da nimb das zu dir.

[*Stosset jhr das Messer durchs Hertz, sie felt tödtlich nieder zu der Erden.*

KÄYSER.

Ach ach Titus Andronicus, seyd jhr auch noch bey Sinnen, wie kömpts, daſs jhr ewer eigen Fleisch vnd Blut ermordet, ach wehe dieses erbärmliche Wesen.

TITUS ANDRON.

Ja Keyser, die grösseste Pein vnd Hellen Angest meines Hertzen, hab ich durch jhr empfangen, aber höre mich recht zu, deine verfluchte vnd hoffertige Keyserin ist eine Vrsache, denn sie meine armselige Tochter durch jhre Söhne, die Hände hat abhawen lassen, auch die Zunge aufsgerissen. Wisse aber nun du verfluchte Keyserin, daſs du jetzt mit grosser Anmuth von deines Söhnes Häuptern gegessen hast, welche ich drinnen gebacket.

[*Keyserin zittert vnd bebet, verschrecket sich grawsamlich.*

Nun aber soltu also keinen Menschen mehr betrüben, wie du mich gethan, nim also dieses dafür.

[*Springet mit dem Messer zu jhr, ersticht sie an des Keysers Seiten beym Tische.*

O mordio wehe.

[*Felt todt zur Erden.*

KEYSER.

O wehe solte ich solche Mordt dulden, das ist mir vnmüglich.

[*Zieht das Schwerdt aufs, ersticht Titum Andron: fürm Tische, felt tödtlich zur Erden, Vespasian: springet vber Tisch zum Keyser.*

VESPASIANUS.

Nun Keyser du must wiederumb sterben, soltu auch tausendt Leiber haben.

[*Ersticht den Käyser, felt todt zur Erden.*

VICTORIADES.

Ach wehe, ach wehe, diſs erbärmliche vnd klägliche Wesen, O wehe nimmermehr werde ich mich können zu frieden geben. Nun Vespasian: das Keyserthumb gehöret euch jetzt zu, setzet die Krone auff ewer Häupt, vñ regierts mit frieden.

VESPASIANUS.

O gnädiger Herr Vetter, was sol ich das Keyserthumb regieren, mein Hertz wil mir im Leibe zerspringen wegen dieser Tragædi, welche nimmermehr mag

unhappy before mine eyes, and my heart is breaking for anguish. Here take this.

[*He stabs her, she falls down dead.*

EMPEROR.

O Titus Andronicus, are you in your senses? how comes it that you murder your own flesh and blood? O poor hapless creature?

TITUS ANDRONICUS.

Ay, Emperor, my heart has been wrung with pain and anguish on her account; but hear the rest. Your accursed and haughty Empress is the cause of this, for it is she who made her sons cut off the hands and tongue of my unfortunate daughter. But know ye now, you accursed Empress, that you have just regaled yourself upon the heads of your sons which I had baked in this pie.

[*The Empress trembles with horror and dismay.*

But you shall no longer afflict any man, as you have done me. Take this in return.

[*He rushes upon her with the knife, and stabs her by the side of the Emperor at table.*

(EMPRESS.)

Help! Murder!

[*She dies.*

EMPEROR.

O horrible! Shall I suffer such murder? no, impossible!

[*He draws his sword and pierces Titus Andronicus, who falls down dead. Vespasian leaps over the table to the Emperor.*

VESPASIAN.

Emperor, now must you die in your turn, and though you had a thousand lives.

[*He stabs the Emperor.*

VICTORIADES.

O woeful, woeful! most harrowing sight. Ah, I shall never be happy again. Now Vespasian the Empire belongs to you; place the crown on your head, and rule in peace.

VESPASIAN.

O my beloved uncle! how can I rule the Empire, when my heart is ready to break at this tragedy, more pitiful than has ever been heard of before? I know

kläglicher erhöret, ich weifs für grofs Betrübnifs nicht was ich sol anfahen, führt jhr nun die Keyserliche Crone auff ewrem Häupte, dann jhr seyd der neheste darzu.

VICTORIADES.

O nein ich begehre sie nimmermehr zuführen, jhr aber seyd ein rechter Erbe dazu, vnd seyd wegen ewer tapffer Thaten beschreyet worden vber die gantze Welt, das ewers gleichen nirgends ist. So wisset jhr, dafs das Keyserthumb viel Anfechtung vnd Feinde hat, auch sehr hoch von nöthen hat einen streitbaren Regenten, derhalben weigert euch nit, vnd empfahet das Keyserthumb, vnd machet darnach allenthalben widerumb Fried, vnd regieret es mit Einigkeit vñ Frewde.

VESPASIAN:

So last vns nun hinein gehen, dafs ich die Krone für jedermänniglich empfahe, aber nimmermehr werd ich können frölich sein.

FINIS.

not what to do in my great sorrow. Place you the Imperial crown on your head, for your claim is the nearest.

VICTORIADES.

O no! I will never wear it. You are the lawful heir, and are so renowned for your brave deeds all over the world, that you have not your equal. Know then that the Empire has many troubles and enemies, and wants a warlike ruler. Therefore resist not, but accept the Empire. Bring about a general peace, and rule in joy and harmony.

VESPASIAN.

So let us then go in, that I may receive the crown in the name of the people; but I shall never be happy again.

THE END.

TRAGEDY OF FRATRICIDE PUNISHED

OR

PRINCE HAMLET OF DENMARK

ACTED IN GERMANY, ABOUT THE YEAR 1603, BY ENGLISH PLAYERS.

The Tragedy of Prince Hamlet has been preserved to us only by a late and modernised copy of a much older manuscript. That copy, bearing the date, "Pretz, den 27. Oktober 1710", has once been in the possession of Conrad Ekhof, the celebrated actor and manager of the Theatre of Gotha, (born at Hamburg, Aug. 12, 1720 — died at Gotha June 16, 1778) after whose death some extracts of it were published in the "*Theater-Kalender auf das Jahr* 1779" Gotha 24mo, pag. 47 to 60, by the care of its editor, H. A. O. Reichard, who in 1781 gave the full text of the play in his Periodical, "*Olla Potrida*", Berlin, 8vo, Part II of 1781, pag. 18 to 68. It is entitled:

TRAGOEDIA.
Der bestrafte Brudermord
oder:
Prinz Hamlet aus Dännemark.

(TRAGEDY. FRATRICIDE PUNISHED, OR PRINCE HAMLET OF DENMARK.)

In the present impression the German text has been given as it stands in the "*Olla Potrida*".

TRAGŒDIA
VON
PRINZ HAMLET AUS DÄNNEMARK.

Personen.

1. Im Prologe.

NACHT in einer gestirnten Maschine.
ALECTO.
THISIPHONE.
MÄGERA.

2. In der Tragoedie.

GEIST des alten Königs von Dännemark.
ERICO, Bruder des Königs.
HAMLET, Prinz des ermordeten Königs.
SIGRIE, die Königin, Hamlets Mutter.
HORATIO, ein hoher Freund des Prinzen.
CORAMBUS, Königlicher Hofmarschall.
LEONHARDUS, dessen Sohn.
OPHELIA, dessen Tochter.
PHANTASMO, Hofnarr.
FRANCISCO, Offizier der Wache.
JENS, ein Bauer.
CARL, der Principal von den Comödianten.
CORPORAL von der Wache.
ZWEI REDENDE BANDITEN.
ZWEI SCHILDWACHEN.
TRABANTEN,
HOFDIENER, } Stumme.
ZWEI COMÖDIANTEN,

PROLOGUS.

DIE NACHT *von oben.*

Ich bin die dunkle Nacht, die alles schlafend macht,
Ich bin des Morpheus Weib, der Laster Zeitvertreib,
Ich bin der Diebe Schutz, und der Verliebten Trutz,
Ich bin die dunkle Nacht, und hab in meiner Macht,
Die Bosheit auszuüben, die Menschen zu betrüben,
Mein Mantel decket zu der Huren Schand' und Ruh',
Eh' Phöbus noch wird prangen, will ich ein Spiel anfangen;
Ihr Kinder meiner Brust, ihr Töchter meiner Lust,
Ihr Furien, auf, auf, hervor und last euch sehen,
Kommt, höret fleifsig zu, was kurzens soll geschehen.

TRAGEDY
OF
PRINCE HAMLET OF DENMARK.

Persons represented:

1. In the Prologue.

NIGHT, in a car, covered with stars.
ALECTO.
THISIPHONE.
MÆGERA.

2. In the Tragedy.

GHOST of the old King of Denmark.
ERICO, brother to the King.
HAMLET, Prince, son of the murdered King.
SIGRIE, the Queen, Hamlet's mother.
HORATIO, the Prince's friend, of high rank.
CORAMBUS, Lord Chamberlain.
LEONARDUS, his son.
OPHELIA, his daughter.
PHANTASMO, the clown.
FRANCISCO, Officer of the guard.
JENS, a peasant.
CHARLES, the principal of the comedians.
A CORPORAL of the guard.
TWO RUFFIANS.
TWO SOLDIERS.
LIFE-GUARDS
SERVANTS } Mute persons.
TWO COMEDIANS

PROLOGUE.

NIGHT, *from above.*

I am the sable Night, all feel in sleep my might.
Of Morpheus I'm the wife, in vicious pleasures rife;
I'm guardian of the thief, I bring to love relief,
I am the sable Night, who have it in my might
All wickedness to do, and cause mankind to rue.
Concealed my veil shall keep the harlot's shame and sleep.
Ere Phoebus lights the sky, I have a game to try.
Ye children of my breast, daughters of lust confessed,
Ye furies, up, arise, come forth and shew your face,
Come listen all to me what shortly shall take place.

ALECTO.
Was sagt die dunkle Nacht, die Königin der Stille,
Was giebt sie Neues an, was ist ihr Lust und Wille?

MÄGERA.
Aus Acherons finstrer Höhle komm ich Mägera her,
Von dir, du Unglücksfrau, zu hören dein Begehr.

THISIPHONE.
Und ich Thisiphone, was hast du vor, sag an,
Du schwarze Hecate, ob ich dir dienen kann?

NACHT.
Hört an, ihr Furien alle drey, hört an, ihr Kinder der Finsterniſs und Gebärerin alles Unglücks, hört an eure mit Mohnhäupter gekrönte Königin der Nacht, eine Gebietherin der Diebe und Räuber, eine Freundin und Klarheit der Mordbrenner, eine Liebhaberin des verstohlnen Gutes, und höchstgeliebte Göttin der Verliebten in Unehren, wie ofte wird mein Laster-Altar durch diese genannte That verehret! Diese Nacht und künftigen Tag müſst ihr mir beystehn, denn es ist der König dieses Reichs in Liebe gegen seines Bruders Weib entbrannt, welchen er um ihrenthalben ermordet, um sie und das Königreich zu bekommen. Nun ist die Stunde vorhanden, daſs er sein Beylager mit ihr hält, ich will meinen Mantel über sie decken, daſs sie beyde ihre Sünden nicht sehn sollen, derowegen seyd bereit, den Saamen der Uneinigkeit auszustreuen, mischet Gift unter ihre Eh', und Eifersucht in ihre Herzen. Legt ein Rachfeuer an, laſst die Funken in dem ganzen Reich herumfliegen, verwirret die Blutsfreunde in dem Lasternetz, und macht der Hölle eine Freude, damit diejenigen, welche in der Mord-See schwimmen, bald ersaufen; gehet, eilet, und verrichtet meinen Befehl.

THISIPHONE.
Ich höre schon genung, und werde bald verrichten
Mehr als die dunkle Nacht von ihr selbst kann erdichten.

MÄGERA.
Der Pluto selbst soll mir so viel im Sinn nicht geben,
Als man in kurzer Zeit von mir bald wird erleben.

ALECTO.
Ich blas' die Funken an, und mach' das Feuer brennen,
Ich will, eh's zweymal tagt, die ganze Lust zertrennen.

NACHT.
So eilt, ich fahre auf, verrichtet euren Lauf.
[*Fährt auf. Musik.*

ALECTO.
What saith the sable Night, the Queen of sleep and rest?
What is her wish and will, what thoughts do move her breast?

MÆGERA.
From Acheron's dark pit, Mægera I, appear,
From thee, ill-omened hag, thy wishes now to hear.

THISIPHONE.
And I, Thisiphone, say on what is thy plan,
Hecate thou dark one, say, I'll serve thee if I can.

NIGHT.
Listen ye furies all, listen ye three, offspring of darkness, messengers of hate, listen to your poppy-crowned Queen of Night, protectress of all midnight thieves and robbers, friend and light to the incendiary, lover of stolen property, and much-beloved goddess of all secret and unhallowed love, how often is my altar honoured by this said deed! This night and coming day I pray your help, for the sovereign of this realm burns in lust to his brother's wife, for whose sake he hath murdered him that he may possess her and the kingdom. Now is the hour at hand in which they consummate their nuptials. I shall cover them with my mantle that they see not their sin. Wherefore be ready to sow the seeds of discord, mingle with poison their marriage vows, envenom their hearts with envy. Kindle the fire of revenge, and scatter the sparks throughout the kingdom, lead blindly brother blood into the snare of incest, rejoice the infernal regions with deeds of ruth and rancorous malice; be gone, speed ye and fulfill my behests.

THISIPHONE.
Enough. I've heard enough, I hie me on my way,
And shall do more than Night e'en of herself can say.

MÆGERA.
Pluto himself, I swear, shall not such things conceive,
As soon performed by me, you shortly shall believe.

ALECTO.
I'll fan the glowing spark, make fiercer burn the flame,
I will, ere day dawns twice, completely spoil the game.

NIGHT.
Make haste, for I ascend, quick to your task attend.
[*Ascends. Music.*

ERSTER ACT.

SCENE I.

(Zwei Soldaten.)

1. Schildw. Wer da?
2. Schildw. Gut Freund!
1. Schildw. Was vor Freund?
2. Schildw. Schildwache!
1. Schildw. Oho, Camerad, kommst du, mich abzulösen, ich wünsche, dafs dir die Stunde nicht möge so lang werden, als mir.
2. Schildw. Ey, Camerad, es ist ja nun so kalt nicht.
1. Schildw. (Ob es gleich kalt ist, so hab ich doch hier einen Höllenschweifs ausgehalten.)
2. Schildw. Wie so zaghaft! das stehet keinen Soldaten an; er mufs weder Freund noch Feind, ja den Teufel selbst nicht fürchten.
1. Schildw. Ja wenn er dich einst bey der Cartause kriegen wird, du wirst das Miserere Domine wohl beten lernen?
2. Schildw. Was ist denn eigentlich deine Furcht?
1. Schildw. Wisse denn, dafs sich ein Gespenst an der Vorderseite des Castels sehen läfst, es hat mich schon wollen zweymal von der Bastey herunterwerfen.
2. Schildw. So lös' ab, du Narr, ein todter Hund beist nicht mehr; ich werde ja sehen, ob ein Geist, welcher weder Fleisch noch Bein hat, mir wird schaden können.
1. Schildw. Siehe nur zu, wenn es dir anders erscheinen wird, was es vor Händel macht; ich gehe nach der Hauptwache. Adieu. [*ab.*
2. Schildw. Gehe du nur hin, vielleicht bist du ein Sonntagskind, die sollen alle Gespenster sehen können, ich warte meines Dienstes.

[*Es werden inwendig Gesundheiten geblasen.*

2. Schildw. Unser neuer König macht sich lustig; sie trinken Gesundheiten.

SCENE II.

Geist *des Königs tritt neben die Schildwache, und erschrickt ihn.* [*ab.*

2. Schildw. Ach heiliger Anton von Padua stehe mir bey; nun sehe ich erstlich, was mein Camerad gesagt. O Saint Velten, wenn nur erstlich die Hauptrunde vorbey wäre, ich lief als ein Schelm von der Post weg.

[*Es wird wieder geblasen und gepauckt.*

2. Schildw. Hätte ich doch einen Trunk Wein von des Königs Tafel, damit ich mein erschrocknes, angebranntes Herz begiessen könnte.

ACT I.

SCENE I.

Two Soldiers.

1. Sent. Who's there?
2. Sent. A friend!
1. Sent. What friend?
2. Sent. Sentinel.
1. Sent. Ho! comrade, you come to relieve me. I wish the hours may not be so long to you as they have been to me.
2. Sent. Nay, comrade, 'tis not so bitter cold.

1. Sent. Cold or no, I have had an infernal fright.

2. Sent. How now so chicken-hearted! that beseemeth not a soldier; he must fear neither friend nor foe, nay, nor the devil himself.
1. Sent. Ay, if he once grip you behind he'll teach you to pray Miserere Domine.

2. Sent. Tell me then, what is it that has frightened you?
1. Sent. Know then that a ghost hath appeared on the platform of the castle; twice it tried to cast me down from the battlements.
2. Sent. Fool, I'm here to relieve you, a dead dog bites not; I shall soon see whether a ghost which hath neither bones nor sinews will do me any harm.

1. Sent. Only look out well, what trouble he may give you, if he appears to you; I go to the guard-house. Farewell. [*Exit.*
2. Sent. Begone with you; — perhaps you were born on a Sunday, and can see ghosts. I'll now mount guard.

[*Healths within drunk, with a flourish of trumpets.*

2. Sent. Our new King takes his rouse right merrily; they are drinking healths.

SCENE II.

Ghost *of the King approaches the Sentinel and startles him.* [*Exit.*

2. Sent. O! St. Anthony of Padua, defend me! Now I see for the first time what my comrade spoke of. O! St. Velten, an the first round were over I'd quit my post like a rogue.

[*Another flourish of drums and kettle-drums.*

2. Sent. O! for a draught of wine from the King's board to bedew my unmanned cowardly heart!

[GEIST *giebt von hinten der Schildwache eine Ohrfeige, dafs er die Musquete fallen läfst.* [*ab.*

2. SCHILDW. Da spielt der Teufel leibhaftig mit. Ach, ich bin so erschrocken, dafs ich nicht aus der Stelle kommen kann.

SCENE III.
HORATIO UND SOLDATEN.

2. SCHILDW. Wer da?
HORAT. Runde!
2. SCHILDW. Was für Runde?
HORAT. Hauptrunde!
2. SCHILDW. Steh Runde! Corporal heraus, Bursche ins Gewehr!

[FRANCISCO *und Wache heraus, geben das Wort auf der andern Seite.*

HORAT. Schildwacht, gieb wol Achtung auf deinen Posten, der Prinz möchte selbst patrolliren; dafs du ja nicht etwan schlafest, sonst kostet es deinen besten Hals.

2. SCHILDW. Ach wenn auch die ganze Compagnie hier wäre, es würde keiner schlafen, und man mufs mich ablösen, oder ich laufe davon, und solt ich auch morgen an den höchsten Galgen gehenkt werden.

HORAT. Was ist denn die Ursach?
2. SCHILDW. Ach, gnädiger Herr, es läfst sich alle Viertelstunde ein Geist allhier sehn, welcher mir so viel zusetzt, dafs ich mir einbilden mufs, als sässe ich lebendig im Fegfeuer.

FRANCISCO. Eben also hat mir die erste Schildwacht auch erzählt, welche in der vorigen Stunde abgelöset.

2. SCHILDW. Ja, ja, verziehet nur ein wenig, es wird nicht lange bleiben.

[*Geist gehet über das Theater.*

HORAT. Bey meinem Leben, es ist ein Geist, und sieht recht ähnlich dem letztverstorbenen König von Dännemark.

FRANCISCO. Er gebehrdet sich kläglich, und läfst, als ob er was sagen wollte.

HORAT. Hierunter ist etwas verborgen.

SCENE IV.
HAMLET.

2. SCHILDW. Wer da?
HAMLET. Schweig!
2. SCHILDW. Wer da?
HAMLET. Schweig!
2. SCHILDW. Antwort, oder ich werde dir was anders weisen.
HAMLET. Freund!

[GHOST *gives the Sentinel a box on the ear from behind, and makes him drop his musket. Exit.*

2. SENT. The devil himself is in this game. O I'm too sore afraid to move from the spot.

SCENE III.
HORATIO AND SOLDIERS.

2. SENT. Who's there?
HORAT. Watch!
2. SENT. Which?
HORAT. First!
2. SENT. Stand, watch — corporal out! to arms!

[FRANCISCO *and watch come out, give the word from the other side.*

HORAT. Sentinel, look well to your post, mayhap the Prince himself will go the rounds; look to it ye be not found asleep, it might cost you the best head upon your shoulders.

2. SENT. Oh! I warrant were the whole company here, not a man amongst them all would sleep at his post; I must be relieved, else I'll run for't at the risk of hanging on the highest gallows to-morrow.

HORAT. And wherefore?
2. SENT. I'faith, your worship, a ghost appears here in this place every quarter of an hour, and frightens me so horribly, I'd think I was all alive in purgatory.

FRANCISCO. The first sentinel, who watched last hour, has just told me the same story.

2. SENT. Ay, ay, tarry but a little while, it will soon appear again.

[*Ghost stalks across the stage.*

HORAT. Upon my life, it is a ghost, and looks extremely like the late King of Denmark!

FRANCISCO. To judge by his gestures, he is miserable, and seems as if he wished to say something.

HORAT. There is some mystery under all this.

SCENE IV.
HAMLET.

2. SENT. Who's there?
HAMLET. Hush!
2. SENT. Who's there?
HAMLET. Hush!
2. SENT. Answer, or I'll teach thee better manners.
HAMLET. A friend!

2. Schildw. Was vor Freund?

Hamlet. Des Reichs Freund.

Francisco. Bey meinem Leben, es ist der Prinz!

Horat. Ihro Durchlaucht, sind Sie es, oder nicht?

Hamlet. Siehe, Horatio, seyd Ihr es! Was macht Ihr hier?

Horat. Ew. Durchl. aufzuwarten, ich habe die Wachen etwas visitirt, ob auch alle Posten wohl besetzt seyn.

Hamlet. Ihr thut, als ein ehrlicher Soldat, denn auf Euch ruhet des Königs und des Reichs Sicherheit.

Horat. Ihro Durchlaucht, es trägt sich ein wunderlicher Casus zu, massen sich allhier alle Viertelstunde ein Geist sehn läfst; er gleicht, meinen Einbildungen nach, recht dem verstorbenen König, Dero Herrn Vater. Er thut auf diesem Rundeel der Schildwacht grossen Schaden.

Hamlet. Das will ich nicht hoffen, denn die Seelen der Frommen ruhen wohl bis zu der Zeit ihrer Erneurung.

Horat. Es ist nicht anders, Ihro Durchlaucht, ich habe ihn selbst gesehn.

Francisco. Mich hat er sehr erschreckt, Ihro Durchl.

2. Schildw. Und mich hat er eine brave Ohrfeige gegeben.

Hamlet. Wie ist es an der Zeit?

Francisco. Es ist recht Mitternacht.

Hamlet. Eben recht, denn um dieselbe Zeit pflegen sich die Geister sehn zu lassen, wenn sie wandeln.

[*Es wird wieder Gesundheit geblasen.*

Hamlet. Holla! was ist dieses?

Horat. Mich dünkt, als wann sie zu Hofe noch lustig Gesundheiten trinken.

Hamlet. Recht, Horatio! mein Herr Vater und Vetter wird sich mit seinen Adhœrenten noch wacker lustig machen. Ach! Horatio, ich weifs nicht, warum nach meines Herrn Vaters Tod ich allezeit solche Herzensangst gehabt; dahergegen meine Königliche Frau Mutter ihn gar bald vergessen, dieser König aber ihn noch eher: denn weil ich in Teutschland gewesen, hat er sich geschwinde zum König in Dännemark krönen lassen, unter dem Schein des Rechtens aber hat er mir die Krone von Norwegen überlassen, und beruft sich auf die Wahl der Stände.

SCENE V.
Geist.

2. Schildw. O wehe, der Geist kommt wieder!

Horat. Sehen nun Ihro Durchlaucht?

2. Sent. What friend?

Hamlet. Friend to the kingdom.

Francisco. By my life, it is the Prince!

Horat. Your Highness, is it you or no?

Hamlet. Ha! Horatio, is it you? What make you here?

Horat. Your Highness, I have gone the rounds, to see that all sentries are at their posts.

Hamlet. You act as an honest soldier, for on you rests the safety of the king and kingdom.

Horat. My lord, a strange thing hath happened, in as much as a ghost appears here every quarter of an hour. To my fancy, he is very like your father the late king. He doeth much harm to the sentinels on the rounds.

Hamlet. I hope not, for the souls of the pious rest quietly till the day of their revival.

Horat. But so it is, my lord; I have seen him myself.

Francisco. He frightened me most horribly, my lord.

2. Sent. And me he dealt a good box on the ears.

Hamlet. What hour now?

Francisco. Midnight hath struck.

Hamlet. 'Tis well, for it is about this time that the spirits are accustomed to shew themselves when they walk.

[*Again healths drunk to sound of trumpets.*

Hamlet. Ho! What does this mean?

Horat. Methinks that at court they are still very merry with their health-drinking.

Hamlet. Ay marry, Horatio! my father and uncle keeps wassail still with his friends and followers. Horatio, I know not wherefore since my father's death so strange a boding doth at all times weigh me down; whereas my royal mother hath so soon forgot him, but this king still sooner; for whilst I was in Germany, he had himself crowned in all haste King of Denmark, and under semblance of right made over to me the crown of Norway appealing to the election of the states.

SCENE V.
Ghost.

2. Sent. Look! where the spirit comes again!

Horat. Doth your lordship see now?

FRANCISCO. Ihro Durchlaucht erschrecken nicht!
[*Der* GEIST *geht über das Theater, und winket Hamlet.*

HAMLET. Der Geist winkt mir; Ihr Herren, Sie treten ein wenig an die Seite, Horatio mache dich nicht zu weit, ich will den Geist folgen und sein Begehren vernehmen. [*ab.*

HORATIO. Ihr Herren, wir wollen ihm folgen, damit ihm kein Leid wiederfahre. [*gehen ab.*

[GEIST *winket bis aufs halbe Theater, und thut etlichemal das Maul auf.*

HAMLET. Rede, wer du bist, und sage, was du begehrest.

GEIST. Hamlet!

HAMLET. Herr!

GEIST. Hamlet!

HAMLET. Was begehrst du?

GEIST. Höre mich, Hamlet, denn die Zeit kommt bald, daſs ich mich wieder an denselben Ort begeben muſs, wo ich hergekommen; höre, und gieb wohl Achtung, was ich dir erzählen werde.

HAMLET. Rede, du seeliger Schatten meines Königlichen Herrn Vaters.

GEIST. So höre, mein Sohn Hamlet, was ich dir erzählen will von deines Vaters unnatürlichem Tode.

HAMLET. Was? unnatürlichem Tode?

GEIST. Ja, unnatürlichem Tode! Wisse, daſs ich den Gebrauch hatte, welchen mir die Natur angewöhnet, daſs ich täglich nach der Mahlzeit zu Mittage in meinem Königlichen Lustgarten zu gehn pflegte, um allda mich eine Stunde der Ruhe zu bedienen. Als ich denn eines Tages auch also thät, siehe da kommt mein Kronsüchtiger Bruder zu mir, und hatte einen subtilen Saft von Ebeno genannt bey sich; dieses Oel oder Saft hat diese Wirkung, daſs, sobald etliche Tropfen von diesen unter das menschliche Geblüt kommen, sie alsobald alle Lebensadern verstopfen, und ihm das Leben nehmen. Diesen Saft goſs er mir, als ich schlief, in meine Ohren, sobald dasselbe in den Kopf kam, muſste ich augenblicklich sterben, hernach gab man vor, ich hätte einen starken Schlagfluſs bekommen. Also bin ich meines Reichs, meines Weibes, und meines Lebens von diesem Tyrannen beraubt.

HAMLET. Gerechter Himmel, wo dieses wahr, so schwör ich dir die Rache.

GEIST. Ich werde nicht eher ruhen, bis mein unnatürlicher Tod gerochen ist. [*ab.*

HAMLET. Ich schwöre, nicht zu ruhen, bis ich mich an diesem Brudermörder gerochen habe.

FRANCISCO. Pray, my lord, be not afraid.
[*The ghost stalks over the stage and beckons to Hamlet.*

HAMLET. The spirit beckons me to go away — Gentlemen stand aside. Horatio, do not go too far. I will follow the ghost and learn his will.
[*Exit.*

HORAT. Gentlemen, let's follow him that no mischief happen to him. [*Exeunt.*

[*The ghost beckons Hamlet to the middle of the stage, and opens his jaws several times.*

HAMLET. Speak, who art thou? say, what thou desirest?

GHOST. Hamlet!

HAMLET. Sir!

GHOST. Hamlet!

HAMLET. What desirest thou?

GHOST. Mark me, Hamlet, for the time draws near when I must return to whence I came: list, and mark thou well what I shall tell thee.

HAMLET. Speak, thou departed spirit of my royal father.

GHOST. Then listen, Hamlet, my son, what I'm about to tell thee of thy father's most unnatural death.

HAMLET. What? Unnatural death?

GHOST. Ay, unnatural death. Know that it was my custom, which nature had made habitual to me, to retire every afternoon within my royal orchard, there to enjoy an hour's repose. One day, when doing this as usual, behold my crown-thirsty brother comes to me, bearing with him a phial of the subtle juice of hebenon; this oil or juice hath this effect, that as soon as a few drops of it mix with the blood of man, it immediately stops up the veins, and takes away life. While I slept, he poured this juice into my ear, which entering my head, I could not but die immediately; whereupon it was given out I had died of apoplexy. Thus was I robbed of kingdom, wife, and life by this foul tyrant.

HAMLET. Just heaven, if this be true, I swear revenge.

GHOST. I cannot rest until my most unnatural murder be revenged. [*Exit.*

HAMLET. I swear I will not rest till this foul murder be revenged.

SCENE VI.

HORATIO. HAMLET. FRANCISCO.

HORAT. Wie stehts mit Ihro Durchlaucht? wie so erschrocken? Haben Sie sich vielleicht alterirt?

HAMLET. Ach freylich, und zwar über die maafsen!

HORAT. Haben Ihro Durchlaucht den Geist gesehn?

HAMLET. Ja! sicherlich hab ich ihn gesehn, auch mit ihm geredet.

HORAT. O Himmel, dieses wird etwas Sonderliches bedeuten!

HAMLET. Er hat mir eine greuliche Sache offenbart, darum bitte ich, Ihr Herren, stehet mir bey in einer Sache, welche Rache erfodert.

HORAT. Meiner Treue sind Sie gewifs versichert, darum offenbaren Sie mir es nur.

FRANCISCO. Ihro Durchlaucht zweifeln an meiner Hülfe auch nicht!

HAMLET. Ihr Herren, ehe und bevor ich Euch solches offenbare, so solt Ihr mir bey Ehre und Treu einen Eid schwören.

FRANCISCO. Ihro Durchlaucht wissen, dafs ich Sie höchst liebe, ich will auch gern mein Leben darbey aufsetzen, wenn Sie sich rächen wollen.

HORAT. Sie fordern nur den Eid von uns, wir wollen Sie getreu beystehn.

HAMLET. So leget Eure Finger auf meinen Degen: Wir schwören.

HORAT. und FRANCISCO. Wir schwören.

GEIST [inwendig]. Wir schwören.

HAMLET. Holla! was ist dieses? Noch einmal, wir schwören.

HORAT. und FRANCISCO. Wir schwören.

GEIST. Wir schwören.

HAMLET. Dieses mufs was Sonderliches bedeuten. Kommt noch einmal, wir wollen auf die andre Seite gehn. Wir schwören.

HORAT. und FRANCISCO. Wir schwören.

GEIST. Wir schwören.

HAMLET. Was ist dieses? Sollte wohl ein Echo den Wiederschall von unsern Worten wieder zurückschicken. Kommt wir wollen noch an einen andern Ort gehen. Wir schwören.

GEIST. Wir schwören.

HAMLET. O ich höre schon, was dieses ist: es scheinet, dafs der Geist meines Herrn Vaters nicht damit zufrieden, dafs ichs offenbaren soll. Ihr Herren, ich bitte, verlafst mich, ich will Euch morgen alles offenbaren.

HORAT. und FRANCISCO. Ihro Durchlaucht leben wohl. [*Francisco ab.*

SCENE VI.

HORATIO. HAMLET. FRANCISCO.

HORAT. How is't, my noble lord? How so terrorstricken? Mayhap you've suffered offence?

HAMLET. Why yes, Horatio, beyond all measure.

HORAT. Have you seen the ghost, my lord?

HAMLET. Ay, verily I have seen it, and held discourse with it too.

HORAT. O Heavens! this bodeth something strange!

HAMLET. He hath revealed to me a horrible thing; therefore, I pray you, gentlemen, stand by me in a matter that demandeth vengeance.

HORAT. Most certainly you are assured of my loyalty; only explain, my lord.

FRANCISCO. Your lordship cannot doubt of my aid in this matter.

HAMLET. Gentlemen, before I make this matter known to you, you must swear an oath by your loyalty and honour.

FRANCISCO. Your lordship knows the love I bear you — and how willingly I would lend my life if you wish to be revenged.

HORAT. Ask us then to swear, and we will stand by you loyally and faithfully.

HAMLET. Then swear by my sword.

HORAT. and FRANCISCO. We swear.

GHOST [*within*]. We swear.

HAMLET. Ha, ha, what's this! Again, we swear.

HORAT. and FRANCISCO. We swear.

GHOST. We swear.

HAMLET. O this is wondrous strange! Come, once more; we will shift our ground. We swear.

HORAT. and FRANCISCO. We swear.

GHOST. We swear.

HAMLET. What is this? Can there be an echo here, to give us back our words? Come, gentlemen, we will go to another spot. We swear.

GHOST. We swear.

HAMLET. O! now I understand what it is. The spirit of my father is perturbed that I should make this matter known. Good friends, leave me — to-morrow I will reveal the whole to you.

HORAT. and FRANCISCO. My lord, farewell! [*Exit Francisco.*

HAMLET. Horatio, komm her.
HORAT. Was verlangen Eure Durchlaucht?
HAMLET. Ist der andre weg?
HORAT. Ja, er ist schon weg.
HAMLET. Ich weiſs, Horatio, du bist mir jederzeit getreu gewesen, dir will ichs offenbaren, was mir der Geist gesagt, nemlich daſs mein Vater eines unnatürlichen Todes gestorben. Mein Vater, der anjetzo auch mein Vater ist, der hat ihn ermordet.
HORAT. O Himmel, was höre ich!
HAMLET. Du weiſst, Horatio, daſs mein seeliger Herr Vater die Gewohnheit hatte, daſs er täglich nach der Mittagsmahlzeit in seinem Lustgarten sich einer Stunde des Schlafs bediente. Solches dieser Bösewicht wissend, kommt zu meinem Herrn Vater, und im Schlaf gieſst er ihm den Saft von Ebeno in das Ohr, daſs er alsobald von diesem starken Gift muſs den Geist aufgeben. Dieses hat der verfluchte Hund darum gethan, die Krone zu erlangen: aber von dieser Stunde an will ich anfangen eine simulirte Tollheit, und in derselben Simulation will ich meine Rolle so artig spielen, bis ich Gelegenheit finde, meines Herrn Vaters Tod zu rächen.
HORAT. Ist es also, Ihro Durchlaucht, so will ich Sie getreue Hand bieten.
HAMLET. (Horatio, ich will mich an diesen Kronsüchtigen, an diesen Ehebrecher und Mörder also rächen, daſs die Nachwelt der Ewigkeit davon nachsagen soll;) ich will itzund gehn, und ihm verstellterweise aufwarten, bis daſs ich Gelegenheit finde, die Rache auszuüben.
[*Gehen ab.*

SCENE VII.
KÖNIG. KÖNIGINN. HAMLET. CORAMBUS *und Staat.*
KÖNIG.³(Obschon unsers Herrn Bruders Tod noch in frischem Gedächtniſs bey jedermann ist, und uns gebietet, alle Solennitäten einzustellen, werden wir doch anjetzo genöthiget, unsere schwarze Trauerkleider in Carmosin, Purpur und Scharlach zu verändern, weil nunmehro meines seeligen Herrn Bruders hinterbliebene Wittwe unsere liebste Gemahlin worden; darum erzeige sich ein jeder freudig, und mache sich unser Lust theilhaftig.) Ihr aber, Prinz Hamlet, gebet Euch zufrieden; sehet hier Eure Frau Mutter, wie traurig und betrübt daſs sie ist über Eure Melancholie. Auch haben wir vernommen, daſs Ihr gesonnen seyd, wieder nach Wittenberg zu reisen, thut solches nicht Eurer Mutter wegen; bleibt hier, denn wir Euch lieben und gerne sehen, wollten also nicht gerne, daſs Euch einiger Schade wiederfahren sollte, bleibt bey uns am Hofe, oder wo ja nicht, so könnt Ihr Euch nach Norwegen in Euer Königreich begeben.

HAMLET. Come hither, Horatio.
HORAT. My lord, what is your will?
HAMLET. Is the other away?
HORAT. Ay, he is away.
HAMLET. I know, Horatio, thou hast at all times been faithful to me, wherefore to thee will I reveal what the ghost hath told me, namely, that my father died an unnatural death. My father, he who is now my father, hath murdered him.
HORAT. O heavens! what do I hear!
HAMLET. Thou know'st, Horatio, that my late father was accustomed to sleep an hour every day after dinner within his orchard. Knowing this, the villain comes to my father and pours the juice of hebenon into his ear while he is asleep; and thereupon, affected by this strong poison, he immediately yields up the ghost. And this the accursed dog hath done to win the crown: but from this hour I will put on the semblance of madness, and play my part so prettily, that surely I shall find occasion to revenge my father's death.

HORAT. My lord, if the matter stands thus, I offer you the hand of faithful fellowship.
HAMLET. Horatio, I swear so to revenge myself on this envious thief, this adulterer, this murderer, that posterity shall speak of it to all eternity; now I go, and with dissembling art will wait upon him till I find an opportunity to take revenge.
[*Exeunt.*

SCENE VII.
KING, QUEEN, HAMLET, CORAMBUS, *and Attendants.*
KING. Though yet of our dear brother's death the memory is green to all and it befitteth us to suspend all joyous demonstrations, yet from this time 'tis meet we change our suits of solemn black to crimson, purple, and scarlet, seeing my sometime late brother's widow has now become our dearest spouse. Wherefore I pray you, let each one show a joyous countenance and share our mirth. But you, Prince Hamlet, content ye; see here your mother, how sad and full of grief she is that ye are melancholy. Likewise we have learned your intent to go back to Wittenberg. We do beseech you remain here for the sake of your mother. Stay with us, for we love you and like to see you, and should not like any harm to overtake you. Stay with us at court, or if not, betake yourself to Norway, to your kingdom.

KÖNIGIN. Vielgeliebter Sohn Prinz Hamlet, es nimmt uns grofs Wunder, dafs Ihr Euch habt vorgenommen, von hier zu reisen, und Euch nacher Wittenberg zu begeben. Nun wisset Ihr ja wohl, dafs Euer Königlicher Herr Vater unlängst Todes verblichen, weswegen uns grofse Traurigkeit und Melancholie zu Herzen gestofsen, und wenn Ihr solltet von uns reisen, würde sich dieselbe ein grofses vermehren; darum, liebster Sohn, bleibt hier: alle Freude und Lust, so Euch beliebt, sollt Ihr ohne Weigerung geniefsen.

HAMLET. Ihrem Befehl will ich von Herzen gern gehorsamen, und vor diesesmal hier bleiben und nicht verreisen.

KÖNIG. Thut solches, liebster Prinz. Aber Corambus, wie ist es mit eurem Sohn Leonhardo, ist er schon hinweg nacher Frankreich verreiset.

CORAMB. Ja, gnädiger Herr und König, er ist schon weg.

KÖNIG. Ist es aber mit eurem Consens geschehen?

CORAMB. (Ja, mit Ober-Consens, mit Mittel-Consens und mit Unter-Consens.) O, Ihro Majestät, er hat einen über die maafsen herrlichen, treflichen, prächtigen Consens von mir bekommen.

KÖNIG. Weilen er mit eurem Consens verreiset, so mag es ihm wohlgehen, und die Götter wollen ihm gesund wieder anhero helfen. Wir aber sind gesonnen, ein Carisell anzustellen, damit unserer liebsten Gemahlin die Traurigkeit vergehe. Ihr aber, Prinz Hamlet, sollet Euch auch nebst andern hohen Personen lustig erzeigen, vor diesesmal aber wollen wir der Lustigkeit ein Ende machen, weil der Tag sich nahet, die schwarze Nacht zu vertreiben. Sie aber, wertheste Gemahlin, werd ich nach Ihrem Schlafgemach begleiten.

Kommt, lafst uns Hand in Hand, und Arm um Arm einschliefsen,
Lafst uns das süfse Pfand der Lieb und Ruh geniefsen.

ZWEYTER ACT.

SCENE I.
KÖNIG. KÖNIGIN.

KÖNIG. Liebste Gemahlin, wie kommt es, dafs Ihr so traurig seyd, Sie entdecke doch die Ursache Ihrer Betrübnisse, Sie ist ja unsere Königin, wir lieben Sie, und alles, was das ganze Reich vermag, ist Ihr eigen, worüber hat Sie sich denn zu betrüben?

KÖNIGIN. Mein König, ich habe grofse Betrübnisse über die Melancholie meines Sohnes Hamlets, welcher mein einziger Prinz ist, und dieses schmerzt mich.

QUEEN. My much loved son, Prince Hamlet, it greatly doth astonish us to learn your intent to leave us and to go to Wittenberg. You know full well your royal father died a short time ago, which causeth us great sadness and heaviness of heart, and should you go from us, it would increase the same; for which reason, dear son, stay with us: you shall enjoy your fill of pleasure at our court without restraint, an it so pleaseth you.

HAMLET. I shall obey you with all my heart, Madam, I will not go, but will remain here.

KING. Do so, dear Prince! Say, Corambus, how is it with your son Leonardo. Is he already gone to France?

CORAMB. Ay, my gracious lord and king, he is.

KING. But had he your consent, Corambus?

CORAMB. Ay marry, your majesty, he got a top consent, a bottom consent, and a middle consent! I'faith he got a rare, a wonderful, a most excellent consent from me.

KING. As he has your consent, I hope he may prosper, and that the gods may speed him hither again in peace and safety. Now for ourself, it is our will to hold a carousal, that an end may be put to our dear spouse's grief. And you, Prince Hamlet, and other noble persons of our court, shew yourselves mirthful; but for this present we shall break up our festivities, for the day is approaching to put black night to flight. You, my dearest consort, shall I follow to your bed-chamber.

Come, let us hand in hand and arm in arm entwine,
Ourselves to the sweet joys of love and rest resign.

ACT II.

SCENE I.
KING. QUEEN.

KING. Dearest consort, whence comes it that you are so sad? Pray tell me the cause of your melancholy! You are our Queen; we love you, and all we have is yours, even to the whole of our Kingdom. What is it then that troubles you?

QUEEN. My gracious lord and master, I am greatly troubled at the melancholy of my son Hamlet, who is my only prince; it is this that grieves me.

KÖNIG. Wie? ist er melancholisch? Wir wollen alle vornehme Doctores und Aerzte in unserm ganzen Königreich zusammen verschreiben, damit ihm geholfen werde.

SCENE II.
CORAMBUS *zu diesen.*

CORAMBUS. Neue Zeutung, gnädiger Herr und König!

KÖNIG. Was ist denn Neues vorhanden?

CORAMB. (Prinz Hamlet ist toll, ja so toll, als der griechische Tolleran jemals gewesen.)

KÖNIG. Und warum ist er toll?

CORAMB. Darum, dafs er seinen Verstand verloren.

KÖNIG. Wo hat er denn seinen Verstand verloren?

CORAMB. Das weifs ich nicht, das mag derjenige wissen, welcher ihn gefunden hat.

SCENE III.
OPHELIA.

OPHELIA. Ach, Herr Vater, beschirmet mich!

CORAMB. Was ist es denn, mein Kind?

OPHELIA. Ach, Herr Vater, Prinz Hamlet plagt mich, ich kann keinen Frieden für ihn haben!

CORAMB. Stelle dich zufrieden, liebe Tochter: aber er hat dich ja sonsten nichts gethan. O nun weifs ich schon, warum Prinz Hamlet toll ist; er ist gewifs in meine Tochter verliebt?

KÖNIG. Hat denn die Liebe eine solche Kraft, einen Menschen toll zu machen?

CORAMB. Gnädiger Herr und König, freylich ist sie kräftig genug, einen Menschen toll zu machen. Denn ich gedenke noch, da ich noch jung war, wie mich die Liebe plagte, ja sie hat mich so toll gemacht, als einen Märzhaasen, anjetzo aber acht ich sie nicht mehr: Ich sitze lieber bey dem Ofen, und zähle meine rothe Pfennige, und trinke Ihro Majestät Gesundheit.

KÖNIG. Kann man aber seine Raserey und Tollheit nicht selbst in Augenschein nehmen?

CORAMB. Ja, Ihro Majestät, wir wollen nur ein wenig an die Seite treten, und meine Tochter soll ihm das Kleinod, welches er ihr verehrt hat, zeigen, so können Ihro Majestät seine Tollheit sehn.

KÖNIG. Liebste Gemahlin, Sie lasse sich belieben, in Ihr Gemach zu gehn, wir wollen unterdessen seine Tollheit in Augenschein nehmen. [*verstecken sich.*

SCENE IV.
HAMLET *und* OPHELIA.

OPHELIA. Eure Durchlaucht nehmen doch das Kleinod wieder, welches Sie mir geschenket.

KING. What! is he melancholy? Then will we gather together all the learned doctors and physicians throughout our whole Kingdom, that they may bring him aid.

SCENE II.
CORAMBUS, *to the above.*

CORAMB. News, news! my gracious lord and king!

KING. What news, Corambus?

CORAMB. Prince Hamlet is mad, aye, as mad as ever the Greek madman was.

KING. And wherefore is he mad?

CORAMB. Because he hath lost his wits.

KING. Where hath he lost his wits?

CORAMB. That I know not, mayhap he knows who hath found them.

SCENE III.
OPHELIA.

OPHELIA. Alas! my father protect me.

CORAMB. How now Ophelia, what aileth thee?

OPHELIA. Alas! my father, Prince Hamlet doth plague me; I can have no peace for him.

CORAMB. Never mind it, my dear daughter. But tell me, he hath not done anything else to you? O! now I know why Prince Hamlet is mad: he is certainly in love with my daughter.

KING. Hath love then so much potency that it depriveth a man of his wits.

CORAMB. My gracious master and king, most assuredly is love potent enough to deprive a man of his wits. I remember when I myself was young, how love plagued me, — nay, but it made me mad as a march hare. But now, I care for it no longer. I prefer to sit by the fire, to count my bright new coins, and drink your Majesty's health.

KING. May we not ourselves be a witness to his distempered fancies?

CORAMB. Yes, your Majesty. We will stand a little on one side, and my daughter shall shew him the jewel which he has given her. Then will your Majesty be able to see his madness.

KING. Dearest wife, we beseech you, go to your chamber. Meanwhile we will be a witness of his madness. [*Hide themselves.*

SCENE IV.
HAMLET. OPHELIA.

OPHELIA. I pray your Highness to take back the jewel which you gave me.

HAMLET. Was, Mädchen, willst du gern einen Mann haben? Gehe weg von mir — doch, komm her. Höre, Mädchen, ihr Jungfern, ihr thut nichts anders, als die junge Gesellen verführen, eure Schönheit kauft ihr bey den Apothekern und Krämern: höret, ich will euch eine Historie erzählen. Es war ein Kavalier in Anion, der verliebte sich in eine Dame, welche anzusehen war wie die Göttin Venus, wie sie nun sollten zusammen zu Bette gehen, ging die Braut vor, und fing an, sich auszuziehen, nahm erstlich das eine Auge aus, welches künstlicherweise war eingesetzt, hernach die Vorderzähne, welche von Elfenbein auch so künstlich waren eingemacht, daſs mans nicht sehn konnte, hernach wusch sie sich, da ging die Schminke, womit sie sich angestrichen hatte, auch fort. Der Bräutigam kam endlich, gedachte seine Braut zu umfangen, wie er sie aber ansichtig ward, erschrak er, und gedachte, es wäre ein Gespenst. Also betrügt ihr die Junggesellen, darum höret mich auch. Aber warte, Mädchen — doch, gehe nur fort nach dem Kloster, aber nicht nach einem Kloster, wo zwey Paar Pantoffeln vor dem Bette stehen. [ab.

CORAMB. Ist er nicht perfect und veritabel toll, gnädiger Herr und König.

KÖNIG. Corambus, verlaſs uns, wenn wir werden euch vonnöthen haben, wollen wir euch schon rufen lassen. [Corambus ab.] Wir haben des Prinzen Tollheit und Raserey mit grofser Verwunderung gesehn, uns dünkt aber, daſs es keine rechte Tollheit, sondern vielmehr eine simulirte Tollheit sey; wir müssen verschaffen, daſs er an die Seite oder gar ums Leben gebracht werde, es möchte sonst was Uebels daraus entstehen. [ab.

SCENE V.
HAMLET. HORATIO.

HAMLET. Mein werther Freund, Horatio, durch diese angenommene Tollheit hoffe ich Gelegenheit zu bekommen, meines Vaters Tod zu rächen. Ihr wiſst aber, mein Vater ist allezeit mit vielen Trabanten umgeben, darum so es etwa mir miſslingen möchte, und ihr etwa meinen Leichnam findet, so laſst ihn doch ehrlich zu der Erden bestätigen, denn die erste Gelegenheit, die ich finde, werde ich mich an ihm wagen.

HORAT. Ich bitte Ihro Durchlaucht, Sie wollen solches nicht thun, vielleicht hat Sie der Geist betrogen.

HAMLET. O nein, seine Worte waren allzuwohl ausgesprochen, ich kann ihm wohl Glauben geben. Was aber bringt der alte Narr Neues?

SCENE VI.
CORAMBUS.

CORAMB. Neue Zeitung, gnädiger Herr! Die Comödianten sind angekommen.

HAMLET. What, maiden! dost thou want a husband? Get thee from me — nay, pr'ythee come back. List girl, you maidens do make nothing but fools of us bachelors, you buy your beauty of the apothecaries and pedlers; listen while I tell thee a tale. There lived once a cavalier in Anion, who fell in love with a lady, who, to look at, was like the goddess Venus. Now when they were to go to bed together, the bride went before and began to undress. First she took out one eye, which had been set in a most artificial manner — then the front teeth made of ivory, likewise wrought with utmost art, whereupon she washed, and the skillfully laid on paint disappeared also. At length came the bridegroom expecting to embrace his bride. But as soon as he caught sight of her, he started back, for he thought he saw a ghost. Thus it is ye deceive us bachelors; therefore listen to me. Pr'ythee tarry maiden — nay go, go thy ways to a nunnery, but not to a nunnery where two pair of slippers stand at the bedside.
[Exit.

CORAMB. Is he not truly and veritably mad my gracious lord?

KING. Corambus leave us now. When we have need of you, we'll send for you. [Exit Coramb.] We have heard the Prince's distempered fancies with great wonder and astonishment. It seems to us no real madness, but rather dissembled. We must contrive to get rid of him, or perhaps indeed put him out of the way altogether, or else some harm may come of it.
[Exit.

SCENE V.
HAMLET. HORATIO.

HAMLET. Horatio, my good friend, I trust by my dissembled madness to hit upon a fitting time for revenging my father's death. (You know my father is at all times surrounded with his guards, for which reason my attempt may fail.) Should you perchance find my body, have it honourably buried, for on the first occasion which present itself, I shall try my chance with him.

HORAT. I entreat your lordship to do nothing of the kind. Perchance the ghost hath deceived you.

HAMLET. No, oh no! the words he uttered were too lucid and distinctly spoken. I believe him, ay, that I do. Ha! what news brings that old fool?

SCENE VI.
CORAMBUS.

CORAMB. News, news! my lord! I have news to tell you. The actors are come, my lord.

HAMLET. Da Marus Russig ein Comödiant war zu Rom, was war da vor eine schöne Zeit!

CORAMB. Ha, ha, ha! Allezeit vexiren mich Ihro Hoheiten.

HAMLET. O Jeptha, Jeptha, was hast du vor ein schönes Töchterlein!

CORAMB. Alle Zeiten wollen Ihro Hoheiten, dafs meine Tochter soll herhalten.

HAMLET. Wohlan, Alter, lafs den Meister von den Comödianten hereinkommen.

CORAMB. Es soll geschehn.   [*ab.*

HAMLET. Diese Comödianten kommen eben recht, denn durch ihnen will ich probiren, ob mich der Geist mit Wahrheit berichtet, oder nicht. Ich habe vor diesem eine Tragödie gesehn, dafs ein Bruder den andern im Garten ermordet, diese sollen sie agiren; wird sich der König nun entfärben, so hat er gethan, was mir der Geist gesagt hat.

SCENE VII.

COMÖDIANTEN. PRINCIPAL CARL.

CARL. Ihro Hoheiten wollen die Götter allezeit mit Seegen, Glück und Gesundheit beschenken.

HAMLET. Ich dank euch, mein Freund, was verlanget ihr?

CARL. Ihro Hoheiten wollen uns in Gnaden verzeihen, wir sind fremde hochteutsche Comödianten, und hätten gewünscht, das Glück zu haben, auf Ihro Majestät des Königs Beylager zu agiren, allein das Glück hat uns den Rücken, der contraire Wind aber das Gesichte zugekehret, ersuchen also an Ihro Hoheiten, ob wir nicht noch eine Historie vorstellen könnten, damit wir unsere weite Reise nicht gar umsonst möchten gethan haben.

HAMLET. Seyd ihr nicht vor wenig Jahren zu Wittenberg auf der Universität gewesen, mich dünckt, ich habe euch da sehn agiren.

CARL. Ja, Ihro Hoheiten, wir sind von denselben Comödianten.

HAMLET. Habt ihr dieselbe Compagnie noch ganz bey euch.

CARL. Wir sind zwar nicht so stark, weilen etliche Studenten in Hamburg Condition genommen, doch seynd wir zu vielen lustigen Comödien und Tragödien stark genug.

HAMLET. Könnt ihr uns nun wohl diese Nacht eine Comödie präsentiren?

CARL. Ja, Ihro Hoheiten, wir sind stark und exercirt genug.

HAMLET. When Marius Roscius was an actor at Rome, what fine times those were!

CORAMB. Ha, ha, ha, how you always do laugh at me, my lord!

HAMLET. O! Jephthah, Jephthah! what a fair daughter hast thou!

CORAMB. Why, my lord, you are still harping on my daughter.

HAMLET. Well, well, old graybeard, let the master of the actors come in.

CORAMB. I will, my lord.   [*Exit.*

HAMLET. These actors come in the nick of time, for through them I shall prove whether the ghost's story is true or no. I have once seen a tragedy wherein one brother murders the other in the garden; this shall they act. And if the king turn pale, then has he done what the ghost has told me.

SCENE VII.

ACTORS. CHARLES, THE PRINCIPAL.

CHARLES. May the gods bestow on your Highness peace, happiness, and health!

HAMLET. I thank you, my friend. What brings you hither?

CHARLES. Pardon, your Highness, but we are strange High-German actors, and were ambitious of the honour of acting at his Majesty's wedding. But Fortune turned her back on us, and contrary winds their face towards us. We therefore beseech your Highness to allow us to act a story, that our long journey be not all in vain.

HAMLET. Were you not some years ago at the University at Wittenberg? It seems to me I have seen you act before.

CHARLES. Yes, your Highness, we are the self same actors.

HAMLET. Have you the whole of the same company still?

CHARLES. We are not quite so numerous, because some students took engagements in Hamburg. Nevertheless we are numerous enough for many merry comedies and tragedies.

HAMLET. Could you give us a play to-night?

CHARLES. Yes, your Highness, we are numerous enough, and well practised.

HAMLET. Habt ihr noch alle drey Weibspersonen bey euch, sie agirten sehr wohl?

CARL. Nein, nur zwey, die eine ist mit ihrem Mann an den Sächsischen Hof geblieben.

HAMLET. Wie ihr zu Wittenberg waret, so agirtet ihr dazumal gute Comödien. Allein, ihr hattet etliche Bursche bey euch, die hatten gute Kleider an, aber schwarze Hemden, etliche hatten Stiefeln an, aber keine Sporen.

CARL. Ihro Hoheiten, man kann oft nicht alles haben, vielleicht haben sie gedacht, sie dürfen nicht reiten.

HAMLET. Doch ist es besser, wenn alles accurat ist: doch höret noch mehr, und bitte zu verzeihen, ihr höret oft nicht gleich, was die Zuschauer urtheilen, denn da waren auch etliche, die hatten seidne Strümpfe und weisse Schuh an, aber auf dem Haupte hatten sie schwarze Hüte, die waren voll Federn, unten bald so voll als oben, die Plomaschen waren, ich glaube, sie musten anstatt der Schlafmützen damit in den Betten gelegen haben, das steht so schlimm, und ist leicht zu ändern. Auch könnt ihr wohl etlichen davon sagen, wenn sie eine königliche oder fürstliche Person agiren, daſs sie doch nicht so sehr gucken, wenn sie ein Compliment gegen eine Dame machen, auch nicht so viel spanische Pfauentritte und solche Fechtermienen, denn ein Potentat lacht darüber, fein naturell ist das beste: der einen König agiret, muſs sich einbilden, daſs er in dem Spiel ein König sey, und ein Bauer auch wie ein Bauer.

CARL. Ihro Hoheit, ich nehme mit unterthäniger Ehrerbietung diese Correction an, und werden uns künftig besser gewöhnen.

HAMLET. Ich bin ein groſser Liebhaber eurer Exercitien, und meine es nicht übel, denn man kan in einem Spiegel seine Flecken sehen: Höret mir nun, ihr agirtet dazumahlen eine Materie in Wittenberg von dem König Pir Pir — es pirt sich so.

CARL. Ach es wird vielleicht von dem grossen König Pyrro seyn?

HAMLET. Mich dünkt es, doch weiſs ich es eigentlich nicht.

CARL. Wenn Ihro Hoheit nur noch etliche Personen nennen, oder etwas von dem Inhalt melden wollten.

HAMLET. Es war so, daſs ein Bruder den andern im Garten ermordet.

CARL. So wird es doch diese Materie seyn. Gieſst des Königs Bruder nicht dem Könige einen Gift in das Ohr?

HAMLET. Recht, recht, eben dieselbe ist es; könnt ihr wohl sie diesen Abend noch präsentiren?

HAMLET. Have you still the three actresses with you? They used to play well.

CHARLES. No, only two, the one stayed behind with her husband at the court of Saxony.

HAMLET. You acted good comedies in Wittenberg at that time. But you had some fellows in your company, who had good clothes, but black shirts, others, who had boots but no spurs.

CHARLES. Your Highness, it is often hard to procure everything; perchance they thought they might not ride.

HAMLET. Still it is better to have everything correct. But listen to another thing or two, and excuse me, for you do not often hear directly what judgments the spectators pass on you. There were also a few who wore silk stockings and white shoes, but had on their heads black hats full of feathers, nearly as many below as on the top; and for my part, I think they must have gone to bed in them instead nightcaps. Now that does not look well, and may easily be reformed. Moreover you may tell some of them, that when they have to act a royal or a princely personage, they should not make such eyes whenever they pay a lady a compliment. Neither should they strut, nor take on such braggart airs; a potentate laughs at such things. Natural ease and elegance is the best. He who plays a king must in the play fancy himself a king; and he who plays a peasant, must fancy himself a peasant.

CHARLES. Your Highness, I accept your Higness' reproof with the deepest respect and will endeavour to do better in future.

HAMLET. I am a great lover of your art, and mean you well, for it is in a mirror that one can best see one's blemishes. I remember you once acted a piece in Wittenberg about a King Pyr, Pyr — Pyr something.

CHARLES. Ah, it was perhaps about the great king Pyrrhus?

HAMLET. Methinks it was, but I am not quite sure.

CHARLES. Perhaps your Highness would name some persons in it, or give me some idea of the matter.

HAMLET. Let me see — one brother murdered the other in the garden.

CHARLES. Ay, ay, I'll swear 'tis the same. Did not the king's brother pour poison into the king's ear?

HAMLET. True, true, the self same story; could you play that piece to-night?

CARL. O ja, das können wir leicht machen, denn es kommen wenig Personen dazu.

HAMLET. So gehet hin, machet das Theater fertig in dem grofsen Saal; was euch an Behölzung mangelt, könnt ihr von dem Schlofsbaumeister fordern; steht euch etwas aus der Rüstkammer an, oder habt ihr nicht Kleider genug, so meldet euch bey den Quatrober oder Intendanten an, wir wollen, dafs euch alles soll gefolgt werden.

CARL. Ich bedanke mich in Unterthänigkeit gegen Eure Hoheiten für diese hohe Gnade, wir wollen zum Anfang eilen. Sie leben wohl.   [ab.

HAMLET. Diese Comödianten kommen mir itzo sehr wohl zu Passe. Horatio, gieb wohl acht auf den König: wo er sich entfärbt oder alterirt, so hat er gewifs die That verrichtet, denn die Comödianten treffen oft mit ihren erdichteten Dingen den Zweck der Wahrheit. Höre, ich will dir eine artige Historie erzählen: In Teutschland hat sich zu Strafsburg ein artiger Casus zugetragen, indem ein Weib ihren Mann mit einen Schuhpfriemen durchs Herze ermordet, hernach hat sie mit ihrem Hurenbuhler den Mann unter die Thürschwelle begraben, solches ist neun ganzer Jahr verborgen geblieben, bis endlich Comödianten allda zukamen, und von dergleichen Dingen eine Tragödie agirten; das Weib, welches mit ihrem Mann auch in dem Spiel war, fängt überlaut (weil ihr das Gewissen gerühret wurde) an zu rufen, und schreyt: o weh, das trift mich, denn also hab ich auch meinen unschuldigen Ehemann ums Leben gebracht. Sie raufte ihre Haare, lief aus dem Schauspiel nach dem Richter, bekannte freywillig ihren Mord, und als solches wahrhaft befunden, wurde sie in grofser Reue ihrer Sünden von denen Geistlichen getröstet, und in wahrer Bufse übergab sie ihren Leib dem Scharfrichter, den Himmel aber befahl sie ihre Seele. — Ach, wo mein Vater und Vetter auch in sich gehen möchte, wo er diese Sache begangen hat! Komm, Horatio, wir wollen gehen, und den König aufwarten; ich bitte dich aber, observire alle Dinge genau, denn ich werde simuliren.

HORAT. Ihro Durchlaucht, ich werde meinen Augen eine scharfe Aufsicht anbefehlen.   [gehen ab.

CHARLES. Oh yes, my lord, we can manage that easily enough, for there are but few personages in the play.

HAMLET. Now go get ready, hasten to prepare the stage in the great hall: whatever wood you may require, you can get from the castellan; if you want anything from the armoury or if you have not dresses enough, make known your wants to the master of the robes or the steward; we wish you should be provided with everything.

CHARLES. We thank your Highness most humbly for your favour, and will hasten to get ready. Farewell.
                                                        [Exit.

HAMLET. These actors come most opportunely. Horatio, pr'ythee watch the king; if he grow pale or alter favour, then oh! most surely hath he done the deed, for play actors with their feigned fables oft hit the truth. Give ear, I'll tell thee a pretty tale. In Germany, at Strasburg, there was once a pretty case. A wife murdered her husband by piercing him to the heart with an awl. Afterwards she buried the man under the threshold, she and her paramour. This deed remained hid full nine years, till at last it chanced that some actors came that way, and played a tragedy of like import; the woman who was likewise present at the play with her husband, began to cry aloud (her conscience being touched) alas! alas! you hit at me for in such manner did I murder my innocent husband. She tore her hair, ran straight way to the judge, freely confessed the murder which being proved true, in deep repentance for her sins she received the holy unction from the priest, gave her body to the executioner, and recommended her soul to God. — Oh that my uncle-father would thus honestly take it to heart an he be the doer of this crime! Come Horatio, let us go and wait upon the King; but pray note all things exactly, for I must play a part.

HORAT. Well my lord, I shall impose on my eyes the duty of keeping a sharp look-out.   [Exeunt.

SCENE VIII.

KÖNIG. KÖNIGIN. HAMLET. HORATIO. CORAMBUS.
OPHELIA. *Staat.*

KÖNIG. Meine wertheste Gemahlin, nun hoffe ich, dafs Sie Ihre Traurigkeit wird verbannen, und der Freude den Wohnplatz einräumen, es soll vor der Abendtafel

SCENE VIII.

KING. QUEEN. HAMLET. HORATIO. CORAMBUS.
OPHELIA. *Retinue.*

KING. Our best beloved spouse, now do we hope that you will banish your sadness, and make it give place to joy; before our evening's repast, there is to be a

Ihr von den Teutschen eine Komödie und nach der Tafel von unsern Landskindern ein Ballet gehalten werden.

KÖNIGIN. Ich will solche Lust gar gerne sehn, ich glaube schwerlich, daſs sich mein Herz wird zufrieden geben, denn ich weiſs nicht, was vor ein bevorstehendes Unglück unser Gemüth verunruhiget.

KÖNIG. Sie gebe sich doch zufrieden. Prinz Hamlet, wir haben vernommen, daſs Comödianten sind anhero kommen, welche uns noch diesen Abend eine Comödie präsentiren wollen: sagt uns, verhält sich das also?

HAMLET. Ja, Herr Vater, sie haben bey mir angehalten, ich habe es ihnen auch permittirt. Ich hoffe, Ihro Majestät werden es auch zufrieden seyn.

KÖNIG. Was ist es vor eine Materie, es ist ja wohl nicht etwa was Widerwärtiges oder was Unhöfliches?

HAMLET. Es ist eine gute Materie; uns, die wir gutes Gewissen haben, denen gehet es nichts an.

KÖNIG. Wo sind sie? laſst sie nur bald anfangen, denn wir wollen zusehen, was die Teutschen thun können.

HAMLET. Herr Marschall, sehet zu, ob die Comödianten fertig, saget, daſs sie anfangen.

CORAMB. Ihr Herren Comödianten, wo seyd ihr? Fort, ihr sollt geschwinde anfangen. Holla, sie kommen schon!

[*Hier kommt die Comödie: Der König mit seiner Gemahlin. Er will sich schlafen legen: die Königin bittet, er soll es nicht thun, er legt sich doch nieder, die Königin nimmt ihren Abschied mit einem Kuſs, und geht ab. Des Königs Bruder kommt mit einem Gläschen, giefst ihm was ins Ohr, und geht ab.*

HAMLET. Das ist der König Pyrrus, der geht nach den Garten schlafen. Die Königin bittet ihn, er soll es nicht thun, er aber legt sich doch. Das arme Weibchen geht weg: sehet, da kommt des Königs Bruder, welcher das Gift von Ebeno hat, giefset ihm ins Ohr, welches sobald das menschliche Geblüthe empfängt, dessen Leib alsobald ertödtet.

KÖNIG. Fackeln, Windlichter her, die Comödie gefällt uns nicht!

CORAMB. Pagen, Lakeyen, brennt die Fackeln an, der König will abgehn: Geschwinde, brennet an, die Comödianten haben einen stumpf gemacht.

[*König, Königin, Corambus und Staat gehen ab.*

HAMLET. Fackeln her, die Comödie gefällt uns nicht — Nun, siehst du, daſs mich der Geist nicht betrogen hat! Comödianten! gehet nur von hier mit diesem Beschluſs,

comedy, played by German actors, and after the same, a ballet given by our own people.

QUEEN. Most gladly shall I behold such merrymaking; still, I hardly believe that my heart will be at peace, for gloomy forebodings of mischief, I know not what, disturb my soul.

KING. Pray, do not be uneasy. Prince Hamlet, we are informed that actors have arrived here, and will perform a comedy to-night. Tell me, is it so?

HAMLET. Ay, my father it is so. They preferred a request to me to that intent, and I have given them permission. I hope your Majesty has no objection.

KING. What is the argument? There's no offence in it?

HAMLET. It is a good argument. We that have a good conscience, it touches us not.

KING. Why do they tarry? Let them begin, we would fain see what the Germans can do.

HAMLET. Marshall, go bid the actors make haste; tell them to begin.

CORAMB. Holla! you actors, where are you? Quick, you are to begin directly. Ah! here they come.

[*The dumb show enters: The King with his spouse. He is going to lie to sleep; the Queen entreats him not to do so. He lies down all the same. The Queen kisses him, and takes her leave. The King's brother comes with a phial and pours something into his ear. Exit.*

HAMLET. That is King Pyrrhus who goes to sleep in the garden. The Queen entreats him not to do so, but he does not harken to her. The poor wife goes away: behold! there comes the King's brother bearing the poisonous juice of hebenon which he pours into the King's ear, and which as soon as it mixes with the blood of man, immediately destroys life.

KING. Ho! torches, lanterns! the comedy offends us!

CORAMB. Pages, lackeys, light the torches! It is the King's will to depart: quick here with the torches! The actors have made a botch of it.

[*Exeunt King, Queen, Corambus and retinue.*

HAMLET. Ho! torches, the comedy offends us. Now didst perceive, good Horatio, the spirit hath not deceived me! Actors, go and understand this, that al-

ob ihr zwar die Materie nicht zum Ende gespielt, und es dem König nicht behaget, so hat es uns doch wohlgefallen, Horatio soll euch meinetwegen contentiren.

CARL. Wir bedanken uns, und bitten um einen Reisepaſs.

HAMLET. Den sollt ihr haben. [*Comödianten ab.*] Nun darf ich die Rache kühnlich fortsetzen. (Sahet ihr, wie sich der König entfärbte, da er das Spiel sahe?

HORAT. Ja, Ihro Durchlaucht, die That ist gewiſs.

HAMLET. Eben also meinen Vater getödtet, wie ihr in diesem Schauspiel gesehn.) Aber ich will ihm den Lohn für seine böse That geben.

SCENE IX.
CORAMBUS.

CORAMBUS. Die Comödianten werden eine schlechte Belohnung bekommen, denn ihre Action hat den König sehr miſsfallen.

HAMLET. Was sagst du, Alter, werden sie eine schlechte Belohnung empfangen? und ob sie schon übel von dem König belohnt werden, so werden sie doch von dem Himmel desto besser belohnet werden.

CORAMB. Ihro Hoheit, kommen denn die Comödianten auch in den Himmel?

HAMLET. Was meynest du, alter Narr, daſs sie nicht auch allda werden ihren Platz finden, darum gehet hin und tractiret mir diese Leute wohl.

CORAMB. Ja ja, ich will sie tractiren, wie sie es verdienen.

HAMLET. Tractiret sie wohl, sag ich, denn es geschiehet kein gröſser Lob, als durch Comödianten, denn dieselben reisen weit in die Welt: geschiehet ihnen an einem Orte etwas Gutes, so wissen sie es an einem andern Orte nicht genug zu rühmen, denn ihr Theatrum ist wie eine kleine Welt, darinnen sie fast alles, was in der groſsen Welt geschieht, repräsentiren. Sie erneuern die alten, vergessenen Geschichten, und stellen uns gute und böse Exempel vor; sie breiten aus die Gerechtigkeit und löbliche Regierung der Fürsten, sie strafen die Laster und erheben die Tugenden, sie rühmen die Frommen, und weisen, wie die Tyranney gestraft wird: darum sollt ihr sie wohl belohnen.

CORAMB. Nun, sie sollen schon ihren Lohn haben, weil es solche Leute sind. Ihro Hoheiten leben wohl!
[*ab.*

HAMLET. Komm, Horatio, ich gehe, und von dieser Stund an will ich darnach trachten, wo ich den König allein finde, ihm das Leben zu nehmen, wie er meinem Vater gethan hat.

though you have not played the piece out, and it has not pleased the King, it has pleased us all the same. Horatio shall bring you your reward.

CHARLES. We thank your honour and beg for a pass-port.

HAMLET. You shall have one. [*Exeunt Actors.*] Now may I go boldly on to vengeance. Did you perceive how the king blenched, when he saw the play?

HORAT. Yes, your Highness; the thing is certain.

HAMLET. My poor father murdered, just as we have seen in this play! But I will reward him for this wicked deed.

SCENE IX.
CORAMBUS.

CORAMB. The actors, I fear, will get a sorry recompense, for their play hath sore displeased the King.

HAMLET. What say you, old man, a sorry recompense? And if they are but ill-rewarded by the King, they will be all the better rewarded by Heaven.

CORAMB. My lord, do comedians then get into heaven?

HAMLET. Think'st thou, old fool, they'll not find a corner there? Wherefore get you gone and see them well bestowed.

CORAMB. My lord, I will use them according to their deserts.

HAMLET. Use them well, I say, for there is no greater praise to be gained than through actors, for they travel far and wide in the world. If they are treated well at one place, they don't know how to praise it enough at the next; for their stage is a little world, in which they represent all that takes place in the big world. They revive the old forgotten stories, and present to us good and bad examples; they publish abroad justice, and the praiseworthy government of princes, they punish the vices, and exalt the virtues, they extol the good, and show the reward of tyranny — wherefore entreat them well.

CORAMB. Well, they shall have their reward, as they are such great folk. Good bye, my Lord.
[*Exit.*

HAMLET. Come Horatio, I am going, and from this hour all my thoughts are bent on finding the King alone, that I may take his life, as he has taken my father's.

HORAT. Ihro Durchlaucht sehen sich aber wohl vor, dafs Sie nicht auch zu Schaden kommen.

Vers.

HAMLET. Ich soll, ich mufs, ich will mich an den Mörder rächen,
Kann ich mit List nichts thun, will ich mit Macht durchbrechen!

DRITTER ACT.

SCENE I.

KÖNIG.

Hier präsentirt sich im Tempel ein Altar.

KÖNIG [*allein*]. Nunmehro beginnet mein Gewissen aufzuwachen, der Stachel der Betrügerey beginnet mich hart zu stechen, es ist Zeit, dafs ich mich zur Bekehrung wende, und dem Himmel mein gethanes Unrecht bekenne. Ich fürchte, dafs meine Missethat so grofs ist, dafs sie mir nicht wird können vergeben werden, doch will ich die Götter inbrünstig bitten, dafs sie mir meine schwere Sünden vergeben wollen.

[*König kniet vor dem Altar.*

SCENE II.

HAMLET *mit blofsem Degen.*

HAMLET. So lange bin ich den verfluchten Hund nachgegangen, bis ich ihn einmal angetroffen, nun ist es Zeit, weil er allein ist, ich will ihn in seiner grösten Andacht ums Leben bringen. [*will ihn durchstechen.*] Doch nein, ich will ihn erstlich sein Gebet thun lassen. Aber ach! wenn ich mich bedenke, meinen Vater hat er nicht so viel Zeit gelassen, dafs er erstlich ein Gebet hätte thun können, sondern hat ihn vielleicht in seinen Sünden schlafend nach der Höllen geschickt, darum will ich ihn auch an denselbigen Ort nachsenden. [*will ihn von hinten wieder durchstofsen.*] Doch, halt ein, Hamlet! Warum willst du seine Sünden auf dich laden? Ich will ihm sein Gebet thun lassen, und vor diesesmal von hier gehen, und das Leben schenken. Zur andern Zeit aber will ich schon meine Rache ausüben. [*ab.*

KÖNIG. Mein Gewissen ist etwas erleichtert, aber der nagende Hund liegt noch unter meinem Herzen. Nun will ich hingehen, und mit Fasten und Allmosen, wie auch durch inbrünstiges Gebet, dem Höchsten versöhnen. Ach verfluchte Ehrsucht, wozu hast du mich gebracht! [*ab.*

HORAT. My lord, be prudent, lest you should come to harm.

Verse.

HAMLET. I shall, I must, I will revenge this bloody deed,
If cunning fail, come force, thou'lt help me in my need!

ACT III.

SCENE I.

KING.

A church and altar.

KING [*alone*]. Now does my conscience begin to awaken, — the sting of my gross deceit begins to prick me. 'Tis time I bethink me of repentance, and confess to Heaven the wrong I have done. I fear my guilt is so great, that it can never be forgiven. But I will pray fervently to the gods, that they will pardon my great sins.

[*Kneels before the altar.*

SCENE II.

HAMLET, *with a drawn sword.*

HAMLET. So long have I dodged the accursed dog, till at last I have found him. Now it is time as he is alone. I will take his life while he is praying [*he is about to stab him*]. But no, I will first let him finish his prayer. Ha! when I think of it, he did not leave my father so much time as to say a prayer first, but sent him to hell in his sleep, perhaps in his sins; wherefore, I'll send him to the same place too [*again about to stab him from behind*]. Nay, hold Hamlet! Why should'st thou take his sins upon thee? I will let him end his prayer, and escape this time, and will give him his life. But I will find another time to wreak my vengeance.

[*Exit.*

KING. My conscience is somewhat lightened, but still the insatiate dog gnaws at my heart. Now will I go and make my peace with heaven by fasting, alms, and fervent prayer. Ah cursed ambition! To what hast thou brought me.

[*Exit.*

SCENE III.
KÖNIGIN. CORAMBUS.

KÖNIGIN. Corambus, saget doch, wie ist es mit unsern Sohn, Prinz Hamlet, beschaffen, läſst seine Tollheit in etwas ab, und will seine Raserey kein Ende nehmen?

CORAMB. Ach nein, Ihro Majestät, er ist eben noch so toll, als er vorhin gewesen.

SCENE IV.
HORATIO.

HORAT. Gnädigste Königin, Prinz Hamlet ist im Vorgemach, und begehret in geheim Audienz.

KÖNIGIN. Er ist uns sehr lieb, darum laſst ihn alsobald hereintreten.

HORAT. Es soll geschehen, Ihro Majestät. [*ab.*

KÖNIGIN. Verberget euch, Corambus, hinter die Tapeten, bis wir euch rufen.

CORAMB. Ja ja, ich werde mich ein wenig verstecken.
[*versteckt sich.*

SCENE V.
HAMLET.

HAMLET. Frau Mutter, habt Ihr Euren ersten Gemal wohl gekannt?

KÖNIGIN. Ach, erinnert mich nicht mehr meiner vorigen Traurigkeit, ich kann mich der Thränen nicht enthalten, wenn ich an denselben gedenke.

HAMLET. Weint ihr? ach, laſts nur bleiben, es sind doch lauter Crocodillsthränen. Aber sehet, dort in jener Gallerie hängt das Conterfait Eures ersten Ehegemals, und da hängt das Conterfait des itzigen: was dünkt Euch wohl, welches ist doch der ansehnlichste unter ihnen? Ist der erste nicht ein majestätischer Herr?

KÖNIGIN. Ja freylich ist es wahr.

HAMLET. Wie habt Ihr ihn denn sobald vergessen können? Pfui! schämet Euch, Ihr habt fast auf einen Tag Begräbniſs und Beylager gehalten. Aber still, sind auch alle Thüren vest verschlossen?

KÖNIGIN. Warum fraget Ihr das?
[*Corambus hustet hinter der Tapete.*

HAMLET. Wer ist es, der uns belauert?
[*sticht ihm nieder.*

CORAMB. O weh, Prinz, was thut Ihr! Ich sterbe.

KÖNIGIN. O Himmel, mein Sohn, was thut Ihr? Es ist Corambus, der Hofmarschall.

SCENE III.
QUEEN. CORAMBUS.

QUEEN. Corambus say, how is it with my son, Prince Hamlet? Does his madness abate at all, or will his ravings never come to an end?

CORAMB. Ah no, your Majesty, he is just as mad as ever he was.

SCENE IV.
HORATIO.

HORAT. Most gracious Queen, Prince Hamlet is in the antechamber, and desires a private audience.

QUEEN. He is most welcome, admit him immediately.

HORAT. It shall be done, your Majesty. [*Exit.*

QUEEN. Conceal yourself behind the arras, Corambus, till we call you.

CORAMB. Ay, ay, your Majesty, I will hide myself.
[*He hides himself.*

SCENE V.
HAMLET.

HAMLET. Mother, did you perchance know your first husband?

QUEEN. O! recall not my former sadness. I cannot restrain my tears when I think of him.

HAMLET. You weep? Pr'ythee weep not, they are but crocodile's tears. But look, in that gallery hangs the counterfeit resemblance of your first husband, and there hangs the counterfeit of your present husband. What think ye now, which hath more dignity and presence? Does not the first bear him with majestic grace!

QUEEN. Nay but he doth, 'tis true.

HAMLET. How then could you forget him so soon? Out upon you! Shame! You celebrated your nuptials almost on the same day with his funeral! But hush! are all the doors locked?

QUEEN. Why do you ask?
[*Coramb. coughs behind the arras.*

HAMLET. Ha! ha! What eaves-dropper have we here? [*Stabs him.*

CORAMB. O! Prince, what have you done! I am slain!

QUEEN. O Heavens! My son, what have you done? It is Corambus, the chamberlain!

SCENE VI.

GEIST *geht über das Theater.* [*geblitzet.*]

HAMLET. Ach werther Schatten meines Vaters, stehe still! Ach! ach! was ist dein Begehren? forderst du Rache? dieselbe will ich schon zu rechter Zeit ausüben.

KÖNIGIN. Was macht Ihr, und mit wem redet Ihr?

HAMLET. Sehet Ihr nicht den Geist Eures seeligen Ehegemals? Sehet, er winket, als wollte er mit Euch reden.

KÖNIGIN. Wie? ich sehe ja nichts.

HAMLET. Ich glaube es wohl, dafs Ihr nichts sehet, denn Ihr seyd nicht mehr würdig, seine Gestalt zu sehen. Pfui, schämt Euch, ich mag kein Wort mehr mit Euch reden. [*ab.*

KÖNIGIN [*alleine*]. Ach Himmel, wie hat doch die Melancholie diesen Prinzen so viele Raserey zugebracht! Ach, mein einziger Prinz hat seinen Verstand ganz verloren! Ach, ach, ich bin viel Schuld daran! Hätte ich meinen Schwager, meines vorigen Gemahls Bruder, nicht zu der Ehe genommen, so hätte ich meinem (Sohn) nicht die Krone Dännemark aus der Hand gespielt. Was ist aber bey geschehenen Dingen zu thun? nichts, es mufs nun so bleiben. Hätte mir der Pabst solche Ehe nicht erlaubt: so wäre es auch nimmer geschehen. Ich will hingehen, und mich aufs höchste bemühen, wie ich meinen Sohn wieder zu seinem vorigen Verstand und Gesundheit helfen kann. [*ab.*

SCENE VII.

JENS *allein.*

Ich bin nun lange nicht zu Hofe gewesen, und meine Zinsen abgegeben. Ich befürchte, wo ich werde hinkommen, ich werde müssen ins Loch kriechen. Könnt ich nur einen guten Freund finden, der ein gutes Wort vor mich redete, damit ich nicht abgestraft werde.

SCENE VIII.

PHANTASMO.

PHANTASMO. Es gehet zu Hofe anjetzo wunderlich zu. Prinz Hamlet ist toll, die Ophelia ist auch toll; in Summa, es geht ganz wunderlich da her, dafs ich auch fast Lust habe, hinwegzulaufen.

JENS. Potz tausend, da sehe ich meinen guten Freund Phantasmo, ich hätte keinen bessern antreffen können, ich mufs ihn bitten, dafs er ein gut Wort vor mich redet. Glück zu, Herr Phantasmo!

PHANTASMO. Grofsen Dank! Was ist dein Begehren, Herr Bauer?

JENS. Ey, mein Herr Phantasmo, ich bin lange

SCENE VI.

GHOST *stalks over the stage.* [*Thunder and lightning.*]

HAMLET. Stay gracious figure of my father, what would'st thou? Dost thou demande revenge? I will execute it at the right time.

QUEEN. How is't with you? With whom do you speak?

HAMLET. See you not the spirit of your departed consort? Look, he beckons as if he would speak with you.

QUEEN. How? I see nothing.

HAMLET. Well, I believe you do see nothing, for you are no longer worthy to look upon his form. Out upon you, I can no longer hold converse with you. [*Exit.*

QUEEN [*alone*]. O God! How has this melancholy brought such madness on the Prince! Alas my only son has entirely lost his wits! And I am much to blame! Had I not wedded my husband's brother, I should not have robbed my son of the crown of Denmark. But what can be done, when things are past? Nothing, they must remain as they are. Had not the pope allowed this marriage, it would never have taken place. I will go and spare no pains to restore my son to his former understanding and health.

[*Exit.*

SCENE VII.

JENS, *alone.*

It's many a day since I have been at court to pay my taxes. I am afraid, go where I may, I shall be put in gaol. O dear! if I had but one good friend to put in a good word for me that I might get off.

SCENE VIII.

PHANTASMO.

PHANT. There are odd goings on at court now. Prince Hamlet is mad, Ophelia is mad too, sum total is, that it's very queer here altogether, so that I have a good mind to take myself off.

JENS. By all that's holy there's my good old friend Phantasmo, the very man I want. I'll beg him to put in a good word for me. Holla! Master Phantasmo!

PHANT. Thank you mightily! What do you want Master clod-hopper?

JENS. Ay, good Master Phantasmo 'tis many a

nicht zu Hofe gewesen, und bin viel schuldig, darum bitte ich Euch, Ihr wollet doch ein gutes Wort vor mich einlegen, ich will Euch auch einen guten Käfs spendiren.

PHANTASMO. Was? meynst du Flegel, dafs ich zu Hofe nichts zu fressen habe?

SCENE IX.
OPHELIA toll.

Ich laufe und renne, und kann doch mein Schätzchen nicht antreffen. Er hat mir Boten geschickt, ich soll zu ihm kommen, wir wollen Hochzeit machen, ich habe mich schon angezogen. Aber da ist mein Liebchen! Siehe bist du da, mein Lämmchen, ich habe dich so gesucht, ja gesucht hab ich dich. Ach gedenke doch, der Schneider hat mir meinen cartunen Rock ganz verdorben. Siehe, da hast du ein schönes Blümchen, mein Herz!

PHANTASMO. O der Teufel, wer nur von ihr weg wäre; sie meynt, ich bin ihr Liebster.

OPHELIA. Was sagst du, mein Liebchen? Wir wollen mit einander zu Bette gehen, ich will dich ganz reine waschen.

PHANTASMO. Ja, ja, ich will dich wieder einseifen und auch auswaschen.

OPHELIA. Höre, mein Liebchen, hast du dein neues Kleid schon angezogen? Ey, das ist schön gemacht, recht auf die neue Mode.

PHANTASMO. Dafs weifs ich ohnedem wohl — — —

OPHELIA. O potz tausend, was hätte ich bald vergessen! Der König hat mich zu Gaste gebeten, ich mufs geschwinde laufen. Siehe da, mein Kütschchen, mein Kütschchen! [ab.

PHANTASMO. O Hecate, du Königin der Hexen, wie bin ich so froh, dafs diefs tolle Ding weg ist; wäre sie länger geblieben, ich wäre mit toll worden. Ich mufs nur gehen, eh' das närrische Ding wiederkommen wird.

JENS. Ach barmherziger Herr Phantasmo! Ich bitte meiner nicht zu vergessen.

PHANTASMO. Nun, komm nur mit, Bruder Hundsfott; ich will sehn, dafs ich dir bey dem Ober-Einnehmer zurechte helfe. [gehen ab.

SCENE X.
KÖNIG. HAMLET. HORATIO. ZWEY DIENER.

KÖNIG. Wo ist Corambus sein Leichnam geblieben? Ist er noch nicht hinweggebracht?

HORATIO. Er liegt noch an den Ort, wo er erstochen ist.

KÖNIG. Es ist leid uns, dafs er so unverhoft um das Leben kommen. Gehet hin, und lasset ihn wegtra-

day since I have been at court, and I am greatly in arrears with my taxes; so pr'ythee put in a good word for me, and I'll bestow a good cheese on you.

PHANT. Eh! Master Clown, think ye I get naught to eat at court?

SCENE IX.
OPHELIA, mad.

I run and run and cannot find my sweetheart. He sent a messenger to me to fetch me to him, — we are to have our wedding, and I am dressed for it already. But ah! there is my love. Is it thou my lamb? Oh! how I have sought thee everywhere, everywhere have I sought thee. Ah, only think the tailor has spoiled me my muslin robe! See! there's a pretty flower for you, my heart!

PHANT. O the devil! I wish I were away! — she takes me for her lover.

OPHELIA. What say'st thou my love? Let's go to bed together, I'll wash thee quite clean.

PHANT. Ay, ay, I'll soap and wash you and wring you out.

OPHELIA. Hark! my sweet one, hast already donn'd thy beautiful new suit? Ay! how finely 'tis made, quite in the new fashion.

PHANT. Well do I know that without — — —

OPHELIA. Alack! alack! what is't I had nearly forgotten! The King has bidden me to supper, I must make haste. Look, there stands my little coach, my pretty little coach! [Exit.

PHANT. O Hecate! thou queen of witches, how glad I am that that mad thing's away; I should have gone mad with her if she had remained any longer. I must be off before the crazy chit come back again.

JENS. Oh kind master Phantasmo! Pr'ythee do not forget me.

PHANT. Come along, brother Bumpkin, we'll see if we can't put you all straight at the custom-house. [Exeunt.

SCENE X.
KING. HAMLET. HORATIO. TWO ATTENDANTS.

KING. Where is the body of Corambus bestowed? Has it not yet been removed?

HORAT. He is still lying in the place where he was stabbed.

KING. It grieveth us that Corambus hath lost his life thus suddenly. Go bear the body away; 'tis our will

gen; wir wollen ihn adlich zur Erden bestätigen lassen. Ach! Prinz Hamlet, was habt Ihr gethan, dafs Ihr den alten Corambus so unschuldig durchstochen! Es ist uns herzlich leid, doch weil es ohngefähr geschehen, ist zwar diese Mordthat in etwas zu entschuldigen; allein ich fürchte, wo es unter den Adel kommt, dafs es bey den Unterthanen leicht einen Aufruhr bringen könnte, und könnten also seinen Tod an Euch rächen. Wir aber aus väterlicher Vorsorge haben ein Mittel erfunden, welches dieses Unglück abhalten kann.

HAMLET. Es ist mir leid, Herr Vetter und Vater! Ich habe etwas mit der Königin in geheim reden wollen, dieser Spion aber hat uns belauert, doch hab ich nicht gewufst, dafs es dieser alte Narr seyn sollte: was meynen aber Ihro Majestät, wie nun am besten mit mir zu procediren sey?

KÖNIG. Wir haben bey uns beschlossen, Euch nacher England zu schicken, weil diese Krone nahe mit der unsrigen befreundet; als könnt Ihr Euch eine Zeit, weil eine gesundere Luft allda, in etwas refrigiren, und zu Eurer Genesung besser als hier gelangen. Wir wollen Euch etliche von unsern Bedienten mitgeben, die Euch begleiten und treulich aufwarten sollen.

HAMLET. Ja ja, König, schickt mich nur nach Portugall, auf dafs ich nimmer wieder komme, das ist das beste.

KÖNIG. Nein, nicht nach Portugall, sondern nach England, und diese beyden sollen mit Euch auf der Reise seyn; wenn Ihr aber in England kommt, sollt Ihr mehr Diener bekommen.

HAMLET. Sind das die Laquaien? Das sind saubere Bursche!

KÖNIG. Höret ihr beyden! [*heimlich zu den beyden Dienern*]. Sobald ihr nacher England kommt, so verrichtet, was ich euch befohlen habe. Nehmet einen Degen, oder ein jeder eine Pistole, und bringet ihn ums Leben. Wo aber dieser Anschlag nicht möchte von statten gehn, so nehmet diesen Brief, und bringet ihn nebst den Prinzen an aufgeschriebenen Ort; derselbige wird wohl dahin bedacht seyn, dafs er nimmer wieder aus England kommen soll. Aber das rathe ich euch, dafs ihr keinem Menschen was offenbaret. Eure Bezahlung sollt ihr haben, sobald ihr zurückkommt.

HAMLET. Nun, Ihro Majestät, welches sind denn die rechten, die mitreisen sollen?

KÖNIG. Diese zwey. Nun, die Götter wollen Euch begleiten, dafs Ihr möget mit gutem Winde an Ort und Stelle kommen.

HAMLET. Nun Adieu, Frau Mutter!

KÖNIG. Wie, mein Prinz, warum heist Ihr uns Frau Mutter?

it should have a noble burial. Ah, Prince Hamlet, what made you stab that poor innocent old man? It grieveth us sorely, still this murderous deed admits of some excuse, seeing it was done unwittingly. Nevertheless I fear that when this gets known amongst the nobles, it may easily excite a rebellion among my subjects, and they may revenge his death on you. This our paternal care hath duly weighed, and we have devised a means to ward this danger from you.

HAMLET. I sincerely grieve this deed, my uncle and my father. I had begged a private audience of the Queen, and this fellow came eaves-dropping; but I did not know that it was this silly old fool. But how does your Majesty think it were best to proceed?

KING. We have determined to send you to England, because this crown is friendly to our own, as if to refresh yourself there for a time, because the air is wholesomer, and may better promote your recovery. We will give you some of our own attendants, who shall accompany you, and serve you faithfully.

HAMLET. Ay ay, King, send me off to Portugal, that I may never come back again, that is the best plan.

KING. No, not to Portugal but to England, and those two shall accompany you on the journey. But when you arrive in England, you shall have more attendants.

HAMLET. Those are the lackeys are they? A pair of nice fellows!

KING. Hark ye [*secretly to the two attendants*]. As soon as ye reach England, do as I have commanded you. Arm yourselves each with a sword or pistol and take his life. But in case your attempt should miscarry, take this letter and the prince to the place indicated thereon; there our prince will be so well cared for that he will never leave England again. Beware that ye make known this plan to no man. Your reward shall be delivered to you on your return.

HAMLET. Well, your Majesty, who are they then that are to bear me company?

KING. These two. The gods be with you, and give you a fair wind to reach the place of your destination.

HAMLET. Now farewell dear mother!

KING. What, Prince! Why do you call us mother?

HAMLET. Mann und Weib ist ja ein Leib, Vater oder Mutter, es ist mir alles gleich.

KÖNIG. Nun so fahrt wohl, der Himmel sey mit Euch. [ab.

HAMLET. Nun, ihr noblen Quantchen, sollt ihr meine Gefährten seyn?

DIENERS. Ja, Ihro Durchlaucht!

HAMLET. So kommt denn, ihr noblen Gesellen, [nimmt sie beyde an jede Hand] lafst uns fahren, lafst uns fahren nach England, nehmt das Bötchen in die Hand, du bist ja ein braver Quant. Lafst uns fahren, lafst uns fahren nach England. [gehen ab.

SCENE XI.
PHANTASMO. OPHELIA.

PHANTASMO. Wo ich gehe oder stehe, da läuft das elementische Mädchen, die Ophelia, aus allen Winkeln mir nach; ich kann keinen Frieden vor ihr haben, sie sagt allezeit, dafs ich ihr Liebster bin, und ist doch nicht wahr. Wenn ich mich nur verstecken könnte, damit sie mich nicht finde. Nun wird der Henker wieder los werden: da kommt sie wieder.

OPHELIA. Wo mag mein Liebchen seyn? Der Schelm will nicht bey mir bleiben, eher vor mir weg — Aber siehe, da ist er. Höre, mein Liebchen, ich bin bey dem Priester gewesen, der will uns noch heute zusammen copuliren; ich habe alles zu der Hochzeit fertig gemacht, ich habe Hühner, Haasen, Fleisch, Butter und Käse eingekauft; es mangelt nichts mehr, als dafs die Musikanten uns zu Bette spielen.

PHANTASMO. Ich mufs nur ja sagen. Komm denn, wir wollen miteinander zu Bette gehn.

OPHELIA. Nein, nein, mein Püppchen, wir müssen erstlich miteinander zur Kirche gehen, hernach wollen wir essen und trinken, und denn wollen wir tanzen — Ach, wie wollen wir uns lustig machen!

PHANTASMO. Ja, es wird lustig hergehn; es werden wohl drey von Einem Teller essen.

OPHELIA. Was sagst du? Wilt du mich nicht haben, so will ich dich auch nicht haben. [schlägt ihn]. Siehe dort, dort ist mein Liebchen, er winkt mir. Siehe da, welch ein schön Kleid dafs er an hat: siehe er will mich zu sich locken, er wirft mit einem Röslein und Lilien auf mich zu; er will mich in seine Arme nehmen, er winkt mir, ich komme, ich komme. [ab.

PHANTASMO. Bey der Nähe ist sie nicht klug, aber weit davon ist sie gar toll. Ich wollte, dafs sie aufgehenkt wäre, so könnte mir das Rabenaas so nicht nachlaufen. [ab.

HAMLET. Man and wife is one flesh — father or mother, it is all the same to me.

KING. Well, fare ye well. May heaven attend you. [Exit.

HAMLET. Eh! you chips of nobility, are you to be my companions?

ATTEND. We are my lord.

HAMLET. Come then, my noble sirs, [taking each by the hand], let's start, let's start for England! Put your best foot forward; you are indeed a cunning fellow. Let's start, let's start for England! [Exeunt.

SCENE XI.
PHANTASMO. OPHELIA.

PHANT. Go where I will, that simpleton, that Ophelia runs after me out of every corner. I've not a moment's peace for her, she fancies day and night that I'm her lover; and that's not true. If I could only hide where she can't find me! The deuce is in it, there she is again!

OPHELIA. Where can my love be? The rogue will not remain with me, he flies me — but ah! there he is. Listen sweet love, I've been with the priest, he will unite us this very day; I have made all ready for the wedding; pullets, hares, meat, butter, cheese, all, all bought — now there is nothing more wanting than that the musicians should play us to bed.

PHANT. I can only say yes. Come then let's go to bed together.

OPHELIA. No, no, my puppet, we must first go to church together, afterwards feast, and then dance — ah! we will be right merry!

PHANT. Ay, ay, merry as crickets; three will eat out of one plate.

OPHELIA. Ha! What do you say? If you will not have me, I will not have you [strikes him]. There, there, is my love, my dearest, he beckons me to him. Look, what a beautiful suit he has on! — look, he wants to entice me to him, he casts a lily and a rose at me; he will embrace me, he beckons to me, I come, I come. [Exit.

PHANT. At close quarters she's lost her wits, but at arm's length she's clean mad. I wish she were hanged, and then the carrion could not pester me so. [Exit.

VIERTER ACT.

SCENE I.

HAMLET. ZWEY BANDITEN.

HAMLET. Es ist hier ein lustiger Ort auf dieser Insel, wir wollen etwas hier verbleiben und speisen: da ist ein lustiger Wald, und da ein kühler Wasserstrom; darum holet mir das beste vom Schiff, wir wollen uns hier recht lustig machen.

1. BAND. Gnädiger Herr, hier ist nicht Essenzeit, denn von diesem Eiland werden Sie nimmer kommen; denn hier ist der Ort, der Ihnen zum Kirchhof bestellt ist.

HAMLET. Was sagst du Schelm, du Esclav! Weifst du wohl, wer ich bin? Sollst du wohl mit einem Königlichen Prinzen also scherzen? Doch es sey dir vergeben vor diesesmal.

2. BAND. Nein, es ist kein Scherz, sondern unser rechter Ernst. Sie präpariren sich nur zum Tode.

HAMLET. Warum das? Was hab ich euch denn Leides gethan? Ich weifs mich ja auf nichts zu besinnen: darum sagt aus, warum kommt ihr auf solche boshafte Gedanken?

1. BAND. Es ist uns von dem König anbefohlen worden: sobald wir Ihro Durchlaucht auf dieses Eiland bringen, sollen wir ihm das Leben nehmen.

HAMLET. Ihr lieben Freunde, verschonet mein Leben; saget, dafs ihrs verrichtet; ich will die Zeit meines Lebens nicht wieder zu dem König kommen; bedenkt es wohl, was ist euch mit einer Hand voll unschuldiges Fürstenblut gedient? Wollt ihr euer Gewissen mit meinen Sünden beflecken? Ach dafs ich zu allem Unglück ohne Gewehr bin! Hätte ich nur etwas in meinen Händen.

[*greift einem nach dem Degen.*

2. BAND. Du, Camerad, nimm dein Gewehr in acht.

1. BAND. Ich werde mich wohl in acht nehmen. Nun, Prinz, macht Euch fertig; wir haben nicht lange Zeit.

HAMLET. Weil es denn nicht anders seyn kann und ich vor euch sterben mufs, aus Antrieb des tyrannischen Königs, so will ichs gern erdulden, ob ich gleich unschuldig, und ihr aus Armuth hierzu erkauft, will ichs euch gerne verzeihen, das Blut aber wird der Bruder- und Vatermörder verantworten müssen an jenem grossen Gerichtstage.

1. BAND. Ey was fragen wir nach jenem Tage; wir müssen verrichten, was uns heute befohlen.

2. BAND. Es ist auch wahr, Bruder! Nur frisch darauf, es mufs doch seyn. Gieb Feuer, ich auf der einen, und du auf der andern Seite.

ACT IV.

SCENE I.

HAMLET. TWO RUFFIANS.

HAMLET. It is a pleasant place here upon this island! Let us linger here a-while and dine. There is a merry green wood, and here a cool spring of water; so fetch the best from our ship, and we will make right merry here.

RUFF. 1. There's no dinner time more for you, my lord, for you will never leave this island again, for here's the spot destined for your grave.

HAMLET. How say'st thou, knave? Know'st thou then who I am? Wouldst thou jest thus with a royal prince? Let it pass this time, I pardon thee.

RUFF. 2. Nay, but 'tis no jest, we are in earnest. Prepare yourself for death, my lord.

HAMLET. Wherefore this? What harm have I ever done you? I cannot recollect any; therefore speak out, why do ye entertain such wicked thoughts?

RUFF. 1. We have received orders for it from the King: as soon as we have brought your Highness to this island, we are to take your life.

HAMLET. Most excellent friends, spare my life! bring word ye have fulfilled the King's commission. I swear nevermore to return to the King, as long as I live. Consider well, what are ye better for staining your hands with the innocent blood of a royal prince? Why would ye pollute your consciences with my sins? Accursed fate that I came here unarmed! Had I but some weapon in my hand! [*Makes an attempt to seize a sword.*

RUFF. 2. Holla! Comrade, look to thy weapon!

RUFF. 1. I will look well to it. Now prince, prepare; our time is short.

HAMLET. If then it must be so, and I must die by your hands, impelled by a tyrannical king, I must submit. And although I am innocent, and poverty hath driven you to this deed, I pardon you from my heart; at the great day this murderer of my father and his brother must answer for my blood.

RUFF. 1. Eh! what is that great day to us? we must execute the commission entrusted to us this day.

RUFF. 2. That's true, comrade! Let us go to work; there is no help for it. You fire from this side, I from the other.

HAMLET. Höret mich noch ein Wort: weil auch dem allerärgsten Uebelthäter solches nicht abgeschlagen wird, sondern wird ihm Zeit zur Bufse gelassen, also bitte ich, als ein unschuldiger Prinz, ihr wollet mich erstlich zu meinem Schöpfer ein andächtiges Gebet verrichten lassen, hernach will ich gerne sterben; ich will euch aber ein Zeichen geben: ich werde meine Hände nach dem Himmel wenden, sobald ich meine Arme ausstrecke, so gebt Feuer, setzt mir beyde Pistolen in die Seite, und wenn ich werde sagen: schiefst! so gebt mir so viel, als ich bedarf, und trefft mich gewifs, damit ich nicht lange gemartert werde.

2. BAND. Nun dieses können wir ihm auch wohl noch zu Gefallen thun, darum macht nur fort!

HAMLET. [*schlägt die Hände voneinander.*] Schiefst zu! [*indem fällt er zwischen den beyden vorwärts nieder, die Diener aber erschiefsen sich selbsten.*] Ach gerechter Himmel, dir sey Dank gesagt vor dein englisches Eingeben, denn diesen Schutzengel werde ich ewig preisen, welcher mir durch meine Gedanken das Leben erhalten hat. Diese Schelme aber, wie gearbeitet, so ist auch ihr Lohn. Die Hunde rühren sich noch, sie haben sich selber harquebusirt, ich aber will zu meiner Revange ihnen den Todesstich vollends geben, es sollte ein Schelm sonsten davon kommen. [*er ersticht sie mit ihren eignen Degen.*] Ich mufs sie besuchen, ob sie auch etwa Steckbriefe bey sich haben. Dieser hat nichts; hier finde ich einen Brief bey diesem Mörder, ich will ihn lesen. Dieser Brief ist an einen Erzmörder in England geschrieben, wenn etwa dieser Anschlag möchte mifslingen, sollten sie mich nur dem überantworten, der würde mir schon das Lebenslicht ausblasen. Allein die Götter stehn doch dem Gerechten bey: Nun will ich mich meinem Vater zum Schrecken wiederum zurückbegeben. Aber zu Wasser trau ich nicht mehr, wer weifs, ob der Schifscapitain nicht auch ein Schelm ist. Ich will den ersten Platz suchen, und die Post nehmen; den Schiffer will ich nach Dännemark wieder zurück commandiren, diese Schelme aber will ich ins Wasser werfen. [*ab.*

SCENE II.

KÖNIG *mit Staat.*

KÖNIG. Uns verlangt zu erfahren, wie es mit unserm Sohn, Prinz Hamlet, mufs abgelaufen sein, und ob diejenigen, welche wir als Reisegefährten ihm mitgegeben, auch treulich werden verrichtet haben, was wir befohlen.

HAMLET. One word more: — as the meanest criminal is not refused his last request for time to repent him of his sins, I, an innocent prince, do beseech you to grant me time to address a prayer to my Creator, which done I will willingly die. I will give you the sign: I will raise my hands to heaven, and fire the moment I spread out my arms. Level both pistols at my sides, and when I call, fire, give me as much as I require, and be sure and hit me that I may not suffer long.

RUFF. 2. Well, we may do that much to please him; therefore let us proceed.

HAMLET. [*Spreads out his arms.*] Fire! [*Meanwhile he falls forward between the two servants, who consequently shoot each other.*] Just heaven! I thank thee for the divine inspiration, and henceforth I will worship this guardian angel, who through my thoughts hath preserved my life. These rogues have received the due recompense of their work. Ha! the dogs, they move still. They have butchered each other, but to satisfy my revenge let them take the coup de grâce from my hand, else one of the rogues might escape. [*He stabs them with their own sword.*] Nay, now I'll search them, it may be I find some writ or warrant on them. There's nothing here, but here I find a letter on this murderer. I'll read it. Ha! this letter is directed to an arch-hangman in England, importing that should this attempt miscarry, I should be handed over to him, and he would make no bones about puffing out my rush-light life! But the gods are ever on the side of the just. Now I will go back again to the terror of my father, but I will not trust myself by water, for who knows whether the captain may not likewise prove a rogue. I will go to the first place and take the post, order the sailors back to Denmark, and cast these dogs into the water. [*Exit.*

SCENE II.

KING, *and retinue.*

KING. We long greatly to hear how it is with our son, Prince Hamlet, and whether the two companions we gave him on his journey, have faithfully fulfilled our commission.

SCENE III.
PHANTASMO.

PHANTASMO. Neue Zeitung, Monsieur König! Hauptneue Zeitung!

KÖNIG. Was ist es, Phantasmo?

PHANTASMO. Leonhardus aus Frankreich ist wieder zu Hause kommen.

KÖNIG. Das ist uns lieb, laſst ihn vor uns kommen.

SCENE IV.
LEONHARDUS.

LEONH. Gnädiger Herr und König, ich begehre von Ihro Majestät meinen Vater, oder die Rache der Gerechtigkeit, weil er so jämmerlich ermordet. Wo dieses nicht geschieht, werde ich vergessen, daſs Ihr König seyd, und mich an den Thäter rächen.

KÖNIG. Leonhardus, gieb dich zufrieden, wir sind unschuldig an deines Vaters Tod. Prinz Hamlet hat ihn unversehenerweise hinter den Tapeten erstochen, wir aber wollen dahin bedacht seyn, daſs er wieder gestraft werde.

LEONH. Weil denn Ihro Majestät unschuldig sein an den Tod meines Vaters, als bitte ich auf gefällten Knieen, mir solches zu verzeihen. Der Zorn hatte mich, wie auch die kindliche Liebe übernommen, daſs ich fast selber nicht gewuſst, was ich gethan.

KÖNIG. Es sey dir vergeben, denn wir können wohl gedenken, daſs es dir sehr zu Herzen gangen sey, daſs du deinen Vater so erbärmlich hast verlieren müssen. Doch gieb dich zufrieden, du solt einen Vater wieder an uns haben.

LEONH. Ich bedanke mich vor diese hohe Königliche Gnade.

SCENE V.
PHANTASMO.

PHANTASMO. Herr Vetter König, noch mehr neue Zeitung!

KÖNIG. Was bringst du wieder vor neue Zeitung?

PHANTASMO. Prinz Hamlet ist wieder kommen.

KÖNIG. Der Teufel ist wieder kommen, und nicht Prinz Hamlet.

PHANTASMO. Prinz Hamlet ist wieder kommen, und nicht der Teufel.

KÖNIG. Leonhardus, höre hier, nun kannst du deines Vaters Tod rächen, weil der Prinz wieder zu Hause kommen; allein du must uns eidlich versprechen, daſs du solches keinem Menschen offenbaren wilt.

LEONH. Ihro Majestät zweifeln an mir nicht; was Sie mir offenbaren, soll verschwiegen seyn, als ob Sie zu einem Stein gesprochen hätten.

SCENE III.
PHANTASMO.

PHANT. News, news, Monsieur King! News spick and span new!

KING. What news, Phantasmo?

PHANT. Leonardo has come back from France.

KING. We are glad of it, admit him to our presence.

SCENE IV.
LEONARDO.

LEON. My gracious Lord and King, I come to demand my father at your hands, or vengeance, just vengeance for his miserable murder. If you do not grant it, I shall forget that you are king, and will revenge myself on the perpetrator.

KING. Be satisfied, Leonardo, that we are innocent of your father's death. Prince Hamlet unwittingly ran him through while behind the arras: but we will see that he is punished for it.

LEON. As your Majesty is quite innocent of my father's death, I humbly crave your pardon on my knees. My anger as also filial love, had so overcome me, that I myself hardly knew what I did.

KING. Let it pass, we can easily believe how it must have cut you to the heart to lose your noble father by such a miserable death. But rest contented, — you shall find another father in ourselves.

LEON. I thank you for your royal favour.

SCENE V.
PHANTASMO.

PHANT. Uncle King, more news still!

KING. What fresh news do you bring?

PHANT. Prince Hamlet has come back!

KING. The devil has come back, and not Prince Hamlet!

PHANT. Prince Hamlet has come back and not the devil, I say!

KING. Leonardo, hear. Now you can revenge your father's death, for the Prince has come home again. But you must swear an oath not to disclose your design to any man.

LEON. Your Majesty may trust me; what you reveal shall be kept as close, as if you had spoken to a stone.

KÖNIG. Wir wollen zwischen dir und ihm einen Wettstreit anstellen, nemlich also: ihr sollt mit Rapieren fechten, und der von euch beyden die ersten drey Stöſse bekommt, soll ein weiſs neapolitanisch Pferd gewonnen haben. Aber mitten in diesem Gefecht sollt ihr euer Rapier fallen lassen, und anstatt desselben sollt ihr einen scharf gespitzten Degen bey der Hand haben, welcher dem Rapier ganz ähnlich gemacht muſs seyn, die Spitze desselben aber must du mit starken Gift bestreichen; sobald du nun seinen Leib damit verwunden wirst, wird er alsdenn gewiſs sterben müssen, du aber sollst doch den Preiſs und hierbey des Königs Gnade gewinnen.

LEONH. Ihro Majestät wollen mir verzeihen; ich darf mich dieses nicht unterstehen, dieweil der Prinz ein geübter Fechtmeister ist, und könnte mir dieses wohl selbst wiederfahren.

KÖNIG. Leonhardus, weigere dich hierinnen nicht, sondern thue deinem Könige solches zu gefallen, um deines Vaters Tod zu rächen, must du dieses thun. Denn wisset, daſs der Prinz als ein Todtschläger eures Vaters solchen Tod verdienet. Allein wir können keine Gerechtigkeit an ihn haben, weil ihm seine Frau Mutter den Rücken hält, und ihn die Unterthanen sehr lieben: dürfte also, wenn wir öffentlich uns an ihm rächen wollten, ein Aufruhr leicht geschehen; daſs wir aber ihn als unsern Stiefsohn und Vetter meiden, geschieht um der heiligen Gerechtigkeit willen, denn er ist mordgierig und unsinnig, und müssen uns künftig selbsten vor einem solchen bösen Menschen fürchten. Thut solches, was wir von euch verlangen, so werdet ihr den König seiner Furcht benehmen, und euch verblümterweise an euren Vatermörder rächen.

LEONH. Es ist eine schwere Sache, welcher ich mich fast nicht unterstehe. Denn sollte dieses auskommen, würde es gewiſs mein Leben kosten.

KÖNIG. Zweifelt nicht; im Fall es ja euch miſslingen sollte, so haben wir schon eine andere List erdacht. Wir wollen einen orientalischen Diamant klein stoſsen lassen, und ihm denselben, wenn er erhitzt, in einem Becher voll Wein mit Zucker süſs vermischt beybringen: so soll er auf unsere Gesundheit doch den Tod saufen.

LEONH. Wohl denn, Ihro Majestät, unter dessen Schutz will ichs verrichten.

SCENE VI.
KÖNIGIN.

KÖNIGIN. Gnädiger Herr und König, liebstes Ehegemahl, ich bringe Euch eine schlechte Zeitung!

KÖNIG. Was ist es, liebste Seele?

KING. We will arrange a match between yourself and him, and on these terms: you shall fence with foils, and he who makes the first three hits, shall have won a white Neapolitan horse. In the middle of the bout you let your foil drop, and instead of it, you must have a sword with a sharp point ready at hand, which must be made quite like the foil, but you must rub the point of it with a strong poison; as soon as you shall wound his body with it, he will certainly die, but you shall win the prize, and your king's favour as well.

LEON. Pardon, your Majesty! I dare not undertake this, seeing the Prince is a practised swordsman, and so might turn the tables on me.

KING. Leonardo, do not refuse but do it to please your King; you must do it to revenge your father's death. For know, the Prince as assassin of your father deserves such a death. But we cannot execute justice against him, because his mother supports him, and my subjects love him. If therefore we would revenge ourselves on him openly, it might easily give rise to a rebellion. The love of holy justice turneth our heart and favour from our step-son and our cousin, for he is bloodthirsty and full of pranks, and for the future we must ourselves be on our guard against such a bad man. If you do what we require, you will relieve your King of his fears, and secretly revenge yourself on the murderer of your father.

LEONH. It is a difficult matter which I scarce like to venture on. For should the truth get wind, my life would be the forfeit.

KING. Nay, doubt not; if this should fail we have already devised another trick. We'll have prepared for him a chalice filled with wine mixed with sugar and the fine powder of an eastern diamond which we will give him, when he is hot: thus shall he drink his death to our health.

LEON. Well then, your Majesty, I will do it under your protection.

SCENE VI.
QUEEN.

QUEEN. My gracious lord and King, my dearest consort, I bring thee woeful tidings.

KING. What are they, dear soul?

KÖNIGIN. Meine liebste Staatsjungfer, die Ophelia, läuft hin und wieder, ruft und schreyt, sie isset und trinket nichts; man meynet, dafs sie gänzlich von ihrem Verstande ist.

KÖNIG. Ach, höret man doch nichts als lauter traurige und unglückliche Zeitungen!

SCENE VII.

OPHELIA *mit Blumen.*

OPHELIA. Siehe da hast du ein Blümchen, du auch, du auch. [*giebt jedem eine Blume*]. Aber potz tausend, was hätte ich schier vergessen: ich mufs geschwinde laufen, ich habe meinen Schmuck vergessen. Ach, meine Fronte; ich mufs geschwinde nach dem Hofschmidt gehn, und fragen, was er vor neue Moden bekommen. Sa, sa, decket geschwinde den Tisch, ich werde bald wieder hier seyn. [*läuft weg.*

LEONH. Bin ich denn zu allem Unglück geboren! Mein Vater ist todt, und meine Schwester ist ihres Verstandes beraubt! Mein Herz will mir vor grofser Traurigkeit fast zerbersten.

KÖNIG. Leonhardus, stelle dich zufrieden, du sollst alleine bey uns in Gnaden leben. Sie aber, liebste Gemahlin, wolle belieben, mit uns hineinzuspatzieren, denn wir haben ihr noch etwas in Geheim zu offenbaren. Leonhardus, vergesset nicht, was wir euch gesagt.

LEONH. Ich werde emsig seyn, solches zu verrichten.

KÖNIGIN. Mein König, wir müssen Rath schaffen, dafs diese unglückseelige Jungfer möge wieder zu ihrem Verstande verholfen werden.

KÖNIG. Man lasse die Sache an unsre Leibmedici gelangen. Ihr aber folget uns, Leonhardus. [*ab.*

QUEEN. The favourite of my retinue, my sweet Ophelia, runs up and down, and crys, and screams, and neither eats nor drinks; they think that she has quite lost her senses.

KING. Alas! one hears nothing but sad and unhappy news!

SCENE VII.

OPHELIA, *with flowers.*

OPHELIA. Ah! hold, there's a flower for thee, and for thee too, and for thee too [*gives a flower to each*]. Well-a-day, what had I not clean forgotten! I must run quick, I have forgotten my jewels. Ha! my diadem. I must go quick to the court goldsmith and ask what new fashions he has got. So, so, spread the table quick, I shall soon be back again. [*Runs away.*

LEON. Am I then born to misery! My father dead, and my sister robbed of her wits! My heart will almost break with its weight of grief!

KING. Take comfort, Leonardo, you shall live in our favour. But you, sweet Queen, be pleased to follow us, for we have something to communicate to you in private. Leonardo, do not forget what we have told you.

LEON. I shall be diligent to do your bidding.

QUEEN. My King, we must devise some means that this unhappy maiden be restored to her senses.

KING. Submit the case to our own physician. Follow us, Leonardo. [*Exit.*

FÜNFTER ACT.

SCENE I.

HAMLET.

Unglückseeliger Prinz, wie lange sollt du noch ohne Ruhe leben! Wie lange verhängst du, gerechte Nemesis, dafs dein gerechtes Rachschwerdt auf meinem Vetter, den Brudermörder wetzest! Ich bin nun wieder anhero gelanget, kann aber noch zu keiner Revange kommen, weil der Brudermörder allezeit mit viel Volk umgeben. Aber ich schwöre, ehe die Sonne ihre Reise von Osten in's Westen gethan, will ich mich an ihm rächen.

ACT V.

SCENE I.

HAMLET.

Unhappy Prince, how long wilt thou know no rest! How long a time, O just Nemesis, dost thou appoint for whetting thy just sword of vengeance against my uncle, this fratricide! Now am I here once more, and cannot yet come to my revenge, because this fratricide is at all times surrounded by so many people. But I swear, that ere the sun hath compassed his journey from east to west, I'll wreak my vengeance on him.

SCENE II.
HORATIO.

HORAT. Ihro Durchlaucht, ich bin von Herzen erfreuet, daſs ich Sie mit guter Gesundheit wieder allhier sehe. Ich bitte aber, Sie wollen mir doch offenbaren, warum Sie sobald wieder zurückgekommen.

HAMLET. Ach, Horatio, du hättest mich bald nicht mehr lebendig gesehn, dieweil mein Leben bereits auf dem Spiel gestanden, wo mich die göttliche Allmacht nicht sonderlich hätte bewahret.

HORAT. Wie, was sagen Ihro Durchlaucht? Wie ist es zugegangen?

HAMLET. Du weist, daſs mir der König zwey Reisegefährten als Diener, mich zu begleiten, mitgegeben hatte. Nun begab es sich, daſs wir eines Tages contrairen Wind hatten, und an ein Eyland, nicht ferne von Dovern anker setzten. Ich stieg mit meinen zwey Dienern aus dem Schiff, etwas frische Luft zu schöpfen. Da kamen diese verfluchten Schelme, und wollten mir das Leben nehmen, und sagten, der König hätte sie dazu erkauft. Ich bat um mein Leben, ich wollte ihnen eben soviel geben, und sollten den König doch unterdessen meinen Tod berichten, ich wollte auch nimmermehr zu Hofe kommen, es war aber kein Erbarmen bey ihnen. Endlich gaben mir die Götter etwas im Sinn: hierauf bat ich sie, daſs vor meinem Ende ich noch ein Gebet thun möchte, und wenn ich rufen würde: schiefst zu! so sollten sie auf mich Feuer geben: indem aber daſs ich rief, fiel ich zur Erden nieder, sie aber erschossen sich selbsten einander; bin also diesesmal noch so mit dem Leben darvon kommen. Meine Ankunft aber wird dem Könige nicht angenehm seyn.

HORATIO. O unerhörte Verrätherey!

SCENE III.
PHANTASMO.

HAMLET. Siehe, Horatio, dieser Narr ist dem Könige viel lieber, als meine Person. Wir wollen hören, was er vorbringt.

PHANTASMO. (Willkommen zu Hause, Prinz Hamlet!) Wisset Ihr was Neues? der König hat eine Wette auf Euch und auf dem jungen Leonhardo geschlagen. Ihr sollt zusammen in Rapieren fechten, und wer dem andern die ersten zwey Stöſse anbringen wird, der soll ein weiſs neapolitanisch Pferd gewonnen haben.

HAMLET. Ist dieses gewiſs, was du sagest?

PHANTASMO. Ja es ist nicht anders.

HAMLET. Horatio, was mag dieses bedeuten? ich und Leonhardus sollen miteinander fechten. Ich glaube,

SCENE II.
HORATIO.

HORAT. My noble Prince, I am heartily rejoiced to see you here again in health and safety. Pray tell me what hath brought you so soon back again.

HAMLET. Alas! Horatio, you were very nearly not seeing me alive again, for my life was already at stake, had not the Almighty taken me under his special protection.

HORAT. What does your Highness say? How did it all happen?

HAMLET. You know that my father gave me two fellows as servants and companions of my travel. Now it chanc'd one day that contrary winds beset us and we cast anchor by an island not far from Dover. I, and my two attendants left the ship to breathe the fresh air. Hereupon the cursed villains came and would take my life, saying, they were hired to do so by the King. I begged for my life, promised to give them as much, and that if they would report my death to the King, I would never show myself at court again. But there was no mercy to be had of them. At length the gods inspired me with a thought: I begged the knaves for time to say a prayer to Heaven before my end, and when I called fire! they were to lodge their bullets in my breast. But when I called, I fell flat on the ground, so that they shot each other. Thus I escaped this time with my life. But my arrival will not be very agreeable to the King.

HORAT. O unheard of treachery!

SCENE III.
PHANTASMO.

HAMLET. Look Horatio, this fool is infinitely dearer to the king than my poor person. Let's hear what he has to say.

PHANT. Welcome to home, Prince Hamlet! Have you heard the last news? The King has laid a wager on you and young Leonardo. You are to measure your skill at fencing, and he who gives his opponent the first two thrusts is to win a white Neapolitan horse.

HAMLET. Are you sure of what you say?

PHANT. Ay, ay, so it is, as I say.

HAMLET. Horatio, what may this mean? I and Leonardo to fight! They have been imposing on this

sie werden diesen Narren etwas weifs gemacht haben, denn man kann ihm einbilden, was man will. Sehet nur, Signora Phantasmo, es ist greulich kalt.

PHANTASMO. Ja ja, es ist greulich kalt —
      [*zittert mit dem Munde.*

HAMLET. Nun ist es schon nicht so kalt mehr.

PHANTASMO. Ja ja, es ist so recht ins Mittel.

HAMLET. Aber nun ist eine grofse Hitze.
      [*wischt das Gesicht.*

PHANTASMO. O welch eine greuliche Hitze!
      [*wischt auch den Schweifs.*

HAMLET. Nun ists nicht recht kalt, auch nicht recht warm.

PHANTASMO. Ja es ist nun eben recht temperirt.

HAMLET. Da siehest du, Horatio, dafs man ihm weifs machen kann, was man will. Phantasmo, gehe wieder hin zum Könige, und sage ihm, dafs ich ihm bald aufwarten werde — [*Phantasmo ab*]. Nun kommt, Horatio, ich will gleichwohl gehn, und mich dem König präsentiren. Aber ach! was bedeutet dieses? mir fallen Blutstropfen aus der Nase; mir schüttert der ganze Leib! O wehe, wie geschieht mir! [*fällt in Ohnmacht.*

HORAT. Durchlauchtigster Prinz, o Himmel, was bedeutet dieses! Ihro Durchlaucht kommen doch wieder zu sich selbst! Durchlauchtigster Prinz, wie ists, was wiederfährt Ihnen!

HAMLET. Ich weifs nicht, Horatio. Indem ich gedachte, nach Hofe zu gehn, überfiel mich eine schleunige Ohnmacht; was dieses bedeuten wird, ist den Göttern bekannt.

HORAT. Ach, der Himmel gebe doch, dafs dieses Omen nicht etwas Böses bedeuten möge.

HAMLET. So sey es wie es will, ich will dennoch zu Hofe gehn, und sollte es auch mein Leben kosten.
            [*ab.*

SCENE IV.
KÖNIG. LEONHARDUS. PHANTASMO.

KÖNIG. Leonhardus, mache dich fertig, denn Prinz Hamlet wird auch bald hier seyn.

LEONH. Ihro Majestät, ich bin schon fertig, und werde schon mein Bestes thun.

KÖNIG. Sehet wohl zu; hier kommt der Prinz schon — — —

SCENE V.
HAMLET. HORATIO.

HAMLET. Alles Glück und Heil warte auf Ihro Majestät!

KÖNIG. Wir danken Euch, Prinz! Wir sind höchsterfreut, dafs Euch die Melancholie in etwas verlassen,

poor fool, for one can make him believe what one likes. Observe, Signor Phantasmo, 'tis horribly cold.

PHANT. Ay, ay, 'tis horribly cold —
      [*His teeth chattering with cold.*

HAMLET. Now it is no more so cold.

PHANT. You're right my lord, just the happy medium.

HAMLET. But now it is very hot.
      [*Wiping his face.*

PHANT. O what a dreadful heat!
      [*Also wiping away the perspiration.*

HAMLET. It seems to me 'tis neither very cold nor very warm.

PHANT. Yes, now it is just temperate.

HAMLET. Do you see, Horatio, one can make him believe what one will. Phantasmo, go get thee to the King, and say I'll wait upon him instantly. [*Phant. exit.*] Come, Horatio, I go this very minute, and present myself to the King. Ha! What does this bode? See, these drops of blood which fall from my nose. I tremble from head to foot! Alas! alas! how is it with me?
            [*Faints.*

HORAT. Most noble Prince! O Heavens! what does this import? Come to your senses my lord! My noble Prince, what is the matter with you?

HAMLET. I do not know, Horatio. When I thought of going to court, a sudden swoon came over me. The gods alone know what it signifies.

HORAT. Heaven grant this be no evil omen!

HAMLET. Be it what it may, I go to court, ay and should it cost me my life.
            [*Exeunt.*

SCENE IV.
KING. LEONARDO. PHANTASMO.

KING. Leonardo prepare, for Prince Hamlet will also be here directly.

LEON. I am prepared, your Majesty, and will do my utmost.

KING. Look well to it; but here comes the Prince in happy time — — —

SCENE V.
HAMLET. HORATIO.

HAMLET. All health and happiness wait on your Majesty!

KING. We thank you, Prince! We are extremely glad, that your melancholy has somewhat abated; where-

derowegen haben wir heut einen Luststreit angestellt zwischen Euch und dem jungen Leonhardo: Ihr sollt mit ihm in Rapieren fechten, und welcher von Euch beyden die ersten drey Stöſse bekommen wird, der soll ein weiſs neapolitanisch Pferd mit Sattelzeug und allem Zubehör gewonnen haben.

HAMLET. Ihro Majestät wollen mir verzeihen, denn ich in den Rappier wenig geübt bin. Leonhardus aber kommt kürzlich aus Frankreich, allda er sich ohne Zweifel wird gut exercirt haben, darum wollen Sie mich entschuldiget halten.

KÖNIG. Prinz Hamlet thut uns dieses zu gefallen, denn wir sind begierig zu erfahren, was die Teutschen und die Franzosen vor Finten haben.

SCENE VI.
KÖNIGIN.

KÖNIGIN. Gnädiger Herr und König, ich werde Ihnen ein groſses Unglück erzählen!

KÖNIG. Der Himmel bewahre uns davor! Was ist es denn?

KÖNIGIN. Die Ophelia ist auf einen hohen Berg gestiegen, und hat sich selber heruntergestürzt und um das Leben gebracht.

LEONH. Ach unglückseeliger Leonhardus! du hast in kurzer Zeit einen Vater und Schwester verlohren! Wohin will doch das Unglück dich leiten! Ich wünsche mir selbsten vor Betrübniſs den Tod.

KÖNIG. Stellet euch zufrieden, Leonhardus! wir sind euch gnädig, fanget nur das Gefechte an. Phantasmo bringe die Rappiere; Ihr aber, Horatio, sollet urtheilen.

PHANTASMO. Da sind die warmen Biere.

HAMLET. Wohlan denn, Leonhardus, so kommet denn an, wir wollen zusehn, wer dem andern die Schellen wird anhängen. Wo ich aber einen Exces begehen möchte, bitte ich zu excusiren, denn ich lange nicht gefochten.

LEONH. Ich bin Ihro Durchlaucht Diener, Sie scherzen nur.

[*In dem ersten Gang fechten sie reine. Leonhardus bekommt einen Stoſs.*

HAMLET. Nun das war eins, Leonhardus!

LEONH. Es ist wahr, Ihro Durchlaucht! Allo Revange! [*Dieser läſst das Rappier fallen, und ergreift den vergifteten Degen, welcher parat lieget, und stöſst dem Prinzen die Quarte in den Arm. Hamlet pariret auf Leonhardo, daſs sie beyde die Gewehre fallen lassen. Sie laufen ein jeder nach dem Rappier. Hamlet bekommt den vergifteten Degen, und sticht Leonhardus todt.*

LEONH. O wehe, ich habe einen tödtlichen Stoſs!

fore we have arranged a fencing match between you and young Leonardo. He who makes the first three hits, has gained the prize, a white Neapolitan horse with saddle and housings complete.

HAMLET. Your Majesty will pardon me, for I am little practised with the foils, while Leonardo comes direct from France, where he has undoubtedly had plenty of practice; wherefore I pr'ythee hold me excused.

KING. Prince Hamlet will do it to please us, for we are curious to learn the feints of the Germans and the French.

SCENE VI.
QUEEN.

QUEEN. My gracious Lord and King, I am the bearer of sad tidings.

KING. Heaven forbid, say on.

QUEEN. Ophelia has ascended a high hill, and cast herself from the top of it, and taken her life.

LEON. Ah, ill-fated Leonardo! In how short a space of time hast thou lost a father and a sister! Whither will mischance lead me! O! that death would come to free me from my woe and misery!

KING. Content ye, Leonardo! You enjoy our favour, only begin the play. Phantasmo fetch the rapiers, Horatio shall be umpire.

PHANT. Here is the warm beer.

HAMLET. Come on, Leonardo, let's see who is to wear the fool's bells. Should I blunder, pray excuse me Leonardo, for I am somewhat out of practice.

LEON. My lord you jest with your servant.

[*During the first bout they fence fairly. Leonardo receives a thrust.*

HAMLET. That was a hit, Leonardo!

LEON. True, your Highness. Now for my revenge! [*He lets his foil fall, and seizes the poisoned sword which is lying ready and deals him a thrust in the left arm. Hamlet parries, so that both drop their weapons. They run to pick them up. Hamlet takes the poisoned sword and mortally wounds Leonardo.*

LEON. Alack! I am mortally wounded! I receive

ich bekomme den Lohn, mit welchem ich dachte einen andern zu bezahlen. Der Himmel sey mir gnädig.

HAMLET. Was zum Teufel ist dieses! Leonhardus, hab ich euch mit dem Rappier erstochen? Wie geht dieses zu?

KÖNIG. Gehet geschwinde, und gebt meinen Mundbecher mit Wein her, damit die Fechter sich ein wenig erquicken. Gehe, Phantasmo, und hole ihn. [*tritt vom Thron. Für sich.*] Ich hoffe, wenn sie beyde von dem Wein trinken werden, dafs sie alsdenn sterben, und diese Finte nicht offenbar werde.

HAMLET. Sagt mir, Leonhardus, wie ist dieses zugegangen?

LEONH. Ach, Prinz, ich bin von dem König zu diesem Unglück verführet worden! Sehet, was Ihr in Eurer Hand habt! es ist ein vergifteter Degen.

HAMLET. O Himmel, was ist dieses! Bewahre mich doch davor!

LEONH. Ich sollte Euch damit verletzen, denn er ist so stark vergiftet, dafs, wer nur die geringste Wunde damit bekömmt, augenscheinlich sterben mufs.

KÖNIG. Holla, Ihr Herren, erhohlet Euch ein wenig und trinket. [*Indem der König vom Stuhl aufstehet, und diese Worte redet, so nimmt die Königin dem Phantasmo den Becher aus der Hand und trinket, der König ruft:*] Holla! wo bleibt der Becher? Ach, wertheste Gemahlin, was thut sie? Dieses, was hier eingeschenket, ist mit dem stärksten Gift vermenget. Ach wehe, was habt Ihr gethan!

KÖNIGIN. O wehe, ich sterbe!
[*Der König stehet vor der Königin.*

HAMLET. Und Du, Tyranne, sollst sie in dem Tode begleiten. [*Hamlet ersticht ihm von hinten zu.*

KÖNIG. O wehe, ich empfange meinen bösen Lohn!

LEONH. Adieu, Prinz Hamlet! Adieu, Welt! ich sterbe auch. Ach, verzeihet mir, Prinz!

HAMLET. Der Himmel geleite deine Seele, weil du unschuldig. Diesen Tyrannen aber wünsche ich, dafs er seine schwarze Sünden in der Höllen abwaschen möge. Ach, Horatio, nun ist meine Seele ruhig, nun ich mich an meinen Feinden gerochen habe. Ich habe zwar auch einen Stofs in den Arm, aber ich hoffe, es werde nichts zu bedeuten haben. Es ist mir leid, dafs ich Leonhardum erstochen habe, ich weifs aber nicht, wie ich den verzweifelten Degen in meine Hand bekommen; doch

the recompense with which I thought to pay another. Heaven, have mercy on me!

HAMLET. What the devil is this, Leonardo? have I slain you with this foil? Say, say, how is this possible?

KING. Go quick, and fetch a cup of wine to refresh our swords-men a little. Go, Phantasmo, and fetch it. [*Descends from the throne. Aside.*] I hope they may both drink and die, and that this trick may not become known.

HAMLET. Tell me, Leonardo, how did this all come about?

LEON. Alas! Prince, I have been seduced to this misfortune by the King! Look at what you have in your hand! It is a poisoned sword.

HAMLET. O! Heavens, what is this! Preserve me from it!

LEON. It was agreed that I should wound you with it, for it is so strongly poisoned, that whoever receives the slightest wound from it, must die.

KING. Ho! gentlemen, take this cup and drink. [*Whilst the King is rising from his chair and speaking the above words, the Queen takes the cup out of Phantasmo's hand and drinks; the King exclaims:*] Ho! where is the cup? Alas! my dearest wife, what are you doing? This drink is mixed with the strongest poison. Alack! alack! what have you done!

QUEEN. Alas! I die!
[*The King stands before the Queen.*

HAMLET. And thou, tyrant, shalt bear her company in death. [*Stabs him from behind.*

KING. Alas! alas! I receive my due recompense!

LEON. Farewell, Prince Hamlet! Farewell, world! I die too. Ah, forgive me, Prince!

HAMLET. May heaven receive thy soul for thou art innocent. But for this tyrant, I wish that he may purge his sins in the hell. Ah, Horatio! now is my soul at peace, I am revenged of mine enemies. 'Tis true I have received a touch upon the arm, but I hope it will be of no consequence. It grieveth me that I have slain Leonardo. I know not how the accursed weapon came to my hand; but as he hath sown, so hath he reaped. He has received his reward. My wretched mother! most

wie die Arbeit, so ist auch der Lohn, er hat seine Bezahlung bekommen. Nichts jammert mir mehr, als meine Frau Mutter. Doch sie hat diesen Tod wegen ihrer Sünden halben auch verdienet. Aber sagt mir, wer hat ihr den Becher gegeben, daſs sie Gift bekommen?

PHANTASMO. Ich, Herr Prinz! ich habe auch den vergifteten Degen gebracht, aber den vergifteten Wein habt Ihr allein sollen austrinken.

HAMLET. Bist du auch ein Werkzeug dieses Unglücks gewesen? Siehe, da hast du auch deine Belohnung!
[*sticht ihn todt.*

PHANTASMO. Stecht, daſs euch die Klinge verlahme!

HAMLET. Ach, Horatio, ich fürchte, es wird nach meiner verübten Rache auch mein Leben kosten, denn ich bin am Arme sehr verwundet. Ich werde ganz matt, meine Glieder werden schwach, und meine Beine wollen nicht mehr stehn; meine Sprache vergeht mir, ich fühle den Gift in allen meinen Gliedern. (Doch bitte ich euch, lieber Horatio, und bringet die Krone nach Norwegen an meinen Vetter, den Herzog Fortempras, damit das Königreich nicht in andre Hände falle.) Ach, o weh, ich sterbe!

HORATIO. Ach, Durchlauchtigster Prinz, erwartet doch Hülfe, O Himmel, er bleibt mir unter den Händen! Ach, was hat doch dieses Königreich eine zeither vor schwere Kriege geführet! Kaum hatte es Friede, so ist es aufs neue mit innerlicher Unruhe, Regier- Streit- und Mordsucht angefüllet worden. Dieser traurige Unglücksfall mag wohl in keinem Seculo der Welt jemals geschehn seyn, wie man leider jetzt an diesem Hofe erlebet hat. Ich will alle Anstalt mit Hülfe der treuen Räthe machen, daſs diese hohe Personen nach ihrem Stande beerdiget werden, alsdenn mich cito mit der Krone nach Norwegen verfügen, und dieselbe übergeben, wie mir dieser unglückseelige Prinz befohlen hat.

Vers.

So gehts, wenn ein Regent mit List zur Kron sich dringet,
Und durch Verrätherey dieselbe an sich bringet,
Derselb erlebet nichts, als lauter Spott und Hohn,
Denn wie die Arbeit ist, so folget auch der Lohn.

ENDE.

do I grieve for her — her sins have brought this just punishment down on her. Say, who gave her the poisoned cup?

PHANT. I, Prince. I have also brought the poisoned sword, but the poisoned wine was intended for you alone.

HAMLET. Hast thou too been an instrument of all this woe and misery? There, take thy due reward?
[*Stabs him.*

PHANT. Run it in, and may your blade grow lame!

HAMLET. Horatio, alas! I fear my revenge has cost me my life, for I am sorely wounded in the arm. I grow faint, my limbs grow weak and refuse to support me, my voice fails, I feel the poison in all my members. Gentle Horatio, take the crown to my cousin, Duke Fortinbras of Norway, that the kingdom may not fall into other hands. Alas! I die!

HORATIO. O! Noble Prince, aid may still come! Heavens! he is dying in my arms. Alas! O! how this Kingdom of Denmark hath been scourged with long wars! Scarce was peace established, when anew internal disturbances, murders, ambition, and contentions fill the land. In no age of the world hath such a tragedy been played as now, alas, at this court. And now, with aid from the faithful counsellors of the kingdom, I will take all fitting measures that these high personages be buried according to their rank. Which done, I will go to Norway with the crown at once, and deliver it as this unhappy Prince commanded.

Verse.

Thus is it when a prince by craft the crown will seize,
And take it for himself by treach'rous practices,
'Tis nothing that he gets but mockery and scorn,
For he shall reap at eve, what he has sown at morn.

THE END.

TRAGEDY OF ROMEO AND JULIET

ACTED IN GERMANY, IN THE YEAR 1626, BY ENGLISH PLAYERS.

The German Text of the TRAGEDY OF ROMEO AND JULIET is printed from the only known Manuscript in the Imperial Library at Vienna. Extracts from it have been published (very incorrectly) in EDUARD DEVRIENT's *Geschichte der deutschen Schauspielkunst,* Band I, Leipzig 1848, 8vo, pag. 408—434. The present impression is the first ever published of the complete play. — The Manuscript has no title-page and bears no date.

TRAGÆDIA
VON ROMIO UND JULIETTA.

Personen.

FÜRST.
CAPOLET.
MUNDIGE.
PARIS.
ROMIO.
MERCUTIUS.
PENVOLIO.
TIPOLT.
PATER.
PICKELHÄRING.
EIN JUNGE.
GRÄFIN CAPOLET.
JULIETA.
AMME (ANTONETA).

ACTUS PRIMUS.
SCENA PRIMA.
FÜRST *mit* KAPOLETH *vnd* MUNDIGE.
Hoffstadt.

FÜRST. Die Sonne schawet an den blaw Saphir glantzenden Himmel den Erdtkreifs nur darumb, damit alles wachse blüe vnd zeitig werde, vnd dem Menschen zu Nutzen diene, wo aber die fünstere Hagelswolckhen mit einer frostnüfs solche berühret, so ist die gefahr vnd der Schad vorhanden. Capolet vnd Mundige weillen in vnserer Regirung nichts Jrrsamber vnd vnleidiger scheinet alfs Euer beyder Heuser vneinigkeit saget vnnfs in was Nutzen bestehet Euer Zorn Hafs vnd Feindschafft alfs dafs Euer Geschlecht gemündert vnd nach der Zeit mit bluetigen Kempfen ausgerodt vnd zergehen mufs vnd ihr habt nichts bessers zu hoffen alfs dafs Euch beyden nichts mehr übrig nach Euren todt, alfs der Nahmb vnd die nachfolgende weldt sagen wir(d) sie sein gewe(sen).

CAPOLET. Gnädiger Fürst und Herr nach dero Belieben zu reden gestehe ich, dafs vnser beyde Heuser von Geschlecht zu Geschlecht in solche Erbfeindschaft

TRAGEDY
OF ROMEO AND JULIET.

Persons represented:

PRINCE.
CAPULET.
MONTAGUE.
PARIS.
ROMEO.
MERCUTIO.
BENVOLIO.
TIBALT.
A FRIAR.
CLOWN (Pickelhœring).
A BOY.
LADY CAPULET.
JULIET.
NURSE.

ACT I.
SCENE I.
PRINCE *with* CAPULET *and* MONTAGUE.
Retinue.

PRINCE. The sun looks at this earth in heaven's azure only that every thing may grow, flower, and mature, and be of use to man: but wherever the dark hail-clouds strike her with a chill, there is danger and loss. Capulet and Montague! since in our reign nothing appears more erratic and intolerable than the quarrel of your two houses, tell us then, what else do you gain by your wrath, hatred, and enmity but that your race dwindle away, and in the course of time become extirpated in bloody fights and disappear, and that you have nothing better to hope, but that after your death nothing remains of both of you, except your names and the saying of future generations: they have been.

CAPULET. Gracious Prince and Lord! To speak according to your pleasure, I confess that both our houses from generation to generation have grown into

gerathen, dafs es scheinet, als ob der Himmel darob ein Wohlgefallen vnd mit seinen influenzen das Kindt in Muetterleib mit der geburthstundt schon feindlich bekleitet. Der Himmel ist mein Zeug, das meine grawe Haar daran keinen gefallen, sondern viel mehr beseufftze den Schadenfohl vndtergang, vnsers so alten Stammen Haufs.

FÜRST. Was sagt ihr graff Mundige, wie gefalt Euch diese meinung?

MUNDIGE. Gnädiger Fürst und Herr diese meinung des Capoleth ist nicht verwerfflich, aber die offt beschehene affront vnd überfallung der Meinigen so sie von den Capoleten erliden ist weldt kündig vnd vnserer Vorfahrer bluetvergiefsung gantze cronicen voll voll (sic) sein ist also meinem bedunckhen nach nicht Rathsamb dafs mein feindt zuesehe dafs mir das wasser in das maul rinnt.

FÜRST. Graff Mundige der tugendtwürdige titul bestehet nicht in hützigen Euffer des Zorns sondern mit Nachlassung des Empfangenen Schaden, der ist Ruhmbwürdig zu nennen, so seinen feindt verzeihen vnd mit freundtschafft obsigen kan.

MUNDIGE. Die Natur lehrent aber viel ein anders gnädiger Fürst und Herr.

FÜRST. Und was dan?

MUNDIGE. Nicht zuelassen, das man von feindt überwunden vnd bezwungen werde.

FÜRST. Es ist wahr was den Krieg vnd landtsverwüstung betrüfft.

CAPOLET. Wan es so währe wolte ich vmb würdiger gleich meine grawe Haar mit Sigesblätter vmb winden, oder einen Ehrlichen todt hoffen, aber dieser Haufs vnd Nahmben Krieg legt mich selber eher in das grab, alfs Hoffnung haben einen friden zu erleben.

FÜRST. Der Himmel kan keinen gefallen an einer einheimbischen Vnruhe oder Stattsverderben haben noch weniger an dem, das zwey so vornehme Stammenheüfser fallen vnd selbst sich zu grundte richten sollen.

CAPOLET. Wie vorgesagt gnädiger Fürst vnd Herr ich liebe die Einigkeit den Frieden vnd hasse das vnrechte Bluetvergiessen.

MUNDIGE. Wer gezwungen das gewöhr zu brauchen, der vergiefst nicht vnrechtes blueth.

CAPOLET. Der fridlich leben will, braucht kein gewähr zu wetzen.

MUNDIGE. Der leichtlich glaubet, wird leicht betrogen.

CAPOLET. Der nicht die Ehre acht, kan leicht ein betrüger sein.

such hereditary feud, that it seems as if heaven taketh delight in it, and by its influences renders the child in the mother's womb hostile from its birth. Heaven is my witness, that my gray hair does not delight in it, but that I sigh over the hurtful ruin of our so ancient stock.

PRINCE. How say you, count Montague? how do you like this sentiment?

MONTAGUE. Gracious Prince and Lord! This sentiment of Capulet is not to be rejected; but the often repeated affronts and attacks which my kinsmen have had to suffer from the Capulets, are well-known to all the world; and whole chronicles are full of our forefather's bloodshed. Therefore methinks it is not advisable, that my enemy should stand by and see the waters rise up to my mouth.

PRINCE. Count Montague! The title to virtue does not consist in heat of anger but in remission of received injury. That man is worthy of praise who forgives his enemy and conquers by kindness.

MONTAGUE. Yet nature teaches something very different, gracious Prince and Lord!

PRINCE. And what?

MONTAGUE. Not to suffer oneself to be conquered and overcome by enemies.

PRINCE. That is true as far as concerns war and devastation.

CAPULET. If it were so, I should all the more worthily at once entwine my gray hair with victorious leaves, or hope for an honourable death. But sooner will the feud of these houses and names lay me in my grave, than there will be hope of my living to see a peace.

PRINCE. Heaven cannot be pleased with civil disturbance or ruin of the state, still less with the fall and mutual destruction of two such noble houses.

CAPULET. As I have said before, gracious Prince and Lord, I love union, and peace, and hate unlawful bloodshed.

MONTAGUE. He who is forced to use his weapon, does not shed unlawful blood.

CAPULET. He who will live peaceably, need whet no weapon.

MONTAGUE. He who easily believes, is easily deceived.

CAPULET. He who does not regard his honour, may easily turn deceiver.

MUNDIGE. Der die meinigen beleidiget, greifft mich vnd meine Ehre an.

CAPOLET. Der mein Herkommen beschimpfet ohne vrsach, ist nicht zu achten.

MUNDIGE. Wan aber die feindtschafft sein vrsach hat?

CAPOLET. Wer feindtschafft haben will, der darf kein vrsach suechen.

MUNDIGE. Die Beleidigung hat kein gedult.

CAPOLET. Der Beleidiget ist straffwürdig.

MUNDIGE. So straff man den so der beleidigung anfenger ist.

CAPOLET. O Mundige, Mundige, ich wintsche das kein beleidiger Nie gewesen wehre.

MUNDIGE. Wan wintschen gültig wehre, so hette ich auch mehr von meiner freundtschafft vnd familia bey leben.

FÜRST. Es gehet vnnſs selbst zu Hertzen, in deme wür bedrachten was thorheit das seyn ein Geschlecht das ander zu verdilgen, die freyheit zu verliehren, täglich vnruhe suechen, sich selbst in vnglickh stürtzen vnd Entlichen übel sterben.

MUNDIGE. Ich wintsche wol zu sterben vnd fridlich zu leben.

CAPOLET. Der Himmel gebe, das es mir auch widerfahre.

FÜRST. Vernehmet, ein König Fürst oder Herr, der da in seiner Regierung sitzet, waſs steht ihm besser an alſs seine Vndterthanen in friden vnd Recht zu erhalten, thuet Er solches so lebt Er glickselig, wo aber in Regirungssachen ein Unruhe vnd Feindtseeligkeit sich sehen lasset, so ist daſs Verderben verhanden, man sehe in allen landten, wo der frid vnd Einigkeit sich vmbhalsen da wohnet lauther frewd. Euer Vndterthanen blueten selbst mit Euch vnter den schwären Joch Euer Feindtschafft, darumb leget ab den Haſs vnd suechet nicht Euer Verderben, wo man nicht mit Schärpffe vnd Statuten des faderlandes mit Euch verfahren soll.

CAPOLET. Gnädigster Fürst vnd Herr, dem die sache angehet der fühlt den Schaden vnd weillen mir gebühren will zu gehorsamben, so setze ich mich nicht wider die gesetz des Verbots.

MUNDIGE. Graff, das guete Vornehmen, so ich an Euch verspühre soll mich nicht hindern den gehorsamb, die gesetz vnd liebe vnsers Vatterlandts zu vollziehen, wo nur der grundtstein Eures willen wohlgelegt.

CAPOLET. Graff, ich will Eurer meinung beyfallen, vnd wan mein will anders alſs der Eure, so verspreche ich hier in gegenwarth vnsers gnädigen Fürstens, das ich alle schuld ertragen, wo Euch vnd den Eurigen von

MONTAGUE. He who insults my kinsmen, attacks me and my honour.

CAPULET. He who defames my extraction without reason, deserves no respect.

MONTAGUE. But if there be a reason for enmity?

CAPULET. He who will have enmity, need not seek for a reason.

MONTAGUE. Offence has no patience.

CAPULET. The offender is liable to punishment.

MONTAGUE. Then let him be punished who began offending.

CAPULET. Oh Montague, Montague! I wish there had never been an offender.

MONTAGUE. If wishing were of any good, I also should have more joy of my friends and family in my life-time.

PRINCE. It makes our own heart ache, to think what folly it is one race destroying the other, losing one's liberty, seeking quarrel day by day, precipitating oneself into misfortune, and in the end dying miserably.

MONTAGUE. I wish to die well and to live in peace.

CAPULET. Would to Heaven that the same be my lot too!

PRINCE. Hear ye! a King, Prince, or Lord who sits in his government, what becomes him better than keeping his subjects in peace and right? If he does that, he lives in happiness; but wherever trouble and hostility appear in matters of government, there ruin is at hand. Look at all countries: where peace and unanimity exist in fond embrace, there is joy. Even your vassals are bleeding from the heavy yoke of your enmity. Therefore discard your hatred and do not court your ruin, unless you would be treated with severity, and according to the statutes of the land.

CAPULET. Most gracious Prince and Lord! He, whose concern it is, feels the injury; and as it behoves me to obey I do not set myself against the law.

MONTAGUE. Count! The good intention I observe in you shall not hinder me from obedience, from following the laws and love of our country, provided the corner-stone of your will be well laid.

CAPULET. Count! I approve of your sentiment; and when my will shall differ from yours, I do here promise, in the presence of our gracious Prince, to take upon myself all responsibility in case you and your

den Capoleten solle eine beleidigung geschehen, vnd hier ist meine Handt.
MUNDIGE. Und hier die meine.
CAPOLET. Zu einer wahren trew.
MUNDIGE. Vnd Rechten freundschafftsbandt.
CAPOLET. Wer dise bricht
MUNDIGE. Verfluechet sey sein Handt.
FÜRST. Dises ist ein werkh, daran wür einen gefallen tragen vnd wintschen
    Euren beiden Stammen
    Die weifse Fridensblüe
    Die waxe Nestors Jahr
    Mit 1000 glickes Nahmen.
MUNDIGE.
Der Himmel hat bifsher gantz zornig aufsgesehen
Nun aber muefs der Krieg vnd Hafs zu Ende gehen.
CAPOLET.
Es hat der Krieges Newd vnfs beyde hart gekrenkt
Jezt vnser will an frid vnd Süfse Ruhe gedenkt.
MUNDIGE.
Die Ruhe nimbt mich ein, die Rach ligt ietzo vnten
Nun ist das vngemach vnd aller Zankh verschwunden.
CAPOLET.
Nun bin ich sorgenfrey vnd sag vonn hertzen recht,
Ich werd mich allzeit nennen sein Diener vnd sein Knecht.
MUNDIGE.
Den ich ertödten wolt nennt mich ietzt seinen freind
Nun mehr hats keine noth, ich weifs von keinem feind.
FÜRST.
Wehe in dem Hertzen dem der da hegt Krieges glueth
Vnd lescht die tugendt aufs, acht weder freind noch blueth
Es will dafs Ilion durch solches Krieges fewer
Dafs Troia muest vergehn in diesem vngehewer
Dafs laster weiche weith aufs Euren tugendt Sinn
Die freindtschafft gebe Euch, die balmen zu gewünn.
[Alle ab.

SCENA 2ᴅᴀ.
JULIETA *vnd* ANTONETA
in garthen.

JULIETA. O grofse Belustigung dieser Frühlings Zeit, wan man sich ergötzen kan in den lustbahren Gärten, felder vnd wälder, wan man höret die rauschende Bächlein die ihren lauff zwischen den Kifselsteinen zerbrechen, welches das gehör ergetzet, wan der zephirus den blätterreichen Bawmen schmeichlet, vnd mit ihnen schertzet, wan die Vögl singen, vnd mit ihrem gefider die lufft durchstreichen, vnd andere tausend anmuethungen die das Hertz erquickhen. Aber sage Julieta wafs frewde genüest du, weil ich wie eine Einsambe turteltaube ein-

people should suffer any injury from the Capulets; and there is my hand.
MONTAGUE. And here is mine.
CAPULET. Unto a true faith —
MONTAGUE. And genuine bond of friendship.
CAPULET. The which whoever breaks —
MONTAGUE. Accursed be his hand!
PRINCE. This is a work therein we delight, and wish
    Both your houses
    The white blossom of Peace;
    May it grow to Nestor's age
    With a thousand lucky names!
MONTAGUE.
The Heavens did as yet anger and wrath portend
But now henceforth must war and hatred have an end.
CAPULET.
War's envy on us both hath grievous suffering brought
To sweet repose and peace our will now turns our thought.
MONTAGUE.
Quiet now fills my heart, revenge lies low too here,
Now does our wrangling all and trouble disappear.
CAPULET.
Now am I free from care, and from my heart I say
I'll call myself your slave and servant from to-day.
MONTAGUE.
He whom I wished to kill now makes a friend of me,
No more I wish his death, I have no enemy.
PRINCE.
Woe to the man whose heart with warlike ardour glows,
Who quenches virtue's light, nor blood nor friendship knows.
'Twas Ilion's fate indeed through just such warlike fire,
That Troy must pass away in monstrous wrong and dire.
Before your virtuous souls may all the vices flee,
And friendship grant to you to gain the victory!
[*Exeunt omnes.*

SCENE II.
JULIET *and* NURSE.
In the garden.

JULIET. Oh! how great is the enjoyment of this spring-time, when one may delight in the merry gardens, fields, and woods; when one hears the murmuring brooks breaking their course betwixt the pebbles, so pleasant to the ear; when the zephyr dallies with the leafy tree; when the birds chant and with their plumage sweep through the air, and a thousand other charms gladden the heart! But say, Juliet, what pleasure dost thou enjoy while I am pent up like a solitary turtle and forced to live like a prisoner, deprived of every enjoyment by

gesperrt, vnd alfs eine gefangene leben muefs indeme mich meiner Eltern Zucht aller frewd berauben, o Italia was für gesetz gibest du dem weiblichen geschlecht, dafs sie nichts genüfsen als die Einsambkeit, sage mir Antoneta soll ich die Blumen besuechen oder schlaffen?

ANTONETA. Schöne Julieta mich wundert selber das sie sich Ihrer Eltern gehorsamb so starkh vnterwürfft, vnd den gehorsamb nicht vberschreidten will, o wehre mir also ich wolte mir schon helffen.

JULIETA. Vnd wie in deme mir nichts mehr erlaubet ist, alfs in disen garthen' vnter den Blumen mich zu erfrewen.

ANTON. Vnd was ist's? Blumen sind blumen, aber ein beth das wäre eine linderung.

JULIETA. Wafs linderung?

ANTON. Linderung der glider.

JULIETA. Wafs glider?

ANTON. Nun der gantze theil defs Menschen, ihr versteht mich ja wohl, wan ihr nur wolt, o wie Einfeldig seht ihr doch aus.

JULIETA. Und wafs dan?

ANTON. Nichts nichts, aber wan ich reden dörffte.

JULIETA. Rede nur frey.

ANTON. Gn. Fräulein, sie verzeihe mir wan ich sagen darf dafs besser währe einen discurs mit einen wackheren gaualier zu führen, alfs sich in die stumme garthenblumen zu uerlieben.

JULIETA. Ach Antoneta wafs redest du?

ANTON. Worumb färbet sie sich schöne Julieta vnd wird roth.

JULIETA. Roth bedeutet lieb.

ANTON. So liebt sie dan.

JULIETA. Worumb solt ich nicht lieben, ich liebe aber weifs nicht wafs.

ANTON. Es muefs was sein dafs sie blagt, dan sie bald roth bald weifs ihr gesicht verendert, sie jagt mir bald ein forcht ein.

JULIETA. Antoneta wisset ihr nicht wer roth vnd weifs erfunden? Habe ichs in meinem gesicht, so ist es nicht ohne vrsach, dan die tugendt lebt in mir, vndt tugendt hats erworben.

ANTON. Tugendt vnd wafs für tugendt?

JULIETA. Tugendt des gemüths.

ANTON. Seit ihr ein Soldat?

JULIETA. Nicht mit waffen.

ANTON. Mit was dan?

JULIETA. Ach!

ANTON. Wie ist Euch?

JULIETA. Ach leider!

ANTON. Leidet ihr?

parental control? Oh Italia! what law givest thou to womankind, leaving them nothing to enjoy but solitude! Say, Antoneta, shall I visit the flowers or go to sleep?

NURSE. Fair Juliet! I really wonder you should pay such strict obedience to your parents, and never transgress it. If I were in your case, I should know how to make shift.

JULIET. And how, since nothing is allowed me but to enjoy myself in this garden among the flowers.

NURSE. And what of that? Flowers are flowers, but a bed would be some comfort.

JULIET. What comfort?

NURSE. For the limbs.

JULIET. Which limbs?

NURSE. Why, for the whole frame. I dare say you can understand me if you choose. How simple you look!

JULIET. And what then?

NURSE. Nothing, nothing. But if I might speak —

JULIET. Speak your mind freely.

NURSE. Pardon me, my lady, for saying, you would do better to carry on a discourse with some gallant cavalier than to make love to the dumb garden-flowers.

JULIET. Oh, Antoneta, what are your talking?

NURSE. Why do you colour, fair Juliet, and blush?

JULIET. Red means love.

NURSE. So you love?

JULIET. Why should I not love? I love, but I know not what.

NURSE. Something must torment you, for you now blush, and now blench. You make me almost afraid.

JULIET. Antoneta, do you not know who invented red and white? If I wear them in my face, there is a reason for it; for virtue lives in me, and colour is virtue's own.

NURSE. Virtue? and what virtue?

JULIET. The virtue of the mind.

NURSE. Are you a soldier?

JULIET. Not in arms.

NURSE. In what then?

JULIET. Alas!

NURSE. How do you feel?

JULIET. Woe!

NURSE. Are you suffering?

JULIETA. Ach nur gahr zu viel.
ANTON. Wessentwegen?
JULIETA. Ich weiſs es nicht.
ANTON. Ich auch nicht.
JULIETA. Waſs sagt ihr?
ANTON. Nichts alſs das mir Ihr Jammer zu Hertzen gehet.
JULIETA. Geduld.
ANTON. Ich sehe eine veränderung an ihr, darumb bitt ich, schöne Julieta, sie verhalte mir nicht ihr anligen, kan ich ihr helffen, ich will nichts vnterlassen ihr zu dienen.
JULIETA. Nichts nichts ist mir, was soll mir sein, ich habe nur geschlaffen, obwohlen mir in den schlaff wunderliche sachen vorkommen, so sein es sachen die nicht wahr können werden, vnd begehr es auch nicht, das es wahr wehre.
ANTON. Warumb dises?
JULIETA. Darumb weil mir vorkommen alſs solte ich einen Mundiqueser lieben, welcher meines Herrn Vatter ärgister feindt, derwegen begehre ich nicht daſs es wahr werde.
ANTON. Feindtschafft kan sich in freindschafft verwandlen wan es den blinden bogen Schütz gefällig währe.
JULIETA. Schweige vnd rede mir nicht von solchen sachen wo du meine gnad nicht verliehren wilst.
ANTON. Ach wann sie nur ein mahl kosten soll die 1000 feldigen frewden die ein verliebtes Hertz genüst sie wurde sagen die Zeit ist vbel verlohren die man nicht auf Liebe wendt.
JULIETA. Wann ich daſs thuen werde, so werden die wässer zurücklauffen, die wölff vor den lämmern fliehen, die Hundt den Haasen weichen vnd der Beer das Meer, vnd der Delphin die gebürg lieben, die Einsambkeit ist meine Kurtzweil.
ANTON. Ach vngesaltzene Kurtzweil vndt widerspenstige tugendt wie sie ietzundt ist so wahr ich auch einmahl aber ich legte meine Zeit beſser an.
JULIETA. Es scheinet Antoneta ihr wollet mich mit Fleiſs zum Zorn reitzen, darumb schweiget mir von der liebe, die nichts bringt alſs stette vnruehe vndt Schmertzen. [*abit.*
ANTON. Ja Ja ich habe sie zornig gemacht, sie gehet daruon, o ihr arme Mägdlein ihr seit wohl Närrisch, das ihr die liebe veracht, vnd denkhet nicht einmahl auf den groſsen Jahrmarkh da ihr müst flederwisch verkauffen, o gütiger Himmel ich habe bald kein Zahn mehr in maul, o wie wohl wirts mir thuen wan du deinen Seegen liest über mich kommen, daſs ich bald einen Mann hette. [*abit.*

JULIET. Alas! only too much.
NURSE. What for?
JULIET. I do not know.
NURSE. Nor I either.
JULIET. What do you say?
NURSE. Nothing but that your misery grieves me to the heart.
JULIET. Patience!
NURSE. I observe a change in you; therefore I pray, fair Juliet, do not keep back from me anything that concerns you; if I can help you I will leave nothing undone to serve you.
JULIET. Nothing, nothing ails me: what should ail me? I have slept, that is all; and though strange things come to me in my sleep, yet are they things that cannot come true, nor do I desire them to come true.

NURSE. And why so?
JULIET. Because it seemed to me as if I was to marry a Montague, who is my father's worst enemy: therefore I do not desire it to come true.

NURSE. Enmity may change to amity, if it were the blind archer's pleasure.
JULIET. Be silent and do not talk to me of such things under pain of my displeasure.
NURSE. Oh, if you were only once to taste the thousand pleasures enjoyed by a heart in love, you would say: the time is ill spent that is not spent on love.

JULIET. Ere I do that, the waters will run up hill, the wolf fly before the lambs, the dog shun the hare, the bear love the sea and the dolphin the mountains. Solitude is my pastime.

NURSE. Ay, saltless pastime and reluctant virtue! As you are now, so have I been once, but I made better use of my time.
JULIET. It seems, Antoneta, you are determined to excite my wrath; therefore do not talk of love, for it brings forth nothing but perpetual trouble and pain. [*Exit.*
NURSE. Forsooth I have made her angry: there she goes. Oh, ye poor damsels, ye are foolish indeed to despise love and not to think of that great fair where ye will have to sell goosewing-dusters. Oh gracious heavens! I have hardly a tooth left in my mouth; what a comfort it would be if you would bestow that blessing on me to let me soon have a husband! [*Exit.*

SCENA 3ᵀᴵᴬ.
Paris. Capolet.

Capolet. Herr Graff die Ehr so sie zu vnseren Haufs tragen ist grofs zu aestimiren, darumb bitt ich noch mahlen, sie wollen ihnen gefallen lafsen die Schlechte tractament, so ihnen zu gefallen bereithet nicht verschmähen, dan was in Capolets vermögen haben sie zu beuehlen.

Paris. Herr Capolet ich bin Niemahlen gewohnet eine solche Ehr zu empfangen, da ich dieselbe nicht mit Ehr belohnen solle, darumb schätze ich sein Haufs preifswürdig mich darinnen zu bewürden.

Capolet. Mein schlechte wohnung wird preifswürdig durch dero gegenwarth.

Paris. Herr Capolet ich bitte.

Capolet. Sie befehlen Herr Graff.

Paris. Mich zu verschonen.

Capolet. Mit was?

Paris. Mit solchen Ehren ceremonien.

Capolet. Sie sein es aber würdig alle Ehre von meinen Hause zu nehmen.

Paris. So wird Graff Paris würdig sein alle Ehre zu ersetzen.

Capolet. Da kompt mein Pickl Häring zu gelegner Zeit. Höre Pickl Häring merkhe aber wohl, wafs ich dir sage.

Pickl Häring.

Pickl. Noch habt ihr mir nichts gesagt, das ich merkhen kan.

Capolet. Du bist ein Narr.

Pickl. Es kan wohl sein.

Capolet. Dises was du verrichten sollst will ich dir sagen.

Pickl. Warumb kans kein gescheider verrichten?

Capolet. Weil ich haben will du alfs der Narr soll es thuen, weillen die anderen bedienten andere verrichtungen haben.

Pickl. Mit Euren schnarchen, ietzt hab ich alles vergefsen, wafs ich thuen soll.

Capolet. Schelm ich habe dir ja noch nichts beuohlen oder gesagt.

Pickl. Ich hab vermeint ihr habt schon ausgeredt.

Capolet. Ich vermeine du bist lustig.

Pickl. A so nicht gar sehr, es thuets wohl aber, gegen 12 Vhr werd ich lustiger werden.

Capolet. Vnd warumb vmb 12 Vhr?

Pickl. Da wird der Koch anrichten.

Capolet. Du halts nur viel von frefsen.

SCENE III.
Paris. Capulet.

Capulet. My Lord, the honour you do our house is to be highly estimated. I therefore beg once more you will be pleased not to disdain the poor treatment provided for you; for whatever is in Capulet's power is at your command.

Paris. Sir! I am not at all accustomed to receive such honour, as I am not able to return it. Therefore I think your house quite worthy to receive me.

Capulet. My poor habitation becomes worthy by your presence.

Paris. Sir! I beg —

Capulet. What is your command, Count?

Paris. To forbear.

Capulet. What?

Paris. Treating me with such honour and ceremony.

Capulet. But you are worthy to receive all honour from my house.

Paris. Then Count Paris will be worthy to repay all honour.

Capulet. There comes my clown in the very nick of time. Hark, clown, and mind what I tell you.

Enter Clown.

Clown. You have not said anything that I could mind.

Capulet. Thou art a fool.

Clown. That may be.

Capulet. I am going to tell thee what thou art to do.

Clown. Why can it not be done by some one in his senses?

Capulet. Because it is my pleasure that thou, as fool, shouldst do it; because the other servants have something else to do.

Clown. With your blustering I have quite forgotten all I am to do.

Capulet. Why, I have not yet commanded nor told thee anything, thou rogue!

Clown. I fancied you had already done talking.

Capulet. I fancy, thou art merry.

Clown. Not overmuch, just sufficient; but near to twelve o'clock I shall be merrier.

Capulet. And why at twelve o'clock?

Clown. Then the cook will serve up the dinner.

Capulet. Thou carest only for feeding.

PICKL. Das halt Leib vnd Seel zusammen.

CAPOLET. Höre Picklhäring nimb disen Zetl, vnd die darinnen aufgezeichnet sein alſs Herr vnd frawen, die lade ein morgen bey mir auf ein Panquet zu erscheinen.

PICKL. Wissen sie schon, daſs sie kommen sollen?

CAPOLET. Nein du solt sie einladen.

PICKL. Wie solt ich sie einladen in Pistollen oder in ein gezogenes Rohr.

CAPOLET. In ein Eſsels Kopff solst du laden du vnuerständiger Schelm.

PICKL. Nun man darf ja fragen.

CAPOLET. Die Zettl wird es weisen wer da kommen soll.

PICKL. So hat der Zettl mehr verstandt alſs ich, so laſst die Zettl hingehen und einladen.

CAPOLET. Ich sage du solt es thuen.

PICKL. Vnd ich sag die Zettl soll es thuen.

CAPOLET. Pickl Häring bring mich nicht zum Zorn, ich laſse dich in die Kuchel führen.

PICKL. Das wäre guet vor mich.

CAPOLET. Warumb?

PICKL. Das ich etwas zu Essen bekomb.

CAPOLET. Nein gestrichen solst du werden.

PICKL. Ich bedankhe mich dauor.

CAPOLET. Gehe vnd verrichte was ich dir befohlen, oder du wirst gestrafft werden.

PICKL. Nu Nu wan ichs thuen mueſs, so thue ichs gehrn, iezt bin ich Herr Latein, o wo werd ich die Heuser abfinden, wo sie wohnen, ich will gehen vnd ein wenig Studiren, wie man die gäst anrädt wan man sie einladen soll — alſs Edl Ehrnuester Insonders Hochgeehrte fraw pfanne Schmidin vnd so. Ey Ihr lacht mich nur aufs ich wils schon machen. [*abit.*

PARIS. In warheit Herr Capolet diſs ist ein lustiger Mensch, damit man die Zeit verkürtzen kann.

CAPOLET. Herr Graff so einfeldig er ist ſo getrew ist er, ich habe ihn von Jugendt an aufferzogen, vnd läst sich brauchen Recht vnd links.

PARIS. Dergleichen habe ich nicht gesehen, wie wird ers aber machen die rechte eingeladene gäst zu finden.

CAPOLET. So guet alſs durch einen gescheiden wird es verrichtet werden. Herr Graff die Zeit verlaufft, will ihme belieben etwas in den garthen zu spatziren, vnd sich der springenden wässer beliebt zu machen vnd andere 1000 annehmbligkeiten zu sehen.

PARIS. Mein Herr Capolet ich folge ihm, ein garthen ist ein belustigung des gemüths.

[*beyde ab.*

CLOWN. Eating keeps soul and body together.

CAPULET. Listen, clown; take this paper and invite those put down thereon, gentlemen and ladies, to appear to-morrow at my banquet.

CLOWN. Are they aware that they are to come?

CAPULET. No, thou shalt charge them.

CLOWN. How shall I charge them? In a pistol or a rifled barrel?

CAPULET. Charge an ass-head, thou silly rogue!

CLOWN. Well, I suppose one may ask a question.

CAPULET. The paper will show who is to come.

CLOWN. Then the paper is cleverer than I am; let the paper go and invite them.

CAPULET. I say, thou shalt do it.

CLOWN. And I say, the paper shall do it.

CAPULET. Clown, don't rouse my anger, or I shall send thee to the kitchen.

CLOWN. That would be a nice thing for me.

CAPULET. How so?

CLOWN. As I should get some victuals.

CAPULET. No, thou would'st get some whipping.

CLOWN. No, thank you.

CAPULET. Go, and do as thou art ordered, or thou wilt be punished.

CLOWN. Well, well, if it cannot be helped, I will do it with all my heart. Now I am Mr. Invite; how shall I find out the houses where they live? I will go and study a little how to address guests that are to be invited, — as, Noble, worshipful Sir; Especially respected Mrs. Tinker, and so forth. You laugh at me? Never mind, I shall manage. [*Exit.*

PARIS. In truth, Sir! a jolly fellow that, with whom one may idle away the time.

CAPULET. As simple as faithful. I brought him up; he makes himself useful right and left.

PARIS. I never saw his like; but how will he manage to find out the right persons to be invited?

CAPULET. As well as a clever man would do it. My Lord, time wears on; would you like to take a walk in the garden and enjoy the fountains and look at a thousand other pleasant things?

PARIS. Sir! I follow you; a garden is a refreshment for the mind.

[*Exeunt.*

SCENA 4ᵀᴬ.
Romio. Penuolio.

Romio. Ach verwundetes Hertz vnd stets brennender Sünne ich, der ich vor disem alle Adeliche gemüeths ergötzung geliebet alſs Reithen Fechten Tantzen vnd was Edl ist, aber Ey laſs. Nun trachte ich allein meiner schönen Rosalina zu gefallen, in dero Diensten zu leben, durch Amors will bin ich ein liebsgefangener worden, o armseeliger Romio wohin bringt dich dein fata? obwohl nur meine Schmertzliche anfechtung mir die augen verdunklen ihr schöne zu bedrachten, dannoch blickt der glantz ihres angesichts in meinen Hertzen herfür wie die Hell glantzende Sonn, ihre augen sein zwey Hell glantzende stern, darin die fewrigen Strahlen verborgen, welche mein Hertz verwundt, ihr athem ist viel Süſser wohlriechender alſs Zephyrus oder angenehme windt von westen, wann Er hin vnd wider durch die bletter rührende beume wehet, die lieblichen blumen so die felder alſs eine tappzerey bekleidet, dises ist noch nichts in vergleichung der erwünschten Süſsigkeit ihres Holdseeligen Munds, ach Rosalina Rosalina!

Penuolio. Wie ists Romio, ich glaub du redest in traum, aber schaw, waſs kompt da vor ein abentheuer.

Pickl Häring auſs.

Gueten morgen oder Mittag ihr Herrn, Mein ich bitte sagt könt ihr lesen?

Romio. Ja wan ich die buechstaben kann vnd verstehe.

Pickl. O Ho Herr buchstabenversteher, wan ich die buchstaben konnt, so wolte ich sie selber wohl lesen.

Romio. Du verstehst mich nit, es möchte vielleicht eine frembde Sprach sein die ich nicht verstunde, laſs mich die Zettl sehen, so will ich dir bald sagen, ob ich es verstehe oder nicht.

Pickl. Ich wolts selber wohl lesen, aber buchstabiren kan ich nicht.

Romio. Ja das verstehe ich vnd es ist zu teutsch, lad ein die fraw Margarita mit ihrer tochter Mellina.

Pickl. Ja ja ich kenne sie sehr wohl, die Muetter ist fast schöner alſs die tochter.

Romia. Lad ein Don Horatio den Jüngeren.

Pickl. Den kenn ich, er gab mir gestern eine guete ohrfeigen vnd einen dugaten daruor.

Romio. So ist die ohrfeigen wohl bezahlt worden, weither lad ein Don Fortuniam vnd seinen bruder Florisell.

Pickl. Daſs sein zwey rechte Eiſsenbeiſser die fangen gleich grachel an.

SCENE IV.
Romeo. Benvolio.

Romeo. Alas! wounded in the heart and burning more and more, now am I immersed in thought, who formerly was so fond of every noble sport, as riding, fencing, dancing, and everything noble. But let that pass. Now my sole endeavour is to be agreeable to fair Rosaline, in whose service to live I am by Cupid's will a prisoner of love. Oh miserable Romeo! whither does thy fate lead thee? Although my painful affliction makes my eyes dull to contemplate her beauty, yet the radiance of her face strikes my soul like the resplendent sun. Her eyes are two splendent stars, the source of those fiery rays that have wounded my heart. Her breath is much sweeter than Zephyrus, or the pleasant breezes from the West, sporting through trees that shake their leaves. The charming flowers that cover the fields like some tapestry, are not to be compared with the coveted sweetness of her lovely mouth. Ah Rosaline, Rosaline!

Benvolio. What is that, Romeo? I suppose you are talking in a dream. But look, what strange thing is that coming here?

Enter Clown.

Clown. Good morning or midday, gentlemen. Pray, can you read?

Romeo. Ay, if I know and understand the letters.

Clown. O ho, Mr. Letter-wise! If I knew the letters I would read them myself.

Romeo. Thou dost not understand me; it might be a foreign tongue, which I do not understand. Let me see the paper and I will soon tell you, whether I understand it or not.

Clown. I would read it myself, but I cannot spell.

Romeo. Yes, I understand this, and it is in German: 'Invite Mrs. Margerita with her daughter Mellina.'

Clown. Ay, I know them well, the mother is almost handsomer than the daughter.

Romeo. 'Invite Don Horatio the younger.'

Clown. Him I know; he gave me a sound box on the ear yesterday and a ducat for it.

Romeo. So the box on the ear is well paid for. 'Further, invite Don Fortuniam and his brother Florisell.'

Clown. Two regular bullies, — they are, always ready for a row.

Romio. Lad ein Don Lucentio vnd Amaranta seine Baſs.

Pickl. Die wohnen in der Schuestergassen gegen den Meykeffer über.

Romio. Lad ein die Schöne Rosalina, o Hönnigſüſser Nahmb dich will ich küssen 1000 mahl.

Pickl. Daſs ist ein Narr er küst das papir, wan er das Mensch hett, er kundt sie küssen, wo ihr ruckgrad ein Ende hat.

Romio. Lad ein Madam Fioleta Catharina.

Pickl. Ist recht, die wohnt in Sauwinkl.

Romio. Lad ein Madam Flora.

Pickl. Hum daſs ist ein Mensch, ist wahr sie tragt allezeit ein flor über das gesicht, das man ihr Nasen nicht sieht, dan die Naaſs steht ihr recht mitts in dem gesicht.

Romio. Lad ein graff Paris, das ist ein wackherer gaŭalier.

Pickl. Ja aber er stinkt zwischen den Zehen wie bauern.

Romio. Aber sage mir wo wird dise Versamblung geschehen?

Pickl. In Meines Herrn Hauſs.

Romio. Wie heist dein Herr?

Pickl. Mein Herr heiſst Capolet.

Romio. Waſs? soll meine liebste Rosalina in meines feindes Hauſs kommen? (*zerreist den Zettl*) diſs will ich nicht haben.

Pickl. O Potz schlapperment was macht ihr? mein ladein Zetl zerriſsen vnd Rosalina ist entzwey gerissen? o du schelm.

Romio. Gehe forth oder ich brech dir den Halſs.

Pickl. Ja brich du mir den podex o du bernheuter du du Mörder, wie viel Herrn vnd frawen hast du entzwei gerissen, vnd vmbs leben gebracht.

Romio. Wilt du gehen oder ich will dir füeſs machen.

Pickl. Vnd wan du mir gleich 6 füeſs woltest machen so darf ich nicht mehr heimb, o Potztausendt die Rosalina hat recht ein ritz in der mitten bekommen, o ich armer ladein was werde ich thuen.

Romio. Ich sag gehe.

Pickl. Ich sag be. [*abit*.

Penuol. Auf disen fest, welches Herr Capolet halten wird, wird deine schöne Rosalina auch sein, die du so sehr liebest, mein ich bitte gehe mit mir ich will dir daselbst solche gesichter weisen, die deiner Rosalina weith vorgehen vnd ich weiſs gewiſs daſs die Jenige so du vor deinen schwanen gehalten, soll bey anderer gegenwarth alſs eine Kree auſssehen.

Romeo. 'Invite Don Lucentio and his cousin Amaranta.'

Clown. They live in Cobbler's Lane, opposite the cock-chafer.

Romeo. 'Invite fair Rosaline.' Oh honey-sweet name! Thee do I kiss a thousand times.

Clown. What a fool! to kiss the paper. If he had got the wench he might kiss her where her spine ends.

Romeo. 'Invite Madam Fioleta Catharina.'

Clown. All right, she lives in Sow-alley.

Romeo. 'Invite Madam Flora.'

Clown. What a wench! she always wears a gauze before her face that people may not see her nose; for her nose stands right in the middle of her face.

Romeo. 'Invite Count Paris?' And a gallant cavalier he is.

Clown. True, but he stinks between his toes like a peasant.

Romeo. But tell me, where is this assembly to be?

Clown. At my master's.

Romeo. What is the name of thy master?

Clown. Capulet is his name.

Romeo. What! is my dearest Rosaline to go to the house of my enemy? (*Tears the paper up.*) I won't have that.

Clown. Odds bobs! what are you doing? tearing up my invitation paper, and Rosaline rent asunder! Oh you rogue!

Romeo. Get along with thee, or I'll break thy neck.

Clown. You may break my podex, you idle fellow, you murderer! How many gentlemen and ladies have you torn in pieces and killed!

Romeo. Wilt thou be off? or I will find thee legs.

Clown. And if you would find me six legs at once, I could not go home. Confound your eyes! Rosaline has got a rent right in the middle. Oh poor messenger, what am I to do?

Romeo. I say, go!

Clown. I say, bo! [*Exit*.

Benvolio. At this feast of Capulet's thy fair Rosaline too will appear, whom thou lovest so much. Pray, go with me, I will there show thee faces far superior to Rosaline's, and am quite sure, she whom thou hast taken for thy swan will look a crow in the presence of others.

ROMIO. Du redest nach deinem Belieben, aber meine Rosalina ist allein der stern meines Hertzens, vnd ihrer schönheit müssen alle weichen.

PENUOL. Sie kompt dir nur so schön vor wan kein schönere darbey ist. Höre Romio komb auf diesen fest will ich weisen die best.

ROMIO. Ich will dir zwar folgen aber du wirst mir hierinnen wenig helffen können. [*beyde ab.*

PICKL HÄRING.

PICKL. Ich habe gleichwohl so viel in meinen Poëtischen Kopff gebracht, dafs ich sie alle geladen habe, aufsgenohmen etzliche haben das Zahnwehe starkh aber schadt nicht es bleibt nur desto mehr frefsen über, ich will schon zerschroden ich habe kein Zahnwehe, aber ich versaume nach Haufs zu kommen dan es wird braff angehen, an frefsen vnd sauffen, dan bin ich gehrn darbey, drumb mufs ich lauffen.

ACTUS SECUNDUS.

SCENA PRIMA.
ROMIO. MERCUTIUS. PENUOLIO.

ROMIO. Ihr Herrn habt ihr vernohmen von den grofsen Panquet defs Capolet, darauf erscheindt der beste Adl vnd die schönsten Damen, darunter sich auch die schöne Rosalina befindet, difs ist der Sporn der mich treibt dahin zu kommen meine schöne zu sehen, die da wird glantzen vnd ein vndterscheid wird machen zwischen allen Damen gleich die Sonn gegen den Mon.

MERCUT. Ihr Herrn ich achte wenig dafs Frawen Zimmer, meine frewd ist schlagen vnd balgen, ich will mich lieber 3 mahl schlagen, alfs einmahl einem weibs bild aufwarthen.

ROMIO. Ach Mercutio lege doch einmahl ab deine dolheit, wo ist der, der durch Kragel reich worden, darumb zähme dich, verehre das Frauenzimmer, so wirst du haben Ehr vnd lob.

PENUOL. Ich halt es mit dem Romio, vnd weil dafs Panquet so státtlich, so will vnnfs gebühren einen Pallet oder Mascara darauf zu praesentiren vnd dafs Frauenzimmer damit verehren.

MERCUT. Ich lafs mirs entlich gefallen, aber was wollen wir tantzen?

PENUO. Eine Masquara wie es breuchlich ist.

ROMIO. Vnd ich will verkleidter die fackl tragen.

MERC. Wafs fackl du muest tantzen deiner Rosalina zu gefallen.

ROMEO. You may talk as you please, but my Rosaline is the only star of my heart, and all must give way before her beauty.

BENVOLIO. She appears so fair to thee only when there is none fairer present. Go to that feast, Romeo, I will point out to thee the best.

ROMEO. I will follow thee, yet in this thou wilt afford me little help. [*Exeunt.*

Re-enter CLOWN.

CLOWN. All the same, I crammed so much into my poetical head that I was able to invite them all, except that some few have got the tooth-ache. But never mind; so much the more victuals will come down — I will mounch away, and have no tooth-ache. However I ought to be on my way home; they will take bravely to eating and drinking and then I like to be one of the party; so I must run.

ACT II.

SCENE I.
ROMEO. MERCUTIO. BENVOLIO.

ROMEO. Gentlemen, have you heard of the great banquet of Capulet's which is to be attended by the best nobility and the fairest ladies, fair Rosaline among them? That is the spur that urges me to go there — to see my fair one, who will outshine all the other ladies as the sun does the moon.

MERCUTIO. Gentlemen, I don't care much for women, my delight is fighting and scuffle. I would rather have three fights than once attend upon a woman.

ROMEO. Nay, Mercutio, pray at last lay aside your folly. Who ever grew rich by quarrelling? Restrain yourself, do homage to woman, and you will earn both honour and praise.

BENVOLIO. I side with Romeo. And as the banquet is so magnificent, it will behove us to represent there a ballet or mascara in honour of the ladies.

MERCUTIO. Well, I agree; but what sort of dance shall we perform?

BENVOLIO. A mascara, as the custom is.

ROMEO. And I will disguise myself and bear the torch.

MERCUTIO. What torch! thou must dance to please thy Rosaline.

Romio. Ich kan nicht.
Mercut. Warumb?
Romio. Mein leib vnd füefs sein gantz schwärmüthig.
Mercut. So entlehne des Cupido flügl vnd fliege, ich schwöre wen ich verliebt währe vnd hette nur ein fues so wolte ich doch hupffen.
Penuo. Ey Er last sich schon bereden dem Frawen Zimmer zu gefallen.
Romio. Ihr Herrn mich taucht wür thuen übel das wür hingehen.
Penuol. Warumb das?
Romio. Ich habe heunt einen schwären traum gehabt.
Mercut. Ich glaub fürwahr die Maphas oder truth hat dich getruckt, ich habe auch einen traum gehabt.
Romio. Wafs war es vor ein traum.
Mercut. Mir hat getraumt, dafs alle traum erlogen sein.
Penuo. Ihr Herrn was wür thuen wollen dafs thuen wir bald, vielleicht seind sie schon von der taffel aufgestanden, so kommen wür zu Spath, ich will Euch folgen aber der Himmel gebe dafs kein vnheil daraufs entstehe. [alle ab.

Romeo. I cannot.
Mercut. Why not?
Romeo. My body and feet are quite melancholy.
Mercut. Then borrow wings from Cupid and fly. I swear, if I were in love and had but one foot, I should hop.
Benvol. Aye, he gives in, and is ready to please the ladies.
Romeo. Gentlemen, methinks, we do wrong to go there.
Benvol. How so?
Romeo. I had a heavy dream last night.
Mercut. Really I suppose Maphas or alp has pressed you. I too had a dream.
Romeo. What was yours?
Mercut. I dreamt that all dreams are lies.

Benvol. Gentlemen, whatever we intend to do, let it be done soon. Perhaps they have risen from table and then we shall be too late. I will follow you, but heaven grant that no mischief come of it.
[Exeunt.

SCENA 2ᴰᴬ.

Capolet, Tibolt, Paris, *alle an der taffl.*

Cappolet. Ihr Herrn mich nimbt wunder dafs vnfs Niemand besuecht bey vnserer Mahlzeit, etwan wie gebreuchlich mit einer masquara, da ich noch jung wahr, wahr ich nicht zu faul wie ietziger Zeit die Jungen gesellen, es dörffte kein Panquet geschehen, ich funde mich alle Zeit darbey mit einer Mascara oder sonsten was lustiges.
Fraw. Ja ich glaub es wohl in Eurer Jugendt seit ihr ein grosser Maufshundt gewesen, aber anietzo miest ihr es wohl lassen.
Tibold. Wie lang ist es wohl Herr Vatter dafs Er keine Mascara mehr getantzt?
Cappolet. Dafs kan ich mich nicht mehr erindern wie viel Jahr es seyn.
Tibold. Es ist so lang nicht das mans nicht wissen soll, ich gedenckhe es noch wohl, dafs der Herr Vatter auf der Mabilia ihrer Hochzeit gedanzt.
Cappolet. Es kan sein, in dem alter ist bald alles vergessen.
Tibold. Aber so mich bedunkt so ist schon eine Mascara vorhanden, willkommen Ihr Herrn.

SCENE II.

Capulet. Tibalt. Paris. *All at table.*

Capulet. Gentlemen, I wonder that nobody visits us at supper, as the custom is, with some masquara. When I was young, I was not so lazy as our young fellows are at the present day. There was no banquet I did not attend with some mascara or other frolic.

Lady (Capulet). I readily believe, you have been a mouse-hound in your youth, but now you must leave it off.
Tibalt. How long is it, father, you have not danced a mascara?
Capulet. I cannot remember how many years.

Tibalt. It is not so long ago that one should not know it. I well remember your dancing at Mabilia's wedding.
Capulet. That may be; in my age everything is soon forgotten.
Tibalt. But it appears there is already a mascara. Welcome, gentlemen!

SCENA 3ᵀᴵᴬ.
ROMIO. PENUOLIO.

CAPPOLET. Ihr Herrn sie seind freindlich willkommen in meiner Behausung.

PARIS. Wür seind ihnen höchlich verpflicht vor dise Ehr so sie hierinnen vnſs beweisen.

[*wird getanzt.*

ROMIO. Schönste Dam die Ehr so ich gehabt mit ihr zu tantzen kan weder meine Zung oder Hertz bezeichen, ich bitte sie vergönne doch einen Schambhafften Pilgramb dero Handt zu küssen.

JULIETA. Gueter Pilgramb ihr entheiliget Euch nicht, dan solche bilder wie ich haben Hände zum fühlen vnd lippen zum küssen.

ROMIO. Die Künheit entschuldiget mich dan [*Küſst sie*] vnd nun bin ich aller meiner Sünden loſs.

JULIET. Wie? so hab ich Eure Sünden Empfangen?

ROMIO. Schönste Dam, wan sie es nicht behalten wil, so gebe sie mir dieselbigen wieder. [*Küſt Sie wider.*]

AMMA. Holla was ist das, die fraw Muetter siehts.

JULIETA. Fahret wohl mein Herr.

ROMIO. Fahre wohl du Zierte aller Damen, ach Romio wie bald seind dein Sünn vnd gedanckhen verendert worden [*bist*].

AMMA. Waſs beliebt den Herrn?

ROMIA. Sagt mir was ist das vor eine Damen so mit mir gedanzet?

AMMA. Mein Herr der sie bekommen, wird an gelt vnd guet keinen mangel leiden, sie ist des Herrn Cappolet sein eintzige Tochter.

ROMIO. O Himmel waſs höre ich, deſs Cappolets tochter, wie geschieht mir, mueſs vnd solle ich nun ein liebes gefangener sein der Jenigen deren Vatter mein ärgister todsfeind ist, in wahrheit sie glantzet vnter andern damen herfür wie ein schöner stern, o Rosalina du bist nur der blaſse Mondt gegen diser glantzenden Sonnen.

TIBOLD. Was höre ich, ist das nicht der verfluchte Hundt Romio mein feind vnd darf sich vnterstehen anhero zu kommen, daſs ist nicht zu leiden. Holla Jung mein stoſsdegen her.

CAPPOL. Vetter Tibold waſs ist Euch, warumb rast ihr so?

TIBOLD. Ha solt ich das leiden, das vnser feind anhero kommen vnser Panquet zu verspotten?

CAPPOL. Wer ist es dan?

TIBOLD. Es ist mein feind der Romio, Holla Jung mein stoſsdegen, du Hurn Sohn wo bleibst du so lang.

SCENE III.
ROMEO. BENVOLIO.

CAPULET. Gentlemen, you are welcome in my house.

PARIS. We are deeply indebted to you for the honour you shew us.

[*Dancing.*

ROMEO. Fairest lady, neither my tongue nor my heart can appreciate the honour I have had of dancing with you. Pray, grant a blushing pilgrim your hand to kiss.

JULIET. Good pilgrim, you do not profane yourself; for saints like me have hands to feel and lips to kiss.

ROMEO. Then boldness excuses me, [*kisses her*], and now all my sin is purged.

JULIET. Why? Then I have taken your sin?

ROMEO. Fairest lady, if you won't keep it, give it me back again. [*Kisses her again.*]

NURSE. Hollah! what is that? your lady mother sees it.

JULIET. Farewell, sir!

ROMEO. Farewell, thou ornament of women! Ah Romeo, how soon have your feelings and thoughts changed! [*Aside.*] Whist!

NURSE. What is your pleasure?

ROMEO. Tell me, who is that lady with whom I danced just now?

NURSE. Sir, the man who carries her off, will not want for money and goods. She is my lord Capulet's only daughter.

ROMEO. O Heaven, what do I hear! Capulet's daughter? What has become of me! Must and shall I henceforth be love's captive to her whose father is my most bitter and most deadly foe? In truth she shines above all other ladies like a beautiful star. O Rosaline! thou art but the pale moon to this resplendent sun!

TIBALT. What do I hear! Is not that that accursed dog Romeo, my enemy? And does he dare to come here? That is not to be endured! Fetch me my rapier, boy!

CAPULET. What is the matter with you, cousin Tibalt? Why are you so angry?

TIBALT. What, should I suffer our enemy to come here to scorn our banquet?

CAPULET. Who is it?

TIBALT. It is my enemy Romeo. Hollah boy, my rapier! Thou whore's son, what makes thee so slow?

CAPPOL. Wofern es Romio ist, so ist er vnſs willkommen vnd wür seind ihm höchlich verpflicht vor die Ehr so er vnſs erweist, darumb seit zufriden vnd machet kein Molest.

TIBOLD. Ich will es aber nicht haben.

CAPPOL. Wie wolt ihr es nicht haben, so will ich es aber haben, wer ist Herr im Haufs ich oder ihr?

AMMA. Ja seit ihr Herr im Haufs oder ist der Herr Cappolet Herr im Haufs?

TIBOLD. Gehe du alte Hex oder ich schlage dich an ein Ohr.

AMMA. Ia ia alle zeit wolt ihr nur die weiber schlagen aber ihr habt nicht einmal das Hertz einen Mann anzurühren.

CAPPOL. Ich sage Vetter Tibold fangt mir nichts an in diser gesellschafft oder da stehet die thier vor Euch offen.

TIBOLD. O himmel, was mueſs ich hören, ein freindt soll hinwekh gehen vnd ein feindt hier verbleiben, wollan ich gehe, aber Romio meine Rach sey dir geschworen.
[abit.

CAPPOL. Ich bitte ihr Herrn sie lassen sich des Tibolds raserey nicht verstören sondern verbleiben gehrn alhier.

ROMIO. Wür bedankhen vns für die Ehre so wür genossen die Zeit fordert vnſs wider von hier zu gehen.

CAPPOL. Ich bitte ihr Herrn sie verbleiben.

PENUOL. Komb forth Romio laſs vnſs gehen vnser kurtzweil ist geendet.

PARIS. Wo es möglich so wollen Sie noch verbleiben.

ROMIO. Wir bedankhen vnſs aller Ehre vnd nehmen also abschied.   [abeunt.

CAPPOL. In wahrheit Romio ist höfflich discret vnd jung, es ist mir leid das ich sein feind mues sein.

PARIS. Ich habe offtermahl gewünscht daſs das Haus Cappolet mit Mundige möchte vereinbahret werden, habe auch vernohmen, daſs sich gar die Herrschafft bemühet diſs lebensstreit beyzulegen.

CAPPOL. Es ist deme also Herr Graff, aber Ihro fürstl. Gn. haben es noch nicht proclamiren lassen, so stehet die feindschafft noch bis dato. Herr Graff er wolle ihme belieben lassen weil die Mahlzeit vorbey vnd alle Vrlaub nehmen mit mir ins Zimmer zu gehen, ich habe mehrers mit dero selben zu reden.

PARIS. Ich folge Herr Cappolet, aber schöne Julieta beliebt ihr mit zu kommen.   [abit.

JULIETA. Ich bin schuldig Ihro Gn. auf den fues zu folgen. — Amma gehe sehe vnd frage wer diser gewesen so mit mir gedanzt.

CAPULET. If it be Romeo, he is welcome, and we are deeply indebted to him for the honour he shews us. Therefore be quiet, and do not make any disturbance.

TIBALT. But I won't have it.

CAPULET. Indeed! You won't have it? But I will have it; who is master of the house, I or you?

NURSE. Aye, are you master of the house or is my lord Capulet master of the house?

TIBALT. Be off, old witch, or I shall box your ears.

NURSE. Aye, aye, you always want to beat the women, but you have not the heart to touch a man.

CAPULET. I say, cousin Tibalt, don't make any trouble in this party or there is the door.

TIBALT. O heavens! what must I hear? a friend must go away and an enemy stay! Well then, I will go, but Romeo, I swear you vengeance.   [Exit.

CAPULET. Pray, gentlemen, do not mind the fury of Tibalt, but stay longer.

ROMEO. We thank you for the honour we have enjoyed; our time obliges us to depart.

CAPULET. Pray, gentlemen, stay.

BENVOL. Come Romeo, let us go, our pastime is over.

PARIS. Pray, remain, if possible.

ROMEO. We thank you for all the honour and take our leave.   [Exeunt.

CAPULET. In truth, Romeo is polite, discreet, and young; I am sorry I must be his enemy.

PARIS. I have often wished, the house of Capulet might become reconciled with that of Montague, and hear that even the Prince endeavours to lay this deadly strife.

CAPULET. So it is, Count Paris, but His Grace has not yet issued the proclamation. Therefore the feud stands to this hour. As supper is over, and all the guests taking leave, may it please you to go with me to my cabinet; I have various things to discuss with you.

PARIS. I follow, my lord; but, fair Juliet, be pleased to go with us.   [Exit.

JULIET. I am bound to follow your Grace instantly. — Nurse dear, go and enquire who the gentleman was who danced with me.

AMMA. Ich glaub fürwahr Julieta ist schon verliebt, aber ich will gleichwohl ihren Befehl verrichten.

PENUOL. Ich habe mich verirrt in disem Haus, saget mir wo geht man hinaufs?

AMMA. Mein Herr verzeihe mir, das ich frage, was wahr das vor einer in den rothen Kleid?

PENUOL. Sein Nahmb heifst Romio.

AMMA. Ist es der Junge Romio? ich bedankhe mich mein Herr, dafs er es mir gesagt.

PENUOL. Habt ihr auch noch etwas mehrers zu fragen?

AMMA. Nein mein Herr.

PENUOL. Und ich in der Wahrheit auch nicht.
[abit.

AMMA. Vnd ich auch nicht.

JULIETA. Amma sage bald, wer wahr er, vnd wie ist sein Nahmb.

AMMA. Schöne Julieta, es wahr der Junge Romio.

JULIETA. Wie der Junge Romio?

AMMA. Ja der Junge Romio.

JULIETA. O ein hönig süfser Nahmb, aber es ist ein vergüffter stachel darin verborgen, ach Romio du hast mein Hertz verwund. [abit.

SCENA 4ᵀᴬ.

ROMIO *allein.* *Hernach* PENUOLIO, MERCUTIUS.

ROMIO. Ach Süfser liebesgott, wie veränderst du die Hertzen deiner leib Eigenen, ich liebte Rosalina, vnd nun bin ich ein liebes gefangener worden der überirrdischen Julieta, ich weifs mir nicht zu helffen in disen Irrgarthen, aber stille Romio, da kompt Mercutius vnd Penuolio, ich will mich verbergen vnd ihr gesellschafft fliehen. [abit.

PENUOL. Romio, Vetter Romio.

MERCUT. Wir föhlen den weeg, da ist er nicht her.

PENUOL. Nein er ging disen weeg. Rueff ihn doch Mercutio.

MERCUT. Wohl ich will ihn rueffen, Romio, liebesgefangener, erscheine vor vnnfs alhier, ich beschwöre dich bey Rosalina augen, bey ihren schönen wangen, bey ihren corallinen leffzen, bey ihren Alabasternen Händen, gerathen leib, schönen brüsten, armen, bein, vnd alles was oben vnd vnten an ihr ist, dafs du alhier erscheinest.

PENUOL. Wofern er dich höret, er wird zornig werden.

MERCUT. Warumb soll er zornig werden, ich sage ja nichts das wider seine Rosalina oder ihn sein kan.

PENUOL. Komb lafs vnfs gehen, er begehrt kein

NURSE. Forsooth I believe Juliet is already in love; but I will do her bidding all the same.

BENVOLIO. I have lost myself in this house: can you tell me the way out?

NURSE. Pardon, Sir, my question; who was the gentleman in the red dress?

BENVOLIO. His name is Romeo.

NURSE. Young Romeo? I thank you, Sir, for telling me.

BENVOLIO. Have you anything more to ask?

NURSE. No, Sir.

BENVOLIO. Nor I indeed. [Exit.

NURSE. Nor I.

JULIET. Tell me quick, who he was, and what is his name?

NURSE. Fair Juliet, it was young Romeo.

JULIET. What, the young Romeo?

NURSE. Yes, the young Romeo.

JULIET. Oh a honey-sweet name! but therein lurks a poisoned sting. Ah Romeo, you have wounded my heart. [Exit.

SCENE IV.

ROMEO *alone. Then* BENVOLIO, MERCUTIO.

ROMEO. Ah, sweet Cupid, how dost thou change the hearts of thy lieges! I did love Rosaline and now I have become the love-prisoner of the heavenly Juliet. I know not where to turn in this maze. But silence, Romeo, there Mercutio and Benvolio are coming; I will hide myself and fly their company.
[Exit.

BENVOLIO. Romeo, cousin Romeo!

MERCUTIO. We have come the wrong way; he is not here.

BENVOLIO. No, he went this way; call him, Mercutio.

MERCUTIO. Well, I will call him. Romeo, captive of love, appear before us here! I conjure you by Rosaline's eyes, by her fair cheeks, by her coral lips, her alabaster hands, her lithe body, her beautiful bosom, arms, legs, and every part of her above and below — appear!

BENVOLIO. If he hear you, you will vex him.

MERCUTIO. Why should I? I say nothing against his Rosaline or himself.

BENVOLIO. Come, let us go. He does not desire

andere gesellschafft, alſs die dunkle nacht, die lieb ist blind, darumb halt sie am meisten von der fünsternuſs.

MERCUT. Ich mueſs ihm noch einmal rueffen, Romio! er ligt gewiſs vnter einen baumb, vnd wintschet, das die früchte Rosalina währen vnd ihme in sein schoſs fallen, o wie anmuethig wäre es ihm.

PENUOL. Ey komb, es ist vergeblich den Jenigen zu suechen, welcher nicht will gefunden werden.

[abit.

SCENA 5ᵀᴬ.

ROMIO *mit einem Jung vnd lautten.*

ROMIO. O angenehme gelegenheit, die sicherheit zeigt mir den weeg, weil der frid geschlossen zwischen meinen Herrn Vatter vnd den Capolet, so weiset mich die liebe zu der himmlischen schönheit der Julieta, deren ich mich schon längsten verpflichtet habe, o Julieta die du mein Hertz gefangen haltest, wan du sehen köntest wie dein göttlicher blickh ein fewer in meinem Hertzen entzündet, du wurdest mit etlichen thränen der Ehrbarmmung begieſsen, du kanst meiner Marter nicht gewahr werden, weil du nicht weiſt, das ich dich liebe, ich weiſs deine vortreffliche schönheit, auch weiſs ich daſs ich liebe aber nicht geliebt werde, so seze keinen fues mehr weither Romio, vnd faſs ein Hertz, o liebe ich rueffe dich an stehe mir bey, an disem orth ist nicht weith ihr Schlafgemach, darumb Jung komb her vnd singe daſs gemachte lied.

Lied.
1.
Ach willkommen schönste blumb, aufenthalt so vieller gaben,
Deine tugendt muſs den Ruhm vor allen schönen haben,
Julieta liecht der Zeit, keine Sonn ist dir zu gleichen,
Deiner Zier vnd trefflichkeit miessen alle Damen weichen.

2.
Ach Julieta dein verstand welcher himmlisch ist zu schetzen,
Gib mir nur ein liebespfandt, daſs mich Ewig kan ergetzen.
Julieta du mein Herzt, Julieta mein behagen,
Stille meiner Seelen Schmertz den ich ietzt so starkh mus tragen.

ROMIO. Aber nun o ihr meine augen, schauet an den orth wo eure Sonnen verborgen, o nacht ziehe vor die schwartze Gardin vnd durch eine dunkle wolkhe

---

any other company but the dark night. Love is blind, therefore he takes most to darkness.

MERCUTIO. I must call him once more. Romeo! I am sure he is lying under some tree, and wishing that the fruits were Rosaline and would fall into his lap. How very agreeable he would think that.

BENVOLIO. Come then; it is in vain to seek a man, that does not mean to be found.

[*Exeunt.*

SCENE V.

ROMEO. *A Page with a lute.*

ROMEO. Oh welcome opportunity! safety points to the way. Since peace is concluded between my father and Capulet, love directs me to the heavenly beauty of Juliet, to whom I have long devoted myself. Oh Juliet, thou who hast taken my heart captive, if thou couldst see how thy divine glance kindles a fire in my breast, thou wouldst quench it by some tears of pity. Yet thou canst not be aware of my torment, because thou dost not know that I love thee. I know thy surpassing beauty, I know too that I love but am not loved. Move not then from here, Romeo, and take heart. Love! I invoke thee, assist me! Not far from this spot is her chamber. Come here then, boy, and sing the song I made.

Song.
1.
Welcome to thee fairest flower, of so many gifts the dwelling,
Fame is thine, by virtue's power over all the fair excelling.
Juliet, the light of days, there's no sun to equal thee,
To thy beauty and thy praise, all must yield the victory.

2.
Ah my Juliet thy mind is indeed a heavenly treasure,
Canst thou no love-token find to afford me endless pleasure.
Ah my Juliet, thou my heart, Juliet my consolation,
Still my soul's devouring smart which now I bear without cessation.

ROMEO. But now, ye eyes of mine, gaze at that spot where my sun is hidden. Oh Night, draw the black curtain, and by a dark cloud prevent me from being

halte zuruck dafs erkhennen meiner persohn, ich sehe liecht, darumb will ich wafs näher hinzuetretten, vnd sehen ob ich Etwas vernehmen kan.

JULIETA. Holla was soll dises bedeuten, ein Music vor meinen Kammerfenster? wer soll sich wohl vnterstehen bey nächtlicher weil mir vnruhe zu machen? mein schlaff ist vnterbrochen, die gedankhen sein verwürt, die Natur verhängnus vnd liebes brunst stürmen alle drey über mich zu samben, vnd suechen mein verderben, die natur vnd lieb halten einen streitt in mir, doch will die liebe Meister sein, die natur aber will, dafs ohne ihre gaben kein ding möglich ist zu vollbringen, wan die Krafft der natur nicht währe, wafs wolte doch die liebe thuen, o Romio warumb heist du Romio, mein traum ist aufsgelegt, du bist der Mundigeser den ich in schlaff gesehen, ach Romio verendere den gehesigen Namen, die verhängnufs stürtzet mich, die liebe reget sich, die natur treibet mich, o Romio wann ich an dich gedenkhe, vor frewd ich dir mein liebe schenkhe.

ROMIO. Das stumme wordt der augen thuet seine meinung. Ach könte meine schönste dises aufs meinem gesicht sehen, mein Hertz wurde noch so fröhlich sein, die Hoffnung wird mich blofs erhalten, weil ich verliebet bin.

JULIETA. Wie? wafs seit ihr vor eine bersohn, vnd wie ist euer Nahmb? das ihr euch vnterstehet bey Schlaffender Zeit vnter mein fenster zu kommen?

ROMIO. Mein Nahmb ist (o ihr Götter soll ich mich offenbahren, es seyn Ja.) mein Nahmb, schönste Julieta, ist zwar ein feindseliger Nahmb vnd heist Romio, aber o schöne, sie verendre denselben nach ihren belieben, wan nur mein Hertz stehts zu dero Diensten sein kan.

JULIET. Wafs Romio! o Himmel wie geschiecht mir, ist Romio vorhanden vnd hat mein Klagen gehört? o liebe, liebe, zu was bringst du mich, Romio Romio, seit ihr noch vorhanden vnd habt meine Reden gehört?

ROMIO. Etwas schönste Julieta.
JULIETA. Ach Romio.
ROMIO. Wafs seuffzet sie meine schöne?
JULIETA. Habt ihr
ROMIO. Wafs gebieth sie?
JULIETA. Mein Clagen vernohmen?
ROMIO. Nicht alles.
JULIETA. Ach Romio ich wolte, das ihr nicht wuste, das ich euch liebe.

ROMIO. Worumb schönste Julieta, veracht sie dan meine getrewe liebe, schönste Julieta, womit soll ich dann genugsamb meine getrewe liebe vnd das Innerliche brennende fewer meines Hertzens bezeugen, oder will sie nicht wissen dafs ich sie liebe? wollan so sterbe

recognised. I see a light; I will draw nearer, and try if I can hear anything.

JULIET. Hollah! What does this mean? Music under my window? Who should dare to disturb me at night-time? My sleep is broken, my thoughts disturbed. Nature, fate, and love's fire are violently rushing upon me, and compassing my ruin. Nature and love fight within me, yet love will conquer. But nature will that without her gifts nothing can ever be accomplished. If the power of nature were not, what could love do? Oh Romeo! wherefore is thy name Romeo? My dream is interpreted, thou art the Montague whom I saw in my sleep. Ah, Romeo! change that loathsome name! Fate strikes me down; love moves within me; nature urges me on! Oh, Romeo! when I think of thee, I give thee joyfully my love!

ROMEO. The dumb word of the eyes discourses. Ah, could my fair one read this in my face, my heart would be far more joyous. Hope alone will keep me up, because I am in love.

JULIET. Why? who are you, what is your name, that you dare come under my window at this hour of sleep?

ROMEO. My name is (*aside:* Ye gods, shall I disclose myself? Well, be it so!) my name, fair Juliet, is a hostile name, is Romeo; but, Oh fair one, change it as you like, provided my heart may be in your service.

JULIET. What? Romeo? Oh Heavens! what hath befallen me? Is Romeo present and has heard my wail? Oh, love, love! what dost thou bring me to? Romeo, Romeo! are you still there, and did you hear my words?

ROMEO. Some of them, fairest Juliet.
JULIET. Ah, Romeo!
ROMEO. Why do you sigh, my fair one?
JULIET. Have you —
ROMEO. What is your behest?
JULIET. Have you heard my wailing?
ROMEO. Not all.
JULIET. Ah, Romeo! I wish you did not know I love you.

ROMEO. Why, fairest Juliet, do you despise my true love? How shall I prove sufficiently my true love and the inward burning fire of my heart? Or do you not choose to know that I love you? Well, let me die, and let my tomb be a monument of your virtue. But

ich, vnd mein grab soll sein ein Denkhmahl ihrer tugendt, aber Ey lafs, mein Hertz ist viel zu wenig auf dem Altar einer so übertröfflichen schönheit aufgeopffert zu werden, ach schönste Julieta, acht sie mich dan nicht würdig ihrer liebe in deme sie dafs selbe wider zuruckh wintschet was sie mir versprochen?

JULIET. Werthester Romio, ich wintsche sie darumb wider zuruckh, auf das ich sie noch einmahl widerschenkhen möchte.

ROMIO. Schönste gebietherin, so lafset vns dan eine Verbindnufs vnserer getrewen liebe anietzo aufrichten, dan ich schwöre alhier bey dem hellglanzenden Mond.

JULIET. Ach schwöret nicht bey den wankelmuetigen vnd vnbeständigen Mond.

ROMIO. Ach bey wemb solt ich den schwören?

JULIETA. Schwöret lieber gahr nicht.

AMMA.

AMMA. Julieta, die fraw Muetter rüefft.

JULIETA. Ich komme. Ach Romio macht euch von hier, der orth ist gefährlich, wofern euch meines Vatters Diener alhier solten gewahr werden, dörfften sie euch das leben nehmen.

AMMA. Dafs euch Sanct Velten hol, so geht forth.

JULIET. Ich komm, ich komm, fahret wohl Romio.

ROMIO. Fahret wohl schöne Julieta, es ist mir unmöglich von disen orth zu gehen, mich daucht ich möchte die gantze nacht alhier verbleiben.

JULIETA. Romio Romio, ach Himmel er ist schon forth.

ROMIO. Nein schönste gebietherin, euer getrewester Diener ist noch hier vnd erwarthet dero selben befehl, welchen er in aller Vnterthänigkeit aufzurichten willens ist.

AMMA. Julieta Julieta, wie wirds werden, habt ihr nicht gehört das die fraw Muetter rüefft?

JULIETA. Amma noch ein kleine geduld, ich komme gleich. Edler Romio, ich habe euch etwas offenbahren wollen, aber es ist mir aus den Sünn entfallen.

ROMIO. Ach schönste Julieta, ich bitte sie befriedige mein Hertz mit einer glickseligen Versprechung ihrer gegenlieb.

AMMA. Ey so blaudert das vnd keins mehr, heist das der fraw Muetter gehorsambt? warth ihr werds kriegen.

JULIETA. Nun ich komme ja gleich. Nehmet hin Romio dises von mir, vnd morgen vmb 9 Vhr will ich euch meine meinung wissen lassen.

AMMA. Potz tausendt Schlaper most seit ihr noch da? Ey was denkt ihr? ist dafs nicht ein schand, dafs man das Mensch nicht heimb kan bringen, so gehts

no! My heart is far too mean to be sacrificed on the altar of so surpassing a beauty. Ah, fairest Juliet, do you not think me worthy of your love, that you would take back what you have promised me?

JULIET. Dearest Romeo! I wished it back that I might give it you again.

ROMEO. Fair lady! let us set up a contract of our true love here. For here I swear by yonder splendent moon —

JULIET. Oh swear not by the fickle inconstant moon!

ROMEO. What shall I swear by?

JULIET. Do not swear at all.

Enter NURSE.

NURSE. Juliet! Your mother calls.

JULIET. Anon, good nurse! Oh Romeo, go, the place is dangerous. If my father's servants were to find you here, they might take your life.

NURSE. Zounds! take yourself off!

JULIET. Coming, coming! Farewell, Romeo!

ROMEO. Farewell, fair Juliet! I cannot leave this place; methinks I would rather tarry here all night.

JULIET. Romeo, Romeo! Oh Heavens, he is already gone.

ROMEO. No, fair lady, your most faithful servant is still here and awaits your commands, which he is ready to carry out in due submission.

NURSE. Juliet, Juliet! How will this end! Did you not hear your mother call?

JULIET. Nurse, have a little patience! I am coming directly. Noble Romeo, I was going to reveal something to you but it has escaped me.

ROMEO. Ah, fair Juliet, pray satisfy my heart with a blessed promise of your love.

NURSE. Oh dear, there's no one for chattering like her! Do you call that obeying your mother? You will catch it.

JULIET. Well, I am coming directly. Take this, Romeo, from me, and to-morrow at nine o'clock I will let you know my mind.

NURSE. Confound you! are you still there? What can you be thinking of? Is it not a shame, one cannot bring that wench home! That is the way with the young

mit den jungen Dirnel, wan man ihnen zueläfst ein finger, so wollen sie die gantze Handt haben. Nun geht oder ich sags.

JULIETA. Nun ich komme ja, lebet wohl Romio.
ROMIO. Vnd sie auch schönste Julieta.
JULIETA. Ach Romio. [abit.
ROMIO. Ach Julieta. — Nun gibe dich zufriden Romio, die weillen du gegenliebe verspührest von der vnvergleichlichen Julieta, ich will mich wider nacher Haufs verfügen, dan ich sehe dafs Aurora ihr langes ligen bey dem alten Titon überdrüssig, vnd Phebus fangt an algemach herfür zu brechen vnd seine erröthete wangen aufszubreitten.

PATER.

PATER. Gueten Morgen Herr Romio, wie so fruhe aus dem Schlaff, doch ein Verliebter hat wenig ruhe wan er stehts an seine geliebte Rosalina gedenkt. Wafs macht die guete Rosalina?

ROMIO. Geehrter Herr Pater, sie wissen wie wunderbahrlich sich der Mensch vnd deren gedankhen verändern, so ists mir armen Romio auch geschehen.

PATER. Wie da, wie da Herr Romio?

ROMIO. Rosalina ist längsten aufs meinen Sünn vnd gedankhen, also dafs ich wenig mehr an sie gedenkhe.

PATER. Solches gefalt mir sehr wohl Herr Romio, das er einmahl befrewet worden von dem liebes Joch.

ROMIO. Frey Herr Pater, o nein, ich habe mein Hertz einer andern geben vnd die selbige mich auch mit gegenliebe belohnet.

PATER. O Himmel kan es wohl möglich sein, das ein Mensch so wankelmüetig vnd übel beständig in der liebe sein kan, aber sagt mir Herr Romio, was ist das vor eine die er liebt?

ROMIO. Es ist die schöne Julieta, des Capolets einige Tochter.

PATER. Solches höre ich nicht gehrn, vnd wie ist es möglich seines feindts tochter zu lieben, doch vielleicht will der Himmel dardurch einen frieden beyden Häusern geben, welches mich von Hertzen erfrewen soll, aber ich halte mich zu lang auf, Herr Romio ich wintsche demselben glickh vnd wohlergehens, hat er meinen geistlichen Rath von nöthen so weifs er schon mein Zelt. [abit.

ROMIO. Der Himmel begleite ihn Herr Pater. Nun ist es Zeit mich auch von hier zu begeben, vnd dises guten geistlichen Rathes werde ich wohl von nöthen haben in allen meinen vorgenohmenen werkhen.
[abit.

girls; if you give them a finger, they want the whole hand. Now do you go in, or I tell your mama.

JULIET. Well, I am coming. Good bye, Romeo.
ROMEO. Good bye to you, fair Juliet!
JULIET. Ah, Romeo! [Exit.
ROMEO. Ah, Juliet! — Now thou mayst be satisfied, Romeo, since thou art aware that thy love is returned by the incomparable Juliet. I will return home again, for I observe that Aurora is tired of lying with old Titon, and Phoebus is beginning to break forth, and display his ruddy cheeks.

Enter FRIAR.

FRIAR. Good morning, Romeo! What, up so early? True, a lover has little rest, when he is always thinking of his beloved Rosaline. How is the good Rosaline?

ROMEO. Honoured father! You know how strangely man and his thought change. The same has happened to me, poor Romeo.

FRIAR. How so, how so, Romeo?

ROMEO. Rosaline has long gone out of my mind and memory; I little think of her.

FRIAR. I am much pleased to hear, sir, that you at last are freed from the yoke of love.

ROMEO. Freed, father? Oh, no; I have given my love to another lady, and she rewards me by returning it.

FRIAR. Oh Heavens! is it possible, that a man should be so fickle and inconstant in love! But tell me, sir, who is it whom you are in love with?

ROMEO. It is the fair Juliet, Capulet's only daughter.

FRIAR. I don't like that at all: how is it possible to love the daughter of one's enemy! But may be that God in this way means to give peace to the two houses, which would gladden my heart. But I am tarrying too long, Sir, I wish you luck and prosperity. If you need my spiritual advice, you know my cell.
[Exit.

ROMEO. Heavens be with you, father. It is time for me also to leave this place; I am likely to need this good father's advice in all my enterprises.
[Exit.

ACTUS TERTIUS.

SCENA PRIMA.
Fraw *mit* Amma.

Fraw. Amma!

Amma. Waſs beliebt ihr gnädige Frau?

Fraw. Sagt mir wo ist vnser tochter Julieta? befindt sie sich noch wohl bey ihrer gesundtheit?

Amma. Sie ist, gnädigste Fraw, bey gueter gesundtheit, vnd thuet nichts alſs büecher lesen.

Fraw. Es ist guet, aber sagt vnnſs Amma soll sie nicht schon alt genug sein einen Mann zu nehmen?

Amma. Ist mir recht gnädige Fraw, so ist sie schon in den 16ten Jahr, dan ich weiſs mich noch wohl zu entsinnen wie lang ich ihr gewarthet hab.

Fraw. Noch nicht gahr 16 Jahr? Amma rueffet sie zu mir, ich hab mit ihr zu reden.

Amma. Alsobald gnädige Fraw will ich rueffen, Julieta süſses turtelteublein, fürwahr ich mag sie wohl so nennen, dan sie ist so fromb vnd angenehmb alſs ein turtelteublein. Julieta kompt herfür, die Frau Muetter puefft euch.

SCENA 2ᴅᴀ.
Julieta.

Julieta. Geliebte Fraw Muetter, in gehorsamb erschein ich, was hat sie mit mir alſs dero gehorsamben tochter zu befehlen?

Fraw. Liebes Kind Julieta, du hast einen sorgfeltigen Vatter.

Julieta. Warumb das Frau Muetter?

Fraw. Darumb daſs dein Vatter sorgfeltig ist gewesen in auferziehung deiner Jugendt, so will er auch sorgfeldig sein in wachstumb deiner Jahren vor dich sorg zu tragen, vnd weil du mannbahr, hat er dir einen wackhern gaualier aufserkoren, den du heyrathen solst.

Julieta. Wie Fraw Muetter, meine Jahr sein noch zu wenig mich in eine würthschafft zu schickhen, vnd einen Mann zu nehmen.

Fraw. Du wirst deines Vatters gebott nicht verwerffen, sondern waſs er von dir haben will in obbacht nehmen, da ist kein entschuldigung gültig deinem Vattern zu widerstreben, er tragt sorg für dich vnd dir einen dapfferen gaualier aufserkoren, nemblich den Graff Paris, darumb sage mir deine Meinung.

Julieta. Wie Fraw Muetter? ich lebe in der gehorsamb, vnd bitte mich mit heyrathen nicht zu zwingen.

Muetter. So lebst du mir vnd deinen Vatter zu wider.

ACT III.

SCENE I.
Lady Capulet *with* Nurse.

Lady. Nurse!

Nurse. What is your ladyship's pleasure?

Lady. Tell me, where is my daughter Juliet? is she still in good health?

Nurse. She is in good health, my lady; and does nothing but read books.

Lady. That is well. But tell me, nurse, don't you think her old enough to take a husband?

Nurse. If I am not mistaken, my lady, she is already turned fifteen; for I remember well how long I have waited on her.

Lady. Not quite sixteen? Nurse, call her, I have something to talk over with her.

Nurse. I will call her at once, my lady; — Juliet, you sweet little dove! — Forsooth I may call her that, for she is as good-tempered and as gentle as a turtle. — Juliet, come! your mother wants you.

SCENE II.
Juliet.

Juliet. Dear mother, in duty I appear before you: what commands have you for your obedient daughter?

Lady. Juliet, my dear child, thou hast a careful father.

Juliet. Why mention that, dear mother?

Lady. Because thy father, careful as he has been in bringing thee up, will be equally so in providing for thee according to thy age; and as thou art marriageable he has chosen for thee a gallant cavalier whom thou art to marry.

Juliet. Why, mother, my years are still too few to fit me for the conduct of a household and the married state.

Lady. Thou wilt not reject the command of thy father, but observe what he requires of thee. There is no excuse for opposing a father. He cares for thy welfare, and has selected a gallant cavalier, Count Paris. Now tell me thy mind.

Juliet. Why, mother, I live in obedience, but pray do not force me to marry.

Lady. Then thou livest in opposition to me and to thy father.

JULIET. Fraw Muetter nein, ich bin geboren zu gehorsamben aber mit heyrathen zu uerschonen.

MUETTER. Wie tochter Julieta? du solst dich glickselig schätzen einen solchen gaualier wie Graff Paris ist zu bekommen.

JULIETA. Liebste Fraw Muetter, verschonet meiner Jugendt vnd schlaget solche gedanckhen aufs den Sünn, dann der gehorsamb meiner Eltern zu folgen, achte ich mehr alfs eine Princessin zu sein.

MUETTER. Julieta du bist halfsstärrig, deiner Sünnen verruckt, aber stille, da kompt dein Herr Vatter, siehe zue wie er deine wörter annehmen wird.   [Abit.

SCENE 3^{TIA}.
CAPOLET.

CAPOL. Wie ists liebes Kind Julieta? Hast du die meinung deiner Fraw Muetter verstanden?

JULIE. Ja gn. Herr vnd Vatter, ich habe es wohl verstanden, aber ich bitte in der Jugendt meiner Jahren mich zu uerschonen einen Mann zu nehmen, dan mir gebühren will noch meinen Eltern zu gehorsamben.

CAPUL. Julieta, mir ist wissendt dein gehorsamb von Jugendt auf, darumb ich dir nicht übel rathen, sondern wohl versorgen will.

JULIE. Herr Vatter, die Meriten des Graff Paris seind nicht verwerfflich, aber ich bitte mit heyrathen mich zu uerschonen.

CAPOL. Wie, widerspenstige tochter, wilst du auch anfangen ein vngehorsambes Kind zu werden?

JULIET. Ach nein gn. Herr vnd Vatter der gehorsamb ist mein glickh, die Ehre mein Reuchthumb, wan es ja nach meiner Eltern willen gehen soll, so bitte ich vmb bedenckh Zeit, damit solches mit wohl bedachtem mueth vnd reiffen verstandt geschehen möge.

CAPUL. Wollan dan, liebe tochter Julieta, bedenckhe dich vndt erfrewe deinen Vatter mit einem frölichen Ja, den Graff Paris zu haben.   [abit.

SCENA 4TA.
AMMA.

JULIET. Fahret wohl Herr Vatter, ich will wafs einer gehorsamben tochter gebühren will, verrichten. Aber Ey, lafs armseelige Julieta, wafs wirstu anfangen in dem du dein Hertz schon den Romio gegeben. Ach Romio komb vnd erledige deine armselige Julieta von den Zwang diser Heyrath, aber Amma ich habe dir eine sach zu offenbahren wofern du mir getrew vnd verschwigen sein wilst.

AMMA. Schönste Julieta habe ich nicht mehr ver-

JULIET. No, mother, I am born to be obedient but also to be excused marrying.

LADY. Why, my daughter, thou shouldst consider thyself fortunate to get a cavalier like Count Paris.

JULIET. Dearest mother, have pity on my youth, and give up all such thoughts; for I think it more to be obedient to my parents than to be a princess.

LADY. Juliet, thou art obstinate, thy mind is perverted. But silence! there comes thy father. Now you will see how he will take thy words.   [Exit.

SCENE III.
CAPULET.

CAPULET. Well, my dear Juliet? Hast thou understood the opinion of thy lady mother?

JULIET. Yes, my gracious lord and father, I have quite understood it, but pray for the sake of my youth that you will excuse me from taking a husband, for it is more fitting that I should still remain under the authority of my parents.

CAPULET. Juliet, I well know thy obedience from childhood; therefore I will not advise thee ill, but well provide for thee.

JULIET. My lord and father, the merits of Count Paris are unexceptionable; but I pray you to excuse me from marrying.

CAPULET. Why, thou headstrong girl, wilt thou also turn a disobedient child?

JULIET. Oh no, my gracious lord and father, obedience is my happiness, chasteness my fortune. If the will of my parents is to be carried out, I pray for respite that the thing may be done with consideration and mature judgment.

CAPULET. Well, my dear daughter, reflect upon it, and cheer thy father with a cheerful assent to take Count Paris.   [Exit.

SCENE IV.
JULIET. NURSE.

JULIET. Farewell, father! I will perform what behoves a dutiful daughter. But, alas, wretched Juliet! what art thou to do, now that thou hast already given thy heart to Romeo? Ah, Romeo, come and deliver thy poor Juliet from the constraint of this marriage. — Look here, nurse, I have something to reveal to you, provided you will be faithful to me and secret.

NURSE. Fair Juliet, do I not enjoy more confidence

trawen bey ihr alſs dises? offenbahret mir was ihr wolt, es wird bey mir sicher verschwigen bleiben, alſs ob ihr es einen stein vertrawet.

JULIE. So wisse dan, seid der Zeit ich mit Romio gedanzt, ist mein Hertz also in liebe gegen ihm verstrickhet, daſs wofern ich nicht heylsambe mittel finden werde, so ist es vmb mich geschehen, darumb sage mir Amma, wilst du mir etwas zu gefallen thuen.

AMMA. Wie Julieta? was gedenkt ihr? Romio ist ja euer Erztfeindt, darumb währe mein rath ihr verläſst ihn, vnd verheyrathet euch mit Graff Paris.

JULIE. Hinweckh mit deinen Rath, gedenkhe nicht mehr daran, dan ich schwöre, wofern ich nicht Romio für einen Mann bekomme, so ist es schon geschehen, vnd ich will mein vnglickh so ich anietzo fühle noch ärger machen alſs es ist.

AMMA. Wollan Julieta, weil ich den ernst bey ihr verspüre, so will ich alles verrichten, waſs sie mir befehlen wird.

JULIE. So gehe alsobald zu Romio, vnd vermelde ihm, daſs er sich vnfehlbar wan er sich meinen Eheman nennen wil vmb 9 Vhr in defs Paters Zelt befinde, alda ich mich mit ihm will vermählen oder trauen lassen, verricht es wol, sey verschwigen, eine guete belohnung wirst du zu gewarthen haben. [abit.

AMMA. Geliebte Julieta, ich bedankhe mich ihrer Zuneigung, ich gehe vnd verrichte waſs sie mir befohlen hat. [abit.

SCENA 5ᵀᴬ.

MERCUTIUS. PENUOLIO.

MERCU. Es nimbt mich groſs wunder daſs Romio nicht anzutreffen sey, sage mir Penuolio, ist er zu Hauſs zu finden?

PENUO. Nein zu Hauſs ist er nicht, ich habe mit seinen Diener geredt, der weiſs eben so viel von ihm alſs ich vnd du.

MERCU. Wo zum Krankheit muefs er sich dan verstekht haben?

PENUO. Tipold, des Capolets Vetter, hat Romio einen Brief geschrieben vnd denselbigen in seines Vatters Haufs geschickht.

MERCU. So ist gewiſs ein duell oder aufsforderungsbrieff.

PENUO. Du hast es errathen, und Romio will ihn beandtwortten.

MERCU. Das glaub ich wohl, ein Jeder der schreiben kan, kan auch einen brieff beandtwortten.

PENUO. Nein, Romio will ihn beandtwortten mit den Degen in der Faust.

with you? Reveal to me whatever it may be: it shall remain as secret with me as if you had confided it to a stone.

JULIET. Know ye then, that since the day I danced with Romeo my heart is entangled in love to him and that I am undone unless some remedy be found. Therefore tell me, nurse, will you do something to oblige me?

NURSE. Why Juliet! What are you thinking about? Romeo is your enemy; therefore my advice is you leave him and marry Count Paris.

JULIET. Away with your advice! don't think of it: for I swear, unless I get Romeo for my husband I am undone, and will make my present misery still worse than it is.

NURSE. Well, Juliet! since I see you are in earnest, I will perform whatever you command me to do.

JULIET. Then go at once to Romeo, and tell him, that if he wants to call himself my husband he should be at the father's cell to-morrow at nine o'clock, where I will be married to him. Do your errand well, be secret, and you may expect a good reward. [Exit.

NURSE. Dear Juliet, I am sensible of your affection, I will go and do what you have ordered.
[Exit.

SCENE V.

MERCUTIO. BENVOLIO.

MERCUT. I am much surprised, that I cannot find Romeo. Tell me, Benvolio, is he to be met with at his own house?

BENVOL. No, he is not at home, I have spoken to his servant, and he knows as much of him as I and you do.

MERCUT. Where the deuce can he be hiding?

BENVOL. Tibalt, Capulet's cousin, has written him a letter, and sent it to his father's house.

MERCUT. It is a duel to be sure or a challenge.

BENVOL. You are right, and Romeo is going to answer it.

MERCUT. Very likely; a man who can write, can also answer a letter.

BENVOL. No, Romeo intends to answer sword in hand.

MERCU. Ach armer Romio du bist schon halbtodt, dan er ist geschossen mit einem pfeil von einen blinden Knaben, vnd wie soll er bestehen mit den Tipold zu fechten.

PENUO. Vnd wafs ist dan Tipold?

MERCU. Nichts mehr als ein Katzen König der

PENUO. Wafs der?

MERCU. Der viel prallens aber wenig Hertz hat.

PENUO. Das ist wahr, aber stille da kombt Romio.

ROMIO.

MERCU. Warth ich will ihm einen grues auf franzesisch bringen, Monsieur Monsieur Romio, das ist franzesisch, Romio, vor den gestrigen Schimpff den du vnfs gegeben.

ROMIO. Ihr Herrn verzeiht es mir, ich weifs nichts darumb.

MERCU. Ja Ja du hast recht sagen deine gedankhen sein nur an Rosalina, ich weifs es gahr zu wohl.

ROMIO. Ja Ja glaub es nur, ich verstehe dein Schertz auch gahr zu wohl.

SCENA 6TA.

AMMA.

MERCU. Wafs zum Henkher kompt da vor eine Hex?

AMMA. Ich gehe lauff vnd renn, vnd sueche den Herrn Romio, kan ihm aber nicht antreffen, aber hier stehen wakhere Herren, die will ich fragen ob sie mich nicht berichten können wo Herr Romio anzutreffen, mein Herr auf ein wordt, ist nicht in diser gesellschafft Herr Romio?

ROMIO. Geehrte Fraw, ich bin es selber nach dem sie fragt vnd mein Nahmb heist Romio.

AMMA. Ach Herr Romio ich bring ihm Zeitung, das er sich bey der Julieta zur Mahlzeit einfinden soll.

MERCU. Wafs will das alte Mütterlein?

PENUO. Sie redt von einer Mahlzeit, sie wird gewifs Romio auff ein Panquet laden.

MERCU. Nichts anders, so mag er kommen nach seinem belieben, ihr Herrn mir falt eine Verrichtung ein, darumb adio, ich gehe von hier.   [abit.

AMMA. Mein Herr wafs gibt er mir vor ein andtwordt, das ich eylents meine botschafft verrichten kan.

ROMIO. Geliebte Fraw, ich werde mich gehorsamb einfinden, vnd gehorsamb aufwarthen.

AMMA. Wollan ich gehe, die Herren werffen kein Vngnad auf mich.   [abit.

ROMIO. Penuolio warumb lachstu?

PENUO. Ich lache nicht sondern weine vielmehr.

MERCUT. Poor Romeo! he is already half killed; for he is hit by an arrow of the blind boy, and how is he to stand a fight with Tibalt!

BENVOL. And what is Tibalt then?

MERCUT. He is nothing more or less than a catsking, a —

BENVOL. A what?

MERCUT. A hectoring fellow with little courage.

BENVOL. True, but there comes Romeo.

Enter ROMEO.

MERCUT. Look here, I will salute him in French. Monsieur, Monsieur Romeo! That is French, Romeo, in exchange for the insult you offered us yesterday.

ROMEO. Pardon, gentlemen, I am not aware of any.

MERCUT. It is all very well to say your thoughts are all with Rosaline; I know it well enough.

ROMEO. Depend upon it, I also understand your joke well enough.

SCENE VI.

NURSE.

MERCUT. What, the deuce is that witch coming here?

NURSE. I am running about to look for Mr. Romeo, but cannot meet with him. But there are some gallant cavaliers; I will ask them where to find him. — Sir, one word; is not Mr. Romeo one of this company?

ROMEO. Madam, I am the person for whom you enquire; Romeo is my name.

NURSE. Ah, Sir Romeo! I bring you a message, that Juliet wants you to dinner.

MERCUT. What does that old woman want?

BENVOL. She talks of dinner; to be sure she has come to invite Romeo to a banquet.

MERCUT. Nothing else; he may go if he likes. Gentlemen, I remember some business; so adio, I will take my leave.   [*Exit.*

NURSE. Sir, what is your answer? Tell me, that I may do my errand without loss of time.

ROMEO. My dear madam, I shall come obediently and wait upon you obediently.

NURSE. Very well, I go, and command myself to your favour.   [*Exit.*

ROMEO. Benvolio, what art thou laughing at?

BENVOL. I am not laughing, — rather crying.

Romio. Warumb das?

Penu. Vmb dafs, das dir dein armes Hertz also geängstigt ist.

Romio. Ach du wurdest es noch härtter kränkhen mich weither zu vexiren, Adieu darumb fahre wohl.

Penuo. Nein, ich will mitgehen, mich also zu uerlassen thuest du vnrecht.

Romio. So schertze nicht mehr, mein Hertz ist ohne dafs mit überflüfsiger betrübnufs überladen.

Penuo. Deine Seuffzer vnd traurigkeit geben zu erkhennen, das dir etwas mangelt.

Romio. Wafs manglen, ich weifs von keinen Seuffzen vnd Klagen.

Penuo. Nein bekhenne vnd sage mir, du bist verliebt vnd dein Hertz ist zertheilt.

Romio. Etwas hast du errathen, dafs mein Hertz nicht mehr mein sondern einer andern gehörig.

Penuo. So viell könt ich wohl merkhen aufs deiner traurigkeit, dafs du verliebt wahrest.

Romio. Ich bestehe dir Penuolio, dafs die Jenige so ich liebe auch schön ist.

Penuo. Ein schönes Zihl, darnach man pflegt zu schiefsen ist am ersten getroffen.

Romio. Ey lafs Penuolio eben dafs quälet mein Hertz, das ich Ihrer Liebe nicht theilhafftig werden kann.

Penuo. So hat sie dan geschworen allezeit keusch zu leben?

Romio. So viel mir bewust so hasset sie viel mehr das Mannsgeschlecht alfs zu lieben.

Penuo. So folge meinen Rath vnd denkhe nicht mehr an sie.

Romio. Nicht an sie gedenkhen? ach so wurde mein leben auch sich bald enden.

Penuo. Herr Vetter gebet euren Augen die freyheit, vnd erwehlet eine andere, dan es gibt ja nicht Händt sondern länder voll weibsbilder.

Romio. Ich sehe dein Schertzen kan mir nicht helffen, drumb verlafs ich dich vnd bleibe der verliebte vnd betrübte Romio. [*abit.*

Penuo. Nein ich folge dir, vnd will mich befleifsen dein Doctor zu sein, bifs ich ein gewisses recept zu deiner traurigkeit finde. [*abit.*

SCENA 7MA.

Julieta. Amma.

Julie. Liebste Amma wafs bringt ihr mir von meinen Romio guete oder befse Zeitung, dan mich verlangt zu wissen, wafs er euch vor eine andtwortt gegeben.

Romeo. What for?

Benvol. For thy poor heart being so tormented.

Romeo. Thou wouldst not mind adding to its torments merely for the sake of chafing me. Adieu then, farewell.

Benvol. No I shall go with thee; thou art wrong to leave me thus.

Romeo. Then leave off joking; my heart is already overburdened with sorrow.

Benvol. Thy sighing and despondency show that there is something the matter with thee.

Romeo. What should be the matter? I know nothing of sighing nor lamenting.

Benvol. No, confess and tell me, thou art in love, thy heart is divided.

Romeo. So far thou art right that my heart is no longer mine, but belongs to some one else.

Benvol. So much I could perceive from thy sadness, that thou art in love.

Romeo. I confess to thee, Benvolio, that she whom I love, is also handsome.

Benvol. A handsome mark to shoot at is most easily hit.

Romeo. Alas, Benvolio, it is just that which torments my heart, that I cannot gain her affection.

Benvol. Has she, then, sworn to remain chaste?

Romeo. As far as I know she rather hates our sex than loves it.

Benvol. Then take my advice and do not think of her any longer.

Romeo. Not think of her! there would soon be an end of my life.

Benvol. Cousin, set thy eyes free and choose another woman; there are handfuls, nay countryfuls of them.

Romeo. Thy playfulness cannot aid me; I leave thee remaining what I am, Romeo in love and in sadness. [*Exit.*

Benvol. No I will follow thee, and try to be thy doctor till I have found out a certain prescription for thy sadness. [*Exit.*

SCENE VII.

Juliet. Nurse.

Juliet. What news, good or bad, do you bring me from my Romeo? I long to know what answer he sends.

AMMA. Er redt gleich wie es einen Ehrlichen Jungen gesellen zuestehet.

JULIETA. Wie Amma, wafs saget ihr? Er redt gleich wie es einen Jungen gesellen zuestehet, pfuy schänet euch er ist ein gaualier vnd kein gemeine persohn.

AMMA. Hoho, verdrüst Euch dises dafs ich ihn einen Jungen gesellen heifs, gehet ein andermahl selber, bringt ihm die bottschafft, hernach mögt ihr ihn nennen wie ihr wolt.

JULIET. Ey liebe Amma nicht so zornig, es wahr nur mein Schertz mit euch also zu reden, drumb sagt mir geschwind, was sagt mein lieber Romio?

AMMA. Ach wafs soll er sagen?

JULI. Wie wolt Ihr mich noch länger aufhalten mich zu quälen.

AMMA. Ey nun er sagt

JULI. Vnd was sagt er?

AMMA. Er weifs selber nicht ob er krankh oder gesundt sey.

JULIE. Ach der Himmel bewahre ihn.

AMMA. Ich muefs euch doch nicht gahr erschröckhen, er sagt, er will nach ihren Befehl zu leben wissen.

JULI. So will er kommen?

AMMA. Ich hab schon gesagt, ja ia er will kommen, seit ihr darmit zufriden?

JULI. Ach ja liebe Amma, bedankhe mich vor dise fröliche Zeitung ich gehe ihn zu erwarthen, vnd euer recompens könt ihr bey mir abholen. [abit.

AMMA. So so, ist das mein Dankh vor mein Mühe vnd lauffen, warth ein andersmahl will ichs bleiben lassen, dan wer das trinkhgelt in Händen hat, da richten sie die bosten selber aus, aber ich gehe vnd will sehen, wafs das verliebte frewlein Julieta noch wird anfangen.
[abit.

SCENA 8.

PATER. ROMIO.

PATER. Herr Romio, die sachen so er mir vorgetragen seind schwär der Vernunfft nach, bedenkh er sich, das ich alfs ein Priester nicht thuen kan mit recht nach seinen begehren, in deme dero Eltern von disen allen keine wissenschafft haben.

ROMIO. Geehrter Herr Pater, es ist aber mein vnd der Julieta willen, vnd ehe sie sich will zwingen lassen den Graff Paris zu ehligen, will sie lieber sterben, darumb were mein bitt, sie wollen alhier ein mittel finden vnd disen gefälligen werkh beyhülff leisten.

PATER. Sohn Romio difs sein schwär sachen zu thuen, dennoch euch zu lieb, wofern Julieta auch zu-

NURSE. He speaks as it behoves an honest young fellow.

JULIET. Why, nurse, how can you talk so? He speaks as it behoves an honest young fellow! For shame! He is a cavalier, not a common person.

NURSE. Oho! If you take it amiss that I call him a young fellow, go yourself another time, be your own messenger; after that you may call him as you like.

JULIET. Ay, dear nurse, don't be angry. It was but my joke. Now be quick and tell me, what does my dear Romeo say?

NURSE. Why, what should he say?

JULIET. How can you keep me in suspense, and tease me so?

NURSE. Well, he says ...

JULIET. What is it he says?

NURSE. He does not know himself whether he is well or ill.

JULIET. May Heaven protect him!

NURSE. I must not frighten you too much. He says he will know how to live according to your commands.

JULIET. He will come then?

NURSE. I told you yes, he will. Are you satisfied?

JULIET. Yes, nurse dear; thanks for these glad tidings. I go to await him; you may call for your reward. [Exit.

NURSE. Ahem! are these the thanks for my trouble and running about? Next time I shall let it alone. For when I have once got my glove-money in my hand, they may do their errands themselves. But let me go and see what that love-stricken girl Juliet is about.
[Exit.

SCENE VIII.

FRIAR. ROMEO.

FRIAR. Sir, the matter you have broached to me is difficult; that stands to reason. Remember that, being a priest, I cannot in duty do what you desire, as your parents are ignorant of all this.

ROMEO. But, Reverend Sir, it is my and Juliet's will; and sooner than marry Count Paris, she will die. Therefore my prayer is you would devise some means, and lend your aid to such agreeable business.

FRIAR. My son, these are difficult things to do. However, to please you, and provided Juliet agrees,

friden, wollen wür sehen, wie der sach zu thuen, dan es will sich gebühren der Julieta freywillige meinung auch zu uernehmen, darumb lasset sie wissen wan sie willens ist mich sambt Euch zu besuechen.

ROMIO. Sie ist, hochgeehrter Herr Pater, willens vmb 9 Vhr alhier zu erscheinen, dan sie mir solches durch ihre Amma hat wissen lassen.

PATER. Wohl dan Herr Romio, so wird er sich der geduld gebrauchen, wie ist die Zeit vorhanden, dan wollen wir sehen, was einen geistlichen Priester wohl ansteht zu thuen, hiermit fahre er wohl Herr Romio, ich verfüge mich in mein Zelt. [abit.

ROMIO. Vnd ich befehle mich in seine freindtschafft vnd wohlgewogenheit. Ach glickhseeliger Romio, will dir dan der Himmel die überirtische Julieta schenkhen, ach ja die gunst ihr schönheit versicheret mich solches, wollan dan ich gehe dem Himmel zu dankhen, dafs dise Himmels Stundt mich der schönen Julieta zu einen Mann beglickhseeligen möge. [abit.

PARIS. CAPULET. JULIETA.

PARIS. Herr Capulet, ihm ist wissendt die lieb vnd affection so ich zu seiner tochter trage, entlich von ihme Herr Capulet ein gewintschtes Ja vnd andtwort zu empfangen, weil mein gröstes Verlangen nichts anders alfs seine Tochter zu meiner Gemahlin empfangen werde.

CAPU. Herr Graff, die' lieb vnd affection so ich zu dero Haufs trage versichert mich, dafs ich meine Tochter Julieta keinem gaualier von Meriten alfs ihnen Herr Graff verehren, vnd schenkhen kan, dardurch mein altes Stammenhaufs glickhseelig zu machen.

PARIS. Herr Capulet, das gewintschte Ja so ich von Ihm empfange, wird ein vrsach sein dafs ich ihm vnd die seinigen ieder zeit auf lebenslang mich verobligiert vnd dienstbahr befinden werde.

CAPU. Ich bedankhe mich Herr Graff, vor dero affection, ich werde thuen, was einem Vatter wohl anständig ist, darumb bitte ich Herr Graff er wolle auch das Jawordt von meiner gehorsamben Tochter Julieta empfangen, welche eben zu rechter Zeit anhero kompt. Geliebtes Kindt Julieta, hier hab ich mit Graff Paris die vndterredung deiner bersohn halber gethan, du wirst dirs gefallen lassen disen tapffern gaualier vor deinen Eheherrn zu erkiesen, dadurch wirst du mich vnd deine Muetter glickseelig machen.

JULI. Wafs mein Herr Vatter thuet, das ist auch mein gehorsamb vnd will.

PARIS. Schönste Julieta, von dero Herrn Vatter vnd fraw Muetter habe ich das Jawordt erhalten sie vor

we will see how to manage it; for it is right that I should learn the free opinion of Juliet. Therefore let her say at what time she would like to come with you to visit me.

ROMEO. She intends, reverend Father, to make her appearance here at nine o'clock: she sent me word to that effect by her nurse.

FRIAR. Well then, Sir Romeo, you must have patience. In due time we shall see what it may become a priest to do. Meanwhile, good bye, Sir Romeo, I will go to my cell. [Exit.

ROMEO. And I commend me to your friendship and goodwill. Ah fortunate Romeo! will Heaven then really grant thee that heavenly Juliet? Ah yes, the favour of her beautiful face assures me of it. Well then, I will go and thank Heaven that that heavenly hour may make me the blessed husband of the fair Juliet.
[Exit.

PARIS. CAPULET. JULIET.

PARIS. Sir, you are aware what love and affection to your daughter makes me long for your consent, since my greatest desire is no other than to obtain your daughter for my wife.

CAPUL. My lord, the love and affection I bear your house is a guarantee that I cannot give away my daughter Juliet to any other cavalier of merit than yourself, if I would ensure the happiness of my ancient race.

PARIS. The much desired Yes which I have received from you will make me your debtor, and place me at the service of yourself and your house for the rest of my life.

CAPUL. I thank you, my lord, for your affection. I shall do what becomes a father; I pray you therefore accept the consent of my dutiful daughter Juliet who is making her appearance just in time. Dear child, I have just conversed with Count Paris on thy behalf. Thou wilt be pleased to choose this gallant cavalier for thy husband, for thus wilt thou make me and thy mother quite happy.

JULIET. What my lord and father does, is also my obedience and will.

PARIS. Beautiful Juliet, I have got the consent of both your father and mother to make you my beloved

meine liebste vnd gemahlin zu nehmen, so verhoffe ich auch das meine lieb vnd affection bey dero Schönheit platz vnd statt finden werde.

JULI. Herr Graff, wie vor vermeld, waſs meiner Eltern befehl, ist auch mein will vnd alſs einer gehorsamben tochter haben Sie mit mir zu befehlen.

CAPUL. Du thuest wohl daran liebe tochter, der Himmel wird dir auch sein gnad vnd seegen geben, vnd hiermit Herr Graff überreiche ich ihm meine Tochter, er empfange sie von meiner Handt.

PARIS. Ich bedankhe mich Herr Capulet vor dises edle Kleinod, vnd sie, schönste Julieta erkhenne ich vor meine Gebietherin, vnd alles, waſs Graff Paris vermag, erwehle ich sie vor eine gebietherin aller meiner Bar vnd Habschafft.

JULI. Herr Graff ich bedankhe mich, ich werde wissen zu leben vnd schuldigste Dienstleistung erzeigen.

PARIS. Wollan dan, ich gehe vnd verlasse sie, damit alle praeparatoria zu vnseren beyläger auf das ehiste verfertiget werden, vnd also adie Herr Capulet. [abit.

CAPU. Herr Graff, ich befehle mich dero selben vnd werde zu disem vorgenohmenen werkh nichts ermanglen lassen. So Adie Tochter Julieta, folge mir vnd erfrewe deine fraw Muetter. [abit.

JULI. Ich folge Herr Vatter. [abit.

PATER. ROMIO. JULIETA.

PATER. Kommet herr meine Kinder, in deme ich von euch nach genügen verstanden wie die sach beschaffen, aber bedrachte solche hoche sachen besser, damit ich mich sambt euch in keine gefahr vnd Vnglickh stürtzen möge.

JULIET. Herr Pater ich habe ihm geoffenbahret meiner Elter Meinung, die gäntzlich haben wollen den Graff Paris zu nehmen, welches ich aber bey mir beschlossen nicht zu thuen, sondern Romio meine getrewe liebe zu schenkhen, darumb bitte ich daſs wür beide durch euere Hülff möchten vermählet werden.

ROMIO. Vnd ich desselben gleichen bitte Herr Pater, er wolle keinen aufschub machen, weillen vnser beyder ein Hertz vnd Sünn, so empfange sie hier o schönste Julieta disen ring, welches ein Zeichen vnd Verbindnus seyn, ihr alſs meinen Schatz biſs in mein grab getrew zu verbleiben.

JULIET. Vnd hier werthester Romio, nehmet disen von meiner Handt, auch das Hertz zugleich, welches euer eigen biſs vnſs der todt scheiden kan, vnd nun Pater mangelt nichts weither, alſs eure mühe der Copulation.

wife; let me hope that my love and affection will find a place also with your beauty.

JULIET. My lord, as I have said before, whatever may be the command of my parents is my will also; you may dispose of me as of an obedient daughter.

CAPUL. In that thou dost well, my dear daughter. Heaven grant thee its grace and blessing! And there, my lord, I give you my daughter; receive her from my hand.

PARIS. I thank you, Sir, for this noble jewel; and you, fair Juliet, do I acknowledge for my mistress, and as far as Count Paris can, do I choose you for the mistress of all my fortune.

JULIET. I thank you, my lord; I shall know how to conduct myself and shew you all my bounden duty.

PARIS. Well then, I will go, and leave you to see all the preparations made for our wedding as speedily as possible. Adieu, my lord Capulet. [Exit.

CAPUL. My lord, I commend me to you, and shall see that there is nothing wanting in the business we have in hand; adieu! Juliet, follow me and gladden the heart of thy mother. [Exit.

JULIET. I follow, my father. [Exit.

FRIAR. ROMEO. JULIET.

FRIAR. Come here, my children; I sufficiently understand from you how the matter stands, but I must give such an important matter more consideration, lest I bring danger and misfortune over myself and you.

JULIET. Father, I have made known to you the opinion of my parents who insist upon my taking Count Paris, while I am resolved never to do that, but, to give my true love to Romeo. Therefore I beg that we may be married by your aid.

ROMEO. I likewise, Sir, beg you not to delay, since both of us are of one heart and mind. Accept then, fairest Juliet, this ring as a token and covenant that I will remain faithful to you unto my grave.

JULIET. And there, dearest Romeo, take that from my hand together with my heart which is yours till death part us. And now, Father, there is nothing wanting but that you take the trouble of uniting us.

PATER. Wollan dan, weil Euer beyder will beschlofsen, vnd es nicht anderst sein kan, so folget mit mir in die Capellen alwohe ich euch vermählen will.

FRIAR. Well, as you have both made up your minds, and there is no help for it, follow me to the chapel where I will join you in marriage.

ACTUS QUARTUS.

SCENA PRIMA.

PENUOLIO. MERCUTIO.

PENUOL. Ich bitte dich Freundt Mercutio, lasse ab von deinem Vorhaben, lafs vnfs von hier gehen, der tag ist worden, die Capuleter finden sich alle zeit vmb diser reuir, wofern wür ihnen begegnen, gehet es ohne schlagen nicht ab, dan in den heifsen tagen das geblüt am hützigsten.

MERCU. Du bist gleich Penuolio den Jenigen, die in ein Wirths Haufs kommen, legen sie ihr gewöhr auf dem tisch, vnd sagen ich will dich in keinem Jahr mehr aufsziehen, sobald sie aber einen kleinen Tummel in den Kopff bekommen, ziehen sie den Degén aufs, hawen in die Stein vnd jauchzen darzue, das einen die Ohren klingen.

PENUOL. Haltest du mich dan auch vor einen solchen Kerl.

MERCU. O schweig, du bist der aller erhitzigste, ich wolte schier sagen in gantz Italia, hast du nicht mit einen gezankt nur darumb dafs er sein wammes vor den Sontag angezogen, widerumb mit einen, der seine alte Schuechband in newe schuech gezogen.

PENUO. Vnd was weither?

MERCU. Auch hast du mit einem gezankt, der nur auf der strafsen gehuest, dieweil er deinen Hundt welcher an der Sonnen lag vnd schlieff, aufgeweckt, vnd gleichwohl wilst du noch von zankhen sagen.

PENUO. Were ich so geneigt zu zankhen alfs du, ich wäre schon längsten in der Erden erkalt. Huy ich schwöre bey meinem Kopff hier kompt ein Capulet.

MERCU. Vnd ich schwöre bey meinen füessen, dafs ich nichts darnach frag.

SCENA 2DA.

TIPOLD.

TIPOLD. Ich bin aufsgegangen vnd gehe noch meinen feindt anzutreffen, aber stille da sehe ich ein paar von meines feindts consorten, ich muefs sie anreden, gueten Abend.

MERCU. Nichts mehr alfs ein gueten Abend, der ist nicht dankhens werth.

ACT IV.

SCENE I.

BENVOLIO. MERCUTIO.

BENVOL. I entreat thee, Mercutio, give up thy enterprise, let us be off. It is day-light. There are always some Capulets in this quarter, and if we should meet any, we should not escape a brawl; for in these hot days the blood is hottest.

MERCUT. Benvolio, thou art like one of those fellows that enter an inn, lay their weapon on the table and say: I will not draw thee for a twelvemonth. But as soon as they are half seas over, they draw their swords, strike the pavement, and shout to make one's ears tingle.

BENVOL. Thou takest me for a fellow like that?

MERCUT. Be silent, thou art the most fiery man, I had almost said in all Italy. Didst thou not quarrel with one man for wearing his Sunday doublet, and with another for tying his new shoes with old riband?

BENVOL. And what else?

MERCUT. And then thou didst quarrel with a man only for coughing in the street because he had wakened thy dog that was lying asleep in the sun. And yet thou talkest to me about quarrelling!

BENVOL. If I were as fond of quarrelling as thou, I should have been cold in the earth ever so long. Halloh, I swear by my head, there comes a Capulet!

MERCUT. And I swear by my feet, I do not care a straw for it.

SCENE II.

TIBALT.

TIBALT. I went out, and am still wandering about to meet my enemy. But stop, there I see a couple of my enemy's consorts. I must accost them. Good evening!

MERCUT. Not more than a good evening? That is not worth a thank.

TIPOLD. Wofern ihr nuir Vrsach gebt, so bin ich bereith zu schlagen.

MERCU. Wie Tipold, muest du erst Vrsach haben, kanst du dich nicht schlagen ohne Vrsach?

TIPOLD. Dises auf die Seith gesetzt, sagt mir wo ist euer mit Consort Romio?

MERCU. Waſs teuffl, meinst du das wür bierfidler sein? Vnd vnſs Consorten nennen darffst, sehe zue daſs kein discord darauſs wird, sonsten ist hier mein fidlbogen.

ROMIO.

TIPOLD. Stillo, stillo, da kompt der eben zu rechter Zeit den ich begehre.

MERCU. Holla hier kompt Romio, Tipold wirst du noch viel von Consorten reden, so ist Romio schon vorhanden.

TIPOLD. Ho ho, die freindtschaft so ich zu den Mundigesern trag ist sehr schlecht, Herr Romio du bist ein schelm.

ROMIO. Wie Tipold, ich habe dir kein Vnrecht gethan, kanst du die Jenigen so dich nicht beleidigen auf der strassen gehen lassen.

TIPOLD. Höre Romio, du kömbst mir vor alſs ein Jung vnd gehest ohne degen, wofern ich dich noch einmahl so antreffe, so will ich dich von meinen laggeien pastiniren lassen.

ROMIO. Lasse mich zufriden Tipold ich erdulde mehr alſs zu viel, ach Himmel ich bin nur vor wenig Stunden sein Schwager worden vnd mueſs dises gedulden. Julieta halt mich zuruckh ihm widerstand zu thuen, ich will mich zwingen vnd von hier gehen. [abit.

MERCU. Waſs, will Romio daſs leiden? ich aber bey meinem leben nicht, Holla Tipold Katzen König, komme hier, sie sagen daſs ein Katz nein leben hat, darumb komb, ich will dir eins daruon nehmen.

TIPOLD. Du, Mercutio, mit mir fechten? Komb komb wan du lust hast in die andere welt, oder ich will dich gahr nach der Höllen schickhen, so komb an.

ROMIO auſs. PENUOLIO.

ROMIO. Haltet ein ihr Herrn, ihr vergesset eures Stands vnd Nahmb.

MERCU. Ja ja, halt ein, halt ein, ich bin schon verwundt.

TIPOLD. So recht, du hast dein theil, fahre nach der Höllen ich aber gehe von hier. [abit.

PENUO. O Himmel, Mercutius ist verwundt!

ROMIO. Wie verwundt, wans nur kein tödtliche wunde ist vnd nicht groſs.

TIBALT. If you give me occasion, you will find me ready to fight.

MERCUT. Why Tibalt, do you require an occasion? can't you fight without any occasion?

TIBALT. This apart, tell me where is your consort Romeo?

MERCUT. What the devil, dost thou take us for fiddlers, that thou call'st us consorts? Take care that no discords arise from it, else here is my fiddlestick.

Enter ROMEO.

TIBALT. Peace, peace! Here comes the very man I want.

MERCUT. Hollah, here comes Romeo. Now, Tibalt, wilt thou talk any more of consorts, there is Romeo!

TIBALT. It is bad friendship I bear to the Montagues. Thou art a villain, Romeo.

ROMEO. How, Tibalt, I never injured thee! Canst thou not let those who do not insult thee walk the street in peace?

TIBALT. Hear me, Romeo, thou appearest to me a mere boy, and carriest no sword. If I meet thee so another time I shall make my lackeys bastinado thee.

ROMEO. Leave me in peace, Tibalt! I suffer more than enough! — Good heavens! it is but a few hours since I became his brother in law, and must forbear. Juliet, restrain me from opposing him! I will control myself, and go from hence. [*Exit.*

MERCUT. What, will Romeo bear this? I will not, by my life! Hollah, Tibalt, king of cats, come here! They say a cat has nine lives, come on, I will take one of them.

TIBALT. Thou, Mercutio, fight me? Come on, come on, if thou hast got a mind for the other world, or I may send thee even to hell. Come on!

Re-enter ROMEO. BENVOLIO.

ROMEO. Stop, gentlemen, you forget your position and name.

MERCUT. Ay, ay, stop! I am hurt already.

TIBALT. Right so, thou hast it, go to hell; I am off. [*Exit.*

BENVOL. Oh Heavens, Mercutio is wounded.

ROMEO. How, wounded? Let us hope not fatally, not seriously.

MERCU. Ich glaub Ihr spottet mein, so grofs ist die wunde nicht alfs ein ochsenmaul oder Stadtthor, aber morgen werdet ihr mich recht gravitetisch begraben helffen.

ROMIO. Ich bitte Penuolio, eyle vmb einen balbirer, damit ihm seine wunde versorget werde.

MERCU. Ey bemühet Euch nicht vor meine wunde zu heylen, doch bekhenne ich, es währe besser ich were in einen arm gestochen alfs durch lungen vnd leber.

ROMIO. O Himmel, ist dan vnser Haus vnd geschlecht mit lauttern vnglickh behafftet? armseeliger Romio was wirst du entlich noch vor widerwertigkeit ertragen müssen?

PENUO. Wie Mercutius, rührst du dich nicht mehr? o Romio Mercutius ist todt, sein geist ist schon nach den wolkhen geflogen.

ROMIO. Wie wafs? Ist Mercutius todt, so trutze ich das ärgiste so mir kommen kan, vnd der Jenige so disen freffl begangen, solle gewifs den schaden fühlen.

TIPOLD.

PENUO. Romio, hier kompt Tipold widerumb.

ROMIO. Es ist guet. Nun Tipold, anietzo ist es Zeit das du zuruckh nehmest den Schelmen so du mir zuuor auferlegt, oder ich halte dich vor einen bifs in deinen todt.

TIPOLD. Ha ha, hast du einmal einen Degen bekhommen, es währe vnbüllich das du vnd Mercutius von einander sollet separirt werden, vnd weil ihr euch in eurem Leben trewlich einander geliebet, so warthe, ich will dir alsobald denselben weg zeigen, den dein mit consort gewandert.

ROMIO. Du vermeinst vielleicht mich mit deinen trutzen zu uerjagen, aber es soll dir föhlen, darumb so komb an vnd brauche dein gewöhr.

[*Fechten. Tipold fält.*

PENUO. Halt ein Romio, Tipold falt zur Erden vnd ist verwundt, drumb ist kein Zeit vor dich vnd mich vnfs länger aufzuhalten.

TIPOLD. O wehe ich bin des todts vnd sterbe.

ROMIO. Penuolio folge mir, lafs vnfs die flucht nehmen meiner liebsten Julieta willen.   [*abit.*

PICKLHÄRING.

PICKL. Wer viel zu thuen hat, hat viel zu schaffen, ich glaube nicht dafs alle Menschen in der weldt so viel zu thuen haben alfs ich allein, ietzt soll ich lauffen vnd sehen wafs vor ein tumult auf der gassen. Aber wafs ligt hier vor ein voller Nafsküttl; potz schlapper-

MERCUT. I believe you are mocking at me. The wound is not so big as the mouth of an ox or a towngate, but to-morrow you will help to bury me right gravely.

ROMEO. Pray, Benvolio, run for a barber to have his wound dressed.

MERCUT. Don't trouble yourself about healing my wound. Yet I must confess, I should rather like to have got a thrust through my arm than through my lungs and liver.

ROMEO. Good heavens! Is our house and race accursed? Miserable Romeo, what misfortune is still in store for thee!

BENVOL. How, Mercutio! thou dost not move? Oh Romeo, Mercutio is dead, his soul has already flown to the clouds.

ROMEO. What? Mercutio dead? Then I defy the worst that can befal me, and he who committed this outrage, shall surely suffer.

Re-enter TIBALT.

BENVOL. Romeo! there is Tibalt again.

ROMEO. Well so. Now, Tibalt, take the villain back again, that late thou gavest me, or I shall take thee for one until thy death.

TIBALT. Hast thou at last got a sword? It would not be right that thou and Mercutio should be separated; and as you truly loved each other in life, I shall soon show thee the same way thy consort went.

ROMEO. Thou mean'st perhaps to scare me by thy bluster, but thou shalt not succeed: come on and use thy weapon!

[*They fight. Tibalt falls.*

BENVOL. Hold, Romeo! Tibalt falls and is wounded. There is no time for thee and me to tarry.

TIBALD. Oh, I am slain, I die!

ROMEO. Follow me, Benvolio; let us fly for my dear Juliet's sake.   [*Exit.*

Enter CLOWN.

CLOWN. Who has much to do has much to manage. I don't believe that all the people in the world have as much to do as I alone. Now I am bid to run and see what is the tumult in the street. But look what a parcel of snot is this? Zounds, it is Tibalt, bleeding like a pig. Hollah,

ment dafs ist Tipold, blut er doch alfs wie ein schwein, holla Tipold, ich befehle dir bey des Herzogs Vngnad, das du aufstehest vnd gehest mit mir, er will nicht andtwortten, ja er ist gahr todt, larmen larmen, Tipold ist todt gestochen, gestorben vnd lebt nicht mehr.

SCENA 3ᵀᴵᴬ.
Hörtzog. Capulet's Fraw.

Hörtzog. Was ist difs vor ein Tumult vnd wer ist Vrsach hieruon?

Pickl. Das weifs ich nicht Herr Hertzog, aber dafs weifs ich wohl dafs ich hier Tipold todt ligend gefunden hab, vnd hier ist der Mann, der so praff post bringen kan.

Hörtzog. Kanst du auch wissen Narr wer dise Mordthat begangen?

Pickl. Ich kan mir leicht einbilden weil er gestochen, es wirts ein Degen gethan haben.

Hörtzog. Schweig du bist ein Narr.

Pickl. Dafs kan wohl sein ich glaub es selber.

Penuolio.

Penuo. Gnädigster Fürst vnd Herr, ich komme die rechte wahrheit zu sagen wie sich difer vnglickseelige Zuefall angefangen, alfs nemblichen Tipold defs Capulets Vetter kam mit scheldtwortten an Mercutium, Mercutius ergriff den Degen vnd wurde erstochen.

Fraw. Gnädigster Fürst vnd Herr, wofern sie gerechtigkeit lieben, so lasset das Jenige bluet widerumb vergossen werden, der Meinen Vetter so jämmerlich ermordet hat.

Hörtzog. Haltet ein Frau, wür wollen erst die gründliche warheit vernehmen, alfsdan der gerechtigkeit ihren lauff lassen.

Fraw. Ach gnädigster Fürst vnd Herr sie geben [?] disen Mundagesen, dan er ist Partheiisch vnd vnsers Haufs geschworner Feind.

Hörtzog. Wofern wür nicht von ihme die warheit wissen, so können wür nicht richten, darumb sagen wür gebet gehör, vnd ihr Penuolio erzehlet den Verlauff dises Mords bey eurem gewissen.

Penuo. Gnädigster Fürst vnd Herr, Tipold kam in einen hützigen Zorn, nannte Romio einen Schelm, Romio aber gantz sanfftmüthig ihm andtworttet, vnd batte, er möchte doch bedenkhen wie vnnöttig diser streitt währe, dardurch Ihro Hochfürstl. Gn. nicht beleidiget wurde, aber alle dise gueten wordt kunten den erzürnten Tipold nicht bewegen, sondern zuge alsobald sein gewöhr aufs vnd ging auf den tapfern Mercutium los, welcher sein gewöhr gleichmäfsig gebraucht, Romio

Tibalt, by the Duke's displeasure I command thee to get up and go with me. He won't answer; dear me, he is dead! Alarm, alarm! Tibalt is stabbed to death, is killed, and lives no more.

SCENE III.
Duke. Lady Capulet.

Duke. What is this tumult about? Who gave rise to it?

Clown. I don't know that, my Lord; but thus much I know, that I found Tibalt lying here dead. And here is the man to give you information about it.

Duke. Can you surmise, fool, who did this murder?

Clown. I can easily imagine since he is stabbed. I dare say a sword did it.

Duke. Hold your tongue, you are a fool.

Clown. That may be; I believe so myself.

Benvolio.

Benvol. Most gracious Prince and Lord! I come to tell the truth how this fatal brawl began. Tibalt, Capulet's cousin, accosted Mercutio with abuse; then Mercutio took up the sword and was slain.

Lady. Most gracious Prince and Lord! As you love justice, shed the blood of him who has so miserably murdered my cousin.

Duke. Hold, my Lady! We will first get to the very truth of the matter, and then let justice take its course.

Lady. Ah, gracious Prince and Lord! You give ear to this Montague who is partial, and the sworn enemy of our house.

Duke. Unless we get the truth from him we cannot judge. Therefore we say: give ear. And you, Benvolio, tell us how this bloody fray happened, upon your conscience.

Benvol. Most gracious Prince and Lord! Tibalt got into a rage, and called Romeo a villain. Romeo spoke him fair, bade him bethink how unnecessary this quarrel was, and urged Your Grace's high displeasure. All these good words had no effect upon the enraged Tibalt, for he drew his sword, and rushed at bold Mercutio, who likewise used his weapon. Romeo cries aloud: Hold friends, for heaven's sake! But it was done already: Mercutio had got a deadly thrust and fell. Romeo, enraged by Mer-

schrier laut, haltet ein vmb des Himmels willen, aber es wahr geschehen, Mercutius hatte einen tödtlichen stofs, füele zur Erden, Romio welcher Mercutii todt nunmehro auch erzürnet wahr, zucket sein gewöhr geschwinder alfs ein plitz, ich aber kunte sobald nicht retten, alfs Tipold durch einen tödtlichen stofs zur Erden fülle, Romio saluirte sich, dises ist wahrhafftig die rechte wahrheit wie es ergangen, vnd soll ichs auch mit meinem leben beantwortten.

HÖRTZOG. Wollan, weil Tipold Mercutium erlegt, ist sein todt durch Romio gerochen, aber dennoch solte Romio nicht sein eigener Richter gewesen sein, weil er aber Tipold erstochen, also verbannen wür ihm von Verona, vnd wird er sich länger alfs 24 Stundt in Verona befinden, so kostet es ihm sein leben, darumb last dises publicirt werden, so geschicht der gerechtigkeit ein vergnügen, vnd ihr fraw von Capulet werd darmit content vnd zufriden leben. [*gehen ab.*

cutio's death, draws his sword as quick as lightning; and ere I could part them, Tibalt was mortally wounded and fell. Romeo fled. This is the exact truth how it all happened, as I am ready to answer for it with my life.

DUKE. Well, Mercutio is slain by Tibalt, his death revenged by Romeo. Yet Romeo ought not to have taken the law into his own hands. As he has slain Tibalt, we banish him from Verona; if he is found in this city in twenty four hours from this time, it shall cost him his life. Let this be published. Thus justice will be fulfilled, and you, Lady Capulet, will be content and satisfied.

[*Exeunt.*

SCENA 4ᵀᴬ.

JULIETA. AMMA.

JULI. Komb liebste Amma vnd saget mir wafs war difs vor ein Tumult in dem Haufs meines Vatters, ist etwan ein Vnglickh geschehen, dan ihr wüst der weiber freyheit ist schlecht in Italia, sie seind eingesperrt gleich den gefangenen, o verdrüfsliche wollust.

AMMA. Ja freylich wahr larmen, aber nicht in eures Vatters Haufs, sondern auf freyer strassen, ach ich wolte ich wuste nichts darumb.

JULIE. Ist dan vnserem Haufs oder freundtschafft ein vnglickh oder leid widerfahren?

AMMA. Ach wehe, ach Vnglickh, ach Romio Romio.

JULI. Wie, wafs sagt ihr mir von Romio?

PICKLHÄRING.

PICKL. Ach Ellend, ach noth, ach barmhertzigkeit, ach Vnglickh, was kan schlimmer sein in der welt alfs zerrifsene Hofsen vnd nichts zu fressen, ich lauff herumb alfs wie ein Jag Hundt vnd sueche Julieta, o wer weifs in wafs vor einen loch oder wünkl sie steckt vnd sich verborgen, vnd etwan weint rotz vnd wasser wegen defs grossen glicks so den Romio begegnet, weither lauff ich nicht sie zu suechen, ich bin so müth von lauffen vnd suechen, dafs ich kein Zahn in maul mehr rühren kan, aber siehe da stehet vnser Amma, Ji Amma was machet Ihr da? wo ist das freulein Julieta? ich bring ihr köstliche Zeitung.

AMMA. Schweig Narr, thue deine Kalbsaugen auf, bist du blind, siehst du nicht hier dafs frewlein Julieta?

SCENE IV.

JULIET. NURSE.

JULIET. Come, dear nurse, tell me what the tumult was in the house of my father? Has there been any accident? You know it is a poor liberty women enjoy in Italy; they are kept like prisoners. Oh melancholy desire!

NURSE. To be sure there was a row, though not at your father's house but in the open street. I wish I knew nothing about it.

JULIET. Has any misfortune befallen our house or friends?

NURSE. Ah woe, ah calamity! Alas, Romeo, Romeo!

JULIET. What? what is it you say of Romeo?

CLOWN.

CLOWN. Oh misery! oh distress! oh pity! oh misfortune! Can there be anything worse in the world than torn trousers and nothing to eat? I am running about like a hound seeking for Juliet. God knows in what hole or corner she hides, shedding tears and snot because of that good luck of Romeo. I won't run any farther to seek her. I am so tired with running and searching, that I cannot move a tooth in my mouth. But look, there is our nurse. I say, nurse, what are you about? Where is your young lady? I bring her precious news.

NURSE. Hold thy tongue, fool. Open thy calfs-eyes. Art thou blind? Dost thou not see Miss Juliet there?

JULI. Der Himmel bewahre mich vor Vnglickh. Wafs bringst du Pickl Häring?

PICKL. So warth, last mich erst zu athem kommen.

JULI. Ist etwan mein Herr Vatter oder fraw Muetter übel auf?

PICKL. Ein treckh, es ist tausendtmahl schlimmer.

JULI. Ach Pickl Häring, halt mich nicht länger auf, ist es ein vnglickh so sag mirs bald.

PICKL. Weither kein vnglickh alfs das er todt ist wie ein stockfisch.

AMMA. Ja frewlein Julieta, dises ist eben was ich nicht sagen wollen, ach Romio Romio.

JULI. Ach Himmel bewahre mich, ist Romio todt?

PICKL. Wan die Amma das sagt, so liegt sie alfs wie ein aufsgestrichene Hex, ich bin der Mann der es besser weifs.

JULI. Ach lieber Pickl Häring, so sage dan was du weist.

PICKL. Dessenthalben bin ich her kommen dafs ichs euch sagen will, Mercutius ist todt, Tipold gestorben, weil ihn Romio todt gestochen, so ist er entloffen, vnd weifs ihn kein Mensch zu finden.

JULIET. So ist meines lebens auch nicht mehr, o du grausamber vnd vnbarmbhertziger Himmel, ach ich Ellende vndt voller trübsaal, soll ich mich dan entlich auch dem todt aufopffern?

PICKL. Gehet lieber nach Haufs vnd legt Euch ins beth, ist gesunder als sterben.

AMMA. O du guter Tipold, wie jämmerlich bist du ermordt.

JULI. Wafs Tipold, wäre nur Romio zu finden.

PICKL. Es ist wahr frewlein Julieta, Romio hat den Tipold erstochen, aber der Hertzog hat ihn verbannt aufs Verona sein Lebtag nicht mehr darein zu kommen.

JULI. Ach all zu vnglickseelige Julieta, ist Romio verbannt so ist mein lebenslicht aufsgelescht, vnd ich mich selbst auch dieser weldt verbannen will.

AMMA. O verflucht sey Rumio, es ist kein Menschen zu trawen wer wolte sagen, das er so falsch seye.

PICKL. O du alter flederwisch, lägst du auff ein scheitter Hauffen, ich wolte selber anzünden vnd mit frewden zueschawen wie du verbrennest.

JULI. Wie Amma, verfluechest du den Jenigen welchen mein Hertz liebt?

AMMA. Wie frewlein Julieta, wollet ihr den Jenigen lieben, der Euch Euren Vetter ermordet hat?

JULI. Wie solte ich den Jenigen hassen der mein leben liebet, ach mein lieber ich will selber sterben.

AMMA. Ach Julieta, verlasset doch den Meineydigen Romio, vnd nehmet graff Paris zu euren Mann.

JULIET. Heaven preserve me from misfortune! What news dost thou bring, clown?

CLOWN. Wait till I have first recovered my breath.

JULIET. Is my father or my mother unwell?

CLOWN. Nonsense! it is a thousand times worse.

JULIET. Don't keep me any longer in suspense; is there any misfortune, tell me at once.

CLOWN. No misfortune except that he is as dead as a stock-fish.

NURSE. Just the thing I did not like to tell you. Ah, Romeo, Romeo!

JULIET. Heaven preserve me! Is Romeo dead?

CLOWN. An the nurse says that, she lies like an arrant witch. I am the man to know better.

JULIET. Sweet clown, tell me what you know.

CLOWN. That is what made me come here to tell you: Mercutio is dead, Tibalt is dead. Romeo has slain Tibalt, and fled, and nobody knows where to find him.

JULIET. Then I have no business to live. Oh cruel, unrelenting Heaven! Oh miserable, afflicted Juliet! Am I too at last to sacrifice myself to death?

CLOWN. You had better go home and lie down; it is far more wholesome than dying.

NURSE. O· dear Tibalt, how miserably art thou slain!

JULIET. What of Tibalt, were but Romeo to be found!

CLOWN. It is a fact, Miss Juliet, Romeo did slay Tibalt, and the Duke has banished him from Verona never to return as long as he lives.

JULIET. Too miserable Juliet! If Romeo is banished, then is the light of my life too extinguished, and I will banish myself from this world.

NURSE. A curse upon Romeo! There is no faith in any man; who should have thought him so false!

CLOWN. Oh you old goose-wing! If you were lying on a pile I myself would set fire to it, and joyfully stand by to see you burn.

JULIET. Why, nurse, you curse the man whom my heart loves?

NURSE. Why, Miss, would you love the man who slew your cousin?

JULIET. How should I hate the man who loves my life! Ah beloved one I will die myself.

NURSE. Juliet, leave the perjured Romeo, and take Count Paris for your husband.

PICKL. Nein Julieta, ich will euch besser rathen, nehmbt sie alle beide, gefallen sie euch, so nehmbt mich vor euren breytigamb.

JULI. Schweig Pickl Häring, hier ist keine Zeit zu schertzen, auch nicht christlich 2 oder 3 Männer zu nehmen.

PICKL. Warumb nicht? Hat doch der türkische Keyser so viel weiber welche nicht alle zu zehlen sein, vnd worumb soll mir oder euch nicht erlaubt werden, 3, 4, 5, 6, 7, 8, 9, 10, weiber oder männer zu nehmen, ich wolte nicht weith, wan ich suechen dörfft, welche in der Stadt Kollschin, Budweifs, Gopplitz, Freystadt, Lintz vnd hier, welche mehr alfs ein weib vnd ein weib mehr alfs einen Mann verlangen oder gahr haben.

JULI. Wollan ich will es thuen, vnd deinen Rath folgen, gehe mit meiner Amma Pickl Häring, vnd sage mein Herr Vatter vnd fraw Muetter, ich liebe den Graff Paris.

AMMA. Dafs ist mir lieb, ich will also bald hingehen vnd solches eurer Fraw Muetter andeuten.

PICKL. Zuruckh alte, dafs währ ein schlechter brauch wan ein Ambasator hinten nach vnd ein altes weib voran gehen solte. [Amma gehet ab.

JULI. Verfluchte Amma, die du mir abradest meinen Ehemann zu lieben, ach mein liebster Romio, dises solle nimmermehr geschehen, aber ach, ach Romio, warumb hast du meinen Vetter ermord, aber recht hast du gethan, weil er dich alfs meinen Ehemann ermorden wollen, aber Romio dein Verbannung schmertzet mich, mein Hertz blutet, vnd gehet mir sehr zu Hertzen, wollan dan, ich will auf mittel vnd weeg bedacht sein, wie ich kan zu ihm kommen, vnd von ihm einen schmertzlichen abschid nehmen, komme hier Pickl Häring, ich weifs du bist getrew vnd verschwigen, drumb vernehme mich wafs ich sage, hier empfange diese etliche Dugaten, vnd bemühe dich den Romio zu finden, welcher noch in Verona wird zu finden sein, vnd kom mit mir in mein gemach, ich will dich mit einem brieff an ihn abfertigen.

PICKL. Ja ia, ihr redt gar recht, frewlein Julieta, ob meine füefs schon so müth dafs ich auf keinen Efsl steigen kunt, so will ich doch den Dugaten zu gefallen gantz Verona durchlauffen, alfs wann ich doll wäre, bifs ich Romio gefunden hab, vnd von Euch alfsdan mehr Dugaten empfangen werde. [abeunt.

PATER. ROMIO.

PATER. Ich bitte liebster Sohn Rumio, er stelle sich doch einmahl zufriden vnd lasse die trawrigkeit bey ihm nicht gahr zu sehr über Handt nehmen, dan es ist noch ein gnädigstes Vrtheil von dem Hertzog aufsgesprochen worden.

CLOWN. No, Juliet, I will give you better counsel. Take them both if you like them; take me for your bridegroom.

JULIET. Hold your tongue, clown; it is no time for joking, nor is it christianlike to take two or three husbands.

CLOWN. Why not? Has not the Turkish Emperor more wives than you can count? Why should it not be permitted to me or you to take three, four, five, six, seven, eight, nine or ten wives or husbands? I should not have far to go if in Kollschin, Budweiss, Gopplitz, Freystadt, Linz, and in this town I would find out husbands or wives who desire, nay who have, more than one wife or husband.

JULIET. Well, I shall follow your advice, clown: go with my nurse, and tell my father and mother I love Count Paris.

NURSE. I am glad of it; I will go at once and inform your mother.

CLOWN. Keep back, old one! It would be a bad custom for an ambassador to bring up the rear, and an old woman to take the lead. [Exit Nurse.

JULIET. Accursed nurse! To dissuade me from loving my husband! My dearest Romeo, this is never to be. But alas Romeo, why didst thou slay my cousin! Though thou wast in thy right as he intended to slay thee, my husband. Yet, Romeo, thy banishment pains me much, cuts me to the heart; my heart is bleeding. Well, I will think of ways and means to join him, and to take a painful leave from him. Look here, clown, I know thou art faithful and secret. Listen then to what I say. Take these few ducats and try to find Romeo, who probably is still to be met with in Verona. Come to my closet; I will charge thee with a letter to him.

CLOWN. Just so, Miss Juliet; you are quite right. Though my feet are so tired that I could not mount a donkey, yet for the sake of your ducats I will run all over Verona like a madman until I find Romeo, and get some more ducats from you. [Exeunt.

FRIAR. ROMEO.

FRIAR. Pray, my dear son Romeo, take comfort at last. Do not allow sadness to get the better of you; it is a merciful judgment the Duke has given.

Romio. Ach Pater ist es leben oder todt? — ist es todt so will ich billich leiden.

Pater. Nein mein liebes Kindt, das wordt todt ist in ein gnädigstes verbannen verendert worden.

Romio. Ach Verbannen viel ärger alfs der todt, o grausamber Himmel, soll ich anietzo scheiden vnd Julieta verlassen? vnd ihrer holdseeligen gegenwarth beraubt sein? ach mehr alfs todtes Schmertzen.

Pater. Ich bitte mein Sohn höret mich.

Romio. Ach Pater wafs soll ich hören, ihr wolt doch widerumb Verbannen sagen.

Pickl Häring *klopfft inwendig.*

Pickl. Holla, ist alles verspert? Niemandt zu Haufs? macht die Thier auf.

Pater. Mein Kindt folge mir vnd verstecke dich, die wacht möchte kommen vnd dich gefänglich nehmen.

Romio. Ich will nicht, sondern hier will ich mich in meinen eigenen thränen ersauffen.

Pater. Ach Himmel, wafs vor ein Dolheit besitzet seine Sünnen.

Pickl. Wo zum Krankheit, werde ich noch lang warthen müssen, macht auf, oder ich werdt doll vnd närrisch.

Pater. Ach Romio, verberget euch, die wacht ist vorhanden.

Romio. Ich will nicht vnd kan auch nicht.

Pater. So stürzt ihr euch selber in gefahr, wer ist da?

Pickl. Der tausendt, macht auf doch ein mahl auf, ich bin gestanden, dafs mir die negel von den Zehen bald weren abgefrohren, ich habe ein Post Herr Pater abzulegen, vnd komme von Julieta.

Pater. Ach fröliger bott, kommet herein.

Pickl. Quos gratias, Bonus dies Domine Pater.

Pater. Grossen Dankh Pickl Häring, wo kompt man her?

Pickl. Aufs der gassen von vnsern Haufs, vnd wolte den Herrn Patribus bitten, er wolle mir sagen, wo ist der Romio?

Pater. Da ligt er vnd ist fast in lauther trawrigkeit, vnd in sein eigenen thränen erstickt.

Pickl. Das sein Narrenbossen, Herr Romio stehet auf, ich komme von Julieta.

Romio. Ach wer nennet den holdseeligen Nahmen Julieta, ach Pickl Häring verfluecht sie mich nicht, dafs ich ihren Vetter Tipold erstochen?

Pickl. Nein da hat sie mir nichts gesagt, ich glaube wan ihr ihn hett gar aufgehenkt, erwürgt, gradbrecht, gespiefst, vnd gahr auf dem Efsl gesezt, sie fragte nichts

Romeo. Ah, father, is it life or death? if death, I will suffer as is reasonable.

Friar. No, my dear child, the word death has been turned into merciful exile.

Romeo. Exile is worse than death. Cruel heavens! am I now to part from Juliet and leave her, and be deprived of her lovely presence? That is more than the pangs of death.

Friar. Pray, my son, hear me.

Romeo. What is the use of hearing! you will speak again of banishment.

Clown, *knocking within.*

Clown. Hollah! everything shut up? nobody at home? Open the door!

Friar. My child, follow me and hide yourself: the watch might come and take you up.

Romeo. I will not do that, but I will rather drown myself in my own tears.

Friar. Good heavens, what madness has got possession of his senses!

Clown. The plague! how long am I to wait? Open the door, or I shall go crazy.

Friar. Romeo, hide yourself; the watch has come.

Romeo. I will not, I cannot.

Friar. Then you are rushing into danger. Who is there?

Clown. The deuce, open the door at last. I have been standing till the nails are frozen off my feet. I have got a message for you, Sir, and come from Juliet.

Friar. Joyful messenger, come in!

Clown. Quos gratias, bonus dies Domine Pater.

Friar. Much thanks. Where does the clown come from?

Clown. From the street, from our house, for the purpose of begging the Patribus to tell me where Romeo is.

Friar. There he lies, almost drowned in sadness and his own tears.

Clown. That is fool's play, Mr. Romeo; get up; I come from Juliet.

Romeo. Who pronounces the lovely name of Juliet? Ah, clown, does she not curse me for having killed her cousin Tibalt?

Clown. She has said nothing of the kind. I dare say if you had hanged him, strangled him, broken him on the wheel, spitted him, nay put him on the ass,

darnach, sondern sie hat mir befohlen euch zu suechen, vnd wan ich euch gefunden hab zu sagen, sie läst euch bitten, daſs ihr dise nacht zu ihr wolt kommen, weil ihr verbannet seit, daſs ualet vnd abschid von euch zu nehmen.

Romio. Ach ist es möglich, vnd solte ich glauben daſs Julieta allein voller Sanfftmuth vnd barmhertzigkeit ist?

Pickl. Freilich ist es möglich, vnd daſs es wahrhafftig ist, so schickt euch Julieta durch ihren Ambasador, als meine persohn, diesen ring, wie auch disen brieff, vnd ich glaube wan ihr nicht kommen wolt zu ihr, sie wurde euch ein Schelmen in den buesen werffen.

Romio. Ach brieff! ach ring! seit mir willkommen, dich mein ring will ich verehrt an meinem finger tragen, biſs der blaſse todt den faden meines lebens zerschneidt vnd enden wird, darumb gehe Pickl Häring, vermelte meiner Julieta daſs ich wan die nacht wird anziehen ihr Schwartzes trauer kleid, will ich mich bey ihr gehorsamb einfinden, vnd den lezten abschid nehmen, hier Pickl Häring empfange vor deine mühe dise wenigen dobulonen vor dein tringgelt.

Pickl. Ich bedankhe mich Herr Romio vor dises wenige, wan es mehr wäre, wär es noch besser. [*abit.*

Pater. Ich bitte ihn Herr Romio, er gehe vnd nehme abschid von seiner liebsten, doch mit solcher Vorsichtigkeit, das er mit anbrechendem tag noch auſs der Statt kommen kan.

Romio. Hochgeehrter Herr Pater, ehe sich der morgenstern retteriret vnd den grossen weldt liecht platz machet, vnd den tag verkhündiget, will ich von hinnen machen, aber mein Vertrawen Herr Pater stehet allein zu ihm, daſs er mir nach Mantua schrüfftlichen bericht ertheile, wie es mit euch vnd meiner Julieta jeder Zeit stehen möge.

Pater. Traget keine Sorg mein Sohn, wan ihr euch in Mantua aufhaltet, solt ihr stets durch brieff ersuechet werden.

Romio. Wollan dan, ich ergebe mich den vnglickh meines Vnsterns, ich reiſse zwar verbannt von hier, mein Hertz aber laſs ich bey Julieta. [*abit.*

Pater. Der Himmel vnd alle Himlische macht geben ihn glickh auf seine Reiſs, vnd Segnen mit solchen glickh, das er bald mit frewden möge Verona sehen, ich aber vnterdessen, will den Himmel frühe vnd spat vor seine wohlfarth bitten. [*abit.*

SCENE 6ᵀᴬ.
Romio, Julieta *in der Kammer.*

Romio. Süſse vnd über die Natur mildreicheste Ju-

she would not mind. No she has commanded me to seek for you, and when found, to tell you she desires you, being banished, to come to see her to-night and bid her adieu.

Romeo. Is it possible? Can I believe that Juliet alone is sweet and merciful?

Clown. To be sure it is possible; and in proof of it, Juliet sends you through her ambassador in my person, this ring together with this letter: and I think, if you would not go to her, she would throw a villain at your face.

Romeo. A letter, a ring! Be welcome both. Thee, my ring, will I wear on my finger till pallid death cut the thread of my life. Go, clown, inform my Juliet, that when night has wrapped herself in her black mourning dress, I shall in due obedience appear and take my last farewell. There, clown, take these few doubloons for thy trouble.

Clown. Thank you for this trifle; if it were more, I should like it better. [*Exit.*

Friar. Pray, Romeo, go and take leave of your sweet-heart, but so cautiously that by the break of day you may yet leave the town.

Romeo. Reverend father, ere the morning-star retires giving way to the world's great luminary, and heralds in the day, I shall be from hence. But my confidence is in you alone that you will send me news in writing to Mantua from time to time how yourself and my Juliet prosper.

Friar. Be under no anxiety for that, my son; while you sojourn in Mantua, there shall never be a letter wanting.

Romeo. Well then, I yield to the fate of my unlucky stars. I go from hence on exile, but my heart I leave with Juliet. [*Exit.*

Friar. May heaven and all heavenly powers grant him good luck on his journey, and bless him with a joyful return to Verona. Meantime I will pray to heaven early and late for his well-being.

[*Exit.*

SCENE VI.
Romeo *and* Juliet, *in the chamber.*

Romeo. Juliet, sweet and more than in nature kind,

lieta, vnd gebietterin meines Hertzens, darf ich mich wol vndterstehen mit schamhafften augen dero holdseeligen Schönheit anschawen? ich bin ein Übelthätter, ich bekhenn'es, mir dennoch vor dero Schönheit vnd bitte vmb perdon, vnd den fähler, so ich gegen ihr begangen mir zu uerzeihen.

JULIE. Ach Romio!

ROMIO. Muefs ich sterben?

JULIE. Nein, stehet auf werther Schatz, vnd empfanget euere Julieta, euere gegenwarth machet, dafs ich euch zu gefallen noch lebe, wiewohlen ich von thränen, vnglickh vnd Schmertzen fast verzehret bin, wafs geschehen, kan man nicht mehr enderen.

ROMIO. Ach ist es möglich, das Schönheit, Tugendt vnd barmhertzigkeit alle in einen solchen zarten Hertzen zu finden, o du all zu grausambes Vnglickh, warumb scheidest du mich von der Jenigen, der gleichen auf den gantzen Erdtboden nicht zu finden.

JULI. Ach liebster Romio, Jammer vnd Hertzensangst wollen mein ermüdetes Hertz ersauffen, wan es möglich ist, so lasse zue mir allein in disen bittern Schmertzen vnd so viel überladene trübsalen, das ich mein Hertz ein wenig trösten kan.

ROMIO. Ach Kummer vnd Vnmueth, ihr herschet nunmehro vnd presset vollkomblich mein vnterdruckte Sünnen, ach lasset nicht zue meine Schöne, das dafs Jenige Hertz möchte aufgeopffert werden so euch zu gefallen lebet, vnd haltet ein mit euren Seufftzen vnd verursachet nicht den todt des Jenigen der euch liebet.

JULI. Ach vnuerhofftes Scheiden, ein kleine weil ist noch dafs gesetz Euch anzuschawen, ach erfrewet doch eure halblebende Julieta mit brieffen zu ersuechen, vnd einen lebenden trost zu geben.

ROMIO. Aller Süfsestes Hertzens Kindt, euer getrewer Romio soll verrichten wafs ihr ihm befehlet, aber ach vnser Scheiden ist verhanden, der tag bricht an, ich werde gezwungen, ach vnglickseelige Zeit, sie zu uerlassen.

JULI. Werthester Schatz, es ist nicht der morgen, der blafse Monschein.

ROMIO. Ach wäre es möglich, das ich den Monschein kunte hoffen ein gantzes Monath zu scheinen, so wurden wür erfrewet, dan der Schein der Sonnen vnfs nichts alfs leid vnd Schmertzen bringt.

JULI. Ach leid, es ist die morgenröth vnd kompt mein Hertz blutig zu färben, ach Phoebus, ach tag, du beraubest mich meines lebenstrosts, ach armseelige vnd verlassene Julieta.

ROMIO. Stellet ein, werther Schatz, eure trawrigkeit, der Himmel wird seinen gefasten Zorn wider vnfs der-

mistress of my heart, may I venture to look with bashful eyes at your lovely beauty? I am a wretch, I confess; yet I appear before you begging pardon and forgiveness for the fault I have committed against you.

JULIET. Ah Romeo!

ROMEO. Must I die?

JULIET. No, rise, dearest, and take your Juliet. Your presence makes me still live to please you, though almost eaten up by tears, misery, and suffering. What is done, cannot be undone.

ROMEO. Is it possible that beauty, virtue, and mercy should be found united in such a tender heart! Oh thou too cruel fate! why dost thou divide me from her who has no equal on this globe!

JULIET. Dear Romeo, wretchedness and anguish will overwhelm my worn-out heart. If you can, leave me to these bitter pains and torture, that I may collect myself in solitude.

ROMEO. Ah! ye Care and Despondency, ye have sway over me now, and oppress my down-cast senses. Ah my fair one, do not allow the heart to be sacrificed that lives to please you! Repress your lamentations, and do not cause the death of your lover.

JULIET. Unexpected separation! A little while does the law allow me to gaze at you still. Comfort your Juliet who is now but half alive, with your letters, and give her living consolation.

ROMEO. Sweet child, your faithful Romeo will perform what you command. But alas! our separation is at hand; the day is breaking; I am forced, oh hapless hour! to leave you.

JULIET. Dearest, it is not the morning, it is the pale moon.

ROMEO. Oh, could I but hope that that moon would shine a whole month, it were a comfort to us; for the sun brings us nothing but grief and suffering.

JULIET. Alas, it is the dawn; it comes to stain my heart with blood. Oh Phoebus! oh day! thou robbest me of the comfort of my life! Ah poor, deserted Juliet!

ROMEO. Restrain your sadness, beloved one; the wrath of heaven will relent one day. I bid thee farewell

mahleins lindern, hiemit nehme ich abschid mit disen Kuſs, vnd sie gedenkhe, das diser Kus die standhafftigkeit vnd ewige trew euer Romio versigle.

JULI. Ach Lippen Kuſs meines Hertzen,
Mich aufssaugen meine Schmertzen.
Meine blücke vnd ihr Kräfften,
Kumb laſs mich sie anhefften
An den Süſsen Zucker Mund
Daſs ich gehe nicht zu grund.

ROMIO. Ach waſs machen, waſs begünnen?
Vnser Hertzen, die voll Schmertzen,
Meine Sünnen seind erfült,
Voller plagen; ach wer stillt
Solches Zagen, waſs mich truckt
Vnd beschwerdt auch gantz verzehrt.

JULI. Das lieben mit betrüben
Ist ein fewer, brennet mich,
Biſs auf den grundt, ach ach weh!
Vnd gantz verwund ich vergeh,
Kumb Seelen Schatz erlaube mir,
Zu Küssen eh du scheidst von mir.

ROMIO. Meiner Seelen Zuckher Speis,
Ich gehe zu begriefsen
Dich, o edle tugendt preiſs,
Ich hoffe zu genüssen
Deine trew vnd bständigkeit,
Biſs vnſs beyd der todte scheid.

JULI. So will ich auch einsamb hier
Wie mir gebührt zu leben,
Vnd die turteltaube thuet
Auf dürn äste so,
[Bis?] mit glickh wird wider geben
Dich mir meinen Romio.

ROMIO. Nun Verona fahre wohl,
Vnglickseeligs Vatterland!
Erhalt mir nur mein Schatz
Biſs ich nicht mehr verbannt
Mein Hertz voll Schmertz bleibt hier,
Ich aber bleib beständig dir.

with this kiss, and remember that this kiss is the seal to your Romeo's constancy and everlasting truth.

JULIET. When kissed by him who has my heart,
His lips at once suck out my smart.
My glances and their power too,
Come let me fix them, love, on you,
Hang on thy mouth in sweet delight,
That I may not perish quite.

ROMEO. Alas! what can we do, what try?
For our hearts are full of smarts,
And my senses too are filled
With sad distress; ah, who e'er stilled
Such wretchedness, as now on me
Its weight doth lay, wastes me away.

JULIET. To love so dear with many a tear
Is a fire that burneth me.
Aye more and more, ah, ah, alas,
Till wounded sore, away I pass.
Come my darling grant to me
To kiss thee ere thou part'st from me.

ROMEO. Sweet food, whereon my soul I feed,
To greet thee now I go,
Thee, thee, O noble virtue's meed,
I hope that I may know
Thy truth and constancy of heart,
Till death's sure dart us two do part.

JULIET. So I then too, all lonely here,
As me beseems will live,
As doeth too the turtle-dove
On branch of leafless tree,
Till fortune once again shall give
My Romeo back to me.

ROMEO. Now Verona, fare thee well,
Most unhappy fatherland!
Only preserve my love
Till I no more am bann'd;
My heart will smart for ever,
But I to thee am faithless never.

ACTUS QUINTUS.

SCENA PRIMA.

CAPOLET. JULIETA. PICKLHÄRING.

CAPUL. Geliebte Tochter Julieta, du weist das ich das Jawordt dem Graff Paris gegeben habe, wie auch schon alles zur Hochzeit bereith vnd verfertiget ist, dennoch ist mein will, das du dem graffen mit aller

ACT V.

SCENE I.

CAPULET. JULIET. CLOWN.

CAPUL. Beloved daughter Juliet, thou art aware that I have promised thee to Count Paris and that everything is ready for the wedding. Therefore I want thee to meet the Count with becoming courtesy and to

Höffligkeit begegnest, dich schmuckest vnd zührest, wie es einer brauth gebührt, dan morgen soll dein Hochzeittag sein.

JULI. Ich weiſs Herr Vatter, das ich den gehorsamb meiner Eltern vnterworffen, aber ach!

PICKL. Huy zue, das Mensch bekompt das Zahnwehe.

CAPUL. Waſs seufſzest du tochter, in deme du volle frewden genüssen kanst.

PICKL. Ein krankher Mensch kan nicht viel frewd haben.

JULI. Ach die Jugendt meiner Jahren!

PICKL. Hab ichs nicht gesagt, sie förcht sich schon vor den sterben.

CAPUL. Die Jugendt deiner Jahren, die du in lauther glickh verzehren kanst.

PICKL. Wan sie viel gelt zu zehlen hat.

JULI. Ach das glickh spöret [störet?] meine lust!

CAPUL. In was?

PICKL. Weil sie das Zahnwehe hat.

JULI. Ach Herr Vatter, in anligenden Krankheiten vnd andern Zuefällen die den Menschen plagen.

PICKL. Mich plagt der Hunger, weil der Koch nicht anrichten will.

CAPOL. Wie Julieta, hast du ein anligen einer Krankheit, so sag es mir.

JULI. Ach es [ist] besser ich schweige.

CAPO. Wo schmerzt es dich.

JULI. In den Hertzen.

CAPO. In den Hertzen?

JULI. Ja vnd leide groſse qual.

PICKL. Herr, Ihr fragt auch närrisch, sie sagt euchs ja, das ihre Schmertzen vmb die brust, bauch vnd nabel vnd umb die angränzenden länder am meisten regieren.

CAPO. Schweig Pickl Häring, oder ich lasse dich in die Kuchel führen, dich zu streichen.

PICKL. Vnd ich habe vermeindt, ihr wolt mir lassen ein fruhestuckh geben.

CAPOL. Tochter, deinen Zuestandt muefs man den Graffen wissen lassen.

JULI. Ach Herr Vatter, es ist besser der graff weiſs nichts von meinen anligen, ich bitte Herr Vatter, er wolle mir zur gnad vmb den Pater schickhen, der sie gewöhnlich besuechen thuet, das er mir einen geistlichen trost gebe, dan ich bin sehr krankh.

PICKL. Krankhe Leuth sollen lustig sein, wer weiſs wie lang sie leben.

CAPOL. Dein Zuestandt Tochter schmertzet mich, doch verfüge dich in dein Zimmer, der Pater soll dich array theeself in bridal pomp; for to-morrow is to be thy wedding-day.

JULIET. I know I owe obedience to my parents: but alas —

CLOWN. Hulloa! the wench has got a toothache.

CAPUL. Why dost thou sigh, my dear daughter, when thou mayest enjoy so many pleasures?

CLOWN. A sick man cannot have many pleasures.

JULIET. Ah, my tender years!

CLOWN. Did I not say so? She is already afraid of dying.

CAPUL. Thy tender years? which thou canst spend in unalloyed good fortune.

CLOWN. Provided she has plenty of money to spend.

JULIET. Alas, my good fortune destroys my happiness.

CAPUL. How so?

CLOWN. Because she has got a toothache.

JULIET. Dear father, in the diseases that may attack me, and other accidents that torment mankind.

CLOWN. As to me hunger is my torment, since the cook won't serve the dinner.

CAPUL. Why Juliet, if thou hast any complaint, tell me.

JULIET. I had better keep silence:

CAPUL. Where hast thou any pain?

JULIET. In the heart.

CAPUL. In the heart?

JULIET. Yes, and I suffer great torture.

CLOWN. Sir, you put foolish questions. Does she not tell you that her pains are principally in the neighbourhood of her breast, belly, navel, and the adjacent demesnes?

CAPUL. Be silent, fool, or I will have you led into the kitchen for a whipping.

CLOWN. I fondly imagined you wanted to give me a breakfast.

CAPUL. My daughter, the Count ought to be informed of thy state.

JULIET. Father, it is better the Count knows nothing of my complaint. For mercy's sake I beg you would send for the father who is in the habit of visiting you, to give me spiritual comfort, for I am very poorly indeed.

CLOWN. Invalids ought to be merry; who knows how long they have still to live!

CAPUL. Thy state grieves me; go to thy chamber, the father shall soon come to see you. Make haste to

bald besuechen, gelange nur bald zue deiner gesundtheit, damit du vnnſs erfrewest mit deinen Hochzeittag, ich gehe vnd verlasse dich. [*abit.*

PICKL. Ich bleib auch nicht mehr da. [*abit.*

JULI. Er lebe wohl Herr Vatter. Ach armseelige Julieta will dan das Verhängnuſs meines Vnsterns nicht aufhören, mich zu quälen? ich soll zwey Männer nehmen, der eine ist verbannt, der andere mich quält, waſs Rath? Der Hochzeittag ist vorhanden, ich liebe Romio vnd nicht graff Paris, meine Sünnen sein verwürt, ich weiſs mir nicht zu helffen, ach Pater niemahlen hab ich Euren Rath besser von nöthen gehabt alſs aniezo, aber siehe zu allen glickh ist er verhanden. Ach willkommen Herr Pater.

PATER.

PATER. Ich bedankhe mich Julieta, wie stehet es mit ihr, sie siehet sehr betrübt auſs, ist ihr waſs widerfahren? oder rühret es von Romio wegen her?

JULIET. Ach Pater, die überheuffige Schmertzen so ich leide machen mich gantz verzweiflen, in deme mein Vatter haben will, ich solte Graff Paris zu einen Mann haben, nun aber weiſs er selber besser, Herr Pater, wemb ich zuegehöre, vnd mit pflicht verbunden bin.

PATER. (Ich will sie ein wenig auf die prob stellen.) Hört mich Julieta, auſs zweyen üblen muſs man daſs beste erwehlen, weilen ihr den Romio nicht zu theil, sondern verbannet wisset, so vollbringet eurer Eltern befelch, vnd nehmbt den Graff Paris, welcher vor gewiſs ein wackherer gaualier ist.

JULI. Wie Pater seit ihr ein geistlicher, vnd wolt mit einem solchen Rath, daſs ich die Ehe vnd meine Ehr befleckhen soll? Nein nein, Pater, nein, ehe 10 mahl gestorben alſs Romio verlassen.

PATER. Anietzo verstehe ich euer beständigkeit, Julieta verzeihet mir, es war nur meine meinung, euch auf die prob zu stellen, weillen ich aber euer Hertz vnuerenderlich gegen Romio sehe, so habe ich ein werkh ersunnen, wo ihr folgen wollet, euch auſs aller gefahr zu helffen, damit ihr Romio erlangen möget.

JULI. Ach Pater, Vatter vnd Erretter meines lebens, wemb solte ich mehr gehorsamben alſs euch, weillen ich alles trosts beraubet bin, vnd mich in meinen Ellend vnd Schmertzen nicht mehr zu trösten weiſs.

PATER. So wisset Julieta, das es hochnöthig euch auf eine Zeit lang zu uerstellen, dardurch ihr nicht gezwungen werdet den Graffen Paris zu eheligen, wisset daſs ich in der Medicin sehr wohl erfahren, darumb schmuckhet vnd ziehret euch auf das beste alſs ein brauth, hernach will ich euch einen Schlafftrunkh be-

recover, that we may rejoice in thy wedding day. I will now leave thee. [*Exit.*

CLOWN. Nor shall I stay. [*Exit.*

JULIET. Good bye, father. Ah, miserable Juliet, will the fate of my unlucky star never cease to torment me? I am to take two husbands: one is banished, the other torments me; what counsel? My wedding-day is at hand; I love Romeo and not Count Paris. My mind is bewildered; I know not what to do. Oh, father, I never stood in greater need of your advice! But fortunately, there he is. Welcome, father.

Enter the FRIAR.

FRIAR. Thank you, Juliet. How are you? You look very sad. Has anything happened to you? or is it about Romeo?

JULIET. Ah, my father, my overwhelming suffering drives me to despair. My father wants me to take Count Paris. You know best to whom I belong, to whom I am in duty bound.

FRIAR. (*Aside:* I will try her a little.) Listen to me, Juliet; of two evils one ought to choose the smaller. As Romeo is banished, and cannot be yours, you had better perform the command of your parents, and take Count Paris, who is certainly a gallant cavalier.

JULIET. How so, my father? You, a minister, want me to contaminate my wedlock and my honour? No, no, father, no! sooner die a hundred times than give up Romeo.

FRIAR. Now I perceive your constancy, Juliet. Pardon me, it was but my intention to try you. But now that I see your heart is unchanged towards Romeo, I have contrived a plan to help you out of all danger, and to win your Romeo, provided you will follow me.

JULIET. Ah, father, saviour of my life! to whom should I pay more willing obedience than to you, bereaved, as I am, of every comfort, and not knowing where to seek for consolation in my grief and misery!

FRIAR. Know then, Juliet, that it is most necessary you should dissemble for a time, to elude compulsion. Understand that I am versed in medicine. Array yourself in bridal attire. After that I will prepare a potion which will make you appear dead for a certain time, and will persuade your parents to have you deposited

reithen, welcher euch ohne schaden auf gewisse Zeit todt vorstellen solle, vnd euere Eltern überreden, das sie euch in dafs Monument legen lassen, das wird ein Vrsach sein dafs beylager zu uerhindern, indessen aber will ich den Romio schreiben, in Eyl verkleidter weifs zu kommen euch zu entführen vnd also von allen Kummer zu entledigen, ist difs euer meinung auch Julieta?

JULI. Ach Schmertz, mein Vnglickh ist zu grofs dafs es mich hinwürfft wo es will, gleich einen ballen, wafs braucht es weither mein Romio ist verbannt, ich gezwungen noch einen zu nehmen, ach aber eher sterben alfs dises gut heifsen, darumb Pater brauchet güfft oder Schlafftrunkh, es ist mir beydes eins, wan ich nur Romio einmahl sehen kunte.

PATER. Sie stelle sich zufriden Julieta, vnd lasset eure Schmertzen bey euch nicht über Handt nehmen, die Hilff ist verhanden, der Schlafftrunkh kan Euch von allen Ellend vnd Schmertzen erledigen.

JULI. Wollan es sey so, euren willen zu folgen verfertiget den Schlafftrunkh, ich bin bereit solchen zu nehmen, es geschehe gleich zum todt oder leben.

PATER. Nein Julieta, sie entschlage sich solcher gedankhen vnd der Himmel behütte sie vor weithern Vnglickh, ich verhoffe durch dises vorgeschlagene Mittel, wird sie allen Kummer vnd Hertzenleid von ihr wenden.

JULI. Pater auf euer Hilff stehet mein Vertrawen, ich gehe euren Befehl zu volbringen.

PATER. Wollan so gehe ich den Schlafftrunkh zu uerfertigen vnd alles zu ihren besten bereithen. [abit.

JULI.
Der Himmel vnd sein Macht geb hiemit seinen Seegen,
Dafs aller Vnglickhfssturm damit sich möge legen.

SCENA 3ᵀᴵᴬ.

FRAW. AMMA. PICKL HÄRING.

FRAW. Amma!

AMMA. Wafs beliebt ihr gnaden?

FRAW. Saget mir, ist alles verfertiget vnd bereith zu meiner tochter beylager?

AMMA. Ich weifs nicht anders gnädige fraw, alfs dafs alles bereith vnd fertig ist.

FRAW. So gehe nach meiner Tochter Zimmer vnd frage sie ob sie geschmuckhet vnd geziehret ist, ihren breytigamb zu empfangen.

AMMA. Es soll geschehen gnädige Fraw.

PICKL. Alte bleib da, Julieta ligt in Schlaff, vnd traumet ihr von sachen, die Niemand wissen soll.

AMMA. Schaw der Narr da, hat viel zu sagen, ey das man nicht thuet was der Herr haben will, Narren

in the vault. Thus will the wedding be delayed. Meantime I will write to Romeo to speed hither in disguise, and to carry you off from this place and from your grief. Do you agree to this, Juliet?

JULIET. Alas, my misfortune is so great that it throws me hither and thither like a ball. There is no need of further reflection: my Romeo is banished, they are driving me to take another husband; I will sooner die than give in. Therefore, my father, let us use poison or the potion you mention, I don't care which, if I only see my Romeo once more.

FRIAR. Make your mind easy, Juliet, and don't allow yourself to be carried away by your grief. There is help at hand; my potion can save you from all your misery.

JULIET. Well, be it so. Prepare the potion, I am ready to take it for life or for death.

FRIAR. No, Juliet, discard such thoughts; Heaven will preserve you from further misfortune. I hope that by the means I propose, you will deliver yourself from your troubles.

JULIET. All my confidence is in your help; I am going to do your bidding.

FRIAR. And I am going to prepare the potion, and to arrange everything for your welfare. [Exit.

JULIET.
That Heaven and its power their blessing grant, I pray,
This tempest of misfortune and misery to lay!

SCENE III.

LADY CAPULET. NURSE. CLOWN.

LADY. Nurse!

NURSE. What is Your Grace's pleasure?

LADY. Is everything prepared and ready for my daughter's wedding?

NURSE. I don't know otherwise, my lady, but that everything is quite ready.

LADY. Then go to my daughter's chamber, and ask her if she is dressed to receive her bridegroom.

NURSE. It shall be done, my lady.

CLOWN. Stay, old girl; Juliet is asleep, and dreaming of things which no one is to know.

NURSE. Look at the fool! He has got much to say. Strange, that people should not do what their master

keren in die Kuchel, zu sehen ob das Essen fertig, vnd nicht mit Frawen Zimmer zu reden.

PICKL. O monstrum horrendum, du ein Frawen Zimmer, o altes Ribeisen vnd altes waffelscheitt, du alte abgeschabene ergötzlichkeit der lieb, was hast du mir zu befehlen?

FRAW. Schweig Pickl Häring vnd zankhet Euch nicht, ein Jedes verrichte was ihme befohlen.

AMMA. Gnädige Fraw der Narr.

PICKL. Gnädige Fraw die Närrin.

AMMA. Halts maul Holtzbockh.

PICKL. Halts maul alter strohsackh.

AMMA. Du bist halt ein Thue kein gut.

PICKL. Vnd du auf der welt nichts nutz.

AMMA. O du sauff aufs.

PICKL. O du alte fledermaufs.

FRAW. Pfuy schämet euch beyde, in gegenwarth meiner solche wordt zu brauchen.

AMMA. Gnädige Fraw, es ist ja nicht zu leiden.

PICKL. Gnädige Fraw, die alte soll mich zufriden lassen.

AMMA. Du werest mir nit gut genug meine Schuhe zu butzen.

PICKL. Vnd du werst mir nicht guet genug wo mein ruckhgrad ein End hat mich zu küssen.

FRAW. Pfuy schämet euch beyde vnd vergesset nicht den respect meiner persohn, gehet Amma, verrichtet was ich euch befohlen.

AMMA. Ich gehe dero Befehl zu uerrichten.
[*abit.*

FRAW. Höre Pickl Häring, du bist etwas grob wan du mit Frawenzimmer redest.

PICKL. Was grob ist, ist auch starkh, ich trauet mirs noch gröber zu machen, wan ich die alte Bockhreiterin nicht wegen Eurer verschonete.

Aufs AMMA.

AMMA. Ach gnädige Fraw was Vnglickh! Julieta ligt in ihrer besten Kleitung aufsgestrecket vnd todt.

PICKL. Das ist erstunkhen vnd erlogen, weil sie aufsgestreckt ligt, so muefs ich gehen vnd sehen was ihr schadt, dan ich verstehe mich tröfflich auf die aufsgestreckte Krankheiten. [*abit.*

FRAW. Der Himmel bewahre mich, Amma, wafs für ein schrocken hab ich eingenohmen.

AMMA. Ich wolte es währe nicht gn. Fraw wafs ich gesagt, aber ich wolt mir die Nasen abschneiden lassen wan Julieta nicht todt ist, dan ich verstehs in keine Kurtzweil mit den Kleidern in Beth zu ligen.

desires. Fools should look in at the kitchen, and see if dinner be ready, not converse with ladies.

CLOWN. O monstrum horrendum! You a lady? you old grater, you old wafer-iron, you worn-out instrument of pleasure, what business have you to command me?

LADY. Silence, don't quarrel; each of you do what he is bidden to do.

NURSE. My lady, that fool of a fellow —

CLOWN. My lady, that fool of a woman —

NURSE. Hold your tongue, you wood-louse!

CLOWN. Hold your tongue, old pad of straw!

NURSE. You are a ne'er-do-weel!

CLOWN. And you of no possible use in the world.

NURSE. You fuddle-cap.

CLOWN. You old bat.

LADY. Fye, you ought to be ashamed to use words like these in my presence.

NURSE. My lady, it is not to be borne.

CLOWN. My lady, why does not the old hag leave me alone.

NURSE. I should not hold you good enough to clean my shoes.

CLOWN. And I should not hold you good enough to kiss me where my spine ends.

LADY. Fye, do not forget the respect due to my person. Go, nurse, do what I told you.

NURSE. I am going to carry out your orders.
[*Exit.*

LADY. I tell thee, clown, thou art somewhat rude when talking to a woman.

CLOWN. Rudeness is strength; I should trust myself to do it more rudely still, if I did not spare the old goat-rider for your sake.

Re-enter NURSE.

NURSE. My lady, what a disaster! Juliet lies here dressed out in her best, stretched out, and dead.

CLOWN. You lie in your throat. As she is stretched out, I must go and see what is the matter with her; I thoroughly understand stretching complaints. [*Exit.*

LADY. Heaven preserve me! Nurse, how you did frighten me!

NURSE. I wish, my lady, what I told you were not true; but I will have my nose cut off if Juliet be not dead. I do not take it for a pastime to lie in bed all dressed.

Pickl Häring.

Pickl. O Ellend, o noth, o barmbhertzigkeit, o mausericordia, Julieta hat sich zu todt gestorben, o erschröckliche bost Zeitung, sie ligt aufs gestreckt mit Händt vndt Füefsen, vnd ist so steuff als ein gefrohrner Stockhfisch.

Fraw. Wie wafs sagst du, Pickl Häring, Julieta todt?

Pickl. Das weifs ich nicht ob sie todt ist, aber sie ligt vnd rührt sich nicht, vnd ihre Seel ist schon in den 24 Elementen.

Fraw. O Jammer, o Ellend, ist Julieta todt so hat mein Frewd ein End, ach armer graff Paris, wafs wird er dar zue sagen, aber hier kompt mein Herr, ach Julieta, armseelige Julieta.

Capulet. Pater.

Capol. Wie ich gesagt, Herr Pater, darbey soll es verbleiben, den wer eine sach vornimbt, soll es beschleinig vollführen.

Pater. Nach dero Befelch, Herr Capolet, soll alles mit höchstem Fleifs verrichtet werden.

Capol. Aber wafs hat difs zu bedeuten, dafs meine gemahlin die thränen abthrukhnet, wie ists liebste gemahlin? was vor eine traurigkeit presset thränen von Euren augen vnd zwinget Euch zum weinen.

Fraw. Ach liebster Herr vnd Gemahl, Vnglickh über Vnglickh.

Capol. Der Himmel bewahre vnfs alle vor Vnglickh, wafs soll dises bedeuten?

Pickl. Herr, der Marder ist ins Tauben Haufs kummen vnd hat 2 junge Tauben zu todt gebissen, ob ers gar gefressen, das weifs ich nicht, vnd dafs ist ja vnglickhs genug?

Fraw. Ach liebster Herr vnd Gemahl, Julieta ist todt.

Pickl. Ist dan das so grofse sach, das ein Mahl ein Mensch stirbt.

Capol. Wie? Wafs? Julieta todt? Das seye der Himmel vor.

Fraw. Es ist nicht anderst, dan die Amma vnd Pickl Häring haben sie beyde todt gesehen.

Capol. Ist es wahr, Pickl Häring?

Pickl. Ich vermeine wohl, es wird wahr sein, dan sie ligt vnd rührt sich nicht, hört vnd sieht nicht, vnd ligt aufsgestreckt wie ein Holtz Klotz, weither brauchts nichts mehr, alfs dafs die Schueler kommen, tragen sie hinwekh vnd singen: mit frid vnd frewd fahr ich dahin, vnd reifse meine strafsen.

Clown.

Clown. Oh misery, oh distress, oh pity, o mausericordia! Juliet is dead. Oh dreadful news! There she lies, hands and feet stretched out, and as stiff as a frozen stockfish.

Lady. What say you, fool, Juliet dead?

Clown. Whether dead or not, I don't know. But the fact is she lies and does not budge, and her soul is already in the twenty-four elements.

Lady. Oh woe, oh misery! If Juliet is dead, there is an end to joy for me. Poor Count Paris, what will he say to it. But there comes my Lord. Ah, Juliet, poor Juliet!

Capulet. Friar.

Capulet. As I said before, father, so shall it be done; for whoever begins a thing ought to carry it out.

Friar. Pursuant to your orders, my lord, everything shall be executed with the greatest promptness.

Capulet. But what does it mean that my wife is wiping her tears? What is the matter, dearest wife? What sorrow brings the tears into your eyes, and makes you weep?

Lady. Dearest lord and husband, misery upon misery!

Capulet. Heaven preserve us all! what does this mean?

Clown. The marten has broken into the dove-cote and killed two young pigeons; I do not know whether he has eaten them too. Is that not misfortune enough?

Lady. Dearest lord and husband, Juliet is dead.

Clown. Is it such a great thing that some one dies?

Capulet. What? Juliet dead? Heaven forbid!

Lady. It is so indeed; both nurse and jester have seen her dead.

Capulet. Is it true, clown?

Clown. I am indeed of opinion it is true. For she is lying, and does not move, nor hear, nor see, and is stretched out like a log. There is nothing wanting but that the students come, carry her away, and sing: With peace and joy I hie from hence, and travel on my way.

Fraw. Ach wehe, es ist nur all zu wahr, helffet, ein ohnmacht überfallet mich.

Capul. Helffet meiner gemahlin vnd bringet sie von hier in ihr Zimmer sie zu laben [*wurd weckh getragen*]. Ach ist Julieta todt? ach ich armer mann, so ist mein trost vnd frewd gestorben. Ach Paris, Paris, dein lieben ist vmbsonst.

Pater. Mein Herr Capolet, er betrübe sich nicht so sehr, wans des Himmels will, dessen Befelch mufs man vollziehen.

Capol. Ach Pater, der Fall ist zu grofs, dafs angesezte Beylager ist verhanden, wafs wird Graff Paris sagen, wan er erfahren, das seine brauth gestorben, sein lieben vmbsonst, anstatt des brauth Krantz soll er todte Cypressen auf ihr grab strewen, ach trawer, Kummer vnd Hertzensangst.

Pater. Mein Herr Capulet, wie schmertzlich es ihme von Hertzen geht, ist leicht zu glauben, aber aufs 2 Übel muefs vnd soll man das beste erwehlen, weillen es geschehen, wer kan es endern. Es währe mein Rath, man lasse es den Graff Paris wissen, Julieta aber in ihr Monument legen, vnd anstatt des Frewden fest ein trawrige leichbegängnufs halten, seine vnd dero Gemahlin bekümmernufs wolle der Herr den himlischen willen aufopffern.

Capol. Ach Pater, weillen es nicht anderst sein kan, so geschehe des Himmels will, last Euch angelegen sein auf dafs Julieta in dafs Monument geleget werde, vnd das man ihr die lezte Ehr erzeigen kan, ich aber gehe den Graffen solches schrüfftlich zu berichten, wofern mich nicht auch der Kummer vnd Hertzenleid in dafs grab leget. [*abit*.

Pater. Es soll alles verrichtet werden Gn. Herr, wollan dan ich Romio geschrieben in höchster Eyl zu kommen, ich hoffe der anfang soll noch einen glicklichen aufsgang erreichen, damit Julieta nicht zwey mahl verheyrathet werde. [*abit*.

[*Traurige Music, Julieta ligt in Monument.*]

Paris *mit ein Korb voll Blumen vnd* Jung.

Paris. Hier ist der orth vnd platz, wo dafs Monument aufgericht vnd Julieta begraben ligt, auf Paris, gehe Julieta zu besuechen, erzeige ihr die letzte Ehr, weil du in ihren leben nicht gewürdiget worden sie zu bedienen, o grausamber vnd tyrannischer todt, wie bald hast du mein gedachte frewd in dafs gröste leyd verändert, wer hette jemahls gedacht, dafs du, liebste Julieta, vor Genüssung meiner getrewen lieb soltest deinen Geist aufgeben, o meineidiges glickh! der ich ver-

Lady. Ah woe, it is but too true! Help, I am going to faint.

Capulet. Assist my wife, bring her to her chamber, give her some cordial. [*They carry her out.*] Juliet dead? Alas, wretched man that I am! With her my joy and comfort are dead too. Ah Paris, Paris, thy love is in vain.

Friar. My lord, do not be so afflicted. What God ordains must be fulfilled.

Capulet. Ah, my father, the case is too hard. The wedding is fixed. What will Count Paris say on learning that his bride is dead, his love in vain, that instead of the bridal wreath he is to strew cypresses on her tomb? Oh sadness, grief, and anguish!

Friar. Sir, I can readily believe how this cuts you to the heart. But of two evils one ought always to choose the least. The thing has happened; who can alter it? I should advise you to inform Count Paris, have Juliet deposited in her monument, and hold a mournful funeral instead of a joyous feast. Your and your lady's sorrow, mylord, must be sacrificed to the will of heaven.

Capulet. As there is no help the will of Heaven be done. Make it your business to have Juliet deposited in the monument, and everything prepared to show her the last honours. I will go and write to the Count, unless sorrow sends me too to the grave.

[*Exit*.

Friar. Everything shall be done, my gracious lord. — And now I am off to write to Romeo to hurry hither. I hope what is begun will end well, and Juliet not be married twice.

[*Exit*.

[*Doleful music. Juliet is seen lying in the vault.*]

Paris, *with a basket of flowers.* Page.

Paris. This is the place where the monument is erected, and where Juliet is buried. Now Paris go and visit her, and show her the last honours as thou wast not found worthy of serving her in life. Cruel, tyrant death, how quickly hast thou changed my anticipated joys to the deepest grief! Who would have ever imagined that you, beloved Juliet, wouldst depart from this world before enjoying my true love. Perjured fate! Having dreamt of all happiness, I come to see this miserable end of my

meint alle glickhseeligkeiten zu genüssen, so sehe ich dafs erbärmliche Endt meiner Liebe! Ist difs köstliche Hochzeitfest meiner frewde, ist difs der Lust Saal, darin ich mich soll ergötzen? wo bleibt der wohl gezierte brauth Crantz? wo die Stein vnd perlen? wo der Kleider Pracht? Ach ach, es ist leider nichts von nöthen, alfs dafs schwähre Seuffzen vnd Clagen. Komme hier, Diener, reiche mir die Blumen, vnd gehe nicht zu weith, damit so Jemand kompt mir ein Zeichen gebest.

JUNG. Es soll geschehen, gnädiger Herr.

PARIS. Ach vnbarmbhertziges Glickh! warumb hast du mir das Jenige entzogen, welches mein Hertz so inniglich geliebet? Wohl, liebste Julieta, also will ich alle tag dir zu Ehren deinen leichnamb mit Blumen ziehren. [*Sträut die blumen auff sie.*

ROMIO *mit* DIENER.

ROMIO. Hier bin ich angelangt, weil mir der Pater geschrieben, ich soll so schnell alfs es möglich alhier anlangen, aber ey lafs, von allen Vnglick übertroffen, weillen Julieta todt, o betrügliche Hoffnung, die du die Menschen zu lockhen weist, vnd versprichst sie nimmer zu uerlassen, wo ist Julieta hinkommen? o grausambe Scheidung! Die vollkombneste Ehe, so jemahls gewesen. Julieta ist todt! vnd alle ihre Schönheiten, Holdseeligkeiten, Süfs vnd liebligkeiten, alle ihr Zucht vnd Keuschheit seint zugleich mit ihr gestorben. Julieta todt? vnd ich schäme mich nicht, länger ein vnglickhseeliges leben auf Erden zu führen? Julieta todt! o tödtliche wordt, weil in disen wenigen wordten all mein vnglickh, Jammer vnd noth begriffen vnd mit der Zeit auch über den armen Romio sollen gesprochen werden, so verstehe mich, Diener, gib her die fackl vndt verlasse mich, dan ich will dafs Monument besehen, vnd den Ehering von Julieta nehmen.

DIENER. Ach gnädiger Herr, ich will hier verbleiben, vielleicht haben Sie meiner von nöthen.

ROMIO. Nein verlasse mich, erwarthe meiner bey dem Pater vnd zeige ihm meine Ankunfft an, dan ich will alhier Julieta beehren.

DIENER. So gehe ich auf Ihr Gn. Befehl. [*abit.*
[*Defs Paris Jung pfeifft.*

PARIS. Mein Jung gibt mir dafs Zeichen, das Jemand muefs vorhanden sein, wer soll sich wohl vnterstehen, vmb dise Zeit in dafs Monument zu gehen? ich sehe ein fackl, ich will mich etwas auf die Seyth begeben, vnd sehen was der anfang sey.
[*Romio geht zum Monument.*

Holla, weiche zuruckh, Vermessener, wer gibt dir Befehl, disen orth zu betretten?

love. Is this the delicious marriage-feast of my joy, this the hall of my revel? Where is the richly ornamented bridal wreath? where are the jewels and the pearls? where the splendid dresses? Alas, nothing is required but heavy sighing and lamenting. Come here, boy, hand me the flowers and stand aloof, but do not go too far, and give me a sign as soon as any one approaches.

PAGE. I will do as you bid, my lord.

PARIS. Ah merciless fate! why hast thou robbed me of what my heart loved so tenderly! Dearest Juliet, thus will I daily strew flowers on thy body in thy honour.

[*Scatters the flowers over her.*

ROMEO. SERVANT.

ROMEO. Here I am, because the friar wrote to me to come as quickly as possible, but alas, overwhelmed by misfortune, for Juliet is dead. Oh deceitful hope! that allures man and promises never to fail him! Where is Juliet? Oh cruel separation! The most perfect marriage that ever was! Juliet dead! and with her all her beauty, charm, sweetness, and loveliness, all her modesty and chastity are dead too! Juliet dead? And I am not ashamed to protract a miserable existence! Juliet dead? Oh deadly word, comprising within itself all my misery, and destined to be pronounced one day also over poor Romeo! Heed what I say, boy! Give me the torch and leave me. I am going to visit the monument, and take the wedding-ring from Juliet.

SERVANT. Sir, I had better stay; perhaps you may need me.

ROMEO. No, leave me and wait for me at the friar's. Tell him I have arrived, while I remain here to honour Juliet.

SERVANT. I go at your command. [*Exit.*
[*The boy of Paris whistles.*

PARIS. The boy gives me warning that something is approaching. Who dares enter the vault at this time? I see a torch; I will retire a little, and watch what happens.

[*Romeo goes towards the monument.*

Hollah, keep off, audacious man! who gave thee authority to enter this place?

ROMIO. Freundt, wer ihr seit, last mich zufriden, vnd saget das ein verzweifelter Mensch Euch Euer leben geschenkhet.

PARIS. Ich sage weiche, verlasse disen orth oder gib dich gefangen.

ROMIO. Diser orth gebührt mir mit recht zu betretten, vnd weil du die Verhindernuſs bist mich zu uerhinderen, so nihme diſs vnd fahre nach der Höllen zue.
[*Ersticht Paris.*

PARIS. Ach Verräther, was thuest du?
Ach wehe ich sterbe hier,
Julieta, liebste brauth,
Jezt komm ich auch zu dir,
Weil du mir warst vertraut.   [*Stirbt.*

ROMIO. Ich muſs gleichwohl sehen wer es ist — ach Himmel es ist der vnglickseelige Graff Paris, ich glaube daſs diser Cörper auch von allen Vnglickh zusammen gemacht, aber o ihr meine vnglickhseelige augen, sehet hier ein rechtes Todten Spectacul, o Julieta, werther Schatz, viel lieber hette ich den todt leiden sollen, alſs dich todt vor mir sehen. Ach biſs in todt geliebste Julieta, weil ich keinen trost mehr weiſs vnd deine Seel schon nach dem Himmel geflogen, ich nur mein Vnglickh alhier beweinen soll, ach nein ich senne mich nach dir, liebste Seele, ey laſs, dein verblichener leichnamb ligt nunmehro ohne gehör, wordt vnd reden, ach warumb verlast du mich mitten in solchen Ellend, o wie komb ich mir selbsten so vnglickseelig vor, vnd waſs? Julieta ist todt vnd ich soll noch leben? Nein, nein, Romio, nein! Nimb den lezten Abschids Kuſs von Julieta vnd bereitte dich zum sterben. Komme, mein gewöhr, durchdringe mein abgemattetes Hertz vnd bringe mich zu meiner Julieta.

Himmel, verzeihe mir,
Waſs ich hier hab gethan.
Ich sterbe willig gahr
Als Julieta Mann.   [*Stirbt.*

Music. Julieta erwacht im Monument.

JULI. O ihr Götter, was ist das? wo befindt ich mich? in einen todten Sarg oder todten Gefängnuſs. Wie muefs das zuegehen, es brennen liechter alſs ob man mich begraben hette, dise anordtnung ist gewiſs von Pater gestellet, dardurch zu glauben, ich seye gestorben, der Schlafftrunkh hat seine würkhung gethan, darumb muefs ich sehen, das ich den Pater antreffe vnd waſs mein wunder Hochzeit noch vor ein Ende gewünnen werde. Aber ihr götter bewahret mich, waſs ligen hier todter leuth? Julieta, faſs ein Hertz vnd sehe wer

ROMEO. Friend, whoever you are, leave me alone, and say, that a desperate man spared your life.

PARIS. I say to thee, give way, leave this spot or give thyself up.

ROMEO. It belongs to me by right to tread this spot: and since you interfere take this and go to hell.
[*Stabs him.*

PARIS. Oh traitor, what hast thou done?
Alas I'm dying here!
Now I too, Juliet, come to thee,
To thee, my bride so dear,
For thou belong'st to me.   [*He dies.*

ROMEO. However I must see who it is — good Heavens, it is the unfortunate Paris. I think, this body too was made up of misfortune. What a spectacle of death are my hapless eyes doomed to see! Juliet, thou treasure of my life, far sooner would I have died myself than see thee a corpse. Ah, Juliet, thou most loved one till death! for I know no consolation more, and thy soul has flown up to heaven. I must bewail my misery here alone. Ah no; I yearn for thee, dearest soul. Alas, thy pale corpse lies now for evermore without hearing, word, or speech! Why dost thou leave me in the midst of so much misery? How wretched do I appear to myself! What? Juliet dead, and I shall still live? No, no, Romeo, no! Take Juliet's last parting kiss, and prepare to die. Out my trusty weapon, pierce my weary heart, and bring me to my Juliet.

Mercy for what I did
In heaven's eye!
Husband of Juliet
Willing I die.   [*He dies.*

Music. Juliet wakes.

JULIET. Oh ye gods, what is this? Where am I? Is it a coffin or a charnel-house? How could this happen? There are tapers as if they had buried me. Certainly this is the friar's contrivance to make people believe I am dead. That potion did its work well. I must try to see the friar, and find out what is to be the end of this wondrous wedding. But ye gods preserve me! what dead men are lying here? Juliet, take heart, see who they are; no greater evil can befall thee than thou art accustomed to bear.

es ist, dan es kan dir kein vnglickh begegnen, das du nicht gewohnet bist aufszustehen.

[*Nimbt ein liecht geht zu Paris.*

Hilff Himmel, hilff, waſs ist dafs? ist das nicht Graff Paris? Ja er ist es, ach er hat sich gewiſs ermord vmb meinetwillen, weillen seine muethmaſsung gewesen, ich sey gestorben, ach armer liebhaber ich beklage deinen todt mit Seufftzen, weil du vmb meinetwillen gestorben — aber waſs ligt hier vor einer — ach gerechter Himmel bewahre mich, waſs sehen meine Augen? ach ihr götter, es ist Romio vnd liget auch ermordet, ach pein, Martter, angst vnd qual, wie muefs dises zuegehen, ich weiſs kein andere aufslegung alſs daſs sie sich beyde vmb meinet willen geschlagen vnd todt verbliben, ach Romio bist du gestorben? so muefs ich dir alfs meinen Mann billich folgen.

Ach Vatter, Muetter, Freundt,
Ich nehmb von Euch Valet,
Ich sterbe voller Schmertz,
Ihr wüst nicht wie mirs geht,
Ach Romio, mein Schatz!
So bist du nun so g'storben,
Du hast durch deinen todt
Mir auch mein todt erworben.
Nimb hin, o Jupiter,   [*stost*
Mein Seel von disen leib,
Damit ich nicht alhier
In stetten Jammer bleib.   [*stirbt.*

Auſs PATER.

PATER. Nunmehro ist es Zeit, daſs ich mich in das Monoment verfüge, dan der schlafftrunkh wird seine würckung verrichtet haben, wan Julieta wider erwacht, daſs ich sie aufs dem Monoment führe vndt errette, damit sie heimlich mit Rumio, ihren Eheman, entweichen kan.

[*Gehet gegen den Monoment.*

Aber gerechter Himmel, waſs ligt hier auf der Erdten, todte Leichnam? Ach weh, ich sehe Julieta todt, Rumio entleibt, Paris in seinen Bluth ligen, ach Freterey, Freterey.

Auſs FÜRST, CAPULET vnd PATER.

JUNG. Es ist nicht anderst, gnädigster Fürst vnd Herr, wie ich berichtet, so wird sich alles fündten.

FÜRST. Holla! Waſs sehen wir, waſs macht der Pater in dem Monoment?

PATER. Ach gnad, gnädigster Fürst vndt Herr, gnadt.

CAPULET. Wie Pater, waſs bittet ihr vmb Gnadt?

[*Takes a candle, and approaches Paris.*

Help, Heaven, help! what is this? Is this not Count Paris? Yes, it is he. No doubt, he has destroyed himself and for my sake, thinking me dead. Poor lover, I bewail thy death, because thou hast died for my sake. But there is another. Ah just Heaven defend me! What do my eyes behold? Ah ye gods, it is Romeo, and he also lies here, murdered! Oh torment, fear, and anguish! How could this happen? No other solution do I know than that they fought on my account, and both have fallen! Romeo, art thou dead? — Then it is right that I follow thee as my husband.

Ah father, mother, friends!
I bid you here adieu.
I die oppressed with grief;
My state ye little knew.
Ah Romeo, my love!
As now thy spirit's flown,
Thy death has been the means
Of bringing me my own.
Take from this frame, I pray,
O Jove, my soul again,   [*Stabs herself*
That I may not alway
In endless woe remain!   [*Dies.*

Enter FRIAR.

FRIAR. The time has arrived to visit the monument. The potion will have had its effect. When Juliet awakes I must lead her from here to some safe place, whence she may fly with her husband Romeo.

[*Approaches the monument.*

But, gracious Heaven, what is this lying here on the ground? Dead bodies! Alas, I see Juliet dead, Romeo slain, Paris weltering in his blood! O treachery, treachery!

PRINCE. CAPULET. FRIAR.

PAGE. It is exactly, my gracious Prince and Lord, as I have said. You will find everything as I told you.

PRINCE. Hollah! What do I see? What is the friar about in the monument?

FRIAR. Most gracious Prince, mercy!

CAPULET. What, friar, are you begging for mercy?

Habt ihr Wisenschafft vmb dise mord, oder selbsten interessirt, saget, redt die wahrheit, damit wir aufs disen Irrthumb kommen.

PATER. Ach gnädigster Fürst vndt Herr, wie auch Herr Capulet, mir als einen geistlichen gebühret nicht zu ligen oder mit der Vnwahrheit vmbzugehen.

FÜRST. Wer mit der Wahrheit handlet, hat sich keiner straff zu befürchten, wir begehren nur zu wissen, wafs Ewere Verrichtung vnd wafs ihr vmb dise Zeit in den Monoment zu thun habet.

PATER. So wissen Sie dan, gnädigster Fürst vndt Herr, wie auch Herr Graff Capulet, dafs Rumio, des Graffen Mundige leiblicher Sohn, sterblich sich in Julieta, Ewere tochter, verliebt, wie auch nicht weniger die Julieta in Rumio, vnd eben damals als Herr Capulet dafs pancket gehalten, vndt Rumio mit Julieta getanzet hat, die Liebe bey ihnen beyden der massen zu genohmen, dafs sie zu mir kommen, vndt vorgaben, wan ich sie nicht in geheimb copuliren wolle, wollen sie ihre erhizte Liebe ohne Ehestandt vollführen. Ich truge ihnen vor die gefahr, darinn sie sich stürzen wurden, aber mein Vermahnen war vmbsonst, endlichen wolte mir als einen Prister gebühren aus zweyen Übeln das beste zu erwehlen, vndt hielte den Ehestandt vor billicher als die vnverheyrate Liebe, gab sie zusammen: Aufs diser Liebe ist leyder dafs erbärmliche Vnglickh erwachsen.

CAPULET. Pater, Ewere Meinung ist nicht in Bösen geschehen, aber leyder übel ausgeschlagen, indeme Niemandt nichts von diser verborgenen Liebe gewust.

PATER. Gnädiger Herr, dafs ich dises gethan ist geschehen, weillen ich wuste die grosse Feindschafft beyder Häuser, nemlichen Mundige vnd Capulet, dafs der Himmel dermaleines durch solche Verbündnufs der Ehe des Rumio vndt Julieta möchte zertrennt[?], vnd die Feindschafft in ewige Freindschafft verkheret werden, weillen es aber leyder anderst ausgeschlagen, bitte ich mich vor entschuldigt zu halten.

FÜRST. Pater, die Fäller der Menschen seindt wunderbahr, wie leicht die Jugend genaygt zu fellen, ist weltkündig, darumb haben die fäller Rumio, Paris vnd Julieta ins grab gelegt, Herr Graff Capulet, was hier geschehen, ist nicht mehr zu endern, er lege ab seine Schmertzen vnd denckhe:

Was hier der Himmel nimbt das kan er widergeben,
Wir müssen sein bedacht dort vor das ewig leben.

CAPULET. Gnädigster Fürst vndt Herr, meine grawe Haar des Alters schmertzen mich nicht so sehr, als diser tödtliche Fall, welcher mich selber zu grabe ziehen soll, aber meine sinnen zeichen mir, das ich disen trawer

Have you cognizance of this murder, or any part in it? Speak, tell us the truth, that we may at last get out of this bewilderment.

FRIAR. Most gracious Lord and you, Sir Capulet, it does not behove me, a man of the church, to lie and deal with untruth.

PRINCE. He who acts with truth, need fear no punishment. All we want to know is, what business you have in the monument at this time of night.

FRIAR. Know then, gracious Prince and you, Count Capulet, that Romeo, Count Montague's son, was enamoured with your daughter Juliet, and Juliet not less enamoured with Romeo. At the time of your banquet, where Romeo danced with Juliet, love waxed so strong in both, that they came to me to tell me that, unless I would unite them in wedlock, they would obey their burning love without matrimony. I represented to them the danger they were going to incur; but my exhortation were in vain. At last, being a priest I had to choose the least of two evils, and prefering matrimony to love without it, I united them. Out of that love has this dire calamity arisen.

CAPULET. What you did was not ill meant, but unfortunately it has turned out badly, because nobody knew anything of this secret love.

FRIAR. Gracious Sir, I did what I did knowing what great enmity existed between the houses of Montague and Capulet, and hoping by this marriage of Romeo's and Juliet's to clear the sky and turn enmity into everlasting friendship. Since, unfortunately, it has turned out otherwise, I crave for mercy.

PRINCE. Father! The ways in which men come to their fall are wonderful. How prone youth is to fall is known to all. Thus have their sad fates laid Romeo, Paris, and Juliet in the grave. Count Capulet, what has happened here cannot be undone; lay aside your grief, and bear in mind:

What Heaven may take here, again can Heaven give,
We must remember that we shall for ever live.

CAPULET. Most gracious Prince and Lord! My gray hairs do not press so heavily upon me as this fatal accident which will drag me to the grave. But reason teaches me to submit to the justice of heaven. I shall

Fall dem gerechten Himmel heimbstellen solle, darum
will ich ihnen zu ehren anstalt machen, dafs sie nach
ihren standt zur erden beygelegt werdten.

O jammervoller Schmertz! Julieta ist gestorben;
O wunderschöne blum! du bist zu fruh verdorben.

HERTZOG.

O groser Trawers Fall! Wie hart gehst du zu Hertzen!
Der hier sie ligen sicht, sicht nichts als lauter Schmertzen.

CAPULET.

Du Liebe hast's gethan! Seind alle drey gefallen,
Die Liebe hat die Schuldt. Seind dafs nicht Hertzens-
      quallen?

PATER.

Die Jugend ist nicht klug, sie liebet vnbedacht;
Die lieb hat sie gar offt zu solchen Fall gebracht.

CAPULET.

Kunt Paris nicht mein Kündt in seinen Leben krigen,
So soll er nach dem todt in ihren grabe liegen.
O werthe schawer Zahl, heist difs nicht recht betrüben,
Ein ieder hütte sich vor solchen Vnglicks Lieben.

ENDE.

prepare the last honours for them, that they may be
buried according to their rank.

O miserable woe! My Juliet is dead.
O loveliest of flowers! Too early droops thy head.

PRINCE.

O mournful spectacle! Thou to my heart dost go;
Who sees them lying here, sees nought but pain and woe.

CAPULET.

Thou hast done this, O love! The death of all these three
Is fault of love alone. Is not that misery.

FRIAR.

Youth is not wise at all, it loves without a thought,
And often love on youth has such destruction brought.

CAPULET.

If Paris during life my daughter could not wed,
In one grave shall he lie with her now that he's dead.
Is't not a sorry sight, O ye spectators all,
Beware that none of you, such ill-starred love befall.

THE END.

INDEX.

Aaron, a dancer. xcvii
Actor, Flemish, at Vienna. 1560. xxi
Actors by profession, earlier in England than in Germany. vii
—— English in Germany etc. *see* Comedians.
—— Flemish, xxix; Foreign, in England. . xi
"Adulteress", The, a tragedy. . . . . xliii, xlvii
"Ahasverus and Esther", a play. cix
Albrecht Frederick, Prince of Prussia. . . . lxxxiv
Allegorical characters in Prologues. . . . cxx
Alleyn, Edward, founder of Dulwich college. xxviii, xxxi
Alleyn, Edward, a player. . . . . . xxvii, xxxi
Alphonsus, Cardinal. xxiii
Altorf, University of. xxxv
"Amadis", a comedy. lxxxiii
Ambassadors, foreign, at the court of Elisabeth. xvii
"Amphitrion", a German play. cxv
Amsterdam, English Comedians in. lxxvi, xc; incident at a play, acted there by English Comedians. cxxii
Ancilla, a character in the "Jew of Venice", a German play. cxviii
Andreae, Valentine. cvi
Andrewes, Richard, a player. xxx
"Angiers, Count of", a German play. . . . cxvi
"Angry Catharine", The, a German play. . . cxix
Anhalt, *see* Ludwig, Prince of, *and* Hans Ernst, Prince of.
Anna, Princess of Denmark. xxxix
"Antonio and Malcida", a play by Marston. . cxx
Antwerpe, city of. xxiii
Apology for actors, by Thom. Heywood. . . xxiii
Aptitude of the English for dramatic entertainments. ix

Archibold, a Capucin friar. xci
Arcial, a King in a play. cx
"Ariodante and Geneuora", a play. lxxiii
"Arrival of the Saints", a play. x
"Art above all arts", a German play. . cxxiv, cxxx
Arzschar [Archer?], a player. lxxxviii
Athletes, English, abroad. xxi
Augsburg, Theatres at. vii
Austrian Minstrels in England. xi
Authorities, Civil and Municipal, the patrons of the stage. vii
Ayrer, Jacob, xlii, lvii, lxi—lxxvii; his comedy of the Beautiful Sidea, lxviii, Part II, 1; his comedy of the Beautiful Phaenicia, lxxi, Part II, 77.

Bale, John, his plays printed abroad. . . . xi
Balge, English Comedians in. xcii
Bamberg, city of. . . . . lxi, lxii
Bandello. . . . . lxvi, lxxii, cxxxii
"Barrabas, Jew of Malta", a German play. . cxvi
"Bartholomew Fair", a play by Ben Jonson. . cxiii
Basle, English Comedians in. cii
"Battle of the senses", a German play. . . . cvii
Bautin, John. xii
Bavarian Minstrels in England. xi
Bear-baiting in London. . . . . xvi, xvii
Beaumont and Fletcher, his "Prophetess". . . cxviii
Beauvois, De, French Ambassador. . . . . xii, xiv
Ben Jonson, cxiii; his „Every Man". . . . xxvii
Bentley, George, a dancer. xcvii
Berlin, English Comedians in, xxiv, xxvii, lxxx, lxxxiii
                                                            lxxxviii, xcii
Betulius, Xystus. cvii

INDEX.

Beyzandt [Bryan], George, a player. xxv
Bible, dramatic subjects taken from the. . . vi
"Birth of the Saviour", a play. x
Bishops, English, at Constance. x
Blackfriar's Theatre. . . . . xxvi, xxvii
"Blanket-washer", a German Droll. . . . cix
Boccaccio. . . . . xxxvii, cxxxiii
Bodmer. cxxxvi
Bora, Käthe von, Luthers wife, ridiculed on
  the stage in London. xii
Borck, Baron von, his translation of "Julius
  Caesar". cxxxvi
Bösslin, John. cii
"Bottom the Weaver", a play. cxxxi
Bouset, John, the clown. . . . . xliii, liii
Brakel, an English merchant in Elbing. . . lxxxii
Brandenburg, John Sigismund Elector of. . . xcii
——— George William Elector of. . . . xcii
——— Christian William of, Administrator
  of Magdeburg. xc
Breadstreet, John, a player. xxviii, xxxiii—xxxv, cxxxv
Brederode, G. A. xc
Breitstrass, see Breadstreet.
Bremen, city of. xv
Breslau, English Comedians in. xciii
Breuningen von Buchenbach, Hans Jacob. . . xiv
"British Kings at war", the two, a German play. lviii
Browne, Edw., a player. . . . . . . xxx, xxxii
——— Robert, a player. . . xxviii, xxx to xxxiii
——— Mrs xxxi
Brone, Robert, see Browne.
Brünighofen, Hans Georg von. xii
Brunswick, city of. xxxv
——— English Comedians in. . . xxxiv, lxxxviii
——— Dorothea, Princefs of. xc
——— a Prince of, at the court of James I. xix
Brussels, English Comedians at. xc
Bryan, George, a player. . . xxiii, xxv, xxvii, lxxvi
Bull-baiting in London. . . . . . . xvi, xvii
Bürger, G. A. lvi
Butzbach, Landgrave Philip of. lxxxix
Buwinghausen, Benjamin von. . . . . . xiv, xix

Caius, Dr., a character in the "Merry Wives
  of Windsor". liii
Cambridge, Count Frederick of Mömpelgard at,
  xiii; Prince Ludwig of Anhalt at. . . . xv
Canterbury. . . . . xii, xv
Capitano, a typic character of the old Italian
  stage. xlvi

Casse, Robert, a player. c
Cassel, English Comedians at. . . . . . xviii, lvii
"Catharina, die böse," a German play. . . . cxxx
Catharine of Navarre. xxxix
"Celide and Sedea", a play. lxxxvii
Cellarius, Johannes. xxxv
Cervantes, his "Curioso impertinente". . . . cxiv
Chalmers. . . . . xxvii, lii
Charles, Archduke and Bishop of Breslau. . xciii
Characters, number of, in early Plays. . . . vii
Chaucer. x
"Christabella", a German play. cxv
Christian I, Elector of Saxony. . . . xxiii, lxxvi
——— His letters to King Fre-
  derick II. of Denmark and Hans Thilo, his
  Steward. xxiv
——— His appointement of the
  English Comedians. xxv
Christian IV, King of Denmark. . . xxiii, xxxix
Christian William of Brandenburg, Administra-
  tor of Magdeburg. xc
Church questions connected with Plays. . . vii
Citizens as actors. xii
Clant, John, the clown. xlii
Classical antiquity revived. iv
Clown, the, in Ayrer's plays. lxv
Cockfights in London. xvi
Cologne, English Comedians in. xci
Comedians, English, on the Continent in 1417, x;
  conjectures respecting them, xx; their wanderings to the Continent, xxii; the earliest
  actors by profession in Germany, xxxvi; charged with corrupting the taste in Germany,
  xxxviii; not allowed to act at Zürich, ciii;
  their Repertoire, civ; the language in which
  they performed, cxxxiv; their costume. . . cxxxv.
Comedians, English, in Amsterdam. . . lxxvi, xc, cxxii
——— in Balge. xcii
——— in Basle. cii
——— in Berlin. lxxvi, lxxvii, lxxx, lxxxiii,
    lxxxviii, xcii
——— in Breslau. xciii
——— in Brunswick. . . xxxiv, lxxxviii
——— in Brussels. xc
——— in Cassel. . . . . . xviii, lvii
——— in Cologne. xci
——— in Copenhagen xxxix
——— in Danzig. xci
——— in Denmark. xxiii
——— in Dordrecht. ciii

INDEX.

Comedians, English, in Dresden. xxiv, xxvii, lxxvi, lxxxiii, lxxxvii, xcv, xcvii, cxiv—cxvi, cxxxv
——— ——— in Elbing. . . . lxxix, lxxxii, xcii
——— ——— in Frankfort. . . . lix, xc, cxxxviii
——— ——— in Gratz. . . . . lxxxiii, xciii
——— ——— in the Hague. lxxix, lxxxi, lxxxiv, lxxxix, xcviii, xcix
——— ——— in Hildesheim. . . . lxi, cxxxv
——— ——— in Königsberg. lxxix, lxxxiv, xcii, xcviii
——— ——— in Leiden. . . . lxxvii, lxxxiii, xc
——— ——— in Memmingen. lxxvi
——— ——— in Münster. cxxxiv
——— ——— in Nuremberg. lxi, lxxxvii, xcviii
——— ——— in Osnabrück. xcix
——— ——— in Poland. xciii
——— ——— in Prague. . . . . lviii, xcvi, cii
——— ——— in Regensburg. . . . lxxxviii
——— ——— in Rostock. lxxx
——— ——— in Strasburg. . . . cii, cxxiii
——— ——— in Stuttgart. . xiv, lxxvii, lxxxiii, cxxxviii
——— ——— in Torgau. xcvii
——— ——— in Ulm. lxxvi
——— ——— in Vienna. . . . . xcv, cii, ciii
——— ——— in Windsheim. ciii
——— ——— in Wolfenbüttel. xxxiii, xliii, lxxxviii
——— ——— in Zittau. . . . . . c, ciii
——— Italian, at Vienna. xxi
Comedies and Tragedies, English, in the German language. . . . . lxvii, civ
Comic element, the, in biblical dramas. . . x
Constance, Council of, x; Plays acted at. . x, xi
Cook, William, a player. xcix
Cooke, Thomas, a player. xxx
Copenhagen, English Comedians in. xxxix
Corambus, the Polonius of the German Hamlet. cxx
Court-Fools. viii
Court-theatres, the first, in Germany. . . xxxvii
Cox, Rob. cix
Crause, Alex. lxxxvi
"Crysella", a German play. cxv
Cupid in Ayrer's "Phaenicia". lxxiii

"Daniel, The prophet", a German play. . . xlii
"Daniel and Susanna", a German play. . . lxxvi
Danzig, English Comedians in. xci
"Daphne", an opera. xcvii
Dekker, Thomas, his "Fortunatus", cix; his "Honest Whore", cxxxiv; his "Jew of Venice", lxxxix; his "Phaeton", cxxxiv; his "Rod for Runaways". xcvi
Denmark, English Comedians in. xxiii
Dethick, Sir Will. . . . . xiv, lxxvi
"Dexterous thief", a German play. cxvi
Dietrich, Master. lxxxvi
Dietrichstein, Cardinal von. . . . . . xciii, cii
"Dioclesian", an English play. cxvii
"Diocletian and Maximinus", a German play. cxviii
Dixon, John, an Instrumentalist. xcvii
Dixon, John, a player. cxxxviii
Docourt, Johann. xii
Dordrecht, English Comedians in. ciii
Dorothea of Brunswick. xc
"Dorothea the Martyr", a German play. . . cxv
Dosin, Christopher. lxxxvi
Dover, city of. . . . . xii, xv
Dowland, John. . . . . xxxv—xxxvi
Drama, the earliest German. iii
——— in six languages performed at Cassel. lvii
Dresden, English Comedians in. . xxiv, xxvii, lxxvi, lxxxii, xcv, cxiv—cxvii
Drolls in German from the English. . . . cviii
Dryden, John, his "Amphytrion". cxvii
"Duke of Florence", a German play. . . . cxv
"Duke of Ferrara", a German play. cxv
"Duke of Venice", a German play. cxvi
"Dukes of Mantua and Verona", a German comedy. cxv
"Dumb knight", by Machin and Markham. . lxvi
Duyck, A. lxxix

Eckard, L. cxvii
Edinburgh. xxxix
"Edward III", a German comedy by Ayrer. . lxvii
Egg, Baron von. xxxv
Elbing, English Comedians in. . . lxxix, lxxxii, xcii
Elisabeth, Princess of Denmark. xxxviii
——— ——— of England. xcvii
——— ——— of Hesse. xxxii
Elisabeth, Queen. . . . . xii, xiv, xxii
Ellidor, a King in a play. cx
Embden, town of. xii
English talent appreciated on the Continent. . xxi
Essex, Earl of. . . . . xiii, xiv
"Esther and Haman", a German play. . . cviii, cxv
"Eucasto" (Hecastus) a German comedy. . . cxviii
Eva Christine, Princess of Saxony. lxxxiii
Eydtwartt [Edward?] John, a player. . . xcvii

INDEX.

Falckenberg, Dietrich von. xviii
Falstaff, his love-adventures. liii
"Faustus", a German play. cxv
Feind, Barthold. cxxxvi
"Felismena", by Montemayor. cxi
Fencers, foreign, at Wolfenbüttel. xl
Ferdinand II, Emperor of Austria. xcv
Ferdinand III, Emperor of Austria. . . . xcix
Fiddlers, English, abroad. xxi
Fiorentino, Giovanni, his "Il Pecorone". . . lii
Flushing. xix
Flutists, English, abroad. xxi
Foltz, Hans, his Shrovetide Plays. iii
Fools, on the early German stage. xlii
Ford, John. cxxxiv
"Fortunatus", an English play. cix
"Fortunatus", a German play. . . . . cviii, cxv
"Four resembling brothers", a German play. . cxix
"Four Royal brothers in England", a German
   play. cxviii
"Four Sons of Aymon", an English play. . . cxxii
Frankfort, English Comedians in. . . . . lix, xc
Frederick, King of Bohemia (previously Frede-
   rick V, Prince Palatine). xcvii
———— Ulric, Duke of Brunswick. . . . xxxv
———— II, King of Denmark. . . xxiii, xxxix
———— of Mömpelgard, Count. . . . . xii, xiii
———— Duke of Wirtemberg. xxviii, xxxix, lii, lxxvi,
                                                  cxxxviii
Friesland. xxviii
Frischlin, N. xxxviii
"Fryer Francis", an English play. cxxii
Fuller, his "Worthies". xxxi

Gallichoraea, the cuckold. xlvii
Garter, Thomas, his comedy of "Susanna". . . xli
George, Landgrave of Hesse-Darmstadt. lxxxix, xcvii
George William, Elector of Brandenburg. . . xcii
Gerando, in Ayrer's "Phaenicia". lxxiii
Gerwalt, in Ayrer's "Phaenicia". lxxiv
Giles (Gellius), Gedeon, a player. c
Globe Theatre. xxxiii
"Godfather, The", a German play. cxvi
Gösslin, John. cii
Gottsched. . . . . cxxxvi, cxxxvii
Gower. cxxi
Gratz, English Comedians in. . . . . lxxxiii, xciii
Gravesend. . . . . xii, xv, xix
Green, John, a player. xcv
Greenwich. . . . . xv, xviii

Grimmelshausen, H. J. Chr. v. ciii
Gryphius, Andr. . . . . cxxx, cxxxvi
Gumpelsheimer. cvii
Guestrow, town of. cxix
Gustavus Adolphus, King of Sweden. . . . xx
———— Duke of Mecklenburg. cxix

Hague, The, English Comedians at. lxxix, lxxxi, lxxxiv,
                                        lxxxix, xcviii, xcix
Hailsbrunn Court at Nuremberg. lxxxvii
Halberstadt, bishopric of. xxxviii
Halle, The "Jew of Venice" acted in. . . . lxxxix
"Hamlet", a German play. cxv, cxix, cxxx, Part II, 237.
Hampton Court. . . . . xiii, xv, lxvii
Hanover. cxxx
Hansa company. xx
Hans Ernst, Prince of Anhalt. xv
Hardydardy, a jester. cix
Harryson, William, a player. xxx
Hathwaye, Richard. lxvii
Helmstedt, University of. . . . . . xxxvi, xxxviii
Helsingör, John Dowland at. xxxvi
Heming, John. xxvii
Henry IV, of France. xviii
Henry V and the Emperor Sigismund. . . . x
Henry VI, professional actors in his reign. . xi
Henry VIII, foreign Minstrels at his court. . xi
Henry Julius, Duke of Brunswick. . xxxiii, xxxviii, lv
———— ———— his tragi-comedy of "Su-
   sanna". xl
———— ———— John Dowland at his court. xxxvi
Henry, Prince of Wales. . . . . . xviii, xix, xcvii
Henslowe, Philip. . . xxxi, xxxii, xxxiii, cix, cxiii
Hentzner, Paul, his description of England. . xvi
Hereswida, Hilda, a British Poetess. . . . i
Hertlein, Christ. lxxxvi
Hes, Henryke, a Minstrel. xi
Hesse-Darmstadt, George II, Landgrave of. . lxxxix
Hesse, William of, Landgrave. xii
"Hester and Ahasverus", an English play. . cix
———— See Queen Hester.
———— See Ahasverus and Esther.
Heugel, treasurer. lviii
"Heurath (die wunderbare) Petruvio mit der bö-
   sen Catharine", a German play. cxxiv
Heywood, Thomas. . . . . xxiii, xxxix, lxxvi, cxxii
"Hieronymus, Marshal of Spain", a German play. cxv
Hilda Heresvida, a British poetess. i
Hildesheim, English Comedians in. lxi
"Historie of Errors", a play. lxvii

INDEX.

Holzhew [Woodhew?] a player. lxxxviii
"Honest Mistress" the, a German play. . . . cxxxiv
"Honest Whore" the, a play by Dekker. . . cxxxiv
Hout, J. van. lxxviii
Howard, C. . . . . xxix, xxxiii, xxxiv
Hrotsvita. i
Humphrey, Laurence. i

"Innocentia", a German play, by M. Kongehl. cxxxiii
Interludes. x
Instrumentalists, English, abroad. xxiii
"Isabella, Queen of Little Britain", a German
   play. xcvii
Italian players in France and Spain, xxii; in
   London. xxii
Jacob, Hans. lxxxvi
James I, King of England. . . xiv, xviii, xxxix, xcvii
James, the Hessian, a player. xcvii
Jeliphur, George, a player. ciii
Jena, University of. xxxv
"Jew of Venice", a German play. . . lxxxix, cxviii
Jöcher, his knowledge of Shakespeare. . . cxxxvii
John Frederick of Wirtemberg, Duke. . . . xix
John George, Markgrave of Brandenburg. lxxvi, lxxxiii
John George I, Elector of Saxony. xcv
John Sigismund, Elector of Brandenburg. lix, lxxxiv, xcii
Johnson, Samuel. lii
Jolifus, Joris, a player. cii
Jones, Richard, a player. . . . xxviii, xxxto xxxiii
"Josepho, the Jew of Venice", a German play. cxv
"Julius Caesar", a German play. cxv
Julius and Hippolyta, a German play. . . cxi, cxxx,
                                                          Part II, 113.
Jumpers and Dancers at Dresden. xxvi
Jünger, Michael, a Minstrel. xi

Keimann, Christian. cxxv
Kid's "Spanish Tragedy". cxx
"King of Arragon", a German play. cxv
"——— of Denmark and Sweden", a German
   play. cxv
"——— of England and King of Scotland", a
   German play. cxv
"——— of Spain and Viceroy of Portugal", a
   German play. cxv
King (Konigk), Thomas, a player. xxv
Kirkmann, his „Wits or Sport upon Sport". . cix
Kite, Jeremias, a player. xcix
Klehe, Henry. lxxxvii
Königsberg, English Comedians in. lxxix, lxxxiv, xcii, xcviii

Koerner, Andrew. lxxxvi
Kongehl, Michael. cxxxiii
Kronenburg, palace of. xxxix
Krosigk, Bernhard von. xv
"Kunst über alle Künste", a German play. cxxiv, cxxx

"Lear, King of England", a German play. . cxvi
Leicester, City of xxx
——— Earl of. . . . . xxii, xxiii
Leiden, English Comedians in. . . lxxvii, lxxxiii, cx
Leipsic. xxxiv
Leopold, Archduke of Austria. cii
Lessing. cxxxvii
Leudegast, Prince of the Wiltau. lxviii
Leupold, Duke. lxix
Lewkenor, Sir Lewis. xix
Lincoln, Earl of, his embassy to Cassel. . . xxxii
Lindner, Michael. liv
Linne in Norfolk, incident in a play acted there. cxxii
"Locrine", a play. cxxi
London, visited by German travellers, xii—xx;
   English actors leaving it, xxi; Danish em-
   bassy at, xxxix; mentioned in the German
   "Fortuuatus", cx; „London Merchant", The,
   a play by John Ford. cxxxiv
Louis Frederick of Wirtemberg, Duke. . . . xix
Louis of Marburg, Landgrave. xviii
Loveday, Thomas, a player. xcix
"Lovers of Pisa", Two, a tale. lii
"Love's Sweetness" etc., a German play. . . xcviii
Lucanus, John. lviii
Ludolff, Prince of Lithuania. lxviii
Ludwig, Prince of Anhalt, his visit to England. xiv
——— ——— ——— present at represen-
   tations of Shakespeare's plays. xv
——— ——— ——— the description of
   his travels to England. xv
——— Duke of Wirtemberg. xii
"Lust's Dominion", a play. cxxi
Luther, his pamphlets against Henry VIII. . vii, xi
——— ridiculed on the stage in London. . . xii
Lydgate, John. cxxxiv

Machin, Lewis. lxvi
Magdeburg, Administrator of lxxxix
"Mahomet", an English play. lxvii
"———", a tragedy by Ayrer. lxvii
"——— and Hiren", by G. Peele. . . . lxvii
Marburg, Landgrave Louis of. xviii
Markham, Gerwase. lxvi

INDEX.

Malone, Edmund. lii
Marlowe, Christ., his "Doctor Faustus". . . cxvii
————— his "Jew of Malta". . . . cxviii
Marston's "Antonio and Malcida". cxx
Mary Eleanor, Duchess of Prussia. lxxx
"Mary, the beautiful, and the old cuckold", a
   German play. cviii
Maurice, Landgrave of Hesse. xviii, xxx, xxxii, xxxvi,
                                                lvii, cxxxv
————— of Orange. xviii
Memmingen, English Comedians in. . . . lxxvi
"Merchant of London", a German play. . . cxxxiv
"————— of Padua", a German play. . . lvii
Merck, John Cam. cvii
Mercoeur, Duke of. xv
Meres, Francis lxxiv
Merry andrews on the German stage. . . . xlii
Minstrels, foreign, in England. xi
Molière. cxiv
Mömpelgard, Count of. xii
Montemayor, his "Felismena". cxi
"Moor of Venice", The, a German comedy. . cxix
Moralities. x
Morell, John and David, players. cxxxviii
Morhoff. cxxxvi
"Mortje", a Dutch play by Brederode. . . . xc
Mülnheim, Hans Jacob von. xii
Münster, English Comedians in. cxxxiv
Munday, Anthony, his "Valentin and Orson". lxvii
Musicians, English, abroad. xxi
————— and actors, English, at Stuttgart. . xiv
————— English, in Stuttgart. lxxvi

Nassau, Count of. lxxviii
Nobility, the German and Dutch, their visits
   to England. xii
Nonsuch, town of. xv
Norway. xxxix
Nottingham, Earl of, his players. xxxiii
Nugent, friar Francis. xci
Nuremberg, town of. xxxv
————— English Comedians in. . lxi, lxxxvii, xcviii
————— theatres at. vii

Oldenburg, city of. xv
Opslo, town of, in Norway. xxxix
Orange, Maurice of. xviii
Origin of the German Drama. iii
"Orlando Furioso", a German play. . . . cxv
Ortelsburg, English Comedians in. lxxxiv

Osnabrück, English Comedians in. xcix
Osterhausen, Hans George von. xcv
Otto, Prince of Hesse. xviii
Oxford. xiii
————— Prince Ludwig of Anhalt at. . . . xv

Pageants at Antwerpe. xxiii
Pamphilus, a character in the "Adulteress". . liii
Papst [Pope], Thomas, a player. xxv
Passion Plays. iv
Pate, Nathan, a player. xcix
Pedel, William, a player. lxxxiii
————— William, Abraham and Jacob, players. xxxviii
Peele, George, his play "Mahomet and Hiren". lxvii
Perst or Pierst, a player. xxv
"Peter Squenz", a comedy acted at Dresden. . cxix
"————— —————", a German play by A. Gryphius. cxxx
"Petruvio and Catharine", a German play. . cxxiv
Pflugbeil, August, a player. lxxxviii
"Phaenicia, the beautiful", a comedy by Ayrer. lxxi,
                                                Part II, 77
"Phaeton", a play, by Th. Dekker. cxxxiv
Philip of Butzbach, Landgrave. lxxxix
"Philolis and Mariana", a German play. . . lxxxvii
"Phoenicia", a German play by M. Kongehl. . cxxxiii
Plautus. lxvii
Poland, English Comedians in. xciii
Politics connected with Plays. vii
Pope, Thomas, a player. lxxvi
Praetorius, Michael. cxxxv
Prague, English Comedians in. . . . . lviii, xcvi, cii
Price, John, a musician. . . . . . . xcvii, cxxxviii
Princes, German and Dutch, their visits to
   England. xii
————— the German, their taste for dramatic
   art. viii
Processions on the stage. viii
"Proculus, old", a German play. cxvi
"Prodigal child", The, a play. cix
"————— Son", a German play. cviii
"Prodigality", a play. cix
Profane scenes in eclesiastical dramas. . . . iii
"Profligate Son", The, a comedy. xliv
"Prophetess", The, by Beaumont and Fletcher. cxviii
"Pyramus and Thisbe", a German farce. . . cxviii

"Queen Hester", an enterlude. cix

Rathgeb, Jacob. xii
Reading, town of. xii

INDEX.

Reformation, the, its influence on the drama. v
Regensburg, English Comedians in. lxxxviii
Rehdiger, Christoph v. xvi
———— Thomas von. xvi
Religious disputes on the stage. xi
Reynolds, John. cxiv
Rheinfelden, Hans Christoph von. xii
Rhenanus, John. cvii
Richard III., entertains foreign Minstrels at his court. xi
"Rich man", The, a German play. cxvi
Riders, English, abroad. xxi
Robert, a player. xcvii
Roberts, James. lxxxix
Röchell, his chronicle of Münster. cxxxiv
Rochester. . . . . xii, xv
Roe, William, a player c
"Romeo and Juliet", a German play. . cxvi, cxxiii, Part II, 305
Rose, David, a painter. . . . . . . lxxxv, lxxxvi
Rose Theatre. cxviii
Rosenblut, Hans, his Shrove-tide Plays. . . iii
Rostock, English Comedians in. lxxx
Rotterdam. xcvi
Runcifax. cx
Runzifall, the devil. lxx

Sachs, Hans. . . . . iv—vi, xxxviii, lvii, lxii
Sackville[Saxfield] Thomas, a player. xxviii, xxxiii—xxxv, cxxxv
Saige, Captain. . . . . xii, xiii
"St. George of Cappadocia", a play. . . . x
Salbert, Christ., a cuttler. lxxxvi
Schampitache, a clown. cxiv
Schetzel, Burkard. xviii
Schlegel, John Elias. cxxxvi
Schmidt, Conrad, a Minstrel. xi
Scholars as actors. vii
Schrämgen, a clown. cxiv
Schütz, Heinrich. xcvii
Schwartzenberg, Count Adam of. xcii
Schwenter, Daniel. cxxxi
Scortum, a character in the "Adulteress". . xlviii
Scottwell, Edward, a player. xcix
"Serule and Astrea", a German play. . . . cviii
"———— and Hyppolita", a German play. . . cxviii
Shakespeare, the London theatres increased by his impulse, xxi; a member of the Blackfriars theatre, xxvii; his connection with Thomas Pope and George Bryan, xxvii; his connec-

tion with Richard Jones, xxxiii; his name unknown in Germany. cxxxvi
Shakespeare, his "Comedy of Errors". . . lxvii
———— his "Cymbeline". . . . . . lvii, cxxxiii
———— his "Hamlet". . . xix, lxxxix, Part II, 239
———— his "Henry VI". cxxi
———— his "Julius Caesar". cxxxvi
———— his "Macbeth". cxxi
———— his "Merchant of Venice". . . lxxxix, cxviii
———— his "Merry Wives of Windsor". . . xlvii, li
———— his "Midsummernigth's Dream". . . cxxx
———— his "Much ado about nothing". xliv, lxxi, cxxxiii, Part II, 79
———— his "Othello". xix
———— his "Passionate Pilgrim". xxxv
———— his "Pericles". cxxi
———— his "Romeo and Juliet". xcviii, Part II, 307
———— his "Taming of the Shrew". . . cxix, cxxiv
———— his "Tempest". . . . xix, lxviii, Part II, 3
———— his "Titus Andronicus". . . xix, Part II, 158
———— his "Two Gentlemen of Verona". cxi, Part II, 115
———— his "Winter's tale" . . . . xix, cxxxiv
Shrove-tide plays, at Nuremberg, iii; their character, iv; obscenities in. xxxvii
"Sidea, the beautiful", a comedy by Ayrer. lxviii, Part II, 1
"Sidonia and Theagene", a German play. . . cviii
Sigismund, Emperor of Germany. . . . . x, xi
"Silvia and Aminta, a German play". . . . cxiii
Simplicissimus. ciii
Skeydell, Peter, a Minstrel. xi
Smyth, Conrad, a Minstrel. xi
Solms, Count Hans Ernst von. xviii
———— Count Philip von. . . . . . xiv, xviii
"Somebody and Nobody", a German play. cviii, cxv
Sommer, John. cxxxv
Sophia, Electress of Saxony. lxxvi
———— Princess of Saxony. xcvii
"Spanish Tragedy", by Thomas Kyd. . . . lxvi
Spencer, John, a player. lxxviii, lxxxiii, lxxxiv, lxxxvi, lxxxvii, xci
Spencer, Sir Robert. . . . . xiv, lxxvi
Starschedel, Otto von. xviii
Starter, a Dutch dramatist. lxxv
Stephen [Stephan], Thomas, a player. . . xxv, xxvi
Stockfisch, Hans von. xcii
Straparola. . . . . xxxvii, lii, cxxx
Strasburg, English Comedians in. . . . . cii, cxxiii
Stuart, Madam Arabella. xix
Stuttgart, English Comedians in. . xiv, lxxvii, lxxxiii
"Susanna", a play. . . . . . . xli, xlii, lvi, lxi

INDEX.

Sussex, Earl of, his players. cxxii
Sydney, Sir Philip. xxii

Taborino, a player. xxi
Tanapfel, Hans, a carver. lxxxvi
Tarlton, his play of the "Seven Deadly Sins." xxvi
Tarleton's "Newes out of Purgatory". . . . lii
Tasso, his "Aminta". cxiv
Thalmüller, Hermann. xviii
"Theagines and Chariclea", a play. . . . cx
Theatre in Germany, its state at the end of the sixteenth cent. ix
Theatres in London increased. xxi
Thilo, Hans, Steward. xxiii
Thomas, a player. xcvii
Thouwasen [?], Edward, a merchant. . . xxxiv
Tieck, Ludwig. . . . . . lxviii, lxix, lxxi, cix
Timbreo, in Ayrer's "Phaenicia". lxxii
"Titus Andronicus", a German play. cv, cxii, Part II, 157
"Titus and Vespasian", an English play. . . cxii
Torgau, English Comedians in. xcvii
Travellers, foreign, to England. xii
Treu, a stage-manager. xcvii
"Troy and Constantinople, Destruction of", a German play. lxxxvii
Trumpeters, English, abroad. xxi
Tunstall, James, a player. xxx
"Two Kings of Britain at war", a German play. cxvii

Ulm, English Comedians in. lxxvi
Union, Protestant, of the German Princes. . xix
Utrecht, city of. xxii

"Valentine and Orson", a play. lxvii
Variscus, Joh. Olorinus. cxxxv
Veltheim, a stage-manager. cxx
"Vincentius", by Duke Henry Julius. . . xliv, lxxi
Vienna, English Comedians in. . . . xcv, cii, ciii
Voelkerling, Pastor. xl
Vulcan in Ayrer's "Phaenicia". lxxiii

Waide or Wayde, John, a player. . . . c, cxix
Wakefield, Edward, a player. xxxiv
Wales, Henry Prince of. xviii
Walpole, Sir Horace. xvii
"War of Wartburg", the first German drama. iii
"Warning for fair women", a play. . . . cxxii
Weise, Christian. cxxx
Wensin, Daniel von. cxxxviii
Whitehall. xix
―――― Shakespeare's plays acted at. . . xcvii
Widemarkter, Caspar von. xviii
Will, a player. xxii
William of Hesse, Landgrave. xii
"Wily beguiled", a play. cxxi
Windsheim, English Comedians in. . . . ciii
Windsor, Count Frederick of Mömpelgard at. xiii
―――― Prince Ludwig of Anhalt at. . . . xv
Wobersnow [?] Arnd von. xxxiv
Wodroff, Vincent, a shoemaker. xcix
Wolffenbüttel, English Comedians in. xxxiii, xliii, lxxxviii
―――― Theatre at. xxxix
Wolframb, Michael. xxxiv
Women, performing on the German stage. . ciii
Wood, John, a player. lxxvii
Woodhew [Holzhew], Behrendt, a player. . lxxxviii
Worcester, Earl of, his players. . . . xxx, xxxii
Worms, city of. cxxx
Wurmser von Vendenheym, Jacob. . . . xix
Wutenau, Albrecht von. xv

Yonger, Mykell [Michael Jünger?], a Minstrel. xi
York, Duke of. xix

Zedler, his knowledge of Shakespeare. . . cxxxvii
Zeland. xxviii
Zittau, English Comedians in. . . . . c, ciii
―――― a German version of the "Taming of the Shrew" represented at. cxxv
Zorn von Bulach, Franz Ludwig. xii
Zürich, city of. ciii

Berlin, printed by A. W. Schade, Stallschreiberstr. 47.